INSIDERS' GUIDE®

INSIDERS' GUIDE® TO

TUCSON

SIXTH EDITION

MARY PAGANELLI VOTTO AND KATE REYNOLDS

INSIDERS' GUIDE®

GUILFORD, CONNECTICUT

AN IMPRINT OF THE GLOBE PEQUOT PRESS

The prices and rates in this guidebook were confirmed at press time. We recommend, however, that you call establishments before traveling to obtain current information.

INSIDERS' GUIDE®

Previous editions of this book were published by Falcon Publishing, Inc. in 1999 and 2000.

Text design by Sheryl Kober
Maps created by XNR Productions, Inc. © Morris Book Publishing, LLC

ISSN 1529-3459
ISBN 978-0-7627-4873-0

Printed in the United States of America
10 9 8 7 6 5 4 3 2 1

CONTENTS

Directory of Maps

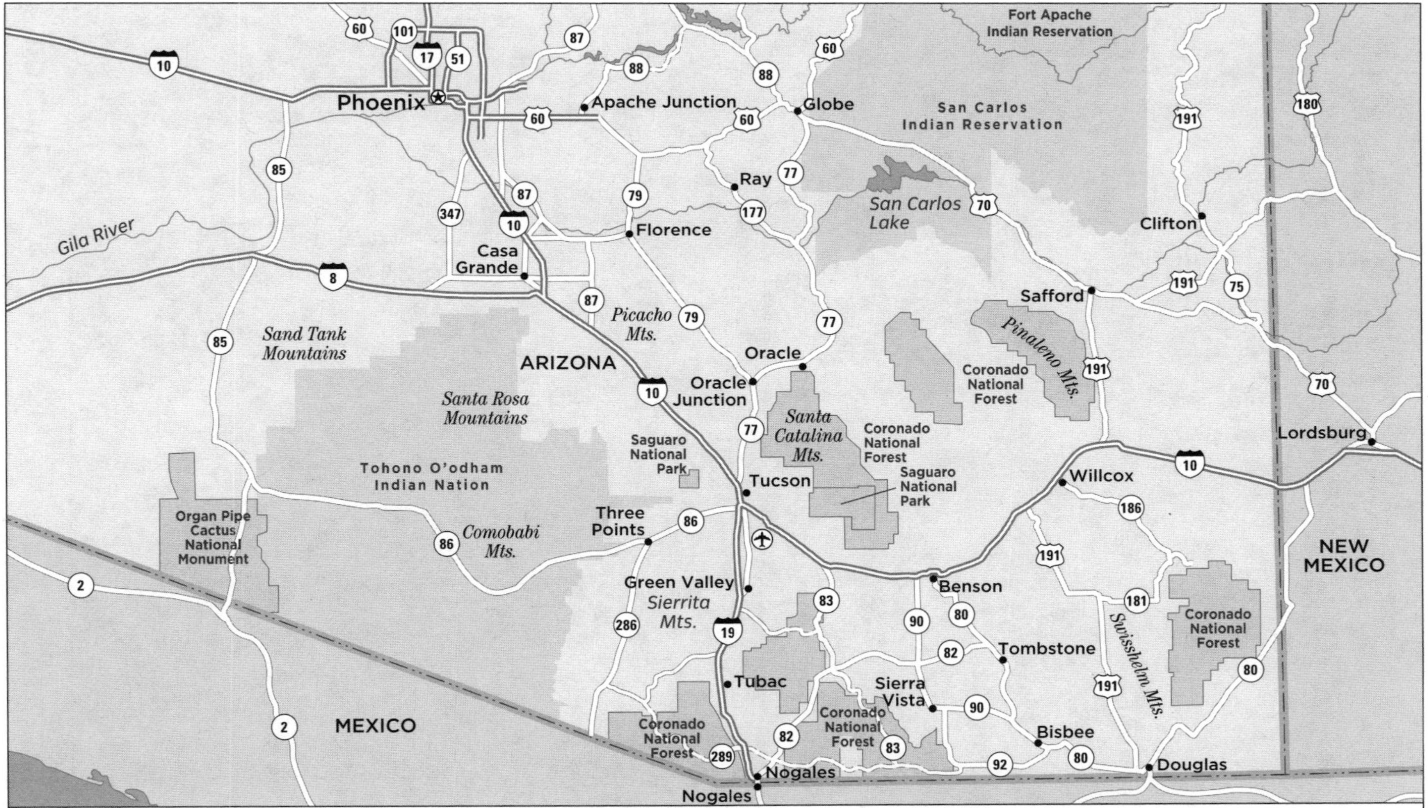

Tucson and Surrounding Area

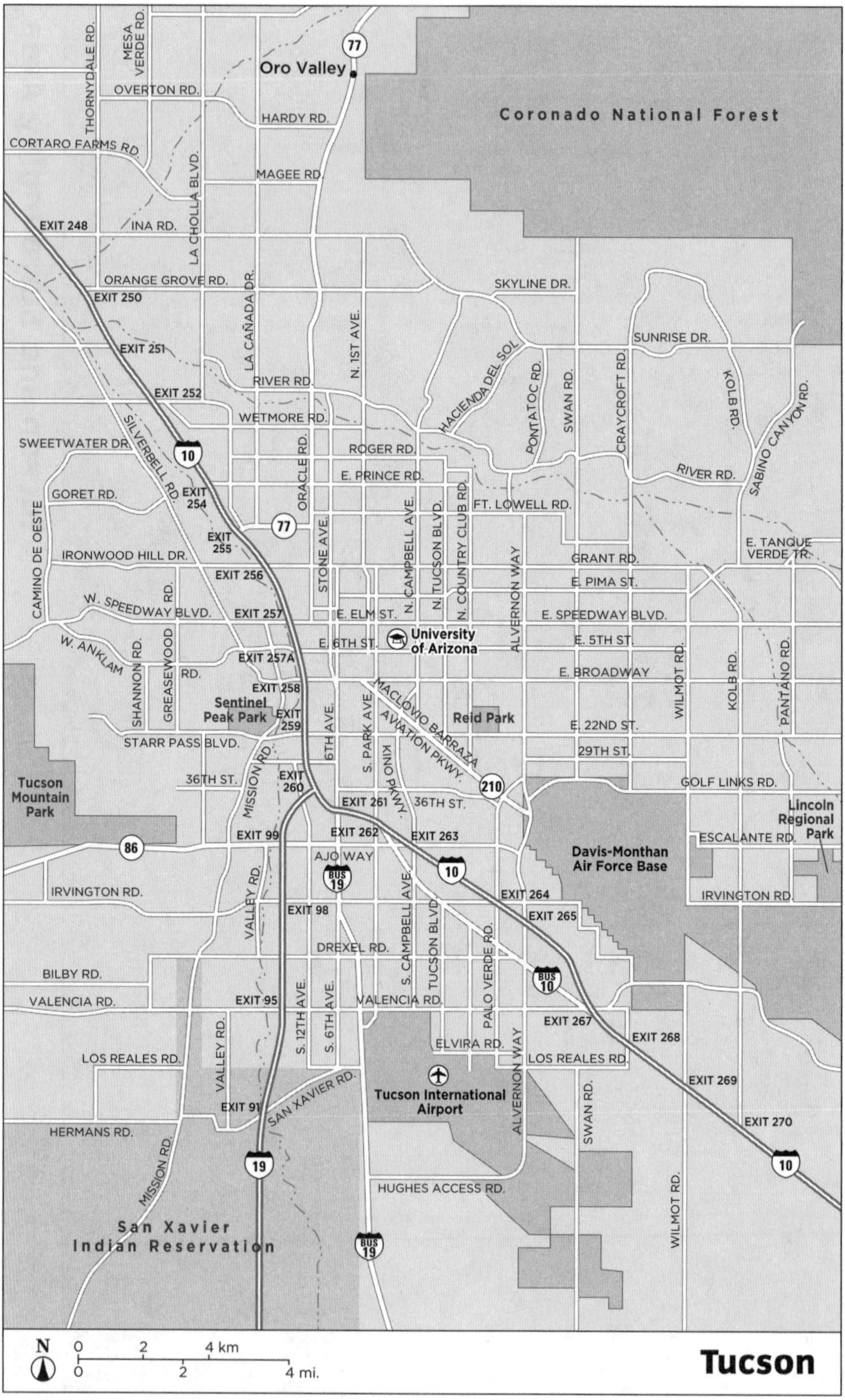
Oro Valley
Coronado National Forest
THORNYDALE RD.
MESA VERDE RD.
OVERTON RD.
HARDY RD.
CORTARO FARMS RD.
MAGEE RD.
LA CHOLLA BLVD.
EXIT 248
INA RD.
ORANGE GROVE RD.
EXIT 250
SKYLINE DR.
LA CAÑADA DR.
N. 1ST AVE.
EXIT 251
SUNRISE DR.
HACIENDA DEL SOL
PONTATOC RD.
SWAN RD.
CRAYCROFT RD.
KOLB RD.
SABINO CANYON RD.
RIVER RD.
EXIT 252
WETMORE RD.
SWEETWATER DR.
SILVERBELL RD.
ROGER RD.
ORACLE RD.
E. PRINCE RD.
RIVER RD.
GORET RD.
EXIT 254
FT. LOWELL RD.
CAMINO DE OESTE
EXIT 255
STONE AVE.
N. CAMPBELL AVE.
N. TUCSON BLVD.
N. COUNTRY CLUB RD.
ALVERNON WAY
E. TANQUE VERDE TR.
IRONWOOD HILL DR.
GRANT RD.
EXIT 256
E. PIMA ST.
W. SPEEDWAY BLVD.
EXIT 257
E. ELM ST.
E. SPEEDWAY BLVD.
W. ANKLAM RD.
SHANNON RD.
GREASEWOOD RD.
E. 6TH ST.
University of Arizona
E. 5TH ST.
EXIT 257A
WILMOT RD.
KOLB RD.
PANTANO RD.
E. BROADWAY
EXIT 258
Sentinel Peak Park
EXIT 259
6TH AVE.
S. PARK AVE.
MACLOVIO BARRAZA AVIATION PKWY.
Reid Park
E. 22ND ST.
STARR PASS BLVD.
29TH ST.
KINO PKWY.
Tucson Mountain Park
MISSION RD.
36TH ST.
EXIT 260
GOLF LINKS RD.
EXIT 261
36TH ST.
Lincoln Regional Park
EXIT 99
EXIT 262
EXIT 263
ESCALANTE RD.
Davis-Monthan Air Force Base
AJO WAY
IRVINGTON RD.
VALLEY RD.
EXIT 264
IRVINGTON RD.
EXIT 98
S. CAMPBELL AVE.
TUCSON BLVD.
EXIT 265
DREXEL RD.
PALO VERDE RD.
BILBY RD.
VALENCIA RD.
EXIT 95
S. 12TH AVE.
S. 6TH AVE.
VALENCIA RD.
EXIT 267
EXIT 268
VALLEY RD.
ELVIRA RD.
ALVERNON WAY
LOS REALES RD.
LOS REALES RD.
SAN XAVIER RD.
Tucson International Airport
EXIT 269
EXIT 91
SWAN RD.
EXIT 270
HERMANS RD.
MISSION RD.
WILMOT RD.
HUGHES ACCESS RD.
San Xavier Indian Reservation
N
0 2 4 km
0 2 4 mi.
Tucson

ADAMS ST.
DRACHMAN ST.
MABEL ST.
HELEN ST.
SPEEDWAY BLVD.
1ST ST.
2ND ST.
UNIVERSITY BLVD.
4TH ST.
5TH ST.
6TH ST.
7TH ST.
8TH ST.
9TH ST.
15TH AVE.
14TH AVE.
13TH AVE.
VAN ALSTINE ST.
ANITA AVE.
CONTZEN AVE.
10
MAIN AVE.
ALDER AVE.
11TH AVE.
QUEEN AVE.
10TH AVE.
PERRY AVE.
9TH AVE.
ASH AVE.
STONE AVE.
ECHOLS AVE.
7TH AVE.
FERRO AVE.
6TH AVE.
ARIZONA AVE.
5TH AVE.
to University Main Gate
HERBERT AVE.
4TH AVE.
HOFF AVE.
3RD AVE.
ST. MARY'S RD.
UNION PACIFIC RAILROAD
Santa Cruz River
El Presidio Historic District
MEYER AVE.
COURT AVE.
4th Avenue Shopping District
Iron Horse Historic District
GRANADA AVE.
FRANKLIN ST.
COUNCIL ST.
WASHINGTON ST.
CHURCH AVE.
ALAMEDA ST.
TOOLE AVE.
PENNINGTON ST.
CONGRESS ST.
BROADWAY BLVD.
UNION PACIFIC RAILROAD
JACKSON ST.
OCHOA ST.
SCOTT AVE.
12TH ST.
Armory Park
CORRAL ST.
Tucson Convention Center
13TH ST.
Armory Park Historic District
McCORMICK ST.
Santa Cruz River Park
CLARK ST.
14TH ST.
CUSHING ST.
Barrio Historico
15TH ST.
SIMPSON ST.
MAIN AVE.
MEYER AVE.
KENNEDY ST.
16TH ST.
N
0 0.25 0.5 km
0 0.25 0.5 mi.
Downtown Tucson

HELP US KEEP THIS GUIDE UP TO DATE

Every effort has been made by the authors and editors to make this guide as accurate and useful as possible. However, many changes can occur after a guide is published—establishments close, phone numbers change, facilities come under new management, etc.

We would love to hear from you concerning your experiences with this guide and how you feel it could be improved and be kept up to date. While we may not be able to respond to all comments and suggestions, we'll take them to heart, and we'll make certain to share them with the authors. Please send your comments and suggestions to the following address:

The Globe Pequot Press
Reader Response/Editorial Department
P.O. Box 480
Guilford, CT 06437

Or you may e-mail us at: editorial@GlobePequot.com

Thanks for your input, and happy travels!

PREFACE

Welcome to Tucson—the Old Pueblo!

One of the "themes" you'll notice as you read through this guidebook is diversity. Tucson is a diverse city—in culture, in history, in recreation, in business, in dining, in lodging, in entertainment, in education, in the arts . . . the list goes on and on. The reason for such diversity is open to much conjecture.

Maybe it all started when a settlement was established in the name of Spain just a stone's throw away from where Native American tribes had lived for centuries.

Perhaps it's because so many people here are from someplace else—places like Milwaukee, Mexico, or Montreal—and they've all brought with them their talents and interests.

Maybe it's the University of Arizona with its mix of people and ideas from all over the world, as well as its outstanding programs in everything from space exploration to creative writing to land management to medicine.

Of course the amazing weather has something to do with our diversity. With more than 350 days of sunshine a year, folks can enjoy all sorts of outdoor activities except playing on a beach (but Tucson does have more than its fair share of places to swim and splash).

Tucson's colorful history—over the years we've lived under five different flags—certainly has something to do with it. Tucson has been a sleepy pueblo, a wild and woolly Western town, a midsize Air Force city, and a growing center of trade with Mexico and Latin America.

Or maybe it's been all those movies and television shows that have been filmed here, bringing glamorous stars and creative film folks.

The best guess would be that all of these factors (and a handful of others that aren't quite so apparent) make Tucson—Tucson. But no matter, you'll soon see that Tucson is a great place to visit or live, no matter what you're into.

Discovering Tucson's many hidden treasures is what makes living and visiting here fun, and you'll find many such gems described in these pages. But as with any city as diverse and growing as Tucson, there is always more to uncover.

So grab this *Insiders' Guide* and explore the Old Pueblo. We know you'll be glad you came.

ACKNOWLEDGMENTS

First a big thank-you to my coauthor, Kate Reynolds, for her enthusiasm, energy, and patience! Kisses and hugs to my family, Eric and Ernie, for continuing to travel Tucson and beyond in search of new information for this great guide. A special thanks to Louise Serpa and the TOCA staff for their support.

Kate wants to add her thanks to the host of people who generously offered time and guidance. She especially wants to thank Bob and Sam Swift for their insightful comments; Greg Lambert for his time and invaluable help; Tom Thivener, whose biking suggestions were super; Lisa Bates for all that she does to help wildlife; Sue Gilsdorf for her adventuring help; and Garland and Carolyn Cox for all their kindness over the years. And she sends a special grateful, heartfelt thanks to coauthor Mary Paganelli Votto for being so easy to work with and so much fun. Kate particularly wants to thank Alan Bomberger, who puts up with last-minute dashes to a ball game and visits to little-known museums with grace and good humor.

We would like to thank Kimberly Schmitz at the Tucson Convention & Visitors Bureau for her up-to-date information and e-mails.

HOW TO USE THIS BOOK

Maybe you're visiting Tucson on a family vacation or business trip. Perhaps you've just relocated to Tucson or plan to soon. Or maybe you're a "snowbird"—the term Southwesterners use for winter visitors who take flight from the snow states to spend all or most of the winter in our inviting valley. No matter why you're here or how long, you'll find this the most thorough and interesting guide to the city and surrounding areas available.

The Tucson area is alive with unique and fascinating flora and fauna; with a multitude of outdoor recreation offerings; with restaurants, attractions, nightlife, and lodgings to suit any taste and budget; and with sports for everyone from bleacher bums to birders to bicyclists. We'll tell you how to get there, what you'll see, how much it will cost, and impart some Insiders' tips (look for the i) and well-founded opinions to help you choose wisely among the vast array of things to do, see, and experience in Tucson. We even give you a complete primer on crossing the border to Nogales, Mexico (not to be confused with its stateside neighbor Nogales, Arizona).

Tucson's city limits are actually rather limited. The city proper comprises only 125 square miles. Therefore, much of what you'll see and do in Tucson is located in the metropolitan area of Pima County that surrounds the city of Tucson. So even though we say "Tucson" on this book's cover and throughout its pages, keep in mind that we are really referring to a metropolitan area of approximately 500 square miles that extends from one mountain range to another. Like most Southwestern cities, Tucson has developed outward rather than upward. You'll find very few high-rises here, but you will find a lot of land to traverse getting from one attraction on the far east side, for example, to another "way out west." Just be patient. With our help you will get there, and it will be worth the trek.

Each chapter of this book covers a specific topic (or combines related topics). We think we've covered every subject that would be of interest and value to any traveler or newcomer. It's easy to zero in on Restaurants if sating your appetite is on your mind, or on our Golf chapter if you're longing to hit the links. If you're just arriving to Tucson by air, turn to our Getting Here, Getting Around chapter and find out how to get where you're going in town—without breaking any rules of the road along the way. Read the Natural World chapter, and you'll soon know as much as Tucsonans do about the strangely fascinating cacti, our summer monsoons, and the four mountain ranges that surround the valley of Tucson. If you're looking for a Spanish-language newspaper or how to find National Public Radio, dial in the Media chapter. And don't skip the History chapter if you want to know the origin of Tucson's name and lots more.

Within each chapter, the information typically is subdivided to help you easily find a specific type of cuisine, a place to shop for Native American jewelry or pottery, or nearby nightlife if you're staying in the downtown area. Places are listed alphabetically within each chapter or subsection of a chapter.

NOTE: Unless otherwise indicated, all listings are in Tucson proper.

You won't be in Tucson long before you hear or see some strange-sounding words. Many of our words for places, streets, and natural things are from the Spanish or Native American languages. You'll want to take the time to learn the correct pronunciation.

If we'd included everything in the Tucson area, this book would be far too weighty to travel with you in a glove compartment, briefcase, or backpack. The philosophy of *Insiders' Guides* is to cover the best and the brightest of what a city has to offer. And while we have made every effort to be accurate and to include all the highlights of Tucson, we're only human. If you find mistakes in our book, if you disagree with something we've said, if you'd like to recommend additions or changes in future editions, or if you'd like to compliment us on a job well done, we would appreciate hearing from you:

Insiders' Guide® to Tucson
P.O. Box 480
Guilford, CT 06437
www.InsidersGuide.com

AREA OVERVIEW

Double rainbows, spectacular sunsets, hot yellow sun and cool pale moon in the same azure sky, towering saguaro and purple mountains majesty, over 350 days of perfect weather—this is Tucson, and it doesn't get much better than this! The city's personality is a combination of great climate, modern metropolitan area, artsy college town, incredible landscapes, ethnic and cultural diversity, upscale resorts, high-tech business, and the Old West.

Many people on their first visit to Tucson are pleasantly surprised by what they find. Shaped by the images of old Western films and television shows, newcomers often expect to see cowboys strutting dusty streets, rattlesnakes under every rock, and townsfolk traveling by buckboard and stagecoach. What they find instead is a bustling city with seasonal bumper-to-bumper traffic, a tall gleaming skyline, and a thoroughly modern, but easygoing, lifestyle.

Tucsonans take great pride in our colorful history and its many cultural influences. Mexico is just 60 miles to the south, and with Tucson's large Hispanic population, its influences are everywhere—from architecture to dining, entertainment to street names.

The Native American population is a small percent, but the Tohono O'odham and Pascua Yaqui tribes have been here for centuries, and their influence impacts Tucson in numerous ways from art to music.

Casual and ***laid-back*** are words that are often used to describe Tucson. You'll find that the lifestyle here is relaxed and sophisticated. There are many terrific hidden treasures in this town alongside the more obvious natural and man-made wonders. Exploring and discovering the secrets and history of Tucson is part of what makes living here special. There's something for everyone.

GEOGRAPHICALLY SPEAKING

Metro Tucson covers approximately 500 square miles reaching from one mountain range to another and sits at 2,389 feet above sea level. The city limits of Tucson cover about 156 square miles. The mountain ranges that surround the area (the Catalinas to the north, the Rincons to the east, the Tucsons to the west, and the Santa Ritas to the far south) contribute to Tucson's wonderful climate. Our location is another contributing factor—the city lies in a zone that receives more sunshine (about 350 days per year) than any other region of the United States.

The city of Tucson is located in the center of eastern Pima County at the intersection of Interstates 10 and 19. Pima County was created in 1864 and included approximately all of southern Arizona acquired from Mexico by the Gadsden Purchase. The county now covers over 9,000 square miles and encompasses not only Tucson but also the separate towns of Marana, Oro Valley, Sahuarita, and South Tucson as well as several unincorporated areas, including Green Valley.

i For great information about Tucson, check with the Metropolitan Tucson Convention & Visitors Bureau. You can call them at (520) 624-1817 or (800) 638-8350, visit their Web site at www.visittucson.org, or go in person to the visitor center located at 100 South Church Avenue, open Monday through Friday from 9:00 a.m. to 5:00 p.m. and Saturday and Sunday from 9:00 a.m. to 4:00 p.m. You'll find tons of maps, brochures, coupons, and an extremely informative staff that knows and loves Tucson.

A modern sculpture and the courthouse dome in downtown Tucson epitomize the seamless melding of old and new in the Old Pueblo. PHOTO BY M. PAGANELLI VOTTO

The average rainfall is 12 inches per year, but that doesn't mean we average an inch a month, as ongoing drought conditions have drastically affected rainfall levels. The summer months bring the monsoon season (see the Natural World chapter), and even in December or January rainfall can be quite heavy. The months in between tend to be hot and very dry, with nary a drop of measurable rainfall. But with an average temperature that hovers near the perfect 81 degrees, Tucson is most attractive to many folks from less-mild climes.

POLITICS AND THE PEOPLE

Tucson is proud of its multicultural heritage (the region has flown the flags of Spain, Mexico, the Confederacy, the Union, and the United States) and diversity (census figures show Tucson is home to several hundred ancestry groups and is one of the largest cities in the country in number of Native Americans). Family friendly, rapidly growing with a healthy developing economy, Tucson attracts people from all walks of life and income. The U.S. Department of Energy listed Tucson as one of the top 13 "Solar American Cities," and Tucson was also included in the book *50 Fabulous Places to Raise Your Family.*

Approximately 50,000 new people move here each year, and almost one-quarter of Tucson residents did not live here five years ago! The median age of a Tucson resident is 35.7, but you'll find all kinds of people here: silver-haired retirees, middle-income families, ranchers, professors, university students, artists, and recent immigrants from all over the world. All are attracted to Tucson for the same reason: its terrific quality of life.

The area is home to two major Indian reservations: the Pascua Yaqui Tribe on 1.87 square miles with about 6,000 members, and the Tohono O'odham Nation on 4,453 square miles with nearly 24,000 members. Each is self-governing, with its own laws and officials. Both nations operate gaming casinos that pour millions of dollars back into their communities in the form of jobs, scholarships, improved health care, and housing.

The city of Tucson operates under a council/manager type of government. This means that both the mayor and city council members are elected by the people to make decisions, and a city manager is appointed by the council to help carry out those decisions. There are six councilpersons, in addition to the mayor, all chosen in citywide elections. The Pima County Board of Supervisors has five elected members (by district) and also appoints a county manager to oversee implementation of laws.

As a nod toward the idea of allowing citizens to have their say, the mayor and council created the Livable Tucson Vision Program, an ongoing effort to develop and implement key goals for the city in areas that include transportation, responsive government, safety and health, education, growth and preservation, and improving the lifestyle of everyone with better jobs, clean air, plentiful water, and more equal opportunities.

GROWTH AND DEVELOPMENT

What started out as a small presidio evolved first into a series of barrios multiplying slowly across the valley and then into a spread-out, medium-size city. Tucson has gone from being a slow-paced, small town to a bustling city. Attractive to families and retirees alike with its great climate and relatively low cost of living, Tucson is practically bursting at the seams.

i Arizona Center for Innovation, located in the Science and Technology Park, assists worthy start-ups with workshops and mentoring. One graduate produced language-learning software. Coccinella Development created a virtual language immersion product called 3DLanguage.

Tucson's cost of living is lower than most other cities in Arizona and remains slightly less than the national average. Add the wonderful weather and laid-back lifestyle, and you get a very popular relocation spot—and they're coming in droves. In November 2006 the population of Pima County vaulted over the "magic million," which leaves Tucson poised to reap enormous business opportunities. As economic advantages expand, Tucson will attract an ever-increasing number of young working families.

And what will they find?

In 2007 total average personal income rose to $30,899, a jump of 7.9 percent from the previous year. Although Tucson was slammed by the 2007 mortgage and housing market debacle, its economic outlook remains strong. *Expansion Management* ranked Pima County as the #1 midsize U.S. county for business recruitment and attraction. Tucson made *Inc.* magazine's list of Top 20 Midsize Cities for Doing Business and grabbed another top slot in *Forbes* magazine's 2007 "Best Cities for Jobs" list. The housing market is still in a state of dynamic change, but in November 2007 the average housing sale price was $269,968. The median price sank to $213,000.

By far the fastest growing area in metropolitan Tucson is the northwest, outside the city limits, in the towns of Oro Valley and Marana. The areas southeast of town and toward the western edge are also expanding rapidly, with new housing developments, master-planned communities, and major retailers moving in. Nevertheless, Tucson retains its slow pace and Western attitude despite it all, and there are still plenty of wide-open spaces, giant saguaros, and cougars roaming residential neighborhoods to remind us that this is still the West.

TUCSON'S CHALLENGES

The biggest challenges that are confronting Tucson in the face of its rapid growth are transportation, development, and conservation. All are critical issues that fuel debate countywide. At issue: how to keep intact the things that make Tucson special but allow development that will foster economic growth and not compromise the natural beauty of the area. It's an issue that many small cities wrestle with, and these are natural growing pains. The good news is that the city and the good citizens of Tucson are not standing still but are facing the challenges of growth and development with the typical forward thinking and independent spirit that make Tucsonans and Tucson special.

Transportation

The lack of a citywide transportation system and the deterioration of major roadways and neighborhood streets continue to be a matter of great concern. Road congestion and traffic gridlock have increased exponentially. Only nine counties larger in population grew at a more rapid rate from 2000 to 2005, and daily vehicle miles of travel jumped from 15.5 million miles per day in 1996 to 22 million in 2005, a daily commute of about half the distance from Earth to Mars. Studies project that this number will reach 36 million miles per day over the next few years. The implementation of a Regional Transportation Authority and Regional Transportation Committee to review and make recommendations is a good start in the desperately needed effort to improve Tucson's roadways.

The battle continues over the development of freeways, and voters have rejected plans for a light-rail system several times. Getting across town from any direction at rush hour is a challenge and, at some major intersections, dangerous. The current roadway system was developed in the 1920s, and it looks like it. Although the city has implemented several strategic plans, including upgrading major thoroughfares and paving side streets, the problem is a big one, which will require foresight, planning, major funding, and citizen support to solve.

Land Use Planning and Conservation

Tucson continues to experience rapid growth, with retirees and others pinpointing this desert paradise as their new home. As a result, much of the desert landscape is being mowed down and destroyed, even though the Sonoran Desert has been identified by The Nature Conservancy as one of the top eco-regions worldwide, deserving of special conservation attention. Both those who have lived here for decades and those who have moved here recently recognize the importance of preserving the unique desert landscape that makes this place special. It's all about choices and trade-offs. It's one thing to be passionate about protecting our environment, but quite another to achieve success. For example, if we use water to grow cotton, that water can't be used to drink. If we use fire to help a forest protect itself, we generate air pollution downwind as the fire burns. Recycling newspapers causes water pollution. Details are always debatable, but what is clear is that trade-offs stand at the center of environmental debate, and the issues are highly complex. How can we protect desert land while continuing to encourage growth?

Local environmental and conservation agencies and organizations like Native Seeds/SEARCH, the Audubon Society, Sierra Club, and The Nature Conservancy are working with city and county governments and developers to address these vital concerns.

Clean air is an absolute must wherever you choose to live. Tucson, like any other growing city, faces issues of pollution. Approximately 60 percent of Tucson's air pollution, such as particulate matter (soot) and carbon monoxide, comes from on-road vehicles.

i The local optics industry pumps about $650 million each year into Tucson's economy. The Optics Cluster represents a broad range of products and services, from fiber-optic components to precision measuring to optoelectronics.

Tucson, like many cities in the Southwest, is vehicle-oriented. The state imposed gas additives in the metro areas of Arizona during winter (October through March). Although this has helped some, it has not drastically reduced the amounts of pollutants in the air. There is a strong push by city leaders to encourage other means of transportation such as city buses, car pools, and bicycles. The acceptance of these alternative forms of transportation is slow and in small numbers, despite the many days when commuters notice the haze that hangs over the city.

A proactive approach to clean air is the city's Trees for Tucson project. As part of Tucson Clean and Beautiful (a city-operated project), trees that thrive in the desert—meaning without needing a lot of water—are planted all over the city. With the help of Tucson Electric Power Company, thousands of trees have been planted in yards and parks and also along roadways.

The city, through various departments, operates several environmental projects, including Adopt-a-Park, where groups and individuals can help maintain not just parks but also streets, washes, and other areas; and Waste Reduction Education, where schoolchildren learn ways to reduce, reuse, and recycle. Tucson Clean and Beautiful offers other programs about recycling throughout the community. Local communities and grants sponsor much of this great community work.

Tucson Vital Statistics

Population (2008 estimate): Pima County 1,016,570; Tucson 534,685

Area and altitude: 156 square miles; 2,389 feet

Nickname: The Old Pueblo

Average temperatures:
July: High 99/Low 74
January: High 63/Low 37

Average number of sunny days per year: 350

Average precipitation: 12 inches

Tucson founded: 1775

Arizona achieved statehood: 1912

Major colleges and universities: University of Arizona, Pima Community College, University of Phoenix

Major area employers: Raytheon Missile Systems, University of Arizona, State of Arizona, U.S. Army Intelligence Center and Fort Huachuca, Davis-Monthan Air Force Base, Tucson Unified School District

Military base: Davis-Monthan Air Force Base

Major airport: Tucson International Airport

Public transportation: Sun Tran bus service

Driving laws: Children under age 5 must ride in car seats. Drivers and front-seat passengers must wear seat belts. Arizona has some of the strictest DUI laws in the nation.

Alcohol laws: Arizona law prohibits anyone younger than age 21 to purchase or consume alcoholic beverages. The purchase, service, or consumption of liquor is prohibited from 2:00 a.m. to 6:00 a.m. Monday through Saturday and from 2:00 a.m. to 10:00 a.m. on Sunday.

Daily newspapers: The *Arizona Daily Star,* morning; *Tucson Citizen,* afternoon

Weekly newspapers: *Tucson Weekly,* Thursday

Sales tax: State tax is 6.1 percent; city tax is 2 percent

Chamber of commerce: Tucson Metropolitan Chamber of Commerce, (520) 792-1212; www.tucson chamber.com

Visitor center: Metropolitan Tucson Convention & Visitors Bureau, 100 South Church Street; (520) 624-1817, (800) 638-8350; www.visittucson.org

Weather: The National Weather Service's local forecast line is (520) 881-3333, or check www.wrh.noaa .gov/tucson.

Daylight saving time: The State of Arizona does not observe daylight saving time. Tucson is on mountain standard time half the year and on Pacific time when other parts of the country are on daylight saving time.

Important dates in history:

1775—The city is established by Spanish soldiers as a walled presidio, the Presidio of San Augustin de Tucson.

1821—Tucson becomes a part of Mexico when Mexico won its independence from Spain.

1853—Tucson becomes a part of the United States as part of the Gadsden Purchase.

1880—The Southern Pacific Railroad reaches Tucson.

1885—University of Arizona established.

1912—Arizona becomes the 48th state.

Famous Tucsonans: Linda Ronstadt; singer; Kerri Strug; gymnast; Stewart K. Udall; former Secretary of the Interior; Barbara Kingsolver, author

ECONOMIC CLIMATE

Tucson has always had a reputation for being a low-wage town, yet people are willing to work for less money just to stay in this fast-growing, sun-drenched Southwestern city. The Eller College of Management Economic and Business Research Center put Tucson's September 2007 non-farm job growth up by 4.8% over the previous year. The average annual earnings per worker here are $43,487, and the median income for a family is $52,400.

According to the chamber of commerce, with more than 1,200 companies employing over 50,000 people in the high-tech industries of southern Arizona, Tucson has become a leader in the new knowledge-based economy. Raytheon Missile Systems leads off as the largest single employer in the city, with over 11,000 employees. The University of Arizona is second, with over 10,000 local employees.

In July 2007 *Fast Company* magazine put Tucson in the top 10 cities for job growth and high-tech industry concentration, dubbing it "Optics Valley." Companies like Raytheon Missile Systems, IBM, Amplimed, DILAS Diode Lasers, OZ Optics, Sion Power Corporation, and Arizona Center for Innovation do business here. Tucson's highly educated workforce has led to a high level of underemployment. Middle-management positions are difficult to come by and have a fairly low turnover. These usually pay a fairly low starting wage compared to other major metro areas—usually in the low to mid $30,000s. Highly skilled positions in the aerospace and optics industries command a more competitive wage, but hourly positions in the hospitality and service industries are fairly low (about $7 per hour). Thus Tucson finds itself with an increasing wage gap; in fact, Arizona has the fourth-highest income gap in the nation. To attract young professional families who will contribute to the community socially and economically, Tucson must actively pursue and attract companies that will pay nationally competitive wages.

In the 2007 Digital Cities Survey, Tucson tied for third place (with Tampa, Florida) on the list of most technologically advanced cities.

Tucson Regional Economic Opportunities (TRED)—a partnership of Pima County, the city of Tucson, and the business community—has targeted specific kinds of industrial clusters for relocation to the area, which has resulted in the creation of thousands of jobs in recent years. These include jobs in aerospace, bio-industry, optics, environmental technologies, and information technology and teleservices. Aerospace is the largest cluster, employing 20,000 to 30,000 people.

The area has become one of the top five locations in the country for teleservices operations and is becoming known as Optics Valley due to the more than 100 innovative optics businesses that have sprouted up in the area. Travel and tourism is an important segment of Tucson's employment scene.

Tucson's proximity to the Mexican border has always had an impact on the region's economy. Tucson was ranked seventh by *Hispanic* magazine in its list of top 10 cities. Since the passage of the North American Free Trade Agreement in January 1994, Tucson's status as a gateway to Mexico and South America has only been enhanced, positioning the area to export its expertise in industrial equipment, telecommunications, electronics, and financial services.

Top 10 Employers in Southern Arizona

1. Raytheon Missile Systems
2. University of Arizona
3. State of Arizona
4. U.S. Army Intelligence Center, Fort Huachuca
5. Davis-Monthan Air Force Base
6. Tucson Unified School District
7. Pima County
8. City of Tucson
9. Wal-Mart Stores
10. Phelps Dodge Mining Company

Source: *Tucson Regional Economic Opportunities,* 2008

The military, too, has always had a strong presence here, and Davis-Monthan Air Force Base is home to the 355th Fighter Wing, the nation's only A-10 training facility. The base hires plenty of civilians, as well as pouring hundreds of thousands of dollars into the local economy.

The University of Arizona has been instrumental in Tucson's high-tech growth, establishing the Science and Technology Park on the southeast side of the metropolitan area just off I-10 near Houghton Road. The site is self-sustaining, with its own water wells, a railroad spur, sewage treatment plant, power plant, a gray water system to recycle water for toilets and landscaping, recreation center, and cafeteria. This complex was built by IBM in the late 1970s and employed 5,000 people at its peak. When IBM pulled out much of its operation in 1989 and 1990, it left behind about 1,000 workers and a $13 million state-of-the-art, 345-acre complex of 12 buildings.

In 1994 the University of Arizona acquired the site (considered the largest real estate deal ever in Tucson), establishing the Science and Technology Park. This networked, 2-million-square-foot technology campus is the sixth-largest university-related research park in the United States. It's home to three Fortune 500 companies: IBM, Raytheon, and Citigroup.

TOURISM

Tourism is a billion-dollar-a-year industry in Tucson. It accounts, directly or indirectly, for one out of 10 jobs in the area and adds more than $1.8 billion per year to the local economy. Restaurants, hotels, tourist sites, and the like are obvious employers. But other companies that benefit from all the tourists include grocery stores, food suppliers, and printing companies. The list goes on and on.

There are really several types of tourists who visit Tucson: those who come for one of the hundreds of conventions held here every year, those who come for family vacations, and of course those who come to escape winter—the proverbial "snowbirds." This last group is made up largely of retirees who "move" here from the Midwest and Northeast for at least half the year to escape winter. Some rent homes; many stay in their RVs (see the Campgrounds and RV Parks and Retirement chapters). A friendly antagonism sometimes can be heard between permanent and these not-so-permanent residents, but the key word there is *friendly*.

Thousands of visitors come to see the area's natural wonders, such as Saguaro National Park (740,000 people per year), Arizona-Sonora Desert Museum (over 470,000 per year), Reid Park Zoo (445,000 people per year), Old Tucson Studios (196,000 people per year), and Mount Lemmon (188,000 people per year). But annual events attract their share of crowds as well. The Pima County Fair normally draws over 250,000 people each year and generates millions for the community. The Fiesta de los Vaqueros Rodeo draws 11,000 people, and its parade—the world's longest nonmotorized parade—sees an estimated 60,000 people line the streets. Baseball's spring training pumps millions into the economy.

After their first taste of all that Tucson has to offer, many folks go back home, pack their bags, and return for good. There haven't been any specific studies to track these people, but tourism ultimately affects Tucson's economy in this roundabout way as well.

DOWNTOWN REVITALIZATION

Like many other cities, the downtown area of Tucson began to lose its appeal for citizens: Shopping had moved out to the far reaches of the city, parking was almost nonexistent, and crime scared many people away.

Business owners in the area became concerned (as did our city leaders), and over time several programs have evolved that share the same goal—bringing people back downtown. Happily, through these various programs things are beginning to turn around.

One response was to focus on the area as an arts district. Created in 1988, the Downtown Arts District is an idea that has taken off, and today hundreds of cultural events are presented in downtown Tucson each year (see the Arts and Culture and Festivals and Events chapters).

Another is the Rio Nuevo, a multimillion-dollar plan for revitalizing downtown. Housing is a major focus of Rio Nuevo, and much has been accomplished downtown, including the IceHouse lofts and the Armory Park del Sol development (see the Neighborhoods, Neighboring Towns, and Real Estate chapter for details). Another notable project is the restored Train Depot (see the Attractions chapter), which has vastly improved Toole Avenue. Future plans include the creation of a major science center, an archaeological park, and a depot plaza.

Business owners in the area have also formed the Downtown Tucson Alliance (520-547-3338; www.downtowntucson.org), a nonprofit group charged with the mission of improving business conditions. The alliance publishes the *Downtown Tucsonan* and promotes area businesses through a variety of events and activities.

SUNNY DAYS AHEAD

The future is bright for Tucson. If we continue to work together and respect our history and natural resources, we can continue to be the place where the Old West meets the New West in a positive and progressive manner.

GETTING HERE, GETTING AROUND

Tucson's rapid growth has had a major impact on all areas of transportation in town. The airport can handle up to eight million passengers per year. The downtown train depot has been restored to its 1941 look with original terrazzo floor and replica of the original ticket counter. Although controversy continues about expansion of the road and freeway system, major thoroughfares are being upgraded, widened, and beautified with public art. A light-rail system is still a dream of many in town, as is commuter rail service to Phoenix.

Planes, trains, cars, and buses will all bring you to Tucson, but when you get here, you really need to have a car. Although there is a bus system, it can be pretty slow going and won't take you to all the attractions in town, not to mention the many not-to-be-missed side trips just a few hours away.

As the second-largest city in Arizona, Tucson is a busy place. But unlike most large cities, there are just two freeways here, and mainly they just circle the city. Although this makes for a much prettier in-town driving atmosphere, it can result in some traffic congestion and tie-ups, especially in prime season (October through May), when visitors and snowbirds flock here to take advantage of the great weather.

Before we tell you the ins and outs and tricks of getting around the metro area, we'll tell you the ways to get here. (Just about the only mode of transportation you can't take to get to the Old Pueblo is a boat.) And we'll tell you how best to get from your arrival point to where you're going in Tucson.

GETTING HERE

By Air

Tucson International Airport is the major air artery into the city. Located just 10 miles south of downtown Tucson off Valencia Road, it's an easy ride from here to just about any part of town. There are also three private airfields serving the Tucson area: the executive terminal of the Tucson International Airport (and just adjacent to it), Ryan Airfield to Tucson's southwest, and Marana Northwest Regional Airport in Marana.

TUCSON INTERNATIONAL AIRPORT
7250 South Tucson Boulevard
(520) 573-8000, (520) 573-8100
www.tucsonairport.org

Many major domestic airlines serve Tucson International Airport, and those that don't can probably get you into Phoenix, a short flight or less-than-two-hour bus or car ride away. **US Airways** (800-235-9292) and **Southwest Airlines** (800-435-9792) are the two major airlines with frequent flights in and out of Tucson, but other major carriers like **American** (800-433-7300), **Delta** (800-221-1212), **Continental** (800-525-0280), **Northwest** (800-225-2525), and **United** (800-241-6522) also provide service to Tucson. One Mexican airline, **Aerolitoral** (800-237-6639), also serves Tucson. The numerous flights each day in and out of Tucson International encompass over 50 cities across the country and major Mexican cities like Hermosillo, Guaymas, and Mexico City. If you're flying to or from Mexico, you'll go through U.S. Customs in the international wing of the airport.

There are some real pluses to arriving at Tucson International Airport. Flights rarely are encumbered by weather delays. The airport is fairly small and uncongested compared to behemoths like Phoenix, Los Angeles, or Chicago, so flight delays are not as common. And passengers can usually get into and out of the airport with ease and minimal hassles.

The airport has both short-term and long-term parking lots, the former very close to the terminal for ease of lugging your luggage or finding an arriving traveler, but even the long-term lot is within walking distance. The short-term lot charges $1 per half hour and $12 per day. The long-term lot charges $1 per half hour then $1.50 per hour and $9 for the day. The garage with 605 spaces offers hourly and daily rates. If you're parking long-term, you'll probably save money at one of the private parking lots just outside the airport, which will shuttle you to and from the terminal. Several of these lots are on Tucson Boulevard, the main road into the airport, and cost about $4 a day. The Park 'N Save lot on Corona Drive between South Tucson Boulevard and South Country Club is fenced and lighted, with 24-hour security.

Ground transportation—taxis, shuttles, limos, or hotel vehicles—will drop you off or pick you up right in front of the terminal, and the locations are well marked with signs as you step out of the terminal's lower (baggage) level.

Airport passengers have several choices for ground transportation. **Sun Tran,** Tucson's public bus system, provides service to and from the airport, so check with the terminal information centers or Sun Tran (520-792-9222) for information. Many hotels provide complimentary airport transportation for their guests, so either ask when you make your hotel reservation or stop at the hotel reservation board in the lower terminal level for direct phone service to some hotels. Although you may have a tough time finding a taxi anywhere else in Tucson, they're plentiful at the airport. They have a flag drop rate that includes the first mile plus a per-mileage charge after that (unless you're going beyond 25 miles of the airport, in which case it would be a flat fee). Expect to pay about $25 between the airport and central Tucson. Taxi fares include baggage and extra persons going to the same location. Arizona Stagecoach (520-889-1000; www.azstagecoach.com) operates a door-to-door van service to and from the airport. You can call them in advance for information or go to the company's reservation desk in the terminal's lower level.

Many car rental agencies are located in or close to the airport. If they're off the grounds, they'll have shuttles to and from the terminal. They include **Alamo** (520-573-4740, **Avis** (520-294-1494), **Budget** (520-573-8475), **Dollar** (520-573-4733), **Enterprise** (520-573-5250), **Hertz** (520-573-5201), and **National** (520-573-8050). It's obviously best to reserve your car before your trip to Tucson, but if you didn't, merely walk up to one of the car rental counters in the building adjacent to the terminal and see if anything's available.

If you want the luxury of limousine service, several in Tucson will transport you to or from the airport. Information on this service is available at the airport as well as later in this chapter.

EXECUTIVE TERMINAL

Tucson International Airport
7081 South Plumer Avenue
(520) 573-8128, (800) 758-1874
www.tucsonairport.org

Operated by the Tucson Airport Authority and connected to Tucson International Airport, the executive terminal is the busiest of the three private fields, primarily because of its proximity to the airport and the city. Open 24 hours, it has access and facilities for all kinds of aircraft, from two-seaters to million-dollar jets. Aircraft services available include fuel, overnight parking, a weather briefing room, and lavatory clean-out, but no aircraft maintenance or repair services. (These are available at neighboring businesses, as is flight instruction.) There's a pilots lounge in the terminal, plus car rentals and taxi and limo services. The terminal can also reserve cars and hotel accommodations. At this airport there are no landing fees for privately owned aircraft, but commercial (cargo or for-hire) craft flying operation 135 or 121 will pay a fee per thousand pounds of the aircraft's maximum gross landing weight capability. The UNICOM number is 122.95. Those in the know say that this is a popular spot for the rich and famous (or infamous) to land and step out of their aircraft into a waiting limousine without curious observers ever seeing them.

RYAN AIRFIELD
9700 West Ajo Way
(520) 883-2921 (maintenance), (520) 883-9800 (general information)
www.tucsonairport.org

Ryan Airfield, also operated by the Tucson Airport Authority, lies at the western end of Valencia Road where it intersects with Ajo Highway in a fairly remote area about 15 miles from Tucson International. Services here include fuel, rental cars, overnight parking at daily and monthly rates, and a restaurant open daily. Maintenance, repair, and lessons are available at private businesses adjacent to the airfield. There are no landing fees. Tower hours are 6:00 a.m. to 8:00 p.m. There is no UNICOM, but radio frequencies are 125.8 for air and 118.2 for ground control.

MARANA NORTHWEST REGIONAL AIRPORT
11700 West Avra Valley Road, Marana
(520) 682-2999, (800) 264-2266
www.tucsonaero.com

Marana Northwest Regional Airport, operated by the town of Marana, is in the town of Marana, about 5 miles west of Interstate 10, and may be most convenient to residents of Tucson's northwest. Services are provided by Tucson Aeroservice Center and include fuel, overnight parking at fees depending on aircraft size, car rental available with advance notice, a restaurant, and a pilots lounge (with showers). There are no landing fees, and a private fixed-based operator on-site provides maintenance, repair, lessons, and charter flights. UNICOM is 122.875.

i If you really must fly into or out of Phoenix instead of Tucson, Arizona Shuttle Service (520-795-6771 or 800-888-2749; www.arizonashuttle.com) operates vans in both directions seven days a week. It's a convenient way to get between the two cities in about two hours. Reservations are required.

Charter Services

If you prefer private to commercial flying and don't have your own wings, several companies operate charter and aircraft rental services. They'll take you to other cities for business or pleasure or on flights of fancy, such as over the Grand Canyon or whale watching in Mexico's Sea of Cortez. **Double Eagle Aviation** (520-294-8214; www.2-eagle.com) is conveniently located near the Executive Terminal and offers a wide range of services for charter and private flying. **Tyconic** (520-883-4823; www.tyconic.com) is based at Ryan Airfield and offers flight instruction and aircraft rentals. Operating out of Marana Northwest Regional Airport, **Tucson Aeroservice Center** (520-682-2999) has full charter services. All three service Mexico and Canada as well as the United States. Located at the Tucson International Airport, **Voyager Flight Services** (520-294-0849; www.flyvoyager.com) offers a variety of helicopter sightseeing tours.

By Train

AMTRAK
400 North Toole Avenue
(520) 623-4442, (800) 872-7245
www.amtrak.com

Tucson's Amtrak station is downtown, in the refurbished 1941 historic train depot at the northwest corner of Fourth and Toole Avenues. Open daily from 10:00 a.m. to 5:30 p.m. and 10:30 p.m. to 5:30 a.m., the station keeps very strange hours, primarily corresponding to trains' arrivals and departures. Amtrak's Sunset Limited passes through eastbound to Orlando, Florida, and westbound to Los Angeles several days a week. The Texas Eagle portion of the line will get you to San Antonio or Chicago. Strangely, Amtrak does not service Phoenix directly but instead stops in Maricopa, about 30 minutes outside Phoenix. Talk continues about light-rail services and commuter service to Phoenix, which would be based at the station.

Parking is available at the station and nearby on the street, but none of it is secured or advisable for the long term. The safest bet for long-term parking is a nearby city garage. Ground transportation from the train station is convenient because it's located downtown and only a stone's throw from Sun Tran's Ronstadt Transit Center at Pennington Street and Sixth Avenue. Beyond the city bus, you're likely to find taxicabs either at the train station or the bus transit center. For a rental car, you'll need to call one for a pickup; none are within walking distance of the train station or in the immediate downtown area.

By Bus

GREYHOUND
471 West Congress Avenue
(520) 792-3475
www.greyhound.com

If you follow the old saying "Leave the driving to us," you'll be arriving or departing Tucson by Greyhound bus.

Greyhound serves all points north, south, east, and west of Tucson, including Nogales and several other cities in Mexico. For example, you can get to or from Las Vegas, Los Angeles, Texas, or Phoenix from Tucson. For the convenience of airline travelers, Greyhound also has several trips a day from its Tucson terminal to its terminal 1 mile from the Phoenix airport. The Tucson station is located at Congress and I-10.

By Car

If you're driving to Tucson from points west, such as California or western Arizona, you'll probably be traveling east along Interstate 8, which meets up with I-10 just south of Casa Grande and about 70 miles north of Tucson. From that point, I-10 east will take you southward right into Tucson. If you're driving from points north like Flagstaff or Phoenix, I-10 eastbound will deposit you in Tucson. If you'd rather take the scenic route than the fast route, exit I-10 early and head for Sacaton or Coolidge, which will take you to Highway 87 and past the Casa Grande Ruins National Monument, then connect with I-10 again.

Mexico is about the only point south of Tucson, so if you're coming from that direction you must be coming across the border, in which case Interstate 19 will carry you north into downtown Tucson. Or take the scenic path, Highway 82 north to Highway 83 north, which will connect with I-10 east of Tucson, then take that west to the city. Traveling from the east, such as from New Mexico, the major route into Tucson is I-10 westbound. This part of I-10 goes through some lovely country, including farmlands around Willcox, Arizona, and a boulder-laden area called Texas Canyon.

If you're traveling from Colorado or northeastern Arizona and its fascinating Indian reservation spots like Canyon de Chelly National Monument or Window Rock, the fast option is to take Interstate 40 east into Flagstaff, then go south along Interstate 17 and I-10 to Tucson. For scenic routes, there are many choices, including Highway 77, which goes through the White Mountains and eventually becomes Oracle Road into Tucson, or U.S. Highway 191, a very scenic road winding through forestlands that eventually connects with I-10 east of Tucson.

GETTING AROUND

OK, you've arrived. Now how do you find your way from one end of the 500-square-mile valley that's metropolitan Tucson to the other, and all points in between? Well, it won't be by boat or by fast transit (like trains), but it could be by car, bus, taxi, or limousine. Here's how to find and use the various forms of in-town transportation and how to get around the streets if you're the driver.

Navigating the Streets

In one sense Tucson is fairly easy to navigate by car. If you get to know the four mountain ranges that are strategically located at the four compass points, you'll be able to ascertain north from south and east from west from nearly any spot in the city. At the very least, learn to recognize the Santa Catalinas and you'll know where north is. And much of Tucson, especially the central area, is laid out in a grid system with streets 1 mile apart and running directly north–south or east–west.

But there are more than a few chinks in this plan, which can confuse even longtime Tucsonan

There are many ways to access Tucson, from modern highways to scenic routes and bridges like the bicycle and pedestrian Basket Bridge. COURTESY OF THE CITY OF TUCSON, TRANSPORTATION DEPARTMENT

drivers. For example, there are the streets that inexplicably change their name somewhere midstream, or natural obstacles such as washes, rivers, or minimountains (and man-made obstacles such as an Air Force base) that simply won't let a street pass through or over them. There are streets that go in any direction but straight and twist and turn until you're almost dizzy trying to stay on course. And then there are the myriad strange names for streets, many of them Spanish—as tricky to read as to pronounce.

To find your way easily through the maze of Tucson streets, we strongly suggest latching onto a good street map and never letting go. Several helpful maps are available in the *Official Visitors Guide* published by the Metropolitan Tucson Convention & Visitors Bureau and available free at the visitor center on 110 South Church Street in downtown Tucson. The rental car company maps are particularly easy to follow and cover most major roads and intersections; pick one up free at any rental car agency. For super detail, Rand McNally has a page-by-page street guide as well as a laminated Easy-Finder version. Another wise piece of advice is to plot out your trip in advance, especially if you're driving to some obscure street that may sound like several other streets.

Keep in mind that many Tucson street names include Spanish words that mean street, way, or place. Among them are *calle, camino, placito, via, avenida,* and *paseo.* Street names can be frustrating to newcomers, but with patience you'll get as proficient at deciphering (or ignoring) them as Tucsonans are.

Downtown Tucson continues its efforts at renovation, resulting in changes to street parking, ramp access, street access, and even possible direction changes. For up-to-the-minute details check the city of Tucson Web site (www.knowyourwaydowntown.info) or contact the **Regional Transportation Authority** (520-770-9410; www.rtamobility.com), the organization that oversees all these projects.

Main Thoroughfares

Our primer on land travel begins with the two biggest arteries, the two interstates or freeways. I-10 comes down from Phoenix heading east (which actually seems like south) into Tucson and skirts the western side of the city. Near downtown, it curves abruptly and actually begins heading directly east, then brushes the very southern part of the metro area to points east, including eventually New Mexico. The other freeway is I-19, which begins about where I-10 curves to go east. From there I-19 heads directly south past Green Valley and eventually to Mexico. (The signs on I-19 give distances in kilometers, not miles.)

Major construction on I-10 is ongoing and affects several on-ramps and access points into the city, frustrating visitors, merchants, and citizens. Be sure to check the local paper (if you live in town) or the Arizona Department of Transportation for up-to-the-minute information on which exits are closed. Their Web site (www.i10tucsondistrict.com/29toP.html) provides details.

The interstates are handy if you're traveling to Phoenix, New Mexico, or Mexico or along the western or far southern parts of the metro area. Beyond that, drivers must tolerate surface streets and lots of stop-and-go traffic, even to get from, say, the far northwest to the east or from the foothills to downtown.

So if the interstates won't get you to where you're going, you might want to know about some of the major streets that cross town. Starting up north, Ina Road will take drivers from the far west, actually I-10 and beyond, all the way to the mountains in the east, but it changes names—first to Skyline Road and then to Sunrise Drive. River Road is another west-to-east option, but it terminates well before the interstate on the west and goes only to Sabino Canyon Road on the east. Nonetheless, it's a good route, albeit curvy in spots, and comes with views. Other major east-west streets are Grant Road, Speedway Boulevard, Broadway Boulevard, 22nd Street, Golf Links Road, Ajo Way, Irvington Road, and Valencia Road, all of which run parallel to one another and are major byways lined with all manner of commercial enterprises.

Major north-south streets, beginning on the west side, include Oracle Road, Stone Avenue, Campbell Avenue, Alvernon Way, Swan Road, Craycroft Road, Kolb Road, and Houghton Road. Some of these streets end abruptly, usually because of natural or man-made barriers. Swan and Craycroft Roads, for example, are stopped in the south by the Air Force base. Tucson International Airport is the southern terminus for streets like Park and Campbell Avenues (which for part of its route is called Kino Boulevard).

A Road by Any Other Name

Quirks are common with Tucson's streets. For example, 22nd Street, a major east-west thoroughfare, changes to Starr Pass Boulevard west of I-10. Fifth Street becomes Sixth Street and then St. Mary's Road and finally Anklam Road as you travel west. Pima Street turns into Elm Street near the Arizona Inn. And there's a Pantano Road and a Pantano Boulevard, and they run next to each other, so who knows which is which. Of all the street quirks in Tucson, however, the strangest may well be the place where Wilmot Road becomes Tanque Verde Road and Grant Road becomes Kolb Road, and they all intersect and go off in different directions. This is a very busy area to boot. Again, consult your trusty map and plan ahead.

And if you're looking for any rhyme or reason to the use of terms such as street or avenue or boulevard, forget it. Many roads are tagged with boulevard, but you may never see one along its length. The use of numbered roads can be confusing also: We have Fifth Street and Fifth Avenue and Sixth Street and Sixth Avenue, for example, and often they intersect. Just remember that in the case of numbered roads, the avenues run north-south and the streets run east-west.

Rules and Warnings

You won't be on Tucson streets long before you notice that most of the main ones have a left turn lane down the center, indicated by yellow lines. This is a fairly easy concept even for newcomers—turn left from the center turn lane. At intersections with a green arrow for left turns, pay attention. The turn signal usually, but not always, comes after, not before, the green light.

And if that's confusing, try figuring out the address numbering system in Tucson. We'll explain it but make no guarantees that it makes sense or that you'll get it. First, the point of origin for addresses in Tucson is Stone Avenue and Broadway Boulevard. In other words, Stone Avenue is the dividing line for east versus west streets and Broadway Boulevard for north and south streets (everything north of Broadway is called north something street, and so forth). That's not terribly difficult, but read on. When you are on an east-west street looking for an east address, you'll find odd building numbers on the north side of the street and even addresses on the south side. But once you cross Stone Avenue and are in the west streets, the exact opposite is true—the odd numbered addresses are on the south side and the even on the north.

i Construction on major and in-town roadways continues throughout Pima County. For a list of all current and future roadway improvements, check www.roadprojects.pima.gov, which lists all road projects with detailed links to each one and provides a map of closures.

And guess what happens to the north-south streets? When you're north of Broadway Boulevard, the odd address numbers are on the west and the even on the east. But south of Broadway Boulevard, the switch takes place and odd numbers are on the east side of the street and even on the west. And making matters worse is the fact that only about every third building (at best) in Tucson even has a visible address number. Finding your destination and driving at the same time can be a real challenge.

Another caution about Tucson streets pertains to rainstorms. We have them infrequently, but they can be fierce. In a flash, a simple dip in the roadway or a low spot where a wash or arroyo crosses the road will fill up with rushing water and can careen vehicles downstream with no warning. So when you see a DO NOT CROSS WHEN FLOODED sign, heed the warning.

As a final caution for driving Tucson's streets, be aware that many downtown streets are one-way, even though they may be two-way streets beyond downtown. Stone Avenue, for example, becomes strictly southbound as it goes through downtown, while Congress Street is westbound and Broadway Boulevard becomes eastbound during their downtown paths. Again, refer to the trusty street map before you turn on the ignition.

Parking

Driving and parking—you can't have one without the other, so here's the mostly good news on parking your vehicle in the Tucson environs. With two primary exceptions, parking is usually very accessible and free. Nearly every business and major attraction has ample parking, and there's almost never a charge. The two notable exceptions are downtown Tucson and the university, where people congregate, buildings dominate, and land for parking is scarce. So if you're attending one of the many events or attractions in either of these areas, you'll probably have to hunt for an available space and pay once you find it. Both areas have metered street parking, but it's not easy to get. Both also have numerous pay parking garages and lots at hourly rates with daily rate specials. Metered parking and some university garages are free on weekends. The university publishes an annual campus parking map, which is also available online (www.parking.arizona.edu), and a guide to downtown parking is available at the city Department of Transportation Web site (www.dot.ci.tucson.az.us/parkwise/downtown.phlp).

Rental Cars

The major national car rental agencies are represented here, and most are located at the airport (see the listing for the Tucson International Airport previously in this chapter) but also have additional locations around town. It's often possible to rent a vehicle in Tucson and drop it off in

Phoenix (or vice versa) without the typical steep drop-off charge, which is a big help if you're using the Phoenix airport. As is true in most large cities, you'll find a number of car rental companies that aren't the "biggies"—they're local but usually offer the same types of vehicles and rates as the national agencies. Some of these are operated out of car dealerships. Check the Yellow Pages under "Auto Renting" and "Auto Leasing" for the many car rental options in Tucson.

If you're renting a vehicle and plan to travel south of the border, however, be advised that you're unlikely to find any rental vehicle that you can take to Mexico. (If the border town of Nogales, Mexico, is your destination, you can easily park in the United States and walk a block or two to the border crossing and into Nogales. Check out the Day Trips and Weekend Getaways chapter for all the details on going to Mexico.)

Riding the Bus

Tucson has only one form of public transit: the **Sun Tran** bus system (520-792-9222; www.suntran.com). It'll get you to and from many places, but it's by no means as frequent or as comprehensive as bus transportation in major cities in other areas of the country. Tucson buses travel mostly within the city limits, even though much of Tucson lies beyond the city. Here are some of the bus basics.

For starters, let's talk about where the buses stop. They only stop at designated bus stops, of which there are over 2,000, indicated by signs. The sign will tell you which route (by number and name) stops there and whether an express bus also stops there. Many stops are covered, which is good news if you're a summer rider or just don't want to wait in the fierce sun, and most are wheelchair accessible.

Sun Tran has several features that make it a usable system for the disabled. Many Sun Tran buses are lift-equipped for wheelchairs and are marked with the international wheelchair symbol on the door. Some buses accommodate people who have difficulty stepping up. Sun Tran produces special guides for people with vision disabilities, operates **TTY/TDD phone service** (520-628-1565), and accommodates guide dogs. If you're in need of special assistance, chances are Sun Tran can accommodate you. Tucson has a special on-call transit service for the disabled, called **Van Tran,** at (520) 798-1000.

Sun Tran also caters to drivers who want to park and ride and bike riders. There are about two dozen locations where you can park a car for free and then take a bus to your destination. They're listed in the *Sun Tran Ride Guide*. For bike riders, Sun Tran buses are equipped with bike racks on the front (although they only carry two, so it's first-come, first-served) at no extra charge. They also rent monthly bike lockers (you need your own lock) at designated locations and have bike racks at designated bus stops.

i Send a scenic e-card of Tucson to friends and family while you're here. There's a great selection of free images on the Metropolitan Web site at www.visitTucson.org/phototour.

Once you've figured out how to find a bus stop, you'll need to know how to get where you want to go. It can be complicated, so your best bet is to call **Sun Tran** (520-792-9222), and they'll give you specific instructions (in Spanish if needed). Or go to their Web site's trip planning page for an interactive guide. You can also pick up a *Ride Guide,* which you can get just about anywhere, including grocery stores and libraries. The guide tells you everything you always wanted to know about Sun Tran. Another option is to go to one of the three transit centers, which have information booths as well as covered waiting areas, restrooms, and telephones. They're also major transfer points for buses. The **Tohono Tadai Transit Center** is located on Stone Avenue just north of Wetmore Road; the **Roy Laos Transit Center** is at Irvington Road and South Sixth Avenue; and the **Ronstadt Transit Center** is downtown at Pennington Street and Sixth Avenue.

Fees

To ride the bus you'll need exact change or a fare pass. The regular fare for ages 6 to adult is $1. Kids younger than 5 with an adult ride free; seniors, disabled, and low-income riders carrying a special ID pay 40 cents. Transfers are free, but you need to request one when you first get on the bus. It's good for two hours in the same direction. In other words, it won't work for a return trip.

If you're a regular rider, the passes may be the way to go. There are several varieties, such as a monthly pass and an economy pass for seniors and qualified low-income riders, as well as monthly express passes, university passes, and booklets of rides. Passes are available at lots of places, including Sun Tran, so call or refer to the *Ride Guide* for where to get one. They're also available by mail.

Close-up

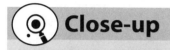

Useful Information

Whether you're here for a vacation or a business trip, there is so much to see and experience in Tucson. No matter how much (or little) planning you've done, there's nothing harder than coming to a new city and trying to find your way around, especially if you don't have a lot of time on your hands. Here are some great local sources that will help you get the best from your trip and give you a sense of what's happening at the moment.

VISITOR INFORMATION

Metropolitan Tucson Convention & Visitors Bureau

100 South Church Avenue, Tucson

(520) 624-1817, (800) 638-8350

www.visittucson.org

Located in the colorful Plaza Placita, the center offers free maps, guides, pamphlets, and brochures for everything in town. The extremely helpful staff can answer questions, suggest walking tours and itineraries, and tell you about any special events taking place in town.

City of Tucson

www.ci.tucson.az.us

The city's Web site will give you a great overview of the city, with visitor information, a live city cam, events, maps, and even job listings.

Pima County

www.co.pima.az.us

The county site offers general county government information and a great page of links to Tucson attractions.

MAGAZINES

Tucson Guide Quarterly

A superhelpful quarterly publication that covers events, restaurants, festivals and fiestas, theater, arts, shopping, golf, and dining. Special sections highlight regional attractions. The "101 Things to Do" is an eclectic guide to lots of unusual and interesting activities and attractions in town, a real keeper.

Tucson Lifestyle

The upscale monthly magazine covers the city beautifully with features, city and dining guides, event calendars, day and weekend trip ideas, and more. Watch for the "Newcomers" edition published annually and bursting with useful information.

NEWSPAPERS

Tucson Weekly

www.tucsonweekly.com

A free weekly newspaper with all the info you need to find out what's happening in Tucson. Comprehensive listings of restaurants, clubs, bars, arts, and music, plus insider articles about Tucson life. Pick one up from bright-red kiosks found all over town at video stores, grocery stores, cafes, and on street corners.

The Arizona Daily Star

www.azstarnet.com

The major daily morning paper in town. The Friday section, "Caliente" (www.aznightbuzz.com), covers the week's activities from music and art to hiking, bicycling, festivals, stargazing, shopping, dining, movies, and special events. It's got it all. Daily events are covered in the Community Calendar in section B of the paper and on the Web at www.dailystarcalendar.com.

Tucson Citizen

www.tucsoncitizen.com

Tucson's afternoon paper, this edition offers a Calendar page on Thursday.

EXCLUSIVELY ON THE WEB

www.dotucson.com

This helpful local Web site offers listings of events, attractions, dining, and nightlife.

Hours and Special Events

Sun Tran buses operate from about 5:15 a.m. to 10:45 p.m. Monday through Friday and from about 6:15 a.m. to 7:00 p.m. on Saturday, Sunday, and holidays. Not all of the bus routes operate all these hours, however, so check the schedule or call Sun Tran.

Even though Sun Tran may not exactly cover the land and may not operate buses every 10 minutes (or even close to that), it does have a number of special runs that make it easy to get to some major events like football and rodeo.

Catching the Cat

Folks who attend or work at the University of Arizona have another transit option—the university's Cat Tran shuttle, its name taken from the school's Wildcat nickname. It operates Monday through Friday from 6:30 a.m. to 6:30 p.m. The NightCat operates Monday through Friday from 6:00 p.m. to 12:30 a.m. but not usually during semester breaks or on school holidays. It's free to riders showing the appropriate ID, and route maps are available at the university. The Web site (www.parking.arizona.edu) offers a full schedule and route maps, or call (520) 626-7275.

Taxis and Van Services

This isn't New York, Los Angeles, or Chicago, folks, so hailing a taxi isn't even in the vocabulary here. About the only places you can expect to see a taxi ready to take on a passenger are the airport, bus and train stations, and possibly major event venues, such as the Tucson Convention Center.

And except for the airport, even these locations aren't a sure bet. So plan on calling for a taxi if you need one.

Tucson has fewer than a dozen taxicab companies, plus several private transportation services operating on-call vans. Taxi rates aren't regulated in Arizona, so they vary widely—we recommend shopping around. Most taxis use a flag drop rate plus mileage charge for shorter trips and a flat fee for longer ones, such as from Tucson to Green Valley. Extra charges usually are not levied for more than one passenger going to the same destination. Several taxi companies can accommodate Spanish-speaking passengers, including Fiesta Taxi and Yellow Cab. Several also have wheelchair-accessible cabs available, including Allstate Cab Company and Yellow Cab. The major taxi companies serving the area are **VIP Taxi Company** (520-881-2227) and **Yellow Cab** (520-624-6611).

As an alternative to taxis, several companies operate private van or car services. Some accommodate either individual passengers or groups, while others are strictly for groups. They typically have flat rates per hour or by destination and may offer tours, special services to businesses, and other limousine-like services. These companies include **Allstate Transportation Service** (520-293-2233), **Diamond Transportation** (520-825-8888), **Ms. Transportation** (520-327-4674), and **Safe Ride** (800-797-7433).

Limousines

If luxury is your lifestyle or if you just want to be pampered on occasion, Tucson has plenty of limousine services—about two dozen. They'll drive you in everything from town cars to Hummers, and some also have vans and minicoaches. The more vehicle and the more amenities you desire, the more it will cost. Some have special rates to and from the Tucson and Phoenix airports. Check the phone book's Yellow Pages under "Limousine" for all the options, but here are a few: **A&A Limousine Service** (520-795-2175), **Tucson Town Cars** (520-884-5997), and **Sunset Limousine** (520-573-9418).

HISTORY

As the oldest continually inhabited region in the Northern Hemisphere, Tucson (pronounced *TOO-sahn*) has been home to an astounding variety of cultures and peoples dating back as early as the first century A.D. The name Tucson is actually a derivation of the Tohono O'odham word *stjukshon* (pronounced *chuk-son*) that translates literally as "spring at the foot of dark mountain" and referred to the Tohono O'odham's original settlement at the foot of the volcanic mountain Sentinel Peak. This area, inhabited for an estimated 3,000 years, is considered the city's birthplace.

Today Tucson is a unique blend of old and new, a city that embraces its diverse cultural heritage and cherishes its natural wonders. Here is a brief look into its fascinating past.

EARLY TUCSONANS

In 1997 archaeologists uncovered the largest Southwest settlement of the Late Archaic period along the Santa Cruz River. The settlement dated back to the Cienega phase (800 B.C. to A.D. 150). The Cienega were farmers in a time dominated by nomadic hunters and gatherers. They grew corn, beans, squash, and tobacco. They traded with others throughout the Southwest for shells and other trinkets that they used in making jewelry. The settlement's 171 pit dwellings, storehouses, and communal structures are believed to have been occupied between 760 and 200 B.C., several centuries before the better-known Mogollon, Anasazi, and Hohokam cultures.

The Hohokam occupied an area along the Santa Cruz River (known then as the Rio de Santa Maria) near what is now downtown Tucson from A.D. 600 to 1450. They irrigated and farmed the area for 700 years. The Hohokam were a dominant culture in the Southwest and built 200 miles of canals around Phoenix to irrigate their crops. They also settled the Tucson area's riverbanks. *Hohokam* is a Tohono O'odham word meaning "those who have vanished," and anthropologists still debate the reason for their disappearance. Some have suggested that the Hohokam may have been the ancestors of the Tohono O'odham, who currently live in the area.

Other Native American tribes followed the Hohokam into the area, settling along the Santa Cruz River and farming the valley. The Tohono O'odham clustered at the foot of Sentinel Peak (now known as "A" Mountain, named for the large whitewashed "A" on its flank that represents the University of Arizona).

SPANISH DISCOVERY

When Jesuit Padre Eusebio Francisco Kino, "the Priest on Horseback," who served as a missionary for the Catholic Church in Spain, arrived in the area from Mexico in 1692, the Tohono O'odham were thriving in a village at the base of Sentinel Peak, farming the fertile valley of the then-flowing Santa Cruz River. Kino, an explorer, cartographer, and scientist, established a mission in the valley. He taught agricultural techniques and introduced Christianity to the Tohono O'odham people.

Father Kino established a number of missions in the Southwest, including Mission San Jose de Tumacacori, south of Tucson near Tubac, and San Xavier del Bac, "the White Dove of the Desert," located 19 miles south of what is now downtown. San Xavier still stands today (see the Attractions chapter). A statue honoring Kino on horseback now graces Kino Boulevard near the Lewis C. Murphy Overpass in Tucson. Duplicate statues stand in the Mexican city and state of

Magdalena and Sonora, and in Italy, which was Kino's homeland.

Amateur archaeologists can experience early Tucson firsthand through the programs at Old Pueblo Archaeology Center. You can volunteer to work on an active excavation, participate in hands-on workshops on pottery and arrowhead making, and help this worthy organization foster the preservation of archaeological and historical sites around town. More information is available at (520) 798-1201 or www.oldpueblo.org.

Present-day Tucson was officially founded on August 20, 1775, when Hugo O'Conor, an Irishman who served in the Spanish army, established the walled Presidio de San Agustin in what is now downtown Tucson. Plans for the presidio included a 12-foot adobe wall for defense against the Apaches. Construction was slow going: By November 1779, the walls were only 4 feet tall.

The walls didn't discourage neighboring Apaches, who launched several attacks on the presidio in the ensuing years. With their failure, however, the Apaches and the Spanish settlers formed a peace that would last until the 1830s.

The Spanish army completed the presidio in 1783. It consisted of a walled garden and more than 20 buildings, including a two-story convent, a chapel, barracks for soldiers, stables, and a granary. The presidio covered about 12 acres and included the area outlined by modern-day Church Street on the east, Washington Street on the north, Main Avenue on the west, and Pennington Street on the south—basically the heart of today's downtown business district. Some historians believe it's the only walled city in our nation's history, and it's from this structure that Tucson gets its nickname, "the Old Pueblo."

MEXICAN RULE

Spain's claim to Tucson ended in 1821 when Mexico gained its independence. For the 65 European settlers in the presidio, it only meant changing their flag—life went on as usual. Farming, sheep and cattle ranching, and trapping in the mountains continued with limited contact with the outside world. What did change was residential development outside the walls of the presidio. Lacking a seaport for the transportation of goods in the early 1800s, the area depended on the Mexican port of Guaymas some 300 miles to the south, from which goods were transported by wagon, creating a new business for "freighters" in the Old Pueblo.

A UNITED STATES TERRITORY

Tucson gained its rough-and-tumble reputation during the early part of the nineteenth century. When the United States signed the Gadsden Purchase in 1853, some 30,000 square miles of Arizona and the Southwest became part of the New Mexico Territory and thus part of the United States. But Tucson remained a Mexican garrison until March 1856, when the Mexican army packed up and left. It wasn't until November that U.S. dragoons rode into town and raised the U.S. flag atop the Miles Mercantile Store. For the next few years, Anglos and American goods began arriving in the area. This was the start of a long and rich cultural mix that thrives today.

In 1858 the Butterfield Overland Route brought the first stagecoaches to Tucson, making it one of 16 stations in Arizona. By 1860 the city's non-Indian population had grown to more than 600, but many were rough characters who had been chased out of California. Tucson quickly gained a reputation as a lawless Western town. Street fights were daily events, and most people carried weapons. Because there was no jail, a plaza whipping post was established to dish out punishment.

Be sure to visit the replica of Tucson's original adobe-walled fortress, the Presidio Wall, on the corner of North Church and West Washington Streets. The site includes a 20-foot-tall lookout tower (*torreón*) and 10-foot-high adjoining walls. There's a tiny museum inside with interpretive information, displays, and artifacts.

A mural on the wall of the presidio museum depicts Tucson's colorful past. PHOTO BY KATE REYNOLDS

The outbreak of the Civil War called Federal troops back East from all over the frontier. Their departure left the settlers defenseless against the Apaches, who had resumed their attacks in the 1830s. Tucson, surrounded by its adobe walls, became one of a few territorial refuges for miners and ranchers in the area. Citizens didn't seem too particular about which side—the Union or the Confederacy—provided protection. When 200 mounted Confederate soldiers arrived from Texas in February 1862, Tucsonans greeted them happily. Soon word came that 2,000 California volunteers would arrive from Yuma, so the Texans retreated home. On May 20, 1862, Union Col. Joseph R. West took possession of Tucson with nary a protest from anyone.

By the time President Lincoln gave Arizona territorial status in 1863 and named Prescott the capital, Tucson's reputation for gambling, prostitution, and filthy streets was common reading in Eastern newspapers. But despite the lawlessness, Tucson had garnered enough political clout by 1867 to force a vote to change the territorial capital from Prescott to Tucson. The Old Pueblo was the capital for 10 years until the power of northern mining interests helped return the title to Prescott.

i **Follow the turquoise line, also known as the Presidio Trail, for a fascinating journey back in time. The self-guided walking tour takes you through downtown Tucson to all major historic landmarks. Grab a free map from the visitor center at La Placita, or download a copy at www.tucsonpresidiotrust.org. The map is chock-full of fascinating information about Tucson's early days.**

During this decade Tucson fast became a genuine "city" and a bustling business and transportation crossroads. The population in 1869 was 3,200. By 1872 a public school had been built. Tucson had two flour mills, four livery stables, and two hotels. Other businesses that thrived included two breweries and numerous saloons. Roulette wheels spun 24 hours a day until 1905.

Just before Tucson became the "Sodom of the Southwest," a new arrival brought some much-anticipated civilization. The first Southern Pacific Railroad train arrived in March 1880. Now goods from the East could be brought in faster and cheaper. Construction materials were a big item, and Tucson's architecture took on the look of sophisticated homes back East. Adobe was no longer the material of choice. You can still see some of these homes today near and around the railroad tracks. Home tours in these historic neighborhoods take place every spring (see the Festivals and Events and Attractions chapters).

The railroad brought other touches of civilization. All kinds of new folks moved in. That same year (1880) also brought the area's first hospital. The Sisters of St. Joseph de Carondelet established St. Mary's Hospital and Sanitarium. A modern St. Mary's Hospital exists today, not far from the site of the original.

The influx of white settlers led to intensified attacks on the surrounding area by the Apaches. U.S. troops constructed Fort Lowell to protect Tucson and nearby ranchers. The raids ended in 1886 when Geronimo, the last great Apache leader, surrendered. The fort was deactivated in 1891. Remnants still stand in Fort Lowell Park in what is now central Tucson. The "fort" is listed on the National Register of Historic Places.

The city's first telephone rang in 1881, and gas-operated streetlights were turned on for the first time in Tucson on March 20, 1882. Suddenly Tucson was a bit less "Wild West." Ironically, that same night Wyatt Earp, avenging his brother Morgan's death in Tombstone earlier that week, shot and killed Frank Stilwell at the Tucson railroad station. Another modern innovation sprang up in 1882: water pipes! Citizens wondered: What could be next?

BUILDING A UNIVERSITY

In 1885 the Thirteenth Territorial Legislature granted Tucson $25,000 to establish a university—the first in a territory that had no high schools. Politicians believed the university would bring economic benefits, but their other purpose was to appease Tucsonans for moving the capital to Prescott. But locals were still more interested in becoming the territorial capital, and, after all, a university might have a negative influence on the city's gambling.

i In 1870 Tucson was the Territorial Capital with 3,224 people. The capitol building was a dirt-floored series of rooms on Ochoa Street, just off Stone Avenue. The population of Pima County was 5,716.

The story of how all this came about is legendary in Arizona. The city's territorial legislators left for Prescott to force a vote to return the capital to Tucson. But in an unfortunate chain of events, inclement weather delayed them. When the legislators finally arrived, they found that a vote had already been held and Prescott had already won. Tucson was tossed money for a university as a consolation prize. This did not go over well with the locals. When the delegates returned to Tucson, they were pelted with rotten fruit and vegetables.

The city fathers convinced a pair of wealthy gamblers and a saloon owner to donate land for the university, which they did—with a catch. The school had to be situated as far away from downtown gambling saloons as possible—to keep any high-minded influences away from the gamblers. The chosen spot was 3 miles across the desert. In 1891 "Old Main," as it's known today, opened its doors to 32 students and 6 faculty members. Today more than 34,000 students are enrolled at the University of Arizona, and the campus, once in the middle of the desert, now lies in the heart of the city.

A NEW ERA AND A NEW STATE

By 1886 Geronimo and his band of renegade Chiricahua Apaches had been exiled to Florida, ending the official Indian Wars (of almost 30 years) with the "Blue Coats" in this part of the West. That was the beginning of the demise of "Wild West" Tucson. In 1896 the first mule-driven streetcars started running, and the following year the first "horseless carriage" sputtered down the dirt streets. By 1906 the mules were replaced with electric streetcars, making a 3-mile loop from downtown to the university.

On a territorial level, Arizona's battle for statehood was driven by lawmakers in the capital, which was finally relocated to Phoenix in 1889. The battle ended on February 14, 1912, when President Taft made Arizona the 48th state. Tucson's population at the time was 13,125.

Along with the new status in the country came a new frontier—flight. Aviation came to Tucson on February 17, 1910, when barnstorming pilot Charles Hamilton flew his biplane a mere 900 feet above the ground to thrill spectators. In 1915 Katharine Stinson, a 19-year-old daredevil pilot, delivered the first airmail to the city. But these were just tastes of what was to come. The aviation age formally arrived in Tucson when the city built the nation's first municipal airport in 1919. In 1927 Charles Lindbergh dedicated the Davis-Monthan Field, which had evolved from that early aviation effort. By the 1930s the U.S. Army Air Corps was using Davis-Monthan Field; they finally took it over completely in 1940. With a state charter and the generosity of 25 local businessmen (each pitched in a $1,000 loan), the Tucson Airport Authority was established in 1948 to operate the municipal airport. TAA still oversees all operations at Tucson International Airport.

By 1920 the city's population had grown to 20,292, and the first of many resort hotels had been built to draw Easterners to Arizona's warm, dry climate. Many came to these elaborate resorts hoping that the climate would cure tuberculosis. In 1931 gasoline-powered buses replaced the electric trolley cars, just like a "real" city.

Hollywood discovered Tucson in 1939, when movie producers built what became Old Tucson Studios as a set for the epic movie *Arizona* (see the Attractions chapter). Since then, hundreds of movies, television shows, and commercials have been made in and around town.

Tucson's population boomed during World War II with the many people who were seeking military employment at Davis-Monthan Field, which had become a military base for training pilots to fly B-17 bombers. After the war, when Davis-Monthan Field became a U.S. Air Force base, it continued providing employment opportunities, both military and civilian (see the chapter on Davis-Monthan Air Force Base).

By 1950 the population was 55,454 in the city and 118,034 in the metropolitan area. The increase in population is attributed to the return of many servicemen and their families to Tucson after the war, as well as the advent of air-conditioning. In the 1960s and 1970s the city focused on developing the arts. In 1967 the Arizona Theatre Company was founded here as the state's only professional resident theater company. The state's only opera company, the Arizona Opera Company, was founded in 1972 and based in Tucson. Three years later the new Tucson Museum of Art was built near the original presidio in downtown Tucson.

During the 1980s high-tech businesses began moving to Tucson, led by aviation-related companies. The metropolitan area's population grew a whopping 22.6 percent to 431,988 in 1993. During this period Madison Avenue advertising agencies began using the saguaro-studded desert to sell everything from cars to beer to jeans to credit cards. The constant romantic image of the West in print and TV ads spurred growth in Arizona's population as many Easterners left their homes to discover the new "promised land."

Tucson is a thriving, ever-expanding city with major military, optic, and hospitality industries keeping the economy strong. Its perfect climate, fascinating history, and incredible desert and mountain landscape keep people visiting and relocating here, making it one of the fastest-growing urban areas in the country. Tucson offers a unique combination of sleepy '50s town and bustling metropolis. With the University of Arizona, several symphonies, dance companies and theaters, spectator sports like baseball's spring training and international bicycling tours in town, along with a huge number of award-winning restaurants, Tucsonans have the best of all worlds.

ACCOMMODATIONS

You'll find just about every kind of place to stay in Tucson—gorgeous mansions, antique adobes, quaint bed-and-breakfasts, luxury spas and resort hotels, and even some old-fashioned dude ranches. Whatever your pleasure, you'll find it here. When making your travel plans, keep in mind that peak season here is between October and April, when the weather is magnificent. February is a particularly popular month with several major conventions in town, so be sure to make reservations well in advance. Summer (May through September) brings some of the best rates and some of the hottest weather.

Visitors who wish to be pampered have a choice of several resorts and spas. You'll pay handsomely for facilities that offer a totally upscale experience, but many feel it's worth the extra cost (most of the resorts do offer fantastic summer rates). Noted for their "elite status" among resorts and spas are Canyon Ranch, Miraval, Starr Pass Marriott, Loews Ventana Canyon Resort, Westward Look Resort, and many more. You may even spot a famous person or two during your stay.

Many Tucson lodgings follow the two-room guest-suite trend geared toward business and family travelers. These accommodations typically have a separate bedroom and living room with a kitchen and two televisions. A continental breakfast is often included (we'll try and let you know which places offer this most welcome amenity). Please note, when we use the word spa at a hotel, we are talking about whirlpools, hot tubs, and the like—as opposed to the spa services you can get at several of the resorts.

For those who prefer to stay at a bed-and-breakfast, we have a separate section in this chapter. Many of the local bed-and-breakfasts are in historic neighborhoods, and the houses' histories are as interesting and colorful. Several others are found on the perimeter of town, surrounded by the desert. Whichever you might choose, be assured that the owners will be able to tell you all about the history of their home and the surrounding area.

If you want an experience a bit more like staying with a large group of friends without the "hotel" atmosphere, a guest ranch may be what you are looking for. Some offer true "cowboy" adventures, with horseback riding and cookouts. Others are more like summer camp, with swimming, tennis, volleyball, and horseshoe tossing, but, unlike camp, offer plenty of pampering. Some ranches have rooms with individual kitchens and telephones, while others offer only the basics for those wanting to escape material trappings.

Most establishments offer the choice of smoking or nonsmoking accommodations as well as rooms that are wheelchair accessible. We've tried our best to note when an accommodation is not the norm. However, we suggest that if you have special needs or requests, you convey them to the accommodation when making your reservations.

We'll note a local number, a toll-free reservation telephone number when available, and a price range symbol (see Price Guidelines).

Price Guidelines

The following price codes indicate the cost of a one-night, double-occupancy stay during peak season. While peak season usually runs from October to April, February brings the highest rates due to all the events that are happening during that month. The price guidelines are therefore most applicable for this very busy month. Rates can be considerably lower during all other months and if you book well ahead of time. The codes do not include a hotel/motel tax within the city limits or a hotel/motel tax in Pima County. Virtually everyone accepts credit cards (we only note the ones that do not), but pets are another story, so it is best to call.

$.................... $76–$115
$$ .... $116–$145
$$$ .... $146–$175
$$$$ .... $176–$215
$$$$$......... more than $215

HOTELS AND MOTELS

Tucson is home to numerous hotels and motels, from small cozy inns, suite hotels, and luxury penthouses to standard motels, and you'll find most major chains here. Most offer free continental-style breakfasts, a morning paper, and a variety of amenities, from heated pools and spas to tennis courts.

BEST WESTERN INN AT THE AIRPORT $$$$
7060 South Tucson Boulevard
(520) 746-0271, (800) 528-1234
www.bestwestern.com

This is the closest hotel to Tucson International Airport (you can watch planes coming and going from the pool), with 149 rooms, free cable, free Wi-Fi, heated pool, spa, and 24-hour exercise facility. A perk for the business traveler: The hotel can arrange for audio, video, and computer equipment in its conference suites. You're also just minutes from spring training and the Pima Air and Space Museum.

BEST WESTERN INNSUITES HOTEL & SUITES $$$$
6201 North Oracle Road
(520) 818-9500, (800) 554-4535
www.bestwestern.com

Located 5 miles east off Interstate 10 at the Orange Grove Road exit in the near northwest side of town, this facility offers 159 one- or two-room suites with refrigerator, microwave oven, coffeemaker, hair dryer, free Wi-Fi, and free HBO. The larger suites have a kitchenette and separate living room, which is ideal for extended stays. Included in the price are a complimentary full breakfast, morning newspaper, and an afternoon social hour at the poolside cafe. You can also enjoy the pool and spa area, two lighted tennis courts, and the fitness center.

BEST WESTERN ROYAL SUN INN & SUITES $$$$$
1015 North Stone Avenue
(520) 622-8871, (800) 545-8858
www.bestwestern.com

Centrally located, this hotel has 79 rooms, including 20 suites with whirlpool tubs. All rooms feature a coffee/tea maker, hair dryer, iron, ironing board, vanity mirror, refrigerator, 27-inch television, DVD player, and high-speed Internet access. Additional amenities include a fitness center, outdoor heated pool and spa, and a full-service restaurant and lounge. Complimentary full, hot breakfast and two-for-one drink specials are offered to hotel guests only.

CLARION HOTEL TUCSON AIRPORT $$$$
6801 South Tucson Boulevard
(520) 746-3932, (800) 526-0550
www.clarionhotel.com

A half mile from the airport, the hotel's 194 units include cable TV, direct-dial phones, and refrigerators. Also available are a heated pool, spa, coin laundry, fitness center, continental breakfast, and complimentary beverages in the evening. The hotel offers transfers to the airport. The dining room offers three meals a day; you'll find some of the city's better hotel dining here.

COMFORT INN SUITES **$$$**
7007 East Tanque Verde Road
(520) 298-2300, (800) 527-1133
www.comfortsuites.com
About half of the 90 rooms here are studio suites, with a microwave oven, refrigerator, king-size bed or two double beds, sleeper sofa, cable with HBO, free Wi-Fi, and free local calls. Each stay includes a complimentary breakfast bar and weekday social hour. You can hang out at the pool or relax in the outdoor spa. Located in the heart of the Eastside Restaurant Row, you have your choice of dining—everything from New Southwest and steaks to a flurry of chain restaurants. For those with business on their minds, this hotel offers a 750-square-foot meeting room that can hold up to 45 people, voice mail and dataport lines, and a free newspaper delivered to your door Monday through Friday.

COUNTRY INN & SUITES BY CARLSON **$$**
7411 North Oracle Road
(520) 575-9255, (800) 456-4000
www.countryinns.com
Most of the 91 suites and 65 studios have kitchenettes. Suites feature king- or queen-size beds. The hotel also has a putting green, pool, whirlpool, and a courtyard for relaxing. On Tuesday enjoy a poolside cookout. Every morning you can expect a free continental breakfast and weekday newspaper. This hotel offers free Wi-Fi.

COURTYARD BY MARRIOTT AIRPORT **$$$$**
2505 East Executive Drive
(520) 573-0000, (800) 321-2211
www.marriott.com
These freshly renovated 149 rooms and suites offer everything you'll need when not lounging by the landscaped courtyard and pool or in the lovely new lobby. A spa, fitness room, laundry rooms, restaurant, and lounge are all on-site. Courtyard has an airport shuttle and two conference rooms that can accommodate up to 40 people each. The on-site business center offers free Wi-Fi.

COURTYARD BY MARRIOTT—WILLIAMS CENTER **$$$$**
201 South Williams Boulevard
(520) 745-6000, (800) 321-2211
www.marriott.com
This midtown spot is right across the street from the busy Williams Center business complex. It's also located right in the heart of town, so families and nonbusiness travelers can easily get to all the attractions with a minimum of fuss. You'll find new rooms (this is one of Marriott's latest additions to Tucson's lodging scene), a pool, a spa, an exercise area, and an in-house breakfast area. You'll also find plenty of other good eats just minutes away (you may not even need to use your car), and getting downtown is just a matter of catching Broadway Boulevard a half block away and heading west for about five minutes.

DAYS INN **$$$**
222 South Freeway
(520) 791-7511, (800) 329-7466
www.daysinn.com
Just off I-10 west of downtown Tucson, this inexpensive facility has 122 rooms and offers guests a free continental breakfast, large pool, laundry, one meeting room for up to 55 people, and another that can hold 950 guests. Days Inn offers a number of discounts to government, military, and AARP members.

i **Beautiful Rex Ranch, situated 30 minutes south of Tucson, offers a perfect wedding setting for that special day. Parties up to 50 people can enjoy the fine dining, spa, and accommodations at this remote guest ranch. There's even an online wedding planner. Visit www.RexRanch.com or call (800) 547-2696 for details.**

DESERT DIAMOND HOTEL AND CASINO **$$$$$**
7350 South Nogales Highway
(520) 294-7777
www.desertdiamondcasino.com
If you like high-tech hotels, then the Desert Dia-

mond is for you. Everything is state-of-the-art, high-end luxury, and you're only steps away from a casino, gift shop, several restaurants, and the Monsoon nightclub. The hotel, freshly opened in late 2007, is owned, operated, and governed by the Tohono O'odham nation. Each of the spacious 149 rooms and suites is tastefully appointed, with your choice of king- or two queen-size beds. You'll find an in-room safe and refrigerator, a desk, a flat-screen plasma TV (the executive suites have 42-inch TVs and a wet bar). The casino operates several restaurants, including one 24-hour grill and a steakhouse that serves top-of-the-line beef. Meeting space is plentiful, with various screens and flexible divisions, all changeable by the flick of a finger. Outside, you can play in the moon-shaped pool, relax in the oversize Jacuzzi, or sit by the fire pit on cool evenings. The hotel and casino are located about a mile from the airport, so it's easy to get in and out. One more bonus—you won't pay any taxes here. The price you see is what you pay.

DOUBLETREE HOTEL **$$$$$**
445 South Alvernon Way
(520) 881-4200, (800) 222-8733
www.doubletreehotels.com

This 10-story, 295-room hotel recently underwent a $10 million refurbishing and now sports new landscaping, new bathrooms, and lots of meeting rooms. It is centrally located to attractions, shopping, the university, and business districts and is across the street from Del Urich and Randolph Park Golf Courses, as well as beautiful Reid Park, where you'll find plenty to do (see the Parks and Recreation chapter). You also get freshly baked chocolate chip cookies upon arrival! The resort-style hotel has three tennis courts, a pool, a spa, two restaurants, a lounge, and a refurbished fitness center.

For business travelers, rooms for meetings and banquets can accommodate between 10 and 1,200 people.

EMBASSY SUITES HOTEL BROADWAY **$$$$$**
5335 East Broadway Boulevard
(520) 745-2700, (800) 362-2779
www.embassysuites.com

Each of Embassy Suites' 142 newly upgraded suites has a private bedroom and separate living room with sleeper sofa, kitchen, microwave, refrigerator, and coffeemaker. Two telephones with dataports and voice mail, as well as in-room movies on two TVs, help you keep in touch with the outside world. A complimentary beverage and cooked-to-order breakfast are included. The lounge offers billiards and a big-screen TV for the times you're not enjoying the outdoor pool, spa, or fitness center. Among the business services is free transportation within 5 miles of the hotel, which includes the University of Arizona and Davis-Monthan Air Force Base.

i Take the family out for an evening of stargazing at Loews Ventana Canyon Ranch. The free programs, offered year-round on Wednesday and Saturday nights, are open to the public. A University of Arizona astronomer is there to help. Times vary, so call ahead (520-299-2020). Ask for the concierge.

EMBASSY SUITES TUCSON—PALOMA VILLAGE **$$$$**
3110 East Skyline Drive
(520) 352-4000
www.embassysuites.com

This 119-room all-suite hotel, opened in 2007, is especially appealing to families, golfers, and business travelers. All suites feature either a king- or two queen-size beds and a 32-inch plasma TV. Each morning you'll eat a cooked-to-order breakfast inside or on a patio with a lovely mountain view. A coin laundry, ATM, and high-speed Internet access are among the features you'll enjoy when not working out in the state-of-the-art fitness center or relaxing by the heated pool. Lots of restaurants are close by, and many golf courses are also easily reached. Four meeting rooms are available; the largest can accommodate 150 people. Outdoor event space and catering are available.

EXTENDED STAYAMERICA **$**
5050 East Grant Road

(520) 795-9510, (800) EXT-STAY (398-7829)
www.extstay.com
This midtown motel is ideal for business travelers or those looking for a no-frills long-term stay. Located across the street from Tucson Medical Center, each room has free local phone calls and voice mail, cable TV, a full kitchen complete with utensils, and access to wireless Internet for a small fee. Fax and mail delivery are perks for the business traveler. Laundry facilities are also available. You have your choice of one queen bed, one king bed, or two double beds. Although there isn't a restaurant on-site, you'll find a great choice of restaurants literally minutes away.

FOUR POINTS BY SHERATON TUCSON UNIVERSITY PLAZA $$$$
1900 East Speedway Boulevard
(520) 327-7341, (800) 843-8052
www.fourpoints.com
Located at the busy intersection of Speedway Boulevard and Campbell Avenue, across from the University of Arizona and down the street from the University Medical Center. You'll find 150 rooms, a pool, spa, a dining room that serves breakfast and lunch, a lounge with a big-screen TV, underground parking, room service, and a variety of convention and banquet services.

HAMPTON INN $$$$
6971 South Tucson Boulevard
(520) 889-5789, (800) HAMPTON (426-7866)
www.hamptoninn.com
With 126 rooms, Hampton Inn also offers suites with a separate bedroom and living room, as well as your choice of executive suites, studios, and standard rooms. All rooms have coffeemakers, hair dryers, and irons and ironing boards for those last-minute touch-ups before your big meeting.

Enjoy the heated pool, spa, in-room movies and cable on the 25-inch TVs, complimentary morning paper, and hot breakfast. The hotel also offers an airport shuttle, and laundry valet services. The businessperson can take advantage of the business center, in-room voice mail, and high-speed Internet access.

HAMPTON INN & SUITES $$$$$
5950 North Oracle Road
(520) 618-8000, (800) HAMPTON (426-7866)
www.hamptoninn.com
Choice is the word when you stay at this near northwest hotel. You have a choice of a king suite, a king room, or a guest room (where you can choose two double beds if that's more to your liking). Some suites include a full kitchen (cooking utensils included) with a dining area and a separate living room.

Business travelers will be delighted with the free local calls and business center, high-speed and wireless Internet access, access to fax and photocopying equipment, a fitness center, evening cocktail hour Monday through Thursday, and meeting rooms. Families can take advantage of the swimming pool, the spa, free cable TV, guest laundry on premises, and the fact that kids younger than 18 stay free when accompanied by parents. In the morning, all can enjoy a complimentary continental breakfast.

HILTON GARDEN INN— TUCSON AIRPORT $$$$$
6575 South Country Club Road
(877) 219-5888
(520) 741-0505
http://hiltongardeninn.hilton.com
Opened in 2008, this three-story, 125-room hotel features the customary swimming pool, but this one is surrounded by a winding "river," where you can float on a raft, enjoying the ambience. Families will appreciate the convenience of a refrigerator, microwave oven, coffeemaker, LCD TV, and freshly prepared daily breakfast. Businesspeople will find a business center, meeting rooms with outdoor terrace, high-speed Internet access, and secure remote printer. There's an on-site fitness center and evening room service to round out the package.

HOLIDAY INN EXPRESS $$$$
2548 East Medina Road
(520) 889-6600, (800) 315-2621
www.hiexpress.com
Conveniently located near the airport, this three-story hotel has 98 rooms with free high-speed

Internet, hair dryer, iron and ironing board, voice mail, speaker phone, coffeemaker, pay-per-view movies, and cable TV. Your room comes with a complimentary newspaper, and you get freshly baked cookies daily. A free buffet breakfast bar is available every morning. The hotel also has a business center, which may be rented as a meeting room for an additional charge and can accommodate 10 people. It includes a computer with free high-speed Internet access, color printer, projector, and dry-erase board. Those of you with furry friends will be pleased to know that pets are allowed with a $50 refundable deposit.

HOLIDAY INN—PALO VERDE **$$$$**
4550 South Palo Verde Road
(520) 746-1161, (800) 315-2621
www.holiday-inn.com

This six-story Holiday Inn near the airport has 301 guest rooms with 53 suites, easy access to most parts of town, and a complimentary shuttle within a 5-mile radius of the hotel. Unlike at other places in town, no continental breakfast is served, but a full-service menu is offered at the in-house restaurant, where kids eat free. Plus you can enjoy a drink or two in the bar. You'll also find a pool, a whirlpool, and a 24-hour fitness center.

Both regular rooms and suites are available. The suites come with a kitchenette, and all rooms have an ironing board, iron, and hair dryer. This is a favorite for many local groups for business or family gatherings thanks to several meeting rooms. You'll also see plenty of military folks, as this hotel is just a few minutes from Davis-Monthan Air Force Base.

HOTEL ARIZONA **$$$$$**
181 West Broadway Boulevard
(520) 624-8711, (800) 845-4596
www.thehotelaz.com

In the center of downtown Tucson, this newly freshened 307-room complex hosts a number of major convention events while still offering individual travelers a homey experience. A heated pool, fitness center, and restaurant are within this high-rise (you'll get some of the greatest views of the city in the topmost floors). The hotel has lots of flexible meeting space, enough for 21 rooms. The Tucson Convention Center is just across the street, as are local, state, and federal government buildings. The Arts District is just a short walk away.

HOTEL CONGRESS **$**
311 East Congress Street
(520) 622-8848, (800) 722-8848
www.hotelcongress.com

Established in 1919, this brick-and-marble building was constructed to provide accommodations to Southern Pacific Railroad passengers traveling through Tucson. Its 40 rooms on the second floor overlook the Downtown Arts District.

One of the many colorful stories about the hotel involves the infamous John Dillinger gang, which was captured here in 1934. Today the hotel's first floor caters to Tucson's artists and writers with The Cup cafe (see the Restaurants chapter) and the locally popular Club Congress, featuring live bands and disc jockeys (see the Nightlife chapter). The rooms were restored in 1985, retaining the original 1920s-era charm. This is not just a historic hotel—it's an experience.

Hotel Congress is in the heart of downtown and also operates a youth hostel.

HYATT PLACE **$$$$**
6885 Tucson Boulevard
(520) 295-0405, (888) 492-8847
www.tucsonairport.place.hyatt.com

If you need to stay near the airport during your visit, this suite hotel is conveniently located right at Tucson International Airport. There are 120 suites, with valet service, complimentary airport shuttle, 42-inch flat-screen TV, complimentary Wi-Fi, refrigerator, wet bar, and coffeemaker. What more could you need?

INN SUITES—TUCSON CITY CENTER **$**
475 North Granada Avenue
(520) 622-3000
www.innsuites.com

You can get just about anywhere easily from this downtown-area hotel, located just off the I-10 Broadway exit. You'll have your choice of room styles here. You can pick a studio with either a king bed or two queens; an executive/family suite with a choice of beds, a sleeper sofa, and a separate living room; or pop for the Presidential Suite with its large spa and extra space. All suites have a microwave, a refrigerator (with complimentary water), and a coffeemaker (with tea or coffee). You can get pretty, too, with the in-room hair dryer. You'll also find free Wi-Fi and a complimentary breakfast and social hour.

This hotel has some of the larger meeting rooms in town. With 13 in all, you can hold everything from a huge wedding in the ballroom (capacity 1,500 people) to a class in one of the smaller facility rooms.

LA POSADA LODGE & CASITAS **$$**
5900 North Oracle Road
(520) 887-4800, (800) 810-2808
www.laposadalodge.com

This three-story adobe-style hotel with teal doors is conveniently located right on busy Oracle Road. All rooms face a serene landscaped inner courtyard with gated pool and spa. The lodge offers 60 deluxe guest rooms in the main lodge and 12 courtyard casitas. The rooms are decorated in various styles, from funky pastel with Jetsons' chairs and lava lamps to sophisticated Southwestern. Eight of the private casitas have front and back patios. Each guest room has a coffeemaker and coffee, hair dryer, iron and ironing board, satellite TV, work desk, and free Wi-Fi. Open-air walkways connect all the floors, along with an elevator. The hotel also features an on-site day spa and the upscale Miguel's restaurant (see the Restaurants chapter).

LA QUINTA INN AND SUITES **$$$**
7001 South Tucson Boulevard
(520) 573-3333, (800) 531-5900
www.laquinta.com

Located one block from the airport, this facility offers 143 rooms and 8 two-room suites with separate sitting and sleeping areas, double vanities, microwave, refrigerator, desk, and speaker phones. All rooms have computer-friendly dataport phones and free Wi-Fi to make your business travel easy. You can also take advantage of the heated swimming pool, spa, exercise facility, meeting rooms for up to 75 people, guest laundry, and same-day dry-cleaning service. The complimentary continental breakfast offers a choice of cereals, fruit, pastries, bagels, and juices.

One nice extra: If you pay for just one night's weekday rate, you can leave your automobile at the hotel for up to seven nights for free (the hotel will transport you to the airport).

MARRIOTT RESIDENCE INN **$$$**
6477 East Speedway Boulevard
(520) 721-0991, (800) 331-3131
www.marriot.com/tusaz

Ideal for those who plan to be here for just a little longer, this modern accommodation offers your choice of 128 suites—studio suites have queen beds and sleeper sofas; the Penthouse Suites have a loft, a Murphy bed, and sleeper sofas. Some have fireplaces.

Both a complimentary buffet breakfast and social hour are part of your stay. Other perks include local restaurant dinner delivery and an on-site fitness center. You can also enjoy the Monday-through-Thursday evening barbecues (in season); the outdoor pool and spa; a sport court ideal for volleyball, basketball, or other sports; and an on-site inexpensive laundry room (one-day dry-cleaning service is also available). Pets are welcome for an additional fee.

And while there isn't a restaurant on-site, you're just minutes from the Eastside Restaurant Row and its plethora of dining choices.

MARRIOTT UNIVERSITY PARK **$$$$$**
880 East Second Street
(520) 792-4100, (800) 228-9290
www.marriotthotels.com/tusup

This nine-story atrium hotel, which features 250 newly upgraded guest rooms and several suites, is near the main gate of the University of Arizona, on the corner of Tyndall Avenue and Second Street. The hotel also has a concierge floor, for those who may need a haven during the relocation process. All rooms are specially equipped with high-speed Internet, workspaces, and voice mail. The Saguaro Grill is in the atrium, and the hotel also has an outdoor pool, whirlpool, sauna, and fitness center. It's just seconds from restaurants and shopping. The Marriott is a perfect choice for parents visiting their young scholars at the university.

PALO VERDE INN SUITES **$**
5251 South Julian Drive
(520) 294-5250, (800) 997-5470
www.starboundinn.com
Just off the I-10 exit at Palo Verde Road, these 153 rooms and 20 two-room suites are just minutes from Tucson International Airport (ask about the hotel's shuttle service) and include a coffeemaker and free Showtime. The comfortable mezzanine overlooks the swimming pool area, where you can enjoy an evening cocktail and meal at the lounge or the restaurant. You'll appreciate the complimentary hot breakfast. There are also four separate courtyards, each with its own heated spa.

QUALITY INN **$$$$**
1365 West Grant Road
(520) 622-7791, (866) 285-3281
www.qualityinn.com
This hotel is conveniently located just off I-10 at the Grant Road exit, making it accessible to downtown, the Arizona-Sonora Desert Museum, Old Tucson Studios, and just about any other attraction in town. A large separate building on the grounds is the site for yearly trade shows.

Guests will welcome the heated pool and spa, in-room coffeemakers, laundry, the deluxe breakfasts, and the free Wi-Fi and airport shuttle. The restaurant and bar are great places to gather after a long, hard day of whatever you've been doing.

QUALITY INN AIRPORT **$$$$**
2803 East Valencia Road
(520) 294-2500, (800) 424-6423
www.qualityinn.com
A 95-room facility just blocks from the airport, Quality Inn offers all the usual amenities, such as a heated outdoor pool and spa, free airport shuttle, free high-speed Internet, cable TV and in-room movies, and a complimentary deluxe breakfast bar. Some suites are available, as are meeting rooms. You get a free newspaper on weekdays.

RADISSON SUITES TUCSON HOTEL **$$$$$**
6555 East Speedway Boulevard
(520) 721-7100, (800) 333-3333
www.radisson.com/suites_tucson
Each of these 304 two-room suites includes an extra-large bathroom, two vanities, two TVs, two telephones, a refrigerator, and a coffeemaker. Two Presidential Suites have fireplaces, dining rooms, and hydro tubs. On the grounds guests can use the oversize heated pool or fitness room. Meeting planners take note of the 14,000 square feet of meeting space.

RAMADA LIMITED **$$$**
665 North Freeway
(520) 622-6491, (800) 272-6232
www.ramada.com
Just off I-10 at St. Mary's Road near downtown, Ramada Limited offers in-room movies and video games, free high-speed Internet, same-day dry cleaning, guest laundry facilities, and a heated swimming pool. All of the 132 rooms have a microwave and refrigerator. The entire hotel underwent a total renovation in 2007. You'll find comfy new mattresses, new bathrooms, and an upgraded free deluxe breakfast, as well as meeting space.

SHERATON TUCSON HOTEL & SUITES **$$$$$**
5151 East Grant Road
(520) 323-6262, (800) 257-7275
www.sheraton.com
With 216 deluxe rooms—108 of which are suites—this is a midtown favorite. It's a great place to relax after a hard day of sightseeing or business meetings, thanks to the outdoor pool, steam room, spa, and sauna. You'll also find a fully equipped fitness center. Get a good night's rest on the Sheraton Sweet Sleeper beds. You can dine at the Garden Room or the Trophies sports bar on-site. Rooms also offer high-speed Internet access for a fee.

VARSITY CLUBS OF AMERICA **$**
3855 East Speedway Boulevard
(520) 318-3777, (800) 521-3131
www.ilxresorts.com

Located a short 2 miles east of the University of Arizona, this hotel is also just minutes from great golf and tennis, outstanding shopping, and many fine restaurants (the in-house restaurant, the Stadium Sports Grill, is filled with university Wildcat decorations). Offering luxury suites, the Tucson branch of Varsity Clubs of America is a favorite of alumni and many other visitors to the university. Spacious suites with full kitchens, a heated swimming pool, a workout center, and a business center are just a few of the amenities that attract visitors.

VISCOUNT SUITE HOTEL **$$**
4855 East Broadway Boulevard
(520) 745-6500, (800) 527-9666
www.viscountsuite.com
A favorite buffet lunch spot (even for nonguests), this four-story atrium hotel includes 216 elegant two-room suites with two TVs, two telephones, dataports, free wireless Internet, and a living room with a desk. The larger Presidential Suites include a refrigerator, microwave oven, two bedrooms, two baths, a bar, and big-screen TVs. Besides the complimentary breakfast buffet, the hotel has a pool, spa, restaurants, and laundry facilities. At the end of your day, enjoy a special guest happy hour.

WINDMILL INN AT ST. PHILIP'S PLAZA **$$**
4250 North Campbell Avenue
(520) 577-0007, (800) 547-4747
www.windmillinns.com
Windmill Inn at Campbell Avenue and River Road offers 122 two-room suites with a wet bar, microwave, desk, three phones, wireless Internet access, two remote-controlled TVs, and refrigerator. Each morning you'll awake to complimentary coffee, pastries, and a daily newspaper. The hotel also offers a free best-seller lending library, guest laundry facilities, meeting rooms for up to 300 people, and an outdoor pool and spa. Bicycles are provided so that guests can explore the nearby Rillito River Park. Stay here and you'll be near some taste-bud temptations: Look for Vivace and Acacia Restaurants in the adjacent St. Philip's Plaza (good shopping, too!).

GUEST RANCHES

A really unique way to experience Tucson is by staying at one of its guest ranches, some of which are still working cattle ranches. You can horseback ride, hike, bird-watch, take roping lessons, and even attend a rodeo at these restored luxury ranches.

C.O.D. RANCH **$$**
P.O. Box 241, Oracle, AZ 85623
(520) 615-3211, (800) 868-5617
www.codranch.com
Thirty-five miles north of Tucson at an elevation of 5,000 feet in the Coronado National Forest, C.O.D. Ranch offers a cool getaway from the city's heat and hustle. Juniper and mesquite trees fill the grounds and keep the casitas and rooms cool and comfortable.

Expert horse people will take you on your choice of trail rides, including everything from a short hour ride to a full-day trek complete with a cowboy cookout. All rates include breakfast, served on-site. Most casitas have queen-size beds and private bath.

Other activities include hiking in the surrounding forest, mountain biking, swimming in the heated pool, horseback riding, guided nature walks, wagon rides, and great bird-watching. You are also welcome to relax in the beautifully restored Main House, which was built in the late 1880s.

C.O.D. Ranch is a great place for a group outing; a wedding can be turned into a weekend event, with guests staying not just for the ceremony but for other planned activities as well. A two night minimum stay is required.

i For an up-to-the-minute list of U.S. dude ranches, head over to www.duderanch.org. A list of Arizona dude ranches can be found at www.azdra.com.

THE FLYING V RANCH **$**
6810 Flying V Ranch Road
(520) 299-0702, (520) 299-4372
www.flyingvranchtucson.com

The oldest continuously operating guest ranch in Tucson, this was once a working cattle ranch with over 250,000 acres. Most of the original property was sold to build the deluxe Loews Ventana Canyon Resort that now surrounds it. The current property exists on 70 of the original acres.

A dude ranch in the 1970s, the Flying V now offers accommodations in six fully self-contained picturesque cottages, several with kitchen facilities and all with heat and air-conditioning, a clock radio, local TV, telephone, and private porches and/or decks. The beautiful property is incredibly private and secluded despite its location. Old cottonwood and mesquite trees provide shade, fruit trees droop with grapefruit and oranges in season, and there is a lovely outdoor pool. No entertainment or meals are provided—this is a spot for introspection, quiet relaxation, and a taste of the Tucson that once was.

There's a minimum-stay requirement, so check the Web site. Credit cards are not accepted.

RANCHO DE LA OSA GUEST RANCH $$$$$
P.O. Box 1, Sasabe, AZ 85633
(520) 823-4257, (800) 872-6240
www.ranchodelaosa.com

Just north of the Mexican border about an hour southwest of Tucson, Rancho De La Osa ("ranch of the she bear") is a bit of a drive but well worth it. You'll pass through some amazing desert country before you discover this gem of a guest ranch with an amazing history: Father Eusebio Francisco Kino and his followers built an adobe mission outpost on the ranch, which is still standing and is reputed to be the second-oldest building in Arizona. Pancho Villa was said to have fired shots at the hacienda during the Mexican Revolution, and there's a cannon ball to prove it!

A guest ranch since the 1920s, there are only 21 rooms, lovingly and simply furnished, each with a private bath and some with a wood-burning fireplace. There's a pool, hot tub, and corrals. Activities include horseback riding, mountain biking, bird-watching, and hiking.

There is a social cocktail hour around 6:00 p.m. every evening. Three gourmet meals are served in the historic Hacienda dining room, on the private outdoor courtyard, or under the stars at a cookout. All meals are included in the room rate. If you love to cook, reserve a spot for the weekend cooking classes or the culinary getaway packages.

Be prepared for serenity and isolation; there are no cars, no stores, and no TVs—in fact, no noise other than birdsong and whistling wind. None of life's stresses intrude here.

TANQUE VERDE RANCH $$$$$
14301 East Speedway Boulevard
(520) 296-6275, (800) 234-DUDE (3833)
www.tanqueverderanch.com

This ranch is in the foothills of the Rincon Mountains on the far east side near Saguaro National Park East and Tanque Verde Falls. Established as a cattle ranch in the 1880s and transformed into a dude ranch in the 1920s, this 640-acre facility offers individual Western casitas, three swimming pools (including one indoors), gourmet dining, five tennis courts, a health spa, and more than 150 horses (Arizona's largest riding stable) for daylong pack trips through the Sonoran Desert. Hiking enthusiasts will also be happy to note that nearby trails can take you to pools of cool mountain water.

Three meals a day are included in your cost. You'll be surprised at the array of choices included in the rate. Weekly activities may include a Southwestern barbecue with a cowboy entertainer/singer, line dancing, and lectures on horse sense and desert wildlife. Parents will appreciate the children's program for ages 4 to 11.

Tanque Verde Ranch is open year-round.

i The Tanque Verde Ranch is a great birding spot, much beloved by members of the Audubon Society who, nonetheless, are rarely allowed access. That means you can enjoy the birds in peace while you stay. Call (520) 296-6275.

WHITE STALLION RANCH $$$$$
9251 West Twin Peaks Road
(520) 297-0252, (888) 977-2624
www.wsranch.com

Step back into movie history at White Stallion Ranch. Located on 3,000 acres of secluded desert near the Tucson Mountains and Saguaro National Park West, the site served as the location for the filming of many scenes from the TV show *High Chaparral*. Many other Western flicks have been shot here as well.

A working cattle ranch, the White Stallion was purchased by the True family in 1965 and has been catering to guests ever since. The house itself was built circa 1939 by David Young, a homesteader. Happily, the True family has retained much of the original look and feel of the old place, with some of the same furniture and accessories from the house.

Dining is as big as the ranch itself. Happy hour munchies and cowboy steaks are served. You can also take a breakfast ride. Recreation choices are abundant, although the emphasis is as it should be—on horseback riding. You'll enjoy a heated swimming pool, indoor hot tub, table tennis, sport court, tennis courts, shuffleboard, billiards, horseshoe courts, hiking (remember the ranch borders Saguaro National Park West), moonlight bonfires with a cowboy singer, and even astronomy programs with several large telescopes. If that's not enough, they have a fitness center with gym and sauna, a movie theater, and a kids' recreation room. A weekly rodeo showcases roping, riding, and steer wrestling. Take some time to explore the petting zoo of miniature horses, deer, emus, and pygmy goats.

Indoors, if you're not hanging out in the large library, you may want to try the saloon on a stool created from a real saddle.

RESORTS AND SPAS

For true self-indulgence, treat yourself to a stay at one of Tucson's luxurious resort hotels or world-renowned spas. Gorgeous views, incredible landscaping, championship golf and tennis facilities, and superb restaurants are just some of the terrific amenities available at these top-notch resorts. There are lots of styles to choose from, from 21st-century modern to historic; you won't be disappointed.

The beautiful and historic Arizona Inn is an award-winning luxury destination. PHOTO BY KATE REYNOLDS

THE ARIZONA INN **$$$$$**
2200 East Elm Street
(520) 325-1541, (800) 933-1093
www.arizonainn.com

This historic hotel, listed on the National Register of Historic Places, not only has a four-diamond lodging rating but is also a local jewel. Built in 1930 by Isabella Greenway, a community leader and Arizona's first congresswoman (1933–1936), and now run by her great-grandson, the first-class inn sits on 14 acres of gardens surrounded by vine-covered walls. The 95 rooms are classy and quiet in one of the city's nicer neighborhoods but still close to everything. The grounds are lush with older established trees, shrubbery, and lots and lots of colorful flowers. Clay tennis courts, outdoor swimming pool, fountains, indoor/outdoor dining, a library in the main sitting room, and a piano lounge add to the inn's elegant atmosphere. It's been listed as one of the "Ten Best Country Inns of America" and Zagat's "Top 50 Small Hotels." Even if you decide not to stay here, at least stop by for a visit. A pianist performs nightly in the dining room. (See the Restaurants chapter for dining information.)

The large neon sign beckoning visitors to spend the night at Ghost Ranch Lodge, near downtown Tucson, was designed by artist Georgia O'Keeffe.

CANYON RANCH HEALTH RESORT $$$$$
8600 East Rockcliff Road
(520) 749-9000, (800) 742-9000
www.canyonranch.com

If a total health and fitness vacation experience is what you want or need, look no further than Canyon Ranch. The world-famous 70-acre complex offers beautifully landscaped grounds, the desert just a step away, and some outrageous views of the surrounding mountains. Besides deluxe accommodations and three gourmet meals a day, the Health and Healing Center has health professionals and full-time physicians who offer more than 50 fitness classes daily. Or you can consult directly with any of the spa's nutritionists, exercise physiologists, movement therapists, and psychologists. Also offered are activities such as boxercise, Tai Chi, yoga, squash, and racquetball. Then treat yourself to a massage, herbal wrap, cleansing facial, or other body treatments. Canyon Ranch offers special Health and Healing packages that range from four- to seven-night stays. No tobacco or alcohol products are allowed at the facility. Also, children must be at least 14 years old to participate in any activities or use the facilities.

HACIENDA DEL SOL GUEST RANCH RESORT $$$
5601 North Hacienda del Sol Road
(520) 299-1501, (800) 728-6514
www.haciendadelsol.com

This resort opened in 1929 as a preparatory school for girls. When it was turned into a guest resort in the mid-1930s, it became the favorite spot for Hollywood types like Clark Gable, Joseph Cotton, and Spencer Tracy. From the 1950s to 1970s, it operated as a private club, and then it was reopened to the public in 1983. The 30 rooms and 3 casitas sit on 34 acres in the Catalina foothills.

Each room is individually decorated, but the general decor and construction follow the 1930s Art Deco style. The guest lobby has a lovely library, bridge tables, and a cozy fireplace. Outdoor activities include horseshoes, tennis, croquet, and horseback riding.

The Grill at Hacienda del Sol is open for dinner daily and Sunday brunch (see the Restaurants chapter).

***Sunset* magazine considers Loews Ventana Canyon Resort a top-10 hotel for nature lovers. Just moments after you leave the grounds, you'll be out into the wilderness.**

On-site Eateries

Diners will glory in the variety of on-site eateries. The Sundance Cafe features daily casual dining (breakfast and lunch only) and "Tucson's Best Sunday Brunch," according to the local authority, the ***Tucson Weekly.*** Strolling mariachis complement the Mexican dishes at the Dos Locos restaurant. Or you might want to just relax by the pool with its up-close view of Pusch Ridge. The swimming pool complex includes a waterslide and kids' splash pool, and kids love it. Here you'll find a great poolside menu at the Desert Spring Restaurant. Lunch is available at La Vista. The Lobby Lounge is a great place to sip a cold one.

HILTON EL CONQUISTADOR GOLF & TENNIS RESORT $$$$$
10000 North Oracle Road
(520) 544-5000, (800) 325-7832
www.hiltonelconquistador.com

The Hilton is one of the largest golf and tennis resorts in the West, with three golf courses, two pro shops, and more than 30 lighted tennis courts, plus horseback riding. With 428 rooms (each with a view of either the desert/mountains or the pool area), 100,000 square feet of meeting space, and five restaurants—four right in the hotel and one at El Conquistador Country Club, located not far away—this resort attracts locals and tourists alike.

Golfers can choose to try the challenging nine-hole Pusch Ridge course or venture over to the 18-hole championship course at the El Conquistador Country Club, just 10 minutes down the road. Hiking, jogging, a fitness center, and spa services can round out your stay. Ask the concierge for a list of planned weekly activities.

THE LODGE AT VENTANA CANYON $$$$$
6200 North Clubhouse Lane
(520) 577-1400, (800) 828-5701
www.thelodgeatventanacanyon.com

This 600-acre private golf resort and lodge has 50 guest suites with a private balcony/patio, a spiral staircase to the two-bedroom loft, and a complete kitchen. Nestled in the Ventana Canyon area of the Santa Catalina Mountains, the two 18-hole golf courses have won *Golf Magazine*'s Silver Medal Award and *Links* magazine's Best of Golf Award. The fitness center is open around the clock, and the 12 lighted tennis courts, saunas, spas, and swimming center with its heated baby pool give guests plenty to do. The resort also has 7,000 square feet of flexible meeting space. The Catalina Room and Ventana Bar & Grill offer panoramic views of the mountain range, golf course, and the desert creatures that make their homes around the resort.

LODGE ON THE DESERT $$$$
306 Alvernon Way
(520) 325-3366, (800) 978-3598
www.lodgeonthedesert.com

You'd never guess as you drive down busy Alvernon Way (just off Fifth Street) that just over the adobe walls lies a peaceful, elegant resort—the Lodge on the Desert. This beautiful in-town resort has been serving guests for over 70 years and in that time has earned a reputation for great service, private getaways, and old-world charm.

Its midtown location is ideal for whatever you've got planned—golfing, tennis, shopping, sightseeing, dining, a game at nearby UA—you name it. If you'd rather spend your day right at the lodge, you can swim in the heated pool.

The adobe-like casitas are charmingly decorated with Mexican tiles and furniture and high-beamed ceilings. Some have wood-burning fireplaces, and one even has its own indoor heated pool. All are easily accessible to the beautiful grounds replete with ocotillo and other desert plants, palms, flower gardens, and lush lawns.

The elegant in-house restaurant serves three meals a day. You should plan to spend one special evening there.

LOEWS VENTANA CANYON RESORT $$$$$
7000 North Resort Drive
(520) 299-2020, (800) 234-5117
www.loewshotels.com

On 93 acres above Tucson, this 398-room golf and tennis resort lies exactly where the Sonoran Desert and the Santa Catalina Mountains meet. The views here are splendid.

For the athlete in you, try one of the eight lighted tennis courts, the two Tom Fazio–designed PGA championship golf courses, fitness center, hiking, biking, horseback riding, two pools, or a waterfall plunge. When you're all done, grab a massage or a facial at the spa. Shops, croquet, and a hair salon are also found right at the resort.

In 2007 the resort added meeting space and boasts a total of 48,000 square feet for business visitors.

Five restaurants offer something for your every mood—casual fare at the Canyon Café, five-diamond dining at the Ventana Room, poolside meals at Bill's Grill, the Cascade Lounge for snacks and drinks, and the Flying V, located at the Spa and Tennis Center, for a taste of the Southwest and a terrific view of the city.

Each of the elegant 398 rooms is decorated to reflect the natural world outside your patio. The bathrooms are a vacation unto themselves. We recommend a lounge in the two-person bathtub. Room service is available 24 hours a day.

MIRAVAL—LIFE IN BALANCE $$$$$
5000 East Via Estancia Miraval
(520) 825-4000, (800) 232-3969
www.miravalresort.com

Staying at Miraval, ranked one of the top spas in the nation, is more than a few nights at a resort. Miraval offers an entire new experience. Here not only will you come away relaxed but also will be enriched by learning to live "mindfully." That is, learning to live for the moment.

Located in the high desert north of the city, Miraval offers guests individual programs to increase their overall well-being. Through yoga, Tai Chi, the Quantum Leap (where you climb a 35-foot pole and take a giant step into the air), horseback riding, fitness programs, swimming, and other recreational activities, you will see yourself in a whole new light. Take an equine therapy class on specially trained horses to gain self-insight. Programs are individualized through the help of experts. There are 104 newly renovated hacienda-style guest rooms on 400 acres that include a Zen garden and labyrinth.

World-class personal services add a special touch. Try a seaweed wrap, a manicure, and a wonderful hot stone massage (only one of several types of massages offered).

Meals at Miraval are an integral part of the process. Both gourmet and healthful, the menu has everything from a fresh fruit smoothie to an elegant dinner of butterflied salmon. Desserts are as beautiful as they are good for you. Wine and beer are available.

Having won rave reviews from *Condé Nast Traveler, Travel – Leisure, Vogue,* and *Harper's Bazaar* (just to name a few), Miraval is a favorite of locals and guests from around the world. Miraval—Life In Balance is an experience not to be missed.

OMNI TUCSON NATIONAL GOLF RESORT AND SPA $$$$$
2727 West Club Drive
(520) 297-2271, (800) 528-4856
www.omnitucsonnational.com

Offering 279 remodeled rooms (some are suites or villas), this boutique golf resort is nestled in the foothills of the far northwest side. The European-style spa and fitness center and the two 18-hole championship PGA golf courses (see the Golf chapter) are outstanding. You'll also enjoy two sparkling pools, two whirlpools, a sauna, a power walk area, and tennis.

Splurge on cocktails poolside at the Cabana Bar, or for a more elegant evening, try the Chic-Urban Steakhouse, new in 2009. For upscale pub fare, try the Legends Bar and Grill. The resort's fine location is just a short drive to many other great choices in dining (see the Restaurants chapter).

STARR PASS MARRIOTT RESORT AND SPA $$$$$
3800 West Starr Pass Boulevard
(520) 792-3500, (800) 535-4028
www.starrpassmarriott.com

This luxury six-floor, 575-room resort (the largest in Tucson) is nestled against the Tucson Mountains in Tucson Mountain Park. Close to downtown (about 5 miles from the convention center) yet in the midst of hiking trails and saguaros, the hotel features a 20,000-square-foot spa with 23 treatment rooms, private lap pool, and Jacuzzis. Every room has a patio or balcony and comes with high-speed Internet, a flat-screen TV, minibar, and coffeemaker. Multiple dining options cover breakfast, lunch, and dinner, including a poolside bar and grill, Southwestern lobby bar, and southern Italian sit-down restaurant. The hotel also offers 88,000 square feet of indoor and outdoor event space, a real plus for the downtown area. Guests have access to the 27-hole Arnold Palmer signature Starr Pass Golf Course (see the Golf chapter). The views are magnificent.

THE WESTIN LA PALOMA RESORT $$$$$
3800 East Sunrise Drive
(520) 742-6000, (800) 937-8461
www.westin.com/westin_la_paloma

This 487-room resort (some of the suites come with wood-burning fireplaces and sunken hot tubs) offers a 27-hole Jack Nicklaus Signature golf course, which was named one of the top 75 resort courses in the country by *Golf Digest*. If golf isn't your favorite physical activity, La Paloma also has a Red Door Spa, 12 tennis courts, indoor racquetball, three swimming pools, a huge waterslide and waterfalls, an aerobics center, Nautilus room, and children's play area. One of the pools even has a swim-up bar for drinks and sandwiches.

Top-rated Janos restaurant and sister J Bar offer scrumptious Southwestern fare (see the Restaurants chapter). The 46,300 square feet of meeting space and new landscaping make it a great place for weddings, conventions, and reunions.

WESTWARD LOOK RESORT $$$$$
245 East Ina Road
(520) 297-0134, (800) 722–2500
www.westwardlook.com

Nestled at the base of the Santa Catalina Mountains on 80 lush acres in the Sonoran Desert, Westward Look was built in 1912 as a private residence. You can see the original sitting room—which has a huge stone hearth, exposed beam and ocotillo branch ceiling, and period furnishings—just off the resort's lobby.

With a facelift encompassing the lobby and all the rooms and baths, this resort offers 244 luxurious rooms with great city or mountain views from cozy private terraces. You can dine on New American Sonoran cuisine in the Gold Room (see the Restaurants chapter) or on casual Southwestern fare in the Lookout Bar and Grille.

Don't pass up a stroll around the lovely landscaped grounds, with tinkling fountains, shade and citrus trees, a Zen-style labyrinth, and an herb, butterfly, and chef's edible garden framed by amazing views.

Tennis is the sport of choice at Westward Look. The 10 championship Laykold courts (four are clay) have helped the resort earn the honor of being named one of the "Top Fifty Tennis Resorts" for more than 20 years by *Tennis Magazine*. Other awards include the Zagat Survey's "Top 10 Resorts" and "Top 5 Restaurants" awards.

Golf isn't neglected, with a 27-hole Jack Nicklaus Signature course garnering a spot in *Golf Digest*'s "Top 75 Resort" courses.

Resort guests have many other options, including five pools, a top-rated spa, horseback riding, a wellness center and fitness club, and meeting rooms accommodating up to 450 people. Small pets are allowed.

BED-AND-BREAKFAST INNS

There are lots and lots of great bed-and-breakfasts of all kinds in Tucson, from historic mansions downtown to cozy adobes in the desert; it's a great way to stay here. We can't possibly cover all of them, so we feature some of the more unique spots in town.

i The Cactus Quail Bed and Breakfast lets you stay for free on your birthday if your visit includes a night or two before or after the big day.

ADOBE ROSE INN $$
940 North Olsen Avenue
(520) 318-4644, (800) 328-4122
www.aroseinn.com

A historic 1933 adobe home, the centrally located Adobe Rose Inn offers six rooms, including a suite and casita. The private Atanacia Room has a striking 6-foot green, blue, and gold stained-glass window, a kiva-style fireplace, high-beamed ceiling, brick floor, and separate entrance. The romantic Sam Hughes Room also features a kiva fireplace, oak floors, and a deep soaking tub—aaah! All rooms have wireless Internet. There are quaint courtyards with bistro tables and evening candlelight, a fountain, and lovely landscaping that includes cactus gardens and potted flowering plants. The whole property is surrounded by thick adobe walls, which make this a private, quiet in-town getaway. The inn also has a pool and a spa, and it serves a three-course breakfast. It's been chosen by BedandBreakfast.com as one of the five best undiscovered inns for romance. This is a great choice for visiting parents, because the university is only a couple of blocks away.

ALTA VISTA BED AND BREAKFAST $$
11300 East Broadway Boulevard
(520) 647-3037, (800) 947-3037
www.altavistabedandbreakfast.com
Hosts Peter and Gaila Smith invite you to their desert oasis near Saguaro National Park East. Voted as having the "most scenic view" by *Inn Traveler Magazine*, the Alta Vista is perched high on a hill with amazing views of the Santa Catalina Mountains to the north and the Rincon Mountains in the east.

The two lovely rooms invite you to kick off your shoes and stay awhile. The White Wicker Room's king-size bed and kiva-style fireplace are complemented by a private bathroom with a shower, satellite dish, television and DVD player, microwave, and refrigerator. The king lodgepole bed in the Santa Fe Room welcomes guests ready for a good night's sleep by the fireplace, while daylight brings wonderful views of the Catalinas. A full homemade breakfast is served in the dining room, complete with farm eggs and homegrown fruit. Customized spa packages are also available.

THE CACTUS QUAIL
BED AND BREAKFAST $$
14000 North Dust Devil Drive
(520) 825-6767, (888) 825-6767
www.cactusquail.com
This Spanish-tiled ranch about 10 miles north of Tucson off Oracle Road offers spectacular views of the Santa Catalina Mountains and rooms decorated with a rustic Southwestern flavor. The largest room (the Bunkhouse), which can sleep four, has a loft and a private bath. The other two rooms (the Pueblo and the Hacienda) have double beds and share a bathroom. You can sit by the cozy fireplace or borrow a book from the inn's library. A four-course sit-down breakfast is served daily. Ask about horseback riding, birding, and hiking in the area.

CASA LUNA $$$
4210 North Saranac Drive
(520) 577-4943, (888) 482-7925
www.casa-luna.com
Located in the northeast part of town, Casa Luna sits in a lovely rural setting with gardens and an outdoor pool. The Picasso Suite offers a private bath and patio and a king or twin beds. The Miles Davis Suite is perfect for easy jazz listening on your private patio; a sleeper sofa accommodates extra guests in this well-appointed room. The Bogart Suite features a rain shower, a 32-inch television with Bose surround sound, and a DVD collection and can be extended to include an additional suite. The Artists Suite is the ultimate in privacy, with a secluded yard, Jacuzzi, and flat-screen television. The Poet's Corner, a cozy suite, sports a queen-size bed, full bathroom, and mountain view.

A full gourmet breakfast is served daily and can be packed to go, and special dietary needs can be accommodated with advance notice.

CASA TIERRA ADOBE
BED AND BREAKFAST INN $$$
11155 West Calle Pima
(520) 578-3058, (866) 254-0006
www.casatierratucson.com
Located on five acres of secluded Sonoran Desert on the western side of the Tucson Mountains, this rustic adobe hacienda offers spectacular views of the mountains and is surrounded by beautiful desert dotted with saguaro cacti. Casa Tierra ("earth house") features more than 50 arches and entryways with vaulted brick ceilings and an interior arched courtyard. The area is only minutes from the Arizona-Sonora Desert Museum, Saguaro National Park West, and Old Tucson Studios. The three rooms and two-bedroom

suite include private baths, small refrigerators, microwaves, patios, and private entrances. In the morning you will be treated to a full vegetarian breakfast, along with home-baked goods, fresh-ground coffee, and a variety of herbal teas. The site is great for birding and hiking or just plain relaxing in the hot tub.

i ***USA Today*** **selected the Royal Elizabeth Bed & Breakfast as among the top five urban bed-and-breakfast establishments for business travelers. Visit www.royalelizabeth.com, or call (520) 670-9022.**

CATALINA PARK INN **$$**
309 East First Street
(520) 792-4541, (800) 792-4885
www.catalinaparkinn.com
This 1927 mansion near the University of Arizona is your chance to vacation in true elegance. The six guest rooms have been lovingly decorated with antiques, and all include a phone, TV, and private bath. Some rooms also have private porches. The rest of the house, with its mahogany doors, is just as beautiful as the rooms. Take some time to enjoy the perennial and rose gardens. Breakfast is delicious, with freshly made pancakes, baked goods, fresh fruit, cereals, and coffee or tea. You can choose to eat in the gorgeous dining room (it's one of the prettiest rooms in the house) or opt for breakfast in bed, complete with the morning paper.

i **If you're looking for a bed-and-breakfast in town (or anywhere in Arizona), check in with the Arizona Association of Bed & Breakfast Inns. This professional association lists over 50 inns that have met their strict standards for inclusion. Go to www.arizona-bed-breakfast.com. For statewide reservations, the Arizona Trails Bed & Breakfast Reservation Service will set you up at any of hundreds of state-inspected B&Bs, inns, hotels, and ranches. Call (888) 799-4284 or go to www.arizonatrails.com.**

DESERT DOVE BED & BREAKFAST **$$**
11707 East Old Spanish Trail
(520) 722-6870, (877) 722-6879
www.desertdovebb.com
This territorial-style adobe is on four acres nestled in the foothills of the Rincon Mountains. The great porches, polished colored concrete floors, and open trusses in the great room, along with the antiques and collectibles, give this B&B a truly unique feel. There are two spacious guest rooms decorated with antiques and collectibles, each with a private entrance, private bathroom, queen-size bed, and seating area. Amenities include Wi-Fi, bathrobes and hair dryers, refrigerator, and microwave. There's no swimming pool, but an outdoor hydrotherapy spa with lovely views of the mountains does just fine. A homemade breakfast in the country kitchen with its 1927 wood-burning stove is served on vintage tableware.

DUNN'S WAY BED AND BREAKFAST **$$$$**
4975 West Via Scaramuzzo
(520) 629-9694
www.dunnswaybb.com
Perched high in the Tucson Mountains, you'll enjoy spectacular city and mountain views from the patio and guest suites at this well-appointed, award-winning B&B owned by Smithie and Jim Dunn. A cozy great room welcomes you to this homey spot where two light and airy private guest suites feature full private baths and patios, refrigerator, microwave, cable TV, phone, and complimentary newspaper. Dunn's Way is especially noted for excellent customer service.

A delicious full-service breakfast is served in the dining room from 8:00 to 9:00 a.m., or you can choose to enjoy an in-room continental breakfast. Closed mid-May to mid-September.

EL PRESIDIO BED AND BREAKFAST INN **$$**
297 North Main Avenue
(520) 623-6151, (800) 349-6151
www.bbonline.com/az/elpresidio
For historic Old Mexico ambience near downtown, consider this 1880s adobe mansion. It's a vacation for all the senses. Eyes and noses are enraptured by the beauty and fragrances of the

gardens; ears and fingers revel at the gentle music and cool current of the fountains. Taste buds are treated to a full breakfast; the menu changes but often has stuffed French toast, bacon, fruit, and juice. Four luxury suites have private baths, TVs, wireless Internet, and phones. El Presidio is within walking distance of the Tucson Museum of Art and the city's historic Presidio District.

HACIENDA DEL DESIERTO BED AND BREAKFAST $$$
11770 Rambling Trail
(520) 298-1764, (800) 982-1795
www.tucson-bed-breakfast.com

This Spanish-style hacienda sits on 16 acres in the Rincon Mountain foothills near Saguaro National Park East. There are three rooms able to accommodate up to four people each. Each room has a queen-size bed and hide-a-beds as well as a private bath, kitchenette, TV/DVD player, telephone, and private entrance. In addition, a large casita has two bedrooms, a full kitchen, living room, bath, and a private outdoor spa. A business center with Wi-Fi access, computers, and printer is available. You'll find shady porches, great views, and a courtyard with fountains and flowers.

Breakfast includes fruit, cereal, hard-boiled eggs, homemade muffins, coffee, and juice. Take a walk on the 0.8-mile nature trail to work it all off.

THE JEREMIAH INN BED AND BREAKFAST $$
10921 East Snyder Road
(520) 749-3072, (888) 750-3072
www.jeremiahinn.com

Located in the eastern foothills near Sabino Canyon, this 3.3-acre desert retreat offers five rooms in a contemporary Santa Fe–style home. Two rooms adjoin to create a suite. All rooms include a queen-size bed, private bath, TV, telephone, and outside entrance. Guests can enjoy nearby golf or horseback riding or take a dip in the pool or spa after a breakfast of a special entree, fruits, and juices served in the dining room, poolside, or in your room. Children age 6 and under stay free and have access to a super game and toy closet and library. This is a very kid-friendly place that serves chocolate milk.

LA POSADA DEL VALLE $
1640 North Campbell Avenue
(520) 795-3840, (888) 404-7113

This elegant 1929 adobe mansion, designed by noted Tucson architect Josias Joesler, is surrounded by gardens and orange trees. Across the street from University Medical Center, the inn has six guest rooms with private baths and entrances. Each room's furnishings are inspired by individual Southwestern themes. The living room has views of the Catalina Mountains. In the morning expect a hearty country breakfast. Tucson's first bed-and-breakfast now offers free Wi-Fi and cable TV.

LA ZARZUELA $$$$$
455 Camino de Oeste
(888) 848-8225
www.zarzuela-az.com

With its stunning desert setting, this five-casita bed-and-breakfast is the perfect rendezvous for romance. Each brightly painted and well-appointed casita features a private bath, private entryway, patio, and mountain view. In addition, all have refrigerators, coffeemaker, hair dryer, TV, video and CD player, and daily fresh flowers. You'll find a shady and welcoming patio, a negative-edge pool, and spa. Your hosts will cheerfully help you plan your visit, including local hikes led by a naturalist. A full gourmet breakfast with home-baked goodies is served daily, and the four-course Sunday brunch tops everything. On Sunday the host puts on an organ recital.

This is a perfect desert oasis for couples or groups up to 50 people, but bear in mind that town is a good half-hour drive away.

PEPPERTREES BED AND BREAKFAST INN $$
724 East University Boulevard
(520) 622-7167, (800) 348-5763
www.peppertreesinn.com

You might not expect Victorian mansions in the Old West, but this 1905 inn is just that. It's an oasis of tranquility near the main gate of the University of Arizona and is within walking distance to shops, museums, and restaurants. The name comes from two large California peppertrees that once dominated the front of the inn. (They were

La Zarzuela is one of only two inns in southern Arizona selected as a Select Registry Inn. PHOTO BY KATE REYNOLDS

lost to one of many summer monsoons some years back.)

The inn comprises four distinct homes. The Annex offers two queen-bedded rooms with sitting rooms, private baths, and full kitchen. The Casita is a king-size suite decorated with a Mexican theme and includes a private entrance, full kitchen, sitting room, king-size bed, and private tiled bathroom. Two private guesthouses (Sunrise and Sunset) have full kitchens, private patios, and separate entrances.

A gourmet organic breakfast, prepared by acclaimed pastry chef (and owner) Jill McCormick, is served daily, usually in the lovely gardens. There's also an in-house gourmet dinner, served in your room or on the patio, available at limited times.

ROCKING M RANCH **$$**
6265 North Happy Trail
(520) 744-2457, (888) 588-2457
www.rockingmranch.net

If you travel with your horse, Rocking M Ranch may be the spot for you. On 10 acres adjacent to miles of trails within Saguaro National Park West, this bed-and-breakfast has five covered corrals with automatic water for keeping your horse ready for a ride at nearby stables or on open trails (no stallions please). Rocking M has four rooms available. Two rooms have a queen-size bed and private bath. The remaining two rooms share a bath; queen or twin beds are available. During the week a continental breakfast is served, and on weekends a full breakfast with eggs, toast, fresh fruit, and coffee begins the day. A boot-shaped pool and heated spa round out the luxuries.

THE ROYAL ELIZABETH BED & BREAKFAST INN **$$$$**
204 South Scott Avenue
(520) 670-9022, (877) 670-9022
www.royalelizabeth.com

A Victorian treasure right in the heart of the Old Pueblo, Anglophiles will love this meticulously renovated 1878 mansion crafted out of adobe. Six spacious guest rooms are beautifully furnished with period antiques, along with satellite

TV, wireless Internet, and a refrigerator. A heated pool and outdoor spa, home theater, lounge, and telescope round out the amenities. Personalized service sets this wonderful desert oasis apart. A two-course gourmet breakfast is served daily. You'll be pampered with organic fresh fruit and healthy options to get a good start to your day. Refreshments such as cookies and biscotti are available throughout the day.

SAM HUGHES INN BED AND BREAKFAST $
2020 East Seventh Street
(520) 861-2191
www.samhughesinn.com

Sam Hughes Inn is a 1931 California mission–style bed-and-breakfast with a red-tiled roof, original oak floors, and Art Deco architectural details. Just 2 blocks from the University of Arizona, this is a historic property located in the National Historic District of Tucson, which also bears the name of a famous early settler: Sam Hughes, an alderman and brother of the governor of the territory of Arizona. You can sleep in Tombstone, Nogales, and Santa Fe without leaving town! The four rooms (two with private entrances) are decorated with antique and contemporary Southwestern furnishings. All come with a private bath, minifridge, hair dryer, and shower robes. A great room with fireplace offers cable TV and a library. Free Wi-Fi is available. In the morning you'll be treated to a delicious full breakfast in the dining room or outside, weather permitting.

THE SUNCATCHER BED & BREAKFAST $$$
105 North Avenida Javelina
(520) 885-0883, (877) 775-8355
www.thesuncatchertucson.com

Owned by Janos Siess (former manager of the top-ranked Cafe Des Artistes restaurant in New York City), this elegant and newly remodeled bed-and-breakfast is furnished with antique Spanish colonial pieces and original period artworks. All but one of the rooms in the SunCatcher has a king-size bed. All have a private bathroom, satellite TV with DVD player, hair dryers, and luxury robes. The deluxe Tucson Suite offers a Jacuzzi tub and private poolside entrance. The smaller Oriental Room has its own Jacuzzi, bidet, and views. There's a heated pool where you can lounge after hiking or biking at nearby Saguaro National Park East. Free Wi-Fi is available throughout the property.

CAMPGROUNDS AND RV PARKS

The best thing about camping in the Tucson area is that, no matter where the campground, it's probably close to, if not surrounded by, some of southern Arizona's most fascinating attractions. The second-best thing is that camping around here offers something to suit just about everyone's taste—from low-lying desert dotted with cacti to high mountains covered with conifer forests and from backcountry camping to fairly posh RV resorts.

In this chapter we cover all the public campgrounds and several of the best private sites close to Tucson, as well as a number of the best camping areas in each direction away from Tucson—except east. Tucson's east—actually the Rincon Mountains—only offers backcountry camping, and it's accessible only by hiking or horseback. (But if that's your style, contact the Saguaro National Park's Rincon Mountain District at 520-733-5153 for details on these campsites and the required permits.) We only include an RV park if it also accommodates the "old-fashioned" type of camper—in a tent. So if you're strictly an RVer, check our Retirement chapter, the Tucson Convention & Visitors Bureau, or the Yellow Pages for additional offerings. And we hasten to add that rates are subject to change and seem to do so quite often.

To get the most out of this chapter, you should use it hand in hand with several other chapters of the book, especially the Natural World, Attractions, and Parks and Recreation chapters. The Natural World chapter, for example, contains lots of additional environmental information on the areas in which you're camping, such as Madera Canyon, the Tucson Mountains, and Mount Lemmon. It can also familiarize you with the unusual flora and fauna you're likely to see no matter where you set up your tent or RV. The Attractions chapter gives details on the many sites you may want to visit from your campground base. And because many of the campgrounds are in or near parklands, the Parks and Recreation chapter will give you a more complete picture of what awaits you in and around these camping areas.

If you're a first-time camper or RVer in Tucson, there are two things you should keep in mind when using the campground descriptions in this chapter. Below the name of the campground is an address or city where it's located. The city listed is the city closest to the camping area. For example, Bog Springs Campground is listed as Green Valley, Arizona; while the campground is near Green Valley, it's also a ways away in the Santa Rita Mountains. So consider the "city" indicator just a general description of the location.

Our second piece of advice relates to the 520 area code. This chapter contains a number of campgrounds that are far enough from the Tucson metro area to be considered long distance by phone, even though they're still in the 520 area code. So be aware that in some cases you'll have to dial the area code even if you're calling from Tucson, and it will be a long-distance call. Although a recording will tell you the error of your ways if you dial only the seven-digit phone number, it may not be helpful enough to tell you the way to correct it—but now you know how.

Now you're ready to dive into the fun part of this chapter—our picks of some of the best places to pitch your tent or park your RV in and around Tucson. So pack up your gear, supplies, and sunscreen, and get ready for your adventure in the great outdoors.

BOG SPRINGS
Forest Service Road 70, Green Valley
(520) 281-2296
www.fs.fed.us/r3/coronado/forest/recreation/camping/sites/bog_springs.shtml

At the western side of the steep Santa Rita Mountains and about 30 minutes south of Tucson—not counting the extra time it might take to traverse up the Forest Service road for 13 miles—sits this 15-acre campground in and operated by the Coronado National Forest. The campground lies just below Madera Canyon, one of the premier birding spots in the Southwest. You'll drive past plenty of century plants, yuccas, and barrel and prickly pear cacti, and if it's spring or fall, they may be in full bloom or showing off their colorful fruits. You'll also wind through pecan groves and across grassland sprinkled with mesquite trees.

At the campground's 5,200-foot elevation, you'll be surrounded by junipers, oaks, and sycamores and hear the soft tumbling of Madera Creek. The many hiking trails leading into the Santa Ritas and the elevation make this a popular spot, especially in summer.

If you're in an RV, keep in mind that the limit is 22 feet and the campground loops, though paved, are steep and twisting. There are 13 tent or RV sites with no hookups at $10 per night per vehicle. Near the campground entrance are several shaded picnic areas with grills, as well as restrooms but no showers. Bog Springs is open all year for 14-day stay limits. Winter nights at this elevation can get quite cold, but summertime camping can be a comfortable diversion from temperatures on the valley floor below. It's a popular place, and spaces cannot be reserved in advance.

If you happen to run out of some basic supplies or food, Madera Canyon even has a small store or two, but it's iffy whether they'll be open (although more likely in summer). Many trails take off from here up toward the Mount Wrightson Wilderness—more than 70 miles of them throughout the mountain range. Or you can save your hiking shoes for another time and simply hike around Madera Canyon and along the creek. Another option is to take the bus tour to the Smithsonian Astrophysical Observatory at the top of Mount Hopkins from the observatory's ground-level visitor center. And nearby you'll find attractions like the Titan Missile Museum and the outstanding golf courses of Green Valley.

To get to Bog Springs, take Interstate 19 south from Tucson to exit 63 (Continental Road/Madera Canyon) and head east on FSR 70 for about 13 miles.

CACTUS COUNTRY RV RESORT
10195 South Houghton Road
(520) 574-3000, (800) 777-8799
www.abtucson.com

If you're looking for the amenities of a resort but still want to bunk in your own tent or RV, Cactus Country RV may be the spot. This private RV complex covers three acres on Tucson's far southeast, close to the Santa Rita Mountains, the Santa Rita Golf Club, and the Pima County Fairgrounds. You can stay for a day, week, month, or a season and have access to electricity, heaters, air-conditioners, cable TV, restrooms, dump station, heated pool, whirlpool, shuffleboard, recreation room, and laundry facilities.

And all of this is in a serene desert setting surrounded on all four sides by state land. Cactus Country sits on a hill from which you can see not only the nearby Santa Ritas but also the Rincon and Santa Catalina Mountains to the north and unobstructed sunset views to the west. The resort offers mature vegetation, paved roads, and gravel-covered spaces.

Of the 265 sites, many of which are tree-shaded, 260 are for RVs at $34 a day and 5 are for tents at $18.50 a day. You'll pay less per day for longer term stays. Many of the extras listed above require an additional fee. Cactus Country is open year-round, and the busiest time is January through March.

From Tucson, take Interstate 10 east, exit at Houghton Road, and go north about 0.25 mile.

CATALINA STATE PARK CAMPGROUND
11570 North Oracle Road
(520) 628-5798
www.pr.state.az.us/parks/parkhtml/catalina.html

The closest campground to Tucson is also one of the best. Located in the Santa Catalina Mountains on Tucson's northwest, Catalina State Park covers 5,500 acres at elevations ranging from 2,650 to 3,000 feet. There are plenty of nature trails in the park and, for the more serious hiker, trails extending up the mountains into the national forest. Highlights of the park include Romero Canyon with its falls and clear pools shaded by sycamore and oak trees, ruins of the pit houses left by Hohokam Indians, and the nearby Pusch Ridge Wilderness, home to desert bighorn sheep. And from this location nearly every attraction in and around Tucson is less than an hour's drive away.

Spacious campsites pleasantly arranged amid groves of mesquite trees await road-weary travelers. There are 120 sites, 95 with water and electric hookups. Facilities include wheelchair-accessible restrooms with showers. Fees vary seasonally, the area is open year-round, and the maximum stay is 14 days. Keep in mind that summer camping here will really feel like summer due to the campground's desert terrain and elevation. Reservations are not accepted, so it's best to show up early in the day (between 8:00 and 10:00 a.m.) during the busy winter season for a campsite. Catalina State Park is about 9 miles north of the city limits on Highway 77 (Oracle Road).

CRAZY HORSE RV CAMPGROUNDS
6660 South Craycroft Road
(520) 574-0157, (800) 279-6279
www.crazyhorserv.com

The owner calls this "a good old down-to-earth RV park with dust." (He means the kind of desert dust a crazy horse would kick up or, in the absence of such an animal, a windy desert day.) In other words, it's comfortable with all the basics but not fancy. The basics consist of 152 sites for RVs, full hookups (electric, water, and sewage), restrooms, showers, a laundry room, and a pool that is heated seasonally. The main road is paved, but the spaces aren't, and trees are few, which no doubt contributes to the dust in the air. Crazy Horse welcomes both kids and pets but does have rules about noise in an attempt to keep the park as peaceful as the surrounding desert.

The daily fee of $28.50 for one to two people is all-inclusive; weekly, monthly, and seasonal rentals are available as well. Crazy Horse is open all year, but the peak season is January 15 to March 15.

Located in the southeast of Tucson 0.5 mile north of I-10 and Craycroft Road, Crazy Horse is close to the Pima Air and Space Museum on Valencia Road and no more than 60 minutes away from any other attraction in the metro area. A truck stop and convenience store are close by.

GILBERT RAY CAMPGROUND
Kinney Road, Tucson Mountain Park
(520) 883-4200, (520) 887-6000
www.pima.gov/nrpr/places/gil_ray/index. htm

Of the two units of Saguaro National Park (east and west), the west unit is the only one with a nearby campground. On the west side of the Tucson Mountains and not very far from downtown Tucson is the vast 20,000-acre Tucson Mountain Park, where this campground is located. Its proximity to Tucson and to some great attractions means that this popular campground, though large, often sports the FULL sign (it's first-come, first-served). In addition to Saguaro National Park, both the Arizona-Sonora Desert Museum and Old Tucson Studios are nearby. So is the 6-mile Bajada Loop Drive, where you'll see Indian petroglyphs. Wildlife is abundant here despite the number of humans around. You'll see the typical varieties of thorny vegetation, lots of birdlife, and probably a coyote or mule deer or two. An excellent visitor center can give you a complete orientation to the park and its trails and sights.

Operated by Pima County Natural Resources Parks and Recreation Department, the campground has 130 sites, with individual 30-amp hookups. There are wheelchair-accessible restrooms and a dump station but no showers. Volunteer attendants are on duty during regular business hours in the winter season but usually not during the slower summer season, when campers are on the honor system to pay at the lock box. The fees are $10 for tenters and $20 for RVs per night for a maximum of seven days, no credit cards accepted.

The easiest way to get here is to take Ajo Way west to Kinney Road and then head north to the campground. The scenic route is Speedway Boulevard to Gates Pass Road, then south on Kinney Road. RVers must take the easy way—RVs are not permitted on Gates Pass Road.

If you love camping out but miss some of the comforts of home, consider renting the rustic adobe cabins in historic Kentucky Camp in the Santa Rita Mountains just 9 miles north of Sonoita. Built in 1904 as the headquarters of the Santa Rita Water and Mining Company, the camp houses five century-old adobe buildings. You can rent the 10-room headquarters building for $200 a night or the cabin for $75 as part of the Forest Service's "Room with a View" program. Watch for white-tailed deer, coatimundis, pronghorns and coyotes, which all make their home here.

LAKEVIEW
Highway 83, Sonoita
(520) 378-0311
www.fs.fed.us/r3/coronado/forest/recreation/camping/sites/lakeview.shtm

Fishing might be the reason you choose this campground, but the camping is also superb. It's located almost at the Mexico border at 133-acre Parker Canyon Lake, where the cottonwoods, willows, and marsh grass—not to mention the sight of water—might fool you into thinking you're not in Arizona. It's not recommended for swimming (algae and reeds would slow your progress across the lake), but bring your fishing gear along and see if you can land any of the lake's rainbow trout, largemouth bass, sunfish, or catfish for a tasty dinner. Lakeside there's a store, a marina, and boats for rent. Pets are allowed on leash only.

Operated year-round by the Sierra Vista Ranger District of the Coronado National Forest, the 65 campsites on 50 acres in the shadow of the hulking Huachuca Mountains accommodate either tents or RVs, with a 32-foot limit. There are restrooms but no showers, dump station, or RV hookups. Maximum stay is 14 nights at $10 a night per vehicle. At an elevation of 5,400 feet, summer nights will be heavenly and winter nights on the cool side.

The easiest way to get here from Tucson is to take I-10 east to the Patagonia/Sonoita exit and then head south on Highway 83 for about 25 miles to Parker Canyon Lake, the last 4 miles over dirt roads.

MOUNT LEMMON

Tucson's own "sky island," Mount Lemmon is also the region's most diverse outdoor recreation area. Along 25 miles of steep and curving roadway up to a 9,000-foot elevation, sights and sounds include full-blown pine forests, see-forever views, biking, skiing, fishing, picnicking, hiking, wildlife watching, and camping. For Tucsonans it's akin to making a short drive to Canada. So it's a very popular place year-round. In summer it's an escape from the heat down below, in fall a spectacular foliage show, in winter a test of winter driving skills and a close place to hit the ski slopes, and in spring a blooming treat for the senses. Designated a scenic byway in 2005, the drive is sublime.

There are several Forest Service–maintained campgrounds. And for the brave among you, wilderness camping is permitted on Mount Lemmon 0.25 mile or more away from campgrounds. All of the Coronado National Forest campgrounds, including those on Mount Lemmon, have a 14-day stay limit. For information on any of the four campgrounds, call (520) 749-8700 or check www.fs.fed.us/r3/coronado. Here are some details on the most popular sites.

MOLINO BASIN

Despite its location in the Santa Catalina Mountains, this campground is actually closed during the summer months (late April through the end of September) due to the heat (no, that isn't a typo). That's because its southern exposure, even at an elevation of 4,500 feet, makes it warmer than, say, Catalina State Park on the northern slope of the same mountain range. Conversely, the same conditions make wintertime camping here quite pleasant at an elevation that normally would be uncomfortably cold.

Molino Basin is the first of several campgrounds on Mount Lemmon operated by the Catalina Ranger District of the Coronado National Forest. About 10 miles up the highway from Tucson, it nests in a deep V between two granite ridges. This is a great area to get the kids treasure hunting for "jewels"—the sandy washes in this basin composed of metamorphosed granite are rich in silvery mica flakes and tiny burgundy "sand rubies," better known as garnets. The area offers great scenic views, rock climbing, and hiking. You'll even spot a few saguaros, which generally don't grow above 3,500 feet.

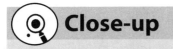

Close-up

Mount Lemmon Rules

Here are some things you should know to keep your Mount Lemmon experience safe and rule abiding.

- Bears live here, too, and they're attracted to food, so keep yours well covered and hidden—that means tightly sealed and in your car or one of the bear barriers.
- Your own pets must be on a leash.
- You can fish at Rose Canyon Lake, but you can't get a license on the mountain, so get one before you come.
- If a summer is particularly dry, the Forest Service may temporarily ban all fires, so have a backup for your charcoal-broiled steaks or hot dogs.
- Gas up your vehicle in Tucson—there are no stations on the mountain.
- At the top in the village of Summerhaven, you'll find a few stores and restaurants.
- Trail maps for the mountain are available at the Sabino Canyon Visitors Center (on Sabino Canyon Road), so get them before you begin your trek up the mountain.
- Some of the campgrounds have daily fees, and all have a 14-day stay limit.
- Most importantly, keep our precious environment clean and undisturbed—a good thing to remember no matter where you're camping.

The Catalina Highway (or Mount Lemmon Highway) begins at Tanque Verde Road about 5 miles east of Sabino Canyon Road. In late 1997 the USDA Forest Service instituted a recreational fee for the Santa Catalina Mountains, which includes Mount Lemmon. If you're camping or otherwise recreating, it costs $5 a day per vehicle, $10 a week, or $20 for an annual pass; often in addition to your campground fees. You can purchase passes at the booth at Milepost 5.5 just before Molino Basin 24 hours a day, seven days a week. Other places to buy the Mount Lemmon passes are the Tucson Convention and Visitors Bureau in La Placita Village downtown and several Walgreens, Chevron gas stations, and CVS drugstores along East Tanque Verde Road. For addresses and telephone numbers go to www.fs.fed.us/r3/coronado/forest/passes/fees/purchase_locations.shtml.

The campground covers 65 acres and has over 30 sites for tents and RVs up to 22 feet for a daily fee of $10, plus you must have a Mountain Pass ($5) to access certain areas. Check with the fee station at Milepost 5.1. There are restrooms but little else, so be sure to have drinking water on hand. Campsites cannot be reserved in advance, but Molino does have a reservable group site.

i Dr. Gordon Hirabayashi was one of only three Japanese Americans to challenge the constitutionality of internment and a curfew imposed on Japanese American citizens. Convicted by the U.S. Supreme Court, he served his sentence at an internment camp in the Coronado National Forest doing hard labor. Ultimately his conviction was overturned, and in 1999 the Coronado National Forest named a new recreation site at the old internment camp after its most famous inmate to honor him and other resisters of conscience who were imprisoned there.

Just 2 miles north of Molino, you'll find the Gordon Hirabayashi area. Formerly an internment camp for Japanese Americans, who helped build the Mount Lemmon Highway during their captivity, this site has 12 units with restrooms but no hookups or water for a $10 per vehicle nightly rate. This area is open year-round. Nearby you'll find an interpretive nature trail with photos and remnants of the old camp.

GENERAL HITCHCOCK

At Milepost 12 and an altitude of 6,000 feet, General Hitchcock is the smallest Mount Lemmon campground; open year-round. The 11 picturesque campsites are not recommended for RVs. Fees are $10 a day and a Mountain Pass ($5) but can't be reserved in advance. There are restrooms but no water, showers, or hookups.

ROSE CANYON

If the idea of lakeside camping and casting for your dinner appeals to you, this is the campground to choose. Only about a block from the campground, the seven-acre Rose Canyon Lake is stocked with several varieties of trout and surrounded by tall green pines. The campground is at Milepost 17.2, with paved loops winding through a number of campground sections and ending at the lake's parking lot. It's only open from mid-April to mid-October, and this oasis at 7,100 feet is very popular with Tucsonans escaping summer's heat. Campsites for tents and RVs number 74. You'll find wheelchair-accessible restrooms and water but no showers, no hookups, and no RVs longer than 22 feet. There is a per-day rate on a first-come, first-served basis. A one-day-use group site can be reserved by calling (877) 444-6777.

SPENCER CANYON

The highest of the mountain's campsites is at Milepost 21.7 at an elevation of 8,000 feet and is only open mid-April to mid-October. It has 60 campsites for tents and RVs shorter than 22 feet, restrooms, and water but no hookups or showers. The fee is $18 a day.

The campground is laid out in four levels, all connected by all-weather roads. Keep in mind that activity at this altitude can be a real strain for lowlanders and confirmed couch potatoes. But if hiking and rock climbing are not your cup of tea, the village of Summerhaven is nearby, along with a few shops, restaurants, and probably a cup of tea that *will* suit you.

PATAGONIA LAKE STATE PARK
Highway 82, Patagonia
(520) 287-6965
www.pr.state.az.us/parks/parkhtml/patagonia.html

Patagonia Lake, not far from Arizona's southern border, offers fun on the water as well as a nicely laid-out campground. The 265-acre lake features fishing, boating, a sandy beach, a store, a marina with boat rentals, and even a high pedestrian bridge with a scenic view. Although rainbow trout are stocked in the lake in winter, you're more likely to hook bass, sunfish, crappies, and catfish in this warmwater fishery. The lake also offers southern Arizona campers a rare treat—waterskiing and windsurfing are allowed here (but only during summer and only on weekdays). As you might guess, Patagonia Lake is a very popular spot for water-deprived folks in this area.

Situated on one of the gentle slopes above the lake, the year-round campground has picnic areas, restrooms, and wheelchair-accessible showers. Of the 115 campsites, 34 have hookups and 12 are boat accessible only. Fees vary, the RV limit is 35 feet, and there is a maximum stay of 14 days. Campsites cannot be reserved in advance.

To get here from Tucson, take I-10 east to Highway 83, go south to Highway 82, and continue south 7 miles past the town of Patagonia. Nearby is Patagonia-Sonoita Creek Preserve, a 312-acre wildlife sanctuary of The Nature Conservancy that's open to the public. The border town of Nogales, Mexico, is only about 40 minutes away.

PEPPERSAUCE
Forest Road 38, Oracle
(520) 749-8700
www.fs.fed.us/r3/coronado/forest/recreation/camping/sites/peppersauce.shtml

This is a superb campground for several reasons, not the least of which is the story (or perhaps tall tale) of how its name originated. The story goes that prospector Alex McKay, who was hooked on pepper sauce—hot sauce—lost a bottle of it in the wash and was upset for the rest of his days at the campsite. And whether you believe that or not, once you see this spot you will surely believe that it's a sight to behold.

i Looking for top-notch camping gear? Head to Summit Hut for a great selection. Call (800) 499-8696 for locations.

Start out in Oracle, which is about 20 miles north of Tucson, and head east-southeast on Mount Lemmon Road, or FR 38. (This is the north side of the Catalinas, not the more famous and traversed Mount Lemmon Highway that goes from Tucson to Mount Lemmon.) After the pavement ends, you'll pass through dry desert laden with ocotillo, cholla, and barrel cacti for about 5 miles. Suddenly you'll top out on a hill, and a few hundred yards below you'll gaze upon a grove of giant sycamores shading the Peppersauce Campground. The roots of this giant green canopy are nourished from Peppersauce Springs, a short distance up the wash, or arroyo, from the campground. This cool retreat from the surrounding heat makes for a great summer camp experience, but it is open all year. It probably comes as no surprise that Peppersauce is a very popular spot.

Peppersauce is operated by the Catalina Ranger District of the Coronado National Forest. There are 19 campsites with tables and fire grills at a daily rate of $10 per vehicle. Trailers are not recommended. Restrooms and water are available but hookups are not, and the stay limit is 14 days. A group campsite with maximum capacity of 10 cars and up to 35 people is also available at Peppersauce for $50 a night. Tents and cars only, no RVs. You can make a reservation by calling (520) 749-8700.

PICACHO PEAK STATE PARK
I-10, exit 219, Picacho
(520) 466-3183
www.pr.state.az.us/parks/parkhtml/picacho.html

Once you see the rocky pinnacle 40 miles north of Tucson known as Picacho Peak, you'll always recognize its dramatic and distinct shape from afar. Along its slope is a state park of the same name. (And speaking of names, the word *peak* could easily have been left out, since that's what *picacho* means in Spanish.) Rising 1,500 feet above the desert floor, the peak is thought to be 22 million years old—four times as old as the Grand Canyon. It is also the site of the westernmost battle of the Civil War, fought between a dozen Union and 16 Confederate soldiers. Rains permitting, in mid-March the park explodes with traffic-stopping displays of wildflowers—acres of golden, purple, and magenta blooms. Within the 4,000-acre park are 7 miles of hiking trails and a scenic drive.

Rest assured that, even though Picacho borders the very busy I-10 connecting Phoenix and Tucson, the campground is far enough removed—about 2 miles west of the freeway—that noise doesn't intrude. Campers have access to 100 sites; fees vary seasonally. The maximum stay is 14 nights. The year-round campground has wheelchair-accessible restrooms, and nearby are showers, a store, restaurant, and gas station. The city of Casa Grande is about 20 minutes away if you have the unstoppable urge to outlet shop or if you need any major services or supplies. At only 2,000 feet, camping is comfortable here in winter but a bit warm in summer.

Drive west from Tucson on I-10 about 40 miles to exit 219—you can't miss it.

VOYAGER RV RESORT
8701 South Kolb Road
(520) 574-5000, (800) 424-9191
www.voyagerrv.com

Located on the far southeast side, this RV resort park might as well be a city. With over 1,576 spaces, 150 acres, 24-hour security, a nine-hole golf course, two heated pools, saunas, spas, classes, and entertainment, many people make this their permanent home. Daily, weekly, monthly, and annual rates are available.

RESTAURANTS

One of the great things about Tucson is the wide variety of restaurants you'll find here, from old-fashioned steakhouses and diners to award-winning resort fare and haute and ethnic cuisine. Tucsonans are very proud of the great variety and quality of their restaurants. You'll still be able to find the best Mexican food this side of the border, and mesquite-grilled steaks continue to play an important role in the restaurant scene. But believe us when we tell you that visitors and residents of the Old Pueblo do not subsist on tortillas and T-bones alone.

Grills, bistros, and cafes are making a strong showing, as does Asian cuisine in all its glorious forms, including some outrageous Pacific Rim offerings. Fine dining is alive and well with continental, American, French, and Italian in the mix. The university is another influence, of course, so you will find enough brewpubs, breweries, coffeehouses, diners, all-American burger joints, and pizza parlors to keep you well fed for months.

Dress for the most part is Tucson casual—comfortable chic for upscale and resort hotels and very casual for most others.

We've divided the restaurants by cuisine, but many of them could easily be placed in more than one category. You may want to scan the entire chapter to get a full view of what the area has to offer.

The categories are All-American; Asian; Breweries and Brewpubs; Burgers, Sandwiches, and Such; Cafes and Bistros; Coffee and Tea Houses; Contemporary American/Contemporary Southwestern; Eclectic Eats; Fine Dining; French; Get It and Go (great places to pick up dinner after a day of fun that should satisfy just about any craving); Greek and Middle Eastern; Healthy, Vegetarian, and Alternative; Italian; Mexican-Spanish; Pizza; Seafood (yep, we do have seafood and very good seafood at that); and Steak Houses (which include places for great prime rib and racks of ribs). Although franchise restaurants can be found citywide, we have included only local chains. Not included in these pages are national restaurant chains, which are rapidly moving into town.

Many of the finer restaurants offer wine-tasting dinners on a regular basis. Check the ***Tucson Weekly*** for the most up-to-date information on these entertaining evenings.

Along with descriptions of the food and the ambience of the establishment, we've added information on the history of the eatery or the building in which it is housed. We'll also advise you about parking for places near the university or downtown, the necessity for reservations, and recommend signature dishes or favorite entrees.

Also, please note that many restaurants in town have a different menu and different hours during summer (some even close for a couple of weeks in summer).

Price Guidelines

The following dollar-sign codes indicate what you will pay for a dinner for two, excluding appetizers, cocktails, dessert, tips, and taxes. You can assume that most restaurants take major credit cards; we only make note of those that do not.

$.................less than $15
$$ .... $15 to $30
$$$ .... $31 to $50
$$$$........... more than $50

ALL-AMERICAN

BOBO'S **$**
2938 East Grant Road
(520) 326-6163

It ain't fancy, just home cooking in a tiny roadside diner, but it sure is good. Especially breakfast, which is served all day. If you're in the mood for real home fries, fresh eggs over easy, and a slab of ham, this is the place for you. Delicious pancakes are bigger than your head—try the blueberry banana. (*NOTE:* Real maple syrup lovers should bring their own.) Hot coffee and the daily paper will start your day off right. Open every day for breakfast and lunch until 2:00 p.m.

GRILL **$**
100 East Congress Street
(520) 623-7621

Grill is a favorite hangout for the young, artsy downtown crowd. The interior is a honest-to-goodness old-fashioned diner, complete with a semicircular counter and booths, an eclectic menu, and 24-hour service. You can get typical diner fare, such as fluffy pancakes, terrific burgers, and American tuna melts, but the Grill also has some upscale choices, including specialty pastas and delicious fresh fish (Friday and Saturday only) prepared a la minute. And ask about the Haystack!

Downtown parking is limited, but you can use either metered spaces (free on weekends) or one of several pay lots within walking distance.

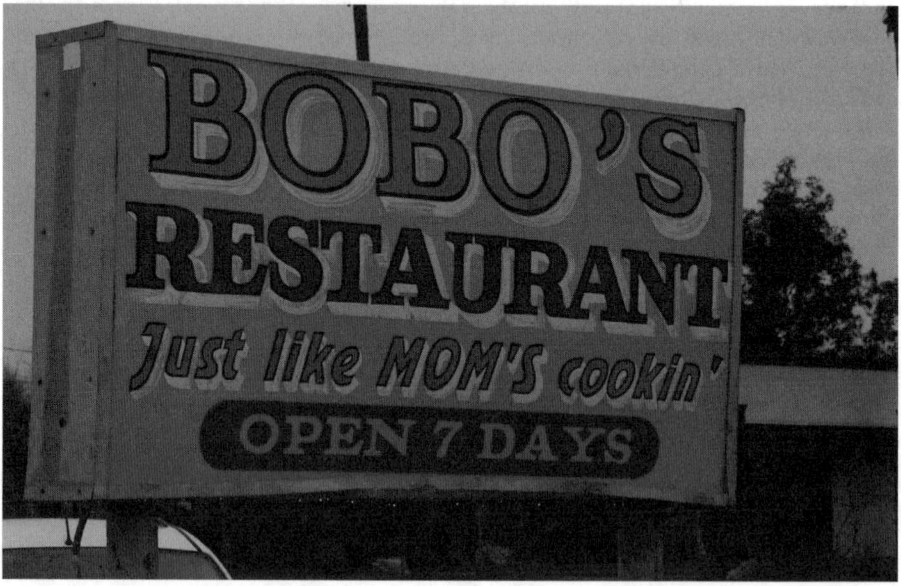

If you're looking for a taste of Mom's cooking, head to Bobo's. PHOTO BY M PAGANELLI VOTTO

GUS BALON'S **$**
6027 East 22nd Street
(520) 747-7788

If you're looking for honest, all-American food, Gus Balon's is the place. All the breads are homemade, the eggs are fried in butter, and every day more than 20 homemade pies are on the menu. Kids can enjoy a jelly omelet or a good old pb & j sandwich. Grown-ups might like to try a breakfast special or a baked ham sandwich. Gus's is open until 3:00 p.m.; closed on Sunday.

HUNGRY FOX RESTAURANT **$**
4637 East Broadway Boulevard
(520) 326-2835

At your first glance at the menu, you might think the prices at the Hungry Fox are a little steep, but on closer examination you'll find out why—all the eggs are double-yolked, which means you get two egg yolks for every one egg you order. What a deal!

The Hungry Fox looks like a cozy country kitchen, with antiques and reproduction pieces on high shelves that run along the walls. The room is bright and cheerful, just like the waitstaff.

Open for breakfast and lunch seven days a week, the Hungry Fox closes at 2:00 p.m.

LITTLE ANTHONY'S DINER **$$**
7010 East Broadway Boulevard
(520) 296-0456
www.littleanthonysdiner.com

Little Anthony's is Tucson's original retro diner. This '50s-style eatery is located at the rear of the Gaslight Theatre, another entity owned by the same family (see the Arts and Culture chapter), and is relatively easy to find.

There will be no surprises here: big juicy burgers (the names are rock 'n' roll related), tasty sandwiches, thick shakes and malts, and even wet fries (french fries served with brown gravy on the side). Pizza, actually Grandma Tony's pizza, another restaurant owned by the same folks, rounds out the menu. The waitstaff is young and friendly, with plenty of energy. Kids get a kick out of the DJ spinning those Golden Oldies at dinnertime while the grown-ups wax nostalgic over all the '50s memorabilia hanging on the walls.

It's a great place to take the kids for a relatively quick something-for-everybody meal. Little Anthony's is open for lunch and dinner on weekdays and adds a breakfast shift on Saturday and Sunday.

i **Both *Tucson Lifestyle* and *Tucson Guide* publish handy free dining guides throughout the year. You'll find them scattered around town at restaurants, shops, and at the Metropolitan Tucson Convention & Visitors Bureau.**

ASIAN

BANGKOK CAFE **$$**
2511 East Speedway Boulevard
(520) 323-6555
www.bangkokcafe.net

For authentic Thai cuisine, head to this unassuming little spot where you'll find a great selection of noodle dishes, steaming soups, fried rice, and spicy curries. The standard pad thai and satay are on the menu, too, but challenge your taste buds with house specialties like Pla Tod Krob Rad Phrik (a crispy trout fillet topped with roasted chili sauce) or Mho Obp Bangkok Cafe (roasted marinated pork tenderloin glazed with chili and served with pineapple and cucumbers). Wash it all down with a cool glass of fresh coconut juice. Closed Sunday.

CAFE PACIFIC **$$**
3607 North Campbell Avenue
(520) 326-5174

Simple, family run, and white-glove clean, this small, immaculately kept restaurant features an eclectic menu of delicious Thai, Vietnamese, Chinese, and Malaysian dishes. It's a well-kept secret in Tucson's Asian community; go for the exotic dinner selections, which include a delectable Vietnamese noodle soup, spicy Indonesian coconut beef stew, and Malaysian satay. Don't miss the mango pudding for dessert, a secret recipe; it's a lovely ending for any meal. Closed Tuesday.

PHO THU **$**
2226 North Stone Avenue
(520) 670-1705
Far, far off the beaten track you'll find Pho Thu, behind a car repair shop just off Stone Avenue and Grant. You'll rarely see a non-Asian person in this funky Vietnamese noodle restaurant. It's all about the food here. The decor runs to pastel-vinyl booths, and the kids love the giant-screen TV showing Japanese cartoons. Noodle soups are the specialty here, and they are delicious. Neon-colored tapioca and fruity gelatin drinks garnished with adzuki beans might look bizarre, but try them! They're strange, sweet, and amazingly refreshing. The soups are great for takeout, too. Closed Monday.

SAKURA **$$$**
6534 East Tanque Verde Road
(520) 298-7777
www.sakuratucson.com
You'll find an interesting combination at Sakura, which is both a sushi bar/teppan-style restaurant and a sports bar. The rooms are separate, but whichever side you choose, we're sure you'll enjoy yourself.

Decorated in traditional Japanese style, the dining rooms offer a show with your dinner: The trained chefs dazzle diners with flashing knives and fire right at the table as they prepare fresh seafood or New York steak teppan-style dinners. Kids will enjoy the show. Prices here are fairly steep, and the show sometimes is better than the food.

The sports bar is a favorite with Eastsiders, offering TVs, dining, and dancing. Open daily.

SAMURAI **$**
3912 North Oracle Road
(520) 293-1963
Samurai is known for Japanese fast food. But don't confuse "fast food" with bland or greasy. Actually, Samurai serves some of the best sushi and teppan-style food around.

The bowls (dons) are the way to go. The yakisoba—beef, chicken, or pork—is hot and tasty, and for sushi try the California roll. If you want a bigger meal, order a bento plate, which is any of the bowl offerings served with gyoza dumplings. Miso soup and green tea ice cream are seasonal favorites.

Samurai may be hard to find, just south of the southeast corner of Oracle and Roger Roads, behind the NAPA auto parts store, but it's worth the search. Samurai is open Monday through Saturday for lunch and dinner.

SERI MELAKA **$$**
6133 East Broadway
(520) 747-7811
www.serimelaka.com
If you want to experience Malaysian cuisine, this is the place to come. Warm and welcoming, and family run, you'll find terrific Malay dishes here alongside familiar Chinese fare. Try the chili crab, a traditional Malay favorite. Giant king crab legs (or whole Dungeness crabs if you call 48 hours in advance) are deep-fried and added to a magnificent sauce made with loads of ginger, garlic, and chilies. The tapioca dessert, buburchacha, is a unique dish made with giant tapioca pearls, sweet potato, corn, and coconut milk. Try it.

TAKAMATSU **$$**
5532 East Speedway Boulevard
(520) 512-0800
You'll find both Korean barbecue and a Japanese sushi bar in this huge barnlike restaurant with a green-shingled roof. As the owners are Korean, be sure to try authentic Korean dishes and order the barbecue for two to cook on your very own grill in the middle of the table. The paper-thin meat is marinated in an exquisite sauce and comes with all sorts of fun condiments you can try, including the incendiary kimchi.

VILA THAI CUISINE **$**
972 East University Boulevard
(520) 393-3489
www.vilathai.com
You'll have to search hard for this little Thai gem. It's hidden away up a flight of stairs at the southwest corner of Park Avenue and University Boulevard. Extremely popular with the U of A crowd for lunch, combination plates offer giant portions at

reasonable prices. Owner Vila Jarrell is passionate about her food and Thai culture and has poured her heart and soul into this venture. The winner here is smoky pad thai with fresh noodles. Wine lovers should try the Monsoon Valley Red from Thailand, available only here. Numerous special events, wine tasting, and art and musical evenings take place weekly. Complimentary valet parking is available, since parking can be a hassle in this part of town. Open seven days a week.

BREWERIES AND BREWPUBS

GENTLE BEN'S BREWING CO. **$$**
865 East University Boulevard
(520) 624-4177
www.gentlebens.com

Located in the heart of the university area, Gentle Ben's is just 2 blocks from the main gate. A downstairs beer garden and an upstairs deck complete with fountains and flowering vines make it a great spot for a bite and a beer.

The restaurant offers great salads, several different burgers, and great brewhouse sandwiches. You'll also find pasta and numerous Southwest specialties.

While you wait for your meal, enjoy a stroll past the glass-enclosed vats of the brews ranging from Red Cat Amber Ale to Tucson Blonde. Some beers are seasonal, and the menu explains each type of beer.

Parking is at a premium. Note that the metered angle parking along the 3 blocks in this area is back-in only!

NIMBUS BREWERY **$**
3850 East 44th Street
(520) 745-9175
www.nimbusbeer.com

Ben Franklin once said, "Beer is living proof that God loves us," and the owners of Nimbus Brewery have adopted this philosophy (the quote is part of their logo).

In a warehouse district off South Palo Verde Road, Nimbus Brewery is a little tricky to find: On 44th Street, head east off of Palo Verde Road and then continue to where 44th Street dead-ends. There, in a large converted warehouse, you'll find the brewery. The atmosphere is very casual.

Food is limited to appetizers, burgers, and sandwiches, which are served at lunch and dinner daily. Live music is featured on weekends. Nimbus beers, which are brewed in small 10-gallon batches, are the only local brews sold at other beer parlors.

THUNDER CANYON BREWERY **$$**
7401 North La Cholla Boulevard
Foothills Mall
(520) 797-2652
www.thundercanyonbrewery.com

Like many of the brewpubs that have cropped up all over America, Thunder Canyon Brewery offers a well-balanced assortment of brews and a menu filled with pub fare (many made with house brews as prime ingredients). But because this brewery is brought to you by the same folks who made the Prescott Brewery (up north in Prescott, Arizona) famous, there is a world of experience apparent at TCB. This is especially true for the service. The staff knows their product and is more than happy to suggest a beer or two or pour you a sample if you so wish. They're also quite happy to offer a menu selection.

Beer-battered fish is a house favorite. Pecan wood–fired pizzas are made with a spent-grain, beer-dough crust. The Bodacious Brownie sundae is served with ice cream and a chocolate whiskey sauce.

A big draw is happy hour. The munchies are delicious, the atmosphere is warm and friendly, and the beer is just waiting to be tapped. The beers are award winners. And you can usually find TCB's four flagship beers on tap daily. Here is where that service we talked about comes in. The bar staff will explain each of the beers and then try to match your cravings with one of the beers. They also can give you the lowdown on the wide single-malt scotch selection that TCB is known for.

Thunder Canyon Brewery is open for lunch and dinner daily. On weekend evenings you can still eat dinner after shopping or a movie at the mall.

BURGERS, SANDWICHES, AND SUCH

BAGGIN'S **$**
Campbell Avenue and Fort Lowell Road
(520) 327-1611

5056 East Broadway Boulevard
(520) 327-8718

6342 North Oracle Road
(520) 575-8878

5407 East Pima Street
(520) 795-7135

2741 East Speedway Boulevard
(520) 327-4342

Church and Pennington Streets
(520) 792-1344

7201 East Speedway Boulevard
(520) 290-9383

3191 East Valencia Drive
(520) 917-5070

Kolb Road and Speedway Boulevard
(520) 290-9383
www.bagginsgourmet.com

Found all over town, these sandwich shops are quick and fairly inexpensive. Turkey is big at Baggin's; in fact, the majority of the sandwiches have turkey as the main ingredient, but you can still get other fresh sandwiches and salads. A regular favorite is the Sundowner, which is stacked high with turkey and all the goodies you might find at Thanksgiving dinner, including cranberry sauce, stuffing, lettuce, and mayo. Nonturkey favorites are the Almost Reuben, a hot pastrami sandwich with coleslaw in lieu of sauerkraut and Baggin's special dressing on marble rye. The chicken salad, which is chunks of chicken in a creamy dressing served on a bed of greens, is another favorite. A recommended side dish is the Chinese sesame noodle salad flavored with soy sauce and sesame seeds. All orders come with a homemade chewy chocolate chip cookie and potato chips.

The decor features Southwestern touches, wooden tables, and saltillo tile floors. Baggin's is open seven days a week for lunch and dinner. The downtown location at Church and Pennington Streets is only open for lunch Monday through Friday.

BEYOND BREAD **$**
3026 North Campbell Road
(520) 322-9965
6260 East Speedway Boulevard, Monterey Village
(520) 747-7477
www.beyondbread.com

Fantastic sandwiches, pastries, cookies, and bread fill this busy cafe and bakery. Daily specials like fresh tomato, basil, and mozzarella on a focaccia; a huge three-layer turkey club made with real turkey; and ripe Brie and rare roast beef on a baguette are only a few of the more than 20 sandwich choices. There's also soup served right in a bread bowl if you have a hearty appetite, and hot breakfast items like cinnamon raisin French toast. The sandwiches are fresh and enormous, the coffee is fresh brewed, and the place is packed. The good news is that you can sample the bread, served alongside a crock of sweet butter, while you wait. Lines are out the door at lunch, so plan accordingly.

BISON WITCHES **$**
326 North Fourth Avenue
(520) 740-1541
www.bisonwitches.com

The sandwiches are really big here and offer more for the taste buds than the usual ingredients. A house favorite is the Green Turkey Sandwich, which has turkey breast, fresh avocado, bacon, cream cheese, alfalfa sprouts, and the house salsa on your choice of white, wheat, or dark rye bread. The Wildcat is piled high with beef, turkey, melted Gouda, lettuce, and a splash of Bison Witches' Russian mustard. For the kid in you, try the grilled pb & j sandwich. Soups are served in bread bowls, and chips come with all meals. After dark, this is more bar than restaurant, so lunch may be a better choice if you've got kids in tow. Lunch and dinner are served daily, and cold beer and mixed drinks are available from the full bar.

BOB DOBBS **$**
2501 East Sixth Street
(520) 325-3767

You won't find any ads for Bob Dobbs. One of Tucson's best-kept secrets, this local sports bar is reputed to have the best burger in town—the Bob Burger. A huge bun with two four-ounce patties (made with a special mix of garlic, Worcestershire, and soy), it's topped with cheddar and comes with tomato and lettuce on the side. Bob's is right next to Rincon Market on Sixth Street.

EEGEE'S **$**
21 locations
www.eegees.com

The story behind eegee's is the American dream come true. In the early '70s, two college students were looking for a way to earn some money when one of them remembered the Italian ices he had loved as a child in New York City. They came up with a recipe for lemon ice, sold the ices from a used vending truck, and the rest, as they say, is history.

The lemon ices remain the mainstay of the menu (there's nothing like an ice-cold eegee's on a hot summer's day). Other flavors are offered monthly. Hot and cold sandwiches, called grinders, are available as well as salads. Open for lunch and dinner daily, there are 21 eegee's locations throughout the Tucson area. Check the Yellow Pages or Web site for a complete listing.

i There are lots of terrific farmers' markets all over town where you'll find fresh produce, farm eggs, local honey, grass-fed beef, and local specialties ranging from emu oil to jams, breads, cakes, and salsas—depending on who's there. For listings see the weekend "Caliente" section of the *Arizona Daily Star*.

JOHNNY ROCKETS **$**
825 East University Boulevard
(520) 622-2245
www.johnnyrockets.com

For a great big burger and a little kitsch, check out Johnny Rockets, where the waiters wear aprons, there's a cool jukebox, and juicy burgers fresh off the grill are served on supersoft buns stuffed with slices of beefsteak tomatoes, mayo, and good old iceberg lettuce, with great fries or onion rings on the side. Thick shakes and malteds and supersize desserts round out this classic menu.

PAT'S DRIVE IN **$**
North Grande Avenue at West Niagara Street
(520) 624-0891

Pat's chilidogs are known citywide, especially by those folks who were teenagers in Tucson during the '50s and '60s. It was a great place to take a date after a school dance or a movie. Today Pat's still serves inexpensive, good food for lunch and dinner daily. Great care is taken to ensure customers get the kind of food they remember. And just because the dogs are the highlight here, don't shun Pat's burgers, fries, or onion rings. All have been named favorites in area polls year after year.

Parking can be tricky. There are a few spaces right on the lot, or you can try parking on a side street.

THE SAUSAGE DELI **$**
2334 North First Avenue
(520) 623-8182
www.sausagedeli.com

University students and faculty flock to this tiny eatery for some of its most unusual sandwiches, made with quality cold cuts, cheeses, and breads (but no sausage). The Susie Sorority is turkey with Havarti on whole wheat with tons of mayo, tomato, and sprouts; the Artichoke Reuben uses chokes instead of sauerkraut to top off the hot corned beef. The regular Reuben is called the Reuben Goldburger. All sandwiches can be served submarine style. Lunch specials come with a choice of chips or one of the deli salads. Beer, sodas, juices, tea, and lemonade are available.

Party subs come as long as 3 feet. Sausage Deli is open six days a week from 10:00 a.m. to 5:00 p.m.

ZIN BURGER WINE AND BURGER BAR **$$**
1865 East River Road
(520) 299-7799
www.foxrestaurantconcepts.com/zinburger.html

Are you a burger fan? If you are, rush over to Zin Burger, THE place in town for upscale burgers and fries. With lines out the door, you'll have to plan your evening—they don't take reservations. The Kobe burger, a zinfully tender burger topped with Vermont cheddar and wild mushrooms is to die for. Hand-cut fries will cost you extra, but they're worth it, hot and crispy. Feel like gilding the lily? Double truffle fries served with truffle aioli and truffle oil will do it. Signature cocktails, 20 wines by the glass, and 12 beer selections will make everything go down easy. Leave room for dessert—shakes, floats, banana cream pie, and the famous Bars of Zin will definitely take you over the edge.

CAFES AND BISTROS

CAFE À LA CARTE **$**
150 North Main Street
(520) 628-8533

Located in the lovely courtyard at the Tucson Museum of Art, this delightful cafe offers great salads, sandwiches, and homemade pastries. You can eat on the patio or inside. Try the popular spinach salad or the tasty salmon club on focaccia with aioli. Open Monday through Friday from 11:00 a.m. to 3:00 p.m. and select Sundays.

CAFFE MILANO **$**
47 West Congress Street
(520) 628-1601

For an authentic taste of Italy, head here. Run by real Italians from Milano, this cozy cafe with bistro tables is a great spot for lunch. Try the grilled focaccia sandwiches filled with real imported proscuitto, handmade mozzarella, and pesto. There are lots of other lunch choices here, along with a great selection of Italian fashion and lifestyle magazines. Don't miss the wonderful cold espresso poured over vanilla ice cream for dessert. Open for lunch Monday through Friday and dinner Friday and Saturday.

i Meat lovers can buy straight from the cow—well almost! The University of Arizona's Meat Science Lab (a USDA-approved meat processing facility that is part of the College of Agriculture and Life Sciences) offers beef of all grades and cuts for sale. Call (520) 318-7021 for a price sheet; open Monday through Friday.

THE CUP **$$**
Hotel Congress
311 East Congress Street
(520) 798-1618
www.hotelcongress.com

For a true sense of downtown Tucson, spend an hour or so at The Cup. Whether it's for breakfast, lunch, or dinner, you will see the full spectrum of the downtown scene, from the city movers and shakers to those who are just passing through.

Featured on the Food Network, this cozy eclectic cafe serves up a fine and feisty menu for breakfast, lunch, tea, and dinner. Looking for a hearty breakfast? Try Eggs and Gunpowder and you'll get a bowl filled with roasted red potatoes, topped with two eggs, and crowned with chorizo and jack cheese. Add a side order of mouth-tingling spicy pinto beans. The lunch menu offers a variety of salads, pasta, tofu, and Mexican-style dishes, while dinner spans the culinary globe with quesadillas and nachos, chicken satay, and katmandu—seasonal vegetables in a rich banana curry, served with coconut quinoa and garnished with banana chips and black sesame seeds. Don't miss the homemade pies and super chocolate chip cookies for dessert.

Parking is typical of downtown—some metered spots, a few pay lots, and very few spaces in back of the building.

CUVEE WORLD BISTRO **$$$**
3352 East Speedway Boulevard
(520) 881-7577
www.cuveebistro.com
High ceilings, picture windows, and warm lighting prepare you for an elegant dining experience. With a menu inspired by "the cuisines of the world," you'll find something for everyone here. Local food-lovers rave about the potato-basil-crusted salmon over a citrus butter sauce with tomato-ginger chutney and sautéed green beans. Pork tenderloin, mahogany roasted duck, and grilled beef tenderloin are also consistent crowd pleasers. Cuvee prides itself on wine pairings, so let them select the perfect wine for you.

THE DISH **$$**
3131 East First Street
(520) 326-1714
www.dishbistro.com
Also a Food Network pick, The Dish is an elegant, sophisticated restaurant serving up delicious gourmet food. Hard to find, it's located inside the Rum Runner Wine and Cheese Company, Tucson's largest wine store. (See the Shopping chapter.)

Creative chefs take common ingredients and turn them into uncommon entrees. The menu is divided into Small Dishes, Green Dishes, Deep Dishes, and Big Dishes. Several evening specialties always include a fresh fish and a meat entree as well as a soup of the day. And here's an Insiders' tip: Sit at the lovely bar and you can order a giant bowl of mussels and a glass of wine for only $10.50 (Tuesday, Wednesday, and Thursday only).

Dinner is served Tuesday through Saturday, and reservations are strongly suggested.

ECLECTIC CAFE **$**
7053 East Tanque Verde Road
(520) 885-2842
www.eclectic-cafe.com
Super busy, this homey place draws them in because its food is delicious, the service is quick, and the prices are reasonable. The interesting menu offers giant stacks of pancakes, eggs every which way, super sandwiches, matzo ball soup, generous salads, and unusual dinner entrees. Open daily; breakfast served only on Saturday and Sunday.

58 DEGREES AT WILLIAMS CENTER **$**
5340 East Broadway Boulevard
(520) 747-5858
www.58degrees.com
If you're an oenophile, head straight to this classy wine bar and shop. You can sip 58 wines by the glass, browse the wine racks in the shop for your favorite vintage, and even store it in a private locker on-site. If you want a bite to eat, you can graze on starters like homemade soup, warm nuts, antipasto, or a salad. Heartier appetites can choose from panini, bruschetta, or several signature entrees. Open Monday through Saturday at 3:00 p.m. The wine shop, featuring hundreds of bottles of fine wine, opens at 10:00 a.m.

TOHONO CHUL TEAROOM **$$**
Tohono Chul Park
7366 North Paseo Del Norte
(520) 797-1222
www.tohonochulpark.org
Sitting on the patio at Tohono Chul Tearoom, you'll forget that just a little more than a block away lies one of Tucson's busiest intersections, Ina and Oracle Roads. That's because the restaurant is set amid the quiet serenity of Tohono Chul Park, a little oasis of desert in the ever-expanding city (see the Attractions chapter).

You have a choice of two patios that are divided by the indoor dining area. On the larger patio you'll find views of the park and some bird-watching. The smaller patio offers the serene sounds of a trickling fountain. The menu is well balanced, including such favorites as chicken salad, quesadillas, club sandwiches, and, for dessert, sorbet and more.

Breakfast and lunch are served daily, as is tea. At tea you'll be offered a choice of teas and little teacakes, scones, and pastries. After your meal take a minute to browse through the gift shop, where you'll find hundreds of handcrafted and imported items.

COFFEE AND TEA HOUSES

BENTLEY'S HOUSE OF COFFEE AND TEA **$**
730 East Speedway Boulevard
(520) 795-0338
www.bentleyscoffeehouse.com
A popular roosting spot for UA grad students, Bentley's is a comfy place for singles or families with kids. Lots of tables, lights, and plugs make it great for work; a kids play area is fun for the younger set. An eclectic menu includes bagels, salads, baked potatoes, soups, and a large selection of coffee drinks, teas, chai, and more. Open daily until midnight.

THE CASBAH TEA HOUSE **$**
628 North Fourth Avenue
(520) 740-0393
www.casbahteahouse.com
Home to a cafe and restaurant, this eclectic spot offers a hefty assortment of coffees. Food is strictly organic vegetarian and vegan with an international twist. Items on the menu include gypsy stew, a homemade red lentil stew spiced with coconut curry and served with pita bread. The Casbah also offers spanikopita, an enchilada plate made with seitan and veggies, and fresh baked goods.

The decor is unlike any you might find around town. The walls and floors are covered with Persian rugs and banners, and the chairs are low, about 4 inches from the ground. The room opens to a cool, shady patio in back.

The Casbah Tea House is open daily for breakfast, lunch, and dinner. Live music, readings, and other events happen daily. Entertainment includes belly dancing nightly on weekends. Parking can be found along Fourth Avenue and on intersecting side streets.

CHANTILLY TEA ROOM **$**
5185 North Genematas Drive
(520) 622-3303
www.chantillytearoom.com
Looking for some respite during a busy day? How about a cup of soothing tea and a bite to eat? Chantilly is the place. This charming little boîte offers lunch, luncheon teas, and a full afternoon tea Tuesday through Saturday starting at 11:00 a.m. Salads, soup, quiche, and a full selection of specialty teas and desserts are offered here. Reservations are strongly suggested.

THE EPIC CAFE **$**
745 North Fourth Avenue
(520) 624-6844
www.epic-cafe.com
Located on the corner of Fourth Avenue and University Boulevard, the Epic has been named the "best cafe for everything" by readers of *Tucson Weekly*.

In addition to lattes, espresso, and other coffee drinks, the Epic has an eclectic array of food such as pita pizzas, tuna with dill and almonds, hummus plates, spanakopita, soups, and salads. Desserts are changed frequently and are always the perfect way to end a meal here.

The Epic is open 6:00 a.m. to midnight daily. Parking can be found on Fourth Avenue or University Boulevard.

JAVALINA'S COFFEE & FRIENDS **$**
9136 East Valencia Road
(520) 663-JAVA (5282)
www.javalinas.com
This friendly little coffeehouse is in a shopping center far, far on the southeast side of the corner of South Nexus and East Valencia in Rita Ranch. Warm and welcoming, you'll find all kinds of java, specialty coffee drinks, Italian sodas, gourmet teas, and fruit smoothies, along with bagels, soup, quiche, and other homemade goodies here. Comfy chairs, chess and checkers, and a little paperback library tempt you to stay awhile. Live music is a draw on Friday and Saturday nights and select weeknights.

LE BUZZ CAFFE **$**
9121 East Tanque Verde Road, # 125
(520) 749-3903
www.lebuzzcaffe.com
Without a doubt, Le Buzz has some of the best pastries in Tucson. This tiny cafe is popular with the bicycling crowd, anxious to fill up on carbs

after cycling Mount Lemmon, and after you eat here you'll see why. Flaky fruit tarts, buttery croissants, crumbly scones, and giant frosted cinnamon rolls are just some of the delicious goodies to come out of the kitchen. They also offer a full breakfast menu, light lunch, and dinner on select evenings.

RAGING SAGE $
2458 North Campbell Avenue
(520) 320-5203
Great coffee and terrific homemade desserts make this tiny coffee shop popular. You'll find lots of people hunched over computers or reading one of the many complimentary newspapers stacked around the place. They use only shade-grown coffee beans to brew up deep, dark, rich java. Non–coffee drinkers will find chai, herbal teas, and Italian sodas on the menu, too. The espresso brownies are the best in town. There's a tiny outdoor seating area. Open daily.

i The Community Food Bank in Tucson (3003 South Country Club Road; 520-622-0525; www.communityfoodbank.com) distributes over 14 million pounds of food annually throughout Pima County. This worthy organization is dedicated to providing food to needy families and senior citizens. They also advocate healthy eating through a variety of educational programs for kids. An all-organic farmers' market takes place Tuesday from 8:00 a.m. to noon. Call for directions; it's hard to find.

7 CUPS TEA ROOM $
2516 East Sixth Avenue
(520) 881-4072
ww.sevencups.com
Tea lovers will adore this beautiful oasis on busy Sixth Avenue. The dark wood lacquer tables were hand-carved in China, and soft lighting comes from Chinese lanterns—a perfect setting to unwind from a hectic day and sip some wonderful teas. And this place is serious about tea. They import numerous varieties directly from China and prepare them in traditional ways—no dipping the tea bag in hot water here. Loose, fresh tea leaves are steeped slowly for full flavor and body by a certified Chinese tea master. Open daily; hours vary seasonally.

CONTEMPORARY AMERICAN/ CONTEMPORARY SOUTHWESTERN

BARRIO FOOD & DRINK $$
135 South Sixth Avenue
(520) 629-0191
www.barriofoodanddrink.com
Soaring ceilings, velvet curtains, picture windows, and a terrific bar set the stage for a wonderful meal here. Excellent bartenders can make any drink you please, from classics to the mixed drink of the moment. The contemporary Southwestern menu offers loads of delicious choices, from huge steaming bowls of fresh pasta to fresh fish and fork-tender beef. Save lots of room for dessert; everything is worth tasting. Centrally located, Barrio is one of the few restaurants that serve dinner until midnight on Friday and Saturday. Open daily, with lunch served Monday through Saturday and dinner Monday through Sunday.

B LINE $
621 North Fourth Avenue
(520) 882-7575
www.blinerestaurant.com
A big draw in the downtown area, B Line is a sleek and sophisticated addition to Fourth Avenue. Serving breakfast, lunch, and dinner, the menu is a mixture of American and Mexican dishes. Sample the buttermilk biscuit sandwiches and homemade crepe cakes with pecan butter for breakfast. Dinner and lunch favorites include a giant bowl of farfalle with pesto and toasted pine nuts and a blackened mahimahi burro with creole sauce. There are also 11 craft beers on tap for the beer connoisseurs among you. Definitely save room for dessert here; it's all good. Rachael Ray of the Food Network loved this place. Open daily from 7:30 a.m.

CAFE TERRA COTTA **$$$**
3500 East Sunrise Drive
(520) 577-8100
www.cafeterracotta.com

Cafe Terra Cotta is one of Tucson's most celebrated restaurants. With reviews in all the major food magazines and accolades such as "One of America's 50 Best Restaurants" according to *Condé Nast Traveler,* Cafe Terra Cotta is in the vanguard of contemporary Southwestern cuisine.

The restaurant's muted Southwestern colors contrast with the bright colors of the art on the walls. High ceilings and large windows create an airy open feeling. The patio offers incredible views of Tucson and the Catalina Mountains.

Chef Donna Nordin has designed a menu based on the fundamental ingredients native to the American Southwest and northern Mexico: chilies, corn, tomatoes, squash, and beans. Her dishes blend American Southwestern and northern Mexican with classical French contemporary cooking techniques and presentation styles with an emphasis on absolutely fresh ingredients. Signature dishes include chipotle-glazed chicken and a stuffed poblano chile relleno platter with shrimp and pork. The margaritas are delicious and unusual; orange agave and blue kachina are two favorites. Unique pizzas are made daily in a wood-burning oven.

Nordin has developed spices, beans, rices, and tea that you can prepare at home. Lunch and dinner are served seven days a week. Reservations are suggested for dinner.

DAKOTA CAFE & CATERING CO. **$$**
6541 East Tanque Verde Road
(520) 298-7188
www.dakotacafeandcatering.com

An innovative mix of New American and Southwestern cooking makes the Dakota a favorite Trail Dust Town dining spot (see the Shopping chapter). The decor is as hip as the menu: Colorful walls are decorated with paintings by local artists, a heavy wooden bar adds a touch of the past, and the small dining room is divided into two areas, which add coziness to the modern atmosphere. You can also dine on the patio. The menu always features a fish of the day as well as appetizers, soups, and salads. Vegetarians will be happy to know that the Dakota serves entrees to suit their tastes, and certain meals can be prepared vegetarian style. The restaurant has a full bar, and espresso and desserts are prepared on the premises daily.

Dress is casual. Lunch and dinner are served Monday through Saturday. Catering is available. Parking can be found on the perimeter at Trail Dust Town.

i In 1912 the Old Pueblo boasted 26 eating establishments, including hotel restaurants, cafes, Mexican restaurants, and the Canton Noodle Shop.

FLYING V BAR AND GRILL **$$$**
Loews Ventana Canyon Resort
7000 North Resort Drive
(520) 529-7936
www.loewshotels.com

A lovely spot in the Catalina foothills, the outdoor patio looks over the golf course, waterfall, and mountains. The indoor seating area features a super bar, comfy chairs, and a fireplace. Don't miss the tableside guacamole, prepared by "guac-amolieres" who expertly fillet fresh avocados and combine them with your favorite ingredients (onion, garlic, jalapeño, tomatoes, cilantro) in a giant volcanic rock molcajete. Best eaten with the signature frozen prickly pear margarita.

THE GRILL AT HACIENDA DEL SOL **$$$$**
Hacienda del Sol Guest Ranch Resort
5601 Hacienda del Sol Road
(520) 299-1501
www.haciendadelsol.com

Superb continental cuisine, elegant Spanish colonial decor, and panoramic views of Tucson and the Catalina Mountains are the hallmarks of this award-winning restaurant. The innovative and seasonal menu features classic dishes with a Southwestern flair. Stunning creations may include grilled lamb, quail, and steak; a variety of tasty and unusual salads; and entrees showcasing local and regional ingredients along with amazing vegetarian options that won't disappoint. Finger-licking tapas are also served at the bar and patio dining areas. And don't miss the amazing desserts.

A terrific Sunday brunch offers fresh-baked pastries, fresh fruit, freshly squeezed orange juice, and coffee or tea served with a choice of appetizer, a choice of entree, and a dessert station. Enjoy dinner in the dining room or at the patio bar Terraza del Sol, with its great view of the sunset. Dinner is offered daily, and brunch is served on Sunday starting at 10:00 a.m.

JANOS AND J BAR **$$$$**
Westin La Paloma
3770 East Sunrise Drive
(520) 615-6100
www.janos.com

Award-winning chef Janos Wilder continues to be a leader in Southwestern cuisine. His Janos and J Bar restaurants feature French-inspired Southwestern cuisine. Produce is the very freshest, purchased from Arizona farmers, and seafood is flown in from around the world, including the Sea of Cortez. The menu is constantly evolving, reflecting seasonal ingredients and international influences. You never know what you'll find on the menu here, but it is guaranteed to be delicious, beautifully presented, and like nothing you've ever had before. Janos is a brilliant chef whose flavor combinations are endless and amazing. Go with lots of friends so you can try everything on the menu, and leave room for dessert; you won't regret the calories!

Here's a tip: Janos offers a special summer tasting menu that's highly affordable and a great way to taste the terrific cuisine without breaking the bank. Watch the local paper for dates. There are also prix-fixe special tasting menus available so you won't have to miss anything. Antiques, colorful walls, and high ceilings all add to the ambience.

J Bar has a lovely outdoor patio for alfresco dining, and the menu here is more casual. It's a great place for a super specialty drink; their margarita is reputed to be the best in town, and the nonalcoholic *liquado del dia* features a different blend of fruits and juices every day.

Janos and J Bar are open Monday through Saturday for dinner only. Reservations are recommended.

JONATHAN'S CORK **$$$**
6320 East Tanque Verde Road
(520) 296-1631
www.jonathanscork.com

A Tucson original, chef Jonathan Landeen has been serving up award-winning Southwestern fare since 1994. You'll find a full bar, an extensive wine list, a patio, and five cozy dining rooms with beehive fireplaces and terrific Southwestern decor at Jonathan's. Specialties include ostrich served charbroiled, blackened, or sautéed with a selection of sauces; selected game meats; and grilled Baja shrimp marinated in a variety of herbs and spices. Steak and prime rib are house specialties. Don't skip the famous mud pie for dessert. Jonathan's is open daily for dinner; reservations are recommended.

METROPOLITAN GRILL **$$**
7892 North Oracle Road
(520) 531-1212
www.metrorestaurants.com

This contemporary grill is owned by Metro Restaurants, a local restaurant group. Beautifully decorated with an open feel—you'll enjoy the comfortable atmosphere as much as the food. Appetizers, entrees, pizzas, and house specialties are wood-fired or spit-roasted. The bar features nightly specials. Cigars are sold and can be smoked in the bar area only.

Metropolitan Grill is in a shopping plaza at the corner of Oracle and Magee Roads. Open for lunch and dinner daily. Reservations are recommended for dinner.

RED SKY CAFE **$$**
2900 North Swan Road
(520) 326-5454
www.redskycafeandcatering.com

Tucked into the Plaza Palomino shopping center, this unassuming, elegant restaurant specializes in cuisine that combines fresh, organic ingredients

Close-up

Janos Wilder, Owner/Chef, Janos and J Bar

Janos Wilder was one of the first chefs to work with local and traditional Native American foods like mesquite flour, prickly pear fruit, tepary beans, and cholla buds and utilize them in his French-influenced cuisine. His efforts have served to define these foods as integral to Southwestern cuisine. Not only does he cook with these ingredients, he also works to sustain them as a board member of the nonprofit Native Seeds/SEARCH and a supporter of local farmers. This unique chef has come a very long way from his first job, as a teenager, in a local pizza parlor. Here he shares his signature recipe for Habañero Pepitas Pesto:

Chef Janos Wilder. COURTESY OF JANOS WILDER

½ cup pepitas (pumpkin seeds)

4 tbsp. sun-dried tomatoes

¼ cup cilantro

¼ cup freshly grated Parmesan cheese

1 fresh habañero chili

4 ounces olive oil

2 tbsp. garlic

salt and pepper to taste

1. Toast the pumpkin seeds to bring out their oils and flavor.

2. In a very hot skillet, blacken the habañero, then, wearing gloves, de-stem, de-seed, and rough chop them.

3. In a food processor, grind the pumpkin seeds with the garlic until fairly fine but not powdery, then add the cilantro until completely combined, followed by the chilies and Parmesan.

4. In a stream, with the motor running, add the olive oil; season with salt and pepper as needed.

Makes two cups. Delicious as a dip or topping for hot pasta.

with California, French, and Southwest styles. The small, secluded outdoor patio with bistro tables and candles is a great place to sit in the evening as you enjoy your meal. Delicious warm bread threatens to fill you up before you even get your appetizers, so watch out!

Chef/owner Steve Shultz is a graduate of the famed Ecole de Cuisine le Varenne of Paris, and it shows in his attention to detail and superb taste combinations. Rack of lamb crusted with pistachios is a signature dish and well worth it—tiny pink chops melt in your mouth. An extensive wine list (four pages long) offers excellent vintages at reasonable prices. Leave room for the delectable Key lime pie (if you're lucky enough to see it on the menu). It's a wonderful sweet/sour creamy filling on a delicate chocolate crust. Service is excellent and solicitous. Open daily for lunch and dinner.

ECLECTIC EATS

CAFÉ 54 **$**
54 East Pennington Street
(520) 622-1907
www.cafe54.org

If you want to do more than just eat, head to Café 54 where your dining experience will provide valuable training and funding to this non-profit downtown cafe. Café 54's primary mission is to provide training and jobs for individuals recovering from mental illness. Working at the cafe provides hands-on training and work experience for these hardworking folks and helps reintegrate them into society. The bistro-style menu changes daily and features a special soup of the day, several entrees and sides, as well as salads and appetizers. Open for lunch only, Monday through Friday.

CANDELA PERUVIAN RESTAURANT **$$**
5845 North Oracle Road
(520) 407-0111

Don't even ask how a Peruvian restaurant ended up in a strip mall in northwest Tucson, just savor the unusual Latin cuisine. Start with the national drink of Peru, a pisco sour made with brandy, egg whites, and citrus juice. If you're not a drinker, ask for a *jugo des frutas,* a fresh fruit drink. Don't fill up on the plate of crunchy fried plantains—save room for specialties of the house including ceviche, empanadas, papa la huancaina (sliced baked potatoes with a feta cheese sauce), and escabeche de pollo (chicken breast cooked with onions and Peruvian spices). For dessert, tres leches cake, made with three kinds of milk and garnished with tropical fruit, will leave you more than satisfied. Open daily for lunch and dinner.

EL CUBANITO **$**
1150 East Sixth Street
(520) 623-8020

It looks a lot like a run-down storefront, but don't be fooled—behind these doors you'll find the only taste of traditional Cuban cuisine in town. Order the Cubanito Special sandwich, a giant mouthful on a 7-inch roll layered with cheese, ham, roasted pork, and pickles. The hearty Ropa Vieja is a specialty; shredded beef is cooked with tomato sauce, garlic, and green peppers and doused with hot pepper sauce, served with black beans and white rice. Open Monday through Saturday until 3:00 p.m. June through August and until 7:00 p.m. the rest of the year.

SOMETHING SWEET DESSERT BAR **$**
5319 East Speedway Boulevard
(520) 881-7735
www.somethingsweet-dl.com

Not on a carb-restricted diet? Got a sweet tooth? Head to this dessert lounge and indulge. Giant slabs of cakes with mouthwatering names like Colossal Chocolate and Chocolate Thunder join creamy cheesecakes, pies, tortes, and tarts. They serve coffee and tea, too. Open daily.

ZEMAM'S **$**
2731 East Broadway
(520) 323-9928

Do you like eating with your fingers? If so, you'll love Zemam's, a tiny little Ethiopian cafe where instead of napkins, all the dishes come with a spongy bread (called injera) used to sop up luscious sauces. Try the doro wat (spicy chicken), spinach wat (spinach and cottage cheese), and any number of thick meat and vegetable stews. Extremely casual; bring your own bottle. Open Tuesday through Sunday for lunch and dinner.

FINE DINING

ACACIA AT ST. PHILIPS **$$$**
4340 North Campbell Avenue
(520) 232-0101
www.acaciatucson.com
Set in the lovely St. Philips Plaza, Acacia offers upscale dining both inside the elegant restaurant and outside on the spacious tree-shaded patio. The menu features contemporary American cuisine, with Latin and Pacific Rim accents. The combination of ingredients and multilayering of flavors make for unusual fare such as the duet of filet mignon and wood-roasted quail in a roasted shallot and wild mushroom half-glaze, with delicious mashed Yukon gold potatoes with roasted garlic and caramelized red onion. Pan-seared Alaskan halibut marries well with a sweet corn and roasted poblano crema and is served over a unique black quinoa polenta garnished with grilled asparagus. Desserts are stellar, with a cheesecake to die for. The presentation and service are always excellent and ingredients top-notch. A popular brunch every Sunday at 11:00 a.m. offers a full menu of classics (French toast, eggs Benedict) and more to the tunes of local jazz musicians. Open daily for lunch and dinner.

ANTHONY'S IN THE CATALINAS **$$$$**
6440 North Campbell Avenue
(520) 299-1771
www.anthonysinthecatalinas.com
A longtime Tucson favorite, Anthony's is continental dining at its best. Nestled at the base of the magnificent Santa Catalina Mountains, it offers you terrific city and mountain views. Anthony's award-winning wine list is considered one of the finest in the world, with over 1,700 selections. Start with a steaming bowl of rich French onion soup topped with melted Gruyère, next a classic roast duckling. Beef lovers will swoon over the incredible chateaubriand served with a red wine sauce and a heavenly béarnaise sauce. Leave room for the ethereal soufflés. Dinner daily.

THE ARIZONA INN **$$$**
2200 East Elm Street
(520) 325-1541
www.arizonainn.com
Casual elegance is the way to describe the ambience in the dining room at this historic inn in central Tucson. The signature breakfast is eggs Benedict and for lunch the classic chilled vichyssoise, but you can also find an eclectic mix of entrees at lunch and dinner, including the fish of the day and usually a wild game offering. The weekly tasting menu offers signature dishes.

The views of the beautiful grounds are legendary. The Arizona Inn dining room is open for breakfast, lunch, and dinner daily and offers Saturday and Sunday brunch.

i If you're an adventurous cook looking for unusual ingredients, don't miss the 17th Street Market (520-792-2588, www.hiddentreasures.com), a huge warehouse space full of every ethnic ingredient possible from Asian to Middle Eastern plus fresh produce, live fish, meat, and tons of frozen things you probably won't even recognize. Located at 830 East 17th Street. Call for directions; it's hidden away and tricky to find.

THE GOLD ROOM **$$$$**
Westward Look Resort
245 East Ina Road
(520) 297-1151
www.westwardlook.com
The award-winning Gold Room at Westward Look Resort has a stunning view of the Tucson valley whether you dine in or eat on the lovely outdoor terrace. Winner of *Mobil Travel Guide*'s Four-Star Award, AAA's Four-Diamond Award, and *Wine Spectator*'s Award of Excellence, the signature cuisine is a fusion of Southwestern and European culinary styles, accented with chilies, herbs, and produce from the on-site Chef's Gar-

den. You'll find a variety of dishes on the seasonal menu. Don't miss Chef Jamie's green chili tater tots. Special features include a Jazz Brunch on Sunday, October through June, and seasonal winemakers' dinners with guest vintners.

Well-prepared food coupled with incredible views and impeccable service make this a good choice for any occasion. Open daily for breakfast, lunch, and dinner.

MIGUEL'S AT LA POSADA **$$$**
La Posada Lodge & Casitas
5900 North Oracle Road
(520) 887-3777
www.laposadalodge.com

Miguel's introduces Nuevo Latino cuisine to Tucson. Housed in the La Posada Lodge & Casitas (see the Accommodations chapter), this lovely open and airy restaurant features an unusual and inventive menu. Chilies of all kinds—chipotle, serrano, poblano, pequin, and more—make a showing on the menu in every category. Homemade salsas grace each table along with multicolored chips for dipping. Mexico meets Italy in the flatiron-grilled filet mignon, which pairs olive oil and garlic with cilantro and Tabasco chilies. The chicken a la brasa in a mole verde comes with a creamy Oaxacan green chili rice. The menu also features fresh seafood dishes like cabrilla and bacon-wrapped Guaymas prawns.

You can sit in the dining room near the fireplace or on the patio and enjoy pool or mountain views. A comfortable semicircular bar with bamboo chairs is a great spot for a drink. Open daily.

VENTANA ROOM **$$$$**
Loews Ventana Canyon Resort
7000 North Resort Drive
(520) 299-2020
www.loewshotels.com

Ranked the No. 1 Restaurant in the Southwest by the *Zagat Survey Restaurant Guide* and *Condé Nast Traveler*, the four-star Ventana Room boasts fabulous views of the mountains and the city, making this a destination and special-occasion restaurant. Housed in the Loews Ventana Canyon Resort (see the Accommodations chapter), you'll find top-notch gourmet cuisine here. White linen tablecloths set with glistening glasses and fancy napkins beckon. The luxury menu offers classic and creative items using indigenous products from local farmers like saguaro cactus syrup and tepary beans. Desserts include innovative soufflés, tarts, and seasonal fruit creations.

You'll have a magical night here. Keep in mind that there are no a la carte selections; three-, four-, and five-course meals are the only option. Open Tuesday through Saturday, dinner only.

Vin Tabla welcomes you in for sophisticated and fine dining. PHOTO BY M. PAGANELLI VOTTO

VIN TABLA **$$$**
Plaza Colonial
2890 East Skyline Drive
(520) 577-6210
www.vintabla.com

The only place in town with a real live sommelier, Vin Tabla is upscale to the max with a wraparound patio and open kitchen. Master Sommelier Laura Williamson is one of only 14 female sommeliers in the United States, so this is the place to explore fine wines. Priced by the two-ounce taster, glass pour, or bottle, you can easily try lots of new selections with your meal. The menu offers New American Small Plates and Share Plates, perfect for grazing, and a wood-burning oven turns out several tasty pizzette. If you just want to pick, a raw/ice bar, salumi bar, cheese bar, and petit four pastry bar are sure to please. Williamson offers wine tasting classes and wine dinners throughout the year for the oenophiles among you.

FRENCH

GHINI'S FRENCH CAFFE **$**
1803 East Prince Road
(520) 326-9095
www.ghiniscafe.com

Ghini's offers a taste of France at a petite price. This small cafe is open for breakfast and lunch only. Ghini's has omelets, sandwiches, salads, and desserts from the adjacent bakery.

The omelets are made with three eggs and stuffed with such goodies as potatoes, onions, cheeses, bacon, garlic, and herbs Provençal. Salads are fresh; both the salade nicoise and wilted spinach salad stand out among several flavorful choices. Chef Ghini's favorite is the eggs Provençal (she confesses to eating them every day). Sides include homemade pâté maison, scalloped potatoes, and French onion soup. And if you're in the mood for just a sweet treat and a latte, Ghini's is happy to accommodate you. The restaurant is open for breakfast and lunch Tuesday through Sunday.

LE RENDEZ-VOUS **$$$**
3844 East Fort Lowell Road
(520) 323-7373
www.lerendez-vous.com

Winning accolades from food critics, dining at Le Rendez-vous is not just a meal but a total "experience." From the impeccable service to the extensive wine list to the fabulous menu offerings, this midtown restaurant brings France to the heart of the Sonoran Desert.

Start with the escargots and then leisurely wend your way through Les Potages, Les Salades, Les Poissons, and Les Viandes to Les Desserts Supreme. All are served in a romantic, intimate atmosphere.

The front door to the restaurant is not directly on Fort Lowell Road. You can park in the attached lot. Le Rendez-vous serves lunch and dinner Tuesday through Friday and dinner only on weekends.

GET IT AND GO

AJ'S FINE FOODS **$–$$**
La Encantada
2805 East Skyline Drive
(520) 232-6380
www.ajsfinefoods.com

Upscale, expensive, and full of great food and drink, AJ's is gourmet to the max. Owned by grocery entrepreneur Eddie Basha, AJ's offers top-of-the-line meats, seafood, a wine cellar, sushi bar, and cafe—all under one roof. Don't feel like cooking? There's a huge selection of prepared entrees. Need some fancy table linens? Fresh flowers for the centerpiece? You'll find all that here and more, along with knowledgeable and helpful staff. Open daily.

FEAST TASTEFUL TAKEOUT
4122 East Speedway Boulevard
(520) 326-9363
www.eatatfeast.com

If you're looking for high-quality takeout, Feast should be your first choice. Chef/owner Doug Levy makes delicious gourmet items to eat in (there's also a tiny restaurant on-site) or take out. Choose from salads, main courses, sandwiches, desserts, and the daily special from the ever-changing menu. Open Tuesday through Saturday.

RINCON MARKET **$$**
2513 East Sixth Street
(520) 327-6653
www.rinconmarket.com

The Rincon Market has been a neighborhood grocery store since 1928. In addition to groceries, Rincon Market has a salad bar, deli sandwiches, baked goods, and a wonderful prepared-meal take-out section. The offerings change on a daily basis, but at any given time you will have a choice of lasagna, tamale pie, dolmas, stuffed cabbage, and an assortment of salads and side dishes. The market's roasted chicken is a favorite of harried mothers all over town: The well-seasoned chickens are cooked daily on a rotisserie. The result is homemade taste without the homemade mess.

Wine and beer are available, and there is a butcher in the grocery store offering quality meats and seafood. The market is open daily.

TONY'S ITALIAN STYLE DELI, BUTCHER SHOP & RESTAURANT **$**
6219 East 22nd Street
(520) 747-0070

This Eastside deli is small but filled to the rafters with Italian goodies. The refrigerator counter holds fresh mozzarella, strings of Italian and German sausages, cold cuts, pepperoncini, and marinated artichokes. There are plenty of deli sandwiches on the menu. Try the Rocky, which is stuffed with mortadella, prosciutto, and provolone and drizzled with oil and vinegar. Or indulge in the house specialties of veal saltimbocca or spaghetti carbonara. For a quick family-style dinner, pick up a Bucket of Spaghetti and Meatballs, which can feed from 2 to 28 people. There are also pans of lasagna. Both come with garlic rolls. They also do catering.

Tony's is open Monday through Saturday from 9:00 a.m. to 8:00 p.m.

WHOLE FOODS MARKET **$$**
3360 East Speedway Boulevard
(520) 795-9860
7133 North Oracle Road
(520) 297-5394
www.wholefoodsmarket.com

Wild Oats/Whole Foods is a gourmet market and so much more—butcher shop, fishmonger, health food store, sandwich shop, bakery, and deli. The list of items you can get here seems endless.

But if you're in a hurry and still want something with homemade flavor, stop in at any one of the markets and pick up a salad to go, veggie lasagna, baked chicken, and a killer brownie from the bakery. Your choice of beverages is wide: everything from juices and bottled water to beers from around the world. You're bound to find something to please your palate. Wild Oats/Whole Foods is open daily.

GREEK AND MIDDLE EASTERN

ALADDIN **$$**
3699 North Campbell Avenue
(520) 320-0468

Craving Middle Eastern cuisine? Take your magic carpet to Aladdin, where you can feast on traditional and delicious dishes from a creamy homemade hummus and deep-fried lamb kibbe to slow-cooked lamb shanks and chicken kebabs. A basket of warm pita bread is on every table. A lovely welcoming interior, pleasant service, and soft music make this a satisfying dining experience. Open for lunch daily, and dinner, seasonally.

i **Several local stores cater to vegetarian palates. Aqua Vita (3225 North Los Altos Avenue; 520-293-7770) and the Food Conspiracy Co-op (412 North Fourth Avenue; 520-624-4821) carry a wide selection of organic produce and frozen vegetarian entrees. For additional resources, check out the Vegetarian Resource Group of Tucson's Web site: www.vrgt.com.**

ATHENS ON FOURTH AVENUE **$$**
500 North Fourth Avenue
(520) 624-6886

Owned by real Greeks, this longtime Fourth Avenue restaurant serves up traditional Greek cuisine. Start with the creamy taramosalata dip with pita bread or the Pikilia combination plate with stuffed grape leaves and kefaloritiri cheese. Avgolemono soup, lemony broth with rice, is a terrific and refreshing starter. Entrees include the standard spanakopita, moussaka, and pastisio; but go out on a limb and try some of the house specialties: sautéed sweetbreads or seafood stew. Enjoy a glass of Greek dessert wine and a baklava on the enclosed patio for dessert. Open Monday through Saturday, dinner only.

HEALTHY, VEGETARIAN, AND ALTERNATIVE

BLUE WILLOW RESTAURANT, BAKERY & POSTER GALLERY **$$**
2616 North Campbell Avenue
(520) 327-7577
www.bluewillowtucson.com

The first part of the name comes from the antique china pattern of star-crossed lovers (their story is on the menu, and the pattern is repeated throughout the restaurant). The second part comes from the nifty cards, posters, and trinkets that are sold in the front shop. On busy days the wait never seems long because the store has so many fun things to look at and play with.

Crepes, omelets, and quiche are the mainstays of the menu. Croissants are excellent, too. Sandwiches, soups, and salads complete the menu. The patio is famous for remaining cool on hotter days; it's tented with netting held up by little balloons.

Expect a wait, especially on weekend mornings. There's a small parking lot and limited free parking on the street. The Blue Willow serves breakfast, lunch, and dinner seven days a week.

CHOPPED **$**
2829 East Speedway Boulevard

4205 North Campbell Avenue
(520) 319-2467
www.choppedtucson.com

Do you like salad? Lots of salad? Chopped is the place for you! A Tucson original, you can choose from over 50 ingredients and 20 dressings and have a "customized" salad chopped and tossed right before your eyes. They also offer soup, panini, sandwiches, and dessert. If your kids are veggie-phobic, no worries! There's a kids menu, too, with salads, pb&j, and grilled cheese.

DELECTABLES **$$**
533 North Fourth Avenue
(520) 884-9289
www.delectables.com

Dining at Delectables is, well, delectable! Open for lunch and dinner seven days a week, this Fourth Avenue staple is still wowing diners of all followings (food followings, that is). You'll find all sorts of choices here: enchiladas, quiche, pasta, an assortment of salads and sandwiches, and lots of yummy desserts, along with vegan and vegetarian options like vegan puttanesca pasta and vegetarian spinach manicotti.

The atmosphere here is casual, and you have your choice of eating in the cool, open dining room or on the patio, where you'll be able to watch Fourth Avenue at its best. Parking can be a problem on the "Ave." Patience usually pays off when you're looking for a spot along the street.

THE GARLAND **$$**
119 East Speedway Boulevard
(520) 792-4221

This cozy little spot on Speedway Boulevard just east of Stone Avenue has a flavor treat for vegetarians and nonvegetarians alike with such delights as fresh fruit crepes and chicken salad. The salad dressings are flavorful without drowning the greens. Rolls and breads are homemade and served warm.

The setting is an older home that has been carefully renovated into a restaurant. The tasteful decorations and efficient, friendly service only add to the comfort zone. The Garland is open for breakfast and lunch Wednesday through Sunday and dinner Friday and Saturday.

GOVINDA'S **$$**
711 East Blacklidge Drive
(520) 792-0630
www.govindasoftucson.com

Located just off North First Avenue—between Glenn Avenue and Fort Lowell Road—in the Caitanya Cultural Center, Govinda's meals, all served buffet style, are consistently good. Dine indoors and enjoy waterfalls, fountains, gardens,

RECEIPT VOID WITHOUT CONFIRMATION ID

CONFIRMATION ID: 266362138

Dealer Name: AMC Communications Inc
Dealer Address: 3132 East Fort Lowell Road
Dealer Location: Tucson,AZ-85716
Phone Number: 520-795-2599
Merchant ID: 71005486

Provider: BOOST RTR TOPUP
Date: 10/17/2011
Time: 5:03 PM PST
Phone Number: 5204617476
Payment: 50.00
Amount Received: 100.00
Change: 50.00
PAYMENTS FOR CRICKET
SERVICE ARE NON-REFUNDABLE
ALL SALES ARE FINAL
This payment was processed by Magicpins

and exotic birds that add serenity to your dining experience. Patio dining is also available.

Lunch and dinner are served Tuesday through Saturday; brunch is offered on Sunday. Thursdays are vegan only.

YOSHIMATSU HEALTHY JAPANESE FOOD $
2660 North Campbell Avenue
(520) 320-1574

A restaurant with the guts to put the word *healthy* in its name has a lot to live up to, and Yoshimatsu succeeds. The funky interior features unusual Japanese pop art and a television running Japanese shows. You'll find a reasonably priced menu with a wide variety of noodle soups, curries, and sushi. Open for lunch and dinner seven days a week.

INDIAN

NEW DELHI PALACE $$
6751 East Broadway Boulevard
(520) 296-8585

New Delhi Palace, a top pick of *Tucson Weekly* readers, specializes in vegetarian and nonvegetarian Indian food. The bread is baked to order in tandoori ovens, and the owner takes pride in the authentic masalas and curries. For the vegetarian, a good bet is the Bengan Bharta, gently seasoned roasted eggplant. Nonvegetarians will delight in any one of the curries, especially satisfying when washed down with one of many varieties of cold beer served from the full bar. New Delhi is open daily for lunch and dinner.

ITALIAN

CARUSO'S $$
434 North Fourth Avenue
(520) 624-5765

Caruso's may well be one of the city's oldest restaurants. In fact, the Zagona family has been serving great southern Italian-American food to Tucsonans at the same location for more than 50 years!

The food is hearty, the ambience charming and very Italian, and the prices reasonable. The Lasagna al Forno, made with homemade noodles and baked to perfection, is a house specialty, and all your Italian favorites are served. Your waitperson can help you choose from the wines offered, which are available by the glass or the bottle. You may dine indoors or on the patio.

Caruso's is a great place to dine after a long day of shopping on Fourth Avenue. The restaurant is open Tuesday through Sunday for lunch and dinner. No reservations are accepted. You'll find limited parking on the street.

GAVI $$
7865 East Broadway Boulevard
(520) 290-8380

Foothills Mall
7401 North La Cholla Boulevard
(520) 209-9200

6960 East Sunrise Drive
(520) 615-1900

Piazza Gavi
5415 North Kolb Road
(520) 577-1099
www.gavifoods.com

Gavi is taking over Tucson! With several Italian restaurants in town, Gavi just keeps adding more. The Piazza Gavi location at Kolb is the most sophisticated of them all, with a softly lit interior, fireplace, two outdoor patios, pizza oven, espresso bar, and comfy couches—you can stay here all day. The menus for all locations feature contemporary Italian cuisine with giant bowls of steaming pasta, lasagna, platters of meat and fish, baskets of bread, pizzas, humongous salads, and enormous desserts.

Gavi has developed a reputation for Italian dinners that offer something more than the usual fare; the servings are large and come piping hot. All four locations are open for lunch and dinner seven days a week. Breakfast is served at the Piazza Gavi and Foothills Mall locations.

NORTH **$$**
La Encantada
2995 East Skyline Drive
(520) 299-1600
ww.tasteofnorth.com
The setting and the decor are top-notch. The food? The "modern Italian" menu features some contemporary takes on traditional dishes, like a pizza topped with proscuitto and melon, and farmer cheese and a "not your typical" chicken lasagna. But there are lots of standard choices too: grilled meats and fish, pastas, and a variety of salads. This is a hot spot for young and hip Tucsonans who enjoy the gorgeous patio and enormous bar. Open daily for lunch and dinner.

PRIMO **$$$–$$$$**
Starr Pass Marriott Resort and Spa
3800 West Starr Pass Boulevard
(520) 792-3500
www.starrpassmarriott.com
Housed in the gorgeous Starr Pass Marriott Resort hotel on the far west side of town (see the Accommodations chapter), James Beard Award–winning chef Melissa Kelly is on board at Primo, where she creates Italian-inspired cuisine. You can eat indoors in the well-appointed dining room or outside on the beautiful patio with its amazing views of the city. The ever-changing seasonal menu offers antipasti (including pizza), pasta, fish, meat (from sustainable and organic sources), and various sides (try the sautéed spinach with pine nuts). Don't get too full—desserts are winners, too. Open daily for dinner.

i Looking for Italian ingredients? Head to Roma Imports. Hidden away on a tiny side street, this huge warehouselike space offers all you can possibly want from pasta to frozen items like meatballs and lasagna. And if you don't feel like cooking, they make sandwiches, too. Located at 627 South Vine Avenue; (520) 792-3173. Open Monday through Saturday. Call for directions!

TAVOLINO **$$**
7090 North Oracle Road
(520) 531-1913
Good things come in small packages, and Tavolino is no exception. With only 12 tables, this little gem is hidden away in a shopping center on the southeast corner of Oracle and Ina Roads.

Get ready for some of the best authentic Italian food in town—chef Massimo Tenino is the real thing, showcasing the homey, delicious cuisine of northern Italy. The homemade linguine alla Bolognese is perfection, with a rich meaty sauce that perfectly coats the strands of rich egg pasta. The lasagna is saucy, with beef, veal, and pork lightly layered with mozzarella and Parmesan cheese. And don't pass up the traditional pesto, a beautiful marriage of fresh basil, virgin olive oil, and Parmesan. The Ravioli di Zucca, a house specialty, is stuffed with butternut squash and napped with a sauce of brown butter and sage. There are several meat and fish entrees, but pasta is definitely the star. A close rival is the amazing Bonet dessert—a chocolate custard topped with crushed amaretti cookies and a sinful bitter caramel sauce.

Open for lunch and dinner. Reservations are essential; they book up early. Closed Sunday and part of August.

VIVACE RESTAURANT **$$$**
St. Philip's Plaza
4310 North Campbell Avenue
(520) 795-7221
While it is an Italian restaurant, with osso buco, polenta, and pastas on the menu, it may better be classified as New Italian for its innovative preparations.

For lunch Vivace has pastas, sandwiches, salads, and various house specialties. Vivace's dinner menu offers several selections. Start with stuffed artichoke hearts for an appetizer, and then try artichoke–goat cheese cannelloni. Vivace has a full bar with an extensive choice of wines by the bottle or the glass. You can dine outside on the lovely patio. Vivace is open for lunch Monday through Saturday and for dinner daily. We suggest reservations.

MEXICAN/SPANISH

CAFE POCA COSA **$$**
110 East Pennington Street
(520) 622-6400
www.cafepocacosatucson.com

Chef/owner Suzana Davila has transformed the ground floor of this rather bleak downtown garage space at East Pennington and North Sixth Avenue into a sleek, comfortable restaurant. Davila creates interesting dishes inspired by different regions of her native Mexico. The menu, listed on a tiny chalkboard, changes daily, but you can always choose the Plato Poca Cosa, which showcases the specials. Closed Sunday.

CASA VICENTE **$**
375 South Stone Avenue
(520) 884-5253
www.casavicente.com

In the mood for some flamenco music? A steaming platter of paella? Head to Casa Vicente, where the kitchen is hopping and the music is lively. Start with tapas, those tiny finger-licking-good appetizers Spain is known for. You'll find a great selection here, over 26 hot and cold choices, from a traditional Spanish frittata to menudo cooked with garbanzos. If you want paella, you need to call at least two hours in advance and bring four hungry friends. Try the Paella Negra, black rice flavored with squid ink and brimming with seafood. Ask about the specials of the day, and don't forget to order a large pitcher of sangria.

Each night features live music—flamenco performances are on Friday and Saturday. Open for dinner Tuesday through Sunday, lunch Tuesday through Saturday.

i **Experience the cuisine of the barrio in comfort on the Gray Line Best of the Barrio tour. You'll get to sample many of the traditional Sonoran Mexican foods available in South Tucson on this four-hour tour that includes stops at five of Tucson's finest family-owned, off-the-beaten-path eateries. You'll feast on handmade pastries and tortillas at La Estrella Bakery, traditional Sonoran-style Mexican entrees at El Menerdero, ceviche and fish tacos at Rodriguez Fish Company, Sonoran hot dogs and carne-asada burritos at El Guero Canelo, and finally "raspados" (shaved ice, ice cream, fresh fruit) at Oasis Fruit Cones. The cost is $59 per adult for tour and food. Call Gray Line at (520) 622-8811, or visit www.graylinearizona.com and go to "Sightseeing Tours."**

EL CHARRO CAFE **$$**
311 North Court Avenue
(520) 622-1922

El Mercado
6310 East Broadway Boulevard
(520) 745-1922

100 Orange Grove Road
(520) 615-1922

4699 East Speedway Boulevard
(520) 325-1922

6910 East Sunrise Drive
(520) 514-1922
www.elcharrocafe.com

Regularly voted Best Mexican Restaurant by the *Tucson Weekly* readers' poll, the original El Charro Cafe is a Tucson treasure. In the historic downtown El Presidio district, the building at North Court Avenue is an 1896 adobe on the National Historic Register. The business is the nation's oldest Mexican restaurant continuously operated by the same family (since 1922), and the food reflects the tradition.

The menu includes topopo jalisciense, a signature chimichanga, carne seca, and baked fish tacos. Carne seca (marinated dried beef) is a house specialty. Try it in the famous, huge chimichanga. For some more unusual items, choose from Carlotta's Creations, which feature interesting combinations of flavors and ingredients. If you just can't decide, they do have a tasting plate, or you can choose from several combination platters that will give you a little bit of everything. They even have their own cookbook, so you can make your favorites at home.

The original location downtown (Court Avenue) has the most charm.

All five sites are open for lunch and dinner seven days a week.

EL GUERO CANELO #1 **$**
5201 South 12th Avenue, South Tucson
(520) 295-9005
www.elguerocanelo.com

It's not at all fancy—in fact, it's just a step above a taco stand—but this south side favorite offers an extensive menu of home-style Sonoran dishes, from giant burros and overstuffed tacos to menudo (served Saturday and Sunday only). Order at the window and serve yourself condiments (lime wedges, cucumbers, shredded cabbage, salsas, and hot sauces). Open daily until midnight for breakfast, lunch, and dinner. This area is somewhat isolated and can be intimidating at night, so consider breakfast or lunch for your first visit. There is a sister location in town, but it has none of the charm of the original.

EL MINUTO CAFE **$$**
354 South Main Avenue
(520) 882-4145

This longtime downtown landmark is known for its carne seca and refried beans. While many restaurants in town serve low-fat cooking, El Minuto has stuck with the traditional methods—maybe not heart healthy, but certainly worth falling off the diet wagon for.

The dining area is decorated with Mexican curios, chili strings, and hand-painted flowered trim on the turquoise and pink walls. Serapes are used for curtains. Eat indoors or sip a Mexican beer as you soak up the historical ambience of the neighboring barrio from the patio at the downtown location.

Located across from the Tucson Convention Center, it's a great place to stop before or after an event. There will be a wait on weekends, so get there early. While you wait, take a short walk to the shrine, El Tiradito, next door. Closed Sunday.

EL MOLCAJETE MEXICAN FOOD **$**
663 South Plumer Avenue
(520) 623-8886

A true Insiders' spot, this mom-and-pop Mexican restaurant is a hidden treasure. Open only for breakfast and lunch, it's a favorite with locals. They, and you, come for the terrific homemade soups, fresh guacamole, the best green corn tamales in town, and the homey, friendly atmosphere. Don't come here if you're looking for fancy food; this is homemade Mexican comfort food. Open seven days a week until 3:00 p.m.

EL TORERO **$$**
231 East 26th Street
(520) 622-9534

Finding this longtime south-side favorite might be a little difficult, but we'll give you an Insiders' tip: As you head south on Fourth Avenue, watch for a mural of a bullfighter, then make the next right onto 26th Street. The second building from the corner is El Torero.

The first things that will catch your eye in this brightly lit restaurant are the long wooden bar, high ceilings, and thick adobe walls. The place may seem a bit noisy, but don't let that change your mind. Even on busy nights, you'll be seated quickly at one of the many tables, and you won't notice the noise.

Anything you order will be outstanding, but try the carne seca plate. You'll get a heap of seasoned shredded beef with Mexican rice and refried beans. A warm flour tortilla accompanies the meal. To eat this in true Mexican style, tear off a piece of the tortilla (making sure you cover it up again to keep it soft and warm), and plop on some carne seca, a dollop of beans, and some salsa. La Bandera (red, green, and white enchiladas) is another favorite, as is the topopo salad, a corn tortilla slathered with beans and topped with a mountain of lettuce, avocado, tomatoes, and your choice of cheese, chicken, or shrimp. It really doesn't need any dressing, but there is vinaigrette available on request.

El Torero is open every day except Tuesday for lunch and dinner. Although a parking lot is adjacent to the restaurant, it's better to park on the street.

JOHN JACOB'S EL PARADOR **$$**
2744 East Broadway Boulevard
(520) 881-2744
www.elparadortucson.com

You might wonder if a Mexican restaurant with a non-Mexican owner could survive the competition in Tucson. But that's exactly what the Jacob family has done, and done well, since 1946.

The food is unique. Try the ceviche or taquitos appetizer, then choose from fajitas, tamales, chiles rellenos, and a carne seca chimichanga with pico de gallo.

Lush plants and a skylight give the feeling of eating in a tropical paradise. Several private dining rooms can be used for meetings or special functions, and El Parador also provides catering services.

The restaurant is open daily for lunch or dinner, and on Sunday a brunch is served. Stop in the Cantina, El Parador's bar, at happy hour on weekday afternoons. Friday and Saturday nights feature a nightclub with live music.

MI NIDITO CAFE **$$**
1813 South Fourth Avenue
(520) 622-5081
www.minidito.net

The wait at Mi Nidito on many evenings can be as long as 45 minutes. Serving Tucson since 1952, Mi Nidito has been voted the best Mexican food in several newspaper polls for many years. Just ask President Clinton. It was here at Mi Nidito that he lunched while in town.

The decor hasn't changed much over the years, nor has the food, a standard take on Sonoran cuisine. Mexican tile, whitewashed walls, and a fake palm tree in the back of the restaurant are not unlike decor in restaurants on the other side of the border. The large and crispy flautas are topped with lettuce, guacamole, sour cream, and a sprinkling of Mexican farmer cheese. The menudo is classic. The chiles rellenos and the burro deluxe are also filling and hearty.

Mi Nidito is open for lunch and dinner every night except Monday and Tuesday.

ROSA'S **$$**
1750 East Fort Lowell Road
(520) 325-0362
www.rosasmexicanfood.com

When Rosa opened her restaurant years ago, patrons could watch her as she cooked meals, waited tables, and kept a watchful eye on her children, who were often at the restaurant when not in school. Today those very same children are grown and continuing the tradition their mom began so long ago.

The refried beans at Rosa's are truly traditional and are some of the best in all of Tucson. The enchiladas, tacos, burritos, chimichangas, and chiles rellenos are all made in the traditional manner as well. The daily sopas (soups) are delicious. If you're not sure which menu item to pick, try one of the family's special combination plates. Don't miss the fabulous salsa, smooth and spicy. Top your meal off with some sopapillas (fry bread) with honey or the almendrado, a unique pudding topped with almond sauce.

Rosa's is open for lunch and dinner seven days a week.

TAQUERIA PICO DE GALLO **$**
2618 South Sixth Avenue
(520) 623-8775

Raised from relative obscurity by a review in *Gourmet* magazine, this tiny taqueria in south Tucson has kept its modest digs and low-key attitude. The only change is that you can now use credit cards to pay for some of the tastiest Mexican food in town. Don't pass up the fabulous shrimp tacos served with homemade corn tortillas or a huge steaming bowl of tortilla soup full of shredded chicken, cheese, and avocado. The whole fried fish is a stunner. Daily combination plates feature whatever's fresh from the sea or the market. Dessert has to be the big plastic cup of fresh fruit the restaurant is named for, pico de gallo: slices of coconut, papaya, pineapple, jicama, and oranges, sprinkled with lime juice and chili pepper. No reservations; open daily for lunch and dinner.

PIZZA

BROOKLYN PIZZA $
534 North Fourth Avenue
(520) 622-6868
www.brooklynpizzacompany.com

Brooklyn Pizza is not the place to take the boss to make a good impression, which is a shame since that means he or she will miss out on great New York–style pizza.

The decor might be called funky. There are a dozen mismatched '50s Formica-topped tables. The walls are painted a deep yellow and covered with artwork. And the music is everything from '50s hits to alternative rock.

When your pizza arrives, you'll swear you're in Brooklyn. The sauce is rich, the toppings are all high quality, and the crust is the perfect blend of crispy and chewy. Toppings include artichoke hearts, chicken, eggplant, feta cheese, ground beef, meatballs, ricotta, spinach, and other more common toppings.

You can also have pasta with marinara sauce, garlic knots, cheese, or any of the pizza toppings. The hero sandwiches are imaginative. Try the Florentine or the Vatican Veggie.

i The Tucson area is home to pecan growers and pistachio groves. At the Pecan Store in Sahuarita (520-791-2062; www.azpecans.com) you'll find 12 sizes of pecans, candies, and more. The Arizona Pistachio Company in Bowie (520-746-0880, 800-333-8575; www.azpistachio.com) is the largest producer of pistachios in Arizona. You can buy their delectable nuts at most local farmers' markets, select stores, and online. They're great plain, but they also offer them flavored.

The restaurant serves lunch and dinner daily and has late-night hours. Beer and wine are available. Brooklyn Pizza delivers to just north of Sixth Street, with a minimum order; it will even deliver beer.

MAGPIE'S GOURMET PIZZA $$
Speedway Boulevard and Swan Road
(520) 795-5977

Broadway Boulevard at Houghton Road
(520) 751-9949

Fourth Avenue and Fifth Street
(520) 628-1661

Ina and Oracle Roads
(520) 297-2712

Sabino Canyon Road and Tanque Verde Road
(520) 546-6521

8295 North Cortaro Farms Road
(520) 572-4300
www.magpiespizza.com

Magpie's was the first pizza place in town to offer gourmet pizza. The restaurant offers several specialty pizzas, such as the Godfather, which has mozzarella, provolone, Swiss, Romano, and cheddar cheeses and Italian sausage, Canadian bacon, and capicolla. Regular crust, sourdough crust, or whole-wheat crust with a choice of sauces—pesto, olive oil and garlic, or regular tomato sauce—are available. Toppings are numerous and include roasted green chilies, sun-dried tomatoes, fresh spinach or zucchini, and pepperoncini. With all of this to offer, it's no wonder Magpie's pies have been named "Best Pizza in Tucson" 17 years in a row.

For the health conscious, Magpie's has light "r" pizzas made without mozzarella or provolone cheeses. Low-fat or cheese substitutes are available at no extra cost. You also have several choices of calzones and fresh salads.

Seating is limited; the majority of Magpie's business is delivery or takeout. A unique feature on the take-out menu is the Take & Bake pizza. Call ahead and order your pizza to be picked up. Then instead of getting a hot pizza at the restaurant and having a cold pizza by the time you get home, you get an uncooked pizza that you can pop into your oven. Magpie's is open for lunch and dinner and has late-night hours.

MAMA'S PIZZA AND HEROS $
7965 North Oracle Road
(520) 297-3993

6996 East 22nd Street
(520) 750-1919

4500 East Speedway Boulevard
(520) 319-8856

50 South Houston
(520) 751-4600
www.mamasfamous.com
With three generations of Mama's children working in the restaurants, you can rest assured that whatever you order will be just like Mama made. The family-size pizza is big enough for a family of four plus any number of relatives and friends who might stop by unannounced. Mama's also serves some great sandwiches. All Mama's are open for lunch and dinner every day.

SAUCE $
Casas Adobes Plaza
7117 North Oracle Drive
(520) 297-8575

5285 East Broadway Boulevard
(520) 514-1122

2990 North Campbell Avenue
(520) 795-0344
www.foxrestaurantconcepts.com
Have a craving for crispy crust pizza? Sauce is the place. Yummy pizzas come topped with pepperoni and cremini mushrooms, rosemary potato, spinach, feta and olive tapenade, or the unlikely prosciutto and melon combo. People chow 'em down in an instant. You can also choose from several tasty salads and lasagna. Wine and beer are available as thirst quenchers. Open for lunch and dinner daily from 11:00 a.m.

ZACHARY'S $
1019 East Sixth Street
(520) 623-6323
Zachary's has a reputation for cold beers and humongous pizzas. The beers come from all over the world. In fact, Zachary's had a large beer selection long before it became trendy. Dress is very casual, and families are welcome.

Pizzas are 2 inches thick and come loaded with toppings, including the standards as well as broccoli, artichoke hearts, fresh tomatoes, jalapeños, spinach, proscuitto, and pineapple. The Big Z is the house specialty. Meat lovers will want to try the T Rex, which comes with pepperoni, sausage, and ham. For veggie lovers, the staff recommends the Uptowner. The salad dressings are homemade. Due to the size of the pizzas, the wait once you've ordered can be almost an hour, especially on nights when there is a UA game. Zachary's is open every day.

SEAFOOD

BLUEFIN SEAFOOD BISTRO $$
7053 North Oracle Road
(520) 531-8500
www.bluefinseafoodtucson.com
A sister restaurant to Kingfisher (see below), this classy seafood bistro is tucked away in the middle of Casas Adobes Plaza. Brick walls and banquette seating are the setting for some super seafood. Oysters, clams, shrimp, clam chowder, and ceviche are just for starters. Specialties include crab cakes, fish-and-chips with house-made tartar sauce, and the grilled salmon melt. A late-night menu is also on tap for the party animals among you (served until midnight). Patio dining is available as well. Open daily for lunch and dinner.

KINGFISHER $$$$
2564 East Grant Road
(520) 323-7739
www.kingfishertucson.com
Kingfisher bills itself as an American regional grill, which means the featured food comes from all regions of America, but the accent is on seafood

in every way, shape, and form. Diners can select from three or four types of oysters flown in daily from the Northwest, the East Coast, and other briny places. And if you don't know one oyster from another, your knowledgeable waitperson will explain the subtle differences.

Fresh fish specials change daily; all are cooked with attention to detail and are free of heavy sauces. Salmon is a staple, but that's not to say the steaks and other entrees aren't good here. The kitchen grills up a pretty mean steak. The wine list is large and varied enough to find a suitable match for any choice of entree.

The decor is modern but cozy. Reservations are suggested. Lunch and dinner are served, and Kingfisher is one of the few places that serves until midnight seven days a week.

MARISCOS CHIHUAHUA **$$**
1009 Grande Avenue
(520) 623-3563

356 East Grant Road
(520) 884-3457

3901 South Sixth Avenue
(520) 741-0361

Cheap, cheap, cheap and tasty, this small chain offers market-fresh seafood and shrimp from the Sea of Cortez. The head on whole fried fish is a wonder to behold. It arrives crispy and flaky on a giant platter along with tortillas and a giant bottle of ranch dressing; ignore the eyeballs and dig in. There's lots of shrimp here: fried or sautéed with garlic and oil are winners. The Seven Seas soup is a must, a rich broth swimming with all sorts of sea creatures. Don't expect a fancy place—you'll find simple tables and chairs and a unique, colorful ocean decor. Open daily.

STEAK HOUSES

EL CORRAL **$$**
2201 East River Road
(520) 299-6092
www.elcorraltucson.com

El Corral has long been a Tucson tradition when it comes to where to take out-of-town visitors for prime rib. There's not an evening any day of the week or season of the year when the outside patio isn't comfortably filled with people waiting for a table. Don't be dissuaded by the wait: It's reasonable, even in peak season. You'll have just enough time for a beer, wine, or highball or two from the bar.

El Corral's claim to fame is prime rib, but the ribs are also a great choice. The prime rib comes in several cuts and sizes, and the ribs come as a full or half rack. Sides include the usuals, such as choice of potatoes or pilaf, but Insiders know that the tamale pie is the way to go. This fluffy, soft corn bread is slightly sweet and studded with mild green chilies and kernels of corn. Top the meal off with a tableside tossed salad with the house Honey Italian dressing and such trimmings as sunflower seeds, croutons, mushrooms, and fresh cracked pepper, and you will walk away more than satisfied.

The ambience here is totally Tucson—casual, comfortable, and slightly rustic Southwestern. Several dining rooms and close tables add comfort instead of a crowded feeling. You'll see diners in their Sunday best and others who look like they just stepped off the golf course. Service is also a plus—quick, knowledgeable, and friendly.

El Corral serves only dinner nightly and does not take reservations..

LIL ABNER'S STEAKHOUSE $$$
8500 North Silverbell Road
(520) 744-2800

Old-timers in Tucson can remember when the drive out to Lil Abner's Steakhouse was a trek. The road was dark, narrow, and winding, but it was always a treat once you arrived. Today the ride doesn't seem so long due to all the development in this part of Tucson and the wider, well-lit road, and there is still a treat at the end. Lil Abner's has some of the best mesquite-grilled steaks around. And the atmosphere is about as cowboy as you can get. Dinner on the patio means beautiful desert views, especially at sunset; the smell of your dinner on the grill; and the twang of Western music, which is offered on Friday, Saturday, and Sunday.

Other entree selections include beef ribs, pork ribs, and chicken, all cooked on the grill of course. Sides include your choice of cowboy beans or potatoes. All meals come with a small salad.

Lil Abner's serves dinner nightly.

MCMAHON'S PRIME STEAKHOUSE $$$
2959 North Swan Road
(520) 327-7463
www.metrorestaurants.com

Voted the best steak house in Tucson by local magazines, McMahon's is famous for its USDA prime aged beef and fresh seafood. Try one of the dry-aged steaks, rare, with a side of creamed spinach, mashed potatoes, and a Caesar salad. Seafood specialties include lobster tails. You'll also find great appetizers, desserts, and over 25,000 wines. Open for lunch and dinner .

OK CORRAL $$
7710 East Wrightstown Road
(520) 885-2373

Don't miss the turnoff to the OK Corral or you'll miss out on great mesquite-broiled steak, ribs (pork and beef), chicken, and some of the best prime rib in Tucson. Stay in the far right lane as you head east on Tanque Verde, and watch for the signs that mark the exit to Wrightstown Road.

OK Corral has been at the same site since 1968. The interior is a slice of cowboy heaven, with large wooden tables covered with red-checked tablecloths, wood paneling, antiques, and, in the center of it all, a huge mesquite grill.

Steaks come in seven sizes and several cuts, and there are four cuts of prime rib. Pinto beans, salsa, salad, and bread accompany each meal. The drinks are hefty, too, and the beer is ice cold.

OK Corral is open Tuesday through Sunday for dinner only. Banquet and catering services are available.

PINNACLE PEAK STEAKHOUSE $$
6541 East Tanque Verde Road
(520) 296-0911
www.pinnaclepeaktuc.com

If you have a friend who has horrible taste in ties, bring him (or her) to Pinnacle Peak. Anyone who walks in sporting a tie will promptly be the center of attention as the waitresses begin clanging cowbells and all action stops. Then, snip! snip! A waitress cuts off the tie and hangs it from the ceiling where it joins hundreds of others. Yep, this place takes casual dress to a whole new level.

Located in Trail Dust Town on Tanque Verde Road, Pinnacle Peak is a Tucson tradition for big mesquite-grilled steaks. A range of steak is offered, from the smaller one-pound T-bone to the monster two-pound porterhouse. Ribs, barbecue chicken, and fish are also available. Sides include the cowboy staples of beans, taters, salad, and bread. Try the apple cobbler for dessert, if you have room that is, and then enjoy a stroll through Trail Dust Town. The shops here are unique, and the kids may want to ride the scale-model train that runs the perimeter (see the Shopping and Kidstuff chapters).

Pinnacle Peak is open nightly for dinner, but expect a wait (especially on weekends); they don't take reservations.

SAM HUGHES PLACE CHAMPIONSHIP DINING **$$**
446 North Campbell Avenue
(520) 747-5223
www.samhughesplace.com

Part sports bar, part sophisticated restaurant, Sam Hughes Place offers "a menu of American favorites," including seafood, salads, and sandwiches, but beef is the thing here, brought in fresh daily and cut in-house. Choose from sterling silver–grade 21-ounce bone-in rib eye, 15-ounce bone-in New York strip, 10-ounce filet mignon, and the gargantuan 23-ounce porterhouse, all accompanied by a giant baked potato with sour cream, butter, bacon, and chives. While you wait for your entree, feast your eyes on the 23 high-definition TVs (usually showing sports) in the main dining room. If you have to use the loo, you won't miss a thing—there are four more TVs in the restrooms. Open daily.

NIGHTLIFE

You'll find a lot happening here, such as great movies, new and old, and great music, from classical to folk to rock and, of course, country! And though Tucson is not a late-night town, you'll find these and other interesting activities to fill your evenings.

If nightlife to you means live music, you'll find a full slate in Tucson, including rock, country, jazz, alternative, dance, blues, and acoustic performances. The major live music clubs are clustered along Fourth Avenue and the connecting downtown area, but other venues can be found in all parts of town. You'll also find plenty of pubs, bars, and the like that may not have live music regularly, but they certainly offer enough entertainment to keep you hopping. Many restaurants offer live music ranging from jazz to piano and classical guitar to strolling mariachis. And, as in most larger cities, several microbreweries and cafes have begun to make their mark as favorite spots to spend some casual time.

To get a taste of both downtown and Fourth Avenue, check out Club Crawl (www.clubcrawl.net), a live music festival with more than 80 bands and musical acts performing on 25 outdoor stages and inside select clubs. All this great music can be yours with a low-cost wristband available in advance or at the door. It's a great opportunity to see downtown's music scene at its best and to mingle with a good cross section of Tucsonans.

For the cinema crowd, in addition to the handful of "regular" movie houses, you'll find the Loft, which shows artsy foreign films, and the Screening Room, specializing in independent productions and the works of local producers. And we have a drive-in theater, the DeAnza, which runs first-run flicks on four screens.

Much of Tucson's nightlife relates to the area's strong arts scene, with numerous theatrical productions, ballets, operas, and symphonic music presentations. We also have a strong literary base that has resulted in a number of regularly scheduled evening poetry readings at various venues, from coffeehouses to bookstores. (See the Arts and Culture chapter for more specific information.)

A FEW GROUND RULES

In the state of Arizona, you must be 21 years of age to consume alcohol, and Tucson's clubs won't let you in the door without a picture ID. Cabs don't really roam the streets here, but if you need one, the clubs are more than happy to call one for you. Arizona's drunk driving laws are very strict and strongly enforced with random roadblocks—especially on holiday weekends—so it's better to pay the money for a cab than spend a night in jail.

Credit card acceptance varies. Cover charges often depend on the popularity of the entertainment and whether or not the band playing is an out-of-town act. Our best advice if you're strapped for cash, or if you just don't believe in paying for entertainment, is to call before you head out the door.

The following listings are broken down into general categories, but nothing in Tucson is written in stone. In any given week, a club could have bands playing rock one night, blues the next, and reggae the following evening. And unless we tell you otherwise, these clubs have full bars.

EASY LISTENING

THE ARIZONA INN
2200 East Elm Street
(520) 325-1541
www.arizonainn.com

One of the city's most elegant and historic spots, the Arizona Inn's classy Audubon Lounge offers overstuffed chairs and sofas where you can listen to a pianist play. (For more information on the Arizona Inn, check the Accommodations chapter.)

LOEWS VENTANA CANYON RESORT
7000 North Resort Drive
(520) 299-2020
www.loewshotels.com

The comfortable Cascade Lounge with big picture windows overlooking the pool area and a huge fireplace offers live music (duos, trios, big bands, and easy listening) on Friday and Saturday till 1:00 a.m. Settle into one of the comfy couches or chairs, nurse a drink (their prickly pear margarita and homemade lemonade are fantastic), and enjoy the sweet sounds in grand style.

MCMAHON'S PRIME STEAKHOUSE
2959 North Swan Road
(520) 327-2333
www.metrorestaurants.com

This popular, upscale steak house has live music nightly in the piano lounge. You'll find duos, trios, vocalists, and pianists performing a wide repertoire of jazz, show tunes, oldies, and standards. Full bar service and restaurant menu are available in the lounge.

CAFES

BENTLEY'S HOUSE OF COFFEE AND TEA
1730 Speedway Boulevard
(520) 795-0338
www.bentleyscoffeehouse.com

A casual, comfortable cafe frequented by UA graduate students, this homey place is a magnet for local songwriters who line up for the Friday-night open mike starting at 7:30 p.m. You might find an a cappella chorus, acid rock band, or classical guitarist on the stage. You'll also find a great atmosphere, sandwiches and desserts, and nonalcoholic drinks.

CUSHING STREET BAR & RESTAURANT
198 West Cushing Street
(520) 622-7984
www.cushingstreet.com

Step back in time at this wonderful downtown bar and cafe housed in a historic landmark. There's a fabulous wooden bar complete with a brass foot rail, floor-to-ceiling cabinets, and antiques. A limited menu of comfort foods (homemade soups, salads, meat and potatoes) is just fine. Come for the ambience and the great bar where the bartenders can make just about anything. (Don't believe it? Ask for a German chocolate cake and see what you get.) There's live music, and concerts take place during the summer in the beautiful enclosed outdoor patio. Call for a schedule. Open Tuesday through Saturday; cover charges for musical events.

EPIC CAFE
745 North Fourth Avenue
(520) 624-6844
www.epic-cafe.com

This casual, funky cafe offers live music and a variety of open-mic nights. A great place to hang out, with high ceilings, great acoustics, and an eclectic crowd, you also get a great view of the Old Pueblo Trolley at night. Performances are spotty, so call first to see who's on the bill. There's free Wi-Fi, too! Open daily.

i **While you're on Congress Street visiting all the clubs, stop in at one of Tucson's oldest music stores—the amazing, the eclectic, the crammed-to-the-ceiling Chicago Music Store (130 Congress Street; 520-622-3341). Filled to the brim with everything musical from instruments to sheet music, they sell, rent, trade, and buy. The staff can find anything from a kid's bongo set to a concertina in this huge store. They're open Monday through Saturday.**

JAVALINA'S COFFEE & FRIENDS
9136 East Valencia Road, #160
(520) 663-5282
www.javalinas.com

Small and cozy, this independently owned coffeehouse is a welcoming hangout on the southeast side. Casual and friendly, you'll find music and conversation over lattes and coffee. There's a limited menu of other goodies. Free Wi-Fi. Live folk music happens here most weekends, along with mixers and other special events. Open daily.

CLUBS

CLUB ASYLUM
121 East Congress Street
(520) 882-8949
www.clubasylum.com

Dark, mysterious, and very Goth, this downtown club covers it all, from industrial and synth-pop to new wave and '80s retro. If you make it inside, check out the giant metal beast above the bar, which is made of scrap motorcycle parts. Open Tuesday through Saturday; cover charge on Friday and Saturday.

i **Hotel Congress was named "One of the Best Bars in America" by *Esquire* magazine, the only bar in the Southwest to make it onto the list.**

CLUB CONGRESS
311 East Congress Street
(520) 622-8848
www.hotelcongress.com

This eclectic club, in the historic Congress Hotel, has risen to the forefront of the downtown night scene. And although it's a favorite of the younger, not-so-tragically hip crowd, older folks can kick up their heels on the dance floor without sticking out like sore thumbs. Club Congress claims to have been "inventing Tucson nightlife since 1985." You'll find lots of live music (local and national) and special events in this funky downtown setting. Weekly events include a '80s dance night. You'll also find considerably calmer live music in the lobby/bar on select weeknights.

i **Nostalgic for the bygone days of vinyl? Don't despair, Twist & Shout (5741 East Speedway Boulevard; 520-290-6600) specializes in 45s, vinyl, and CDs from the '60s, '70s, and '80s. They buy, sell, and trade. Open daily.**

LEVEL BAR AND LOUNGE
St. Philip's Plaza
4280 North Campbell Avenue
520-615-3835
www.leveltucson.com

A hot spot for the upscale, well-dressed, and well-heeled, Level is a small but hip spot for seeing and being seen. A cozy dance floor, flat-screen televisions, curtained VIP room, sleek wooden bar, and outdoor patio with a fire pit brings them in all night long. Dress codes are strictly enforced—you won't find shorts or work boots on this well-turned-out crowd. Open Wednesday through Saturday until 2:00 a.m.

PEARL
445 West Wetmore Road
(520) 888-8084
www.pearltucson.com

Billing itself as "Tucson's first Las Vegas–style entertainment venue," this 20,000-square-foot club features a full-service restaurant and lounge, an oxygen bar, a dance club, an "omni-sex" restroom, and a 2,000-square-foot outdoor patio with hookah pipes. If you're in the money, spring for the $5,000 Pink Pearl cocktail that comes in two Swarovski crystal champagne glasses you get to take home. Open Wednesday through Sunday. Get out your fancy clothes, the dress code prohibits baggy clothes, flip-flops, beanies, and T-shirts.

THE SHELTER
4155 East Grant Road
(520) 326-1345

Open since 1994, Shelter bills itself as a go-go boot wearing, martini drinking, swanky, groovy lounge. The crowd is very eclectic. They sip drinks at the bar or in booths while a strange collection of tunes plays on the stereo, and the television runs classic flicks such as '60s James Bond movies. There are DJs on the first Sunday of every month and pool tables, but the draw here is the ambience and the cocktails. Drinks are serious business here: Bartenders only offer top-of-the-line libations and never use prefab mixes or disperse alcohol from a gun. Open daily 3:00 p.m. to midnight.

THE WILDCAT HOUSE
1801 North Stone Avenue
(520) 622-1302
www.thewildcathouse.com
Named for the Arizona Wildcats, this cavernous, low-lit club packs 'em in for all sorts of dance nights, including R&B, hip-hop, and Tejano. Peopled mostly by a younger crowd, the three bars keep the drinks coming, and the large-screen TVs are usually on the sports channel. Happy hour is Monday through Friday from 4:00 to 8:00 p.m. If you get hungry from all that dancing, they have an extensive menu of bar food, steaks, salads, sandwiches, and excellent burgers. It's located at the northwest corner of Stone and Lester. There is a cover charge. Open Monday through Saturday.

BARS

CHE'S LOUNGE
350 North Fourth Avenue
(520) 623-2088
Not much to look at, this friendly neighborhood bar on Fourth is not out to impress. No cover, dollar beers, excellent bartenders, and a terrific jukebox make this a great place to hang out. Live entertainment most weekends.

FAMOUS SAM'S
3010 West Valencia Road
(520) 883-8888

7930 East Speedway Boulevard
(520) 290-9666

2320 North Silverbell Road
(520) 884-7267

1830 East Broadway Boulevard
(520) 884-0119

7129 East Golf Links Road
(520) 296-1245

2048 East Irvington Road
(520) 889-6007

8058 North Oracle Road
(520) 531-9464

3933 East Pima Street
(520) 323-1880

2480 West Ruthraff Road
(520) 292-0429

3620 North First Avenue
(520) 292-0314

8058 North Oracle Road
(520) 531-9464
www.famoussams.com
If you're looking for a dark spot with ice-cold beer, great background music, lots of TVs, and friendly service, Famous Sam's is the place (or should we say places, as there are now multiple Famous Sam's scattered throughout the city). Sam's started over 25 years ago with one little bar on the east side of town. It quickly became "famous" for killer hot pastrami sandwiches and a friendly, casual atmosphere. Today any one of the Sam's offers much the same (happily, the pastrami sandwiches are still very good, while the menu has been expanded some). These are great sports bars. Evening drink and food specials can be found, although each entity may have different daily specials. Live entertainment is also found at some of the bars on weekends.

O'MALLEY'S
247 North Fourth Avenue
(520) 623-8600
With a very large bar, late-night snacks, and a separate club for live bands, this is a popular weekend college hangout. Live music is featured Thursday through Saturday, but O'Malley's sees business all week long. Patrons are drawn in by

the airy high ceilings (the building was once home to a highly successful lumber company), outside patio, and several pool tables. On weekends don't be surprised to see people waiting in line to get in. O'Malley's charges a cover when there's a band.

THE RED GARTER SALOON
3143 East Speedway Boulevard
(520) 325-0483
Smoke-filled outdoor patio, raspy-voiced waitresses hoisting pitchers of beer, darts, pool, crispy fried chicken wings, and juicy burgers, what else can you ask of a real bar? The Red Garter pulls in folks of all stripes—bikers, actors, students, they all come in for the homey atmosphere and great bar food. Drinks are cheap, too. Check it out. Open daily 11:00 a.m. to 2:00 a.m.

THE RED ROOM AT THE GRILL
100 East Congress Street
(520) 623-7621
You'll find live music weekends starting at 10:00 p.m. at the Grill's eclectic Red Room. No cover, ever! This funky diner is the only thing in Tucson that's open 24/7. Grab some grub (see the Restaurants chapter) and a drink from the full bar, and settle in for a night of unique entertainment.

THE SHANTY
401 East Ninth Street
(520) 623-2664
This place has been packing them in for over 30 years, so much so that many of today's patrons are children (and even some grandchildren) of earlier generations.

There are several reasons for the continued popularity of the Shanty. One is its location—just blocks from the UA and right in the heart of the Fourth Avenue/Downtown scene. Another is the large selection of imported beers. The third is the casual atmosphere where students and professors can meet and mingle. Summer nights find the patio abuzz with activity.

JAZZ

THE GRILL
Hacienda del Sol Guest Ranch Resort
5601 North Hacienda del Sol Road
(520) 529-3500
www.haciendadelsol.com
Thursday through Saturday you'll find live music on the outdoor patio, where you can sip delicious drinks, indulge in tasty appetizers, or order a complete dinner while you enjoy the high-energy rhythms at one of Tucson's premier historic hotels.

RIC'S CAFE
5605 River Road
(520) 577-7272
Friday and Saturday nights at Ric's you'll find delightful contemporary jazz performed in the evening by a variety of professional musicians. You can sit under the softly lit palms at the bistro tables and enjoy both the music and dinner in the lovely outdoor courtyard.

17th Street Market Live Music

It may seem strange at first to hear live music in a grocery store. But once you settle in, you'll love the eclectic musical offerings scheduled by **17th Street Market** music consultant Harvey Brooks, a composer, producer, and performer (he performed with Bob Dylan, Richie Haven, The Doors, and Miles Davis). Performances take place most weekends. There's even a music shop here with drums, Chinese gongs, and kalimbas for sale. Call (520) 624-8821, extension 147, or visit the Web site at www.hiddentreasures.com for directions and a schedule of events.

WESTWARD LOOK RESORT

245 East Ina Road
(520) 297-1151
www.westwardlook.com

You'll find a terrific Sunday jazz brunch at this elegant resort hotel served every Sunday from 11:30 a.m. to 2:00 p.m. Relax and enjoy a great meal to the soothing sounds of a variety of professional musicians. The Lookout Bar and Grille also offers live music on the weekends.

MARIACHI/LATIN

BAR ¡TOMA! AT EL CHARRO CAFE

311 North Court Avenue
(520) 622-1922

Mariachi music fills the courtyard Saturday evenings and Sunday around noon at this downtown bar and restaurant known for its Mexican cuisine. The restaurant opens at 11:00 a.m. Monday through Saturday and at noon on Sunday. Enjoy the funky cowboy-hatted fountain while you listen to the bouncy, upbeat tunes.

Sonoran Mexican cuisine and live mariachi music can be yours at El Charro's ¡Toma! PHOTO BY KATE REYNOLDS

EL PARADOR

2744 East Broadway Boulevard
(520) 881-2744
www.elparadortucson.com

Every Friday and Saturday night the leafy large entry area is hopping with a live salsa band. Salsa lovers 21 and over can join in the fun for a mere $7 cover charge. Don't miss the salsa lessons for $5.

LA FUENTE

1749 North Oracle Road
(520) 623-8659
www.lafuenterestaurant.com

You'll find authentic mariachi music at La Fuente Wednesday through Sunday year-round. The talented singers roam the restaurant and perform onstage right up until closing.

i **For a wonderful evening, head downtown to colorful La Placita Village for a free outdoor movie. Held every Thursday at 7:30 p.m., you'll find a series of great classic films, from *Dr. Strangelove* to *Lolita*, under the stars. You can grab a bite at one of the many tiny eateries, take-out shops, and cafes or bring your own. Call (520) 326-5282 for more information. La Placita Village is at 110 South Church Avenue.**

ROCK AND BLUES

BOONDOCKS LOUNGE

3306 North First Avenue
(520) 690-0991
www.boondockslounge.com

You can't miss this place—a giant wine bottle sits in front of the building. This funky club has two bars, a dance floor, and several pool tables. Live music runs Wednesday through Sunday, with a variety from rock to blues. It's dark, and the crowd varies depending on who's playing. This is a great little place to shoot some pool on an off night or hear some of Tucson's best local bands. You'll pay a cover to get in the door when there is a band.

THE CHICAGO BAR

5954 East Speedway Boulevard
(520) 748-8169
www.chicagobartucson.com

With bands seven nights a week, this has been one of Tucson's most popular spots since its beginnings as a blues club in 1972. A widely mixed crowd packs the place almost every night. The dance floor is well used (as are the pool tables), and Tucson's most popular bands play this venue, including rock, metal, reggae, blues, and R&B. There is a cover.

DV8
5851 East Speedway
(520) 885-3030
DV8 is one of Tucson's hippest clubs. Get ready for hip-hop, R&B, '80s, '90s, and today's music. The bartenders are friendly and the drinks cheap. Foosball and billiards will keep nondancers busy. Open Tuesday through Saturday.

Tucson night owls head to DV8, a happening place.
PHOTO BY M. PAGANELLI VOTTO

FROG & FIRKIN
874 East University Boulevard
(520) 623-7507
www.frogandfirkin.com
This is a real college hangout, and live music begins blasting out of the doors around 6:00 p.m. on select weeknights and weekends. The Frog is always packed—indoors and out—with kids downing beers and enjoying traditional pub fare and pizza.

PLUSH
Fourth Avenue and Sixth Street
(520) 798-1298
www.plushtucson.com
A great atmosphere with comfy couches, deep red walls, and big windows that look out on the Fourth Avenue scene, Plush offers live music ranging from jazz to alternative, Southwestern, country, rock, and blues.

RIALTO THEATRE
318 East Congress Street
(520) 740-0126
www.rialtotheatre.com
The historic Rialto Theatre hosts some of the biggest names in town, with live performances from punk to salsa to rockabilly. It's quite a scene.

VAUDEVILLE CABARET
110 East Congress Street
(520) 622-3535
www.vaudevillecabaret.com
Velvet curtains screen the view from the street, but don't be intimidated—go on in. With great lighting and sound, you'll find all sorts of gigs from local musicians to touring acts on the stage at this downtown spot. Open daily until 2:00 a.m.

GAY AND LESBIAN BARS

AIN'T NOBODY'S BIZNESS
2900 East Broadway Boulevard, Suite 118
(520) 318-4838
www.thebiztuc.com
This popular little pub is primarily a lesbian bar, but lots of straight people come here just for the great DJ music. There's a bar and a dance floor (which is always packed). People in the know refer to this place as The Biz.

IBT'S
616 North Fourth Avenue
(520) 882-3053
www.ibts.net
If you're looking for the young, hip, gay crowd, head to IBT's (It's 'bout Time). Located downtown on Fourth Avenue, they've got it all here: dancing, drinks, drag shows, live DJs, jazz night, outside patio bar, friendly bartenders, an automatic teller machine, video games, human Jenga, bingo for fun, patio barbecues, and more. Open daily.

WOODY'S BAR
3710 North Oracle Road
(520) 292-6702
This friendly spot on the west side of town has a nice vibe. There's a bar, flat-screen TVs, DJs,

and occasional live music. A spacious outdoor patio and grassy lawn is home to barbecues and casual conversation. Karaoke, Havana Night, a chilidog buffet, and more take place throughout the week, so come on down. Special events include an annual Jell-O wrestling fund-raiser. Open daily.

MAKE 'EM LAUGH

LAFF'S COMEDY CLUB
2900 East Broadway Boulevard
(520) 323-8669
www.laffscomedyclub.com
In the tradition of New York comedy clubs, Tucson's nightspot for a good chuckle is open Thursday through Saturday. A full dinner is provided. The club hosts both touring and local up-and-coming comics. There is a cover charge.

CASINOS

CASINO DEL SOL
5655 West Valencia Road
(800) 344-9435
www.casinodelsol.com
The huge 5,000-seat amphitheater here plays host to a variety of concerts during the year. Past shows have featured Sheryl Crow, Don Henley, Tony Bennett, and James Taylor.

Stage 21 and Zeboz offer additional live music, shows, and special events.

CASINO OF THE SUN SUNSET PAVILION
7406 South Camino de Oeste
(520) 883-1700
www.casinosun.com
This more intimate venue (600 seats) hosts a variety of local and national events from concerts to boxing.

DESERT DIAMOND CASINO
Interstate 19 and Pima Mine Road at exit 80
(520) 294-7777
www.desertdiamondcasino.com
The 2,400-seat Diamond Center at this state-of-the-art casino run by the Tohono O'odham Nation has a whole slew of acts throughout the year, from male strippers to boxing to old-time singers and rock groups. The Sports Bar also offers live local entertainment seven days a week.

The classy Monsoon Nightclub offers a huge dance floor and all types of music. Call or check their Web site to see what's coming up.

ROOTIN', TOOTIN' GOOD TIMES

CACTUS MOON
5470 East Broadway Boulevard
(520) 748-0049
This hot top-40 country music dance club does not offer live music, but it does offer nonstop country hits, line dancing, a Friday happy hour (starting at 5:00 p.m.), and a variety of drink specials. If you're a little unsure of your dancing capabilities, line dance lessons are offered on Wednesday, Thursday, and Saturday nights. All this can be yours for a low cover. The Moon doesn't shine Monday or Sunday.

THE MAVERICK
6622 East Tanque Verde Road
(520) 298-0430
www.mavericktucson.com
The Maverick is one of the true country bars in town. Bands are pure country, and dancing is as much a part of the scene here as the drinking. It's been said the Maverick is the kind of place a country gal can walk into alone and not feel intimidated. You can even take dance lessons on select nights.

The dance floor is smooth and can get quite crowded on nights when the bar offers two-for-one drink specials. Service is great, as are the drinks (you'll also be pleased with the reasonable prices). Live music four nights a week. Open Tuesday through Saturday.

THE RIVER'S EDGE LOUNGE
4635 North Flowing Wells Road
(520) 887-9027
The River's Edge Lounge is your basic country-and-western dance club with line dancing and live music Friday and Saturday. It's a good spot

to break in those cowboy dancing boots you just bought. Open until 2:00 a.m.

BREWING UP A STORM

GENTLE BEN'S BREWING COMPANY

865 East University Boulevard
(520) 624-4177
www.gentlebens.com

Located one block west of the UA Main Gate, Gentle Ben's Brewing Company is Tucson's favorite place for fresh microbrews, food, and fun. Ben's is two stories of an award-winning brewery, a full-service restaurant, and two neighborhood bars. It's a great place for lunch, dinner, special occasions, private parties, catering, and partying. This continues to be a favorite of the college crowd, basically because of its prime location. Lunch and dinner are served daily. (See the Restaurants chapter.)

NIMBUS BREWERY

3850 East 44th Street
(520) 745-9175
www.nimbusbeer.com

This converted warehouse may be a bit tricky to find. From Palo Verde Road, turn east on 44th Street and continue to its very end. There you'll find a very casual, wide-open brewpub. Weekend evenings will find music and special events. If you get hungry, you can chow down on a selection of beer-battered appetizers, chicken fingers, quesadillas, or the (in)famous fried bologna sandwich. Pool tables are also available.

THUNDER CANYON BREWERY

Foothills Mall
Corner of La Cholla Boulevard and Ina Road
(520) 797-2652
www.thundercanyonbrewery.com

You'll find a great ambience, food, and choice of home brews here. Friday afternoon happy hours are usually quite crowded, as are weekend evenings when people who go to the mall's movie theater stop in for a drink before or after a flick. Also known for its wide selection of scotch, you'll find the food holds up against any and all of the beer offerings.

i **Attention all film buffs! Do not miss Tucson's greatest video store, Casa Video. Located at 2905 East Speedway and open 9:00 a.m. to 1:00 a.m. every day, this store has one of the most incredible collections of videos in town, if not the country. You'll find classics, foreign, documentaries, and wonderful theme collections (Favorite Directors, Oscar Winners). You could spend days here just exploring and you won't go hungry; bags of freshly popped popcorn are free to all. Call (520) 326-6314 or visit their Web site at www.casavideo.com.**

ALTERNATIVE CINEMA

Tucson has two theaters that offer foreign, art, and independent films. The University of Arizona also presents a number of films and documentaries at various locations on campus, and when it does, the shows are usually well advertised in the local newspaper calendar sections.

THE LOFT CINEMA

3233 East Speedway Boulevard
(520) 795-7777
www.loftcinema.com

With three screens, this is where you can satisfy your urge for foreign and art films, including a regular midnight screening of *The Rocky Horror Picture Show* on Saturday. Become a member and get super discounts and free popcorn.

THE SCREENING ROOM

127 East Congress Street
(520) 622-2262
www.azmarc.org

A small, 90-seat theater with an art gallery in the lobby, the Screening Room is known for independent productions, both from local producers and internationally known filmmakers. The theater, in the heart of the downtown Arts District, sponsors a weeklong film festival every April that screens everything from full-length films to short documentaries (see the Festivals and Events chapter). Ticket prices vary.

IN THE STARS

For a more mellow way to spend an evening, Tucson offers great stargazing opportunities. You can take a drive to the outer limits of the city and do your own, or try one of these more formal (and more up-close) looks at the stars. (See the Attractions chapter for more about both observatories.)

FLANDRAU SCIENCE CENTER AND PLANETARIUM
Cherry Street and University Boulevard
(520) 621-7827
www.gotuasciencecenter.org

Although they plan to move downtown in 2011, you can still catch a glimpse of the stars from the observatory's 16-inch telescope on Wednesday through Saturday nights from 7:00 to 10:00 p.m. A knowledgeable guide will explain in detail what you are seeing. The stargazing is free.

KITT PEAK NATIONAL OBSERVATORY
Highway 386
(520) 318-8726
www.noao.edu

The Kitt Peak National Observatory is open to the public daily from 9:00 a.m. to 3:45 p.m., except Thanksgiving, Christmas, and New Year's Day. Guided tours are offered daily at 10:00 a.m., 11:30 a.m., and 1:30 p.m.; group tours are available by appointment. Guided tours last approximately one hour and are led by trained docents who know the history and interesting facts regarding each telescope. Normally the tours go to the following telescopes: 10:00 a.m., the world's largest solar telescope; 11:30 a.m., the 2.1-meter telescope; and 1:30 p.m., the 4-meter Mayall Telescope (this tour lasts 90 minutes). Tour locations are subject to change due to maintenance and safety issues. Visitor center admission is free. Guided tours cost $4 per adult, $2.50 for children 6 to 12; children under 6 are free.

You can also stargaze at Kitt Peak at night with the reservation-only Nightly Observing Programs. Hours for the popular stargazing programs vary throughout the year based on sunset times and space is limited. The nighttime stargazing is not available from July 15 through September 1. (See the Attractions chapter for details.)

A few suggestions that will make your visit more enjoyable. Wear warm clothing to tolerate the 15- to 20-degree temperature difference (Kitt Peak's elevation is 6,875 feet). Also wear walking shoes, as you'll traverse steep paths on your way to the scopes. It is recommended that those with cardiac, respiratory, or other health problems notify the visitor center ahead of time.

SHOPPING

The best thing about shopping in Tucson is exploring the hundreds of small shops that carry items uniquely Southwestern. And most folks who visit here or live here are looking for just that—things Western, Mexican, cowboy, or American Indian. In this chapter we emphasize the gifts, clothes, food, art, and home furnishings that people want to see and buy when they come to Tucson.

We also have malls, and we do have major department stores that are every bit as complete as those in cities of the East and West Coasts.

If you're not quite sure what "Southwestern" or regional specialty items are, here are a few tips. Chilies are big (as in popular) here and come in all forms and shapes, from the many varieties of fresh ones ready to be added to a recipe to the dried ones hanging on strings, known as ristras. Hanging a ristra on your door is said to bring good luck. But you can also get good luck from a dream catcher, which is an American Indian form of art made of yarn, usually crafted in a circular shape and embellished with beads, feathers, and/or leather. Southwest Indians also make kachinas, which are dolls but probably unlike any you've ever seen. They are wood carvings, from tiny to more than a foot high, lavishly decorated with bright colors, feathers, spears, and masks, bearing names such as Eagle Dancer or Crown Dancer. Other Indian art forms popular in Tucson shops are baskets, rugs, pottery, and sterling silver with turquoise.

Popular items from south of the border include Spanish colonial furniture, characterized by thick natural wood and intricate carvings, clay pottery, stoneware, iron and tin ornaments, wool rugs, and colorful blankets. Much of the food considered regional has its origins in Mexico as well, such as tortillas, spices and flavorings, and salsas. Tucson also has some food specialties that grow locally, including pecans, pistachios, mesquite honey, citrus fruits, and sweets made from cacti.

With this briefing on regional specialties, you're ready to put on your walking shoes and explore the shopping scene in Tucson.

NATIVE AMERICAN

Below we highlight some of the shops dealing in Native American arts and crafts, but check other categories, such as "Malls, Plazas, and Shopping Centers," "Shopping Districts," and "Southwestern Shops," for more places to find these popular regional items.

BAHTI INDIAN ARTS
4330 North Campbell Avenue, Suite 73
(520) 577-0290
www.bahti.com

This store on the north side of charming St. Philip's Plaza offers fine Indian arts and crafts. You'll find rugs, pots, sand paintings, weavings, kachinas, fetishes, sculpture, and baskets by contemporary Southwest Indian artists. The shop also has books, tapes, and CDs on and by Native Americans.

DESERT SON
4759 East Sunrise Drive
(520) 299-0818
www.desertson.com

This shop specializes in Southwest Indian items such as art, pottery, vases, kachinas, Navajo rugs, sand paintings, and jewelry. Desert Son is closed on Sunday.

GALLERY WEST
6420 North Campbell Avenue
(520) 529-7002
www.indianartwest.com
Serious collectors will appreciate the museum-quality antique Native American art here, including rugs, weavings, baskets, pottery, and beadwork. Gallery West is closed on Sunday (and Monday during summer).

GREY DOG TRADING COMPANY
2970 North Swan Road
(520) 881-6888
www.greydogtrading.com
You'll find Grey Dog in the lovely Plaza Palomino, along with its selection of Hopi kachinas, Pueblo pottery, Zuni fetishes, Navajo weavings, jewelry, baskets, and sand paintings. The store is closed on Sunday.

MAC'S INDIAN JEWELRY
2400 East Grant Road
(520) 327-3306
This shop boasts a large selection of well-priced Native American jewelry but also has kachinas, pottery, rugs, carvings, and sand paintings. It's closed on Sunday.

MORNING STAR TRADERS
2020 East Speedway Boulevard
(520) 881-2112
www.morningstartraders.com
Morning Star Traders offers baskets, pottery, Navajo rugs, kachinas, and a large selection of old and new jewelry in a charming Spanish Colonial Revival building. Closed Sunday.

SAN XAVIER MISSION SHOPS
1959 East San Xavier Road
(520) 295-1350
While visiting the historic San Xavier Mission, you'll have a chance to shop for not only religious items pertaining to the mission but also items such as pottery, art, and baskets representing Southwest Indians, particularly the Tohono O'odham, on whose reservation the mission resides.

SILVERBELL TRADING
7119 North Oracle Road
(520) 797-6852
www.silverbelltrader.com
Set in Casas Adobe Plaza, this shop offers native arts from both American and northern Mexican Indians, among them the Mayo, Yaqui, Tarahumara, Zuni, and Hopi. It features contemporary and antique baskets, pottery, and jewelry. Silverbell Trading also has a selection of children's books primarily by and about Indians and books about the Southwest for all ages. The store is closed on Sunday.

i The Tohono O'odham are renowned for their exquisite baskets, woven by hand from a variety of native plants. They are so finely made that some can actually hold water. Baskets were also used for cooking and were prized as trading items. They can range in size from 1 inch to several feet high and feature designs that incorporate spiritual as well as natural themes. Some lovely examples can be viewed at the Arizona-Sonora Desert Museum. The best place to purchase an authentic basket is through the Tohono O'odham Basketweavers Organization (520-383-4966), on the Tohono O'odham Reservation in Sells, about an hour outside Tucson. You can also view and purchase baskets at their online gallery at www.tocaonline.org. The distinctive look, incredible craftsmanship, and smell of grass and desert air make for more than a wonderful souvenir.

TURQUOISE SKIES
4410 South Mission Road
(520) 578-1673
www.turquoiseskies.com
It's a bit off the beaten path and seems forlorn all by itself, but Turquoise Skies is across the street from two huge adult RV and mobile home communities. The store sells items by Navajo, Hopi, and Zuni Indians and over 35 other tribes,

including rugs, jewelry, baskets, and kachinas. It's closed Sunday and Monday.

GOURMET FOOD AND SPIRITS

Tucson offers a number of specialty food items that are great for both chowing down and gift giving—goodies such as tortillas and other Mexican favorites, medjool dates, locally grown pistachios, prickly pear cactus candies, and all manner of Mexican and Southwestern flavorings. Here are some of the best spots for finding food items for which Tucson is famous, as well as some of the more unusual places to go for other taste treats.

AJ'S FINE FOODS
La Encantada
2805 East Skyline Drive
(520) 232-6340
www.ajsfinefoods.com
You'll find lots of terrific gourmet fare here along with a sushi bar, cafe, wine cellar, and boulangerie. Prepared foods to go include super salads all made in-house, pastas, pizzas, and more. It's expensive, but you get what you pay for. The produce section is a work of art. Open daily.

ALEJANDRO'S TORTILLA FACTORY
5330 South 12th Avenue
(520) 889-2279
The retail part of this wholesale operation offers customers not only tortillas but also bagged spices and prepared foods such as tacos, tortas, and pastries. They also serve burritos with a variety of fillings, including chorizo. Menudo is available daily.

CARAVAN MIDDLE EASTERN MARKET
28217 North Country Club Road
(520) 323-6808
This store stocks Middle Eastern ingredients of all kinds: Egyptian rice, Israeli couscous, coffees, teas, nuts, canned foods, frozen meats, delicious pastries, and some of the best olives in town. Open daily.

EL RIO BAKERY
901 North Grande Avenue
(520) 882-9457
www.elriobakery.com
Located in a heavily Hispanic area west of downtown and Interstate 10, El Rio has great Mexican baked goods plus some traditional ones. Here you'll find pan de huevo (egg bread), empanadas, pan dulce, cochinitos (gingerbread pigs, a favorite), delicious Mexican cookies, and tortillas. El Rio also has some prepared take-out food such as burritos with machaca and beans, plus a small selection of grocery items.

EUROPEAN MARKET & DELI
4500 East Speedway Boulevard
(520) 512-0206
europeanmarketanddeli.com
Folks hungry for items from Russia and other Eastern European countries always find a treat here. The market carries 30 different kinds of sausage in addition to canned goods, bakery items, and a variety of candies and chocolates.

G&L IMPORT EXPORT
4828 East 22nd Street
(520) 790-9016
Tucsonans need not go to the Far East to find anything Asian—it's all right here at this large store specializing in Asian imports. It's filled with Japanese, Chinese, and Middle Eastern food products in bottles, boxes, cans, and bags, including soy sauces, pastas, wines, seasonings, and vegetables. There's also a large selection of cooking tools such as woks, tea utensils, strainers, chopsticks, and even a few Asian furnishings and accessories.

GRANDE TORTILLA FACTORY
914 North Grande Avenue
(520) 622-8338
This area of Grande Avenue, just west of downtown, is a small pocket of authentic Mexican food offerings. The Grande Tortilla Factory is one of the best-known shops and has been operated by the same family for over 50 years. The tortillas are still stretched by hand, and you'll definitely notice the difference from machine-made ones.

Other goodies here include masa (ground and kneaded corn kernels used in tamales), crushed pepper, dried chili pods, empanadas, manzanilla tea, and menudo. The factory is closed Wednesday and Sunday.

INDIA DUKAAN
2754 North Campbell Avenue
(520) 321-0408
This shop offers a wide variety of Indian foods, from papadums to rice of all kinds. You'll find unusual condiments, spices, curries, naan, dals, sweets, nuts, frozen dinners, and ayurvedic medicines along with a library of original "Bollywood" videos and DVDs to rent. Not sure how to cook up these fragrant ingredients? There's a selection of cookbooks, too. Open daily.

LA BUENA MEXICAN FOODS
234 East 22nd Street
(520) 624-1796
You'll find great Mexican food prepared daily here, such as flour and corn tortillas, taco shells, green corn and red chili tamales, plus the ingredients to make your own, such as masa and nixtamal. The store has fresh menudo daily.

LA MESA TORTILLAS
7823 East Broadway Boulevard
(520) 298-5966
Folks on the east side don't have to be deprived of homemade tortillas, because La Mesa makes them fresh daily. Other offerings include burros with a variety of fillings, tamales by the dozen, and even a complete lunch served from 11:00 a.m. to 2:00 p.m. The store is closed on Sunday.

RINCON MARKET
2513 East Sixth Street
(520) 327-6653
www.rinconmarket.com
This corner market and deli in central Tucson is almost an institution and a favorite of locals. The store specializes in spit-roasted chicken and has other deli delights as well, plus a complete market with butcher shop. You can take your deli food to go or dine on the outdoor patio.

ROMA IMPORTS
627 South Vine Avenue
(520) 792-3173
www.romaimports.com
If you're cooking Italian and want authentic ingredients, shop at Roma's, where you'll find pastas, cheeses, sauces, sausages, pancetta, prosciutto, biscotti, cannoli, tiramisu, olive oils, sun-dried tomatoes, olives, and lots more, all imported or made on-site. You can also get a great sandwich to eat in or take out. And to make you feel even more Italian, Roma's carries novelty items such as aprons and T-shirts emblazoned with a bit of Italy. The shop is closed on Sunday. Make sure to get directions; it's hard to find.

RUM RUNNER WINE AND CHEESE COMPANY
3131 East First Street
(520) 326-0121
www.rumrunnertucson.com
Wines and cheeses are definitely the specialty of this upscale shop, but it carries other things as well, such as homemade deli items, gift baskets, breads, and regional food products. The wine selection is one of the best in the area. The shop also has a full-service bistro and wine bar. The new location is just down the street from the old.

17TH STREET FARMERS MARKET
830 East 17th Street
(520) 792-2588
www.treasureshidden.com
This huge market is hidden away on 17th Street between Euclid and Park. It's stuffed with every ethnic ingredient imaginable. They also have tons of fresh organic produce, a huge selection of seafood (some swimming in tanks), and fresh meats. You can spend days roaming the aisles here. Closed Sunday.

TANIA'S TORTILLAS AND MEXICAN FOOD
2856 West Drexel Road
(520) 883-1595
For a selection of prepared food that's as large as any Mexican restaurant's menu, stop by Tania's. This tiny shop has soups, red and green chilies,

machaca, carne asada, menudo, flour tortillas, and lots more.

TED'S COUNTRY STORE
2760 North Tucson Boulevard
(520) 325-3122
This place is like a homey old-time country corner store that has an updated style and an upscale selection of products. They have a great wine selection, a deli with sandwiches made to go, and regional food products such as spices, jellies, and honey. You'll also find the basics here. Closed Sunday.

VIRO'S REAL ITALIAN BAKERY
8301 East 22nd Street
(520) 885-4045
If you have a hankering for Italian baked goods like those sold in ethnic neighborhoods back East, try Viro's. Along with all kinds of breads, Viro's has sweets such as biscotti, panettone, and pizzelles. The bakery is closed Monday.

WHOLE FOODS MARKET
3360 East Speedway Boulevard
(520) 795-9844

7133 North Oracle Road
(520) 297-5394
www.wholefoodsmarket.com
This chain of upscale organic grocery stores carries lots of regional and local specialty products in addition to their normal grocery items. You'll find locally made prickly pear juice and syrup, Tucson-made salsas, homegrown olives, Arizona pistachios and pecans, wines and beers from local vineyards and microbreweries, along with cotton clothing, hats, unusual gift items, and Southwestern-themed kitchenware. If they don't have it, they'll go out of their way to order it for you.

GROWING THINGS (OR DESERT FLORA)

In this section we concentrate on nurseries that specialize in things that grow in the desert, which are popular items not only for folks who live here but also for visitors who want to take a bit of Mother Nature's unusual desert life back home.

B&B CACTUS FARM
11550 East Speedway Boulevard
(520) 721-4687
www.bandbcactus.com
On Tucson's far east side, B&B features more than 600 species and varieties of cacti and succulents from all over the world in its greenhouses and outdoor displays. You'll find desert-garden kits, container cactus gardens, Mexican pottery, and hanging baskets for the patio. Take your camera along, and you can photograph some amazing blooms. B&B packs plants for traveling and shipping and also has mail-order selections. The nursery is closed on Sunday and Monday.

BACH'S GREENHOUSE CACTUS NURSERY
8602 North Thornydale Road
(520) 744-3333
Located in the far northwest, Bach's has hundreds of species of cacti to choose from. Whether you're looking for a cactus for your home or yard or an unusual one for a gift, you'll surely be able to find it here. The nursery sells planted cacti gardens and will pack your selections. Bach's is closed on Sunday.

DESERT SURVIVORS
1020 West Starr Pass Boulevard
(520) 884-8806
www.desertsurvivors.org
This is a favorite spot for locals for two reasons: Desert Survivors has a great selection of desert "greenery," and it's a vocational rehab program for mentally challenged adults, so your purchase helps these people maintain active and productive lives. Although you won't find cacti here, you will find nearly everything else that grows in these parts, including trees, yucca plants, agave, and succulents. The nursery is open year-round, Tuesday through Sunday, and has very popular semiannual sales in April and October.

NATIVE SEEDS/SEARCH
526 North Fourth Avenue
(520) 622-5561
www.nativeseeds.org

As unusual as the store's name is what it sells—seeds and more seeds. This nonprofit shop is heaven for the desert gardener. The shelves are lined with thousands of seeds, some of which are endangered species. And if Native Seeds doesn't have what you want, it can probably be ordered (hence the "SEARCH" in the name). The mission is to preserve and promote the traditional crops, seeds, and farming methods that have sustained native peoples throughout the American Southwest and northern Mexico. (Native Seeds/SEARCH also maintains a conservation farm in Patagonia.) If you're looking for the unusual, such as blue speckled tepary beans or blue corn, or the more common desert lupine, sunflower, or evening primrose seeds, you'll find them here, along with baskets, jewelry, and lots of food products including all kinds of dried chilies, bean soup mixes, mesquite meal, and salsas. You'll also find a great selection of books about gardening and the Southwest. Native Seeds is open daily.

TANQUE VERDE GREENHOUSES
10810 East Tanque Verde Road
(520) 749-4414

This desert nursery on the far east side has six large greenhouses with thousands of plants and hundreds of varieties of cacti and succulents. The selection includes euphorbia from Africa, mammillaria from Mexico, and organ pipes from Arizona. You can buy a ready-to-go dish garden of cacti or have one custom designed. Employees carefully pack the cacti for air or road travel or mail them (fully guaranteed) if you prefer. If you don't have a green thumb but still want a cactus memento, the greenhouses also have sweet treats made from cacti, such as candies and jellies. Closed Sunday.

MEXICAN IMPORTS

For locals and visitors who don't want to make the trek south of the border for authentic Mexican goods, Tucson has plenty to offer right here. We list some of the more popular ones, but check in other sections of this chapter because nearly every mall or shopping plaza has a store carrying some items imported from Mexico. One of the best spots is the Lost Barrio shopping district on South Park Avenue, where most of the shops specialize in Mexican imports. Mexican products that seem to be very popular stateside include Mexican (or Spanish) colonial furniture, pigskin furniture (called equipale), rugs, blankets, handblown glassware, framed mirrors, tin and metal light fixtures and lamps, pottery, stoneware, religious statuary, Talavera (the brilliantly painted ceramics made in the city of Puebla), and colorful wooden animals made in Oaxaca.

ANTIGUA DE MEXICO
3235 West Orange Grove Road
(520) 742-7114

Mexican goods offered here include equipale furniture, glassware, carved wood furniture, lighting fixtures, stone fountains and statuary, clay pottery, tin items, folk art, and sterling silver jewelry.

AQUI ESTA
204 South Park Avenue
(520) 798-3605

This shop in the Lost Barrio shopping district specializes in handcrafted Mexican-style furniture and accessories. They also import and sell Mexican tile, Talavera pottery, Equipale furniture, and ironwork. Closed Sunday.

AZTECA MEXICAN IMPORTS
1111 South Kolb Road
(520) 290-0024

You may not see a sign proclaiming that it's Azteca, but you will see a huge collection of pottery, fountains, and chimineas at this outdoor location just north of 22nd Street. Open daily.

BORDERLANDS OUTLET STORE
309 East Seventh Street
(520) 622-3476

Chock-full of wonderful Talavera pottery, tiled mirrors, glass, furnishings, Mexican paper flowers, and unusual knickknacks, this rustic shop offers a multitude of imported products in all price ranges. Open daily.

LA BUHARDILLA
2360 East Broadway Boulevard
(520) 622-5200
In English it means "the attic," and finds here include colonial and Spanish baroque furniture, wrought iron, pottery including Talavera, silver, and paintings. The store also carries hand-carved wooden doors and materials for restoring or building haciendas. La Buhardilla is closed on Sunday and Monday.

QUE BONITA
6934 East Tanque Verde Road
(520) 721-1998
This shop specializes in Old Mexico and Santa Fe furniture and boasts a large showroom with new arrivals weekly. There's also an extensive selection of Southwestern decorative accessories, pottery, and Zapotec rugs. The shop has a unique collection of southwestern clothing and jewelry too. It's open daily.

SOUTHWESTERN SHOPS

A chapter on shopping in Tucson just wouldn't be complete without a section devoted to regional, or Southwestern, items. Tucsonans and visitors are always interested in things grown or made in the Southwest—chilies (whether real or artificial), salsas, sweets made from cacti, locally grown pecans and pistachios, minerals, turquoise, and Mexican and American Indian arts and crafts. Here are some ideas of where to look, but many more are included in other sections of this chapter.

CACTUS CARDS & GIFTS
5975 West Western Way Circle
(520) 883-5930
If you happen to be visiting the many attractions on the western side of the Tucson Mountains, you'll be near this shop that offers lots of southwestern goods, from T-shirts to sweets and cards to pottery and souvenirs. Closed Sunday.

WESTERN WEAR

Both real cowboys and wannabes have a good choice of Western wear in Tucson, from hats and chaps to bolo ties and belt buckles.

ARIZONA HATTERS
2790 North Campbell Avenue
(520) 292-1320
This store carries a large selection of name-brand hats, including Stetson, Resistol, and Milano, for both men and women, plus a selection of men's Western shirts and belts. They'll custom-fit and shape the hat of your choice.

BOOT BUNKHOUSE
5126 East Pima Street
(520) 322-9044
Off the beaten track between Swan and Craycroft, this old-time family-owned shop specializes in boots of all kinds: Western, hiking, work, hunting, and uniform. Not only is there a huge selection to choose from, but they are also famous for their sizes, which range from 3 to 17 and AAAA to EEE. They sell accessories, wallets, belts, straw hats, and T-shirts as well. Personalized service is superb. Owner Chuck Siegfried promises, "We're about service; we get you what you want." Open Monday through Saturday.

CORRAL WEST RANCH WEAR
4525 East Broadway Boulevard
(520) 322-6001
www.corralwest.com
This store, part of a chain out of Cheyenne, Wyoming, has a complete line of Western clothes, including boots and hats from manufacturers such as Justin Boots, Tony Lama, Stetson, Rocky Mountain Clothing Company, and Wrangler.

COWTOWN BOOTS
5190 North Casa Grande Highway
(520) 888-0290
www.cowtownboots.com
If you can figure out how to get here, you can choose from about 10,000 pairs of boots for

both men and women made by Cowtown Boot Company, Durango, Dingo, and others. It also carries Western clothing for children and adults. It's located on the Eastside frontage road of I-10 just north of the Ruthrauff Road exit.

WESTERN WAREHOUSE
6701 East Broadway Boulevard
(520) 885-4385

3776 South 16th Avenue
(520) 622-4500

3719 North Oracle Road
(520) 293-1808
www.westernwarehouse.com

Claiming to "dress the West for less," this store also claims to have the biggest selection of boots, hats, clothes, and accessories for the whole family. (Employees speak Spanish.) The huge selection of straw and felt hats includes names such as Resistol and Stetson, plus they'll steam and shape your hat for free. The collection of boots represents practically every size and color imaginable, from cowhide to exotic leathers.

MALLS, PLAZAS, AND SHOPPING CENTERS

Tucson has malls and an abundance of plazas and shopping centers—sometimes it seems like there's one at every intersection. We cover a number of the more unusual ones here.

BROADWAY VILLAGE
East Broadway Boulevard at Country Club Drive
no phone number

Built in 1932, this Joesler-designed Mission-style complex was one of Arizona's first shopping centers. You can still see parts of the original whitewashed adobe brick and inlaid tile structure that today surrounds a brick courtyard with trees all around. Among the unusual shops here is Clues Unlimited, a bookstore of mystery and intrigue, while Primitive Arts is a gallery with fine pre-Columbian and ethnographic finds. A bakery/cafe delights the senses of smell and taste with great baked goods and interesting lunches to take or eat there. You'll also find here the acclaimed Elle, A Wine Country Restaurant. Just across the street to the west of the main structure is a row of shops, also part of Broadway Village, including Table Talk for all manner of housewares.

CASAS ADOBES PLAZA
North Oracle and Ina Roads
no phone number
www.casasadobesplaza.com

When this Spanish-style plaza was built in the 1940s, it was a shopping hub out in the boonies. Today it's at a busy intersection, but strolling here can still be pleasant. The plaza also houses a boutique, beauty salons, Marshall's Jewelers, Old Brazil, a Whole Foods Market, Maya Palace, Silverbell Trading, and Chico's. For food there's Sauce, Wildflower Grill, and Bluefin Seafood Bistro.

CROSSROADS FESTIVAL
Grant and Swan Roads
no phone number

This plaza meanders from Swan Road around the corner and east along Grant Road for the equivalent of several blocks. It's an eclectic mix ranging from upscale apparel stores to discount hair salons and everything in between. It houses a major grocery store, a bank, a French bakery, jewelry and gift shops, fine apparel stores, Bed, Bath & Beyond for housewares, and Mrs. Tiggy Winkle's Toys (see the Kidstuff chapter). If you're looking for the only Tucson jeweler that carries Tiffany products or a certified Rolex watch dealer, Marshall's Artistry in Gold is the spot. Several restaurants are here, including the very popular Good Egg and Buddy's Grill. There's also the Grand Cinemas Crossroads movie theater, which offers discounted recently released movies, but you'll need to hunt for it because it's hidden in back.

EL CON MALL
3601 East Broadway Boulevard
(520) 795-9958
www.elconmall.com

El Con was Tucson's first mall and occupies a large parcel of what is now very valuable land in a central Tucson location. Although spread out, it's all one level and therefore not as overwhelming as the many more modern malls. At press time, lots of the larger stores had moved to other locations, leaving the future of the mall in doubt. Home Depot and Target are still active and popular. You'll also find a Century 20 theater complex and a small food court. The mall is easily accessible by bus.

EL MERCADO
Wilmot Road at Broadway Boulevard
no phone number

Designed to resemble a Spanish open-air mercado (market), this plaza features a number of unusual shops plus salons and restaurants. Here you'll find a store with all kinds of delicious handmade chocolates and Maya Palace. The El Charro Cafe is an offshoot of El Charro, Arizona's oldest Mexican restaurant (see the Restaurants chapter).

FOOTHILLS MALL
Ina Road and La Cholla Boulevard
(520) 219-0650
www.shopfoothillsmall.com

Foothills Mall is distinguished by its wide Saltillo tile corridors and architectural features that give it the feeling of a village mercado. An upscale outlet and entertainment mall, it houses a Saks Fifth Avenue outlet, Barnes and Noble, Linens and Things, Levi's outlet, Old Navy, and Ross and Dress Barn outlets, among others. For food there are several sit-down restaurants, a brewery, and a food court with several vendors. For entertainment, the mall has a 15-screen movie theater and GameWorks Studio. There are plenty of special events and entertainment at the mall as well. It's a pleasant place to shop, be entertained, or just people watch.

JOESLER VILLAGE
River Road and Campbell Avenue
no phone number

Named for Josias Joesler, Tucson's premier architect, this upscale shopping plaza on the northwest corner of this intersection is home to boutiques, clothing stores, several galleries, and a number of casual and sophisticated restaurants.

KAIBAB COURTYARD SHOPS
2837 North Campbell Avenue
(520) 795-6905

Kaibab (meaning "mountain lying on its side" in the Paiute Indian language and pronounced *ki-bob*) Courtyard is actually a cluster of three shops totaling about 13,000 square feet and specializing in Southwestern and Native American goods. One is the Nambe Foundry Outlet, offering Nambeware, a shiny silverlike metal that's formed into functional art such as vases and bowls. The two others, Desert House and Kaibab Shops, sell everything from Hopi kachina dolls, Navajo rugs, and Zuni fetishes to Mexican dinnerware. You'll also find clothing, furniture, and folk art from Mexico, and art, gifts, and home accessories by local artists. If you're in the market for something reflecting the region, these shops should be on your list.

LA ENCANTADA
2905 East Skyline Drive
(520) 299-3556
www.laencantadashoppingcenter.com

Big, beautiful, and full of wonderful stores, this lovely outdoor mall sits at the crest of Campbell Avenue at Skyline. Open courtyards, fountains, balconies, and gardens make this a great spot to stroll and shop. Shops include Tucson's only Crate & Barrel, Williams-Sonoma, and Pottery Barn. You'll also find specialty clothing and stores like Tommy Bahama and Cole Haan, and a phenomenal Apple retail store. Upscale restaurants offer options from barbecue to northern Italian; AJ's Fine Foods has gourmet groceries. Spend the day.

The restful indoor garden and patio at La Encantada provide a respite after a long day of shopping. PHOTO BY M. PAGANELLI VOTTO

PARK PLACE
5870 East Broadway Boulevard
(520) 748-1222
www.parkplacemall.com

This attractive mall is built on all one level in a close-in Eastside location. The large stores are Sears, Macy's, and Dillard's, which are accompanied by more than 100 shops and restaurants plus a movie theater. For books there's Borders Books and Music; for moviegoers, a huge 20-plex theater. The information booth is located just inside the mall's main entrance, which is at the center of the building on the south side facing Broadway Boulevard. Park Place is wheelchair accessible and rents strollers. There's also a kids' playground at the food court.

PLAZA PALOMINO
2970 North Swan Road
no phone number
www.plazapalomino.com

This is one of the loveliest places to shop in Tucson, although it definitely leans toward upscale. Elegant shops, galleries, and restaurants constructed of adobe with Spanish-tiled roofs surround a tiled courtyard with fountains, foliage, and singing birds. Plaza Palomino is located near the Fort Lowell historic district, full of old Spanish charm and a peaceful break from hectic malls. You'll find a number of boutiques, jewelry, art, and home decor shops, and several restaurants with patio seating so you can enjoy the surroundings. Shops specializing in Southwestern goods include Native American arts and crafts at Grey Dog Trading; and jewelry, art, and handcrafted gifts at Enchanted Earthworks. It's also host to a great farmers' market on Saturday. You can arrive here in luxury for free by using the plaza's courtesy shopping shuttle that's available by calling Black Tie Limo at (520) 488-8621.

RIVER CENTER MERCHANTS ASSOCIATION
5605 East River Road
no phone number

At the base of the Catalina foothills, River Center is a pretty setting for its two dozen shops and restaurants, including a branch of the Pima County Library. A fountain, outdoor dining, and views of the city lights below add to the ambience. In addition to a major drugstore, you'll find boutiques, Tucson Trunk (a card and gift, not luggage, shop), a beauty salon, and several small businesses. Restaurants include Ric's Cafe, with outdoor dining.

When it's time to wind down your shopping day, drop by Plaza Liquors at 2642 North Campbell Avenue. They've got nearly 100 different kinds of beer, most available in single cans.

ST. PHILIP'S PLAZA
River Road at Campbell Avenue
(520) 529-2775
www.stphilipsplaza.com

Set in a Joesler-designed Mexican-style plaza, this is an upscale shopping center in a pleasant (but congested) location. The plaza itself is a series of Spanish-style brick courtyards, which make for a picturesque stroll with shade trees, lovely tiled fountains, and gardens. One of Tucson's finest beauty salons and day spas, Gadabout, is located here (they have several other locations, too). Shops include the hip Changes. There are art galleries, jewelry stores, and several of Tucson's top eateries. Also located at St. Philip's is Windmill Inn, an all-suite hotel. Watch for special doings that take place here, such as jazz concerts and a Sunday farmers' market.

TRAIL DUST TOWN
6541 East Tanque Verde Road
(520) 296-4551
www.traildusttown.com

To find this hidden gem of a shopping and entertainment area, look for a three-story stack of boulders with a small covered wagon on top. Trail Dust Town offers regional items in a handful of small shops that line a bricked courtyard, complete with gazebos, grass areas, colorful flowers, and plenty of shady spots and benches for people watching. You'll see facades and memorabilia

Yee-ha! Trail Dust Town offers great eats, cowboy shows, and lots of boutique shops. PHOTO BY KATE REYNOLDS

of the Old West all around—a bank, apothecary store, jail, barbershop, hotel, saloon, train depot, wagon parts, posters, and signs. The real stores include Dry Heat Trading Co., T-Line Leathers, and AZ Gold. Trail Dust Treasures features Southwestern gifts and novelties, while Dad Pfeenerbar's Old Time Photos will deck you out in Western wear and snap your photo. There's also a chocolate shop and the very fascinating General Store, which sells everything from old-time candy and nostalgia items to fine totem poles. For fun, take a ride on the train that circles the shopping area or on the carousel. And kids and grown-ups alike enjoy the Wild West stunt shows that take place periodically. Dining options here include the cowboy steak house Pinnacle Peak and Dakota Cafe, with patio dining and Southwestern-style food (see the Restaurants chapter).

i **Tired of shopping and feeling in need of a little pampering? You're in luck. Over at Qi Nail Spa, the owner often serves pork or shrimp egg rolls to weekend clients. You can have a pedicure and a treat all at once. It's at 3900 West Costco Drive. Call for an appointment. (520) 742-0597.**

TUCSON MALL
4500 North Oracle Road
(520) 293-7330
www.tucsonmall.com

We're not talking megamall like the ones in Chicago or Minneapolis, but this is certainly Tucson's largest. Its two levels contain more than 200 department stores and specialty shops, including Dillard's, JCPenney, Sears, Macy's, Mervyn's, Frederick's of Hollywood, Gap, Guess?, Footlocker, Lane Bryant, Eddie Bauer, Victoria's Secret, Disney Store, and a number of shops specializing in gifts, jewelry, home furnishings, athletic wear, and shoes. There's something here to suit anyone's taste and budget. Kids (and adults) will enjoy riding the dragons, horses, and reindeer on the carousel, while indoor fountains add a bit of tranquility to the frenzied shopping. The food court has more than a dozen food booths and plenty of inside seating to accommodate famished shoppers. Next to the food court is Arizona Avenue, a row of shops specializing in regional items from Indian and Mexican rugs to pottery to food. Don't miss the See's Candies Store and your free sample. There's also a colorful children's play area. The mall has strollers and wheelchairs (free) available as well as TDD phones. And just across Stone Avenue on the mall's east side is a major Sun Tran bus transit center.

SHOPPING DISTRICTS

They can't really be classified as malls, plazas, or shopping centers, so we've labeled them shopping districts—areas around town that have a concentration of commercial establishments, mostly retail shops, that shouldn't be overlooked. These are places where you'll get a taste of Tucson history and culture along with your purchases.

Downtown

Also known as the Tucson Arts District, the downtown area is a hub of cultural, social, and commercial activity, bounded roughly by Cushing Street on the south, Granada Avenue on the west, Franklin Street on the north, and Scott Avenue on the east. You'll find an amazing array of shops, many of them quite unusual—everything from plumbing supplies to tattoo parlors—along with galleries and eateries. The main thoroughfare bisecting this area is Congress Street, where many of the stores are concentrated. As with many downtown areas, however, the shops here tend to come and go. Nonetheless it's worth exploring this eclectic area for the unusual and for the experience. A focus of the city's downtown renovation efforts, this area is a bit off-putting, as many storefronts are empty or undergoing renovation. Things not to miss include the historic **Hotel Congress** (311 East Congress; 520-622-8848), the eclectic shop **Got All Your Marbles** (220 East Congress; 520-628-1433), with jewelry and accessories made with marbles; **Chicago Store** (130 East Congress; 520-622-3341), stuffed to the brim with instruments of all shapes and sizes; and the renovated **Fox Theatre** (17 West

Close-up

Fourth Avenue Should Be on Your List

Fourth Avenue is a great shopping and people-watching destination. This historic district runs for 6 blocks along Fourth Avenue south from University Boulevard to Ninth Street. It's a real mix of funky, fun, and eclectic shops, galleries, boutiques, restaurants, and unusual secondhand stores. Free street parking is available all along the avenue and the side streets, or you can take the Sun Tran bus.

A great way to start your tour of the area is to hop on the restored trolley car at Fourth Avenue and Eighth Street and ride it all the way to the end of the line, 1 block from the University of Arizona's Main Gate (about 10 minutes). This fun, old-fashioned ride will give you a bird's-eye view of what there is to see and do along the avenue! It runs Friday evening, Saturday noon to midnight, and Sunday noon to 6:00 p.m. for $1 one way (and only 50 cents for seniors and kids 6 to 12; it's free for younger ones). The all-day fares are cheap, too: $2.50 for adults and $1.25 for kids over 6.

Once you disembark, take a leisurely stroll and wander in and out of the more than 100 shops that line Fourth Avenue. Thrift shopping here may be about the best in the city. You can buy, sell, or trade everything from bicycle parts and washers to old lace and vintage clothing. If you're going to a shindig and need a costume, Fourth Avenue can outfit you. Other old stuff you'll find here includes furniture, jewelry, antique dolls, vintage musical instruments, and funky sunglasses. Even if you're not in the market for old things, you'll take a trip down memory lane at secondhand stores like **The Other Side, Kanella's,** and **How Sweet It Was.**

In need of a grass skirt, Hawaiian lei, a costume, or bolo tie? You'll probably be able to find them all somewhere along Fourth Avenue. Care for some light? You'll find dragon's blood-scented candles at the **Rustic Candle** company. **Creative Ventures** craft mall showcases the clever wares of many local artisans and crafters. **Del Sol International Shop** has a huge array of Mexican products, from glassware and jewelry to clothing and rugs. The unique **Native Seeds/SEARCH** shop here shouldn't be missed. You'll also find one-of-a-kind jewelry, ceramics, glass and metal shops, unusual bookstores (including Antigone Books, profiled in this chapter), art galleries, and lots more on this avenue.

There's no shortage of places to stop or shop for food: coffeehouses; sweet shops; the **Food Conspiracy,** a natural grocery and specialty foods store; **Caruso's,** featuring Italian food; **La Indita Restaurant,** combining Mexican and Indian tastes; **Chocolate Iguana;** the always popular **Delectables; Brooklyn Pizza Company;** and even **Dairy Queen.**

And if all of this isn't enough to satisfy your shopping urge, twice a year Fourth Avenue closes to traffic and puts on a huge street fair with hundreds of booths offering a mind-boggling array of arts and crafts, food, entertainment, and other types of fun. You'll find Fourth Avenue guides at many of the shops on the avenue. For more information call the **Fourth Avenue Merchants Association** at (520) 624-5004 or (800) 933-2477 or visit their Web site: www.fourthavenue.org.

Congress; 520-624-1515). **Santa Theresa Tile Works** (440 North Sixth Avenue; 520-623-1856) offers ceramic works of art. **Flanagan's Celtic Corner** (222 East Congress; 520-623-9922) a newcomer to the downtown scene, sells just about everything Celtic, from glassware to coats of arms. The colorful **La Placita Village** (110 South Church) is home to the **Tucson Visitors Center** (open daily) and several shops, cafes, and restaurants. A great time to visit is during the Club Crawl event (see the Nightlife chapter).

This area is accessible by Sun Tran bus, and parking is available on the street or in public lots or garages.

LOST BARRIO
200 South Park Avenue
no phone number

A barrio that became a warehouse district is now a shopping district—one of the most interesting in Tucson if you're in the market for imports. Located on the southwest corner of Park Avenue and 12th Street, these warehouse buildings along a 2-to-3-block area aren't fancy, but they're packed full of furniture and accessories in wood, iron, metal, stone, fabric, and glass. Much of it is from Mexico, but you'll also find work from Native American, African, and other cultures, and nearly everything is warehouse-priced. Stores here include Aqui Esta (520-798-3605), Rustica (520-623-4435), and Magellan Trading (520-622-4968). Some of the shops will also provide custom work in wood, iron, and upholstery. If you want to experience a bit of Nogales, Mexico, without crossing the border, this may be the spot, but not on Sunday. Parking is free on the street.

OLD TOWN ARTISANS
201 North Court Avenue
(520) 623-6024, (800) 782-8072
www.oldtownartisans.com

This 1850s restored adobe structure fills an entire city block in the heart of the historic El Presidio neighborhood. Reputedly the original buildings on this site were dwellings and shops for early settlers. In keeping with Spanish tradition, the exterior wall was built on the property line with a central courtyard inside. Today the buildings surrounding the courtyard are shops offering Southwestern folk art, American Indian tribal art, and imports from Mexico. Many of the items are handmade by some of Tucson's finest artisans, yet it's all reasonably priced. If you're looking for regional items, you'll find one of the best collections all in one spot here. Old Town Artisans also houses La Cocina (Spanish for "kitchen") and its delightful patio garden. While shopping, ask for a walking-tour map and visit all the nearby sites reflecting Tucson's history and culture. You can park at meters on surrounding streets or in nearby public lots.

University Area

Although there's shopping almost all around the university, the most concentrated area is on University Boulevard extending about 2 blocks west from the main gate at Park Avenue. As one might expect, the shops and businesses here are student-oriented, but they also appeal to most anyone. Besides, it's an interesting place to watch university life.

Among the shops on this street are **Diva, Pitaya, American Apparel, Urban Outfitters,** and **Landmark Clothing and Shoes,** which carries popular brands such as Bass, Teva, Polo, Timberland, and Birkenstock. The shopping area just wouldn't be complete without a store selling everything University of Arizona, from clothing and hats to school supplies and calendars, and it's got that in the **Arizona Bookstore.** The eateries in this area, many with outdoor seating facing the street, offer a varied selection of food and refreshments with a view. There's the popular **Gentle Ben's** (see the Restaurants and Nightlife chapters), several gourmet pizza places, and eclectic restaurants and bars. For a comprehensive listing go to www.maingatesquare.com.

The Old Pueblo Trolley runs down the center of University Boulevard and connects with the Fourth Avenue shopping district. (See this chapter's Close-up.) Metered parking is available on University Boulevard.

BARGAIN AND OUTLET SHOPPING

Tucson has a number of places devoted to outlet shopping and other bargain merchandise. And if you want even more choices, head to Casa Grande, Arizona, about an hour north of Tucson.

BUFFALO EXCHANGE

2001 East Speedway Boulevard
(520) 795-0508

6170 East Speedway Boulevard
(520) 885-8392

Buffalo Kids/Little Traders
6216 East Speedway Boulevard
(520) 881-8438
www.buffaloexchange.com

This is the place for great bargains on gently used clothing and accessories. You can bring in items for trade or cash on the spot, or just browse the clean and hardly used clothing on the racks. The kids' location, Buffalo Kids/Little Traders, also has used toys, books, and videos. Open daily.

OLD PUEBLO TRADERS

5851 East Speedway
(520) 747-0800

Known locally as OPT, you might want to head here when your sore feet won't make it to another shopping spot, but you desperately need a comfy pair of Hush Puppies or Grasshoppers. OPT is like a warehouse of clothes and shoes for women, the latter including hard-to-find sizes. Brands you'll find here, in addition to the aforementioned shoes, include Koret, Sasson, Jantzen, Playtex, and Easy Spirit.

TANQUE VERDE SWAP MEET

4100 South Palo Verde Road
(520) 294-4252
www.tanqueverdeswapmeet.com

Put on your walking shoes and grab a hat and a jug of water so you'll be all set for a morning or evening of swap meeting. It's called the Tanque Verde Swap Meet because it started out on the corner of Tanque Verde and Grant Roads in the days when there used to be enough land to accommodate it. It moved but retained its name.

There's plenty of parking and dust, but buyers can find some good bargains and interesting items here. Most days you'll even find vendors selling some great produce from Mexico such as tomatoes, watermelons, limes, peppers, avocados, and mangos. The swap meet is open from 3:00 to 11:00 p.m. Friday; 7:00 a.m. to 11:00 p.m. Saturday. Sunday hours are from 7:00 a.m. to sundown.

VF FACTORY OUTLET

I-10 at South Palo Verde Road
(520) 889-4400
www.vffo.com

Compared to more modern outlet centers, VF Factory Outlet is small. But that may be a blessing for folks who don't want to walk a mile to shop. There are no more than a dozen indoor stores, carrying apparel, accessories, luggage, housewares, and party and paper products. Brand names include Vanity Fair, Wrangler, Lee, Healthtex, and Jantzen. It's a bit tricky to get to, however, so look for the Palo Verde Inn on South Julian Drive—you'll see the outlet building almost adjacent to it.

BOOKS, ETC.

Although Tucson has its share of national bookstore chains, which are often located in malls, you'll also find many other bookstores, both new and used, all around the metro area. Here are just a few of the more notable ones.

ANTIGONE BOOKS

411 North Fourth Avenue
(520) 792-3715
www.antigonebooks.com

This shop in the Fourth Avenue shopping district offers books by and about women and has a unique selection of nonsexist books for children. Antigone Books also has music, cards, and T-shirts on related topics.

ARIZONA BOOKSTORE
845 North Park Avenue
(520) 622-4717

501 North Park Avenue
(520) 622-6169
www.arizonabookstore.com
University of Arizona and Pima College students frequent these stores because they buy and sell college textbooks. They also have a great selection of UA items, as well as school and engineering supplies, computer books and software, and technical and general interest books. Validated parking is available.

BOOK STOP USED BOOKS
214 North Fourth Avenue
(520) 326-6661
This hole-in-the-wall bookstore has a little bit of everything, from general fiction paperback and hardcovers to fascinating Native American and Arizona history books to a unique children's book collection with lots of classic titles. With over 100,000 volumes stuffed into floor-to-ceiling shelves, bookworms will love this place.

BOOKMAN'S
1930 East Grant Road
(520) 325-5767

3733 West Ina Road
(520) 579-0303

6230 East Speedway Boulevard
(520) 748-9555
www.bookmans.com
The three Bookman's locations account for over 50,000 square feet of fabulous new and used books. The 20,000-square-foot shop on Grant Road is a favorite of locals and university students because it's centrally located, an interesting place, open until 10:00 p.m., and full of great used materials. You'll find both hardbound and paperback used books here on nearly any subject and new books on subjects of local interest, such as the desert and hiking. They also deal in used CDs, videos, and software and have a great selection of old and rare magazines, as do the other two locations in town.

BORDERS BOOKS AND MUSIC
4235 North Oracle Road
(520) 292-1331

5870 East Broadway Boulevard
(520) 584-0111
www.borders.com
Borders stores have an extensive selection of both books and music. They offer discounts on *New York Times* best sellers and have a large children's section. You'll also find specialty magazines and out-of-state newspapers. While browsing, you can relax in the cafe.

i You really have to drop by Clues Unlimited to meet Emily. She's a Vietnamese potbellied pig who sits in the store daily greeting her numerous friends. Call (520) 326-8533 or e-mail Emily at emily@cluesunlimited.com. She may or may not write back, depending on her mood.

CLUES UNLIMITED
123 South Eastbourne Avenue
(520) 326-8533
www.cluesunlimited.com
This specialty bookstore stocks over 10,000 titles in mystery and detective fiction, including the latest releases, hard-to-find and unusual titles, collectors' editions, and signed firsts. They also offer an extensive backlist and ship anywhere in the United States and overseas. One nice feature: They offer home delivery service in Tucson. Open Monday through Saturday.

KID'S CENTER
1725 North Swan Road
(520) 322-5437
www.e-kidscenter.com
You'll find a great selection of children's books for all ages here, from baby classics like *Pat the Bunny* to the ever-popular *Magic Treehouse* series and chapter books for the older set. Kids love to hang out in this comfortable and welcoming store,

which also carries a range of games and toys for all ages. Kids ages 1 to 10 can sign up for the Birthday Club and get a discount coupon.

MOSTLY BOOKS
6208 East Speedway Boulevard
(520) 571-0110
www.mostlybooks.biz
This general bookstore has thousands of terrific new and used books covering all topics, including fiction, recovery, and children's, along with hundreds of used audiobooks. They also have a large selection of greeting cards and gifts.

SINGING WIND BOOKSHOP
700 West Singing Wind Road, Benson
(520) 586-2425
OK, so it's not in Tucson. But you should not miss this amazing store. You'll find it off exit 304 in Benson, at the end of Singing Wind Road. Owned by the feisty and extremely knowledgeable Winn Bundy, the place is a treasure trove of books about the Southwest and Americana. The vast collection includes travel guides, fiction, nonfiction, photography, anthropology, poetry, religion, and more, all organized in Winn's unique style. There's a great children's reading room. The store also hosts special musical events and readings; call to find out the schedule. Cash or check only; open daily.

TUCSON'S MAP AND FLAG CENTER
3239 North First Avenue
(520) 887-4234
www.mapsmithus.com
This is the top source in town for maps, from street atlases of Tucson and Phoenix to topographical maps and charts. The center has travel maps of Mexico, plus an excellent selection of travel guides for the entire planet. If it has to do with geography or topography, you'll probably find it here, but not on Sunday, when the store is closed.

FASHIONS

You'll find lots of fashionable clothing stores in Tucson in plazas, malls, and shopping centers all around town. Here we offer some of the more eclectic and unusual stores in town, which cater to every taste.

CELE PETERSON'S
4811 East Grant Road, Suite 155B
(520) 323-9413
Cele Peterson's is practically a Tucson fashion institution, having opened the first store in 1931. The remaining store carries sophisticated but pricey clothing for women in both dressy and casual styles. The shop has a large collection of Pandora and Troll jewelry. It's closed on Sunday.

CHANGES
4300 North Campbell Avenue
(520) 577-8055
Tres chic. Changes offers lots and lots of casual and sophisticated clothing for all occasions, accessories, shoes, and jewelry. Located in St. Philip's Plaza.

CHICO'S
7003 North Oracle Road
(520) 797-1200

4811 East Grant Road, Suite 107
(520) 325-2422
www.chicos.com
Part of a national chain, you'll find these women's clothing stores in the Casas Adobes and Crossroads Festival shopping centers. With a motto of "easy wear, easy care," clothes here are stylish and comfortable and cater to a variety of tastes and sizes. You'll also find all kinds of accessories here, from jewelry to shoes.

Extremely helpful staff can assist you with putting together an outfit for casual or fancy occasions.

FIRENZE BOUTIQUE
2840 East Skyline Boulevard
(520) 299-2992
Located in a small shopping plaza in the foothills, Firenze sells Giorgio Armani clothes, accessories, and shoes for both men and women. The boutique is open daily.

THE KAIBAB COURTYARD SHOPS
2837–41 North Campbell Avenue
(520) 795-6905
Here you'll find a great selection of upscale Southwestern clothing for women, along with fashionable all-cotton dresses and separates that you can mix, match, and layer for a comfortable, sophisticated look.

MAYA PALACE
El Mercado
6332 East Broadway Boulevard
(520) 748-0817

Casas Adobes Plaza
7057 North Oracle Road
(520) 575–8028

Plaza Palomino
2960 North Swan Road
(520) 325-6411
www.mayapalacetucson.com
This unusual fashion store for women has three locations. They specialize in fashions and accessories from around the world, along with a selection of handcrafted gift items. If you're looking for a unique, exotic, brightly colored outfit in flowing fabrics such as cotton, rayon, and silk, this is the place to shop. The salespeople are friendly and will help you coordinate a total look, right down to the jewelry. The El Mercado and Casas Adobes stores are open on Sunday.

PICANTE BOUTIQUE
2932 East Broadway Boulevard
(520) 320-5699
The accent here is on comfortable women's cotton and natural fiber, easy care–easy wear clothing. You'll also find jewelry from glittery to tribal to funk, hand-painted silk and batik scarves, and an unusual collection of ethnic shawls from Mexico, Guatemala, and Bolivia.

SAVVY BOUTIQUE
5675 North Swan Road
(520) 577-9733
This boutique in a small plaza in the foothills offers women upscale, casual contemporary clothing and accessories. Labels the boutique carries include Flax, Eileen Fisher, Stephanie Schuster, Go Silk, and Sigrid Olsen. It's closed on Sunday.

OUTDOORS AND RECREATION

In addition to national chain stores offering outdoor and recreation gear and clothing, Tucson has a few specialty stores that cater to the outdoor lifestyle.

AUDUBON NATURE SHOP
300 East University Boulevard
(520) 629-0510
www.tucsonaudubon.org
Affiliated with the Tucson Audubon Society, this shop in the university area has a wide selection of natural history books and gifts. Book subjects include astronomy, geology, birds (of course), mammals, insects, reptiles, plants, and oceans. It also has educational materials and children's books on nature subjects and supplies for birders and hikers, such as binoculars, field guides, and hiking maps. For gift giving or for personal use, you'll find games, greeting cards, maps, tapes, and records, all with a nature theme. And for your feathered friends, you'll find bird feeders. The shop is closed on Sunday.

SUMMIT HUT
5045 East Speedway Boulevard
(520) 325-1554, (800) 499-8696

605 East Wetmore Road
(520) 888-1000
www.summithut.com
This is a local favorite for all kinds of outdoor equipment and advice, including a great selection of books and pamphlets on outdoor and southern Arizona subjects. In addition to all the outdoor stuff for sale, Summit Hut also rents gear such as tents, packs, sleeping bags, and climbing boots. And if you need a present for someone who's into nature, it has T-shirts and cards and funky gift items.

YESTERYEAR'S TREASURES

Tucson has some great antiques shops and secondhand stores. Antiques fairs, shows, and auctions take place here year-round with great prices and wide variety. You'll find everything from furniture and kitchenware to glass and toys. The main "antiques district" is on Grant Road between Campbell Avenue and Craycroft Road. You can pick up a free antiques guide at most of the antiques stores in town—just ask.

AMERICAN ANTIQUE MALL
3130 East Grant Road
(520) 326-3070
www.americanantiquemall.com
Voted the "Best of Tucson," this is the largest antiques mall in the city and offers everything from A to Z. You'll find pre-Columbian artifacts, vintage clothing, glassware, turn-of-the-twentieth-century pottery, Navajo rugs, artwork, and more right in the heart of the antiques district. Closed Tuesday and Wednesday.

THE ANTIQUE PRESIDIO
3024 East Grant Road
(520) 323-1844
www.theantiquepresidio.com
Packed floor to ceiling with goodies, this huge, multiroomed antiques store has a wide selection of everything from funky furs to vintage clothes and hats to rows of many-colored Pyrex kitchenware to a fair share of kitsch, including a large collection of goofy salt and pepper shakers. A mixed bag of wooden furniture might delight refinishers out there. Check the Web site for discount coupons before you go. Open daily.

CANYON STATE COLLECTIBLES
5245 East Pima Street
(520) 795-1922
Whether you're hunting for movie and movie-star memorabilia or political and military collectibles, Canyon State probably has it. It also offers sports cards, old jewelry, collector plates, old toys and dolls, postcards, animation art, stamps, coins, Native American jewelry and artifacts, and Hummels, Royal Doultons, and Lladros. Lots and lots of amazing goods are found here. The store is closed on Sunday and Monday.

CHRISTINE'S ANTIQUE SHOP & DOLL COLLECTION
4940 East Speedway Boulevard
(520) 323-0018
Nearly every square inch of this large store is crammed full of old things, including glassware, lamps, furniture, dolls, dollhouse miniatures, and antique linens. It's fascinating and a real find for doll collectors. Closed on Sunday.

i **The Freecycle Web Network, started in Tucson in 2003, is a Web-based community swap program. You can donate your used items or find something you need. Visit http://groups.yahoo.com/group/freecycle. You'll have to join the group, but it's free.**

FIREHOUSE ANTIQUE CENTER
6522 East 22nd Street
(520) 571-1775
Nearly 40 dealers occupy this mall, buying and selling antiques and collectibles that include books, estate jewelry, linens, sports items, furniture, and vintage clothing. The Firehouse also provides services such as furniture restoration, repairs, and appraisals and estate liquidations. Open daily.

MUSEUM SHOPS

Many of Tucson's major attractions and museums also have gift shops where you'll find lots of unique Southwestern, Mexican, and other gift items. Here are some of the more outstanding ones.

ARIZONA-SONORA DESERT MUSEUM GIFT SHOP
2021 North Kinney Road
(520) 578-3008
www.desertmuseum.org
You'll find everything you ever wanted with a Sonoran Desert motif at this terrific shop. T-shirts,

hats, books about desert and plant life created exclusively for the museum, desert artifacts and collectibles, jewelry, cards, stuffed animals—you name it, they've got it! Open daily.

TOHONO CHUL PARK GIFT AND MUSEUM SHOPS
7366 North Paseo del Norte
(520) 742-6455
www.tohonochulpark.org

This lovely park is home to two shops bursting with a wonderful collection of gifts and collectibles. Lovely one-of-a-kind pottery by local artists, traditional and native crafts, unique gift items like saguaro cactus cookie cutters, hummingbird ceramic tiles, wind chimes, regional specialty food items, books, plants, and much, much more. The shops are open daily. There is a $7 admission fee for adults to enter other parts of the park. Seniors and active military pay $5; students with ID pay $3; children ages 5 to 12 pay $2.

TUCSON BOTANICAL GARDENS GIFT SHOP
2150 North Alvernon Way
(520) 326-9686
www.tucsonbotanical.org

Plant lovers will find all sorts of goodies here, such as botanical books, wildflower seeds, whimsical garden art, and unusual jewelry. The shop is open daily.

TUCSON MUSEUM OF ART SHOP
140 North Main Avenue
(520) 624-2333
www.tucsonarts.com

This elegant shop carries all sorts of work by regional artists, including beautiful blown-glass bowls and pitchers, Mexican-style tiled mirrors, jewelry by local artists, painted furniture, and a wonderful selection of cards, prints, and books from around the world. Closed Monday.

ATTRACTIONS

There is so much to see and do in Tucson. You'll find it all here: sophisticated art museums and galleries, cowboy ghost towns, an internationally renowned desert museum, and spectacular natural wonders like Colossal Cave, Saguaro National Park, and Sabino Canyon. There are many hidden treasures here, too, like tiny shrines, historic buildings, and hummingbird gardens. We cover lots of them in this chapter, but it's just the tip of the iceberg. Plan to take a lot of time in Tucson to do justice to the many amazing natural and man-made attractions in and outside of town. (See the Kidstuff chapter for activities geared more toward the younger set.)

Price Guidelines

The following price codes indicate what you will pay per adult for general admission. If an attraction is free, it will not have a price code. If the attraction offers free admission on certain days, it will be indicated in the listing.

$	**less than $5**
$$	**$5–$10**
$$$	**$11–$20**
$$$$	**more than $20**

ARIZONA HISTORICAL SOCIETY $-$$
949 East Second Street
(520) 628-5774
www.arizonahistoricalsociety.org

The historical society is actually four museums, with the main one near the UA campus on Second Street. Its three branch museums are the Sosa-Carrillo-Frémont House, the Wells Fargo Museum, and the Fort Lowell Museum. (The last is covered separately in this chapter.)

Entering the historical society's lovely old building is to take a walk through Arizona's history. Permanent exhibits include authentically decorated period rooms depicting life in the Arizona Territory, artifacts from Arizona's frontier life and its Native American populations, and a full-scale re-creation of underground mining. Numerous temporary exhibits focus on specific times or topics in Arizona's past. And for anyone doing research on nearly anything pertaining to Arizona or Tucson, the historical society maintains an excellent library, which includes rare and unique maps and photos, that's open to the public. Docent tours are offered by appointment, and the museum is wheelchair accessible. There's also a gift shop specializing in authentic Southwestern arts and crafts and books. The historical society conducts special events and lectures year-round. Admission is $5 for adults, $4 for seniors and students 12 to 18 years of age, and free for children under 12. Admission is free on the first Saturday of the month. Hours are 10:00 a.m. to 4:00 p.m. Monday through Saturday. The library is open from 10:00 a.m. to 3:00 p.m. Monday through Friday and from 10:00 a.m. to 1:00 p.m. on Saturday. Parking is available at the multistory garage at Euclid Avenue and Second Street, where there is a special section set aside for visitors to the historical society; watch for a small sign at the entrance. Take your parking ticket to the society for validation and your parking is free.

At the Sosa-Carrillo-Frémont House, 151 South Granada Avenue (520-622-0956), hours are 10:00 a.m. to 4:00 p.m. Wednesday through Saturday. The historical society has turned this house, one of Tucson's oldest adobe buildings, into a museum. It's named for the families that occupied it from the 1870s and today is furnished in late-nineteenth-century fashion, with rotating displays of territorial life. Admission is $3 for adults, $2 for students and children 12 to 18. Children under 12 get in free. The museum is free the first Saturday of each month. (See the Arts and Culture chapter for more details.)

The society's Wells Fargo Museum (520-770-1473) is located at 140 North Stone Avenue in the historic Wells Fargo Bank Building. This museum specializes in the history of downtown Tucson and offers a variety of permanent and rotating exhibits. It's open Monday through Friday from 10:00 a.m. to 4:00 p.m. Admission is $3 for adults, $2 for seniors and children 12 to 18. Admission is free on first Friday of the month.

ARIZONA-SONORA DESERT MUSEUM $$$
2021 North Kinney Road
(520) 883-2702
www.desertmuseum.org

This fabulous "museum" is actually a combination zoo, museum, and botanical garden. Here you will learn everything you ever wanted to know about the Sonoran Desert. Exhibits re-create desert habitats of all varieties of plants and animals.

Allow yourself at least three hours. The natural landscape is re-created so realistically that you find yourself eye-to-eye with mountain lions, prairie dogs, Gila monsters, hawks, and hummingbirds. Every inch of this mostly outdoor museum is packed full of fascinating plant and animal life. One exhibit features nocturnal desert dwellers. Another gives visitors an underwater view of beavers, river otters, and fish. A walk-through cave leads to a fine collection of rare and beautiful regional gems and minerals. And you'll see all varieties of reptiles and spiders safely tucked away behind glass. In the hummingbird aviary, one of the museum's most popular spots, hundreds of tiny birds hover about, showing off their colors and flying skills. All during your walk you'll find volunteers giving fascinating demonstrations about the creatures and plant life of the desert.

From late October through mid-April, the Desert Museum offers unique raptor free-flight demonstrations that showcase hawks, falcons, owls, and other birds. Showtimes are typically at 10:30 a.m. and 1:30 p.m., but call first to check.

The museum is clean, meticulously cared for, and exquisitely laid out to give the best views possible of the plants and animals. It's wheelchair accessible and stroller friendly, and both are available for free. The museum also has excellent eateries; shops that shouldn't be missed for natural history books, native crafts, bird feeders, and much more; and an art gallery of artists' Sonoran Desert interpretations in a variety of media.

It's open daily from 8:30 a.m. to 5:00 p.m. October through February and 7:30 a.m. to 5:00 p.m. March through September. From June through August, the museum is open Saturday nights with special doings. There are shade ramadas, drinking fountains, and restrooms in several locations, but be prepared to protect yourself from the sun, especially in summer. Admission prices vary seasonally; children under 6 are free. Discount coupons are usually easy to find at the Tucson Convention & Visitors Bureau, in the Tucson Attractions Passport booklets (available at the visitors bureau), in local publications, and in some stores and banks.

The museum is located on the west side of the Tucson Mountains, about 14 miles from downtown Tucson, and can be reached via either Ajo Way or Speedway Boulevard. RVers must take the Ajo Way route to Kinney Road.

i Leapin' lizards, Batman! The Arizona-Sonora Desert Museum's newest highlight, called Life on the Rocks, is great fun. You can see lizards and gophers and snakes (oh, my!) and other rock-dwelling creatures (some are alive, and some are life-size) in the narrow canyonlike display. It's set up so you can actually see underground. Look for it between the two loop trails.

ARIZONA STATE MUSEUM
Park Avenue and University Boulevard
(520) 621-6302
www.statemuseum.arizona.edu

Enter the main gate of the University of Arizona

campus and you face a lovely tree-lined street bordered by some exquisite old buildings. Two of these are the Arizona State Museum's north and south buildings. As the oldest and largest anthropology museum in the Southwest, its collections are recognized as some of the world's most significant resources for the study of Southwestern cultures. Included are 100,000 artifacts from archaeological excavations of the Hohokam, Mogollon, and Anasazi cultures; more than 25,000 ethnographic objects documenting the cultures of both historic and living American Indians; and 175,000 historic and contemporary photographic images.

Through the museum's exhibits, visitors discover the wonders of ancient civilizations and the contributions of living Native American cultures. Anyone with an interest in the Southwest will also appreciate the museum's library of 40,000 volumes (open to the public Monday through Friday, 9:30 a.m. to 4:30 p.m.), including many rare titles. In the gift shop browsers or buyers will find an excellent selection of pottery, kachina dolls, rugs, carvings, jewelry, baskets, cards, posters, and books reflecting the museum's theme.

Hours are Monday through Saturday 10:00 a.m. to 5:00 p.m. and Sunday noon to 5:00 p.m. Admission is free ($3 donations are suggested and appreciated), and both buildings are wheelchair accessible. Metered street parking is available to the west of the main gate on University Boulevard, Second Street, and First Street; several pay parking lots located in the same area will cost no more than a few dollars and are free on weekends.

ASARCO MINERAL DISCOVERY CENTER $$
Interstate 19 and Pima Mine Road, Sahuarita
(520) 625-7513
www.mineraldiscovery.com

Folks who are interested in minerals or copper mining will see and learn all about them at this attraction 15 miles south of Tucson. Dubbed the largest man-made attraction in southern Arizona, visitors have a choice of seeing just the Mineral Discovery Center, which is free, or also taking the open-pit mine tour, for which a fee is charged for anyone older than age 4 ($5 for kids age 5 to 12, $8 for adults, and $6 for seniors).

The Mineral Discovery Center has a variety of hands-on exhibits about mining and minerals, from how ore deposits are formed and how they are discovered and mined to how the land is reclaimed after mining. A multimedia theater has presentations on mining, mineral resources, and reclamation. There's also a display of historic and present-day mining equipment. The tour takes visitors by air-conditioned bus to an operating open-pit copper mine nearby. You'll see how the land is excavated, the massive machinery that mills the earth and extracts and processes the minerals, and the reclamation process designed to restore the landscape.

Tours take about an hour, and flat shoes are recommended because some walking will be required. Call ahead if you need arrangements for wheelchair access. The center is open Tuesday through Saturday from 9:00 a.m. to 5:00 p.m. Tour times vary seasonally, so call ahead. Reservations are recommended; call (520) 625-8233. It's operated by ASARCO Inc., a worldwide mining company whose copper operations are based in Tucson.

BIOSPHERE 2 $$$
Highway 77 at Mile Marker 96.5
(520) 838-6200
www.bio2.com

We all live on Biosphere 1 (Earth), and Biosphere 2 was created to be a model of Earth—an experiment to duplicate Earth's environment and lifeforms and enhance knowledge of its ecosystems. When this $150-million-plus model opened in 1991, eight biospherians lived here self-sufficiently in the world's largest glass-enclosed ecological laboratory, and visitors could only tour the outside areas. No one lives inside Biosphere 2 today, and visitors can now tour the human habitat, the once-sealed environment where the biospherians lived and worked. The building covers more than three acres and resembles something from a science-fiction movie. Visitors will see a million-gallon ocean with above- and underwater view-

Biosphere 2 is a one-of-a-kind attraction. COURTESY OF THE METROPOLITAN TUCSON CONVENTION VISITORS BUREAU, GILL KENNY

ing, a tropical rain forest, plus five other biomes (self-sustaining communities of living organisms) replicating Earth. It's like taking a trip around the world in an afternoon.

It's best to start at the visitor center to get your bearings of the 250-acre campus, a map, and a filmed overview of the project. Be sure to have comfortable shoes and plan on at least two hours to see everything. Along the way guides can answer questions and point you in the right direction. Or you can take a tour. Tours begin at 9:30 a.m. and are offered every 45 minutes thereafter until 3:30 p.m. There are several specialty tours available for an extra charge. You'll also find shops selling mementos of your Biosphere visit and the Lions Den Cafe for snacks.

Admission prices vary. Discount coupons are often available at the Tucson Convention & Visitors Bureau, at other spots around the city, and in local publications. Biosphere 2 is open daily from 9:00 a.m. to 4:00 p.m. except Thanksgiving and Christmas. Most exhibits and presentations are wheelchair accessible, and strollers and wheelchairs are available for rent at the admission gate; rental fees vary. This is not the best attraction for toddlers.

To get here take Oracle Road north about 15 miles and watch for the sign pointing to Biosphere 2.

CASINO OF THE SUN
7406 South Camino de Oeste
(520) 883-1700, (800) 344-9435
www.casinosun.com

Casino Del Sol
5655 West Valencia Road
(520) 838-6506, (800) 344-9435
www.casinodelsol.com

The Pascua Yaqui Tribe was one of the last Native American peoples to gain federal recognition by the U.S. Congress. In 1964 the tribe was deeded about 200 acres of desert land southwest of Tucson and acquired an additional 590 acres in 1988. Today about 13,000 members of the tribe live in the area, which also houses the tribe's casinos, a source of revenue and employment for tribal members. Casino of the Sun, built in 1989, boasts casino games, slot machines (including nickel machines), live-action card room, blackjack, video poker, and more. There are over 500 games to choose from.

The tribe's second casino, Casino Del Sol, built in 2001, offers live entertainment in an outdoor amphitheater (see the Nightlife chapter) and has 22,500 square feet of gaming space, featuring nearly 1,000 multidenominational slot machines, plus live blackjack and poker. Casino Del Sol has several dining options, including a fine-dining Italian restaurant, several casual and quick restaurants (from tacos to pizza), and a bar/lounge in the center of the gaming floor. Players clubs are available at both locations. The casinos are open every day except on certain days during the Holy Week of Easter.

As with casinos all across the United States, these places really draw the crowds, particularly on weekends. Parking is free, with plenty of wheelchair-accessible spots. From Tucson go west on Valencia Road about 5 miles past Interstate 10—you won't miss the signs pointing the way. Both casinos are open 24/7 and offer $5 shuttle service, with pickups all over town.

COLOSSAL CAVE MOUNTAIN PARK $$
16721 East Old Spanish Trail, Vail
(520) 647-7275
www.colossalcave.com

This attraction is one of the most unusual and fascinating in southern Arizona. Colossal Cave was formed somewhere between 12 and 20 million years ago by the welling up of hot sulfur–laden brine. It is the largest dry, or dormant, cave in the United States. The cave has a fascinating history: It was used by prehistoric peoples around A.D. 900 for shelter and storage, and in the 1800s train robbers used it as a hideout.

The tour route is 0.5 mile long and takes about 50 minutes. It's led by a guide who relates the cave's history, legends, and geology. You'll walk down and back up about six stories (and some 360 steps) to see amazing stalactites, stalagmites, flowstone, and other formations, not to mention a few prehistoric markings. It's always 70 degrees and dry in the cave. Unfortunately, this is not an attraction for people who are in wheelchairs or who have difficulty walking.

Tours are given daily year-round. They're not prescheduled, but the wait is 30 minutes at most. Part of the 2,000-acre Colossal Cave Mountain Park, there are lots of other things to do here. You can visit the 120-year-old La Posta Quemada Ranch; browse in the terrific gift shop that has rocks, minerals, and unusual souvenirs; take a horseback ride along the historic stagecoach route; or just enjoy the spectacular view from the stone terrace.

The cost is $8.50 for those 13 and older, $5 for ages 6 to 12, and free for younger ones. You will also pay a fee of $5 per car just to enter the park. Summer hours, in effect March 16 through September 15, are 8:00 a.m. to 6:00 p.m. Monday through Saturday and 8:00 a.m. to 7:00 p.m. Sunday and holidays. Winter hours are 9:00 a.m. to 5:00 p.m. Monday through Saturday and 9:00 a.m. to 6:00 p.m. Sunday and holidays. To get here from Tucson take scenic Old Spanish Trail for about 17 miles or I-10 east to exit 279 and then north for about 6 miles.

i Colossal Cave Mountain Park offers hayrides and stagecoach rides. The cost is $7 per person for a ride of about 15 to 20 minutes. Call (520) 647-7275 to book.

DAVIS-MONTHAN AIR FORCE BASE
Craycroft and Valencia Roads
(520) 228-4717
www.dm.af.mil

You can read all about Davis-Monthan Air Force Base, located on Tucson's south side, in our separate chapter of the same name. But unless you have official business there or otherwise have access to the base, you'll only be able to see it by taking a tour. The tours of the base are now operated by Pima Air and Space Museum and embark from that site, 6000 East Valencia Road. (There will be a security check of the bus before it enters the grounds.) The one-hour tour goes through the base, including down the flight line for a view of the array of planes using the 14,000-foot runway, but it focuses on the intriguing aircraft storage facility (or "boneyard"). Photos are allowed. If you're at all interested in the military or in vintage and modern aircraft, we highly recommend the base tour. (*NOTE:* Everyone over age 16 will need a government-issued photo ID.) Details are in the air base chapter.

DESERT DIAMOND CASINO/NOGALES HIGHWAY
7350 South Nogales Highway
(520) 294-7777, (866) 332-9467

DESERT DIAMOND CASINO/I-19
1100 West Pima Mine Road
Exit 80 off I-19, Sahuarita
(520) 294-7777, (866) 332-9467
www.desertdiamondcasino.com

Casinos are hot in Tucson, bringing in revenue for several indigenous tribes. The Desert Diamond Casinos, with three locations (two in Tucson and one in Why, Arizona) are among the largest moneymakers. Owned and operated by the Tohono O'odham Nation, they have over 1,200 employees.

Opened in 1993, the original Desert Diamond Casino on Nogales Highway hosts more than 800 fast-paced slot machines, live blackjack, poker, a large bingo center, and keno. The casino also offers a full-service bar, grill, and a 24-hour snack bar for late-night munchies.

The location at Pima Mine Road just south of Tucson opened in 2001 to great fanfare. The Santa Fe–style architecture, fountains, exhibits of Native American crafts, and open plazas are a delight just to wander through even if you're not into gambling. The complex is home to the upscale Agave Restaurant as well as lunch and dinner buffets, a grill, and a sports bar. The gaming area looks like it has descended from outer space and features 500 slot machines plus live blackjack and keno. The 2,400-seat Diamond Center serves as a venue for live acts (see the Nightlife chapter). Free shuttles are offered at various locations around town; call (520) 393-2749 for reservations. Open 24/7, you must be 21 to enter the gaming area.

FLANDRAU SCIENCE CENTER AND PLANETARIUM **$$**
Cherry Avenue and University Boulevard
(520) 621-7827
www.gotuasciencecenter.org

The center plans to relocate downtown in 2011 in a completely new setting. (Plans include an IMAX theater and tropical vivarium to view spectacular butterflies.) Exhibits in place here now are a living and working laboratory designed to offer the ultimate in sensory exploration, with prototype exhibits and planetarium programs for the public to experience and evaluate. It's a great opportunity to put in your two cents about what you and the kids would like to see in the new space.

You can view the stars at the outdoor observatory and, with the assistance of a guide, look through a 16-inch telescope, gazing at planets, galaxies, and star clusters. The observatory is open year-round on clear nights Wednesday through Saturday, and viewing is free.

Back inside Flandrau, take in a show at the dome-shaped theater of stars, where you'll be mesmerized by special effects, panoramic projections, and a state-of-the-art video projection system. You'll sit in comfortable reclining seats as the virtual reality shows on astronomy, sky lore, exploration, and ancient cultures take you back through time or forward into the future of space travel. Downstairs, the Mineral Museum, home to one of the finest university-owned collections, features a fascinating display of Arizona minerals, gems, and specimen rocks. And finally, Flandrau has a wonderful science store featuring science kits, posters, puzzles, star charts, books, toys, games, and more—all designed to make learning about science fun.

Admission to Flandrau is $5 for anyone over the age of 4. Kids under 4 get in free. Admission includes exhibits, the Mineral Museum, and one planetarium show. There are no planetarium shows offered Thursday or Friday. Metered parking is available on the streets.

Close-up

Unique Spots in Town

Tucson is home to so many hidden treasures; these are unique and worth a stop:

History of Pharmacy Museum

The College of Pharmacy at the University of Arizona

1703 East Mabel Street

(520) 626-1427

www.pharmacy.arizona.edu/museum

The weirdest thing here is a wad of John Dillinger's gum (yes, really!). The rest of the collection takes up four floors of the pharmacy building and includes over 60,000 bottles; 18 show globes (the symbol of the profession of pharmacy) of various shape, size, and color over 100 years old; original drug containers; books; and artifacts from Arizona circa 1880–1950, including several large drug store fixtures from Arizona's territorial days. Open Monday through Friday 8:00 a.m. to 5:00 p.m. Free admission.

Postal History Foundation

920 North First Avenue

(520) 623-6652

www.postalhistoryfoundation.org/

This Tucson jewel opens a door into the fascinating world of western postal history. Inside, you'll find a library containing 30,000 books and U.S. Post Office publications, a collector stamp sales office, a museum with turn-of-the-twentieth-century fittings, and a working post office. The library has been honored for its noteworthy architecture and is open to anyone wanting a quiet place to study. The museum claims to have over a million stamps, and staff operates an extensive youth education program. The coolest thing about this museum is the volunteers who love showing people around. Few Tucson residents are even aware of the existence of this museum—shhhhh. Open Monday through Friday from 8:00 a.m. to 3:00 p.m. Free admission.

Southern Arizona Transportation Museum

Downtown Train Depot

414 North Toole Avenue

(520) 623-2223

www.tucsonhistoricdepot.org

Housed in the beautifully restored 1942 historic train depot, this small museum focuses on the history of the railroad in southern Arizona, which roared into town in 1880. You can check out Locomotive No. 1673, which had a starring role in the movie *Oklahoma!* and is one of only eight mogul-type steam engines in the country. It's permanently parked in the back of the depot near the tracks. Call to check museum hours. Free admission.

FORT LOWELL MUSEUM **$**
2900 North Craycroft Road
(520) 885-3832
www.arizonahistoricalsociety.org
Take a trip into Tucson's past and have a family day at the park, all for free. The small museum operated by the Arizona Historical Society is located in the pleasant surroundings of Fort Lowell Park, once the site of a Hohokam Indian village. Centuries later a cavalry fort was erected here. From 1873 to 1891 soldiers were stationed at Fort Lowell to protect Tucson settlers from Indian raids. The museum is actually a reconstruction of the commanding officers' quarters. Here you'll find period furnishings, a photographic story of the 75 former occupants of Fort Lowell, and frontier artifacts. It's open Wednesday through Saturday from 10:00 a.m. to 4:00 p.m. Adults pay $3 entrance fee. Seniors and students are admitted for $2. Kids under 12 get in free.

GARDEN OF GETHSEMANE
West Congress Street and Bonita Avenue
(520) 791-5890
This little gem is tucked away behind a gate in a small downtown park at the corner of Congress Street and Bonita Avenue. Called the Garden of Gethsemane, the park contains life-size carvings of the Last Supper, the Crucifixion, and the Holy Family, along with several smaller shrines. The carvings were created by Spanish sculptor Felix Lucero, who vowed to do the work as a tribute to God when his life was spared on a WWI battlefield. A restful and contemplative place in the midst of heavy traffic, the gates are open daily from 8:00 a.m. to 3:30 p.m. and there's no admission fee. The garden may be reserved for special occasions.

HISTORIC OLD PUEBLO
The downtown area of Tucson is home to historic homes, museums, specialty shops, and some of the oldest and most interesting architecture in town, ranging from adobes to ornate mansions. The downtown is also known as the Tucson Arts District, with a number of eclectic galleries, funky restaurants, and sophisticated shops. After all, this is the area of town where Tucson began. Here you'll find remnants of the original presidio wall, look up at the striking mosaic tile dome of the Pima County Courthouse juxtaposed against Tucson's few high-rises, and wander along narrow streets lined with colorful restored adobes. It's a unique combination of old and new.

Unlike many bustling downtowns, Tucson's downtown area retains a sleepy, low-key atmosphere. You won't find hordes of tourists thronging the shops or pouring into the museums. It's relaxing and invigorating with lots of interesting sights to see around every corner. Take your time, carry lots of water, and just stroll through this unique part of Tucson's past and present.

Streets in these neighborhoods weren't created with car traffic in mind, so it's best to tour through history the old-fashioned way: on foot. There are four distinct districts, each with its own attractions.

One is defined by what once was the old presidio wall, which today is bounded by Pennington Street, Church Avenue, Washington Street, and Main Avenue and represents over 130 years of the city's architectural history. This area offers more than two dozen attractions, including the Gardes Footbridge; the Pima County Courthouse; La Casa Cordova, one of the oldest homes in Tucson and now a museum; and other historic houses open to the public, including the Stevens House and the Edward Nye Fish House. In the center of the more modern Tucson Museum of Art lies the Plaza of the Pioneers, honoring Tucson's early citizens.

Just to the north is the second area to tour, the El Presidio Historic District, bounded by Washington and Sixth Streets and Granada and Church Avenues. Although some of the old mansions here are still private residences, they're worth just walking by. You'll also find several, like the territorial-style 1907 Manning House and Steinfeld Mansion, that have been converted into offices but still hold their allure. And be sure to take a peaceful break in the Alene Dunlop Smith Memorial Garden on the east side of Granada Avenue.

Downtown and Barrio Historico comprise the third area to tour, which is south of the presidio wall district and bounded by Simpson Street,

Church Avenue, Congress Street, and Granada Avenue. Here you'll find the lovely 1880s town house, Sanmaniego House, now a restaurant; El Tiradito, the wishing shrine; and the Sosa-Carrillo-Frémont House, one of Tucson's oldest adobe structures and the only barrio building spared when the convention center was built.

Just to the east of the barrio area is the Church Avenue District, extending to Fifth Avenue. This area encompasses the lovely Temple of Music and Art; the former Carnegie Library, now housing the Children's Museum; and St. Augustine Cathedral, one of central Tucson's most striking structures dating from 1896. At the northeast corner of this area, you'll find the old Congress Hotel and the renovated historic Southern Pacific Railroad Depot, now operated by Amtrak.

INTERNATIONAL WILDLIFE MUSEUM $$
4800 West Gates Pass Road
(520) 617-1439
www.thewildlifemuseum.org

Both kids and their parents have an opportunity to see and often touch more than 400 kinds of mounted animals from around the world here. Bighorn sheep, for example, are perched along a large boulder display, showing how they live and interact in the mountains around the Sonoran Desert. Another display graphically shows the huge size difference among bears, from the smallest black bear to the grizzly. The nocturnal area depicts desert creatures of the night. Other species on display include reptiles and birds. Visitors can also watch award-winning nature films in the 100-seat theater, learn about wildlife through interactive computer displays, or shop for unique gifts from around the world.

Except for major holidays, the museum is open Monday through Friday from 9:00 a.m. to 5:00 p.m., Saturday and Sunday 9:00 a.m. to 6:00 p.m., and is wheelchair accessible. Admission is $7 for adults, $5.50 for seniors and students, $2.50 for kids 4 to 12, and free for younger ones.

It's located 5 miles west of I-10 via Speedway Boulevard to Gates Pass Road. Until about mid-2010, when extensive freeway renovation is complete, the I-10 exit for Speedway is closed. If you are traveling west on I-10, exit at 29th Street and use the frontage road to Speedway. If you are traveling east on I-10, exit at Prince Road and use the frontage road to Speedway.

i For an unusual and fun way to tour Tucson, try an hour or two on a battery-powered Segway. The company offers several tours of the downtown area, ranging from one-hour rides to several hours on the Presidio Trail. Everyone gets a lesson first. For more information call (800) 979-3370 or visit http://tucsonsegway.com/tours.html.

KARTCHNER CAVERNS STATE PARK $$$
Highway 90, Benson
(520) 586-4100 (information line),
(520) 586-2283 (reservations)
www.pr.state.az.us

Discovered by two cavers in 1974 and kept secret for many years, this amazing natural attraction is now part of an extensive park area. Guided tours of the Throne Room (all ages welcome) and Big Room (children under 7 not permitted) are available seasonally year-round and are led by knowledgeable rangers.

You will enter through hermetically sealed doors developed to maintain the humidity levels in these magnificent wet caves and preserve them in their original state. You won't find garish colored lights, just natural phenomena more amazing than you can imagine. It's a tough tour for kids—there's no touching and lots of walking and talking—and no strollers or baby backpacks are allowed. However, kids will enjoy the trails, nature walks, and the great interactive discovery center.

Reservations are required; make them well in advance, as tours book up early. Fees vary, but you will pay a park entrance fee per vehicle as well as a separate fee to tour the caves. (See the Parks and Recreation chapter for more details.) The park is located 9 miles south of I-10, off Highway 90 at exit 302.

Kitt Peak offers all-night advanced observing programs for anyone interested in serious astronomy. Guests are treated as visiting astronomers and have access to center resources. You'll use high-quality eyepieces and digital cameras to snap great shots as your souvenir. To make reservations call (520) 318-8728 or (520) 318-8733. Costs start at $425 per night for two people.

KITT PEAK NATIONAL OBSERVATORY
Highway 386
(520) 318-8726, (520) 318-8200
www.noao.edu

Visit the world's largest collection of optical telescopes at Kitt Peak. At an elevation of 6,875 feet above the Sonoran Desert floor, Kitt Peak is in the Quinlan Mountains, which are part of the Tohono O'odham Indian Reservation, on land leased to the federal government. The location is so appealing to astronomers because it's under some of the finest night skies in the world.

To see this amazing collection of observatories (one of which is 18 stories tall) and telescopes, start at the Kitt Peak Visitor Center and learn the history of optical astronomy and the role Kitt Peak has had in shaping astronomical research. Then take a one-hour guided tour (10:00 a.m., 11:30 a.m., and 1:30 p.m.) to see the facilities and learn how astronomers use telescopes to unlock the mysteries of the universe. At the National Solar Observatory exhibit gallery, you'll be able to watch astronomers operate the world's largest solar telescope. All of this takes place daily (except Thanksgiving, Christmas Eve and Day, and New Year's Day) from 9:00 a.m. to 3:45 p.m. There's no admission charge, but donations are suggested.

For a totally different experience and the chance to actually view the skies through some of the equipment, visit Kitt Peak at night or plan your daytime visit so you can stay until dark. But be aware that reservations are a must for the nighttime program (the limit is 34 people). Called the Nightly Observing Program, it's conducted nightly by tour guides and costs $39 for adults or $34 for students, active military, seniors, and anyone younger than 18. It lasts for three and a half hours, but you must arrive one hour before sunset, so the starting time varies. (To limit the effect of bright lights at night, drivers are escorted down the peak using only parking lights for about a mile.) The stargazing program uses the visitor center telescope dome, which is equipped with binoculars and a state-of-the-art 16-inch telescope to view planets, the birth and death of stars, nebulae, and galaxies. Keep in mind that temperatures are 10 to 20 degrees cooler than in Tucson, so on winter nights it will actually be frigid. Also be aware that walking paths to several of the telescopes are steep and may pose a problem to people with cardiac and respiratory troubles.

There are no food or gas facilities at Kitt Peak. Public restrooms are adjacent to the parking lot, while wheelchair-accessible restrooms are in the visitor center. Kitt Peak is 56 miles southwest of Tucson, a 90-minute drive, via Ajo Way (Highway 86) to Highway 386, which is Kitt Peak Road.

MISSION SAN XAVIER DEL BAC
1950 West San Xavier Road
(520) 294-2624
www.sanxaviermission.org

Also referred to as the White Dove of the Desert, this incredible structure, built between 1777 and 1797, is a wondrous sight to behold. The oldest Catholic church in the United States, the full name means "mission for the Saint Francisco Xavier at the place where the water appears." (The reference is to the place where the underground Santa Cruz River rose to the surface.) But you need not know the correct way to say it or what it means to appreciate the splendor of this luminous white structure rising out of the desert floor on the land of the Tohono O'odham Indians.

Pronounced *Sahn-hav-yair,* for two centuries it has stood as a symbol of religion brought to Native Americans by missionaries traveling from Mexico. It was the O'odham who became the skilled masons and laborers who erected the domed, vaulted, and arched building of fired

The magnificent San Xavier del Bac is known as the White Dove of the Desert. COURTESY OF THE METROPOLITAN TUCSON CONVENTION VISITORS BUREAU, GILL KENNY

bricks, stone, and lime mortar (or stucco) under the direction of missionary priests who had seen great edifices in Spain and Italy. From Father Kino's initial work on the foundation in 1700, it took 97 years before the church was opened for services, and even then it was not actually completed. (Look closely and you'll see that the east bell tower has never been completed.)

Today it remains the parish church of the O'odham of the San Xavier District of the Tohono O'odham Nation. But by the thousands, people of all faiths come through the mission's old dark doors of mesquite wood to appreciate its beauty and the labor of love it so obviously took to construct it.

Six generations of the same family have worked to maintain the mission's exterior, using a mixture of sand, lime, and cactus juice for stucco. An interior restoration taking six years and $2 million (mostly donated) was completed to mark the mission's 1997 bicentennial. An international team of experts refurbished 54 polychrome wall paintings and 44 statues, many made in Mexico more than 200 years ago, as part of their task. Nearly every area of the baroque-style interior is covered with elaborate paintings and sculpture created by unknown artists. Throughout the small rooms of the mission there are photos, documents, and artifacts showing its history. A gift shop, craft store, museum, and refreshments are available on the premises.

The mission is open to visitors daily from 8:00 a.m. to 5:00 p.m., and Masses are held at various times. Admission is free, but donations are welcomed. It's located 19 miles south of downtown Tucson via I-19. Words can't adequately describe the mission; it must be seen.

i **Be sure to look carefully down and to the left or right of the altar at Mission San Xavier del Bac. You'll see small paintings of saints and Southwestern desert creatures such as mice, snakes, and rabbits.**

MOUNT LEMMON SKI VALLEY SKYRIDE **$$$$**
Mount Lemmon
(520) 576-1321 (live), (520) 576-1400 (recorded information)

Many chapters in this book discuss Mount Lemmon, Tucsonans' playground in the sky in the Santa Catalina Mountains. All along the 30-mile ride to the top, activities include hiking, picnicking, camping, fishing, climbing, and just enjoying the diverse scenery and topography as it changes from desert to pine forest through five distinct vegetative zones. At the highway's end, just past the village of Summerhaven, lies Ski Valley, but you need not be a skier to enjoy the lift, or skyride, to the summit. The 30-minute round-trip ride of about 1 mile operates year-round both weekdays and weekends. It departs at the base of the ski area at an 8,200-foot elevation and travels to 9,157 feet with spectacular views of the valley below and mountains as far away as Globe and Phoenix. At the base you'll find a gift shop, mountainside patio where snacks and beverages are served, and a restaurant. For folks who'd rather glide down the slopes than ride, this is a complete ski area—the southernmost in the United States—with 22 ski runs at beginner, intermediate, and expert levels; equipment rental shop; and ski school (see the Parks and Recreation chapter).

If you're taking the skyride for pleasure, the ticket prices vary seasonally. The Mount Lemmon, or Catalina, Highway begins at Tanque Verde Road about 5 miles east of Sabino Canyon Road. For road conditions (weather or construction delays), call (520) 547-7510. Although there is a per-car user fee for Mount Lemmon, the fee does not apply if you're going to Ski Valley.

OLD PUEBLO TROLLEY **$**
Fourth Avenue and Eighth Street
(520) 792-1802
www.oldpueblotrolley.org

Don't miss a ride on Tucson's historic Old Pueblo Trolley. Introduced in 1906 (when trolleys replaced Tucson's mule-drawn streetcars), trolleys ferried passengers until 1930, when they were replaced by buses. Sixty years later (in 1990), thanks to the efforts of volunteers who restored cars and lines of track, trolley service started again. The wood-paneled interiors, velvet seats, and live engineer make for a great trip into the past on several antique cars from Japan (1953), Belgium (1930s), and Portugal. The trolley currently takes passengers on a 1-mile journey through some of the most historic and diverse areas of Tucson. It runs between Tyndall Avenue and Fourth Avenue and Eighth Street, and riders can catch it at either end and hop off along the way. At the end of the line on Eighth Street, there's a car barn where you might see other trolleys being restored. An extension that hooks the trolley up with the downtown area is scheduled to open mid-2009. The extension will run from Fourth Street, go west on Congress Street and south on Fifth Avenue, turn east on Broadway, and then head north again to reconnect at Fourth Avenue for the return trip. The trolley operates Friday evening from 6:00 to 10:00 p.m., Saturday from noon to midnight, and Sunday from noon to 6:00 p.m. Kids younger than 6 ride free, kids 6 to 12 and seniors pay 50 cents, and adults pay $1 for a one-way trip. All-day fares are only $2.50 for adults and $1.25 for kids 6 to 12. Sunday all fares are 25 cents one-way.

OLD TOWN ARTISANS
201 North Court Avenue
(520) 623-6024, (800) 782-8072
www.oldtownartisans.com

This unique marketplace in a historic 1850s adobe is one of the highlights of the downtown area. Tucked away in the El Presidio Historic District, it is now home to galleries and all sorts of shops offering pottery, glass, Southwestern and Native American jewelry, clothing, accessories, and much more. This is a great place to shop. You'll also find a lovely patio with tables, a restaurant, and a coffee bar (see also our Shopping chapter).

OLD TUCSON STUDIOS **$$$**
201 South Kinney Road
(520) 883-0100
www.oldtucson.com

To see a re-creation of a Western town in the 1880s, Hollywood style, head on out to Old Tucson Studios. This Tucson-area attraction started out in 1939 as an elaborate set for the movie *Arizona* and was eventually turned into a frontier town replica for the public, although it continues its former life as a set for movies and TV shows. (While there, you may even see some movie or TV show being filmed.) Old Tucson Studios suffered a serious fire in 1995 and some of the original structures and memorabilia were destroyed, but it has been rebuilt and expanded. All the buildings in this town are meticulously constructed and adorned to reflect the Old West, and you'll really feel taken back in time as you saunter by or enter saloons, dance halls, a jail, a general store or mercantile, corrals, stables, and wooden sidewalks. But there's lots more to do here than soak up the atmosphere and dream about the famous movie stars who may have stood on the same spot. Activities range from historical to modern day—gunfight shows, stagecoach rides, saloon revues, a gun museum, an antique Reno locomotive exhibit, gold panning, amusement rides, petting farms, magic shows, shops, and restaurants.

Admission prices vary, but it's free for kids age 4 and under. Discount coupons are easy to find at the Tucson Convention & Visitors Bureau, some grocery stores and banks, and other locations. Old Tucson Studios' hours vary seasonally; they are closed Thanksgiving and Christmas Day. Of the two ways to get here from Tucson—west on either Ajo Way or Speedway Boulevard to Kinney Road—the Ajo Way route is easiest to travel. The other route leads to Gates Pass Road through the Tucson Mountains, which offers breathtaking views and scenery but is a narrow cliff-hugging road often referred to as "white-knuckle pass." RVers must take Ajo Way to Kinney Road.

i A new exhibit at Pima Air and Space Museum, called The Spirit of Freedom Hangar, houses 10 rare aircraft and an Arizona Aviation Hall of Fame. Check out the Cold War spy plane called the Blackbird.

The entrance to the Pima Air and Space Museum captures the spirit of the place "where history takes flight."

PHOTO BY M. PAGANELLI VOTTO

PIMA AIR AND SPACE MUSEUM **$$**
6000 East Valencia Road
(520) 574-0462
www.pimaair.org

History and aircraft buffs, along with everyone else, will be enthralled by this indoor and outdoor museum displaying one of the largest collections in the world of vintage and current flying machines. Visitors will see everything from an exact full-scale replica of the Wright flyer, the first machine to fly, to the fastest, the SR-71 Blackbird, a sleek machine that flies at more than 2,000 miles per hour (or Mach 3-plus in flying lingo). You'll see just about every type of aircraft flown by the U.S. military branches over the years, plus many types of private and commercial aircraft, including an Air Force One plane used by Presidents Kennedy and Johnson. Visitors can go inside many of the larger aircraft and see navigation equipment, gunnery bays, and cargo holds. Throughout the museum, interpretive exhibits inform visitors about the aircraft and about aviation's past, present, and future. The museum has a space artifacts gallery containing early space items such as mock-ups of the X-15 and Mercury space capsule. The museum also houses the Challenger Space Center, which is open to the public daily for tours.

The museum is open daily except Thanksgiving and Christmas from 9:00 a.m to 5:00 p.m., but there's no admittance after 4:00 p.m. Kids 6 and under get in free; admission prices vary seasonally, with discounts for seniors and military personnel. Wheelchair accommodations and tours are available. If you plan to visit both Pima Air and Space Museum and the Titan Missile Museum near Green Valley, ask for a combination deal to save a couple of bucks. Pima Air and Space Museum is also the place from which to take a bus tour of Davis-Monthan Air Force Base and its aircraft boneyard, AMARC. (See the separate Davis-Monthan listing in this chapter.) Combination tickets for the air base tour and/or Pima Air and Space and Titan Missile Museums are available.

i **The *Tucson Attractions Passport* booklet gives you two-for-one admissions and other savings at lots of area attractions. You can buy your passport on the Web at www.visittucson.org or pick one up at the visitor center, Tucson Mall, or Park Place. Have your passport stamped and get two admissions for the price of one at participating attractions. You can save hundreds of dollars. And the passport's good for a year.**

REID PARK ZOO **$$**
1100 South Randolph Way
(520) 791-4022
www.tucsonzoo.org

Among the 400 exotic animals you'll see at the zoo is the strange-looking, long-nosed giant anteater, an animal for which Reid Park Zoo has the most successful captive breeding program in the world. But you'll see lots more at this terrific small-scale zoo: bears, llamas, tortoises, giraffes, zebras, elephants, and lions, plus several types of exotic and more common birds, reptiles, and fish. All the animals live in environments approximating their natural habitat. Maybe you'll even be lucky enough to be in town when one of the female residents has just given birth. (The zoo staff is great about announcing these arrivals and will gladly let you know.)

To help visitors learn about the animals, there are a few roving interpretive stations as well as docents leading impromptu tours. On weekends the zoo offers several special events. The zoo has a gift shop, wheelchair-accessible restrooms, snack bars, and free parking. All of this takes place in the middle of centrally located Reid Park, where the facilities and fun include walking and biking paths, picnic ramadas, swimming pools, tennis courts, a lake with pedal boats for rent, a formal rose garden, and a band shell.

The zoo is open 9:00 a.m. to 4:00 p.m. daily except Christmas. Try to go early, because the morning is the best time to see the animals being active. Admission prices are $6 for those age 15 and older, $4 for seniors, $2 for kids 2 to 14, and

Close-up

Public Art Treasures

Keep your eyes peeled as you travel throughout town, as there are numerous public art projects, big and small, sprinkled around, from bridges and sculptural bus stops to gorgeous murals and tile work. Some of the more notable include the amazing Diamondback Bridge conceived by Simon Donovan that spans Broadway west of Euclid Avenue. Just look up as you drive on Broadway Boulevard heading downtown—you can't miss it.

The enormous mural on the sound barrier wall dividing Barrio Anita from I-10 is another visual pleasure. Commissioned by the Arizona Department of Transportation and designed by artists Joshua Sarantitis and William Wilson, it features tile mosaics as well as painted images depicting neighborhood people and barrio life. There are two sections located on North Contzen Avenue just off Speedway Boulevard and I-10.

Smaller in scale, but equally interesting, is the mural on the side of an old adobe home at 555 Meyer Avenue between 16th and 17th Streets. Created by Franklin, it's a great example of "primitive art" a la Grandma Moses with its burro, street scene, and angels. And for gorgeous tile work, check out the lovely wall sprouting ceramic saguaro flowers on Tenth Avenue between 36th and 37th Streets.

A small portion of the spectacular 21-foot-high mural in Barrio Anita. PHOTO BY M. PAGANELLI VOTTO

A gentle giraffe at Reid Park Zoo; kids can feed them special biscuits on designated days. MARY PAGANELLI VOTTO

free for younger kids. All children younger than 14 must be accompanied by an adult.

SABINO CANYON RECREATION AREA **$$**
5900 Sabino Canyon Road
(520) 749-8700, extension 0
www.sabinocanyon.com

One of Tucson's most popular and spectacular natural attractions, Sabino Canyon is not to be missed. Located on the extreme eastern border of the Sonoran Desert, the area is visited by over one million people a year. You'll see incredible rock cliffs, running streams, and terrific views of the Catalina Mountains, along with many varieties of cactus and other indigenous plants. The best way to experience the canyon is to take one of the two 45-minute shuttle-bus narrated tours, offered 365 days a year, weather permitting. You can also hike, bike, picnic, or just walk through this pristine desert landscape. The park is open every day, 24 hours a day. Entry fee is $5 per vehicle, or you can buy an annual pass for $20 also good for Mount Lemmon and Madera Canyon. (See the Parks and Recreation chapter for additional details.)

TITAN MISSILE MUSEUM **$$**
I-19 and Duval Mine Road, Sahuarita
(520) 625-7736
www.titanmissilemuseum.org

This museum is a National Historic Landmark because it displays the only remaining Titan II missile that wasn't dismantled after the cold war ended and the Strategic Arms Limitation Treaty took effect. For more than 20 years, from the mid-1960s to the mid-1980s, this nuclear Titan II was on 24-hour alert ready for launching from its underground silo. This site near Green Valley was transformed into a museum and is operated by the Arizona Aerospace Foundation.

Except for the propellants and nuclear warhead, the missile and its huge launching arena are just as they were years ago. Some of the displays are above ground, while others are 35 feet underground, so walking shoes are required to descend the 55 steps. (People in wheelchairs or those who have difficulty walking can make arrangements to use the elevator.) Underground, you'll walk through the 200-foot-long cableway to the silo containing the Titan II missile and see the launch control center. Aboveground, you'll get another look at the missile through the glass covering where the massive 750-ton roll-back silo door is partially open. You'll also see the rocket engine that propelled the 330,000-pound missile from launch to an altitude of 47 miles in just two and a half minutes, plus the reentry vehicle, a favorite subject of photographers (picture taking is allowed).

Guided tours are offered daily beginning at 9:00 a.m., with the last tour at 4:00 p.m. They take one hour and start on the half hour. No reservations are taken, except for large groups. The museum is open daily (except Thanksgiving and Christmas) from 9:00 a.m. to 5:00 p.m. Kids 6 and under are free, ages 7 to 12 are $6, and adults are $9.50, with discounts for seniors and military personnel. Ask about a combination ticket if you also plan to visit Pima Air and Space Museum or take the tour of Davis-Monthan Air Force Base. To get here, take I-19 south to exit 69 west, then go past La Canada Drive to the museum's entrance.

i The Titan Missile Museum hosts a terrific annual spring fund-raiser. The event is held at night and, for a nominal donation, you get unlimited access to areas not usually shown during regular tours, including the crew rooms and Level 7 below the missile.

TOHONO CHUL PARK $$
7366 North Paseo del Norte
(520) 575-8468, (520) 742-6455
www.tohonochulpark.org

Step into this 49-acre oasis, and you'll forget that the sights and sounds of the bustling city are a mere stone's throw away. Tohono Chul, meaning "desert corner" in Tohono O'odham, envelops visitors with its solitude and beauty. It's a place to experience and learn about the flora and fauna of the rich Sonoran Desert in a pleasant and attractive environment.

Nature trails of 0.25 and 0.75 miles, shaded by lush paloverde trees, meander through gardens, pools, exhibits, and washes. Rabbits, lizards, and Gambel's quail scurry around, while hummingbirds and many other varieties of birdlife fly overhead in this "aviary without walls." Plant life native to the desert surrounds the trails, much of it labeled with their common and scientific names, so you'll actually be able to identify these strange-looking growing things. Several gardens on the grounds include the hummingbird garden, designed to attract these small hovering birds, and the ethnobotanical garden, showing crops grown by early Indian settlers and introduced by Spanish and Anglo arrivals.

The park's Exhibit House is a 1937 restored adobe building with art and cultural exhibits and a gift shop. Another building, a hacienda-style former residence, provides a lush plant-filled courtyard and patios for relaxing or a meal, snack, or afternoon tea replete with scones, jam, and cream in the Tea Room. There's also a gift shop. At the Greenhouse you can ask questions about desert plants and gardens and purchase native plants. The park conducts a variety of tours and holds special events like the Wildflower Festival in spring and the night-blooming cereus event in early summer. (See the Natural World chapter to read about this unusual flower and other desert flora you'll see at the park.)

Admission to this desert preserve is $7 for adults, $5 for seniors and military, $3 for students, $2 for children ages 5 to 12, and free for kids under 5. Free parking is available. The wheelchair-accessible grounds are open daily from 8:00 a.m. to 5:00 p.m. except major holidays. The gift shop hours vary. Admission is free on the first Tuesday of the month. You'll find Paseo del Norte at the first stoplight on Ina Road just west of Oracle Road.

TUCSON BOTANICAL GARDENS $$
2150 North Alvernon Way
(520) 326-9686
www.tucsonbotanical.org

One of Tucson's treasures, this small but exquisite in-town garden presents a complete primer on the amazing plants that thrive in southern Arizona. Its five and a half acres offer a shady and peaceful spot to view and learn about plants indigenous to the area plus some that normally would grow only in the tropics if not for the environment and care provided by the Tucson Botanical Gardens staff.

Walking paths and garden oases are surrounded by cacti of all types, native trees, wildflowers, flowering plants that attract birds, and even plants imported from tropical climates. Although the gardens are open year-round with plenty to see, there are specific times of the year that certain garden areas thrive. For example, the herb garden is prolific April through June, the wildflower garden blooms March through May, cactus plants show their colorful blooms April through August, and the Native American crops garden has its yield May through August. The folks at the botanical gardens will tell you what's in bloom if you call. They'll also tell you what special events are coming up, such as herb or plant sales held during the year. There's a gift shop with books and other items focusing on southern Arizona's flora and even a picnic area where visitors can bring their own refreshments and dine among the cypress, citrus trees, and roses.

Tucson Botanical Gardens is open from 8:30 a.m. to 4:30 p.m. except on New Year's Day, July 4, Thanksgiving, and Christmas. Admission is $7 for ages 12 and older; children 4 to 12 are $3, and kids 3 and under are free.

TUCSON MUSEUM OF ART AND HISTORIC BLOCK $$

140 North Main Street
(520) 624-2333
www.tucsonarts.com

The cornerstone of this historic arts district is the contemporary Tucson Museum of Art, home to 6,000 pieces of art in its permanent collection, a gift shop, and one of the loveliest courtyards in town, with sculpted benches, fountains, and a chic cafe. The rest of the block consists of four historic homes dating from the 1800s. Each one has a colorful history and contains fascinating period exhibits. Docent-led tours are available October through April (call for specific times); they are free with the price of museum admission. The museum is open 10:00 a.m. to 4:00 p.m. Tuesday through Saturday and noon to 4:00 p.m. on Sunday. Closed Monday and major holidays. Admission is $8 for adults; children under 12 are free. Senior and student admissions are discounted. Admission is free on the first Sunday of the month. (See the Arts and Culture chapter for additional information.)

UNIVERSITY OF ARIZONA MINERAL MUSEUM $$

Cherry Avenue and University Boulevard
(520) 621-4227
www.flandrau.org

In the basement of the Flandrau Science Center and Planetarium (described previously in this chapter) is the university's Mineral Museum. Rock hounds or other folks interested in gems and minerals will appreciate this small but excellent exhibit of more than 2,000 rock and gem samples, some of which are rare and most of which were excavated in Arizona. Call for admission prices and hours.

WHIPPLE OBSERVATORY TOUR $$

Mt. Hopkins Road, Amado
(520) 670-5707
http://cfa-www.harvard.edu/facilities/flwo/visit_center.html

It's customary to associate the Smithsonian Institution with our nation's capital, so most folks are surprised to find the Smithsonian linked with Arizona. But that renowned organization does have a facility south of Tucson—the Fred Lawrence Whipple Observatory on the top of Mount Hopkins in the Santa Rita Mountains. A number of telescopes and meteorological instruments are located on a half-mile ridge at 7,600 feet, while the mountain's summit at 8,550 feet houses the world's fourth-largest multiple-mirror telescope. The latter is a joint project of the Smithsonian and the University of Arizona.

At the base of the mountain stands the Whipple Observatory visitor center (open Monday through Friday), which also happens to be a lovely area with walking trails, desert flora, and picnic tables. From there it's 10 miles up the mountain to the observatory on a narrow switchback road. Although the road can be traversed, at its end drivers will discover a locked gate, so the only way to visit the observatory is by taking a tour, which the observatory conducts by bus. From mid-March through November, public tours are operated on Monday, Wednesday, and Friday starting at the more down-to-earth visitor center, which opens at 8:30 a.m. weekdays.

The tour begins at 9:00 a.m. with a video presentation, after which the bus travels up the mountain, returning at 3:00 p.m. Tour-takers should be aware of the elevation, which can pose a problem to people with certain health problems. Also, some uphill walking, stair climbing, and standing for 15 to 20 minutes are required during the tour. And if you're squeamish about narrow mountain roads with few guardrails, it's best to pass on the tour and learn about the observatory at the visitor center. Reservations are a must for the tour, and only 30 people can be accommodated. Children younger than age 6 are not permitted because of the tour's duration. And even if you have a reservation, it's best to call whenever weather conditions are poor, as the tour could be canceled. Bring a lunch along, because you'll only find a soft-drink machine and drinking water at the top. They do have picnic tables. And don't forget sunglasses, a hat, and possibly even a jacket—the summit is 15 to 20 degrees cooler than down below. The tour fee is $7 for adults and $2.50 for kids ages 6 to 12.

Finding the visitor center is a bit tricky, but you won't be disappointed, even if your plans don't call for a tour. From I-19 south take exit 56 (Canoa Road) to the Eastside frontage road; head south for 3 miles to Elephant Head Road, then turn right onto Mt. Hopkins Road and drive 7 miles to the visitor center.

KIDSTUFF

Kids thrive in Tucson, with its fresh air, sunny skies, beautiful parks, and wildlife galore. There aren't many places left where you can see coyotes, hawks, owls, quail, snakes, and javelinas all right in your own backyard. You'll find lots and lots of things to do here indoors and out. One-of-a-kind museums, stargazing, cowboy towns, kid-friendly art, music, theater, and many more unique hidden treasures are here for children of all ages.

YESTERDAY, TODAY, AND TOMORROW

The following attractions transport kids into the past or the future as well as show them the world around them today. They're mostly educational, but that will be our little secret. Your kids will be having too much fun to realize they're actually learning something.

ARIZONA HISTORICAL SOCIETY, MAIN MUSEUM

949 East Second Street
(520) 628-5774
www.arizonahistoricalsociety.org

Say "We're going to the historical society" to your kids, and you'll probably hear a loud moan. But say "Let's go see what an old Tucson fort was like," and the response should be an enthusiastic "Yeah!" The society, which is actually a museum, is fun for kids as well as adults. Youngsters can climb aboard a restored stagecoach; see a replica of El Presidio, a fort that was Tucson's first settlement; hunker down inside a traditional brush hut; view a Tohono O'odham Indian village; try on serapes; and lots more. One favorite is the mine display, complete with a walk-through underground mine tunnel, that shows how early settlers here drilled for gold and silver. It's history with a fun slant, and it's free (donations are appreciated, however).

The historical society is smack in the midst of the university area, so street parking can be tough. However, you can park free at the big garage at the northeast corner of Euclid Avenue and Second Street, about 1½ blocks from the society; just be sure to get your ticket validated by the receptionist before you leave the museum to head for your vehicle. Hours are 10:00 a.m. to 4:00 p.m. Monday through Saturday. (See the Attractions chapter for more adult-oriented features of the historical society.)

BIOSPHERE 2

Highway 77 at Mile Marker 96.5
(520) 838-6200
www.bio2.com

Kids love the surreal, futuristic structures of Biosphere 2, the world's largest glass-enclosed ecological laboratory. It used to be that researchers lived inside for years, so visitors could only tour the outside and peek in. Now visitors can actually go inside and see how the crews lived and how this miniature of our own biosphere, Earth, runs. The main tour starts with the "human habitat" where the scientists lived. From there you go through an airlock into the wilderness areas, including a steamy tropical savanna. A wooden trail travels along the 40-foot ocean cliff where you can look down into the million-gallon tropical ocean. A special kids' area teaches them about sound, light, and conservation. The on-site University of Arizona research program offers kid-friendly programming and hands-on activities. This is a better bet for older kids (over 6). Toddler types might find it frustrating, because beyond viewing the fascinating architecture, there isn't too much for younger kids to do and not all areas are accessible via stroller. High-energy kiddies can run around the extensive grounds (250 acres).

There's also a shop, snack bar, and hourly guided tours. Only the exterior grounds and not the guided tours of Biosphere 2 are accessible by stroller, wheelchair and walker.

Admission is fairly steep, but kids younger than 5 are admitted free. Discounts are available for AAA members, seniors, and college students, plus you can usually get discount coupons at lots of local places, including in the newspaper or from the Tucson Convention and Visitors Bureau. No pets or picnicking is permitted. Biosphere 2 is about 45 minutes north of downtown Tucson on Oracle Road. Open daily from 9:00 a.m. to 4:00 p.m.; closed Thanksgiving and Christmas Day. (See the Attractions chapter for more information.)

COLOSSAL CAVE MOUNTAIN PARK
16721 East Old Spanish Trail, Vail
(520) 647-7275
www.colossalcave.com

The dry cave at this extensive park about 30 minutes east of Tucson is a great family destination. Forty-five-minute guided tours take you deep into the cave, once home to ancient peoples and desperados. Strollers are not permitted, but kids 5 and older will enjoy the spooky shadows and stories. A park admission fee of $5 per car plus guided cave tour admission fees apply. (See the Attractions chapter for additional information, including fees and hours.)

There are no eating facilities here, so be sure to fill up or take your own snacks. If you're not into spelunking, the on-site museums have several kid-friendly exhibits. You can also pan for gold and gemstones and visit Henry and Big Nasty, two resident desert tortoises. There are daily trail rides available for an additional fee. The park also sponsors many family-friendly weekend events; check the newspaper or Web site for a schedule.

FLANDRAU SCIENCE CENTER AND PLANETARIUM
Cherry Avenue and University Boulevard
(520) 621-7827
www.gotuasciencecenter.org

This terrific science center on the University of Arizona campus is a real kid-pleaser. The center plans to relocate downtown in 2011 in a completely new setting, so exhibits in place here now will be prototypes as they test what works best for kids and grown-ups alike. It's a great opportunity to put in your two cents about what you and the kids would like to see in the new space.

The Mineral Museum housed downstairs holds case upon case of fascinating rocks of all kinds and sizes. Budding scientists will love the store, where they can take home science kits, posters, books, and learning toys. Or they can look for planets, galaxies, and star clusters in the observatory's 16-inch telescope, which is open year-round 7:00 to 10:00 p.m. on clear Wednesday through Saturday nights for free. Flandrau is open Thursday through Sunday with varying hours. Admission to Flandrau is $5, which includes a planetarium show; kids under 4 are free. Parking can be tough here in the middle of the university, especially during evening athletic events. On weekends and after 1:00 p.m. weekdays, there is free parking for Flandrau visitors along Hawthorne Street (north of the Science Center). Paid parking is available at Cherry Avenue Garage near McKale Center and Second Street Garage located on Second Street west of the Flandrau.

GADSDEN-PACIFIC DIVISION TOY TRAIN OPERATING MUSEUM
3975 North Miller Avenue
(520) 888-2222
http://hometown.aol.com/ienglish/index.htm

Their hours are irregular, but if your child loves toy trains, this is THE place to go. This huge warehouse space is home to five tabletops of operating miniature train layouts and displays. From the intersection of North Romero and West Roger Roads, go north to Price Street and turn left (west). Go 2 blocks to Miller Avenue. Call ahead for hours of operation; admission is free, but donations are welcome.

Close-up

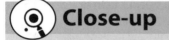

Docent Program for Kids

Do your kids love animals? Are they interested in the desert world that surrounds them? If so, they might be the perfect candidates for the Junior Docent program at the fabulous Arizona-Sonora Desert Museum (see this chapter's listing and the Attractions chapter for information on the museum). This unique program offers kids ages 12 to 16 a chance to work behind the scenes and with visitors at this world-famous museum. Junior Docents receive training on the plants, animals, and geology of the Sonoran Desert region and participate in field trips and live animal encounters. Applications are accepted year-round for 12 positions. You can download the application and recommendation forms at www.desertmuseum.org or call (520) 883-3083.

A rare bighorn sheep at Arizona-Sonora Desert Museum. COURTESY OF METROPOLITAN TUCSON CONVENTION & VISITOR'S BUREAU, GILL KENNY

INTERNATIONAL WILDLIFE MUSEUM
4800 West Gates Pass Road
(520) 617-1439
www.thewildlifemuseum.org

Housed in a very cool-looking fort, the International Wildlife Museum features over 400 kinds of mammals, insects, and birds from around the world. There's just one thing—they're all stuffed! But kids seem to love this friendly, easily accessible museum nonetheless. Especially because they can touch just about everything here (a real plus), including hairy buffalo, a life-size lion, bear, and crocodile. You can also watch some terrific nature films in the comfortable 98-seat theater. There's also a gift shop and restaurant on the premises. The museum is open every day except Thanksgiving and Christmas, Monday through Friday 9:00 a.m. to 5:00 p.m., Saturday and Sunday

9:00 a.m. to 6:00 p.m. Admission is $7 for adults, $5.50 for seniors, $2.50 for kids 4 to 12; children under 4 are free.

OLD PUEBLO TROLLEY
Fourth Avenue and Eighth Street
(520) 792-1802
www.oldpueblotrolley.org

The historic Old Pueblo Trolley is a great ride for everyone, not just kids. The restored antique electric trolleys rumble along the tracks on their route from the main gate at the University of Arizona along University Boulevard to Eighth Street with lots of stops along the way (extensions to the line are anticipated). The velvet seats and wood-paneled interior complete with uniformed conductor transport you back to an age gone by. Kids love to stomp on the bell (ask the conductor). The 1-mile ride takes about 25 minutes and is a great way to explore this unique downtown area, home to funky shops, eclectic restaurants, cafes, and the UA crowd. You can also visit the trolley car barn and museum at the end of the line at Eighth Street. On your way off take a minute to check out the lovely wrought-iron trolley stops.

One-way fares are $1 for adults, 50 cents for kids 6 to 12 and seniors, and free for kids younger than 6. But the best deal is on Sunday, when a ride is only a quarter. Or you can get all-day fares for a mere $2.50 (adult) and $1.25 (child) and stop, shop, and sightsee in this fascinating area. It operates Friday evenings from 6:00 to 10:00 p.m., Saturday from noon to midnight, and Sunday from noon to 6:00 p.m.

OLD TUCSON STUDIOS
201 South Kinney Road
(520) 883-0100
www.oldtucson.com

Little broncobusters (and big ones, too) will be thrilled by the sights and sounds at this slightly hokey replica of an old frontier town. Kids can see spectacular stunts, musical revues, and gunfights (all pretend, of course), hear old Southwestern lore, and pan for gold. They also can ride a miniature train or an antique car (these have a varied schedule, so call ahead).

Old Tucson Studios started out in 1939 as a movie set and later was turned into a theme attraction. It's been the site for hundreds of Western movies and TV shows. There are shops, rides, restaurants, and saloons along with all the trappings of the Old West. It opens at 10:00 a.m. daily; closing hours vary seasonally. Gate admission is $16.95 for ages 12 and older, $10.45 for ages 4 to 11, and free under that. Discount coupons are easy to find around town at the visitors bureau and some banks and grocery stores. (See the Attractions chapter for more information.)

PIMA AIR AND SPACE MUSEUM
6000 East Valencia Road
(520) 574-0462
www.pimaair.org

What kid isn't enraptured by flying machines? Within Pima Air and Space Museum's 100,000-square-foot building and 150 acres of surrounding land, there are more than 250 examples of nearly every type of flying machine ever invented. A 42,000-square-foot hangar is home to the Aviation Hall of Fame and rare aircraft. There's a perfect replica of the very first airplane, the Wright flyer; an SR-71 Blackbird that flies at Mach 3-plus and set the speed record; presidential airplanes; World War II bombers; helicopters; and ultralights. (The museum is fortunate to be across the street from the airplane graveyard at Davis-Monthan Air Force Base, so it can get unusual planes that are retired there.)

There are numerous hands-on exhibits for kids, including a cockpit they can climb into and work the flight controls and a control tower where they can turn on runway lights and listen to radio transmissions. The museum's Challenger Learning Center specializes in educational programs for children. Here kids can check out a training version of an Apollo space capsule, see a real moon rock, and learn all about the Phoenix Mars mission. For an extra fee, kids will love the Flight Simulator ride, located in Hangar 1 North, (you must be 38 inches tall to ride).

Hours are 9:00 a.m. to 5:00 p.m. daily, except Thanksgiving and Christmas (last admission at 4:00 p.m.) Admission prices vary seasonally, but it's free for children 6 and under. A grill in Hangar

Kids of all ages love the Pima Air and Space Museum—you can even have your birthday party here! PHOTO BY M. PAGANELLI VOTTO

1 serves up kid-friendly fare. (See the Attractions chapter for more information.)

T-REX MUSEUM
3835 North Oracle Road
(520) 888-0746
www.trexmuseum.org

Fossils, colorful pictures, models, and 300 live insects from around the world are bound to fascinate kids of any age. Touching is encouraged; from six kinds of dinosaur poop to a live python. Admission is $5 and includes a fossil dig and movie theater admission. Open Monday through Saturday 10:00 a.m. to 5:00 p.m. and Sunday noon to 5:00 p.m. The cool gift shop offers the largest selection of dinosaur-related toys, games, puzzles, books, and more in the state.

TUCSON CHILDREN'S MUSEUM
200 South Sixth Avenue
(520) 792-9985
www.tucsonchildrensmuseum.org

Housed in the historic Carnegie Library in downtown Tucson, this museum is a real hit with kids, and although many of the exhibits are a bit weary and well worn, the kids don't seem to mind. You'll find a wide variety of hands-on exhibits, a fire engine, police motorcycle, a music room, and an Ocean Discovery Center with an underwater sea video. Kid-size computer workstations offer simple interactive software programs, and dinosaurs roam (not really) in the robotic animation exhibit. There's also a giant bubble room where kids can surround themselves with a 5-foot cylindrical bubble. Special areas include an art studio, music performance area, and the hands-on Electri-City Gallery, which shows how electricity works.

Special events take place throughout the year, and there are always fascinating kid-friendly activities happening, like making prints from a fresh apple, creating stationery with twigs and leaves, fashioning Mexican paper flowers, and making slimy bugs—all included in the price of admission.

Admission is $5 for ages 2 to 18, $7 for adults, and $5 for seniors. Hours are 10:00 a.m. to 5:00 p.m. Tuesday through Saturday and noon to 5:00 p.m. Sunday. Kids younger than 16 must be accompanied by an adult.

CREATURES, CRITTERS, AND CACTI

Kids are enthralled with things that crawl, growl, bite, and sting, so here are some great places where they can see wildlife without Mom or Dad worrying about having to administer first aid.

ARIZONA-SONORA DESERT MUSEUM

2021 North Kinney Road
(520) 883-2702
www.desertmuseum.org

If there's only one place you have time to visit, this probably should be it. Don't be fooled by the name "museum"—actually it's a unique combination of zoo and natural museum that's truly world-class.

Kids will be enthralled by just about everything they see—reptiles, desert insects such as scorpions and tarantulas, and wild cats such as bobcats. The beaver and otter pond is fun to watch from above but even more exciting from below, where observers can see all the underwater antics of these furry swimmers. There's also prairie dog town, bighorn sheep climbing around their mountain caves, and huge walk-in aviaries, including one devoted exclusively to hummingbirds. "Life on the Rocks—Leapin' Lizards" is a terrific kid-friendly exhibit highlighting some of the smaller species found in rocky environments. Not all the animals here are real, see if you can tell! Volunteer docents conduct hands-on shows throughout the museum daily. Kids will like the cafeteria-style restaurant and especially the ice-cream shop located along the trail. The gift shop has lots of books and learning tools on the desert life presented at the museum.

The museum is primarily a walking experience, with 2 miles of paths on 21 acres. Strollers are available for free. It's hot here in summer, so be prepared or plan your visit for early in the day or the evening or go during Summer Saturday Nights (June through August), when special activities are scheduled. It's open every day, and admission prices vary seasonally; kids 5 and under are free. (See the Attractions chapter for more information about this museum.)

CHILDREN'S DISCOVERY GARDEN AT THE TUCSON BOTANICAL GARDENS

2150 North Alvernon Way
(520) 326-9686
www.tucsonbotanical.org

A great way to introduce kids to nature, this tiny garden created just for them is a lovely oasis in the middle of the larger botanical garden. A giant bee and butterfly hover above touchable and edible plants, a worm farm, and a beautiful water wall made of exquisite ceramic tiles that you'll have trouble dragging your kids (and yourself) away from.

Butterfly Magic is another big draw for kids. For an extra admissions fee, you can walk through a greenhouse full of fluttering live tropical butterflies and view their stages of development from pupa on in a special exhibit, only on display October through May. (See the Attractions chapter for details on the Tucson Botanical Gardens.)

PICTURE ROCKS MINIATURE HORSE RANCH

6611 North Taylor Lane
(520) 682-8009

Run by fourth-generation Arizonans Connie and Al Kazal, this working ranch is home to over 55 miniature horses and colts, 45 tiny Nigerian goats, 300 multicolored bantam chickens, and 200 loose ringneck doves and turtledoves. Kids will adore this open, friendly (educational even!) place. You can feed the chickens (bring lots of loaves of cheap wheat sandwich bread) and pet the horses and goats. Bring your camera and lots and lots of film (or memory cards) for some great photo ops!

There's a $5 per person entry fee (all monies go to feed and care for the animals). Special rates are available for groups and schools. Open daily by appointment. Reservations are necessary, so do call ahead. There is no minimum group size, and the Kazals are happy to arrange a tour or birthday party for anywhere from 1 to 65 people.

Keep in mind that morning is best (between 8:00 a.m. and noon), as that's when the animals will likely be awake and alert. Wheelchair accessible and walker friendly, there's a shaded picnic area and wheelchair-accessible restrooms but no restaurant facilities. Take Ina Road West and pass under Interstate 10, go left on Wade to Picture Rocks to Taylor Lane (approximately 10 miles), then turn left on Taylor Lane.

REID PARK ZOO
1100 South Randolph Way
(520) 791-4022
www.tucsonzoo.org
Though small, this well-designed zoo offers everything from long-nosed giant anteaters to lions, tigers, and rhinos—it's the perfect size for kids. There are also jaguars, pygmy hippos, elephants, zebras, giraffes, and all manner of birds in aviaries. The South American section features bears, llamas, tapirs, and the carnivorous piranha, plus a lush aviary. Kids love baby animals, so be sure to ask what's been born recently. All of the 500 or so animals here live in modern, naturalistic settings, but the snack bar and gift shop are reserved for their human guests. The zoo sits in the middle of Reid Park, so it's a great place to have a picnic, ride a bike, or play on the playground. There are lots of special activities for kids here—you can even feed a giraffe on designated days.

The zoo is open daily from 9:00 a.m. to 4:00 p.m.; closed on Christmas. If you go in the summer, go early in the day when animals are active. Parking is free, which also happens to be the admission price for children younger than 2. The older crowd has to pay a modest fee—$2 for kids up to 14, $6 for adults, and $4 for seniors. The family membership for two adults and their children is a great deal at $48. All children younger than 14 must be accompanied by an adult. Strollers and double strollers can be rented for the day. (See the Attractions chapter for more information.)

GET A LITTLE CULTURE

Introducing kids to a little culture may not be tops on their list of things to do, but it works better if the attraction is specifically geared to youngsters. So in this section we present culture your kids might actually enjoy, plus places where the little hams you have at home can take a stab at real acting.

ARTS FOR ALL/THIRD STREET KIDS
2520 North Oracle Road
(520) 622-4100
www.artsforallinc.org
Although it focuses on kids with disabilities, this nonprofit performing arts group welcomes all children. Funded by grants and various charities, it offers youngsters the chance to learn and perform dance, music, drama, opera, and improvisations. In addition to classes, usually held after school during the school year or via a summer camp, the organization has two performing components. One is the ensemble company that performs at various private functions and has traveled to Australia, performed at the White House, and appeared in a movie filmed in Tucson. The other component is open to kids who audition for Third Street Kids' public performances, which are sometimes original plays and other times popular ones: opera, drama, comedy, or musical. Watch the newspapers for information on where and when a Third Street Kids play is appearing, or call the organization. It provides a great opportunity for kids to learn skills in the arts and to perform.

i The Reid Park Zoo offers two very popular annual events for kids (not to mention tons of great special events throughout the year). Put Howl-O-Ween on your calendar in October with trick-or-treating, decorations, and haunted caves. Zoo Lights is a must for December with light displays, snow, live entertainment, and refreshments to happily ring in the holiday season. Call (520) 837-8200 or check the Web site at www.tucsonzoo.org for details.

TUCSON SYMPHONY ORCHESTRA
Tucson Symphony Center
2175 North Sixth Avenue
(520) 882-8585 (box office)
www.tucsonsymphony.org

The Tucson Symphony Orchestra offers six informal, interactive "Just for Kids" concerts designed to introduce quality classical music to children of all ages. Each concert highlights an ensemble of the orchestra in a presentation combining humor, storytelling, demonstrations, and audience participation. They're held at the Tucson Symphony Center on the first Saturday of the month from October through March. Call for the exact dates and times. There is a suggested donation of $2.

MUNCHKINS IN MOTION

You certainly don't need us to tell you that kids love to move. From roller-skating to tumbling, Tucson's got them covered.

CELEBRATE
7830 East Wrightstown Road
(520) 751-9898
www.celebrateintucson.com

Kids bouncing off the walls? Head to this super indoor playground, open for ages 2 to 12. You'll find inflatables of all shapes and sizes here, including an obstacle course, slide, and basketball game. There is a snack bar on the premises; no food or drink can be brought in. Open play is Monday through Friday, 10:00 a.m. to 6:00 p.m. Call for Saturday and Sunday hours and availability—they can be booked with private birthday parties. Admission is $10 per child. Socks are required.

J.W. TUMBLES
6546 East Tanque Verde Road
(520) 722-8987

7942 North Oracle Road
(520) 544-8987
www.aztumbles.com

Gymnastics, tumbling, and sports skills are some of kids' favorite things, and they're all available at J.W. Tumbles. This isn't a free-for-all place, but a structured way for kids between 4 months and 9 years old to develop skills, build confidence, and learn teamwork while having fun (and getting rid of some excess energy). Classes are structured by age and are kept to fewer than 12 kids. Infants as young as 6 months can sign up for the "Squeakers" movement class (parents, of course, must accompany them). You can even throw a birthday party here.

Close-up

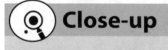

Skyride at Mount Lemmon's Ski Valley

For a great day trip with the kids, take a drive to Mount Lemmon's Ski Valley and ride the chairlift to the top. Just an hour from Tucson, the drive is gorgeous, the lift exhilarating, and the scenery beautiful. The kids will love every minute! Once at the top you can hike a series of trails (in summer months), and from May to October you'll see millions of ladybugs clustered all over trees, flowers, twigs—just about everywhere. The bright red, black-spotted insects hibernate here every year, and it's an incredible sight. You can bring your own picnic feast to eat atop the mountain, or stop in the snack bar or the slightly more formal (there are real tables) Iron Door Restaurant with patio dining and a kid-friendly menu that won't break the bank. (Try the famous chili and homemade corn bread with warm honey.) The Skyride is open year-round. Take Catalina Highway off Tanque Verde Road in Tucson. Drive 4.2 miles to the forest boundary, and continue 26 miles to the Ski Valley turnoff. Turn right and drive 1 mile to the ski area. Call (520) 576-1400 for recorded information.

RANDOLPH SKATEPARK
200 South Alvernon Way
(520) 791-4560

Twisting and high-flying bodies along with scrapes and bangs of skateboards are what you'll see and hear at this facility right behind the Tucson Parks and Recreation Department's Randolph Center. Kids—mostly teens—now have a 16,000-square-foot asphalt-paved area to call their own and strut their skateboarding skills. It includes two Bauer boxes, which for the uninitiated are platforms with ramps leading up to them and a rail along the back; one flat-top pyramid; two 6-foot quarter pipes (tall ramps used for launching maneuvers); and two grind rails. Skateboarding isn't permitted in other city areas the kids seem to gravitate to, such as downtown sidewalks and the Tucson Convention Center pavement, so this is a safe and legal alternative. In-line skating is also popular here. It's free and open daily (except holidays). During the school year hours are 2:00 p.m. to dark Monday through Friday, 8:00 a.m. to 6:00 p.m. Saturday, and noon to 6:00 p.m. Sunday.

SKATE COUNTRY
7980 East 22nd Street
(520) 298-4409
www.skatecountry.com

Kids who like loud music and light shows accompanying their roller-skating will love Skate Country. But it's not just for kids—entire families can have a blast here. For starters, quad skate rentals are one price for any age: $2; if you use in-line skates, bring your own. The rink, which has good supervision, is open daily year-round, but skating hours and admission prices vary. Monday through Thursday at designated times is called Cheap Skates because it's only $4. But if the whole clan is going, Sunday Family Night may be the best deal—a family of up to six pays only $12 to skate from 6:00 to 9:00 p.m. Saturday mornings are reserved for "tiny tots," when kids younger than 12 skate from 10:00 a.m. to noon for $4. There's also an adult skate Thursday night from 8:00 to 10:00 p.m. for anyone age 18 or older for $5. A video arcade and snack bar are available.

Tug on your skates and zoom around the smooth wood floor of Skate Country to your favorite music. PHOTO BY M. PAGANELLI VOTTO

JUST ADD WATER

Water parks are great finds in Tucson's desert and in summer's heat, when the whole family needs to find a cool place.

BREAKERS WATER PARK
8555 West Tangerine Road
(520) 682-2530
www.breakerswaterpark.com

Kids can actually catch a wave in Tucson, but only at Breakers Water Park, which boasts one of the largest wave pools in the world. Unlike almost everything else in Tucson, however, water parks are summer season attractions, so Breakers is only open late May through Labor Day. But that's precisely the time a splash in the cool water is most welcome. The 20-acre park in the far northwest also has five waterslides and a toddler pool, so it's fun for kids of all ages. Don't forget the waterproof sunscreen.

It's open summer Tuesday through Sunday from 10:00 a.m. to 6:00 p.m. Admission prices vary; there is a season pass, and kids under age 3 are free. Admission is reduced after 3:00 p.m. No outside food or beverages can be brought into the park.

Dive-in Movies

During the summer months, luxe resort Loews Ventana Canyon shows free outdoor movies at their spectacular pool. Open to anyone (you don't have to be a hotel guest) the family-friendly movies are shown on an outdoor screen at the pool Saturday night at dusk. Grab a tube, float on the warm water, and enjoy a great night out. Grown-ups can order a drink or dinner from the poolside grill and enjoy the show, too. Call (520) 529-7936 for the schedule.

JUST PLAIN FUN

These are our picks for places kids will love while they get to pretend to be racecar drivers, baseball champs, golf pros, or even fairy-tale characters.

FUNTASTICKS
221 East Wetmore Road
(520) 888-4653
www.funtasticks.com

If your kids are way too full of energy, give them a couple of hours here and you might tire them out, at least momentarily. The stuff to keep kids entertained and exercised runs the gamut. In addition to Tucson's largest kiddie arcade, there are two 18-hole miniature golf courses, bumper boats, single- and double-seat go-karts, rookie go-karts, laser tag, batting cages, and a video arcade. These attractions usually cater to older kids and teens, but Funtasticks has lots of stuff geared to the littler ones—baby bumper boats, kiddie cars, and a small roller coaster, to name a few.

Funtasticks is open daily, but hours vary for activities. Call ahead for times. The rates for each activity also vary.

Funtasticks is located across the street from Tucson Mall and is surrounded by shopping and places to eat. It's also less than a half block from a Sun Tran bus transit center that is a major transfer point with an information booth, covered waiting area, and restrooms.

GOLF 'N STUFF
6503 East Tanque Verde Road
(520) 296-2366
www.golfnstuff.com

This is a lot like Funtasticks (see above) but on the far east side. In Little Indy, kids can maneuver their own miniature racecars along a twisting track. Or they can bump around in bumper cars or bumper boats, bat a thousand in the batting cages, aim for a hole in one on the miniature golf courses, or test their skills in the huge video arcade. Older kids will love the rock climbing and laser tag. Some of the attractions have minimum age requirements, so you might want to call ahead instead of seeing the look of disappointment on little faces once you're there. It opens daily at 10:00 a.m. and closes at 10:00 p.m. Sunday through Thursday and 1:00 a.m. Friday and Saturday. Rides open at various times seasonally. Prices are per activity.

VALLEY OF THE MOON
2544 East Allen Road
(520) 323-1331
It's wild, wacky, and weird—and kids love it. The spirit of childhood was embodied by one man in this little hidden wonder. Long ago he created rock cliffs, caves, pools, and miniature gardens among the desert flora on his piece of land and called it Valley of the Moon. Then he added fantasy fairy tours and Bunnyland Theater, with trained rabbits. Playing the mysterious mountain gnome, he gave tours, told stories, and performed magic shows that captivated his young audiences. All of this happiness he gave away for free. Now operated as a nonprofit organization, the Valley of the Moon continues the tradition of entertainment with a variety of special events. Hours vary, and donations are welcome. Call to find out when activities and events are scheduled. Valley of the Moon also books parties.

PICK A PARK

Parks aren't just for playing Frisbee or flying kites. Tucson has dozens of parks with tons of fun things for kids—and parents—to do. Many of the parks have swimming pools, so put on those swimsuits and jump in; some of them are open year-round, but most are especially inviting in the heat of summer. Swing, jump, climb, and slide on the jungle gym equipment. Hit tennis balls, toss footballs, or play softball. Have a family picnic under a ramada. It's all free, except for a nominal charge to swim—or perhaps use the courts. (For a complete list of parks and what they offer, see the Parks and Recreation chapter.)

BRANDI FENTON MEMORIAL PARK
3482 E. River Road
(520) 877-6000
www.pima.gov/nrpr/places/brandi/index.htm
Great for a family outing, this 56.7-acre park is located north of the Rillito River at East River Road and North Alvernon Way and offers a multitude of activities for kids of all ages. Everyone loves the brightly colored splash park, a terrific way to cool off on hot Tucson days. The splash park is open April 22 to October 31 from 7:00 a.m. to 7:00 p.m. Two covered playgrounds offer slides, rock climbing walls, and bouncy, rubbery pavement. Three soccer fields, covered basketball courts, and an equestrian arena are perfect for sports fans of all ages.

Dogs are welcome here, too, at the off-leash dog runs at the east entry to the park. You'll also find walking paths, a fitness course, and a memorial garden at the visitor center. Named for 13-year-old Brandi Fenton, who was killed in a fluke car accident, this park is a wonderful memorial to her young life. The park is open from 7:00 a.m. to 10:00 p.m.

THE SPORTING LIFE

There's plenty of opportunity for kids to both watch a sport and be a sport around Tucson.

If your little baseball or softball player is jumping at the chance to see a real pro baseball team, several of them do their spring training right here in Tucson, so it's a great opportunity for kids and adults to get a preview of the year's up-and-coming players. The spring training season takes place in February and March, but tickets can be tough to get, so plan ahead. (See the Spectator Sports chapter for details on spring training baseball.)

The University of Arizona has teams in men's basketball, women's softball, baseball, football, and hockey, so there's likely to be some sort of college game going on any time of the year. See the Spectator Sports chapter for all the details, call the university (520-621-2287), or check the Web site at www.arizonaathletics.com to see who's playing when.

Kids also love watching a rodeo, and Tucson has one of the best in the West—La Fiesta de los Vaqueros, held the last weekend in February. It's a several-day event complete with a major parade that kids will love, too. (See the Festivals and Events chapter for more information about the rodeo.)

For kids who want to get in on the action, Tucson parks offer junior golf clinics in May and June; then kids have unlimited free golf at city courses after completing the clinic. Call the city's Parks and Recreation Department (520-791-4653) or see the Golf chapter for more details. Randolph Park has junior tennis on Saturday for kids ages 5 to 17 that includes instruction and practice time on the courts. You must register in person, but you can get information from the Parks and Recreation number above. And several Tucson parks have a Saturday-night teen basketball league, also called Late Night Hoops, for 13- to 19-year-olds (520-791-4870).

Pima County Parks and Recreation (520-877-6000) offers lots of sports and classes for kids—swimming, BMX bicycle racing, gymnastics, Tae Kwon Do, track, golf, and soccer, plus TOTS recreation for the young ones. They're held at various times of the year and at locations around the county. Check the program guide and class catalog available at rec centers around town for details.

ENTERTAINING EATS

Finding good food for kids is always a challenge. Tucson has its share of family-style restaurants, but many upscale restaurants are offering healthy kid-friendly cuisine as well. Here is just a sampling of the kid-centric choices around town.

CHUCK E CHEESE'S
6130 East Speedway Boulevard
(520) 745-8800
www.chuckecheese.com

The pizza, burger, and salad menu isn't really the main draw here; it's the fun and games. It's a madhouse with kids everywhere, and lots of noise. Young ones love crawling through the tubes and watching Chuck E Cheese in the mechanical stage show. Older ones gravitate toward the Skeetball or video games. Kids can win prizes, while parents can get package deals covering food and tokens (or "bags of gold" as they're known here). Chuck E Cheese's is open daily during afternoon and evening hours.

LITTLE ANTHONY'S DINER (MAIN LOCATION)
7010 East Broadway Boulevard
(520) 296-0456
www.grandmatonyspizza.com

We guarantee moms and dads will like this place as much as, if not more than, the kids do. It'll take you back decades to the real diners that are almost extinct now, complete with oldies on the jukebox and black-and-white-checkered floors. It's got a great atmosphere, with happy servers who sing and dance and give a great rendition of "Happy Birthday" to those celebrating. At any moment someone will spring up from a booth and swing to the oldies on the dance floor. There's a video room with pinball machines, and outside you'll usually find at least one beautifully preserved auto from the '50s plus a few rides for the kids. The food choices are many and reminiscent of yesteryear's diners—from burgers, salads, and pizzas to old-time blue-plate specials such as turkey, meat loaf, and fried chicken. The kids' menu has burgers, peanut butter and jelly sandwiches, corn dogs (on a stick), and mac n' cheese. Little Anthony's is open Tuesday through Thursday from 11:00 a.m. to 10:00 p.m., Friday 11:00 a.m. to 11:00 p.m., Saturday from 10:30 a.m. to 11:00 p.m., and 11:00 a.m. to 9:00 p.m. Monday and Sunday. This busy and popular spot is behind the Gaslight Theatre.

MIMI'S CAFE
4420 Oracle Road
(520) 690-9544

120 South Wilmot Road
(520) 747-7273
www.mimiscafe.com

Finally, a restaurant that offers more than chicken fingers for kids! This family-friendly place has lots to choose from, even for picky eaters (their kid-size burgers are served plain—no pesky lettuce or tomato). The children's menu even offers a turkey dinner and soup and salad. Open daily for breakfast, lunch, and dinner from 7:00 a.m. to 11:00 p.m.

OREGANO'S PIZZA BISTRO
4900 East Speedway Boulevard
(520) 3278955
www.oreganos.com

A Chicago-based chain, Oregano's offers a blob of raw pizza dough to every table with kids, which keeps them amused and happy throughout the meal. And the food is pretty good, too! You'll find lots of pizza, giant salads, onion rings and fries, toasted ravioli, garlic bread, and soup along with kid-friendly pizza slices and bowls of pasta. You'll have to drag them away!

TRAIL DUST TOWN
6541 East Tanque Verde Road
(520) 296-4551
www.traildusttown.com

This isn't just one restaurant but several places to chow down and shop while the kids have fun. It's a lovely little plaza of shops and restaurants in authentic Old West replica buildings surrounding a trellised courtyard. It's pleasant to just stroll around, but the kids are more likely to want to ride the narrow-gauge railroad and do the mine tunnel tour, go panning for gold, see the gunfight shows, or ride the antique restored carousel. There's an ice-cream and candy shop, a general store with all kinds of old-fashioned trinkets and goodies, a cowboy steak restaurant (Pinnacle Peak), and another restaurant with pleasant outdoor seating (Dakota Cafe). As the name Trail Dust Town implies, the theme is Western, but there's no dust here—just pretty walkways, real shade trees, and benches for watching the goings-on or the kids. Get the details on the eating establishments in the Restaurants chapter, though the kids will probably be just as happy with the ice-cream and candy shops.

TOYS AND OTHER NECESSITIES

ALDRICH BABY NEWS
5665 East Speedway Boulevard
(520) 795-2400
www.aldrichbabynews.com

This is not a magazine or a publishing company, but rather a huge retail store specializing in baby products and some children's furniture. You'll find just about everything here from toys to furniture, clothes, books, cards, strollers, and car seats—all top-of-the-line manufacturers and prices and all in one place. If you can't find it here, they'll happily order it for you; they'll deliver it, too (for an extra charge).

ANGEL THREADS
La Encantada Mall,
2905 East Skyline Drive
(520) 299-3221

This lovely shop offers clothing, shoes, and accessories for young girls and boys from infant to girls 8 and boys 4, in both casual and dressy styles. You'll also find stuffed animals and a selection of diaper bags.

BABY'S AWAY
no address
(520) 615-9754
www.babysaway.com

This business is more for moms and dads than babies, because it rents all kinds of things parents might find a need for, especially when vacationing. If you're looking for a stroller, high chair, playpen, crib, car seat, or even a tub of toys while you and baby are away from home, here's where to call. There's no retail shop, but Baby's Away delivers just about anything to help take care of baby. Strollers, for example, rent for $5 a day, while a full-size crib, including linens, is $9. If you're traveling with a baby, keep this number handy.

BUILD-A-BEAR WORKSHOP
Tucson Mall
4500 North Oracle Road, #135
(520) 888-9218

Everyone loves teddy bears, and what's better than making your very own! Build-a-Bear Workshop lets kids big and small pick out their very favorite stuffed animal friends, stuff it, stitch it up, and select its special outfits. It's a favorite spot for birthday parties. Open Monday to Saturday 10:00 a.m. to 9:00 p.m. and Sunday 11:00 a.m. to 6:00 p.m.

CARTER'S FOR KIDS
Foothills Mall,
Ina Road and La Cholla
Boulevard
(520) 742-7501
www.carters.com
This is an outlet store for all the famous Carter's kids' clothes that have been outfitting youngsters for generations.

THE GYMBOREE STORE
Tucson Mall, 4500 North Oracle Road
(520) 293-2119

La Encantada Mall, 2905 East Skyline Drive
(520) 615-1183
www.gymboree.com
This is a private-label clothing store for kids from birth to age 7. It sells shoes and accessories. The clothing is mostly casual, mostly cotton, and always bright and colorful.

i **Looking for things to do in town with your kids? The Tucson edition of *Bear Essential News for Kids* has tons of listings: best places for birthday parties, guide to summer camps, and coupons for just about every kid-friendly place here. This free newspaper is available around town at convenience stores, fast-food restaurants, and kiosks and online at www.bearessentialnews.com.**

KID'S CENTER
1725 North Swan Road
(520) 322-5437
www.e-kidscenter.com
Tired of giant toy stores dizzyingly full of junky stuff? Head for this terrific shop full of educational, interesting toys and tons of wonderful books and puzzles.

LIL' TRADERS
6216 East Speedway Boulevard
(520) 881-8438
www.liltraders.com
A children's resale shop, this is patterned after the successful Buffalo Exchange for adults. The kids' version is a great place for quality used clothing plus toys, athletic equipment, and some furniture. Lil' Traders buys, sells, and trades.

MAX & MAUDE'S
7111 North Oracle Road
(520) 297-2079
www.maxandmaudes.com
Nestled in the Casas Adobes Plaza, this upscale shop offers trendy, brand-name designer clothing for children, newborn to age 12. You'll also find a great selection of infant accessories and blankets, diaper bags of the moment, and a limited selection of classic toys and books.

MILDRED AND DILDRED
La Encantada Shopping Center
2905 East Skyline Drive
(520) 615-6266
www.mildredanddildred.com
Don't worry about touching in this bright, colorful toy store—it's encouraged! Chock-full of high-end specialty toys for the up-to-10 set, this place focuses on toys that encourage children to use their imagination. (Remember that?) You'll find kid-friendly play tables and a fanciful sky mural on the ceiling along with dress-up clothes, collectible dolls, old-fashioned board games, stuffed animals, books, and more at this popular kid-magnet. They also offer story times several days a week.

MRS. TIGGY WINKLE'S TOYS
4811 East Grant Road
(520) 326-0188
www.tiggytoysonline.com
A unique, independent toy store with a heavy emphasis on fun, this shop offers all sorts of toys from the gross to the silly right alongside educational (think Scholastic) and classic (Beatrix Potter, Mother Goose) material. The store sponsors lots of special events (a Fairy Festival, yo-yo lessons, readings, and more). You'll find it in the Crossroads Festival shopping center.

SANTA FE KIDS
Tucson Mall,
4500 North Oracle Road
(520) 293-4050
Little cowboys and cowgirls will like this store that carries Western and Southwestern stuff for kids—such as clothes, rocks, leather pouches, boots and belts, bows and arrows, and accessories and toys.

STARIZONA
5757 North Oracle Road
(520) 292-5010
www.starizona.com
Starizona is an unusual local astronomy shop that, in addition to having a large stock of telescopes and accessories for sale, offers a slew of free viewings through its high-tech telescopes. Starting at sunset on Monday, Wednesday, Friday, and Saturday nights, you can check out the incredible heavens. On Friday, Saturday, and Sunday days, you can look through a special solar scope for solar viewing. Best of all, it's free! This is a great way to learn the sky, how to use your new telescope, try out scopes or accessories, or just have a great time!

YIKES TOYS
2930 East Broadway Boulevard
(520) 320-5669
Looking for a unique gift for the person who has everything? You'll definitely find something at Yikes Toys, which specializes in eccentric toys for all ages. There are tons of little goodies here great for party grab bags, like realistic plastic and rubber animals, funky whistles, nose flutes, lots of gag gifts, jokes, tricks, and odd things like rubber monster women and a lovely selection of old tin toys.

FESTIVALS AND EVENTS

For a small city, Tucson is extremely busy year-round with special events and festivals that showcase our multicultural heritage. No matter what month you plan to visit, you'll always find an interesting or unusual event to check out. From film festivals to rodeos, carnivals to bike races, golf tournaments to music under the stars, Tucson has a diverse—and fun—mix of entertaining events.

Cinco de Mayo festivities celebrate a victory for the Mexican army in 1862, while Pow Wow Days gives visitors insight into Native American culture. But that's not to say that we don't hoist a stein or two during Oktoberfest or don't celebrate a wearing o' the green on St. Paddy's Day. In fact, we have two Oktoberfests, and St. Patrick's Day is celebrated with a parade followed by daylong activities.

Film buffs can also find several film festivals in town. Music fans, whether they applaud an aria or jazz, will be thrilled at the number of choices. Cyclists can ride in some of the nation's finest races, including the 111-mile El Tour de Tucson, which traces the perimeter of town. The Old Pueblo hosts several rodeos, La Fiesta de los Vaqueros being the most renowned. Sports fans won't be left wanting either with three golf tournaments, a tennis tournament, and a Senior Olympics, just to name a few events. Foodies will be happy to note that whatever festival they attend, they will be able to enjoy a delicious assortment of goodies—goodness knows an abundance of food festivals can be found, too.

Thanks to our consistently beautiful weather—some 350 days of sunshine a year—few events will be canceled due to rain or cold (although once in a while a summer monsoon will cause an event to be postponed or canceled). In fact, the majority of events take place outdoors except during summer, when the 100-degree-plus temperatures send everyone scurrying indoors.

February and March are the busiest months, something that should be noted when making hotel reservations. February alone hosts two of the biggest events—the aforementioned La Fiesta de los Vaqueros Rodeo and parade and the world-famous Tucson Gem and Mineral Show. Add a major golf tournament, a fiddlers' contest, and the Renaissance fair—just to name a few—and your slate should be quite full.

For those of you who can't imagine spending the winter holidays in the desert, you'll be put in the holiday mood with several light festivals, a celebration of a Mexican Christmas, our popular Fourth Avenue Street Fair—where you can get some nifty gifts for friends and family—and enough musical celebrations to get you in the spirit.

So hang on to your hats. Here are plenty of great ways to have fun in the Old Pueblo.

JANUARY

SENIOR OLYMPIC FESTIVAL
4208 South Santa Rita Avenue
(other venues throughout town)
(520) 791-3244
www.tucsonseniorgames.org

The Tucson Parks and Recreation Department (see the Parks and Recreation chapter) is known for the wide variety of programs it offers, especially those created with seniors in mind. One of the best examples in the varied slate is the Tucson Senior Olympic Festival for participants over age 50.

Modeled after the real thing, complete with a celebratory opening ceremony and lighting of the torch, the Olympic Festival brings together senior athletes from all over the Southwest for nine days of competition and camaraderie in mid-January. The festival attracts thousands of senior athletes competing in nearly 90 events and 33 sports at venues all over town. Competitions are held in aerobics, racquetball, swimming, cribbage, a wide variety of card games, cycling, horseshoes, boccie, and much more.

The public is invited to watch (and maybe get a little inspiration to get into shape). Watch the newspaper or call the City of Tucson Parks and Recreation Department for a complete rundown of times, places, and events. There is a registration fee to participate.

i Two great sources for current festivals and events are the *Tucson Guide* (520-322-0895) and *Tucson Lifestyle Magazine* (520-721-2929). The *Guide*, published quarterly, offers comprehensive listings of festivals and events in Tucson and southern Arizona. Every issue of the monthly *Tucson Lifestyle* includes an arts and events guide that covers 50 events and exhibits in town. Both publications are available at local newsstands, bookstores, grocery stores, and by subscription.

DILLINGER DAYS
Various locations downtown around Congress Avenue
www.downtowntucson.org/dillingerdays

Downtown Tucson transforms into the 1930s for this annual event commemorating the capture of John Dillinger and his gang in 1934 in Tucson. The Hotel Congress offers tours and lectures. You'll find reenactments of the shootout on the street corners, along with live music, walking tours, film documentaries, and food all along Congress Avenue for this one-day event in mid-January. If you're into it, dress in 1930s clothes and join in the fun. Companion exhibits are featured at the Arizona Historical Society Museum, Postal History Foundation, and Southern Arizona Transportation Museum at the train depot (see the Attractions Chapter for details on these locations).

JEWISH FILM FESTIVAL
Jewish Community Center
3800 East River Road
(520) 299-3000
www.tucsonjcc.org

This annual festival, which runs for about two weeks starting in mid-January, features films by award-winning Jewish directors, producers, and writers. A wide assortment of films is shown, and pre- and postfilm receptions are held. Often the director or subject of the film will attend. Ticket prices depend on the time of the showing, with discounts available for seniors and students. (Tickets to special showings may be higher.) There is also a festival pass that will get you into all the films.

Parking at the JCC is easy and free in the front lot.

ANNUAL QUILTER'S GUILD SHOW
Tucson Convention Center
260 South Church Street
(520) 547-5463
http://tucsonquiltersguild.com

Whether you love quilts for their historic value or enjoy the intrinsic beauty that is the art of the quilt, you won't want to miss this show. The

Tucson Quilter's Guild sponsors this annual event, which features more than 200 quilts, quilted garments, quilting demonstrations, antique displays (including a short history of each quilt), product vendors, and even a raffle. Visitors to this three-day event in the middle of the month also have an opportunity to vote for the best quilt of the show, which then receives the "Viewer's Choice" award. There is a fee for admission and parking in the TCC lot.

FAMILY ARTS FESTIVAL
La Placita Village and the Tucson Convention Center
(520) 624-0595
www.familyartsfestival.org

There's something for every family member at this lively downtown festival in mid-January. Four stages provide continuous entertainment, including live theater, dance and instrumental music, and performances by local artists. You'll also find hands-on, interactive workshops from Latin dance basics to chalk art and bonsai demonstrations. This is a great place to learn about the diverse arts and cultural groups in town, who all have display tables with lots of information for the taking. If you get hungry, foods from around the world are available at the food booths. An arts and crafts market showcases local artists' work in various media. Best of all, it's all free!

SOUTHERN ARIZONA SQUARE/ROUND DANCE AND CLOGGING FESTIVAL
Tucson Convention Center
260 South Church Street
www.sardasa.com

Thousands of square and round dancers kick up their heels to calling by the finest callers, cuers, and clogging instructors at this annual event. With all-wood floors and three dance halls, this annual event takes place over several days in mid-January at the Tucson Convention Center and offers dancing for all levels, from basic to experienced to challenge. There are registration, ticket, and spectator-only fees, which change annually.

Appropriate dress is required at all evening sessions. There is no alcohol, and all smoking is done outdoors, so families can feel comfortable whether they decide to dance or just watch. Parking at the TCC is available for a separate fee. This event attracts many RVers; call ahead for special parking arrangements for your recreational vehicle. The event is sponsored by The Square and Round Association, which has folk dancing classes and dances citywide just about any time of the year.

WINGS OVER WILLCOX
Willcox Chamber of Commerce
1500 North Circle I Road, Willcox
(520) 384-2272, (800) 220-2272
www.wingsoverwillcox.com

A must for bird lovers everywhere, this wonderful weekend event, held in mid-January, is devoted almost entirely to birding. There are so many things to do that you won't know where to begin! Among the highlights of the weekend are several opportunities to view the amazing sandhill cranes that winter in the Willcox area by the thousands. The weekend also includes lectures, field trips, tours, a banquet, an all-you-can-eat country breakfast, and seminars by experts. You can attend a daylong photography tour, join other beginning bird-watchers and learn how to identify common bird species, explore the Dragoon and Chiricahua Mountains, or go on a hawk stalk in Sulpher Springs Valley to spot the more than 15 species of hawks, eagles, and falcons that live there. Advance registration is required for all activities. Fees vary by event.

FEBRUARY

ARIZONA RENAISSANCE FESTIVAL
U.S. Highway 60, 7 miles west of Florence Junction
(520) 463-2700
www.renfestinfo.com

Although time travel hasn't been perfected just yet, you may want to try the next best thing: the Arizona Renaissance Festival. For eight weekends from February through the end of March, costumed folk, be they kings or commoners, stroll the 30-acre grounds entertaining the crowds in much the same way they did at a sixteenth-century marketplace. This includes jousting, jesters, Renaissance music, and dancers. The food sold is much the same as it was in days of yore. Craftspersons create and sell their wares. Bring your wallet; most rides cost extra.

The fair is held rain or shine from 10:00 a.m. until 6:00 p.m. Take Oracle Road north to Pinal Pioneer Parkway—Highway 79—to Florence Junction, where you catch US 60 for 7 miles.

Tickets prices vary; kids under age 5 are free. Discount coupons are available at all Arizona Fry's Food Stores.

SPRING TRAINING
Tucson Electric Park
2500 East Ajo Way
(520) 434-1367

Hi Corbett Field
3400 East Camino Campestre
(520) 327-9467
www.cactus-league.com

Tucson is the only city in the country to host three major-league teams during spring training. The Arizona Diamondbacks, Colorado Rockies, and Chicago White Sox all practice here during late February and March. Games are played at Hi Corbett Field and Tucson Electric Park. Hurry up—future plans call for a move to other Arizona ballparks.

COCHISE COWBOY POETRY AND MUSIC GATHERING
Buena Performing Arts Center and Buena High School, Sierra Vista
(520) 458-9759, ext. 210
www.cowboypoets.com

If you're a fan of cowboy music and poetry, this is the place to be. Poets, singers, and musicians perform some of the best stuff you'll ever hear. On Saturday you can move from room to room at Buena High School and listen in on free open-mic sessions starting at 10:00 a.m. Headliner performances take place on Friday and Saturday evenings and Sunday afternoon at the 1,300-seat Buena Performing Arts Center. Ticket prices vary. Don't miss this unique event. It's held on the first consecutive Friday, Saturday, and Sunday in February.

LA REUNION DE EL FUERTE
Fort Lowell Park
2900 East Craycroft Road
(520) 318-0219
www.oflna.org

Go back in time to when the West was young! The Old Fort Lowell Neighborhood Association sponsors this free event that showcases the neighborhood and its fascinating history in early February. History buffs will love the cavalry drills, period reenactments, and self-guided walking tour (with free map) of the ancient Hohokam site, military camp, and historic homes and chapels. Band performances take place throughout the day, along with a series of lectures that feature local historians and experts. Food, drinks, and souvenirs are sold along Fort Lowell Road.

TUCSON GEM AND MINERAL SHOW
Tucson Convention Center
260 South Church Street
(520) 322-5773
www.tgms.org

The Tucson Gem and Mineral Show really sparkles! Held the second week in February, this amazing event is the largest gem and mineral show in the world. Begun nearly 50 years ago, the show attracts the finest dealers, jewelers, and lapidary artists from around the world, plus thousands of visitors every year. Specialty exhibits are some of the big draws. Lectures are also an integral part of the weekend. And although it has spawned hundreds of satellite exhibits all over town—some beginning as early as the middle of January—the Gem and Mineral Show is a separate entity and is held exclusively at the TCC. It is open to the public for the entire four days and not to be confused with the adjacent dealer show, which is open to gem dealers only.

Food is available at the TCC food stands. There is an admission fee and a fee for parking on-site in the TCC lot. The show runs Thursday through Sunday. Check the newspaper for

The annual Gem and Mineral Show attracts thousands of visitors to Tucson. COURTESY OF METROPOLITAN TUCSON CONVENTION & VISITORS BUREAU, GILL KENNY

a comprehensive map, list of show locations, times, and costs.

OLD-TIME FIDDLE CONTEST
DeMeester Outdoor Performance Center
Reid Park, 22nd and Country Club
(520) 791-4079
www.ci.tucson.az.us

Old-time music lovers rejoice! Come hear some of the finest fiddlin' in town. Begun in the 1940s, pickers and pluckers have competed for the honors (and prizes) at this free all-day, outdoor event.

Contestants as young as 4 years old start this the event in mid-February, with local musicians and professional fiddlers continuing throughout the day. The competition is stiff, but still a whole lot of fun, especially for the audience. You can pack a picnic lunch to be enjoyed on a blanket on the grass hill in front of the band shell or buy goodies from the many food vendors.

Enter the park from Country Club Road, between Broadway Boulevard and 22nd Street.

THE ACCENTURE MATCH PLAY CHAMPIONSHIP
The Gallery Golf Club
14000 Dove Mountain Boulevard, Marana
(520) 571-0480, (866) 942-2672
www.worldgolfchampionships.com

The Accenture Match Play Championship takes place at the end of February at the Gallery Golf Club in Marana, just north of Tucson. The world's top 64 golfers will participate in this exciting five-day tournament that features a multi-million-dollar purse. Headliners include top pros such as Tiger Woods, Vijay Singh, Phil Mickelson, and Stewart Cink.

LA FIESTA DE LOS VAQUEROS
Tucson Rodeo Grounds
4823 South Sixth Avenue
(520) 741-2233
www.tucsonrodeo.com

Begun in 1925, La Fiesta de los Vaqueros (the feast of the cowboys) has been a highlight of the winter season in Tucson. Held the last full weekend in February, the festivities kick off for the public with the world's longest nonmotorized rodeo parade.

The parade begins at South Park Avenue and Ajo Way and then travels south on Park Avenue to the rodeo grounds on Irvington Road at South Sixth Avenue. Crowds begin to line the route in the early morning—the parade starts around 9:00 a.m.—and parking can be at a premium, so it's best to plan ahead.

Grandstand seats are available for reasonable rates, but you can get a great view for free on any of the streets on the route. Shuttle service from various locations will take you to the parade site for a separate charge.

The parade features bands from all the local schools, local celebrities, real cowboys on their mounts, Mexican dancers, the Buffalo Soldiers from a nearby Visionquest program, horse-drawn carriages, and the requisite clowns.

Time was that so many families were involved in the rodeo that attendance at schools in the area dropped considerably during the event. Eventually the school districts conceded to the issue and closed for the Thursday and Friday of the rodeo. Happily for schoolchildren citywide, that tradition continues so that everybody can attend some or all of this event. Kiddies can join in on the rodeo fun, too, with the Mutton Bustin' competition—the littlest cowboys and cowgirls see how long they can ride on the back of a sheep—and the Arizona Junior Rodeo competition.

The rodeo itself is a five-day event, beginning on Wednesday and culminating on Sunday afternoon. Preliminary events are held on previous days. The public can watch such happenings as the Tucson Pro Roping contest and qualifying events for the rodeo.

Officially recognized by the Professional Rodeo Cowboy Association, the rodeo offers prize monies to the tune of hundreds of thousands of dollars.

One of Tucson's oldest and most popular events, the rodeo brings bucking broncos, steer roping, and loads of entertainment to town every year. PHOTO BY M. PAGANELLI VOTTO

Ticket prices vary depending on the day and the event. Parking on all days will cost you and is available on the rodeo grounds. Events usually end around 4:30 p.m. each day. You can buy tickets at the rodeo grounds or by calling (520) 741-2233, (800) 964-5662. Get your tickets in advance to ensure seating and avoid long lines.

MARCH

WINTER CHAMBER MUSIC FESTIVAL

Leo Rich Theater, Tucson Convention Center
260 South Church Street
(520) 577-3769
www.arizonachambermusic.org

One week a year, in early March, the Leo Rich Theater at the TCC comes alive with the sounds of chamber music. Sponsored by the Arizona Friends of Chamber Music, the festival features top musicians and promising young talent playing everything from classic to modern pieces. A short introduction is given before each concert. The concerts are held on opening Sunday night; Tuesday, Wednesday, and Friday nights, and the closing Sunday afternoon. The Gala Benefit Dinner is held on Saturday evening. Tickets are available for individual concerts, with discounts to students with IDs. A package for all of the concerts is also available. The gala is priced separately. Chamber music is a part of the evening, of course. And take a little bit of the evening home with you by buying a CD of previous years' concerts. The Friends of Chamber Music also hold a series of concerts throughout the year.

CLIMB "A" MOUNTAIN

Pima Community College West Campus
2202 West Anklam Road
(520) 321-7989, (800) 227-2345
www.community.acs.events.org/ctctucson

Held the second week in March, this walk may not seem much of a challenge, but remember, most of it is uphill. Beginning at Pima Community College West Campus, this 3.1-mile round-trip walk allows for some of the prettiest views of Tucson. When you reach the top of "A" Mountain, you'll find food vendors, a jumping castle, massages, music, information booths, and plenty of fun. Proceeds benefit the American Cancer Society.

As part of the festivities, you can purchase a commemorative flag honoring a loved one who has battled cancer. The flags are placed alphabetically along the route and can be taken home after the event. Registration begins early in the morning, followed by a group warm-up—no one wants to get injured here. Prizes are offered for those who earn the most money from pledges. There is a registration fee; all registered walkers receive a T-shirt.

SAN XAVIER WA:K POW WOW

San Xavier del Bac Mission
Interstate 19, exit 92
(520) 294-5727

The Tohono O'odham Indians invite hundreds of Native American dancers and craftspeople from the United States and Canada to gather at the San Xavier Mission grounds 12 miles south of Tucson for intertribal competitions in drum and dance techniques, including gourd, team, round, grass, hoop, and two-step dance. Exhibitions and native crafts enrich the festival. Local families cook and sell traditional foods. Though still cameras are allowed, video cameras are not.

The festival costs $8 for adults, $6 for children 7 and up, and is free for younger ones. There is also a parking fee. All monies go to benefit the San Xavier community. (Read more about the mission in our Attractions chapter.)

APRIL

FOURTH AVENUE SPRING STREET FAIR

Fourth Avenue between University Boulevard and Ninth Street
(520) 624-5004
www.fourthavenue.org

If you're in town on one of the two weekends—one in April, the other in December—that the Fourth Avenue Street Fair is being held, consider yourself lucky, and then put on a pair of walking shoes and head for this longtime Insiders' favorite. The 6-block area—which on any given day is a great place to shop, dine, and have fun—is closed to traffic during the fair.

Artisans and craftspersons offer one-of-a-kind clothing, handcrafted jewelry, handmade toys, pottery, unique household items, essential oils and aromatherapy goods, dried flowers, and much, much more. You can have your palm read or your face painted. You can watch jugglers do their thing, dance to the beat of a reggae band, or just enjoy some of the best people watching Tucson has to offer. Food booths on the side streets offer goodies from all over the world. Merchants stay open and sometimes have special sales or giveaways.

Sponsored by the Fourth Avenue Merchants Association, this is an event not to be missed. Parking is at a premium on the side streets, but patience will pay off, even if it means a short walk to "the Ave." (See the Close-Up in our Shopping chapter.)

i When you visit Fourth Avenue during the street fair, check the side streets for easy parking; locals also offer their driveways and yards for a fee.

BLESSING OF THE VINES FESTIVAL
Village of Elgin Winery
471 Elgin Road, Elgin
(520) 455-9309
www.elginwines.com

Have you ever dreamed of stomping grapes? (Anyone remember *I Love Lucy* episode 150?) Your dream will come true at the Elgin wine festival, where the grape-stomping competition is only one of many activities. The festivities go on for two days in early April and include wine tastings, lunch, music, and arts and crafts. Elgin is about 90 minutes south of Tucson. Take Interstate 10 to exit 281, go south, and turn left onto Elgin Road. The winery is about 4 miles on the right. There is an admission fee, which gets you entrance into the grape-stomping competition and a souvenir wine glass.

COUNTRY THUNDER
Canyon Moon Ranch, Florence
(520) 868-9711
www.countrythunder.com

Over 150,000 fans head to this four-day event, one of the biggest events in country music, which takes place in early April. Headliners have included Leann Rimes, Brooks & Dunn, and Randy Travis. Held at Canyon Moon Ranch off Highway 79 in Florence, get ready for lots of music and food. You can camp nearby or stay at one of the limited number of local hotels. Admission is daily, or you can purchase a pass for the whole shebang.

SOUTHERN ARIZONA HOME BUILDERS ASSOCIATION (SAHBA) HOME & PATIO SHOW
Tucson Convention Center
260 South Church Street
(520) 795-3025
www.sahba.org

With more than 400 exhibitors and thousands of visitors, this is the home show of all home shows in the area. Twice a year—in early April and October—the cavernous Tucson Convention Center Exhibit Hall is packed so full of exhibits and booths that it spills over onto the floor of TCC's arena. You'll find ideas for any project you may be contemplating, and some that you didn't even know existed. Exhibits can be found on landscaping, barbecuing, skylights, garage doors, kitchen projects, innovative flooring, spas, swimming pools, and much more.

You'll also enjoy guest speakers and daily demonstrations, and you may even win one of the many door prizes offered by exhibitors.

There is an admission fee, but kids under 12 get in free. Parking is plentiful in the TCC lots and will cost a fee for all day.

TOUR OF THE TUCSON MOUNTAINS
Throughout the mountains
(520) 745-2033
www.pbaa.com

More than 1,000 bicycle riders tour the Tucson

Mountains west of the city in 27- and 70-mile races that start at Town Hall in Marana. This race usually takes place on the last Sunday in April and includes a kids' and family fun ride. Registration forms are available the first week of January, and fees vary depending on which course you choose.

UNIVERSITY OF ARIZONA SPRING FLING
Rillito River Park
North First Avenue and River Road
(520) 621-5610
www.uaspringfling.com

Although the Spring Fling, the country's largest student-run carnival, attracts thousands of students, it's a great family-fun activity. That's because in addition to the usual carnival rides, live music, food booths, and games, families will find the Kid's Kingdom—an area of the fair filled with special exhibits and events and rides. Wildcat athletes can often be found shaking hands and signing autographs.

This four-day event in early April is manned by some 3,000 student volunteers and helps raise money for the 120 clubs and organizations on campus. (Spring Fling is also the name of the nonprofit organization that puts the whole thing together.)

Thursday through Saturday the event is open to midnight. On Saturday gates open at noon. Sunday hours are from noon to 6:00 p.m.

ARIZONA INTERNATIONAL FILM FESTIVAL
Various venues
(520) 628-1737
www.azmac.org

Tucson has long been a mini-Hollywood (see the History chapter), with many movies filmed right here in the Old Pueblo. Film buffs in Tucson launched the Arizona International Film Festival to bring to light the talents of independent filmmakers from around the world. In its short history the festival has grown from a four-day event with a handful of films to a 10-day extravaganza featuring dozens of films from a variety of countries.

Held in late April and sponsored by the Arizona Center for the Media Arts—which operates the Screening Room, 127 East Congress Street (see the Nightlife chapter)—the event also features workshops, a Festival-in-the-Schools Program (where movies from the festival are screened at local high schools by local high school students), and the Reel Frontier Film and Video competition. Films are shown throughout the festival at the various venues around the city.

Since the first festival in 1990, it has premiered over 400 films (both world and U.S. premieres), had 40 countries represented, featured over 150 Arizona works, and has been attended by almost 50,000 people. Films are shown on different dates at the different venues, which allows for catching the film you might have missed or getting to see a favorite another time. The sites are found all around town, so no matter where you are, a showing is just minutes away. Sites include the Screening Room, the Loft, and several other "regular" movie theaters.

Tickets for single events can be purchased two hours before each screening on-site. Special events, such as the Opening Night Reception and the Award Night Reception, and certain screenings will run you extra, depending on the event. There are Saver, Producer, and Student passes available. These give you entry into a plethora of events depending on the type of pass you purchase. Passes can be bought ahead of time (check the local papers for specific information on where to buy them). Parking, of course, varies depending on the film site.

PIMA COUNTY FAIR
Pima County Fairgrounds
11300 South Houghton Road
(520) 762-9100
www.swfair.com

Annually in late April, the Pima County Fair is the biggest draw in attendance in Tucson. Each year over 400,000 people attend the fair to enjoy the farm exhibits, the food, and the nightly entertainment.

Throughout the 10-day run, you'll find the usual contests, exhibitions, games, and carni-

The Pima County Fair offers thrills for kids of all ages; there are tons of rides, lots of games and shows, and plenty of food. MARY PAGANELLI VOTTO

val rides—and plenty of extra touches, such as the interactive children's exhibits and a fine art exhibit, that go beyond the standard offering of a county fair.

Entertainment includes nationally known bands as well as local favorites. Local students show and sell their carefully tended livestock, poultry, and even rabbits. Ribbons are awarded for every kind of homemade goodie (or craft project) you can think of. There is an entrance fee.

LA FRONTERA TUCSON INTERNATIONAL MARIACHI CONFERENCE
Tucson Convention Center
260 South Church Street
(other venues throughout town)
(520) 838-3908
www.tucsonmariachi.org

This annual event in late April celebrates the blend of Hispanic music and culture that has influenced Tucson since its beginnings. The conference offers a chance to hear the best mariachi bands in the world, enjoy folk dancing, and observe artisan exhibits of Mexican arts and crafts.

Tucson's International Mariachi Conference showcases performers from all over the world. COURTESY OF METROPOLITAN TUCSON CONVENTION & VISITORS BUREAU, GILL KENNY

MAY

CINCO DE MAYO
Kennedy Park
Mission Road and Ajo Way
(other venues throughout town)
(520) 791-4873

This holiday—which translates as "fifth of May"—celebrates the victory of the Mexican army over the French at Puebla, Mexico, in 1862. Festivities can be found citywide, especially at the many Mexican restaurants in town. You'll find music, dancing, crafts, and food at this lively fiesta.

TUCSON FOLK FESTIVAL
El Presidio Park area
115 South Church Street
(520) 319-8599
www.tkma.org

This music festival, sponsored by the Tucson Kitchen Musicians Association, includes major national acts as well as continuous music featuring contemporary folk, blues, bluegrass, folk rock, ragtime, and gospel groups. Local and regional acoustical musicians play on multiple stages. Booths sell crafts and food. The free event is held the first weekend of the month.

IRONWOOD FESTIVAL
Mason Audubon Center
3835 West Hardy Road
(520) 744-0004
www.tucsonaudubon.org/masoncenter

Held on the second weekend in May at the Mason Audubon Center on the northwest side of town, this one-day festival celebrates the centuries-old ironwood trees in the park by focusing on nature and preservation. Open only by appointment during the rest of the year, this is a great opportunity to explore this lovely 20-acre preserve full of saguaro and cholla cacti, grapefruit trees, and meandering paths. The festival features educational activities, interpretive walks, cultural presentations, food, music, live animal presentations, and many more activities. You'll find booths and information for most of the local and regional parks and many environmental organizations. It's a great event to take the kids to; they love touching the live snakes, desert tortoise, and lizards.

Parking is at a premium; you can park on the roadside or at nearby Tortolita Middle School and catch a ride on free shuttles provided by Tucson Electric Power. The center is located on the southwest corner of Hardy and Thornydale Roads. There is an admission fee.

WAILA FESTIVAL
Bear Down Field
Cherry Avenue and Fourth Street
(520) 628-5774
www.arizonahistoricalsociety.org

Held in mid-May and sponsored by the Arizona Historical Society, this free outdoor event showcases Waila (pronounced *why-la*), or Chicken Scratch, music (the traditional social dance music of the Tohono O'odham) with bands, Native American artisans demonstrating their crafts, and various food venders. The Tohono O'odham are southern Arizona's largest Indian tribe, and this festival is a fine way to learn about their traditions. Admission and parking are free.

i **Try some traditional Tohono O'odham foods at the Waila festival. You may find sautéed cholla cactus buds, traditional giant-size tortillas, a hearty corn and chili pepper stew called ga'iwsa, and more at this celebration of Tohono O'odham culture.**

JUNE

JUNETEENTH FESTIVAL
Kennedy Park
Mission Road at Ajo Way
(520) 225-2670
www.juneteenth.com

In celebration of the day Texas slaves heard about their emancipation (two months after the Civil War ended), Juneteenth festivities include athletic events, gospel music at churches around the city, and a one-day festival at Kennedy Park (see the Parks and Recreation chapter). You can listen to gospel music and a wide variety of musical entertainment throughout the day on Saturday, plus visit an assortment of food booths, all in celebration of Afro-American culture. Take Ajo Road west to La Cholla Boulevard and watch for signs. This event is free.

HA:SAN BAK: SAGUARO HARVEST CELEBRATION

La Posta Quemada Ranch at Colossal Cave Park
(520) 647-7121
www.colossalcave.com

Saguaro cactus fruit (bahidaj) has been harvested by the Tohono O'odham people for centuries. Learn the details of how the harvesting is done and what the fruit is used for in workshops and demonstrations by tribal members. The event includes an all-day workshop (reservations strongly suggested), beginning at 6:30 a.m., where you get to pick saguaro fruit and prepare it for syrup making. Public activities from 11:00 a.m. to 2:00 p.m. include music, traditional dancers, craft making, and food. Workshop costs vary, and there is an entry fee per car to enter the park. Dates can change depending on the weather, so be sure to call first.

JULY

FOURTH OF JULY FIREWORKS

Various locations

Many of the major resorts tucked away in the foothills of Tucson sponsor their own well-executed fireworks, but the main event for residents is the massive light show launched from "A" Mountain just west of downtown. This free spectacle can been seen from around the city, and many people gather for tailgate parties around the Convention Center downtown. But here is an Insiders' tip: Find someone who has a home with a flat roof (there are lots of them around here). From there you'll be able to catch not just the fireworks downtown, but probably one or more of the many other displays going on.

TOUR FOR TUCSON'S CHILDREN

Tucson Convention Center
260 Church Street
(520) 791-4969
www.cityoftucson.org/parksandrec

This family-oriented cycling event held on the Fourth of July raises money for bike helmets for local kids. Judging from the money that has been raised in previous years, this is quite a popular event. The most challenging is a 27-mile pledged race, but families can enjoy some time together with the Family Fun rides and runs of varying lengths. The race starts at the TCC parking lot on Church Street. There are varying entry fees.

AUGUST

TOMBSTONE VIGILANTE DAYS

Various locations, Tombstone
(888) 457-3929
www.tombstone.org

Any visit to Tombstone, "The Town Too Tough to Die" (see the Day Trips and Weekend Getaways chapter), means strolling down the wooden sidewalks, touring the historic buildings, and soaking up some of that Old Wild West atmosphere. During this three-day festival, the citizens of Tombstone go all out to celebrate the history of their hometown. Along with the usual gunfights and hangings (mock, of course), you can enjoy a chili cook-off and a period fashion show. And if you're up to it, try the Vigilante 10K run. Take I-10 east to the Benson exit, Highway 80, and follow the signs to Tombstone.

SEPTEMBER

MUSIC UNDER THE STARS

Reid Park
22nd Street and Country Club Road
(520) 791-4079

The Tucson Pops Orchestra began playing in 1955. Today the 50-piece group presents numerous concerts each year, and it continues a tradition of offering free concerts under the beauty of Tucson's night sky each Sunday at 7:00 p.m. during the month. Bring a blanket or lawn chair and sample the various refreshments sold by local vendors, or come early with the family and enjoy a picnic before the show.

GREEK FESTIVAL

Greek Hellenic Community Center
1145 East Fort Lowell Road
(520) 888-0505

Old-world charm meets modern-day fun at this popular event held in mid-September. (The festival has drawn upwards of 20,000 people in past years.) It's easy to do because admission is nominal, with kids under 12 free.

Along with a dazzling array of Greek foods, you'll be able to learn Greek dances; sip ouzo, metaxa (Greek brandy), or Greek beer; buy Greek handcrafted items; or ride an assortment of carnival rides.

This is one of the area's most popular events, so parking is at a premium. It might be best to park on one of the side streets nearby and walk a short way to the festival. The Hellenic Community Center is located just off the corner of Fort Lowell Road at Mountain Road. The festival runs from Thursday through Sunday nights.

MOUNT LEMMON OKTOBERFEST

Mount Lemmon Ski Valley
10300 Ski Run Road, Mount Lemmon
(520) 885-1181, (520) 576-1400

While it isn't Bavaria, Mount Lemmon is the closest thing to it in the area and offers some respite from the lingering heat that may still be present in late September. The festival is usually held for four weekends in late September and early October. You'll find German food, music, and dancing at this free event. There is a charge for parking.

OCTOBER

REX ALLEN DAYS

Various locations, Willcox
(520) 384-4583, (877) 234-4111
www.rexallenmuseum.org

The last of the singing cowboys is a native of Willcox, a large farming community about an hour and a half east of Tucson. Featuring a carnival, a rodeo and a parade, arts and crafts, and Western music and dancing, this annual event in early October hearkens back to the good old days. Rex Allen Jr. performs two special shows on Saturday, late afternoon and evening. There is a charge for tickets to his show and the rodeo, but just about everything else is free.

Take I-10 east to the Willcox exit and head south.

TUCSON CULINARY FESTIVAL

Loews Ventana Canyon Resort
7000 North Resort Drive
(520) 299-2020
www.tucsonculinaryfestival.com

There is no better way to experience the amazing culinary variety in Tucson than to attend this annual event. Every major chef, food vendor, and food- and wine-related retailer in town are here. For a set admission fee, you'll have access to wine tastings, food samples, seminars, and cooking demonstrations. Extras include a Sunday brunch hosted by a top chef.

TUCSON MEET YOURSELF

El Presidio Park
349 West 31st Street
(520) 792-4806
www.tucsonmeetyourself.org

Despite its odd name, this three-day festival in early October is a great place to experience the cultural diversity of Tucson. You'll find booth after booth of foods from every ethnic background: Danish, Laotian, Greek, Korean, Mexican, Southern, and Native American. Try an iced Japanese green tea, sweet potato pie, lamb kebabs, prickly pear juice, Mexican horchata, and Indian fry bread. The variety is overwhelming, so bring a hearty appetite. The festival also features music of all types, a children's program, and folk art demonstrations.

El Presidio Park is located in the heart of downtown between Alameda and Pennington Streets on Church Street. Look for the beautiful domed courthouse off Alameda Street. Paid parking can be found at the El Presidio underground garage, which can be entered off Alameda Street. There is also a public works garage at 50 West Alameda Street.

TUCSON POETRY FESTIVAL
Various venues, Tucson
www.tucsonpoetryfestival.org

Started in 1981, this festival celebrates the beauty of language. The four-day festival takes place in early October and includes open-mic readings and special performances featuring regional talent. Readings, workshops, and presentations by acclaimed poets also take place. Call or check the Web site for exact times, locations, and admission prices.

DESERT THUNDER PRO RODEO
Tucson Rodeo Grounds
4823 South Sixth Street
(520) 721-1621
www.desertthunder.com

Here's a chance to see real rodeo cowboys at work. This qualifying event runs for two days in mid-October and features bull riding, barrel racing, calf roping, and the like. You'll also enjoy team roping, steer wrestling, women's drill team, and, for the younger set, mutton busting, junior bull riding, pony rides, and a jumping castle. Goodies are available—you might want to purchase a real cowboy hat to take home with you.

Ticket prices vary. Kids are free with one paid general admission ticket.

TUCSON BLUEGRASS FESTIVAL
Desert Diamond Casino
Interstate 19 and Pima Mine Road
(520) 296-1231
www.desertbluegrass.org

Held at the Desert Diamond Casino in late October, the festival features workshops in guitar, bass, banjo, and song construction. You'll also find music and craft vendors and performers at the plaza stage. The action starts at 9:00 a.m. There is an admission fee; kids under 16 are free. If you're into bluegrass, this is the place to be!

NOVEMBER

EL TOUR DE TUCSON
Congress Street and Granada Avenue
(520) 745-2033
www.pbaa.org

November brings ideal cycling weather and with it this world-famous perimeter bicycling race. Held on the Saturday before Thanksgiving, the ride starts in the heart of downtown and then continues around the city, returning to downtown for the finish. The route covers dirt paths, traveling through washes, and plenty of riding up- and downhill. For the less hardy souls, or bodies as the case may be, there are start-up points at 109, 81, 66, and 35 miles. And kiddies can join in for fun rides. This race is sanctioned by the Perimeter Bicycling Association of America, which is headquartered right here in Tucson.

Spectators can watch El Tour for free anywhere along the route. All registered riders receive a poster and a medallion. This event is supported by University Medical Center and presented by Diamond Ventures.

THANKSGIVING FIESTA
Singing Wind Bookshop
700 West Singing Wind Road, Benson
(520) 586-2425

The indomitable Winn Bundy, former librarian and a font of information about writers, poets, and musicians in the region, hosts this annual fiesta at her delightful Singing Wind Bookshop in Benson. It attracts hundreds of book lovers. Authors read from their latest books, and there's lively music and lots of fun. It's held on the Sunday preceding Thanksgiving Day. (See the Shopping chapter for more information about Singing Wind.) Take I-10 to exit 304, and drive north 2.25 miles on Ocotillo Road. Go right onto Singing Wind Road, and follow it to the ranch house that serves as the bookshop.

DECEMBER

NACIMIENTO

Tucson Museum of Art Complex
140 North Main Street
(520) 624-2333
www.tucsonarts.com

A nacimiento is a Mexican nativity scene. You'll be able to see one of the finest examples of this beloved holiday tradition at the Cordova House, which is part of the Tucson Museum of Art complex downtown.

A creation of Maria Louisa Tena—who began the nacimiento as a tribute to her mother, who always had a nacimiento in their house—the finely detailed scene includes tiny angels, animals, the manger, trees, moss, fairy lights, and even running water. Scenes from the life of Christ, Mexican ranches, African villages, and Bible stories complete this wondrous exhibit. The entire scene fills the room and even reaches the ceiling in some places.

The exhibit starts in November and runs through March, but to get the authentic affect of a true Feliz Navidad, stop by the Cordova House before Christmas. You can enjoy the terrific Holiday Craft Market at the same time. There is no admission fee for viewing the nacimiento. Parking is available in the museum parking lot or on any of the side streets nearby.

FOURTH AVENUE WINTER STREET FAIR

Fourth Avenue between University Boulevard and Ninth Street
(520) 624-5004
www.fourthavenue.org

Along with the Fourth Avenue Spring Street Fair in April, this is the area's second-largest event in attendance, some 250,000 people a year. And it's no wonder! Artisans and craftspersons offer some of the most unique items around in early December. The musicians and performing artists are abundant. And the food . . .

The Winter Fair is a great place to find presents, whether it's jewelry, clothing, or pottery, for those special someones on your list, and while you're at it, buy something special for yourself. You can also have your face painted, take part in a political discourse, or have your fortune told—maybe you'll find out that you'll be returning to the Street Fair next year.

LUMINARIA NIGHTS

Tucson Botanical Gardens
2150 North Alvernon Way
(520) 326-9686
www.tucsonbotanical.org

The stars of the show at this two-day event near the beginning of the month are the more than 2,000 luminarias (candles nestled in sand inside a paper sack) that light the paths throughout the gardens. For years families have delighted in the glow of the night and the accompanying music by a variety of musical groups that perform at locations throughout the garden grounds. The candles are lit from 5:30 to 8:00 p.m.; admission prices vary. Come and enjoy complimentary cookies and cider at this 5.5-acre oasis in the heart of Tucson.

TUCSON MARATHON

Start locations vary, Oracle
(520) 320-0667
www.tucsonmarathon.com

Runners in this marathon will drop 2,500 feet in elevation from the start of this race (in Oracle) to the finish line (they'll also enjoy some outrageous desert and mountain views along the way).

The majority of this race is downhill, so if you are a diehard marathoner, you'll be delighted with your time—this is, after all, the nation's fastest USA Track and Field marathon in America. Please note, it is recommended that you train your quadriceps to avoid serious aches and pains after your downhill run. For the not-so-experienced, a half-marathon is also held, and if you can round up four friends, you all can enter as a relay team, with each leg of the relay a different length.

Finishers receive a medallion. Entry fees vary depending on time of registration (call the Tucson chapter of Roadrunners Club of America at 520-326-9383 or go to www.azroadrunner.org for info on this race and many others in the area).

Both the Tucson marathon and the half-marathon are certified by USA Track and Field. Marathoners will also be happy to know that this race is a Boston Marathon qualifying race, and proceeds earned go to a local charity.

During the Christmas season you'll see many stands along the roads selling ristras (pronounced *ree-stras*)—ropes and wreaths made from dried red chili peppers. These make great Southwestern holiday decorations when hung from doors and windows.

MUSIC IN THE CANYON
Sabino Canyon
5700 North Sabino Canyon Road
(520) 749-1900
www.sabinocanyon.org

In the eastern foothills of the Santa Catalina Mountains, Sabino Canyon is a favorite spot for local hikers and outdoor enthusiasts. But during the second week of December, music lovers come from all over town to hear a Saturday-evening concert from a variety of performers, including the Tucson Boys Chorus, local singing groups and jazz bands, and local guest celebrities. Santa and Smokey Bear (this is part of the national forest) are typically in attendance, and light refreshments are for sale. Some 600 luminarias line the quarter-mile path to the stage area. Though there are no tickets required, donations are appreciated, and canned food is collected for the Tucson Community Food Bank. For those who may have difficulty making the quarter-mile walk, call ahead to arrange to be taken by wheelchair.

ZOO LIGHTS
22nd Street between Country Club Road and Alvernon Way
(520) 791-3204
www.tucsonzoo.org

During the Festival of Lights, the zoo comes alive with lights, music, and holiday cheer. For two weeks in mid-December, over 50 local organizations decorate Christmas trees in celebration. Live music on weekends and holiday munchies are available. The fun starts at 6:00 p.m. and runs until 8:00 p.m. Admission prices vary; bring a new, unwrapped toy for each free admission. The toys help the Toys for Tots drive. After a visit you'll agree—Christmas can be fun in the desert.

WINTERHAVEN FESTIVAL OF LIGHTS
Fort Lowell Road between Country Club Road and Tucson Boulevard
www.mywinterhaven.net

This long-standing Tucson tradition is just the event to get you into the holiday spirit. For 10 days, just before and shortly after Christmas, the residents in this older, midtown neighborhood—clearly defined by Prince Road on the north, Fort Lowell Road to the south, Country Club Road to the east, and Tucson Boulevard to the west—go all out in decorating the exteriors of their homes. Nearly everyone gets involved (rumor has it that when you move into the neighborhood, you must agree to participate in decorating your home). Some folks stick to the traditional Christmas themes, but you're just as likely to find an extraterrestrial or two or a cowboy Christmas scene. Some homes also honor Kwanzaa and Hanukkah.

Admission is just a few dollars or a couple of nonperishable food items for the local food bank. You can choose to take a hayride or horse-drawn carriage tour, which saves waiting to enter the area, or ride the city buses. Certain nights are designated walk-through only (no cars). Check the local newspapers. Prepare for long waits to get in and lots of traffic. Parking is limited on the perimeter of the neighborhood but is usually free.

ARTS AND CULTURE

Back in the 1860s, when Tucsonans wanted a little culture—and entertainment—they'd attend one of the many Mexican puppet shows or circuses that traveled through town. Performances would be outdoors, of course, and in order to enjoy the evening show, the audiences had to build bonfires using old cacti.

The arts scene in Tucson is quite different these days. Today you'll find symphony orchestras, jazz, bluegrass festivals, the state opera, ballet companies, folk and modern dance companies, art museums that rival bigger cities in scope, numerous art galleries, and several diverse local theater companies.

Venues have changed, too. Although we still enjoy many fine productions under the stars, Tucson audiences can attend performances at everything from a large arena setting to a small intimate theater. Indeed, Tucson has lived up to the ***Wall Street Journal*** calling it "a mini-mecca of the arts."

The Tucson-based Arizona Opera Company, Arizona Theater Company, and Tucson Symphony all have multimillion-dollar budgets. Many of the smaller companies' budgets are well over $100,000—all of which makes for a lively and creative arts scene.

The focal point of the city's art scene is the Tucson Arts District. In 1986 the Tucson City Council approved a $5.6 million allocation to create the Arts District and save the Temple of Music and Art on Scott Avenue as the anchor facility of the district. Located in historic downtown Tucson and clustered around Congress Street, the district is populated by galleries, cafes, and artists' studios.

Each season, through its UA Presents series, the University of Arizona's Cultural Affairs Department brings in world-famous performers in theater, dance, music, ballet, and multicultural performances for the entire community to enjoy. This is one of the most anticipated concert series in Tucson due to the quality and diversity of the acts the university brings to the Old Pueblo. Various season-ticket packages (some where you can create your own mix and match) and single tickets are available through the UA Box Office. Major acts also perform at the Tucson Convention Center each season.

Among all these various arts and culture–related organizations, you will also find many other art, theater, and music organizations.

Music lovers will be thrilled at the options available. Tucson supports annual blues, jazz, bluegrass, reggae, mariachi, Western music, and folk festivals. Local support organizations make sure that each of these types of music can be heard year-round, many times for free. And the bar and club scene in town (see the Nightlife chapter) offers all types of live music just about any night of the week.

Tucson theater audiences can enjoy productions that range from major Broadway plays and musicals by professional touring companies to original works, experimental plays, multicultural works, and classical theater staged by local professional and community groups. The stage could be a park, a concert hall, the University of Arizona, or a small, experimental theater that seats 20 people. Pima Community College also plays an active role in the dramatic arts. The

University of Arizona Theater Arts Department, with its Repertory Theatre, is one of the nation's oldest theater departments, and Tucson's Parks and Recreation Department puts on Shakespeare in the Park at the DeMeester Outdoor Performing Arts Center (Parks and Rec is also a sponsor of the Tucson Pops Orchestra). Dance offerings range from a classical ballet troupe to Afro-American/Latino, Native American, and Mexican folk dancers.

Art galleries and museums are plentiful. Many of the art galleries are located in and around downtown, but others can be found citywide. The Tucson Museum of Art, the University of Arizona Art Museum, and the Center for Creative Photography, which is located on the UA campus, boast many fine exhibitions and collections. Pima Community College's Art Museum, located at the Center for the Arts on campus, is another fine example of the diversity of sites where art is exhibited.

Tucson has long been recognized as a creative and prolific center for the literary arts. For more than 30 years, the University of Arizona Press has been publishing award-winning books. The university's creative writing program also boasts the country's largest, in size as well as scope, writing program (it's been rated among the top 10 in the nation). The UA's Poetry Center and Tucson's annual Poetry Festival have done wonders in bringing poetry out of the literary closet and into the public's ear. Tucson has fast become a haven for regional and national writers alike. The late Edward Abbey and Joseph Wood Krutch are writers in Tucson's past. Today nationally prominent writers such as Barbara Kingsolver, N. Scott Momaday, Alberto Urrea, Nancy Mairs, Tom Miller, Charles Bowden, Richard Shelton, Leslie Marmon Silko, Peter Wild, and Jane Miller are just a few of the names associated with Tucson's writing community. Pima Community College has a variety of creative writing programs, both credit and noncredit, for those who wish to expand their skills in all forms of writing.

The Tucson performing arts season typically runs from September to May. During this period the University of Arizona and Pima Community College are in session, and the snowbirds—winter visitors escaping the snow of the Northeast and Midwest—become temporary residents of the Old Pueblo, making for larger audiences. In the summer major events decrease; though the literary scene remains constant, many smaller theaters continue to perform, and the art galleries and museums remain open.

What follows is an overview of the arts scene in Tucson. We have included several of the support organizations because they are extremely influential when it comes to championing local art and artists.

i For a whole new perspective on Tucson, pick up a copy of the magazine *110 Degrees—Tucson's Youth Tell Tucson's Stories*. Featuring original, heartfelt stories by low-income Tucson youth, the magazine is published by the community-based nonprofit VOICES, whose mission is to mentor low-income youth to tell their personal, family, neighborhood, tribal, and community stories so that they can strengthen their cognitive, artistic, emotional, leadership, and higher education skills. Order issues at www.voicesinc.org, or call (520) 622-7458.

SUPPORT ORGANIZATIONS

ARIZONA COMMISSION ON THE ARTS

417 West Roosevelt Street, Phoenix
(602) 771-6501
www.azarts.gov

The Arizona Commission on the Arts, established in 1967, is the state agency that connects artists and communities across the Grand Canyon State. Their Web site includes extensive information on programs, grant opportunities, advocacy, and resources and includes both in- and out-of-state opportunities and resources in the areas of jobs, arts education, arts organizations, and artists.

ARIZONA MEDIA ARTS CENTER

P.O. Box 431, Tucson, AZ 85702-0431
(520) 628-1737
www.azmac.org

This service and resource organization encourages the study, production, appreciation, and use of all forms of film and video. It has a research library and offers programs, classes, and conferences. An international film festival and art film presentations are held at the Screening Room, 127 East Congress Street in the Tucson Arts District (see the Festivals and Events chapter).

THE CENTRAL TUCSON GALLERY ASSOCIATION

(520) 629-9759
www.ctgatucson.org

This is a member-based gallery association of 10 top Tucson galleries. The association organizes six First-Saturday Art Tours in and around downtown Tucson. An Art Safari is held in February, a Summer Art Cruise in June, and The Big Picture in October.

TUCSON/PIMA ARTS COUNCIL

10 East Broadway Boulevard, Suite 106
(520) 624-0595
www.tucsonpimaartscouncil.org

The council, a nonprofit organization, was established in 1984 and is recognized as the official arts agency of the city of Tucson and Pima County. Recipient of the 2003 Governor's Arts Award for Service to the Community, the council provides arts and cultural development services through direct funding, technical assistance, commissions, and contracts to both individual artists and arts organizations. Numerous workshops are offered throughout the year.

VENUES

BERGER PERFORMING ARTS CENTER

1200 West Speedway Boulevard
(520) 770-3690
www.asdb.state.az.us/berger

Known locally as "The Berger," this auditorium offers cozy seating for 496 with an elevated stage. A state-of-the-art facility, it's a favorite site for acoustic music and for Celtic, eclectic, folk, and traditional music concerts. Located on the campus of the Arizona School for the Deaf and Blind, the Berger is one of the city's premier venues for smaller, yet popular events.

CENTENNIAL HALL

University of Arizona
1020 East University Boulevard
(520) 621-3341
www.uapresents.org

Originally the Main Auditorium, Centennial Hall, which dates back to 1937 and is listed on the National Register of Historic Places, was renovated in 1986 and rededicated and renamed Centennial Hall in honor of the 100th anniversary of the University of Arizona. The space blends the charm and formality of the old theater with state-of-the-art technical and acoustic advances. Today the facade of the building looks just as it did back in 1937, yet the back of the theater soars five stories high and easily accommodates big Broadway productions.

UA Presents, the university's performing arts series, offers numerous performances here between September and May. Independently produced shows, mostly in music and dance, continue at the hall year-round. On-street parking is free after 5:00 p.m., with paid covered parking available in various parking garages on the campus. Reserved parking for handicapped patrons is also available.

DEMEESTER OUTDOOR PERFORMING ARTS CENTER

Reid Park, 22nd and Country Club
(520) 791-4873
www.tucsonaz.gov/parksandrec

The DeMeester is a most eclectic, and perhaps the most casual, performance venue in the area. Performances are year-round and include concerts, dramas, and special events. The natural amphitheater offers lawn seating, and patrons are encouraged to bring lawn chairs or blankets. Often food vendors will be on-site, but picnics are allowed.

PIMA COMMUNITY COLLEGE CENTER FOR THE ARTS

2202 West Anklam Road
(520) 206-6986
www.pima.edu/cfa

Located at Pima Community College's West Campus, the Center for the Arts has several venues. The Proscenium Theater is a plush, state-of-the-art facility with box seats along the walls. With 425 seats, it's the college's largest and most used venue for both college and outside community productions and concerts. Considered to be "Tucson's finest midsize performing arts venue," its blend of high-tech equipment, superb acoustics, and classical aura is appreciated by performers and audiences alike. When events are happening at PCC, they usually happen here. Other arts organizations also use this venue.

The Black Box Theater, the college's space for experimental theater, seats 75. The stage can be manipulated into either a traditional setting, a thrust stage, or a theater in the round. Lighting and acoustics are state of the art.

Offering another intimate venue is the Recital Hall. Here the amphitheater seating offers a great view of the stone-backed stage no matter where you sit. This is an ideal spot for smaller groups to perform. The hall seats 75-plus.

The Center's Amphitheater and Courtyard allow for outdoor performances. This venue also used for receptions.

RIALTO THEATRE

318 East Congress Street
(520) 798-3333 (event line), (520) 740-1000 (tickets)
www.rialtotheatre.com

Constructed in 1919, the Rialto Theatre was the most elegant and luxurious playhouse west of the Mississippi. Its unique architecture made it a dramatic showcase for plays, films, and vaudeville. The stage was the largest in the western states. The Sistine Choir sang from it, Ginger Rogers danced on it, and Tucson's first talking picture was shown from it. As the oldest performance theater in Tucson, its opening served notice that Tucson was on the nation's cultural map.

In 1948 the Rialto changed its name to the Paramount. For the next 15 years the theater was Tucson's premiere movie house, but changes in economics and society caused the Paramount to close its doors for the last time. A decade later, the theater where once orchestras played overtures to discriminating audiences had become a porno palace.

Known then as the Cine Plaza, the theater cleaned up its act in 1978 with a switch to first-run Spanish-language films, but a fire in 1981 and a boiler explosion in 1984 bolted its doors again. Unused for a decade and in disrepair, the Rialto was scheduled for demolition.

Concerned Tucson citizens, recognizing the importance of preserving this architecturally unique structure, negotiated the purchase of the theater property. The nonprofit Rialto Theatre Foundation was established in 1995 to raise the funds necessary for the theater's restoration.

Partially restored, the Rialto is now home to big-name acts alongside eclectic blues, rockabilly, and many trendsetting music groups.

TEMPLE OF MUSIC AND ART

330 South Scott Avenue
(520) 884-8210, (520) 622-2823 (tickets)
www.arizonatheatre.org

This is truly the flagship of Tucson's downtown performance venues. In 1907 a women's civic organization called the Saturday Morning Musical Club decided the city needed a "temple" for music and art. It took longer than they expected, but their dream came true in 1927, when the Temple of Music and Art was completed. Over the years and through the misuse of many owners, the Temple fell into disrepair. A very vocal group set about to save it—one woman even stood between the building and the bulldozers to prevent its destruction. Her efforts and those of many others were rewarded when the demolition was called off and the restoration began. The Temple's $2.6 million restoration was completed with an official grand opening on October 13, 1990.

The Temple is the home of the Arizona Theatre Company, which performs in its 622-seat Alice Holsclaw Theater. The theater also hosts a variety of other performances, including music, dance, and contemporary rock acts.

Upstairs, along an outdoor balcony walkway, is the Cabaret Theater (which seats about 90) as well as the Temple Gallery, where various contemporary works are exhibited.

TUCSON CONVENTION CENTER
260 South Church Street
(520) 791-4266
www.ci.tucson.az.us/tcc

The arena, which seats up to 9,000-plus people, hosts huge events, such as home shows, conferences, circuses, and concerts by big-name stars who make a stop in the Old Pueblo. But there are two more artistic venues: the Music Hall and the Leo Rich Theatre. The Music Hall seats 2,200-plus and is the home of the Tucson Symphony Orchestra, the Arizona Opera Company, and Broadway in Tucson. The much smaller Leo Rich seats 511, making it an ideal spot for chamber music recitals and concerts by contemporary and pop artists.

THEATER

ARIZONA REPERTORY THEATRE
Fine Arts Complex
University of Arizona Campus
Park Avenue and Speedway Boulevard
(520) 621-1162
http://web.cfa.arizona.edu/theatre

Arizona Repertory Theatre is the professional training company of the University of Arizona's Department of Theater Arts. One of the nation's oldest theater departments, it has offered performances to the community for more than 60 years. Plays and musicals are produced from August through April, with several productions a year.

i Learn all about Chinese culture at the lovely Chinese Cultural Center (1288 West River Road; 520-292-6900; www.tucsonchinese.org). There's a soothing outdoor pavilion with chimes, but most of the activities take place inside. Special events include a New Year's dinner and the Autumn Moon festival. Classes cover the Chinese language, cooking, watercolor, calligraphy, and Tai Chi.

ARIZONA ROSE THEATRE COMPANY
Berger Performing Arts Center
1200 West Speedway
(520) 888-0509
www.arizonarose.cc

Founded in 1986, this theater company offers productions throughout the year, primarily at the Berger Performing Arts Center (see Venues above). The company is committed to presenting high-spirited and upbeat productions that offer positive statements. It also performs at local schools throughout the year.

ARIZONA THEATRE COMPANY
Temple of Music and Art
330 South Scott Avenue
(520) 884-8210, (520) 622-2823 (tickets)
www.arizonatheater.org

This group has been designated "The State Theatre of Arizona." Founded in 1967 as the Arizona Civic Theater, the company staged its first productions in a small hotel in Tucson for a small number of theatergoers. In 1972 the company went professional and changed its name to the Arizona Theatre Company. Later in 1978 ATC began performing in both Tucson and Phoenix.

Theater is alive and well at the University of Arizona's sculptural patio at the School of Theater and Dance.
PHOTO BY M. PAGANELLI VOTTO

Today ATC mounts several professional productions per year during the regular arts season, ranging from Shakespeare and classical and contemporary dramas to musicals and works by new artists.

BIANCO CHILDREN'S THEATRE
4475 North Summerset Drive
(520) 886-0860
Kids ages 6 to 16 make up this band of thespians that performs several times a year. They learn the tricks of the trade—vocal, choreography, and acting skills—and dazzle their young and young-at-heart audiences at the Gaslight Theatre, 7010 East Broadway Boulevard.

BORDERLANDS THEATER
40 West Broadway Boulevard
(520) 882-7406, tickets
www.borderlandstheater.org
This professional company presents theater and educational programs that reflect the cultural and racial diversity of the Southwest border region. Through its work, Borderlands seeks to generate a better understanding of the multiethnic diversity of the border that contributes to this region's unique character through play production and development with a focus on the Chicano/Latino voice. Education outreach programs include mentoring, school visits, and community collaborations.

GASLIGHT THEATRE
7010 East Broadway Boulevard
(520) 886-9428
www.thegaslighttheatre.com
Tucson's only live, old-fashioned musical melodrama theater, the Gaslight is well known in the area for its lighthearted, rip-roaring comedies. Audiences can enjoy hissing at the villains, cheering the heroes, and tapping their toes to the music. The majority of these year-round productions are written by local playwrights (including the song parodies) especially for Gaslight Theatre.

It's good family entertainment, where one can also dine on a wide variety of snack foods like pizza, hot dogs, and nachos, and enjoy fountain treats, beer, wine, and soft drinks. The food is provided by Little Anthony's Diner, which is located at the back of the theater. It's one of the best-run operations in town.

INVISIBLE THEATRE
1400 North First Avenue
(520) 882-9721
www.invisibletheatre.com
A very visible force in Tucson's cultural community, Invisible Theatre is the city's original experimental theater (affectionately known as "The I.T."). Susan Claassen established the I.T. in 1971, and for the first few years of productions, it offered works from local writers. Since the late 1970s it has become better known as a "director's theater," presenting adaptations of classics, off-Broadway plays, musicals, comedies, and original scripts. The I.T. also supports Project Pastime, an educational program for developmentally delayed students. The 80-seat theater's season runs September through June.

LIVE THEATER WORKSHOP
5317 East Speedway Boulevard
(520) 327-4242
This production company offers a full schedule at its theater on Speedway, as well as an educational program for aspiring artists and special acting classes for kids 6 to 18. Since its founding in 1994, LTW has become an important element of Tucson's community theater groups. Its 90-seat air-conditioned theater offers intimacy and comfort. LTW offers drama classes as well. Audiences appreciate the reasonably priced tickets.

REDONDO MUSIC THEATRE
Leo Rich Theatre
(520) 615-1130 (tickets)
http://redondomusictheatre.com
A former casting director in Hollywood, Director Hal Hundley brings his keen eye for talent and savvy production skills back to Tucson to produce classic Broadway musicals with the Redondo Music Theatre. Productions have included *Pump Boys and Dinettes, Cabaret, South Pacific,* and *Guys and Dolls.* All performances are held in the Leo Rich Theater at the Tucson Convention Center.

THIRD STREET KIDS
2520 North Oracle Road
(520) 622-4100
www.artsforallinc.org
Arts for All, Inc., a nonprofit organization, runs this program that began in 1985 as an after-school theater program for children with disabilities. Students ages 3 to 21 come from throughout greater Tucson and meet five times a week at the above address. There are also weekend workshops and a summer camp of the arts. The students have represented Arizona at several national and international events. (See the Kidstuff chapter.) Founder and executive director Marcia Berger has won numerous awards for her work leading this group. A day program for adults with developmental disabilities is another major part of Third Street's programs.

DANCE

BALLET ARIZONA
3645 East Indian School Road, Phoenix
(602) 381-0196
www.balletaz.org
No, you didn't read the address wrong. Tucson and Phoenix share the professional state ballet company, which was developed when three rival ballet companies joined together. Ballet Arizona creates, performs, and teaches classical and contemporary ballet, primarily in Phoenix.

BALLET FOLKLORICO TAPATIO
2100 South Fourth Avenue
(520) 622-2898
www.dancingtapatio.com
Swirls of colorful costumes, enthusiastic dancers, and toe-tapping Mexican folk music make this dance troupe a visual and musical delight.

A professional dance group, dancers perform all the traditional Mexican folk dances. (Each state in Mexico has a particular dance that they call their own; costumes are specific to each region as well.) The dancers also perform traditional dances of the Southwest during their many shows around town.

BALLET TUCSON
200 South Tucson Boulevard
(520) 903-1445
www.ballettucson.org

Ballet Tucson is an energetic company of professional dancers and apprentices ranging in age from 16 to 35. Many of its members have danced professionally with companies of national stature such as New York City Ballet, American Ballet Theatre, San Francisco Ballet, Ballet West, Alvin Ailey, Boston Ballet, and Dance Theatre of Harlem. The company presents classics as well as innovative contemporary works. In addition, an exceptional children's company of more than 100 performs alongside Ballet Tucson's professionals in family-oriented productions such as *The Nutcracker, Cinderella,* and *A Midsummer Night's Dream.*

BARBEA WILLIAMS PERFORMING COMPANY
P.O. Box 2775, Tucson, AZ 85702
(520) 628-7785

This multidisciplinary community performance company promotes African-American and Latino culture. The range of the group's work spans traditional and contemporary theater, dance, music, and even poetry. Performances are held at community centers, schools, and other venues throughout the city. You can also catch this troupe at various festivals throughout the year, usually for just the price of admission to the festival. The company also promotes Afrocentric art in its gift shop, which offers hair design, gourds, and unique decorative items for the home. The shop is located in a private home and is open by appointment only. Please call ahead.

O-T-O DANCE
300 East University Street
(520) 624-3799
www.orts.org

Established in 1985, O-T-O Dance is one of Tucson's largest touring modern dance companies. Also known as Orts, it performs historical, avant-garde, and contemporary dance works and has a full home season, which runs year-round. They also work with several of the local schools. Orts is one of the only dance companies in the nation to have its dancers fly on single-point trapezes. The low-flying, single-point trapeze not only swings the dancers but also allows them to spin in a circle. The group brings master teachers and choreographers to town to conduct workshops and set choreography at the historic Y Hall. All ages are welcome. Performances are at various venues around town.

REDHOUSE DANCERS
6932 East Fourth Street
(520) 886-7651

This Native American cultural performing arts group was formed in the Monterey Peninsula area in 1965. The family group moved to Tucson in 1973. Along with the Navajo Nation Dancers, the Redhouse Dancers conduct informational and craft classes. The group performs spectacular and colorful dances at a number of festivals, fiestas, schools, and conventions throughout the area, all aimed at providing a better understanding of Native American traditions and customs.

UNIVERSITY OF ARIZONA DANCE DIVISION
School of Dance
Ina Gittings Building, Room 121
(520) 621-4698
www.arts.arizona.edu/dance

The dance program at the University of Arizona offers the study of dance as an art form and as a performing art. The philosophy of the program is that dance leads to an understanding of human movement. Jazz, ballet, and modern dance are offered with equal emphasis so students can experience and appreciate the diversity. As a performance group, UA dancers have been recognized for their professional productions and performances at the Ina Gittings Dance Studio Theater.

LITERARY ARTS

OLD PUEBLO PLAYWRIGHTS

P.O. Box 64914, Tucson, AZ 85728
(520) 321-0072
www.oldpuebloplaywrights.org

Founded in 1989, Old Pueblo Playwrights is dedicated to the nurturing of fledgling playwrights and screenwriters. Members bring their first-draft scripts to weekly Monday-evening meetings at the Temple of Music and Art for feedback from other members. Many members have sold screenplays and gone on to win national theater awards or have had their works produced by one of Tucson's many theater companies. Each January the group presents a Festival of New Plays to showcase members' works.

SOCIETY OF SOUTHWESTERN AUTHORS

P.O. Box 30355, Tucson, AZ 85751
(520) 546-9382
www.ssa-az.org

A nonprofit organization with more than 600 members, the society is open to poets, novelists, nonfiction writers, essayists, playwrights, and screenwriters who are published or aspire to be. The group has monthly meetings where general topics are discussed, and an occasional mixer offers a chance to network. Once a year it sponsors a large writers conference where attendees meet and talk with nationally known authors, publishers, agents, and other regional writers. Keynote speakers at past conferences have included Ray Bradbury and Tony Hillerman. There are membership fees.

UNIVERSITY OF ARIZONA POETRY CENTER

University of Arizona
1508 East Helen Street
(520) 626-3765
www.poetrycenter.arizona.edu

Established in 1960, this is a nationally acclaimed resource of over 50,000 books, periodicals, and audio/video recordings. Currently in temporary quarters, a new home for the center is in the design phase. The 17,000-square-foot facility at the corner of Helen and Vine Streets provides a rare-book room, quiet areas for reading, audiovisual listening and viewing spaces, guest accommodations, and a welcoming outdoor courtyard for presentations and receptions.

The center's mission is to provide a welcome environment that will "maintain and cherish the spirit of poetry" for students and the community. The library and most reading events are free and open to the public.

MUSIC

Tucson's music scene offers everything—classical music, opera, folk, chamber music, country, bluegrass, Western, blues, jazz, and New Age. A variety of vocal groups and choirs ranging from professional to "kitchen musicians" are also active. So whether you are a professional musician, a part-time music maker, or a member of an appreciative audience, you can find fellow music lovers with ease.

It would be almost impossible to list all the support groups and music organizations in this chapter (Tucson's large mix of music offerings could be a book unto itself). Here we give you a look at some of the area's larger and more active groups. Should your tastes run to a more particular type of music, one these groups can steer you in the right direction.

ARIZONA OPERA COMPANY

3501 North Mountain Avenue
(520) 293-4336
www.azopera.com

In 1971, 15 local musicians and actors came up with the idea of founding a professional opera company in Tucson. The following spring the city witnessed its first classical production of Rossini's *The Barber of Seville.* Today it's the state's only professional grand opera company. Between October and April the company presents seven performances of five productions at the Tucson Convention Center's Music Hall. Past productions have included *Aida, La Boheme, Carmen,* and *La Traviata.* This is the only opera company in the United States to perform regularly in two cities (Tucson and Phoenix) and is one of only a few American opera companies to have produced the entire Wagner Ring Cycle.

ARIZONA REPERTORY SINGERS
P.O. Box 41601, Tucson, AZ 85717
(520) 792-8141
www.arsingers.org
This 40-plus-voice mixed ensemble brings a wide variety of choral music to venues throughout southern Arizona. Founded in 1984, the chorus specializes in a cappella choral music from numerous eras and countries. Concerts number about 20 per year. The group is known for its musicianship and high-energy performances. All the concerts take place at a variety of locations.

ARIZONA SYMPHONIC WINDS
5201 North Rocky Ridge Place
www.azsymwinds.org
A community ensemble of some 60 musicians, the group has been performing at a variety of venues throughout Tucson since 1986. Most winter concerts are held at the auditorium of Rincon University High School. Arizona Symphonic Winds regularly presents outdoor concerts at Udall Park. This group allows emerging artists a chance to develop their talents through performance and education.

CIVIC ORCHESTRA OF TUCSON
P.O. Box 42764, Tucson, AZ 85733
(520) 798-0062
www.cotmusic.org
Founded in 1975, this volunteer symphony orchestra offers free concerts at a variety of sites throughout the city. It also sponsors an annual Young Artists competition, a competition open to Tucson-area high school students, and conducts a musical education outreach program at area schools. The afternoon performing season runs October through May and offers several concerts.

DESERT VOICES
P.O. Box 270, Tucson, AZ 85702
(520) 791-9662
www.desertvoices.org
Established in 1988 as the Metropolitan Community Chorus, today the choral ensemble produces three major concerts between December and June. Though the group is dedicated to promoting a positive gay and lesbian, bisexual, and transgendered presence in southern Arizona, membership is open to anyone who is supportive of gay/lesbian and alternative lifestyles. Four major concerts are held at various venues throughout Tucson.

THE FOOTHILLS PHIL
2101 East River Road
(520) 577-5090, ext. 1910
www.cfsd16.org
This philharmonic offered through the Catalina Foothills School District brings adults and students together to share their love of music and seeks to motivate students to pursue the study of stringed instruments. It offers a complete orchestral experience. The orchestra presents concerts at Catalina Foothills High School Theater, 4300 East Sunrise Drive, in December and May. Tucson's own Lázló Veres conducts!

OLD ARIZONA BRASS BAND
(520) 990-6386
www.oabb.homestead.com
This terrific brass band really takes you back to the old days. Founded in 1997 by Ray Hicks, the band's mission is to provide a living representation of the military and civilian brass bands of territorial Arizona from 1872 to 1912. The music, uniforms, and musical instruments are authentic to the cavalry and town bands of this period. They perform throughout southern Arizona and at several historical celebrations and reenactments, including the annual Reunion de El Fuerte Festival (see the Festivals and Events chapter).

i **Do you like drums? Do you like to dance? Head out to one of the Dambe Project's "Let's Dance" events where you can whirl and twirl to your heart's content to the deep, strong beat of West African drumming. This nonprofit organization also offers performances and drumming and dance classes. For more information check www.dambeproject.org, or call (520) 245-4547.**

SONS OF ORPHEUS—THE MALE CHOIR OF TUCSON
P.O. Box 31552, Tucson, AZ 85751
(520) 621-1649
www.sonsoforpheus.org
A nonprofit, nonsectarian community men's choir, Sons of Orpheus includes men of all walks of life. Founded in 1991, the choir presents concerts throughout southern Arizona, nationally, and internationally that range from classical to popular and span all periods, styles, and languages. Director Grayson Hirst encourages any man who enjoys singing to join.

SOUTHERN ARIZONA SYMPHONY ORCHESTRA
P.O. Box 43131, Tucson, AZ 85733
(520) 323-7166
www.sasomusic.org
Established in 1979, the symphony is a blend of professional and amateur volunteer musicians who offer a rich diversity of classical performances. Critics rave over the intensity of this company's performances. Over the years the orchestra has premiered several new works by American composers in Tucson and southern Arizona, while still maintaining a balance of the classics such as works from Rossini, Beethoven, Haydn, and more. SASO performs several concerts between October and June. Performances are usually at the Desert View Performing Arts Center and other local venues. Season tickets and single tickets are available. Discounts are available for seniors and students.

TUCSON ARIZONA BOYS CHORUS
5770 East Pima Street
(520) 296-6277
www.boyschorus.org
Founded in 1939 and known as "America's singing ambassadors," this well-established group has become internationally recognized and tours extensively throughout North America and overseas. The chorus has performed for presidents, kings, and heads of state. Dedicated to providing boys 8 to 14 in the area with an educational opportunity as well as performance experience, the group offers many local concerts in Tucson at various venues between October and May. Their Musicale Regale, Winter Holiday, and Pops concerts are truly delightful.

TUCSON CHAMBER ORCHESTRA
P.O. Box 13925, Tucson, AZ 85728
(520) 401-4369
www.tucsonchamberorchestra.org
Established in 1991, the 35-member orchestra was formed to provide an outlet for the area's professional musicians as well as talented amateurs. Each season the group performs a range of traditional and contemporary works for small orchestra. Prominent area soloists are featured, and new compositions by area composers are regularly introduced. The orchestra has also released several CDs.

TUCSON GIRLS CHORUS
4020 East River Road
(520) 577-6064
www.tucsongirlschorus.org
Founded in 1985, this nonprofit organization provides an environment where girls grades 2 through 8 develop self-esteem, discipline, and music literacy. Today there are more than 200 girls involved in four choruses. The chorus usually offers many concerts at different venues around town.

TUCSON PHILHARMONIA
P.O. Box 41882, Tucson, AZ 85717
(520) 623-1500
www.tpyo.org
A full symphonic youth orchestra, Tucson Philharmonia rehearses at the Armory Park Center. It provides symphonic training and performance opportunities to southern Arizona youths in a professional environment. Membership in the orchestra is determined each year by audition (this is considered an all-star group) and currently comprises approximately 100 high school–age musicians from schools around southern Arizona. The young musicians travel from as far away as Douglas and Nogales to practice each week. Fall and spring concerts are held between November

and April at various venues. The philharmonia offers coaching sessions with Tucson Symphony Orchestra musicians and scholarships for instruments and education. A sampler series of concerts takes place throughout the year at Armory Park; this series is free.

TUCSON POPS ORCHESTRA
P.O. Box 14545, Tucson, AZ 86732-4545
(520) 722-5853
www.tucsonpops.org

This professional pops orchestra has been offering southern Arizona Music Under the Stars for free since 1955. The concerts take place at Reid Park's DeMeester Outdoor Performance Center, which is named in honor of the violinist founder of TPO. The orchestra offers several concerts each season that feature old favorites and popular classics. The concerts are held in May, June, and September.

TUCSON SYMPHONY ORCHESTRA
2175 North Sixth Avenue
(520) 882-8585 (tickets)
www.tucsonsymphony.org

The oldest existing professional symphony orchestra in the Southwest, TSO was founded in 1929. During the year TSO offers world-class guest artists and several concert series, including Classics, Pops, and Masterworks. Concerts are held between September and April at the Tucson Convention Center Music Hall, Catalina Foothills High School, Tucson Symphony Center, and many other local venues.

UNIVERSITY COMMUNITY CHORUS
University of Arizona College of Fine Arts
(520) 621-1301
www.arts.arizona.edu

This exciting 100-plus chorus is made up of university students, professors, and professional and amateur singers from the community. The chorus performs several concerts a year, including a popular holiday songfest. Works range from Handel to Orff. No auditions are necessary.

UNIVERSITY OF ARIZONA COLLEGE OF FINE ARTS
1017 North Olive Road
(520) 621-1301
www.arts.arizona.edu

Numerous events are held during the school year at the College of Fine Arts, which has existed for more than 100 years. With the help of its world-renowned faculty (who are highlighted during the Faculty Artist Series) and its 500 music majors and 100 dance majors, the School of Music presents more than 300 concerts per year, almost on a daily basis. Concerts feature everything from classical recitals, jazz, and opera to steel drum bands.

MUSIC SOCIETIES AND ORGANIZATIONS

No matter what your musical taste, there is probably a local organization you can join, a newsletter you can receive, limited discounts on concerts you can take advantage of, or like-minded enthusiasts you can mingle with. Below is a sampling of the music societies and organizations in the area.

ARIZONA EARLY MUSIC SOCIETY (AEMS)
P.O. Box 68512, Tucson, AZ 85737
(520) 297-3448
www.azearlymusic.org

This nonprofit group's mission is to present concerts of early music and promote related activities such as classes about various forms of early music, including harpsichord, lute, harp, and violin. Smaller, more intimate concerts are a part of the Haus Musik series. Private homes serve as the venue, and food and drink are served. Tickets, which include the meal, are $25.

DESERT BLUEGRASS ASSOCIATION
www.desertbluegrass.org

A nonprofit group of pickers gets together once a month and produces a monthly newsletter to inform members of upcoming bluegrass music events and news. Dues are annual and include the newsletter. Pickers and players gather several times per week at local eateries to jam. Listeners are more than welcome (bring your banjo if you want to join in). These jam sessions are free. They also sponsor an annual festival in October. (See the Festivals and Events chapter.) Membership will get you a newsletter, info on upcoming events, and discounts on events statewide.

TUCSON FRIENDS OF TRADITIONAL MUSIC
P.O. Box 40654, Tucson, AZ 85717
(520) 293-3783
www.tftm.org
These Tucson friends promote participation in and appreciation of traditional music and dance. The year-round calendar of concerts, dances, and workshops features American, Celtic, South American, and other "World Music" traditions. With a substantial membership, it offers a monthly newsletter (*TFTM News*) and sponsors contra dances with live music and callers. Family and other memberships are available, which get you the newsletter and discounts on some concerts.

TUCSON JAZZ SOCIETY
6262 North Swan Road, Suite 185
(520) 408-6181
www.tucsonjazz.org
Of all the nonprofit support organizations in Tucson, the Jazz Society presents the greatest number of organization-produced concerts in the area (about 40 per year). Founded in 1977, the society sponsors the Tucson Jazz Orchestra and Jazz Werx, an education program for young people. Two of the major events the group sponsors are the Plaza Suite Series at St. Philip's Plaza seasonally and Primavera, the oldest women's jazz event in the world, in March. During the rest of the year, it presents or copresents many other events. Family and individual memberships are available, which include concert ticket discounts as well as the bimonthly newsletter.

TUCSON KITCHEN MUSICIANS ASSOCIATION
P.O. Box 26531, Tucson, AZ 85726
(520) 792-6481
www.tkma.org
This nonprofit group's primary focus is to promote acoustic and folk music in the area. TKMA produces the annual Tucson Folk Festival, a two-day event held each May that presents a variety of acoustic music styles by local and national performers (see the Festivals and Events chapter). It also produces or coproduces a number of other concerts year-round at venues around town. As a member you'll receive discounts on concert tickets as well as a monthly newsletter.

TUCSON MUSICAL ARTS CLUB
www.nfmc-music.org
Established in 1953, this affiliate of the National and Arizona Federation of Music Clubs promotes individual and community growth and understanding of all forms of musical arts. It encourages young musicians through scholarships, special awards, and workshops. Miniconcerts are given the first Sunday of the month at Borders Books on North Oracle Road.

VISUAL ARTS

Galleries

It's not unusual to stroll into a cafe or restaurant in Tucson and see original artwork hanging on the walls for sale, especially downtown and on Fourth Avenue. Art is everywhere in Tucson, and the number of galleries and original art shops—close to 150—increases each year. Some may not hang around for long, but they are quickly replaced with others.

BLUE RAVEN GALLERY
3054 North First Avenue, Suite 5
(520) 623-1003
This small, rustic gallery showcases Mata Ortiz pottery, Tohono O'odham contemporary and traditional baskets, original silk paintings, bronzes, and sculptures. The focus is on innovative work featuring Sonoran Desert culture and wildlife and Sonoran sea life expressed in various media. The gallery also offers classes. Open seasonally Thursday through Saturday and by appointment. Hours vary, so be sure to call ahead.

CONRAD WILDE GALLERY
210 North Fourth Avenue
(520) 622-8997
www.conradwildegallery.com
In the heart of the Fourth Avenue arts scene, this gallery shows contemporary painting, sculpture, and works on paper from emerging and established artists. Open Tuesday through Saturday.

DAVIS DOMINGUEZ GALLERY
154 East Sixth Street
(520) 629-9759
www.davisdominguez.com
Located in the up-and-coming Warehouse District, this well-known gallery is the largest (in square footage) contemporary gallery in the city. It has been in Tucson since 1976 and features modern paintings and major sculpture. Open Tuesday through Saturday.

DEGRAZIA GALLERY IN THE SUN
6300 North Swan Road
(520) 299-9191
www.degrazia.org
High above the city, at a site that was once quite remote, stands this unusual gallery that celebrates the life and work of the late Ted DeGrazia. More than 125,000 people a year visit this site to view some of the more than 10,000 DeGrazia paintings that deal with Spanish exploration of the Southwest, Indian lore, legends, celebrations, rodeos, and bullfighting. DeGrazia even designed the floor tiles, light fixtures, and other decorative features throughout the gallery. Signature works are of Indian children with round faces and flowing black hair. The prolific artist also worked in bronze, ceramics, stone lithographs, serigraphs, glassware, and jewelry.

Down a path from the main building is the small, open-roofed Mission in the Sun—a chapel DeGrazia designed and built himself. The chapel's walls are decorated with DeGrazia murals.

Before his death in 1982, DeGrazia created the DeGrazia Art and Cultural Foundation to keep the site operating. Since that time the foundation has also supported other arts organizations, including public broadcasting, within Tucson.

The gallery is open daily. You can purchase DeGrazia posters, cards, and gifts at the charming gift shop located in the main building. There is no admission fee.

DESERT ARTISANS' GALLERY
6536 East Tanque Verde Road
(520) 722-4412
www.desertartisansgallery.com
Desert Artisans' Gallery was founded in 1987 by local artist Sarah Rankin. The gallery is a fine art co-op gallery featuring Southwestern art from Tucson Arizona and the Southwest. It features contemporary works in oil, pastels, acrylic, photography, watercolor, ceramics, glass, and more. As a co-op gallery, they offer great values on beautiful art by allowing you to buy directly from the artists. Open seven days a week.

DINNERWARE ARTSPACE
264 East Congress Street
(520) 792-4503
www.dinnerwarearts.com
Named for its original location in a market selling ceramic dishes, this nonprofit membership gallery has been in operation since 1979. Committed to the presentation of high-quality contemporary art by emerging and established local, national, and international artists, the gallery features experimental work not normally available in Tucson. Open Wednesday through Saturday.

THE DRAWING STUDIO GALLERY
33 South Sixth Avenue
(520) 620-0947
www.thedrawingstudio.org
Founded in 1992, this not-for-profit gallery is affiliated with the artists' cooperative the Drawing Studio. The picture-windowed, sleek gallery space on Fourth Avenue features the work of students and professional artists in a variety of media. There are continuous year-round exhibitions here, and the studio offers weekly drawing and studio practice open to the public, a wide variety of workshops, and courses ranging from drawing to printmaking and calligraphy.

Ted DeGrazia is famous for his depictions of angels. The lovely gallery and gardens are open to the public at no charge. PHOTO BY MARY PAGANELLI VOTTO

EL PRESIDIO GALLERY
186 North Meyer Street
(520) 299-1414
www.elpresidiogallery.com
This small gallery in the Old Town Artisan block offers works by the Southwest's finest artists in a wide variety of subjects and mediums, which include oil, watercolor, clay, bronze, glass, and wood. Open daily.

ETHERTON GALLERY
135 South Sixth Avenue
(520) 624-7370
www.ethertongallery.com
Specializing in Native American vintage photographs and classic photography, this 3,500-square-foot gallery also exhibits contemporary paintings, prints, and sculptures. Etherton operates the Temple Gallery on the second floor above the courtyard at the Temple of Music and Art as well. The main gallery downtown is open Tuesday through Saturday. You'll find it above Barrio Grill.

THE GALLERY AT 6TH & 6TH
439 North Sixth Avenue
(520) 903-0650
www.sixthandsixth.com
Located in the downtown Warehouse District, this gallery specializes in American modernism from the 1940s forward, as well as contemporary art continuing that tradition. The emphasis is on nonobjective art that celebrates line, texture, form, and color. The gallery is also the exclusive representative of the estates of Ulfert Wilke (1907–1987) and Michio Takayama (1903–1994). Open Tuesday through Saturday.

GROGAN GALLERY OF FINE ART
2890 East Skyline Drive
(520) 577-8787
www.ggrogangallery.com
This upscale gallery in the foothills features local and nationally recognized artists in various media who are in their midcareer. Special events take place throughout the year highlighting featured artists. Open Monday through Saturday.

i **Experience life backstage with Arizona Theatre Company at the historic Temple of Music and Art. Backstage tours of the 623-seat concert hall are offered Saturday during the ATC season, September through April. More information on both the shows and the tours is available from ATC at (520) 884-8210 or www.arizonatheatre.org.**

LA PILITA MUSEUM GALLERY
420 South Main Avenue
(520) 882-7454
www.lapilita.com
For a unique experience in one of Tucson's most historic downtown districts, head to La Pilita in Barrio Viejo, next to the El Tiradito Shrine and El Minuto Cafe (see the Restaurants chapter). A small museum and gallery, exhibits here change monthly and focus on regional history. A permanent exhibit of historic photos of early Tucson is worth a look, and don't skip the store full of unusual gifts. Open Monday through Saturday; closed in summer.

LOUIS CARLOS BERNAL GALLERY
Center for the Arts
Pima Community College, West Campus
2202 West Anklam Road
(520) 206-6942
www.pima.edu/performingarts/bernalgallery
Housed in Pima Community College's Center for the Arts, the Louis Carlos Bernal Gallery is dedicated to a longtime PCC instructor and celebrated photographer. The gallery features the work of international, local, and regional artists. Special exhibits highlight student competitions showing works in ceramics, drawing, fibers, metals, mixed media, painting, photography, prints, and sculpture. Open Monday through Friday.

MADARAS GALLERY
3001 East Skyline Drive, #101
(520) 615-3001
1535 East Broadway Boulevard
(520) 623-4000
www.madaras.com

These galleries feature local artist Diana Madaras's pastel watercolors of desert scenery. These very popular works are featured on prints, cards, and calendars available in gift shops around town. Here you can find her work all in one place along with fine art originals. Open Monday through Saturday; Skyline location is open Sunday.

MEDICINE MAN GALLERY EAST
7000 East Tanque Verde Road, Suite 16
(520) 722-7798

Mark Sublette Modern
2890 East Skyline Drive, Suite 190
(520) 299-7798
www.medicinemangallery.com

These galleries display one of the finest collections of early American and Western art. Specialties focus on the life work of Maynard Dixon and the Taos Society of Artists. You will also find antique American Indian art, which includes Pueblo pottery, Navajo textiles, kachina dolls, and jewelry. They also offer a wonderful assortment of antique furniture, including Stickley, Mission, Arts and Crafts, and Spanish Colonial furniture. Hours vary.

OBSIDIAN GALLERY
4320 North Campbell Avenue, Suite 130
(520) 577-3598
www.obsidian-gallery.com

Specializing in fine contemporary crafts, works in clay, fiber, metal, jewelry, glass, wood, and mixed media are featured at this well-known gallery. Past rotating exhibits have included El Dia de los Muertos (Day of the Dead), a multimedia exhibition featuring works by more than 30 local artists. Open Monday through Sunday.

PHILABAUM GLASS STUDIO AND GALLERY
711 South Sixth Avenue
(520) 884-7404
www.philabaumglass.com

This working studio and gallery is internationally known for its contemporary blown-glass pieces. Artist Tom Philabaum's works are exhibited throughout North America, Europe, and Mexico. Here at his studio you will be mesmerized by Tom and his team as they shape molten glass into sculptures. Call for specific times.

The gallery shows a wide assortment of contemporary glass art by studio artists from across the country. A featured artist exhibition changes every few months. The gallery is open Tuesday through Saturday.

RAICES TALLER 222 ART GALLERY & WORKSHOP
218 East Sixth Street
(520) 881-5335
www.raicestaller222.org

Raices (roots) and Taller (workshop) is both a gallery and a workshop. The brainchild of a group of local artists, it's the only Latino-based nonprofit cooperative contemporary gallery in the city. Located in the historic Warehouse District, this is a terrific and vibrant art space. The gallery offers workshops in silk-screening, silver sand casting, and papier-mâché and is renowned for its unique Dia de los Muertos (Day of the Dead) exhibits. Open Friday and Saturday or by appointment.

RANCH HOUSE GALLERY AT AGUA CALIENTE PARK
12325 East Roger Road
(520) 749-3718

Located in the original ranch house in the Roy Drachman Agua Caliente Park, this small gallery in a beautiful setting features works by artists from Pima County with a focus on Southwest themes. The shows change every six weeks and have included photography, oil, watercolor, and sculpture. Admission is free. The gallery is open

Close-up

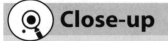

Louise Serpa—Rodeo Photographer

A Vassar girl, Louise Serpa never imagined that she would spend most of her adult life in dusty rodeo arenas all over the Southwest. So how did this self-described NYC debutante become the most well-known and respected female rodeo photographer in the country?

One of the world's most renowned rodeo photographers, Louise Serpa is a Tucson treasure. PHOTO BY M. PAGANELLI VOTTO

A divorced mother with two young daughters, Serpa moved to Tucson in 1960. While watching a friend's child compete in Junior Rodeo she grabbed a camera, started taking photos, and got bitten by the shutterbug. Fascinated by the athleticism of the rodeo riders and drawn to the endless energy of the arena, she started following the circuit, taking pictures as a hobby. What started out as a hobby, however, became a necessity after one of her daughters came down with severe rheumatoid arthritis. Her first paying shots were taken with a $27 Argus C3, and she sold the photos for pennies apiece to make money to cover medical expenses. In 1963 she was the first woman photographer permitted to shoot inside any professional arena and that was the beginning of a stellar career that has spanned several decades.

Serpa was inducted into the Cowgirl Hall of Fame in Fort Worth in 1999 and is the recipient of numerous awards. Her photographs are exhibited at museums and galleries worldwide. Her highly acclaimed book, *Rodeo* (Aperture Press), is a real insiders' look at the world of rodeo illustrated by her amazing photographs. Her work can be purchased via her Web site: www.louiselserpa.com.

Wednesday through Sunday. The ranch house itself is a piece of Tucson history, completely furnished with period antiques and wonderful historic photos of the surrounding park area.

i The large neon sign beckoning visitors for a night's stay at Ghost Ranch Lodge near downtown Tucson was designed by artist Georgia O'Keeffe.

SANTA THERESA TILE WORKS SHOWROOM
439 North Sixth Street
(520) 623-1856
www.santatheresatileworks.com

Santa Theresa artisans make one-of-a-kind handcrafted and painted tile works at this working studio. Located in the historic Firestone Building, it's amazing to see the creativity at work here—from individual custom tiles to full-scale artworks and murals in fantastic designs and colors. Here you can browse the showroom and see the works in progress at the studio. Santa Theresa has also produced several public artworks in town; ask for a copy of the guide listing locations. If you're creative, the studio offers many workshops throughout the year. Open Monday through Saturday.

SETTLERS' WEST GALLERIES
6420 North Campbell Avenue
(520) 299-2607
www.settlerswest.com
Settlers' West has been around since the early '70s and in that time has earned a reputation for beautiful and unique works that represent Arizona (wildlife and Western works predominate). Open Monday through Saturday.

TOHONO CHUL PARK GALLERY
7366 North Paseo del Norte
(520) 742-6455
www.tohonochulpark.org
Tohono Chul Park's small gallery rotates works of regional artists with about 16 changing exhibits each year. Past exhibits have included American Indian art, photography, and Mexican tile art. The desert-garden park also has a gift shop, with one-of-a-kind items by local artisans, and a restaurant with two outdoor patios. High tea is served in the afternoon. (See the Restaurants chapter.) There is a charge to access the gallery.

Art Museums

CENTER FOR CREATIVE PHOTOGRAPHY
University of Arizona campus
1030 North Olive Road
(520) 621-7968
www.creativephotography.org
Established in 1975 and located across from the UA Museum of Art, this one-of-a-kind photographic center and museum is known throughout the world for its extensive archives and collections of works by important twentieth-century photographers. The center contains more than 60,000 photographs, galleries, research facilities, and a library. The library covers all aspects of photography and includes more than 10,000 monographs, catalogs, books, periodicals, and microfilms. Hundreds of hours of videotaped interviews and lectures by noted photographers are also available for viewing in the library. The museum store carries the largest selection of photography books in Arizona, along with photography-related gift items.

Southwest photographer Ansel Adams and Dr. John P. Schaefer, then president of the university, conceived this center, which now houses the late photographer's complete archives, in 1974. The other several dozen archival collections housed at the center include Richard Avedon, Ernest Bloch, Dean Brown, Wynn Bullock, Harry Callahan, Louise Dahl-Wolfe, Andreas Feininger, Sonya Noskowiak, Marion Palfi, Aaron Siskind, W. Eugene Smith, Frederick Sommer, Paul Strand, and Edward Weston. Prints of archival work can be viewed with reservations.

The center is open Monday through Friday from 9:00 a.m. to 5:00 p.m. and Saturday and Sunday from noon to 5:00 p.m. Admission and events are free.

MUSEUM OF CONTEMPORARY ART (MOCA)
191 East Toole Avenue
(520) 624-5091

MOCA on the Plaza
149 North Stone Avenue
www.moca-tucson.org
Founded in 1977, MOCA exhibits the work of avant-garde contemporary artists with 8 to 12 temporary exhibitions each year, some solo exhibitions, and some thematic group exhibitions. The museum offers a variety of education and outreach lectures and events designed to educate the community about issues and ideas in contemporary art. MOCA is Tucson's only public institution devoted exclusively to the art of our time. The Toole Avenue location is open Thursday through Sunday; the Plaza location is open Monday and Thursday through Saturday. There is an admission fee.

TUCSON MUSEUM OF ART AND HISTORIC BLOCK
140 North Main Avenue
(520) 624-2333
www.tucsonarts.com

Founded in 1924, the Tucson Museum of Art was housed at several sites in the city before the current museum was built in 1975 on the site of Tucson's original Spanish presidio. The complex takes up an entire city block in the heart of downtown.

Besides the modern main building, the site has towering shade trees, a bubbling fountain, outside sculptures, and courtyards. The complex also includes five distinctive homes built between 1850 and 1906. La Casa Cordova, a restored 1850s-era home that is believed to be the oldest house in town, replicates life during that time and contains a small presidio museum. Casa Romero House is now a pottery studio, library, and part of the museum's art school. The Hiram Stevens House, built in 1866, is now the home of the Cafe a la Carte. The historic Edward Nye Fish House houses the Goodman Pavilion of Art of the American West. J. Knox Corbett House, a 1907 restored mission revival home, is furnished with period pieces and is open for tours.

The Tucson Museum of Art houses a permanent collection of more than 6,500 works of art. The focus is the Americas, including pre-Colombian, Spanish, colonial, Western American, and contemporary American art. Each year it hosts 8 to 10 changing and traveling exhibitions of work in all media.

The noncredit Art School has operated for over 50 years and offers classes in ceramics, sculpture, painting, drawing, theater arts, mixed media, art history, and art criticism for students 5 through 105.

Inside the main building is a gift shop offering many one-of-a-kind handcrafted ceramic, wood, fabric, and jewelry items from local artists, as well as posters, books, and greeting cards from around the world. The outdoor area hosts concerts, block parties, art festivals, the fall Holiday Craft Market, the spring Artisans Market, and more. You'll also find an adorable cafe, Cafe à la Carte (see the Restaurants chapter), with outdoor seating at umbrella-covered tables or indoor seating at cheerful bistro tables.

You could spend all day here, especially if you plan on venturing off into the surrounding Historic Block, where other small artsy shops abound.

Labor Day through Memorial Day, the museum is open Tuesday through Saturday from 10:00 a.m. to 4:00 p.m. and Sunday from noon to 4:00 p.m. It's closed on Monday from Memorial Day to Labor Day, as well as for major holidays. Admission fees vary; free to those 12 and younger. First Sunday of the month is free.

UNIVERSITY OF ARIZONA MUSEUM OF ART
Park Avenue and Speedway Boulevard
(520) 621-7567
www.artmuseum.arizona.edu

Located on the University of Arizona campus, this museum is open to the public throughout the academic year, with limited summer hours. The permanent collection has more than 4,000 works, including Rembrandt, Pontormo, Degas, Arp, Piranesi, Picasso, O'Keeffe, and Rothko. It also houses one of the Southwest's most complete collections of art from the Renaissance to the present day, thanks to a donation by Samuel H. Kress in the 1950s of more than 50 works. Most noteworthy are the collections of European and American nineteenth- and twentieth-century paintings and sculptures. Most of the permanent collections are displayed on the second floor and are rotated several times a year. The first floor features changing exhibits.

The museum is open Tuesday through Friday from 9:00 a.m. to 5:00 p.m. and Saturday and Sunday noon to 4:00 p.m. Closed on university holidays. There is no admission fee.

Murals and Public Art

Though wall paintings have been found in the ruins of prehistoric Indian kivas dating back 1,000 years, Tucson's modern mural movement began in the 1950s and 1960s when a number of local banks commissioned interior murals—painted and mosaic—featuring historic images of Tucson and Arizona. By the 1970s murals began showing up in different neighborhoods. The artists who produced them were influenced by such artists as José Orozco and Diego Rivera. Many murals rich in Mexican American images were created on the outside walls of neighborhood centers, beginning with the El Rio Neighborhood Center. Five more were created at other centers, incorporating imagery from other cultures including Yaqui, Tohono O'odham, and African-American.

During the 1980s financial support from the city of Tucson, Pima County, community service organizations, and private businesses helped create dozens more murals in the area. Today Tucson sports hundreds of murals and public art throughout the community, with more created each year. Schools, realizing that getting students involved in mural projects was great for the students' self-esteem, sought funds to create murals on playground walls, ramadas, and inside the school buildings. The Arizona Commission for the Arts responded with funding to send artists to schools to help the students create these murals, and today there are more than 66 murals at more than 40 schools.

One of the most visible pieces is Tucson artist Simon Donovan's $2.4 million **Diamondback Rattlesnake Bridge,** created for the city of Tucson. This magnificent footbridge spans Broadway just west of Euclid Avenue. A companion bridge completed in 2007, the 240-foot **Basket Bridge** spans Park Avenue where it becomes Euclid. Designed by Rosemary Lonewolf, the metalwork features designs of coyote tracks and lizards. Nearby, where the Barraza-Aviation Parkway meets East Broadway, you'll see black-and-white historical images on ceramic tiles conceptualized by graphic designer Stephen Farley.

The fanciful Sun Tran bus stops downtown include a 1956 Chevy near the corner of East Broadway and Fourth Avenue, while the stop on North Church Avenue and West Pennington Street blooms with giant purple flowers. Farther uptown on North Stone Avenue, you can't miss the 630-foot colorful mural by Pasqualina Azzarello. Many major thoroughfares in town are sprinkled with beautiful ceramic artworks, tiles, and wrought-iron sculptures of desert plants and animals, much of it funded by the Department of Transportation.

Other public art is very visible, too. From the sculpture dubbed *Sonora,* which stands in front of the downtown library, to the rock work that lines either side of Mountain Avenue, Tucsonans don't even have to cross the doors of a museum to see art. Most of the works come from the city and county One Percent for Art budget and have met with public approval. The UA campus and PCC campus also display many types of public artworks.

With numerous murals and public art scattered citywide, it's a good idea to have a guide. The **Tucson/Pima Arts Council** (520-624-0595) offers a select listing at their Web site: www.tucsonpimaartscouncil.org; click on "Public Art Collection." These works have become a vital part of Tucson's art scene and heritage. Hunting down this unique art makes for an interesting and out-of-the-ordinary afternoon tour of the Old Pueblo.

Historical Museums

ARIZONA HISTORICAL SOCIETY
Tucson Main Museum
949 East Second Street
(520) 628-5774
www.arizonahistoricalsociety.org

This museum is much more than dusty exhibits tracing the history of the state. Here you'll find hands-on exhibits, most notably the period rooms where you can see how Arizonans lived and worked through the decades. The museum also houses an extensive photo exhibit, a research library, and a Mining Hall, where visitors can learn about the impact this industry made in Arizona. The gift shop is great, too. The Downtown Museum, in the Wells Fargo Bank, 140 North Stone Avenue, highlights Tucson history with rotating exhibits. There are varying admission fees. (See the Attractions chapter.)

ARIZONA STATE MUSEUM
University of Arizona campus
Park Avenue and University Boulevard
(520) 621-6302
www.statemuseum.arizona.edu

In this museum you'll find items that made Arizona what it is today. The exhibits detail Native American life from prehistoric times to the present. You'll find pottery, baskets, clothing, and all the other artifacts that made up daily life, all with detailed information on how they were used. The gift shop offers Native American arts and crafts. Open to the public Monday through Saturday 10:00 a.m. to 5:00 p.m. and Sunday noon to 5:00 p.m.

FORT LOWELL MUSEUM
2900 North Craycroft Road
(520) 885-3832
www.arizonahistoricalsociety.org

This small but unique museum features exhibits about military life on the Arizona frontier and is located in the reconstructed commanding officers' quarters, which were established in 1873. You'll find it in Fort Lowell Park at the corner of Craycroft and Fort Lowell Roads. Open Wednesday through Saturday 10:00 a.m. to 4:00 p.m. Lots of special activities take place throughout the year, including walking tours, lectures, and living history events. Admission fees vary.

SOSA-CARRILLO-FRÉMONT HOUSE MUSEUM
151 South Granada Avenue
(520) 622-0956
www.arizonahistoricalsociety.org

Built in the 1870s, this hidden treasure is located in the Tucson Convention Center complex between the music hall and the arena. The museum features exhibits about Tucson's Hispanic pioneer families, period room settings, a museum shop, and special exhibits. The museum also offers fabulous walking tours of downtown historic areas, lectures, and special activities. It's open Wednesday through Saturday from 10:00 a.m. to 4:00 p.m. There is an admission fee, but it's free on the first Saturday of each month.

THE NATURAL WORLD

Few cities on Earth have natural settings as spectacular as Tucson's. Going from Tucson on the desert floor to its highest surrounding mountain peak is equivalent to going from Mexico to Canada in one hour, so varied are the flora, fauna, and climates. It isn't man-made trappings like buildings that characterize Tucson, it's nature. You'll get to know the real Tucson in this chapter.

The Sonoran Desert covers approximately one-third of Arizona, from Tucson west into California and south into Mexico and the Baja Peninsula. Out of this desert grow several mountain ranges and a remarkable array of plants, animals, and natural resources—not to mention several million people in cities like Tucson, Phoenix, and Yuma and in Mexico. The Sonoran Desert floor lies 3,000 feet above sea level but rises to more than 9,000 feet in the mountain ranges surrounding Tucson. The city of Tucson occupies 150 square miles of this desert, while metropolitan Tucson covers 550 square miles. Pima County, wherein the bulk of the metropolitan area lies, occupies 9,240 square miles, almost half of which is Indian reservation.

But before you venture into this desert region, take a few moments to review the Pronunciation Guide. Many of our words for plants, animals, and places come from Spanish and Native American languages. Here's a sample of some you might need to know. Learning how to pronounce these strange-looking words will be of great benefit as you travel in and around Tucson and through this chapter.

PLANT LIFE

Perhaps the most remarkable aspect of our desert is its plant life. Contrary to popular opinion, the desert teems with plant life, ranging from the most majestic of them all, the saguaro cactus, to carpets of spring wildflowers. That's because, for a desert, the Sonoran is fairly wet, averaging more than 11 inches of rainfall and only 17 short-lived freezing lows a year in the Tucson area.

Pronunciation Guide

agave	uh-GAH-vee	ocotillo	oak-oh-TEE-yo
Ajo Way	AH-hoe Way	paloverde	pah-lo-VER-day
arroyo	ah-ROY-oh	Pima	PEEM-ah
cholla	CHOY-ya	Rillito	ree-EAT-oh
Cruz	cruise	Sabino	sah-BEAN-oh
gila	HEE-la	saguaro	sah-WAH-ro
Ina Road	EYE-nuh Road	Tanque Verde	tank-ah VERD-ay
javelina	have-a-LEEN-uh	Tohono Chul	toe-HOE-no CHEWL
Mam-a-gah	MOM-uh-ga	vaquero	vak-CARE-oh
mesquite	m'SKEET	yucca	YUCK-uh
nopalito	no-pah-LEE-toe		

Cacti are perhaps the most unusual and most noticeable of the desert plants. Cacti are succulents, meaning that they have an uncanny ability to store water. They also typically have a built-in defense mechanism, thwarting predators and the curious with their almost-indefatigable needles. Some of these prickers are so tiny they appear invisible, but one slight touch and the uninitiated will painfully learn otherwise. One of the neat things about cacti is their constancy. Day after day and year after year, they remain green and stable and sturdy.

It's the Gila woodpecker and the gilded flicker who make those nest holes in the saguaros. The Gila woodpecker creates a new nest annually. When that hole is later abandoned, other creatures, such as lizards or even pygmy owls, move into the cool interior. Gilded flicker cavities tend to be on the north or northwest side of the saguaro.

Saguaro

Say the word *cactus* and what usually comes to mind is the saguaro. Saguaro means "giant cactus" in Latin, and it grows only in the Sonoran Desert. A protected species, it has come to be a symbol of Arizona and even the entire West. Saguaros can reach an amazing 50 feet in height and weigh more than two tons, most of it stored water. It takes 75 years for a saguaro to even begin to grow its first arm or two, and they can grow up to 20 or more arms.

The saguaro is home to a number of desert dwellers, as evidenced by the many holes you'll see in them. Hole makers include pack rats, Gila woodpeckers, and other birds. When tenants move out, others take occupancy, including elf owls, purple martins, and sparrow hawks. The saguaro's insulation keeps its internal temperatures about 20 degrees cooler than the outside air, which makes it a mighty inviting dwelling to the little ones. In April or May the saguaro cactus blooms with waxy white flowers at the tip of its arms or main trunk. The flowers eventually give way to crimson-colored fruit. For centuries Native Americans have harvested the fruit for food.

It has become quite popular to incorporate saguaro ribs into furniture or other home accessories, but anyone who does so can only use saguaros that are already dead and felled—and even then only with a permit. Landscapers and developers can obtain permits to relocate saguaros, but in truth those over 12 feet rarely survive the transplant, taking three to five years to die. Although you can see saguaro cacti anywhere in the Tucson area, including many front yards, Saguaro National Park (east and west units) has thousands, many of them giants, and is easily accessible. (Read all about the national park—actually a preserved parkland with units on either side of Tucson—in our Parks and Recreation chapter.)

The nonprofit Arizona Native Plant Society is a great resource for learning more about indigenous plants. They sponsor field trips and workshops and distribute a statewide newsletter with articles on native plants, landscaping, and conservation. For more information, go to www.aznps.org.

Compared with the saguaro cactus, made famous in movies, paintings, and postcards, the desert's other cacti are relative unknowns. Cacti are native to the Americas and encompass over 1,000 species; in southern Arizona, we have 100 of them, each one more odd-looking than the next.

Ocotillo

The ocotillo cactus appears as a stand of tall, spindly sticks spreading upward and outward forming a V shape. And though the cactus may seem dead, a good rain will produce hundreds of tiny bright-green leaves up and down each of its spindles. In spring the ocotillo sprouts gorgeous red blooms several inches high at the tops of its spindles. Under the right conditions, the ocotillo is truly a beauty of the desert.

Prickly Pear

Another common cactus is the prickly pear, so named because its dark red fruits resemble pears. Those brave enough to tackle the fruit make it into a variety of prickly pear edibles like jelly and candy. The prickly pear cactus itself looks like a collection of green oval pads stuck on one another. These pads are a favorite Mexican vegetable, called nopalito, albeit quite tricky to harvest. Prickly pears can be green or a lovely purple hue.

Organ Pipe

The organ pipe cactus is so called because it sprouts a clump of tall slender arms that reach skyward, resembling the pipes of an organ. From afar, it has much the same coloration and riblike appearance of a saguaro, but its shape is different and its arms much thinner and straighter.

Cholla

Another cactus is the cholla, of which there are many varieties. Any cactus that looks like a miniature tree—with trunks and lots of squiggly little branches covered with prickers—is probably a cholla. One type of cholla is called jumping cholla because its spiny protrusions supposedly leap off and attach themselves to unwary passersby. This is quite an exaggeration, but they will attach if bumped; then it's the victim who jumps. Another is the teddy bear cholla, named because its needles resemble a fluff of teddy bear–like fleece, but don't be deceived by its appearance. Other cacti include the barrel and the hedgehog, both of which sprout brilliantly colored blossoms in springtime. Remember that all cacti have needles, some more visible and ferocious than others, so it's wise to look but don't touch.

Agave

Cacti are not the only strange-looking things that grow in our desert. The agave, also a succulent, is another signature plant of the Southwest. It sprouts a rosette of thick, hard, sharp-tipped leaves out of the ground. But the agave's most amazing feature is a stalk that grows straight up from the center of the leaves, sometimes reaching 15 to 20 feet, with smaller branches near the top that sprout large clusters of flowers. Protruding majestically out of the scrubby desert landscape, this plant can easily be mistaken for a tree because of its mammoth height and shape. It has earned the nickname "century plant" because it takes so long for the plant to bloom—up to 30 years. Some species bloom only once after all that work and then die. Beyond its striking looks and amazing life cycle, the agave has another claim to fame—it's an ingredient in tequila, a liquor produced primarily in Mexico and made famous by a tasty frozen concoction as well as a song (hint: "Margaritaville").

i Care for a fascinating stroll around the University of Arizona campus? Click on over to http://arboretum.arizona.edu/plantwalks.html and find the downloadable plant walk and bird habitat maps. Along your self-guided tour you'll see a baobab tree, a boojum, and lots of native flora.

Yucca

And then there's the yucca, which looks like it might have stepped out of a science fiction movie set. Unlike the agave, yuccas have a stem or trunk on which the leaves grow—long, thin daggerlike leaves that are more often brown than green nearer the ground, giving the impression the plant is wearing a hula skirt. Nicknamed "Spanish dagger" for obvious reasons, the yucca also sprouts a stalk from its center that bears a large cluster of wheat-colored flowers in spring. Native Americans use the tough and fibrous yucca leaves for weaving baskets, sandals, and rope and its roots for soap. Although not unique to the Sonoran Desert, yuccas do seem to like it here. One of the larger and more famous varieties is the Joshua tree, which can have a life span of 500 years and is more commonly found near the California border.

Close-up

The Saguaro Harvest

When the beautiful white flower of the saguaro ripens in summer, it is harvested by the Tohono O'odham (desert people) who have made their home in the Sonoran Desert for thousands of years. The fruit is harvested using a pole (kuipad) about 12 feet long made of saguaro ribs with a pointed stick made of mesquite tied to the end. The end of the stick is used to knock the ripe fruit (called bahidaj in the O'odham language) from the cactus. The pod is split open to reveal the magenta flesh and tiny black seeds inside. The harvest is a very spiritual event that reflects the O'odham's respect for nature; no fruit is picked until the saguaro is asked to give its blessing to the harvest, and great care is taken to pick only the ripest fruit.

The pulp is collected in baskets, cooked, and strained to make a delicious syrup and jam, and the seeds are dried and ground to make nut butter. The O'odham also collect any sun-dried pulp (gune) that has fallen on the ground or stuck on surrounding trees. This crunchy sun-dried fruit is eaten like candy. The syrup is also fermented to make wine that is drunk during the annual rain dance ceremony (Nawait I'i). You can participate in this unique seasonal event through the Arizona-Sonora Desert Museum (520-883-2702). Reservations are critical.

Ripe fruit bursts from the saguaro in late June. COURTESY OF TOHONO O'ODHAM COMMUNITY ACTION

Creosote Bush

One of the oldest living things on Earth makes its home in the Arizona desert—the creosote bush, which has been around for about 11,000 years. But to be honest, most longtime residents of Tucson wouldn't recognize one if they tripped over it. That's because the creosote is more known by smell than by sight. Accompanying almost the first drop of desert rain are two distinct aromas—one is earth (or dirt or dust to some noses) and the other is the almost tarlike fruity smell emitted by the creosote that actually comes from a resinous coating on its stem and leaves. It's a smell we've grown to love and appreciate, for it signals rain.

Cereus

It may not be fair to introduce you to this next plant, because your chance of seeing it is slim to none. It is the night-blooming cereus, a nocturnal flower with delicate white petals and a baby's breath–like center of yellow stamens that blooms only during a single night in June. If you happen to be in Tucson during June, contact the Tohono Chul Park (520-575-8468) and you may be lucky enough to be there when this rain plant unfurls its flowers. (You'll find Tohono Chul Park listed in the Attractions chapter.)

i Visit the lovely and serene Tucson Botanical Gardens at 2150 North Alvernon Way to get a close look at Tucson's amazingly varied plant life. The garden offers tours, lectures, classes, workshops, and numerous special events. The small but impressive Edmund L. McGibbon Reference Library contains more than 2,000 books and periodicals on regional horticulture, botany, gardening, and natural history for on-site use and is open Monday, Wednesday, and Friday from 1:30 to 4:30 p.m. Call (520) 326-9686, ext. 20, for more information.

TREES

Yes, trees do grow in Tucson. Two of the most prominent native trees are the paloverde and the mesquite. The latter has become popular among barbeque aficionados and fireplace owners as a wood with great burning qualities and a pleasant aroma. In fact, that delicious smoked steak you dined on last week in Seattle or Chicago may well have owed its distinctive flavor to an Arizona mesquite tree.

Botanically, the mesquite tree is a legume (yes, bean). It has a dark bark with twisting branches and small fernlike evergreen leaves. Many mesquites never become more than scrub due to lack of water. Like many other desert dwellers, it has been a source of food, fuel, medicine, and containers for Americans, Native and otherwise, for centuries. And the bees use the blossoms to make a delicious edible honey. It is a protected tree, and cutting is allowed by permit only. There are several bosques of mesquite around Tucson providing lovely shaded neighborhoods for the lucky residents. (Check out our Neighborhoods, Neighboring Towns, and Real Estate chapter for some tips on finding them.)

Prolific in the desert, the paloverde tree (paloverde means "green stick" in Spanish) is named for its beautiful lime-green bark. It doesn't have leaves and doesn't need them because photosynthesis takes place throughout the tree, but it does have thin needles (long or short, depending on the variety). The paloverde is at its most glorious in spring when it is covered with a cascade of golden yellow fleecelike blooms. A street lined with paloverdes is a sight not to be missed in the Tucson spring.

Many nonnative trees grow here as well, often with a little help from a garden hose. Local favorites are citrus trees—grapefruit, orange, lemon, and lime. You will see at least one of these lush green-leafed beauties growing in many a back or front yard, particularly in the midtown neighborhoods like Sam Hughes and El Encanto and in some foothills areas. (See the Neighborhoods, Neighboring Towns, and Real Estate chapter for a description of these neighborhoods.) These trees give Tucsonans three precious commodities—shade, undeniably the best-tasting fruit to be had, and in spring the wonderful smell of the citrus blossom.

No discussion of local plant life would be complete without mention of the desert broom. The desert broom seems to be green even when everything around it is browning from lack of water. It goes to seed around November or December, and each plant produces hundreds, possibly thousands, of fluffy white seeds. Its branches were used as brooms by the pioneers, and some Native Americans chew the stems to ease a toothache.

ANIMALS AND OTHER THINGS

The first thing you should know is that our animal life is prolific, in part because the desert is relatively wet and in part because it produces so many things for the animal population to consume and live in or under. The second thing you should know is that most of the scary sagas you've heard about the animal life are quite exaggerated. Many of our four-legged and feathered inhabitants are certainly unusual, though, and will no doubt pique your curiosity.

Birds

Among the most fascinating bird dwellers of the Tucson area are the roadrunner and Gambel's quail. The television cartoon characterization of the roadrunner is not too far off base. It usually travels by foot rather than by flight; in fact, the roadrunner is the fastest American bird afoot, traveling at least 15 miles an hour when racing away from predators. It can reach 2 feet in length, mostly tail and legs with a silly-looking feathery topknot. Perhaps it comes as no surprise that the roadrunner is a member of the cuckoo family. Although you won't likely find one sprinting across a city street, they are fairly easy to spot in less built-up areas.

i The Tucson Audubon Society offers a wide variety of free day trips to get you acquainted with the birds of Arizona. Visit www.tucsonaudubon.org for further information.

Gambel's quail also seems to prefer feet to flight. (Fortunately for the bird and for us, this is not the quail sought after by hunters and treasured for its flavor.) Its primary mark is a reddish teardrop-shaped plume atop its head. To see how popular this bird is with the human population, just enter any Southwest or Arizona specialty shop and you will find numerous replicas of it—from mailbox flags to lawn ornaments to T-shirt art. But seeing them for real, especially as a family unit, is quite a remarkable sight. After the chicks are born in spring, the family travels around the desert on foot—an adult, followed by perhaps a dozen tiny young, followed by the other adult—all in a row. Be careful when driving along county streets lest you disturb and perhaps even injure this marvelous procession.

The Sonoran Desert has more species of birds—about 500—than any other arid region on Earth, making it a top spot for birders. You may not be a master spotter, but you will easily recognize hummingbirds, ravens, pigeonlike mourning doves, wrens, owls, and woodpeckers.

Mammals

As for furry friends, you might expect to see chipmunks and squirrels only in heavily treed areas. Don't be surprised when you see them in the desert, too. Other animals you're likely to spot in the rural environs include coyotes, 10-inch-high kit foxes, mule deer—so named because of their floppy, mulelike ears—and jackrabbits with elongated ears and legs. In higher elevations you may see bobcats, mountain lions, bighorn sheep, black bears, and a strange-looking piglike creature called a javelina. A member of the peccary family, this animal has an elongated snout and caninelike teeth and travels in herds for protection.

Reptiles

But it's the reptile population that visitors to our desert find most fascinating and often most frightening. Those squiggly, sure-footed, and speedy lizards can be as small as an inch and as large as several feet in length. The variety of

Close-up

Wilbur & Wilma: Romance in the Desert

Once upon a time—and not so very long ago—a Tucson bobcat named Wilbur suffered a head injury when a bulldozer accidentally demolished his den. His mother and sister died in the accident, but young Wilbur caught a break. Rescuers rushed him for emergency care to the Tucson Wildlife Center.

There Lisa Bates, director of the center, and her team of volunteers saved Wilbur's life. He still has occasional seizures and will need to remain at the center the rest of his days because of his need for daily meds, but he is safe and well cared for.

The Tucson Wildlife Center is a nonprofit volunteer organization that focuses on a special sort of three Rs—the rescue, rehabilitation, and release of wild animals. They take in large mammals, raptors, and other large birds. Patients stay only until strong enough to be released. Clients include orphans, some just hours old, and trauma victims. A partial list of patients includes Bubbles the javelina, who endured a gunshot wound; Cochise the eagle, who ate a rodent that had been poisoned; and Igor the black vulture, who was captured for use in religious cult ceremonies.

Since the center opened in 2000, the volunteers have saved countless lives—coyotes, gray foxes, javelinas, bobcats, raccoons, red-tailed hawks, herons, great-horned owls, elf owls, Harris hawks, and falcons. About 50 percent of their charges have been struck by a car, and about 30 percent have been poisoned from eating rodents tainted with rat poison. Few people realize that poisoning a rat can mean death to more than just the rodent.

The Tucson Wildlife Center, tucked away on five acres on the far eastern side of town, is owned and run by Lisa Bates and her husband, Pete Lininger. Lisa got her start caring for wildlife back when she was a kid. Her first rescue was a baby javelina, shot by a hunter. In later years she studied plant pathology and received her masters degree from the University of Arizona. When she later retired from the Environmental Research Lab, she knew exactly what she wanted to do with the rest of her life: Rescue the wild animals she loves. Her dream now is to build the first wildlife hospital in southern Arizona.

At the Tucson Wildlife Center, Peanut the baby javelina recuperates from a leg injury. PHOTO BY KATE REYNOLDS

The story of Wilbur the bobcat has a delightful ending. About a year after his arrival at the center, a baby girl bobcat got into serious trouble. This baby—later named Wilma—had been mistaken for a domestic kitten while still in the wild. When a lady picked her up, baby Wilma bit her. It's the law in Arizona that a wild animal who bites a human must be put down, but Lisa went to bat to save Wilma's life. With the help of the Pima Animal Care Center, a deal was struck. Lisa promised to house Wilma forever at the center, and the baby bobcat kept her life.

So they put young Wilma in a cage next to Wilbur, just to . . . well, to get acquainted. Yes, you guessed it. Wilbur and Wilma fell in love. Really. And they will have a home together forever.

Volunteers at the Tucson Wildlife Center are on call 24/7. If you spot a wild animal in trouble, please call (520) 290-WILD (9453). They can also be reached at P.O. Box 18320, Tucson, AZ 85731 or www.tucsonwildlife.com.

lizards in the desert is almost endless, and most seem to blend in invisibly with the landscape. Some have hard spinelike intrusions covering their body, or great folds and wrinkles. The Gila monster, the largest lizard known to the United States, is a protected species recognizable by its black-and-yellow beadlike skin. It definitely has the worst reputation among lizards. Despite being the only venomous lizard in the United States, it is slow and timid and has to chew into its victim to inject poison. Odds are you will not even catch a glimpse of this shy creature, let alone be bitten by one.

Another Arizona reptile with a bad reputation, albeit a bit more deserved, is the rattlesnake. Few people realize that rattlers can be found in nearly all of the contiguous 48 states. They're simply more visible here because we spend so much time outdoors treading in their territory. In truth, however, a human stands a greater chance of being struck by lightning in these parts than being bitten by a rattlesnake. And many snakebites happen because of carelessness or bravado or even intoxication. The snake's rattle is a forewarning—listen up!

Pima County is home to eight venomous snakes, including seven varieties of rattlesnake, which can be found from the high mountains to the low desert (and occasionally in a homeowner's garage). The other poisonous snake is the small and rare coral snake, with colorful bands of red, yellow, and black. Snakes are most active in spring through fall but can be seen anytime of the year. They are more likely to wander into urban settings when searching for water during prolonged dry spells.

Spiders

Our desert is home to another well-known and often misunderstood type of fauna—spiders. One of these has been the subject of horror movies and strikes fear in the hearts of most. Yes, it's the dreaded tarantula. But unless you suffer from arachnophobia, you have no reason to fear it. Their reputation is totally unfounded and no doubt exacerbated by both Hollywood's portrayal and their sheer size. They can reach a diameter of 4 inches or more and stand several inches high. But they don't jump and typically don't even sprint very far. They do have fangs but don't often bite; if they did, it would feel like a bee sting and be no more dangerous. Tarantulas are most often seen in late summer. Females stay close to the burrows they dig, so you would be more likely to see a male as it wanders around in search of a mate. In B movies the monster tarantulas only live about 90 minutes; in real life they have unusually long life spans—males up to 10 years and females up to 25.

Of all the spiders found in the desert—including the female black widow spider, whose bite is venomous and can cause complications but is not usually deadly, and the wolf spider, which can be quite large and amazingly fast but doesn't bite—the only variety whose bite can lead to really serious complications is the brown recluse, which is not unique to this area. This spider's shape is similar to a black widow's except it is brown and, other than that, not very distinctive.

Scorpions

The scorpion is another desert creature with a fearsome reputation that's largely unfounded. Its most identifying characteristics are two claws in front and a slender whiplike tail that curves upward. They come in all sizes, from quite small to 3 inches or more in length. The smaller the scorpion, the more potent the sting. While a scorpion's sting won't really hurt a human, it can be dangerous to domestic animals like cats and small dogs—and also to small children and seniors. And because scorpions like to find comfort in air-conditioned buildings during the summer heat, they often turn up in living rooms or bedrooms, contributing to a thriving exterminating business in southern Arizona.

THE MOUNTAINS

Rising from the Tucson valley floor are four mountain ranges that ring the city. (Actually, a fifth range is sometimes included, the Tortolitas to the northwest, but we don't want to overwhelm you.) Although they are within the Sonoran Desert, the mountains differ greatly from the desert floor that's nearly 6,000 feet below them. To the north are the Santa Catalinas, east are the Rincons, south are the Santa Ritas, and west are the Tucson Mountains. The stark Tucson Mountains are so close that they almost spill into the downtown business district, while the spread of Tucson's population has reached right into the foothills of the other three ranges. But even if you never actually get up into the mountains, you certainly will notice their beauty and ever-changing hues, especially at sunrise and sunset.

Because of their elevation, the mountains provide cooler temperatures as well as flora and fauna different from the desert floor's. Here you will find the southernmost ski area in the United States at the top of Mount Lemmon in the Catalinas. You will also find cacti and giant century plants giving way to oak, aspen, and pine trees. And wildlife to be found here but not in the valley includes mountain lions, black bears, peregrine falcons, and bighorn sheep. You may even see some very unexpected un-wild life, such as cattle roaming the open ranges of the lower mountain elevations. The proximity of these mountain ranges to the city makes Tucson a place of wonder, delight, and diversity for residents and visitors alike. Each of these mountain ranges has its distinct characteristics and people playgrounds, so here is an overview of what you might see.

Santa Catalina Mountains

The name Santa Catalina, meaning Saint Catherine, comes from Father Kino, a famous discoverer whom you can read all about in our History chapter. The highest point of this 200-square-mile range is Mount Lemmon at 9,157 feet. The Mount Lemmon Highway, or Catalina Highway, is a dramatic road of steep canyons on one side and mammoth granite spires on the other, with many scenic stops along the way. We're not talking New England here, but the fall foliage show is still a sight, with golden aspens and red oaks displaying their vivid hues among towering green pine and fir trees. (For details on how to get to Mount Lemmon and what to do and see there, turn to the Attractions chapter.)

Also in the Santa Catalinas is Tucsonans' own "special oasis." It's called Sabino Canyon and is easily accessible from the city's northeast side. Actually, Sabino is just one of several exquisite canyons in this area of the Santa Catalinas, and if you've seen one canyon you haven't seen them all, because they are all very different. But Sabino is the closest, and it will satisfy nearly anyone's craving for a taste of the wilderness. The canyon is a well-developed riparian woodland of cottonwood, willow, and other native trees along a cool creek (complete with waterfalls and swimming holes) and with bountiful wildlife, all meandering along the mountainside for almost 4 miles. (Details on Sabino Canyon, including tram information, are in the Parks and Recreation chapter.)

Other attractions in the Catalinas, but not accessible by road, include rock formations known as Prominent Point, Finger Rock, Thumb, and Rosewood Point—all of which rise above the city to the north of Alvernon Way. Areas of the Catalinas that are a bit more accessible via easy hikes are Pima Canyon and the Pusch Ridge near Catalina State Park on Tucson's northwest side. (Look for details on these in our Parks and Recreation chapter.)

Rincon Mountains

To Tucson's east lie the three peaks of the Rincon Mountains, with a top elevation of 8,666 feet. Unless you are an accomplished hiker, there is no easy way to ascend this range. Because the Rincons run north to south, they do offer some spectacular sights viewed from the city: glorious reflections of the sun's colors at sunset, fierce-looking clouds rumbling toward the city during summer's monsoon storms, and a massive blanket of bright white when dusted by a rare winter snow.

The most popular way to experience the Rincons is at Saguaro National Park East (see the Parks and Recreation chapter), which offers excellent views of the mountains, not to mention its

Mule and white-tailed deer make their home in the mountains around Tucson. COURTESY OF THE METROPOLITAN TUCSON CONVENTION & VISITORS BUREAU, FRED HOOD

own amazing attractions and great spots to watch the sun setting over Tucson's western mountains. Another option is to take Reddington Pass, a rugged and dusty road that offers great vistas and some Arizona cattle-country scenes as well. Reddington Road is also the way to access the trail to Tanque Verde Falls. When running at full tilt after winter or summer storms, the falls in this narrow granite canyon are awesome, but the force of the water and the slippery rocks can create a dangerous combination. Watch your step!

The Rincons are also home to Colossal Cave, a massive underground labyrinth that indicates Arizona was once covered by ocean. It is one of the largest dry caverns in the world, and its end has yet to be discovered. Other than a movie theater, it also may be the only place around to experience a constant 70 degrees during summer's unrelenting heat. (Read about Colossal Cave in our Attractions chapter.)

Santa Rita Mountains

Have you ever heard of a mountain range without an "Old Baldy"? Neither have we. Ours can be found in the Santa Rita Mountains to Tucson's south. Its other name is Mount Wrightson, and it tops out at 9,453 feet. With no road, this Old Baldy is definitely best left to the serious hiker. The second peak of the Santa Ritas is Mount Hopkins, and located at its pinnacle is the Smithsonian's Whipple Observatory. Although accessible by a narrow switchback road, there is no point in driving it because the observatory is behind locked gates. Instead visit the observatory's visitor center at the south base of the mountain, and make a reservation for the bus tour to the observatory. (See the Attractions chapter for details.) A more down-to-earth and car-friendly way to enjoy the Santa Ritas is the beautiful Madera Canyon at about 5,000 feet elevation. Here you will find easy hiking, a cool stream, nature trails, and picnic spots. And the birding in Madera Canyon is exquisite, with species that are not seen elsewhere in the United

States. You might see elf owls, trogons, flycatchers, and up to a dozen species of hummingbirds.

Tucson Mountains

Last but not least, we visit the Tucson Mountains on the west. This range is the smallest of the four in both girth and height, but in many ways it's both more dramatic with its volcanic peaks and more people friendly with roads, trails, and other attractions. These mountains have much to offer in rich flora and fauna. At the Mam-a-gah Picnic Area, accessible by a 20-minute hike from the King Canyon trailhead across from the Arizona-Sonora Desert Museum, you will find the Tucson Mountains' only permanent source of water. Continue downstream on the wash and you will find extensive petroglyphs—ancient carvings in rock.

i Don't miss the annual night-blooming cereus event at Tohono Chul Park. This otherwise sticklike cactus produces beautiful white waxy flowers between May and August that bloom for only one night. The park has one of the largest collections in the world of these plants, and when there are enough of them blooming at one time, the park calls a "bloom night." The flowers have a highly unusual smell that attracts the sphinx moth. To find out when bloom nights are happening, call (520) 742-6455, ext. 210.

The closest spot to traverse this range, however, is at "A" Mountain, the conical little mountain that overlooks downtown Tucson. Viewable from almost any high ground in Tucson and accessible by car, it derives its moniker from the big letter "A" painted on it by each year's University of Arizona frosh class. Officially named Sentinel Peak, this is also the sight of Tucson's annual July fourth fireworks, funds and weather permitting (see the Festivals and Events chapter for details). The Tucson Mountains can be accessed from three roads: from Ina Road to Picture Rocks Road on the north side, through Gates Pass Road from Speedway Road near downtown, or on the south side via Ajo Way. This is also where you'll find Old Tucson Studios, home of many Western film shoots; Saguaro National Park West; and the exquisite Arizona-Sonora Desert Museum.

Speaking of the Arizona-Sonora Desert Museum, you may find it comforting to know that you need not necessarily spend weeks, months, or even years attempting to see firsthand the vast Sonoran desertscapes described in this chapter. It's all re-created—from birds to cacti to coyotes—in magnificent form at the museum, so if your visit to our fine city is short, make this one of your first stops. (Get the details on this world-class museum in our Attractions chapter.)

THE RIVERS

"Where the river runs dry" is a saying that really befits Tucson, because our rivers usually run nothing but dry. Remember, folks, this is the desert. Tucson boasts two "major" rivers: the Rillito and the Santa Cruz. The Rillito River runs east to west across what seems to be almost the center of Tucson. But in fact it forms the northern boundary of the city; to its north actually lies Pima County, where Tucson's population continues to spread. Rillito translates to "little creek" in Spanish (we take what we can get in these parts). The Santa Cruz River runs along what is today Interstate 19, except the river was there first. In fact, it's been used as a transportation route between Mexico and points north for centuries; the fact that the river is usually dry just added to the convenience. The strangest thing about this river, however, is that it starts its course in southern Arizona, runs south into Mexico, then makes an abrupt turn and flows back north into Arizona near Nogales. It then continues as a north-flowing river for 180 miles until it reaches the Gila River.

About the only time water runs in the rivers is after heavy rains—the summer storms of July and August and winter rains in January and February. In the interim, the riverbeds are great for walking the dog, horseback riding, or mountain bike riding. In fact, many miles right along the Rillito and the Santa Cruz have been turned into river parks for safe and scenic fun.

In addition to the rivers, dry washes, also called arroyos in Spanish, dot the landscape. These are natural or man-made pathways for rainwater. Tucson's soil is made up primarily of sand, clay, and rock, none of which have great absorption qualities. So instead of going down, water travels along the surface, entering into smaller washes, then larger ones, and eventually into the rivers. Within several days or even hours after the rains subside, the rivers and washes again run dry. Conversely, only a few hours of torrential rain will overflow these same washes and rivers, causing flooding, road closures, and property damage.

Our dry washes and riverbeds perform a vital function beyond channeling the rain. They are home to much of our desert plant and animal life.

NATURAL RESOURCES

The riches of nature abound in and around Tucson, and our two most prominent natural resources are water and minerals. Stand on nearly any high ground in Tucson and look toward the southwest, beyond the buildings of the city. You will see a large expanse of light-colored earth; this is a copper-mining plateau near Green Valley. Unlike the traditional method of underground mining, pit mining requires removing all the rock layer before sifting the earth under it to mine the copper; it's obvious the growth in this industry has not come without taking its toll on the land.

Since the dawn of time, rocks and minerals have fascinated people, providing both utility and adornment. Native Americans of the Southwest gathered turquoise and other stones for ceremonies and weaponry. Spaniards came into the Southwest in search of mineral wealth, although they dug only gold and silver, overlooking deposits of base metals like copper. Gold prospectors scoured "them thar hills" looking for the precious metal, and Tombstone was founded as a silver-mining town. Arizona towns like Bisbee and Globe still thrive on copper mining. And Tucson is host to the greatest gem and mineral event in the country, and probably the world, each February—the Tucson Gem and Mineral Show (see the Festivals and Events chapter).

Butterflies are attracted to the numerous varieties of wildflowers that grow in the area. COURTESY OF THE METROPOLITAN TUCSON CONVENTION & VISITORS BUREAU, FRED HOOD

With an annual average rainfall of only 11 inches and nearly constant sunshine, it's no wonder that water would be a precious resource in Tucson. Our desert flora and fauna generally make do with the water nature provides—plants by storing it internally for months and animals by resting during the day and foraging at night, often for the very plants that hold moisture. But what do people do?

In Arizona two-thirds of the water people use comes from underground, and in Tucson practically all our water needs are met with groundwater. It's been said that even if Tucson didn't have a rainfall in five years, no one would have to turn off the tap. But as the population increases and we look for more ways to green up our surroundings, the supply will diminish. Billions of dollars have been spent by federal and state governments, including Arizona's, to divert Colorado River water as an alternate source of water. The Colorado River no longer reaches to its outlet in the Gulf of California—we are using it up. But for now, at least, Tucson's water supply is adequate.

The reality is that no matter where one lives, water is a precious natural resource and water conservation is a wise human practice. Unlike some other cities in the arid Southwest, Tucson's population has largely accepted desert landscaping as opposed to trying to re-create Kentucky in their backyards. Grass lawns are still visible in older midtown neighborhoods, but newer housing communities are adopting desert landscaping, or Xeriscaping, whereby native and low-water-usage plants are grouped according to their water needs to conserve water.

Natural resources have long formed the backbone of Pima County's economy, often referred to as the four Cs: climate, copper, cotton, and cattle. Climate has produced a healthy tourism industry, while the mines of Pima County now produce over 70 percent of the copper mined in the United States. You may be surprised about the cotton, but drive north of Tucson, such as on Interstate 10 toward Phoenix, and you will see acres and acres of it growing with the help of irrigation. Cattle ranching has been an important part of southern Arizona since Father Kino first introduced the tame beasts in the 1690s. The first Arizona cowboys, or vaqueros, were Native American or Mexican. Although much diminished from earlier days, cattle ranches, complete with the "cowboys" who tend them, still exist, mostly in higher elevations. The flavor of the cowboy West remains strong in Tucson—from cowboy boots and Stetson hats to horseback trail riding and world-class dude ranches for cowboy wannabes.

STARGAZING

Tucson is known as the astronomy capital of the world. With nights that are nearly always clear, stars as bright as beacons, and unobstructed mountain peaks to hold our formidable astronomy tools, the Tucson area offers some of the best possible conditions on Earth for viewing outer space.

Three major astronomical observatories are located near Tucson: the University of Arizona's facilities in the Santa Catalina Mountains; Kitt Peak National Observatory, 56 miles west of Tucson; and the Smithsonian Astrophysical Observatory on Mount Hopkins, in the Santa Rita Mountains. These sites hold the most sophisticated and advanced telescopes and tracking devices ever created, some parts of which were developed by the University of Arizona. And in a more down-to-earth location, right in Tucson, sits the university's Flandrau Planetarium. (For information on visiting these places among the stars, turn to the Attractions chapter.)

Meanwhile, as you glance upward at Tucson's star-filled night skies, remind yourself that some of the world's foremost astronomers are doing the same, trying to unravel the mysteries of endless space and perhaps our own humble beginnings.

i Flandrau Science Center at the University of Arizona will help you give a star party for you and your friends at the Tucson location of your choice. The center will send out one or two student astronomers, a pair of giant binoculars, and a telescope. You and your friends can learn about the Tucson skies. Call (520) 621-STAR (7827) for more information.

THE WEATHER

In case you haven't already noticed or heard, Tucson has sunshine—more, it is reported, than any other place in the United States. The actual count is 350 days a year. (Lest you feel deceived, this refers to any day on which the sun shines at some time rather than days on which it shines all day.) To be sure, there are days in the summer months when Tucsonans look skyward, urgently pleading for just one cloud to pass by.

The average yearly high is 82 and low is 54. The hottest months on average are June and July at 99, and the coolest are December and January at 65. If this sounds too good to be true, remember that these are averages. It is just as likely that Tucson will have a number of 100-plus (or even 105-plus) days and a number of winter nights with temperatures below freezing, at least for a few hours.

Temperatures are the subject of a lot of talk in Tucson, but so is rain. In summer a word you'll hear often is monsoon—as in "When are the monsoons getting here?" or "Here come the monsoon clouds, so where's the rain?" The climatologists say using monsoon is a misnomer; a monsoon is what India or Southeast Asia experiences. But Tucsonans like its descriptive quality and aren't likely to give it up.

About mid-July, just when Tucsonans are sure they can't survive another day of 100-plus temperatures, months without rain, and rising humidity, the late-afternoon clouds begin building up—huge, rapidly moving white and dark gray clouds, tinged with reds and golds by the sun's rays still shining in the western sky. But these are fickle clouds. For days they may release no rain, or just a smattering of rain on some lucky sections of the mountains or valley. Eventually, they give us what we long for, along with ferocious winds, thunder, displays of lightning that are unparalleled, and maybe even a sky-sweeping rainbow or two or three. With the lightning also comes the fear of fire, particularly in the mountains and foothills that have been parched for months. As inaccessible as some of these places are, the mountain fires can burn for days or even weeks, fueled by high winds and not at all affected by dribbles of rainfall.

By nightfall or shortly thereafter, the rains subside and the desert is cooled off and somewhat watered down, at least briefly. Mother Nature repeats this scene, often several days a week, through July and August and often into September. And whether on any given day she will produce rain or just its trappings, only Mother Nature knows for sure; that's the way of our monsoon season. We do get a bonus with these late-summer rains: Plant life that has seemed to all but die suddenly resurrects, and birds and animals of all sorts come out of hiding to enjoy the rain and have a feeding frenzy. It's like having a second spring.

Tucson may also have a second "rainy" season, typically in December and January, when average amounts are 0.84 and 0.75 inch, respectively. (Yes, you read those numbers right—less than an inch.) These are the rains that will sometimes produce a blanket of mountain snow and, ever so rarely, a dusting of valley snow. At Mount Lemmon, however, the average annual snowfall is 175 inches, which makes downhill and cross-country skiing possible a mere hour's drive from the city. When these winter rains are normal and are followed by rains in March and April, we can expect a great spring show of blooms from the desert that lasts into early summer.

Tucsonans boast about the dry heat that results from our very low humidity levels much of the year. And indeed it is a benefit of our climate. On even the coolest winter days, one rarely feels cold or chilled during the daylight hours. For eight months of the year—October through May—you can simply count on beautiful weather for almost any outdoor activity.

Although Tucson has many attractions that make it a great place to recreate and reside, our weather certainly tops the list. It is the weather that makes possible so much of what we do, see, and enjoy in and around Tucson.

PARKS AND RECREATION

With nearly 350 days of sunshine a year and a fascinating array of recreational options, you'll find plenty of fun in the sun in Tucson! Parks and forests can be found in just about any direction—although some forests aren't quite the traditional forests you'll find elsewhere. State parks offer hiking, fishing, camping, bird-watching, and more. Pima County and the city of Tucson both maintain outstanding parks and recreation departments. Because of the location of many of the parks, there has been a great deal of cooperation among the federal, state, county, and city governments. This cooperative effort has resulted in preservation of the natural beauty of the area as well as quality service for visitors. And, if all that isn't enough, many local recreation-oriented businesses offer everything from skydiving and rock climbing to hot-air balloon rides and mountain goat pack adventures. You can even be a true city slicker by taking part in a cattle drive.

Federal land includes our most beautiful Saguaro National Park—both east and west divisions—and the Coronado National Forest, where some of the "trees" are really saguaro cacti. The national forest encompasses Mount Lemmon, which offers a cool respite in summer and snow skiing in winter, and Sabino Canyon, probably the best place around to truly experience the beauty of the area.

State parks also preserve the area's beauty. Catalina State Park on the far northwest side is a favorite for school field trips, and at Lake Patagonia (see the Day Trips and Weekend Getaways chapter) you can boat, fish, swim, or camp.

And if you think there are no urban green spaces in the Old Pueblo, you'll be happy to know that Pima County supervises more than 30 parks and recreation sites, and the city parks system is made up of several large urban green spaces, tiny little pocket parks that are just big enough for a couple of park benches, and everything in between—more than 120 sites in all. Both entities offer numerous leisure activities, classes for all ages and interests, and annual events (see the Festivals and Events chapter).

Businesses that revolve around recreation are plentiful. You'll find the expected horseback riding and hayrides (after all, Tucson was once a wild and woolly cowtown). But you'll also find caving, swimming, and hot-air ballooning.

CORONADO NATIONAL FOREST

Encompassing more than 1.7 million acres in southeast Arizona and southwest New Mexico, this forest is home to many types of cacti, as well as pine tree forests in the mountainous area, known in these parts as "sky islands." A total of 12 mountain ranges with elevations ranging from 3,000 to 10,720 feet are within the boundaries of this spectacular, biologically diverse forest.

Wildlife covers everything from roadrunners and jackrabbits to mountain lions and bears. These larger wild creatures tend to shy away from humans, so don't let that deter you from enjoying the many marvelous sites within the Coronado National Forest.

The following areas are all located in the Coronado National Forest, and most are within an hour's drive from town.

Mount Lemmon

As you travel the winding highway (designated a scenic byway in 2005) to the top of Mount Lemmon, you'll notice several changes in the vegetation. In all, five climate zones exist on this mountain. That's why there is a 20- to 30-degree temperature difference between the bottom (desert) and the top (pine forest). Camping, picnicking, skiing, hiking, fishing, and bird-watching are just a few of the recreational activities available to visitors.

As a short stop, park your car at Windy Point. The view will show you where you were just a short while ago. You might also want to take another rest at Rose Canyon Lake. Here among the whispering pines, you can enjoy a picnic, a short hike, or a little bit of fishing. As you continue to the top, follow the signs that will take you to the tiny village of Summerhaven, where a few shops, a restaurant, and a cafe can be found. And then continue on just a bit and visit Ski Valley, our lone skiing spot in the immediate area. The lifts are open year-round.

A day pass costs $5 per car, but if you plan on camping you might want to buy the weekly pass for $10 or a yearly pass for $20, available for purchase on the mountain or at locations around town.

Ski Valley on Mount Lemmon is the southernmost ski resort in the United States. PHOTO BY M. PAGANELLI VOTTO

The road can be closed due to weather or construction. Before you go, check the Mount Lemmon construction hotline at (520) 547-7510 or the USDA Forest Service Web site at www.fs.fed.us/r3/coronado.

Sabino Canyon and Bear Canyon

If you were to ask a hundred Tucsonans what THE place to take out-of-towners is, the answer would likely be . . . Sabino Canyon. Each year more than one million people visit this lovely spot. Tucked into the Catalina Mountains (it's the largest of the three major canyons in the range), Sabino Canyon is a perfect example of the ecosystem that makes up the Sonoran Desert and surrounding area. A tour of Sabino gives you a respect and love for the desert, whether it's your first time or your fifteenth.

This magnificent canyon is one of the most visited spots in Tucson. Part of the Santa Catalina Mountains, it has streams, waterfalls, various desert flora and fauna, saguaros and other types of cacti, trees, and wildlife. You can access all this beauty either by foot or tram or both. The motorized covered trams have benchlike seating and will take you on a wonderful guided tour. Drivers are volunteers well versed in the canyon flora and fauna. You'll ride on roads and over bridges built in the 1930s by the Civilian Conservation Corps (CCC). Get ready for some magnificent vistas. You can also hop on and off the tram at any of the stops along the way if you want to get a closer look or just sit at one of the many picnic spots and enjoy the hot sun and the cool breeze. Take Sunrise Drive east to Sabino Canyon Road and turn left, heading north for about 0.25 mile. Parking is $5 per day per vehicle or $20 for a yearly pass. Call (520) 749-8700 for information about Sabino Canyon and the Coronado National Forest.

Starting at the visitor center, you'll find there are several ways to enjoy the canyon. The Forest Service runs the visitor center, which also houses a gift shop. Friendly folks will give detailed information on both Bear Canyon and Sabino Canyon. The guides provide interesting narration and often can spot a bird or an animal that an untrained eye may not catch. Many people choose to ride up and walk down; because the tram also makes stops along the way, you can hop off—or back on—as long as you show the driver your ticket. The round-trip takes about 45 minutes. The tram operates 365 days a year. From December through June trams run every 30 minutes between 9:00 a.m. and 4:30 p.m. seven days a week. From July through November they run once an hour, 9:00 a.m. to 4:00 p.m. Monday through Friday. It costs $7.50 for adults and $3 for kids between the ages of 3 and 12.

Whichever way you choose, you'll be awed by the canyon's raw beauty. You'll see tall crags that reach heavenward (some intrepid folks choose to climb these high tors); running water from mountain streams; stately saguaros; hundreds of ocotillo, barrel, prickly pear, and cholla cacti; and mesquite and cottonwood trees. You may even catch a glimpse of wildlife and most certainly will see all types of birds. Picnic areas are plentiful.

i Volunteer naturalists at Sabino Canyon offer wonderful free Wednesday-night walks, a chance to get out and enjoy the beautiful Tucson evenings. Summer hikes start at 6:00 p.m. and begin half an hour later in other seasons. Call (520) 749-8700 for a schedule.

From the Sabino Canyon Visitor Center, you can also walk or ride the tram 2 miles through Bear Canyon, where you can then hike the trail to Seven Falls, a favorite of local hikers (see the hiking section in this chapter). The tram to Bear Canyon (strictly for hikers) will cost $3 for adults and $1 for children 3 to 12. Call (520) 749-2861 for recorded information about tram tours or (520) 749-2327 for a live operator.

SAGUARO NATIONAL PARK

More than 80,000 acres of land make up the two sections of this one-of-a-kind park. The area was established as a national monument in the 1930s and then upgraded to national park status in 1992. There are hiking and nature trails throughout for all ages and abilities. You'll find thousands of saguaros, plus stands of ocotillo, cholla, prickly pear, and barrel cacti. Creosote bushes and mesquite trees are also plentiful.

i For a unique adventure, take an exciting off-road jeep tour of the Sonoran Desert. These four-wheel-drive, open-air jeeps will take you on special trails designed to give you a great feel for the desert. The experienced drivers are great guides and will tell you everything you ever wanted to know about desert flora and fauna. Most tours offer day, sunrise, and sunset tours. You can also request the driver bring along some exciting wildlife (tarantulas and snakes, for example) for closer viewing. You never know what you might see on this great ride. Be sure to make reservations in advance. Try Trail Dust Adventures (520-747-0323; www.traildustadventures.com) or Sunshine Jeep Tours (520-742-1943; www.sunshinejeeptours.com).

Saguaro National Park East

When you visit this beautiful national park for the first time, you will be amazed at the sheer number of saguaro and other types of cacti found here. Cactus Forest Drive, an 8-mile tour, is astounding. This is the older of the two sections, so the saguaros are mature and may be more than 200 years old. Also known as the Rincon Mountain District because it's in the Rincon Mountains, the park is made up of more than 67,000 acres of cacti, rock formations, and desert. Wildlife residing here includes javelinas, coyotes, Gila monsters, bobcats, deer, and lizards and birds galore. You may not see all of these creatures, but if you stay until sunset, you may hear the mournful serenade of the coyote population.

Camping and hiking are allowed, but you must have a permit, available at the visitor center. Hikers are warned that this is considered wilderness hiking, which means, in this case, that it is very rocky and steep, and elevations run from 3,000 feet to more than 7,000 feet.

Vegetation changes from desert scrub to various pine trees. Bring plenty of water and a friend. Picnic areas are also available along the Cactus Forest Drive. There will be an admission fee per vehicle to the park, which is also good for Saguaro Park West. The visitor center is free and open daily (except for Christmas and New Year's Day).

Take Broadway Boulevard east to Old Spanish Trail, and then follow the signs to the visitor center. Here you can find plenty of useful information about the park. Call (520) 733-5153 for more information, or visit www.nps.gov/sagu.

Saguaro National Park West

There are two approaches to the Tucson Mountain District part of the park. The long, and not quite as interesting, way is to take Ajo Way west to Kinney Road then head north to the visitor center. This way is for the faint of heart and those pulling trailers or driving recreational vehicles. The road is flat and only slightly winding. The other way, more beautiful and just a little challenging, is to take Speedway Boulevard to Gates Pass Road. Here's where your heart will start pumping as the road narrows and the edge drops quite a distance to the desert floor. Follow the road past the Arizona-Sonora Desert Museum for about another 2 miles. The visitor center has information about the flora and fauna found in the park, as well as lovely exhibits and a bookstore.

Hiking trails snake through the area (see the hiking section in this chapter). The shortest of these trails is Cactus Garden Trail, which is only 100 yards; the longest is the Hugh Norris Trail, which is 4.9 miles one-way. Several of these trails link together or meet with longer trails in the park if you're looking for an extended day hike.

Indian petroglyphs can be found at the northern end of the park via the Signal Hill Trail. Ask for directions at the visitor center.

As in the east section of the national park, you'll find many saguaro cacti (although the saguaros here are younger than the ones in Saguaro East), beautiful rock formations, and stunning scenery. The park has wonderful hiking and biking adventures. Take the paved Bajada Loop Drive, a total of 6.0 miles, for a real taste of what the park has to offer. Picnic sites can be found along the way. There's no charge to enter this part of the park. Call (520) 733-5100 for more information, or visit www.nps.gov/sagu. The visitor center is open daily, except on Christmas and New Year's Day.

IRONWOOD FOREST NATIONAL MONUMENT

Declared a national monument by President Clinton in 2000, this wide-ranging area about 25 miles southwest of Tucson covers 129,000 acres. Included in this amazing swath of land are the desert mountain ranges of Silver Bell, Waterman, and Sawtooth; desert valleys; and one of the richest stands of ironwood trees in the Sonoran Desert. But you'll have to be equipped with a sturdy SUV or, better yet, four-wheel drive to access these wonders of nature, as the roads are unpaved, rough, and rutted. There are no facilities of any type here, just pure unadulterated nature. There are no admission, parking, or camping fees. Camping is permitted for up to 14 days, but there are no official campground sites.

If you're a nature lover who hates visitor centers, guided tours, and lots of people, this is the place for you, and it's gorgeous any time of year. There are two main points of entry for the area: Interstate 10 at Marana Road, and I-10 from the Red Rock exit, southwest on Sasco Road to Silverbell Road. A cautionary note: Many parts of the monument are very isolated; be sure to bring adequate food and water. For more information call the Bureau of Land Management at (520) 258-7208.

i For some real fun, join the Tucson Orienteering Club, which meets the third Sunday of every month. You'll learn to navigate by foot in the great outdoors, using only a topo map and compass. Visit www.tucsonorienteering.org to learn about lots of events for every skill level.

STATE PARKS

In addition to Catalina State Park, other state parks of interest in the Tucson area include Patagonia Lake State Park and Tumacacori National Historic Park (see the Day Trips and Weekend Getaways chapter). State park fees may be higher during peak seasons.

Catalina State Park

You'll find camping, hiking, picnicking, horseback riding, and some of the prettiest up-close-and-personal experiences with desert life at Catalina State Park. Located 9 miles north of the city off Oracle Road, the park covers some 5,500 acres at the foot of the Catalina Mountains. Although a state park, it's still part of the Coronado National Forest and is maintained cooperatively by the USDA Forest Service and the state of Arizona.

With its easy accessibility, over 100 picnic areas, 120 campsites, and numerous hiking trails, it's easy to see why this is such a popular spot (more 135,000 visitors a year take advantage of the diverse recreational activities).

Birders can enjoy the 1.0-mile nature loop that travels through a heavily wooded mesquite stand. The area provides shelter for many birds, including golden eagles and various falcons.

For hikers, seven additional trails lead to wooded areas through canyons; natural pools, and the ruins of a prehistoric Hohokam village. During the rainy season running water is plentiful. Elevation changes are minimal. Campers should note that wood fires are not allowed, so bring charcoal or your camp stove. Horseback riders are also welcome, but they must stay on the nature trails (see Horseback Riding later in this chapter).

Park at the visitor center for a fee of $6 per car. For more information, call (520) 628-5798 or visit www.pr.state.az.us/parks/parkhtml/catalina.html.

PIMA COUNTY NATURAL RESOURCES, PARKS, AND RECREATION

Pima County Natural Resources, Parks, and Recreation Department maintains parks and neighborhood recreation centers throughout the entire county, several of which are at public schools. In addition to the usual services, classes, sports programs, and swimming pools, the department also is responsible for a caving area (see Caving later in this chapter), operating a professional baseball complex, distributing a variety of health services, maintaining an archery range, overseeing a horseracing track (see the Spectator Sports chapter), and maintaining a campground and several hiking trails.

Kids of all ages can find something to do—whether it's the Teach Our Toddlers Skills (T.O.T.S.) program, the various teen-oriented programs, or the many senior programs and classes. Middle-agers need not feel left out. They, too, can grab a bit of fun or learning with the programs and services available at the neighborhood centers.

With more than 15 recreation centers and numerous parks, the county has something for everybody. Whether you want to learn how to speak Spanish, make your own holiday gifts, or trace your family tree, the county parks and recreation department has it.

Teens can learn babysitting skills, arts and crafts, or architecture. Little ones can learn social skills or just have fun. The department's after-school program is a big part of the county's work. Through this program, both elementary and middle school children have a safe, educational, and fun place to go after school. Fees are minimal, and the staff-to-kiddie ratio is 1 to 20.

i For an unforgettable evening, head to Gates Pass for the sunset. Tucson's desert sunsets are remarkable for their vividness and colors, and you'll get the best-ever view here. Take someone you love and a great bottle of wine, a picnic maybe.

Seniors can join the neighborhood senior centers and take classes in such things as painting or clogging. They can also join in group activities such as guided group hikes or softball. Many special activities are also planned year-round.

Health services include Well Woman Check, mobile health services, family planning, immunizations, and health evaluations for children.

Aquatics, golf, boxing, tennis, archery, hiking, and numerous other recreational activities can also be found in county parks. Classes and activities vary from season to season, and not all are offered at every recreation facility. The department publishes *Leisure Times* twice a year, which includes a complete listing of all the happenings and where they are happening. Call (520) 877-6000 for more information or check the Web at www.pima.gov/nrpr.

Pima County Parks

COLOSSAL CAVE MOUNTAIN PARK
(520) 647-7275
www.colossalcave.com

Located less than 25 miles from the city, Colossal Cave was first explored by Anglos as far back as 1879 and used by prehistoric peoples long before that. It is considered a "dry" cave, which means the formations have stopped "growing" due to lack of water. The temperature is always a comfortable 70 degrees.

At the 2,500-acre park that surrounds the cave, families can have some fun with trail rides, a riparian area for some great hiking, a museum, and several picnic sites. You can tour the working La Posta Quemada Ranch, which is also part of the park. The ranch has cookouts for large groups, and little ones get the opportunity to "pan" for gold and "rope" a steer. Birders will find the riparian area a heaven on earth.

There is a fee to enter the park and fees for the various activities. Hours differ by the season, so call ahead. Take I-10 to exit 279 and then travel 6 miles north or take the Old Spanish Trail (catch it off Broadway Boulevard). (See the

The Pima Canyon Trail features scenic mountain vistas and a rewarding but rugged hike. PHOTO BY M. PAGANELLI VOTTO

Attractions chapter for more information about Colossal Cave.)

RILLITO RIVER PARK
(520) 877-6000

Originally constructed as part of the reclamation of the riverbanks after several years of serious flood damage, this park is one of the prettiest places to exercise anywhere.

Stretching from I-10 to Campbell Avenue, this linear park is a favorite outdoor place for many Tucsonans. It's also the site of many "walks" for charitable organizations throughout the year.

Paved and unpaved paths run along either side of the river, with both sides available for skating, jogging, and walking. Cycling is limited to the north bank, and horseback riders are limited to the south side (although you'll find some great riding in the riverbed itself). The only other rules concern right-of-way. Signs are posted along the way to remind you who gives way to whom. Water fountains, restrooms, picnic areas, and parking can be found at certain cross streets, and a few picnic areas with grills are scattered throughout. Footbridges cross the river at various halfway points between the street entry points.

The landscaping is complemented by beautiful public art, mainly metal and tile work. Midway along the route is Children's Memorial Park, dedicated to hundreds of area children who have died. A large plaque engraved with the names of the children and a statue stand in tribute. The park area also has a small playground and picnic sites.

Enter the park at any major cross streets. Parking for cars can be found at the access ways.

ROY P. DRACHMAN-AGUA CALIENTE PARK
(520) 749-3718
www.pima.gov/nrpr/places/agua_pk/index.htm

The phrase oasis in the desert may be highly overused, but in the case of Agua Caliente Park, it rings true. This 101-acre park, located at 12325 East Roger Road in northeast Tucson, features a natural spring that feeds into three large ponds. Palm trees and beautiful Santa Catalina Mountain views add to the pleasures of this lovely park. Walking, wildlife viewing, birding, and picnicking in the shade are all activities open to the public. Some of the large mesquite trees are thought to be over 200 years old, and the site was first occupied as early as 5,500 years ago. Rarely crowded, the park is a terrific spot for a picnic or for lounging with a great book.

SANTA CRUZ RIVER PARK
(520) 877-6000

Beginning at Grant Road on the north and traveling to 29th Street/Silverlake Road—with a short break between Silverlake Road and Ajo Way—cyclists, joggers, walkers, and skaters take advantage of this linear park for recreation and transportation.

Sites along the way include the Garden of Gethsemane, a huge stone monument with various religious figures (see the Attractions chapter), a disc golf course, beautiful ceramic work by local artist Susan Gamble, and Tucson's largest tree—a huge eucalyptus measuring 4 feet in diameter located just under the Congress Street Bridge. Picnic sites are also available.

At El Paseo de los Arboles, a park within a park, trees can be planted in a grove as a living remembrance of a loved one or for a special occasion. This tiny park has won national recognition for planning and implementation. Planting is done on a scheduled basis.

Parking with access to the east side of the park can be found north of Speedway Boulevard or near the 22nd Street Bridge where each street intersects the bike path. Parking with access to the west side can be found just south of Speedway Boulevard.

TUCSON MOUNTAIN PARK
(520) 877-6000

Located west of the city, Tucson Mountain Park, a 20,000-acre desert preserve, has thick stands of saguaro cactus; great hiking, biking, and camping; and, some say, the best place in the Tucson Basin to see a sunset. Maintained by the county, the park borders Saguaro National Park West. Enter the park at Ajo Way and Kinney Road.

CITY OF TUCSON PARKS AND RECREATION

The city of Tucson maintains an award-winning Parks and Recreation Department. Not only does the department operate more than 125 parks (many with swimming pools, tennis courts, and picnic areas), but Parks and Rec also has year-round classes, arts and crafts shows, a zoo, an outstanding after-school and summer program, senior programs, fast-pitch and slow-pitch coed softball leagues, adult volleyball and basketball leagues, and swimming programs. The city also runs more than a dozen rec centers that serve as neighborhood meeting places for young and old alike.

The *City of Tucson Parks and Recreation Program Guide and Class Catalog* is available at any of the city's centers or area libraries and select retailers. You can also check the Web at www.ci.tucson.az.us/parksandrec for a comprehensive listing of parks, centers, and events or call (520) 791-4873 for more information.

You'll find an assortment of public art in city (and county) parks, thanks to forward-thinking local government leaders. One percent of the city's park department budget for capital improvements from bond funds is earmarked for public art. Works are chosen with the help of the Tucson/Pima Arts Council.

i For a lovely new hike in Tucson Mountain Park, try the 2.0-mile Hidden Canyon Trail. You'll enjoy lots of expansive views. Go west on 22nd Street (it becomes Starr Pass Boulevard). Just before the Starr Pass Resort, turn right onto the service drive. Wind around another 0.25 mile to the trailhead on the right. Parking is allowed along the road.

Programs, Classes, and Leisure Activities

KIDCO

(520) 791-4877

Designed with the elementary school kid in mind, this safe, creative program will please both children and parents. Arts and crafts, games, and a citywide carnival are just a few of the elements that make up this model program for participants ages 5 through 11. (See the Education and Child Care chapter.)

LATE NIGHT HOOPS

(520) 791-4870

Found at various sites throughout the city, this program gives teens 13 to 19 a place to go on Friday and Saturday nights. They can get a good workout while establishing friendships and learning sportsmanship. There are men's, women's, and coed leagues available.

SENIOR PROGRAMS

(520) 791-4121

Recognizing that many of the retirees in Tucson are anything but retiring, Parks and Rec has developed an extensive array of activities for seniors. From the Senior Olympic Festival (see the Festivals and Events chapter) to a friendly game of bridge at one of the designated senior centers, those over 50 can attend classes in everything from Tai Chi to tennis, join a collectors club or a hiking group, or just plain socialize.

THERAPEUTIC RECREATION CENTER

1000 South Randolph Way

(520) 791-4504 (TDD and voice)

Individuals with disabilities can find an assortment of recreational activities in this unique program. Monthly dances, field trips, arts and crafts classes, and special events that include the whole family are just some of the activities offered. Support groups, summer day camps, and adapted aquatics programs are also offered as part of the Therapeutic Recreation Program.

TUCSON CITY PARKS

CHRISTOPHER COLUMBUS PARK

4600 North Silverbell Road

Site of one of three city parks with a lake, Christopher Columbus Park offers sailboating—use the launch ramp—and fishing on Silverbell Lake (no swimming allowed). Picnic areas with grills, ramadas, and a playground are also in the park. Model airplane fans can enjoy their hobby at the park's model airplane facility.

Plans are under way for major upgrades and renovations at this city park. Funding is available for improvements near the lake, along the Santa Cruz and just south of Camino del Cerro. The funded improvements include a soccer field, parking, a trail staging area, and a new entrance off of Camino del Cerro; a river trail along the Santa Cruz with an equestrian trailhead; a path around the lake; and a maintenance facility. Construction is projected for completion in late 2008.

A popular feature of this west-side park is a leash-free dog run. The 14,000-square-foot area is open from dawn to two to three hours after dusk and features a Fido fountain.

FORT LOWELL PARK

2900 North Craycroft Road

A trip to this midtown lovely is more than just a walk in the park. Here you will also find a history lesson or two and see the remains of buildings that were once part of historic Fort Lowell, an outpost that guarded the town of Tucson. (See the Attractions chapter.)

Tennis courts, a swimming pool, a playground, a jogging path, an assortment of fields with and without lights, handball and racquetball courts with lights, and both sand and grass volleyball courts attract visitors all week long. A pond attracts ducks and other waterfowl. Parking and picnic spots with ramadas can also be found.

The entrance to the park and parking is just east of the intersection of Glenn Street and Craycroft Road.

Close-up

Dog Friendly Parks

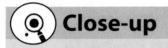

Tucson is a dog paradise—great weather and lots of places to walk—but there is a leash law, so our friendly Fidos need to head to Tucson's dog parks for off-leash exercise. Here are a few top picks with the canine set to go along with the Christopher Columbus Park dog run.

Udall Park

7290 East Tanque Verde Road

This fenced, double-gated, 43,560-square-foot area offers water fountains for dogs, picnic tables, and a few shade trees but not much grass. Open daily from 6:00 a.m. to 10:30 p.m.

Reid Park

Country Club Road and 22nd Street

This nicely fenced dog park was recently moved to the area behind the parking lot off Country Club Road. It has been refurbished and has partitioned areas for large and small dogs, water, grass, and sheltered areas and is lighted at night. Open from 7:00 a.m. to 9:00 p.m.

McDonald Park

4100 North Harrison Road (off Catalina Highway)

This grassy, hourglass-shaped 2,800-square-foot space, with separate areas for large and small dogs, offers a doggie drinking fountain and numerous plastic bag dispensers. Open sunrise to 10:00 p.m.

GOLF LINKS SPORTS COMPLEX

2400 South Craycroft Road

This wide-open recreation area is the site of many soccer games in the evening and on weekends. Four softball fields with lights are also a busy part of this park. Trees are plentiful.

HIMMEL PARK

1000 North Tucson Boulevard

With a great number of tall, mature shade trees and a gorgeous swimming pool and kids' pool, Himmel Park is one of the "coolest" spots in town. Athletes young and old can enjoy the exercise course, the Little League and soccer fields, and the tennis courts. The courts are lit at night, and the park serves as one of the sites for the city's USTA tennis league program.

For a more leisurely choice, you can always pack a lunch to munch at one of the picnic sites or grab a book from the public library on-site (don't forget to apply for your library card first).

Located just 1 block south of Speedway Boulevard on Tucson Boulevard, Himmel Park is easily accessible with plenty of free parking.

JACOBS PARK

3300 North Fairview Avenue

Jacobs Park offers all the amenities of a large city park while still maintaining the feel of a cozy neighborhood park. Located on the near west side (3 blocks south of Prince Road on Fairview Avenue), this urban green space has a new play pool, a swimming pool, a YMCA, ball diamonds, soccer fields, swings, slides, grills, picnic areas, and acres of open space where the kids can frolic; or let them cool down under the shade of one of the large old trees in the park. Weekdays will find the locals enjoying a quiet respite, while the weekends are filled with soccer league games, picnickers, and city league baseball and softball.

A YMCA, which is housed in the recreation center, is the site of many senior activities.

J. F. KENNEDY PARK

Ajo Way at Mission Road

Kennedy Park is known for its well-stocked fishing lake and as the site of some of the city's festivals, which take place in a grassy amphitheater with seating for 7,500 (see the Festivals and Events chapter). This popular south-side park also offers picnic sites with ramadas, soccer fields, multiple-use courts, Little League fields, a grassy volleyball area, and a swimming pool, in addition to the outdoor fiesta area. Kennedy Park is easy to find. Take either Ajo Way west or Mission Road south. The park is at the southwest corner of the intersection of Ajo Way and Mission Road.

LAKESIDE PARK

8300 East Stella Road

Boaters and anglers will be pleased with the fishing and boating at this east-side favorite. Boating is restricted to small sailboats, rowboats, and canoes. But Lakeside Park has much more to offer than just water sports.

All fields, with the exception of the Little League field, have lights. Picnic sites, with and without ramadas, can be found. Joggers can take a turn along a pleasant path, and kiddies can spend some time on the playground equipment.

MCCORMICK PARK

2950 North Columbus Avenue

At first glance McCormick Park (named for Ada McCormick) may appear to be one of the many tiny parks that dot the city, but on closer inspection you'll notice a baseball field, an exercise course, a grassy volleyball area, a rec center, a playground, and a fair share of picnic ramadas with grills.

Located in midtown, McCormick Park is near the Central-Lighthouse-City YMCA, a YMCA that houses a pool. The park is located about a block and a half south of Fort Lowell Road on Columbus Avenue.

MORRIS K. UDALL PARK, UDALL CENTER

7290 East Tanque Verde Road
(520) 791-4931

One of the larger and most popular Parks and Recreation centers, Udall offers the latest in recreational facilities and a senior center. The rec center has workout rooms, racquetball courts, an indoor track, arts and crafts rooms, meeting rooms, and a heated pool. The center offers myriad programs and activities. Hundreds of leisure classes are held here throughout the year. The center is open daily.

The park area is also top-shelf, with an outdoor amphitheater, lighted volleyball courts, a playground, and fields for all kinds of organized sports. Take a jog on the well-maintained jogging path, or enjoy a picnic in one of the shady ramadas.

RANDOLPH RECREATION COMPLEX

200 South Alvernon Way
(520) 791-4560

This is the city's main recreation center and will please athletes and nonathletes alike. Encompassing a gymnasium, a swimming pool, a tennis center, and performing arts and arts and crafts buildings, you can be assured there is always something going on here. Parking is plentiful.

RANDOLPH ARTS AND CRAFTS BUILDING

A complete lapidary shop, ceramics room with kilns, children's crafts room, and painting studio make the Arts and Crafts Building one of the most popular recreation sites in Tucson. The pottery shop and photo lab are located adjacent to the Arts and Crafts Building. A wide variety of classes include drawing, calligraphy, enameling, and jewelry.

RANDOLPH PERFORMING ARTS BUILDING

Dance, music, and dramatic art classes are offered here along with a dance room, music studio with piano lab, and fully equipped auditorium.

RANDOLPH RECREATION CENTER COMMUNITY BUILDING

Randolph Center's central information desk, offices, and meeting rooms can be found in this building. City basketball leagues, youth leagues, Late Night Hoops, and aerobics classes are just a few of the activities that are held in Randolph Gym. Gymnastics classes for infants through teens are held in a well-equipped gymnastics room along with a slew of great leisure classes. Check the *Tucson Parks and Recreation Program Guide and Class Catalog* for more details. The building is open Monday through Friday from 6:30 a.m. to 10:00 p.m., Saturday from 8:00 a.m. to 6:00 p.m., and Sunday from noon to 6:00 p.m. Closed holidays.

RANDOLPH SWIMMING POOL

This wonderful pool is open seasonally. Call to check on hours and programs.

RANDOLPH TENNIS CENTER

50 South Alvernon Way
(520) 791-4896
www.randolphtenniscenter.com

The United States Tennis Association (USTA) awarded Randolph Tennis Center a National Facility of the Year Award. This terrific center offers 25 lighted tennis courts, a pro shop, 10 racquetball courts, and year-round instructional programs for all ages. Monthly open tournaments for all ages and levels, tennis leagues, and racquetball clinics round out the program.

REID PARK

22nd Street and Country Club Road

You'll hear old-timers (those who've lived in Tucson for more than 20 years) still calling this beauty Randolph Park. That's because until the Parks and Rec Department decided to honor Gene C. Reid, a longtime Parks and Rec director, the park was called Randolph Park. Today the moniker Randolph is used for the Randolph Recreation Complex located adjacent to Reid Park (see separate listing above for details).

This gem in the parks department crown comprises the city zoo, a beautiful rose garden, a large pond, ball fields, picnic areas with grills and some ramadas for shade, a sports complex/baseball field, a performing arts amphitheater, and the Randolph Rec Complex.

Mature trees and plenty of grass make this an ideal spot for a family picnic. Evenings and weekends are filled with city league slow-pitch softball and volleyball games.

DEMEESTER PERFORMING ARTS CENTER IN REID PARK

22nd Street and Country Club Road
(520) 791-4873

This lovely little band shell is one of the nicest touches in Reid Park—the site of Shakespeare in the Park, numerous music concerts, and other live performances. Seating is, for the most part, on the grass. Bench seating is available for 60 to 100 people. You'll notice a molded-concrete sculpture on the band shell. The six figures represent all aspects of the arts, and the sculpture is appropriately named *Celebrate the Arts*. This was the first piece of public art commissioned under the city's One Percent for Art program.

HI CORBETT FIELD AT U.S. WEST SPORTS COMPLEX IN REID PARK

Randolph Way and Camino Campestre
(520) 791-4873

Located in the northeast corner of Reid Park, the lovely Hi Corbett Field is home to USA Baseball and the Colorado Rockies spring training. The field seats 10,000 and has snack bar facilities.

REID PARK ROSE GARDEN

22nd Street and Country Club Road

Here you'll find more than 100 varieties of roses. Cosponsored by the Rose Society of Tucson and All-American Rose Selections, Inc., the garden is located west of Reid Park Lake. (Insiders know the best blooms can be found in April.)

Reid Park Zoo offers a variety of specialized tours. One example is a behind-the-scenes tour in which you can visit the zoo kitchen and health center and other off-limits places. Check the Web site at www.tucsonzoo.com for current programs.

REID PARK ZOO
1100 South Randolph Way
(520) 791-4022
www.tucsonzoo.org

Reid Park Zoo is a highlight of any visit to the park. With 400 animals—the South American Habitat Loop features 11 habitats within three ecosystems—the zoo is a source of both education and fun for the whole family. Trained docents can answer just about any question posed, and an impressive graphics system acts as another source of information about the zoo and its denizens. As part of the public art-in-the-parks program, a series of bronzes that are modeled to scale is scattered throughout the zoo. Information about each animal is on the sculptures. It's also in braille.

Throughout the year numerous special events take place, including the Zoo Lights in December (see Festivals and Events chapter), Zoocson, A Valentine's Day Woo at the Zoo, and a Howl-O-Ween Party.

The zoo also maintains a well-respected captive-breeding program. The giant anteater breeding program is considered the most successful of its type in the world. Classes are also available, as is a great gift shop.

Admission fees vary. The zoo is open from 9:00 a.m. until 4:00 p.m. (See the Attractions and Kidstuff chapters.)

RECREATION

Archery

Pima County operates an archery range, which is located in Tucson Mountain Park, just west of the city. Open from 7:00 a.m. until dark, the range offers targets from 20 to 70 yards and three 14-target units. The more challenging units are laid out in several choices—animal, hunter, and field.

Day use is $3. Take Ajo Way west to Kinney Road. Turn north on Kinney Road and then go past Old Tucson Studios, continuing for approximately 1.5 miles.

Boating and Urban Fishing

Three city lakes offer boating (small sailboats, rowboats, and canoes only, please!) and fishing: Kennedy Lake in Kennedy Park, Lakeside at 8300 East Stella Road (at the corner of Stella and Sarnoff), and Silverbell Lake in Christopher Columbus Park.

Stocked by the Arizona Game and Fish Department, the lakes will satisfy any angler, but a fishing license is required for people over the age of 14. All boats must also be registered if motorized. Call (520) 628-5376 for more information.

LAKE PATAGONIA
400 Patagonia Lake Road, Patagonia
(520) 287-6965
www.pr.state.az.us/parks/parkhtml/patagonia.html

This 265-acre lake is very popular with desert folks—and with good reason. In addition to the swimming and hiking, fishers can angle for trout in the winter and a variety of other game fish in the other months.

Boaters can bring their own (only small boats are allowed), or you can rent a canoe, rowboat, or pedal boat for a fee plus a refundable deposit. Call the marina (also the retail store) at (520) 287-5545 for rates. There is an entry fee per vehicle for the park.

Boxing

BOXING INC.
1240 North Stone Avenue
(520) 882-8788

6121 East Broadway
(520) 829-7969

4165 West Ina Road
(520) 744-7333
Boxing is not just for guys—think *Million Dollar Baby*! A great way to get fit fast, these gyms offer over 42 classes a week, including kickboxing, muay thai boxing, grappling, sparring, and judo. The facilities at the Stone Avenue location include a full gym, cardio equipment, weights, a boxing ring, boxing bags, and wrestling mat. The smaller West Ina Road location offers free weights. Open daily except Sunday; most classes are one hour long. There is a monthly membership fee. Not sure if boxing is for you? You can try it for just $15—they'll provide gloves and wrappings.

CENTRO DEL SUR COMMUNITY CENTER
1631 South 10th Street
(520) 792-3937
At Centro del Sur Community Center, boys and girls can learn the fundamentals of boxing, get physically fit, and develop good sportsmanship. There is no fee for boxing training, but to compete you must join the U.S. Amateur Boxing Association. Equipment is provided.

Caving

CAVE OF THE BELLS
Coronado National Forest
(520) 388-8300
Part of Coronado National Forest, the Cave of the Bells with its underground lake is located in Sawmill Canyon at the end of a four-wheel-drive road on the eastern slopes of the Santa Rita Mountains. The cave entrance is gated and protected, accessible only with a key that is available at the Nogales Ranger District or in Tucson at the Coronado National Forest Supervisor's Office, 300 West Congress Street. It's better to pick up a key at the West Congress address, because they have more keys. A $50 refundable deposit is required. Call for detailed directions.

COLOSSAL CAVE MOUNTAIN PARK
I-10, exit 279, Vail
(520) 647-7275
www.colossalcave.com
Colossal Cave has a colorful history, having been used by prehistoric peoples—and by train robbers. Some say the thieves' stolen booty still lies hidden deep within the cave.

Colossal Cave tours are offered daily, but it's a good idea to call ahead, as the times change. A guided tour is a short 0.5 mile. In addition to this 45-minute tour—no reservations needed—you also have your choice of other, more "in-depth" tours.

For a slightly spooky, some might say romantic, experience, try the candlelight tour. The tour is held after hours and groups vary between 10 and 20 people, so you are afforded a more personal touch. Reservations are needed for this tour because they are only given on the second and fourth Saturdays of the month. Children under 10 cannot take this tour.

Or for a more out-of-the-way experience, dare to take the Ladder Route Tour. Donning a helmet with a headlight, you'll climb ladders, cross bridges, and crawl through narrow passageways. As with the Candlelight Tour, there is an age limit here—10 years of age. (See the Attractions chapter for details on Colossal Cave.)

CORONADO CAVE
Coronado National Memorial
(520) 366-5515
www.nps.gov/archive/coro/cave.htm
Located at the end of the Coronado Cave Trail (0.75 mile one-way) in Coronado National Memorial, this is a live cave with tunnels, stalagmites, and stalactites that is easy to explore. Two flashlights per person are required; helmets are optional. To enter the cave you must get a free visitor's permit at the visitor center. Take I-10 east and exit south on Highway 90 to Sierra Vista, then south on Highway 92 to South Coronado Memorial Drive. (From Bisbee take Highway 92 west.) Follow South Coronado Memorial Drive 5 miles to the visitor center.

KARTCHNER CAVERNS STATE PARK
Highway 90, Benson
(520) 586-4100 (information line), (520) 586-2283 (reservations)
www.pr.state.az.us

Discovered by amateur spelunkers in 1974, this incredible living cave was kept secret for 14 years until it was opened to the public in 1988 by the Arizona State Parks Department. Now the central attraction in the 550-acre park, Kartchner is a wet, or live cave, meaning that the calcite formations are still growing. You'll see amazing 70-foot-tall ceilings dripping with many-colored stalactites and stalagmites along with rare quartz needles that form birds nests and thin stalactites called soda straws that extend like spaghetti. You have to see it to believe it. The cave's relative humidity averages 99 percent year-round, and the temperature stays around 67 degrees. You'll also find a 23,000-square-foot Discovery Center full of exhibits. Reservations are critical. The park is about 50 miles south of Tucson on Highway 90. (See the Attractions chapter.)

Hiking

The Sonoran Desert and the surrounding mountains offer outstanding hiking opportunities. Some are user-friendly; others offer challenges that should only be attempted by experienced hikers. But no matter your status as a hiker, there are several important things you should do when you take a hike. One, always bring more water than you think you'll need. The desert heat can surprise you. Two, always tell someone where you're going and how long you expect to be there. Better yet, take a friend along—and make sure someone knows where the both of you are going! No matter how tempting it may be to spend several hours alone in the desert, it's best to ask a friend or two along. One more caveat: Stay on the well-marked trails to avoid getting lost.

Pima County maintains numerous trails throughout the area, many of which cross state and federal land. You may need to purchase a state permit to hike through some of these areas. During the cooler times of the year, the county also offers group hiking and nature walks. Your four-footed best friend is only allowed on certain trails and then only on a leash. Call the county parks and recreation department for details at (520) 877-6000, or check the Web site at www.pima.gov/nrpr/places/trails.htm.

Saguaro National Park's east and west divisions both have great trails that take you through various terrain from desert floor to mountaintop. The visitor centers at each part of the park have information and maps on the specific trails to be found. There are quite literally thousands of hiking areas and trails in the area, so the best bet is to stop by one of the local camping supply stores, like Summit Hut (see listing in the Shopping chapter), to purchase one of the many hiking guides available. Or contact local hiking groups and organizations (see the Insiders' tip in this chapter) for suggestions. Here are just a few of the many beautiful trails to explore in the area.

ASPEN TRAIL–MARSHALL GULCH LOOP
Mount Lemmon

Mount Lemmon offers many scenic hiking trails, including the gorgeous Aspen Trail–Marshall Gulch Loop, located just minutes from the tiny village of Summerhaven.

This hike will take you through lofty pines, lush ferns, and other cool foliage. Altitude starts at about 7,500 feet and proceeds at a leisurely pace to around 8,000 feet. Because this is a mountain trail, the best times to enjoy it are spring, summer, and fall. Running water is not uncommon in winter.

Take the Catalina Highway north out of Tucson toward Mount Lemmon and Summerhaven. When you reach the junction with the turnoff for the ski area, continue straight for another 1.3 miles (do not take the Mount Lemmon Ski Valley turnoff) through Summerhaven, following signs to the Marshall Gulch area. The trailhead is at the end of the road. The total hike is about 3.7 miles. At the Marshall Gulch Ridge the elevation is 8,000 feet. Views along the way are spectacular.

CATALINA STATE PARK

This state park north of the city is ideal for family hikes. The elevation changes are minimal, while still offering some great views and desert scenery. Several well-marked trails can be found in the park area. The Canyon Loop Trail is a 2.3-mile loop trail from the main trailhead. It goes through some of the lower foothills of the Santa Catalinas. There are several other options, including the Romero Canyon Trail, which leads into Pusch Ridge, and the Sutherland Trail, which heads into Cargodera Canyon. (See the section on Catalina State Park at the beginning of this chapter for more information.)

Looking for folks to go hiking with? Check out these local organizations.

Southern Arizona Hiking Club
(520) 751-4513
www.sahcinfo.org
Founded in 1958, this nonprofit, volunteer hiking club leads hikes almost daily. Their monthly bulletin (free to members) lists every hike.

Sierra Club, Rincon Chapter
www.arizona.sierraclub.org/rincon
This local chapter of the Sierra Club leads hikes almost every weekend, and you don't have to be a member to go.

Ramblers Hiking Club
www.clubs.arizona.edu/~ramblers
Open to the public, this is the University of Arizona hiking club. There is no membership fee. The club organizes a variety of activities as well as all sorts of hiking and camping trips locally and beyond.

DAVID YETMAN TRAIL EAST

Tucson Mountain Park

This moderately difficult trail is named for a former county supervisor who was big on desert preservation. Located in Tucson Mountain Park, the trailhead starts at the west end of Camino del Oeste near the end of Anklam Road. The trail meanders for approximately 5.5 miles through chollas, saguaro, and other desert vegetation. You can catch the shorter, tougher uphill climb of the John Krein Trail about three-quarters of the way along. Elevation runs from 2,000 to 5,000 feet. You will cross a wash, just past the Krein Trail turnoff. Remember, if there's a lot of water, proceed with extreme caution: You don't want to get swept away. The only way back is the way you came, for an 11.0-mile round-trip.

To get to the trailhead, take Speedway Boulevard west. Notice the name change to Anklam Road. Follow Anklam Road until Camino Del Oeste and turn left, then travel to the trailhead.

FINGER ROCK

This hike in the Santa Catalinas is really three very different hikes ranging from very rugged to user-friendly. All three basically begin at the north end of Alvernon Road.

The Finger Rock Trail gives hikers, appropriately enough, a magnificent view of Finger Rock. At the 3.0-mile point, you will cross Linda Vista Saddle, a great place to pause and catch the linda vista (beautiful view). From here you can then continue 1.5 miles to a junction where you can continue to Mount Kimball (turn left/west) or head up to the Window (turn right/east). This is considered by local hiking experts to be rugged and steep.

Two hundred feet from the Finger Rock trailhead, you will pick up Pontatoc Canyon Trail. This 6.0-mile round-trip hike will take you to pools of cool water during the rainy season. One mile into Pontatoc Canyon Trail, you can pick up the Pontatoc Ridge Trail, which has stunning views of the city, the desert, and the mountains. It's considered an easy hike of about 3.8 miles round-trip. Elevation at the trail's end is about 6,000 feet. At the end of the Ridge Trail are several old mine holes; use extreme caution and avoid this dangerous area.

GOLDEN GATE LOOP

As you hike this easy trail, look up—you may experience déja vù. The ridges along this part of the Tucson Mountains have appeared in many a Western movie.

The trail begins at the David Yetman West trailhead at the pullout designated G3, on the west side of Gates Road as you descend from the summit. You'll hike for about 0.5 mile and then follow the sign to the loop trail. The elevation ranges from 2,700 feet to 3,000 feet, making this an easy hike for even the novice hiker. About 0.75

mile along the way, you will come to a fork in the trail. Either direction will loop you around to where you are standing.

Views along the way are great, but vegetation stays about the same, with plenty of saguaros and other low-desert vegetation. One note: At the far end of the loop you will walk awhile along Kinney Road. Be careful of the traffic, and keep an eye out for the return trail marker.

MILLER CREEK TRAIL

The Rincon Wilderness Area rises to some 8,486 feet, offering intense hiking and some of the most beautiful views you will ever see. This 16.2-mile round-trip hike is only one of five that lead into the mountain wilderness. Take I-10 east to the J-Six-Mescal Road exit (exit 297), and head north on Forest Road 35 for about 17 miles. Look for the trailhead on the left. The trail is well signed, so getting to the top will be easy to find (although the rugged hike will prove challenging for even experienced hikers). Beginning at the gate—please close it behind you—the trail follows Miller Creek into Saguaro National Park East. The terrain changes from desert to scrub to oak woods. As you pass though the oak stands, the trail begins to get steep. At the Happy Valley Saddle, take the Heartbreak Ridge Trail. Here you'll notice the change to pine forest (by this time you've climbed some 1,900 feet in a little over 5.0 miles).

Following the trail, you'll come to the signed junction to Rincon Peak. Follow along until you reach the top. Take at least 6 quarts of water.

PIMA CANYON

This challenging hike in the Santa Catalinas will take you close to 5,000 feet in elevation, high enough to perhaps catch a glimpse of bighorn sheep.

The northern trailhead starts at the east end of Magee Road. Although there's some public parking, it should be noted that parking on the road could result in a hefty fine. The first one-third mile passes through a subdivision, and it's best to stay in the fenced corridor. The only drinking fountain and emergency phone will be found at the entrance.

The canyon, with its rocky walls, still allows for great views of the valley. About 3.0 miles into the hike, the vegetation changes and you might see running water. Another 2.0 miles takes you to an elevation of about 2,500 feet. Hike another 2.0 miles and you will reach 4,500 feet in elevation. You'll be at Mount Kimball.

Camping is allowed with a permit. And to protect the bighorn sheep that reside near here, no dogs are permitted. Campsites must be set up at least 400 feet from the trail.

SABINO BASIN

A hiker's visit to Tucson isn't complete without a trip to the heart of Sabino Canyon. Whether you start at the visitor center and walk the paved road to the trailhead or take the tram to the trailhead, you will walk away from the hike enriched by a deeper understanding of the way Mother Nature has designed the area.

The hike from the trailhead has been called easy, and you will see everything from saguaro and cholla cacti to Mexican oaks, cottonwoods, and sycamores at the trail's end. You may even find some running water. About halfway through the hike, you can catch the trail to Hutch's Pool, a popular local swimming hole.

At the trail's end, in Sabino Basin, several canyons join together. You can meet up with other trails at this point, one of which leads 1.6 miles to Mount Lemmon. Choose to take another canyon trail, or turn around and hike back the way you came, for a 5-mile round-trip. (See the Sabino Canyon section at the beginning of this chapter for more information.) Contact the visitor

i If you're not into serious hiking, head to Tohono Chul Park for one of their Walk in the Park tours. These fascinating docent-guided tours meander through the 48 spectacular desert acres of the park and are offered at 9:00 a.m. and 1:00 p.m. on Tuesday, Thursday, and Saturday. The pace is slow, the terrain easy and fairly flat. Call (520) 742-6455 or check the Web at www.tohonochulpark.org for more details.

center before you head out, as sometimes trails are closed due to wildlife sightings.

SEVEN FALLS

People love this hike, and it's no wonder. Located in Bear Canyon, the trailhead is easily accessible and the 4.0-mile hike is doable for just about anyone with good hiking boots and stamina. The views along the way are some of the most spectacular you'll ever see.

And yes, waterfalls can really be found, along with lovely natural pools for swimming. The amount of water you'll find, though, depends entirely on the time of year and the amount of recent rainfall. Sometimes, in fact, when there is an abundance of rain or snowmelt, the water can be quite deep and fast moving. It can also be quite cold, so come prepared, and be careful.

Catch the trailhead via Sabino Canyon to Bear Canyon. Follow the well-marked trail to the base of the falls and then proceed, carefully, to the top of the falls. The hike, or climb, as it may better be called, can be tricky, so proceed with caution. For the return trip, retrace your steps. Check with the visitor center to be sure the trail is open. (See the Sabino Canyon section earlier in this chapter.)

Horseback Riding, Hayrides, Cattle Drives, etc.

COCORAQUE RANCH CATTLE DRIVES
3199 North Reservation Road
(520) 682-8594
www.cocoraque.com

To experience the true West, why not check out a real working cattle ranch? Family run since the 1890s, Cocoraque Ranch offers several ways to relive the life of a real cowboy. You can do the work that ranch hands and cowboys have been doing for decades by taking a two- or three-hour or all-day trail ride where you'll check the cattle, fences, and watering holes along the way. If you can band together 15 or more people, you can do a real cattle drive, during which you'll be in the saddle for two and a half hours driving the herd from different pastures, then back to the ranch house for a real outdoor cookout with cowboy beans, steak, chicken, and tortillas.

PURPLE MOUNTAIN PACK GOATS
P.O. Box 1345, Tucson, AZ 85702
(520) 403-4056
www.azpackgoat.com

And now for something completely different . . . custom-guided hikes with alpine pack goats carrying all equipment, food, and beverages. You can bring your own food, but co-owner Tom DiMaggio has been known to serve up some delicious gourmet grub on hikes.

Each trip is planned with the customer in mind. The DiMaggios use information regarding size of party, physical capabilities, and interests to design a one-of-a-kind tour for you and your group. You can traverse any of a number of gorgeous trails in Madera Canyon, the Dragoons, and throughout the Coronado National Forest.

Prices vary and are per person per day (the cost varies depending on your choice of a prepared meal, the number of folks in your party, and distance of the trek). Bring your camera to take pictures, because friends back home may not believe you when you tell them about this adventure. As with any desert hike, don't forget your water.

PUSCH RIDGE STABLES
13700 North Oracle Road
(520) 825-1664
www.puschridgestables.com

Offering a full slate of horse-related activities, this stable is adjacent to Catalina State Park and other areas of the Coronado National Forest. There are 10,000 acres here for your enjoyment, whether you decide to take the usual horseback ride with a guide or one of the many other options available. Pusch Ridge Stables has breakfast rides, which begin at dawn, so you can experience the beauty of a desert sunrise. Or opt for an evening steak ride, where your meal is cooked over an open fire in real cowboy fashion. To add a little romance, moonlight rides are also on tap. One- and two-hour horseback rides are also available daily.

The stable's hayrides will carry you and your party over desert trails via horse-drawn carriages. At one of the stops you can enjoy a picnic or steak dinner. Entertainment, such as a hoedown or recreational games, can be included. The costs vary per person for horseback rides and hayrides.

Take Oracle Road north to Milepost 84, then make an immediate right turn and follow the signs to the stable.

ROCKING K STABLES
13401 East Old Spanish Trail Road
(520) 647-0040
This stable on the east side offers trail rides through 5,000 acres bordering Saguaro Park East. The working ranch also hosts cattle drives complete with fireside Western cookouts. Hayrides and sunset rides are popular here. All levels of riders are welcome. Call for rates and schedule.

WALKING WINDS STABLES
10000 North Oracle Road
(520) 742-4422
Trail rides at these stables will take you through beautiful desert and mountain scenery. The ride through the national forest will afford you some of the best views of the area. Both novice riders and those with a little more experience in the saddle will enjoy rides of one or one and a half hours. They also offer sunset rides for spectacular beauty.

Take Oracle Road north to the Hilton El Conquistador Resort; the stables are on the grounds.

Hot-Air Ballooning

BALLOON AMERICA
(520) 299-7744
www.balloonrideusa.com
Balloon America's pilots will float you over the magnificent Catalina foothills. Options include a one-hour ride at 6:30 a.m., the Desert Sunrise Tour, at altitudes from treetop level to 3,000 feet, which takes you toward Sabino Canyon and the base of the Santa Catalina Mountains. This flight includes a flute of real or nonalcoholic champagne. The Catalina Mountain Tour is a 75- to 90-minute flight that includes a full preflight gourmet breakfast.

There's a digital camera on board so you can document your flight. Passengers must be age 3 and over. Call for prices and special packages. There are no flights during summer months.

Baggage and smoking are not allowed, but you are encouraged to bring your camera.

Early reservations are also a must. And you'll pay a fee if you cancel 14 or more days prior to your flight (any later than 14 days will result in your being charged the full price). If the company has to cancel for any reason, you will receive a full refund. The price for the Desert Sunrise Tour is $225. The Catalina Mountain Tour is $475 a person. Allow up to three hours for the tours.

The balloons take off from La Mariposa Resort at North Houghton Road between Speedway and Tanque Verde Road. Closed June through September.

BARNEY BRENNER BALLOON ADVENTURES
(520) 743-7300
Get set for the thrill of a lifetime. You'll begin your adventure early in the morning when you arrive at the launch site to watch the inflation of the balloon. When guests are settled in the comfortable gondola, you'll take off and experience stunning desert vistas as the wind whispers through your hair. Take your camera. Each flight is unique and depends on wind direction and conditions of the day. An experienced FAA-certified balloon pilot will check the conditions and choose the best option.

The flight will be followed by a celebration in which you'll sample a variety of treats. The entire experience usually lasts about three hours and costs about $195 per person. Gift certificates are available. The launch site is about 1.5 miles west of I-10 and El Camino del Cerro. Call for specific directions and to reserve your spot.

Rock Climbing

With all the mountains that surround Tucson, there are plenty of sites for rock climbing, no matter what your level of skill. Favorite spots include Windy Point, on the Mount Lemmon Highway; Esperero Spires, a 500-foot climb near Sabino Canyon; Table Mountain, near Pusch Ridge, north of the city; and Leviathan Dome in Oracle, also north of town.

ROCKS & ROPES
330 South Toole Avenue, Suite 400
(520) 882-5924
www.rocksandropes.com

For all you rock-climbing hounds out there, this indoor rock-climbing gym has plenty to offer. Thirty-five-foot walls with 125 routes, measuring in various degrees of difficulty, fill the converted warehouse. Fifty-three top ropes can also be found.

Lessons are offered for newcomers. The $30 first-time fee includes lessons, use of gear, and plenty of information. Monthly memberships are also available. Nonmembers can access the gym. Hours run from 3:00 to 10:00 p.m. weekdays and from 11:00 a.m. until 8:00 p.m. weekends. The doors open to members only at noon during the week.

Singles Organizations

EQUALLY YOKED
5125 North 16th Street
(520) 882-9778
www.equallyyoked.com

Equally Yoked is the largest social club for Christian singles in the nation, with 30 member centers and over 35,000 members. The Tucson location organizes social activities and outings of all kinds.

TUCSON FUN & ADVENTURES, INC.
3255 East Grant Road, PMB #144
(520) 256-3866
www.tucsonfun.com

The more than 400 members of Tucson Fun & Adventures agree: This is a great way to meet other single professionals in the Tucson area. A staff of event coordinators plans the events—large and small—including hiking, travel, barbecues, wine tastings, whitewater rafting, theme parties, archery, dancing, investment seminars, tailgate parties, progressive dinners, camping, theater, cooking classes, and more. Event coordinators take care of everything; all you have to do is show up and enjoy yourself at their activities.

Tucson Fun & Adventures offers free informational meetings once or twice a week. Call to find out about their next meeting and to get more information about the services they offer.

Skiing

SKI VALLEY, MOUNT LEMMON
(520) 576-1321 (live), (520) 576-1400 (recorded information)

Ski Valley is the southernmost ski area in North America. At an elevation of 9,100 feet, skiers have their choice of 15 runs ranging from beginner slopes to expert ones. Ski Valley allows for snowboards. Lift ticket prices vary, and rental equipment is available at the ski-lift complex. You can also take a learn-to-ski lesson.

Days of operation are truly limited, and if it's been a dry winter, skiing will be minimal. Call the 24-hour recorded info line for details and conditions. If you are skiing, you will not need to pay the user fee to drive Catalina Highway up the mountain.

Skydiving

SKYDIVE ARIZONA
4900 North Taylor Drive, Eloy
(520) 466-3753
www.skydiveaz.com

For a view of Arizona that is literally above all the rest, take the 45-minute drive north to SkyDive Arizona. There novice and veteran skydivers alike will find all levels of skydiving instruction and fun.

If you're not quite ready to solo jump, opt for a tandem dive with an experienced diver. And for those who appreciate the beauty of skydiving but would rather keep their feet on the ground, spectating is free. Prices vary on lessons and jumps.

Indoor skydiving at SkyVenture Arizona in Eloy is a once-in-a-lifetime experience. PHOTO BY MARY PAGANELLI VOTTO

Take I-10 west toward Phoenix and exit at Sunshine Boulevard. Turn right and go about a mile to Frontier Road, where you will turn left. Driving 2 or 3 more miles takes you to Tumbleweed Road. Turn right and proceed for another 2 miles to the school. Closed Tuesday and Wednesday.

SKYVENTURE ARIZONA
4900 North Taylor Drive, Eloy
(520) 466-4640, (888) BODYFLY (263-9359)
www.skyventureaz.com
Afraid to jump out of a plane? Try the next best thing—indoor skydiving. Just an hour north of Tucson, this vertical wind tunnel is a terrific way to defy gravity. Just take a quick lesson, suit up, and you're flying. Open to ages 3 and up, there is a 250-pound weight limit. Be sure to make reservations in advance; they book up quickly.

Swimming

As you might have guessed, swimming is a year-round activity in Tucson. To accommodate swimmers of all ages, public pools can be found citywide. The city swim program offers free swimming lessons for children during the summer.

For older water bugs, there are also adult swim classes (for a mere $10), adapted aquatics for those with disabilities, competitive swim leagues, aqua exercise, synchronized swimming teams, diving classes, and special times for family swims.

Hours vary from park to park and season to season, with Archer, Catalina, Fort Lowell, Sunnyside, and Udall pools open year-round. It's best to call ahead to check hours and times.

Pools may close at the first sight of lightning during a summer monsoon. For information call (520) 791-4245.

BREAKERS WATER PARK
8555 West Tangerine Road
(520) 682-2530, (520) 682-2304
www.breakerswaterpark.com
The giant wave pool is the big attraction at this fun spot. But the five waterslides come in a close second. Located on the far northwest side, Breakers is open during the summer season, roughly from the end of May until Labor Day. You'll find a kiddie pool and acres of running-around room as well. No outside food and beverages are allowed, but there is a snack bar. Trees and ramadas offer much-needed shade.

Open Tuesday through Sunday 10:00 a.m. to 6:00 p.m. Admission prices vary, but anyone under age 3 gets in free.

Tennis, Racquetball, and Handball

Tucson has more than 200 tennis courts among the city, county, schools, private resorts, and clubs. While most of the resorts require a stay, the city and county courts are available to everyone.

Adult tennis and racquetball lessons are held at Randolph, Udall, Himmel, and Fort Lowell Parks. The city's USTA tennis league can also be found at these sites. In addition, multiple-use courts are available at many city parks. Fees vary. Call (520) 791-4896 for information. No reservations are accepted.

Tennis clinics are available for all ages, with the Junior Tennis Program offering competitive camps and leagues. The Junior Tennis Program has lessons and games for youngsters on Saturday and after school.

Tucson is also the home of the Handball Hall of Fame and the United States Handball Association. There is an annual membership fee, and with it you get a monthly newsletter and information on tournaments and league play. Contact the USHA at (520) 795-0434. Handball public courts can be found at Reid, Udall, Pima College West, and Fort Lowell Parks.

Public courts also host a diverse mix of local, state, and national tournaments year-round.

GOLF

Yes, there is grass in Tucson! And you'll find most of it on the superb golf courses that dot the city. Lush green grass, mountain views, bright blue skies, and over 25 courses in the city alone make Tucson a golfer's dream come true. You can literally hit the links here 365 days a year on courses designed by top architects like Tom Fazio, Arthur Hills, Robert Trent Jones Jr., and Tom Weiskopf. You can choose from a vast variety of course types, locations, and prices—from posh resorts charging up to $225 in peak season for a round with cart to municipal courses at less than $40 with cart. The county course and five municipal courses are maintained at standards that in most parts of the country are reserved for the best country clubs, so even if you're on a budget, you can play on truly superb courses.

Summer golfing in Tucson offers some outstanding values, with prices up to half the peak winter season rates and tee times that you don't have to scramble to get. You may not want to drive, chip, or putt golf balls in the midday heat, but courses are open sunrise to sunset, so you can play when temperatures are more bearable.

For visitors or newcomers to Tucson, the hardest part of the game may well be finding the golf course. Many of the courses have obscure addresses—they're on streets named just for the golf course, for example, and the street names give no clue as to where they really are. So to help you find the links you're looking for, we include some major cross streets or other directions that will get you there with a lot less frustration. Except for the day-trip courses at the end of the chapter (which are listed geographically), the courses are listed strictly in alphabetical order, but we tell you where in the area each is located to help you decide which to play when. We also tell you which courses are semiprivate, meaning that you'll need to be a member of the club or guest at the resort to play them. Courses that are strictly private are not listed here.

Most Tucson courses have four seasons for determining fees. The peak season usually runs from early January to mid or late April, when the fees are steepest. Prices are lower in the fall or early winter season, usually October through December, and in the spring or early summer season (mid or late April through May or June). Lowest rates—often more than 50 percent off the peak rates—are offered in summer, generally running June or July through August or September. Most courses offer "twilight" rates year-round, typically beginning around 2:00 p.m. Nearly every course is open sunrise to sunset, which means longer playing hours in summer than in winter. At the municipal courses, driving range hours are sunrise to 10:00 p.m., with a nominal fee charged for buckets of balls.

If you're a golfer who prefers the old-fashioned way of golfing—walking rather than riding a cart—you'll need to select your courses carefully. Most courses in the Tucson area just aren't made for walking and won't even permit it; the desert terrain is too rocky and hilly or the courses are too long to reasonably walk them. If you're looking for a course to walk, watch for those that say traditional (although even that's not a guarantee you can walk it). The best ones would be most of the municipal courses, plus Crooked Tree, Dorado, Quail Canyon, and Green Valley's Haven and Tortuga. But not to worry, you can still get lots of walking in at other courses by keeping your cart on the cart path and walking to your shots.

TIPS ON PLAYING CITY COURSES

You may not need a golf lesson, but if you're planning to play any of the five excellent Tucson municipal courses, we offer this lesson in how best to navigate them. It's critical that you know about the reservation system, and you also may want to know some of the great ways to save money.

There are three ways to make reservations at Tucson municipal golf courses. You can call (520) 791-4336 to speak with a live customer service representative 24 hours per day, you can log on to www.tucsoncitygolf.com and book a tee time six days in advance, or you can visit www.golfnow.com and reserve there.

If you are a Tucson resident, your best bet is to get a resident's card, which you can do by showing your Tucson driver's license to the folks at Randolph Golf Course's Pro Shop at 600 North Alvernon Way. This resident program (also called the "Affinity" program) will entitle you to discounts at certain times of the year and also to certain rewards.

Nonresidents can get the same discounts by purchasing a $75 reward card, entitling you to resident rates at the municipal golf course. In either case, you will need to reserve by providing a credit card number.

Another great way to save money if you're age 62 or older is the senior's card. Its discounts are slightly less than the resident's card, but you'll save a couple of bucks—even more if you have both cards. Inquire about this card at the Tucson City Golf number or office listed above or at any of the municipal courses. Senior rates do not apply January through March.

GOLF COURSES

ARIZONA NATIONAL GOLF CLUB

9777 East Sabino Greens Drive
(520) 749-3636
www.arizonanationalgolfclub.com

Robert Trent Jones Jr. designed this beauty of a classic desert golf course at the foot of the Santa Catalina Mountains to be as challenging as the rugged natural flow of the land. Instead of carving up the terrain, the design meshes with the land and its natural hills, arroyos, rocks, and stands of giant saguaro cacti. So although it tests the limits of your ability, it also offers the tranquility of spectacular scenery, including the rare beauty of nine natural desert springs. Accuracy is a hallmark of this course. It will take your best and biggest hits to play the 625-yard number 11, for example.

From the longest of three tee positions, the par 71 course is 6,776 yards and rated 72.4. Arizona National Golf Club has a great driving range as well as a putting green and clubhouse. In peak season the rate is $175 on weekends for 18 holes with a cart. Take Tanque Verde Road northeast to Catalina Highway. Go left onto Catalina Highway and take a left onto Houghton going north. Take a left on Snyder and a right onto Sabino Greens Drive.

THE CROOKED TREE GOLF COURSE AT ARTHUR PACK REGIONAL PARK

9101 North Thornydale Road
(520) 744-3322

Located on the northwest side of town, this county-owned golf course recently underwent extensive remodeling. The result is a beautifully rejuvenated 18-hole course, designed to be difficult, yet friendly. Greens are true and quick, while fairways have also been upgraded. The practice facility is superb, and walkers will enjoy the scenic mountain and desert vistas. Championship tees have been lengthened and improved, leading to more challenging play for the low handicapper.

City and county amateur championships are often played here, and it's often possible to just walk onto the course without advance reservations, especially in summer. For 18 holes in peak season, the weekend cost is $49 with a cart. Seniors are eligible for a small discount on the playing rates. Facilities include a driving range, renovated clubhouse, chipping green, and putting green. The views of Pusch Ridge at the base of the Santa Catalina Mountains are a real bonus.

DELL URICH MUNICIPAL GOLF COURSE
600 South Alvernon Way
(520) 791-4161
www.tucsoncitygolf.com

This course was redesigned, renovated, and renamed in 1996. It used to be the south course to Randolph North, and they were both known by the name Randolph. They are the most centrally located courses in Tucson if you're staying in the downtown area or anywhere nearby and want a great golf course with a midwestern feel that you can get to quickly. Both courses are accessed from Alvernon Way just north of 22nd Street, and they share facilities such as practice green, driving range, and clubhouse. As with the other municipal courses, it would be hard to find a better golfing venue for the money, or even for more money. Of the two side-by-side courses, the 18-hole, 6,633-yard (70.8 rating), par 70 Dell Urich is shorter and less challenging, but the renovation did add more contours. Its straightforward layout and smooth terrain make Dell Urich (pronounced *YOU-rick*) great for novices or a quick round of golf. Like all the municipal courses, discounts are available for residents and seniors, and you must use the automated central phone system—explained in detail earlier in this chapter—to reserve tee times.

Winter rates (November through May) range from $16 to $70. Reservations are necessary during the peak season—sometimes weeks in advance.

i **The First Tee program, intended for kids ages 5 to 17, teaches kids core life values as well as golf skills. Kids sign up for three- or six-week classes and have a ball. The program is funded and sponsored by the Tucson Conquistadores, so the registration fee is only $5 per year. Classes are taught year-round. To learn more, call (520) 628-1555.**

DORADO GOLF CLUB
6601 East Speedway Boulevard
(520) 885-6751
www.doradogolf.com

This par 62 public course is conveniently located on the near east side of town right off a main byway. But it's also nicely secluded in the midst of a lovely, quiet residential community. Dorado is a traditional grassy course and well maintained with bent grass greens. You can play 9 or 18 holes quickly on this executive course and only pull out your driver once or twice. Long yardage is 3,900 at a rating of 58.9. During the winter peak season, it's best to call several days to a week ahead for reservations. The best deals at this course are reduced fees after noon, available year-round. There's a chip-and-putt area and a snack bar. The course is close to several hotels.

The winter weekend rate for Dorado is $30 for 18 holes with a cart.

EL RIO MUNICIPAL GOLF COURSE
1400 West Speedway Boulevard
(520) 791-4229
www.tucsoncitygolf.com

A favorite for both locals and visitors, this city course is close to downtown on the near west side just beyond Interstate 10. Ideal for the short knocker, this par 59 course measures from 5,824 to 6,418 yards and is rated 69.6. It has a fairly flat terrain with tight fairways, lots of trees, and two small lakes. The greens are famous for being small and hard—a pitch-and-run setup.

Facilities include a practice green, well-lit driving range, and clubhouse. The oldest municipal course in Tucson and one of the oldest courses in Arizona, it dates back to the 1930s and was the original site of the Tucson Open. Discounts are available for residents and seniors, and tee times can be made only through the central Parks and Rec number.

For prebooked 18 holes with a cart, the winter prime time (after 7:00 a.m.) resident rate is $40.

FRED ENKE MUNICIPAL GOLF COURSE
8251 East Irvington Road
(520) 791-2539
www.tucsoncitygolf.com

You'd have to look hard to find a better desert course than this one run by the city. Located on the southeast side of town on a main thoroughfare, this is a limited turf course with substantial teeing areas, large greens, well-calculated bunkers, and tricky sand traps. It's target golf, calling for accuracy over distance. You can choose from four teeing areas. White tees are 6,072 yards, rated 69/126. If you play from the back tees and plan to get a good score, you'd better be a good golfer. The heavily bunkered 455-yard, par 4 number 9 hole will challenge anyone. The course offers a practice green, well-lit driving range, and a bar and grill for après golf. From a couple of spots on this course you can see the Davis-Monthan Air Force Base's aircraft boneyard, a pleasant scene if you're into flights of fancy.

The resident winter rate (November through May) for 18 holes prebooked with a cart is $40.

THE GOLF CLUB AT VISTOSO
955 West Vistoso Highlands Drive
(520) 797-9900
www.vistosogolf.com

Located northwest of Tucson in Oro Valley, the Golf Club at Vistoso was voted the best public golf course in Tucson by *Golf Digest* magazine. Designed by the famous Tom Weiskopf, the longest of four tees plays to 6,932 yards at par 72 and a rating of 71.8. With views of the Tortolita Mountains to the northwest and the Catalinas and city to the south, the fairways are surrounded by natural washes, giant saguaros, and mesquite trees, producing a stunning and challenging target golf course.

Each of the 18 holes is named—Prickly Pear, Double Cross, Waterfall, Hidden Green, Risky, and Sidewinder are a few that will give you a clue about what to expect as you play them. A unique feature at Vistoso is that all carts are equipped with uplink GPS systems. Facilities include a clubhouse, driving range, and putting green. The peak-season rate for 18 holes on the weekend with a cart is $140 before 1:00 p.m. Check the Web site for specials. You can get to the Golf Club at Vistoso from Oracle Road by going west on First Avenue to Tangerine and continuing on to Rancho Vistoso Boulevard. Take a left on Vistoso Highlands Drive, and watch for signs in the center divider.

HERITAGE HIGHLANDS GOLF CLUB
4949 West Heritage Club Boulevard
(520) 579-7000
www.heritagehighlands.com

Opened in 1997, this Arthur Hills–designed, semi-private course is part of a country club retirement community on Tucson's far northwest side. Set amidst lush natural vegetation, it's situated at the base of the Tortolita Mountains with views of the whole valley and every mountain range. The course is a loosely formed semicircle of long, angled fairways. With its variety of tee boxes and fairway angles, every game can seem totally different. It's almost like two courses in one—the front nine are flatter and the back nine more challenging and hilly. This par 72 championship course challenges the best without being too intimidating for the average player. The course measures 6,904 yards from the back tee at a rating of 72.2. Its signature hole is number 13 (a blind tee shot to a plateau about 35 feet high, dropping to a long green behind an outcropping of rocks), and there are four challenging par 5s. Facilities include a clubhouse with bar and grill, driving range, and putting green.

The cost for 18 holes prebooked with a cart is $89 January through April. Go west on Tangerine Road from Oracle Road (or east on Tangerine from I-10) to Dove Mountain Boulevard and head north until you come to the gated community that is home to the course.

HILTON EL CONQUISTADOR RESORT AND COUNTRY CLUB
10000 North Oracle Road
www.hiltonelconquistador.com

This resort on the far northwest side (in Oro Valley) offers one 9-hole and two 18-hole courses set amid the dramatic natural landscapes and rolling elevations of the Santa Catalina Mountains. Also available is a comprehensive golf academy.

PUSCH RIDGE COURSE
(520) 544-1770

This nine-hole par 70 course gets its name from the dramatic granite ridge adjacent to the Hilton El Conquistador Resort that towers 2,000 feet above the course. The course winds around and above the resort (on the east side of Oracle Road), offering some of the best city and mountain views to be had. A tight course that golfers describe as the best nine-hole course in the area, it runs the gamut from fast greens to long driving holes to short par 3s. Yardage from the longest of three tees is 2,788 with a rating of 65.6. The course features dramatic elevation changes and some risk/reward holes that offer fun choices for players of all levels. A putting green, plus the resort's restaurants, are available to golfers. In peak season with a cart, 9 holes will cost $39 and 18 holes $49.

CONQUISTADOR AND CAÑADA
(520) 544-1800

The Hilton El Conquistador's two 18-hole courses are located not at the resort but about 3 miles away at the Country Club, 10555 North La Cañada Drive. (From the resort or from Oracle Road, take First Avenue to Lambert Road to La Cañada.) Facilities include a driving range, putting greens, and a restaurant and lounge.

Both the golf and the views from these desert courses are spectacular. The peak-season fee is $125 for 18 holes with a cart on weekends.

i For golf club collectors or anyone looking to score a nice but inexpensive set of clubs, have we got a deal for you! Check out the large collection of used golf equipment at Copper Country Antique Mall & Collectibles, 5055 East Speedway Boulevard (520-326-0167). Clubs can run anywhere from $5 to $50.

THE LODGE AT VENTANA CANYON GOLF AND RACQUET CLUB
6200 North Clubhouse Lane
(520) 577-4061
www.thelodgeatventanacanyon.com

The Lodge at Ventana Canyon Golf and Racquet Club is just south of Loews Ventana Canyon Resort, and both are just north of the intersection of Kolb Road and Sunrise Drive in the close-in northeast foothills. (In other words, if you get to the resort entrance, you've gone too far.) The lodge offers two distinct courses nestled against the dramatic backdrop of the Santa Catalina Mountains. In an 1,100-acre enclave, half the terrain is preserved open space providing a natural habitat for deer, rabbits, Gambel's quail, and other native creatures amid the saguaros and mesquites. Winding through this secluded hideaway are two 18-hole championship courses—Canyon and Mountain—designed by Tom Fazio.

Unless you're a member of the lodge, you may play only the resort course. In peak season you can reserve only seven days out unless you're a member or lodging guest. It's rather complex, in case you haven't noticed, so call for an explanation if you're still confused. Whichever course you do play, you'll be playing on one of the best courses around, but it will cost $225 per player (peak season), including a cart, for 18 holes.

CANYON COURSE

Area golfers say it can easily take six hours to play a round of 18 on this course that offers both some incredible golfing and views amid fine desert scenery. It winds through the beautiful Esperrero Canyon and incorporates the massive rock formation known as Whaleback Rock, where at night bobcats emerge from the desert to snooze along the green. The fairways are lush on this 6,818-yard par 72 course with a rating of 72.7. This is definitely a target course where many balls are lost to the desert rough. You'll be impressed by the dramatic finish on the par 5, number 18 island green, where patrons of the restaurant may offer a round of applause if you manage to keep the ball in play.

MOUNTAIN COURSE

This second course at Ventana Canyon is more difficult. The obstacles inherent in its natural desert landscape make the Mountain Course one of the most formidable in the area. At 6,926 yards and par 72, it's rated 74.2. The course's renowned 100-yard, par 3 number 3 signature hole is hit from a peak over a ravine to the green on another peak, and the tee offers a breathtaking panorama that stretches for 100 miles across the Sonoran Desert into Mexico. This is reputed to be the most photographed hole (other than the Grand Canyon, we presume) west of the Mississippi.

OMNI TUCSON NATIONAL GOLF RESORT AND SPA
2727 West Club Drive
(520) 575-7540
www.omnihotels.com

This top golf resort and spa is home to two 18-hole courses: the Tom Lehman–designed desert-style Sonoran golf course and the championship Catalina course. The Sonoran course features steep elevation changes and magnificent views of the surrounding Sonoran Desert. At 6,418 yards, length is not the primary challenge. Rather, Lehman's design incorporates strategic fairway bunkering that requires players to place their tee shots carefully, while a set of green complexes call for thoughtful approaches and a deft short game. The Catalina course has been home to the PGA Tour's annual Chrysler Classic of Tucson since 1976.

Facilities include a driving range, short game area, and putting green, as well as a restaurant and lounge. Peak-season weekend play here is $185 for 18 holes with a cart. It's located in the northwest near the intersection of Cortaro Farms and Shannon Roads. Or from I-10, exit at Cortaro Farms Road east to Shannon Road, then go north.

i Don't miss golfing at twilight, offered year-round here. The soft night air, indigo skies, and some of the most incredible sunsets are an unforgettable Tucson experience.

THE PINES GOLF CLUB AT MARANA
8480 North Continental Links Drive, Marana
(520) 744-7443
www.playthepines.com

This course is located in the far northwest, where the town of Marana is rapidly expanding southward toward Tucson. The Pines is situated in a sprawling industrial/residential development called Continental Ranch, and the course itself abuts the west side of I-10 from about Cortaro Farms Road northward. Tucson's first quarry course, the back nine holes of this 18-hole course are built on the original 90-acre, 100-foot-deep sand and gravel quarry. The front nine is a links-style course. The course was designed by the Phoenix architectural firm Gilmore Graves and offers a mix of dramatic elevation changes and stunning mountain views. Course length is approximately 6,300 yards. Men's gold tees are rated 69.2, par 71. There's a clubhouse, restaurant, and full-service pro shop. The peak-season weekend rate is $74 including cart and range balls. Exit I-10 at Cortaro Road west, then to Arizona Pavilions Way north.

QUAIL CANYON GOLF COURSE
5910 North Oracle Road
(520) 887-6161
www.quailcanyon.com

This course is the place to get your short game in shape. It's more of a recreational than professional course, with 18 par 3 holes totaling 2,311 yards. Hole number 4 is longest at 165 yards, number 7 the toughest (it's long with natural obstacles), and number 14's pond is usually home to local ducks. In winter this course charges $26 for 18 holes and a cart. It's easy to find on a major thoroughfare in close-in northwest Tucson.

RANDOLPH NORTH MUNICIPAL GOLF COURSE
600 South Alvernon Way
(520) 791-4161
www.tucsoncitygolf.com

Randolph North is the longest of Tucson's municipal courses. A favorite of locals, it's a nice course with a midwestern feel. The course features a traditional country club design and is noted for its mature vegetation, tall trees, and wide, expansive fairways. Greens vary from relatively flat to severely sloped or tiered and from large to small. Two outstanding holes are the 15th, a lovely hole of 200 yards surrounded by water, and the 18th, with two ponds that carry over from fairway to green. Long yardage is 6,863 with a rating of 71.9. Facilities include a well-lit driving range, practice green, and clubhouse. This is a superb course located almost in the heart of Tucson and surrounded by city parks and recreational offerings.

The prebooked 18-hole resident fee with cart is $46 in winter (November through May).

SANTA RITA GOLF CLUB
16461 South Houghton Road
(520) 762-5620
www.santaritagolf.com

This course is at the foot of the Santa Rita Mountains on the far southeast side of the valley, about a 30-minute drive from central Tucson. Every one of the 18 holes features beautiful views of the mountains, and many offer Tucson valley views as well. The course also boasts some of Arizona's most outstanding bent grass greens. And because it's nearly 1,000 feet above Tucson, it's slightly cooler and a good choice for summer golf. Be forewarned, however, that wind is a factor here on almost every hole.

You can tee off from any of three teeing positions, with the longest at 6,523 yards, on this par 72 course rated 70.2. Five of the holes are very challenging par 3s; the 250-yard number 12 is reputed to be the most challenging par 3 in Arizona, with hazards all the way and a very narrow layout. Santa Rita has a clubhouse and full practice facilities.

Weekend rates are very affordable here: $35 for 18 holes with a cart in peak season.

Golf Courses in Tucson

Tucson offers a wide variety of courses for all abilities. From top resorts and private clubs to easily accessible public courses, you'll find it all here in this increasingly popular golfing destination. Check our individual alphabetized listings for details on each course.

Municipal Courses

The following public courses are operated by the city of Tucson and Pima County:

- Crooked Tree
- Dell Urich
- El Rio
- Fred Enke
- Randolph North
- Silverbell

Private and Resort Courses

Tucson is also home to the following select luxurious private and resort courses that are open to the public:

- Arizona National Golf Club
- Dorado Golf Club
- The Gallery at Dove Mountain
- The Golf Club at Vistoso
- Heritage Highlands Golf Club
- Hilton El Conquistador Resort and Country Club
- The Lodge at Ventana Canyon Golf and Racquet Club
- Omni Tucson National Golf Resort
- The Pines Golf Club at Marana
- Quail Canyon Golf Course
- Santa Rita Golf Club
- Starr Pass Golf Resort

Silverbell Golf Course, one of Tucson's several municipal golf courses, offers challenging sport and beautiful desert vistas. PHOTO BY KATE REYNOLDS

SILVERBELL MUNICIPAL GOLF COURSE
3600 North Silverbell Road
(520) 791-5235
www.tucsoncitygolf.com

Silverbell Golf Course is a championship layout located high upon the west bank of the Santa Cruz River. It's been totally redesigned by golf course architect Ken Kavanaugh, who molded the old Silverbell course into a more demanding mix that has undulating fairways that meander among stands of mature pine trees, strategically placed bunkers, and two large lakes that come into play on five holes. All the holes have been redesigned and are challenging and fun. A par 70 golf course consisting of five par 3s and three par 5s of varying lengths and strategies will test and excite golfers of all abilities from beginner to professional. It's still a young course but may prove to be Tucson's finest municipal golf course. Amenities include a practice green, well-lit driving range, and bar and grill. In winter (November through May), the cost to residents for prebooked 18 holes with a cart is $40. The course is situated close to downtown at the foot of the Tucson Mountains just west of I-10 and north of Grant Road on a main byway.

STARR PASS GOLF RESORT
3645 West Starr Pass Boulevard
(520) 670-0400
www.starrpass.com

This newly redesigned 27-hole Arnold Palmer signature design course is a favorite among visiting pros. Perched in the foothills of the Tucson Mountains, the rocky, cactus-covered desert terrain surrounds the lush green fairways and bent grass greens of these three nine-hole courses. The courses are kept at PGA standards all year. There are tricky but fun holes at all three courses. The Coyote course is the longest, the Roadrunner nine is the shortest, and the Rattler is considered the toughest. The desert-style layout challenges players at any level.

The golf club has great teaching facilities and practice areas. In addition to a lovely territorial-design clubhouse, Starr Pass has a great driving range and putting green. The peak-season rate for 18 holes with a cart is $205. The course is 3 miles west of I-10 on Starr Pass Boulevard (which is actually 22nd Street for most of its length) and very close to the downtown area.

PRACTICE RANGES

If you're interested in taking a whack at some balls with your driver or putter but don't have the time to get to a golf course, you'll find several nicely equipped practice ranges around the city. All are open year-round and have hours generally from early morning to 9:00 or 10:00 p.m. but tend to close earlier in winter months. Most have clubs you can rent or just use for the practice, and some actually sell clubs and give you a chance to demo them before you buy. Some also offer lessons. Unless otherwise noted, there is a fee for a bucket of balls, depending on the size, and the putting and chipping areas are free whether you're paying for a bucket of balls or not.

LA MARIPOSA CLUB
1501 North Houghton Road
(520) 749-1099
www.lamariposaresort.com

This is a membership sports and fitness center that happens to also have a golf practice range that's open to the public. You'll find a driving range as well as private lessons and golf clinics at this east-side spot on Houghton between Speedway Boulevard and Tanque Verde Road.

THE PRACTICE TEE
4050 West Costco Place
(520) 544-2600

This northwest facility is called "upscale" by those in the know and indeed does seem to have lots to offer, starting with 100 all-grass tee stations from which you can hit to actual greens. You'll find putt, chip, and sand trap practice areas as well as lessons; clubs to rent, buy, or demo; and club repair. Ball buckets come in four sizes. Look for this facility behind the Costco/Home Depot where Orange Grove Road meets Thornydale Road.

ROLLING HILLS GOLF COURSE
8900 East 29th Street
(520) 298-2401
Part of a members-only golf course on the southeast part of town near Camino Seco Boulevard, the driving range and chipping and putting areas here are open to the public. Clubs are available for rental, and you can buy large and small baskets of balls.

i Tucson plays annual host to the World Golf Championships–Accenture Match Play Event, one of four World Golf Championship events. Eligibility for the Accenture Match Play Event is limited to the top 64 worldwide players. Past champions include the great Tiger Woods. The event takes place at the Gallery Golf Club at Dove Mountain each February.

DAY TRIP GOLF COURSES

Just 30 minutes down Interstate 19 from downtown Tucson is Green Valley, a bustling and expanding retirement community that's also become a hot spot for golf. It offers beautiful scenery set in the rolling terrain of the Santa Cruz River valley plus a number of spectacular golf courses to choose from within a short distance of one another. And after you've played to your heart's content in Green Valley, just take a swing farther south down I-19 to find courses in Tubac, Rio Rico, and Nogales. You can play for days in this area south of Tucson and never play the same course twice. Good golf packages are available if you prefer to stay in the area rather than drive down from Tucson. Plan on riding, not walking, these courses. You'll also find a new course, Del Lago, in Vail, a rapidly growing area in the southeast part of town.

HAVEN PUBLIC GOLF COURSE AND TORTUGA GOLF COURSE
110 North Abrego Drive, Green Valley
(520) 625-4281
www.havengolf.com
This was Green Valley's first golf course, built in 1967, and is also one of the easiest to find. Just exit from I-19 at Esperanza Boulevard (exit 65), go west, look for the large sign to the left of the Green Valley Social Center, and untrunk your clubs. Ideal for players of all skill levels, Haven is 18 holes totaling 6,867 yards (rated 71.6) from the back tees or 5,811 yards from the forward tees. The Tortuga Golf Course is a nine-hole pitch-and-putt course. This course is an excellent choice if some of your traveling companions are just not ready for the big 18—you can play the par 72 Haven course and your traveling companion can keep busy on Tortuga, and everybody is happy. The Haven course is a traditional design with grass throughout and mature vegetation. In fact, you may be surprised to see large pine trees interspersed with eucalyptus and palm trees. Panoramic views of the Santa Rita Mountains may lull you into a sense of calm, but don't get too relaxed or you'll miss some shots requiring both distance and accuracy.

The facilities include a driving range, putting green, and chipping green, plus the Overpar lounge. For Tortuga the peak-season fee is $15 (no carts). Haven's peak-season rate is $45 for 18 holes, including use of a cart.

TORRES BLANCAS GOLF CLUB
3233 South Abrego Drive, Green Valley
(520) 625-5200
www.torresblancasgolf.com
One could say that this course rose out of the ashes like the legendary phoenix. When developers began digging out the course in 1994, they actually uncovered a nearly complete golf course that had been abandoned due to the economic conditions of the early 1980s. Under the dirt was what course developers discovered to be a masterpiece layout by Trevino Designs that needed only an irrigation system and a few refinements. The result is a 165-acre course with a traditional design reminiscent of the PGA Tour courses—the fairways are expansive and considerably wider than most modern golf courses. It stretches along the west bank of the Santa Cruz River and eventually into one of the state's largest pecan

tree orchards. Three lakes add to the beauty and challenges of the par 72 course that plays to 7,000 yards at a rating of 69.9.

The peak-season weekend fee is $79 for 18 holes with a cart. There's also a full-service gourmet restaurant, the Madera Room. Torres Blancas is located within one of Green Valley's residential communities, Santa Rita Springs Development on the east side of I-19, and its Mediterranean-style clubhouse with a tower can easily be seen from the highway. Take exit 63, Continental Road, east to the frontage road, then south to the course.

SAN IGNACIO GOLF CLUB
4201 South Camino del Sol, Green Valley
(520) 648-3468
www.sanignaciogolfclub.com

Designed by Arthur Hills in 1989, San Ignacio has earned accolades for its excellence. To get there, exit I-19 at Continental Road (exit 63), take the west-side frontage road south to Camino Encanto, and follow the signs. The four teeing areas range from the 6,288-yard professional tees rated 72.8 to the 5,200-yard forward tees.

No matter which teeing position you choose, intelligent decisions and accurate shots are de rigueur. San Ignacio was designed to use the natural terrain to its best possible advantage, and its superb layout makes it possible for golfers to see everything they will encounter from every tee, including the best route to the green. The fairways and rough are Bermuda grass, and the greens are bent grass. The signature hole is number 13, a 522-yard double-dogleg par 5 featuring elevated tees and a double lake along the left side. And San Ignacio offers some of the most popular dining in Green Valley as well at the Coyote Grill.

In peak season, 18 holes with a cart run $77.

CANOA HILLS GOLF COURSE
1401 West Calle Urbano, Green Valley
(520) 648-1880
www.canoahillsgolfclub.com

This par 72 course is a good 18-hole choice for anyone who wants a challenge, yet is fair to the average golfer. Surrounded by the natural terrain and stands of mesquite trees, the fairways are tight yet inviting. Accuracy in placing the ball is key here. The greens are generous, and their bent grass always in immaculate condition. From the men's black tees the course plays to 6,088 yards with a 67.9 rating. Facilities include a practice range, putting green, and restaurant and lounge. The rate for 18 holes with a cart in peak season is $77. To get here, exit from I-19 at Continental Road, take the west-side frontage south to Camino Encanto Road, and follow the signs.

CANOA RANCH GOLF CLUB
5800 South Camino del Sol, Green Valley
(520) 393-1966
www.canoaranchgolfcourse.com

This 18-hole course, designed by the team of Schmidt-Curley, offers gorgeous views of Elephant Head and Green Valley. You'll find dramatic elevation changes and beautiful desert surroundings. Note especially the rock wall carved right out of the mountain on hole number 2. There are six par 3s here—and they're tough. It's been featured in *Golf Digest* as one of the top courses in the world. Some say that if you can only play one course in the area, this would be a good choice. The Canoa Ranch Grill is a great spot for a delicious postgame lunch or dinner. A greens fee of $85 gets you a golf cart and use of the practice areas.

Take I-19 south to exit 56, Canoa Ranch Road. Take the frontage road north about 0.25 mile to Calle Tres. Turn west and go 0.5 mile to Camino del Sol, then turn south and follow the road to the clubhouse.

DEL LAGO GOLF CLUB
14155 East Via Rancho del Lago, Vail
(520) 647-1100
www.dellagogolf.com

Located about 15 miles southeast of Tucson in the fast-growing area of Vail, this Nugent Group–designed course offers 120 feet of elevation change, a combination of links and desert golf with wide sweeping fairways, and seven lakes with spectacular mountain views. The first hole begins at the peak of the course, while other holes play down to the valley. Back tees at 7,206 yards carry a rating of 73.9 and a slope of 135; par is 72. With an elevation of 3,500 feet, it can be cooler than Tucson-area courses. The course surrounds the master-planned community of Rancho del Lago and has a driving range, practice bunker, 12,000-square-foot practice green, and a clubhouse with a full-service pro shop and a bar and grill. This is a Tucson gem, with a great layout and plenty of dimension that helps pull out your best golf.

From Tucson take I-10 to the Vail Road–Wentworth exit (exit 279) and go north on Vail Road for 3.5 miles; the course is at the top of the hill. Peak weekend rates for 18 holes with a cart are $89.

TUBAC GOLF RESORT
One Otero Road, Tubac
(520) 398-2021
www.tubacgolfresort.com

If you're a movie buff as well as a golf buff (or even just a golf-movie buff), you may recognize this golf venue as one of the sites for Kevin Costner's *Tin Cup*. In fact, the lake on the 16th hole was created just for the movie (we hope it poses less trouble to you than it did to Mr. Costner). Located south of Green Valley on the east side of I-19 at exit 40, Tubac is a traditional championship course that winds along both sides of the Santa Cruz River. At this spot, however, the dry riverbed to the north becomes a viable stream feeding the beautiful, stately cottonwood trees that contribute to this course's appeal. The setting seems more quaint and rural than Southwestern. Nine new holes, designed by local golf architect Ken Kavanaugh, were added in 2006, bringing the total to 27.

The original 18 holes were the work of pioneer golf course architect Red Lawrence. This par 71 course plays to 6,533 yards from the back tees with a 71.8 rating. Its signature hole is the charming and picturesque number 18. You'll find a driving range, practice greens, and restaurant and lounge at the resort, plus it's just minutes away from the delightful Tubac Village (see the Day Trips and Weekend Getaways chapter). A new clubhouse, golf pro shop, and practice facility round out the package.

It's $109 for 18 holes with a cart in peak season on weekends.

i Tucson is host to several pro tournaments. The Chrysler Classic of Tucson, one of the PGA's longest-running tournaments (begun in 1945), is held annually at the Omni Tucson National Golf Resort in February. The LPGA Championship takes place in March of every year at the Randolph North Municipal Golf Course. Both events attract thousands of golf fans and lots of pros to town.

RIO RICO RESORT GOLF COURSE
1069 Camino Caralampi, Rio Rico
(520) 281-8567, (800) 288-4746
www.rioricoresort.com

Continue south down I-19 to exit 17, take a left at the stop sign, follow the large terra-cotta markers, and you'll find Rio Rico Golf Course, one of Arizona's lesser-known gems. Although the resort itself is on the west side of the interstate, the course is on the east side, meandering through rich pastureland. Golfers here have been known to think they actually were playing in the lush and rolling hills of Arkansas or Tennessee. Fairways are lined with mesquite and cottonwood trees. The classic 18-hole layout designed by Robert Trent Jones Sr. welcomes every player with its rolling fairways and large open greens, plus enough sand traps and water hazards to challenge the best. From its longest tees the course measures 7,119 yards, par 72, and rating of 72.9. Food and beverages are available at the course, as are a practice range and putting green. The cost for 18 holes with a cart in peak season is $69. The resort also has popular golf packages.

BICYCLING

Tucson is a bicyclist's paradise. Miles of scenic trails and terrific weather year-round are just a couple reasons *Bicycling Magazine* ranked Tucson as one of the top three North American cities for bicycling. Whether you're a professional or just looking for some great exercise, this bicycle-friendly city is the place to ride.

HISTORY

Tucson has a long history of bicycle-friendly legislation and planning. At the forefront of bikeway development, the city designated its first bikeways in 1971, totaling some 8 miles. This was the nation's first community plan for a bikeway system, a series of designated bike routes designed to assist cyclists in connecting with other routes around the city.

In 1975 the first Tucson Regional Bikeways Plan was approved by the Pima Association of Governments, and over the next two years more than 56 miles of bikeways were added. The policy was so successful that the Bicycling Federation of America used it as a national model.

The next expansion of this transportation plan was completed in 1981. It called for all new road construction and reconstruction projects to include bike lanes. This direction has helped install over 630 miles of bike lane in the Tucson region to date. To answer the growing interest in what Tucson had to offer bicyclists, the Pima Association of Governments began publishing the Tucson Bicycle Map in 1986.

All of the planning and policies paid off in 1994 when Tucson was officially designated a "Bicycle Friendly Community" by the League of American Bicyclists.

Now the city and county and Pima Association of Governors each have full-time bicycle coordinators along with a host of nonprofit bicycling groups, advisory committees, and cycling clubs. Plans to expand bike lanes, increase motorist-biker education programs, add more bicycle-friendly facilities and bike parking will only enhance this already pro-bicycling city.

HITTING THE STREETS

The free Tucson Bicycle Map can be found at all retail bike shops and public libraries around the area. This multicolored map lists shared-use paths, bike lanes, residential bike routes, and just about everything else a cyclist needs to know to peddle around Tucson. We strongly recommend getting one. That way you can pick the best way to get around town on your bicycle.

Out on the roadways, many of the official routes are marked with large green Bike Route signs, and most have 4- to 5-foot-wide sections with white lines painted to mark the bicyclist's designated roadway. On other busy routes, streets have separate bus lanes that are shared with bicyclists.

When riding within the city, remember that bicyclists have the same responsibilities as motorists. Those responsibilities include riding on the right with traffic, obeying traffic signals, having lights on after dark, and signaling before turning. There's also one additional responsibility: If you're younger than 18, you're required to wear a helmet. (And if you're older, it may not be the law, but it's a very good idea.)

In many areas, even those with good biking systems, riders still have to exercise great care when crossing major thoroughfares. However, the city has alleviated that problem in some areas. For example, the city has two bicycle boulevards that crisscross the University of Arizona and extend in each direction, providing bike commuters a safe way to get to work, school, and entertainment destinations. If you're going to campus from north of Speedway Boulevard, a main east-west thoroughfare makes crossing simple. Three bicycle and pedestrian tunnels have been installed at Olive Road, Highland Avenue, and Warren Avenue, all between Campbell and Park Avenues.

BIKE AND RIDE

Sun Tran, the city's bus system, has made it easy to bicycle and ride the bus with its Bike & Bus program. Bike racks are mounted on the front of all buses. Passengers unfold the rack and mount their own bikes, but it's on a first-come, first-served basis because the racks only carry two bikes.

Sun Tran also rents weatherproof bike-storage lockers at a number of locations and all transit centers for a fee. A number of bus stop locations have bike racks for people who want to leave their bikes at the stop. All these locations are listed in the Sun Tran information guide. (See the Getting Here, Getting Around chapter.)

BIKE PATHS

As part of the effort to maintain safe and accessible bicycling for residents, the city has created a series of great bike paths. Each route has its own charm, and all are shared with walkers, joggers, and in-line skaters. As an extra bonus, you'll find many beautiful public artworks along the way.

THE BARRAZA-AVIATION BIKEWAY/GOLF LINKS PATH

A cyclist can take the path from Escalante and Kolb all the way downtown, crossing the gorgeous bicycle and pedestrian bridges—the Diamondback and Basket. The entire stretch of path is about 10 miles long!

i A phantom rider known as the "Grey Wolf" is said to ride forever in the Tucson area. He's been spotted, wearing a pink jersey, on the McCain Loop, Helmet Peak, Main Gate Square, and Old Nogales Highway. Have you seen him?

DAVID BELL BIKE PATH

This bike path is right in the heart of the city. The 3-mile "loop" makes this a great spot for a quick jaunt either before or after work. The pathway circles a good portion of Reid Park, traveling parallel to Randolph Way on the west, Broadway Boulevard on the north, Alvernon Way on the east, and 22nd Street on the south. Access is easy from any one of these roadways. Those who choose to drive can leave their cars in any one of the park's parking lots.

MOUNTAIN AVENUE BIKE BOULEVARD

Mountain Avenue is a north-south primary collector that leads to and from the University of Arizona. The Mountain Avenue corridor was chosen to encourage and facilitate the use of alternative, nonpolluting modes of transportation. Six-foot bike lanes, separated by a rideable 3-foot buffer area, and reduced travel lanes of 11 feet for vehicles effectively make this a bicycle boulevard that provides a connection from the University of Arizona to the Rillito River Linear Park and Pima County Trail System. South of campus, the bikeway continues along Highland Avenue and connects to the Aviation Bikeway.

OLD SPANISH TRAIL BIKE PATH

Another route on the east side, this one presents a little more of a challenge with its slight hills and dales. The pathway boasts some of the nicest scenery due to its proximity to Saguaro National Park, a great place to park and start your ride. This pathway has been improved with new bike lanes added to make the entire ride easier, with continuous bike lanes all the way to Colossal Cave. An underpass at Old Spanish Trail and Harrison helps cyclists and pedestrians avoid the traffic at the Target Shopping Center.

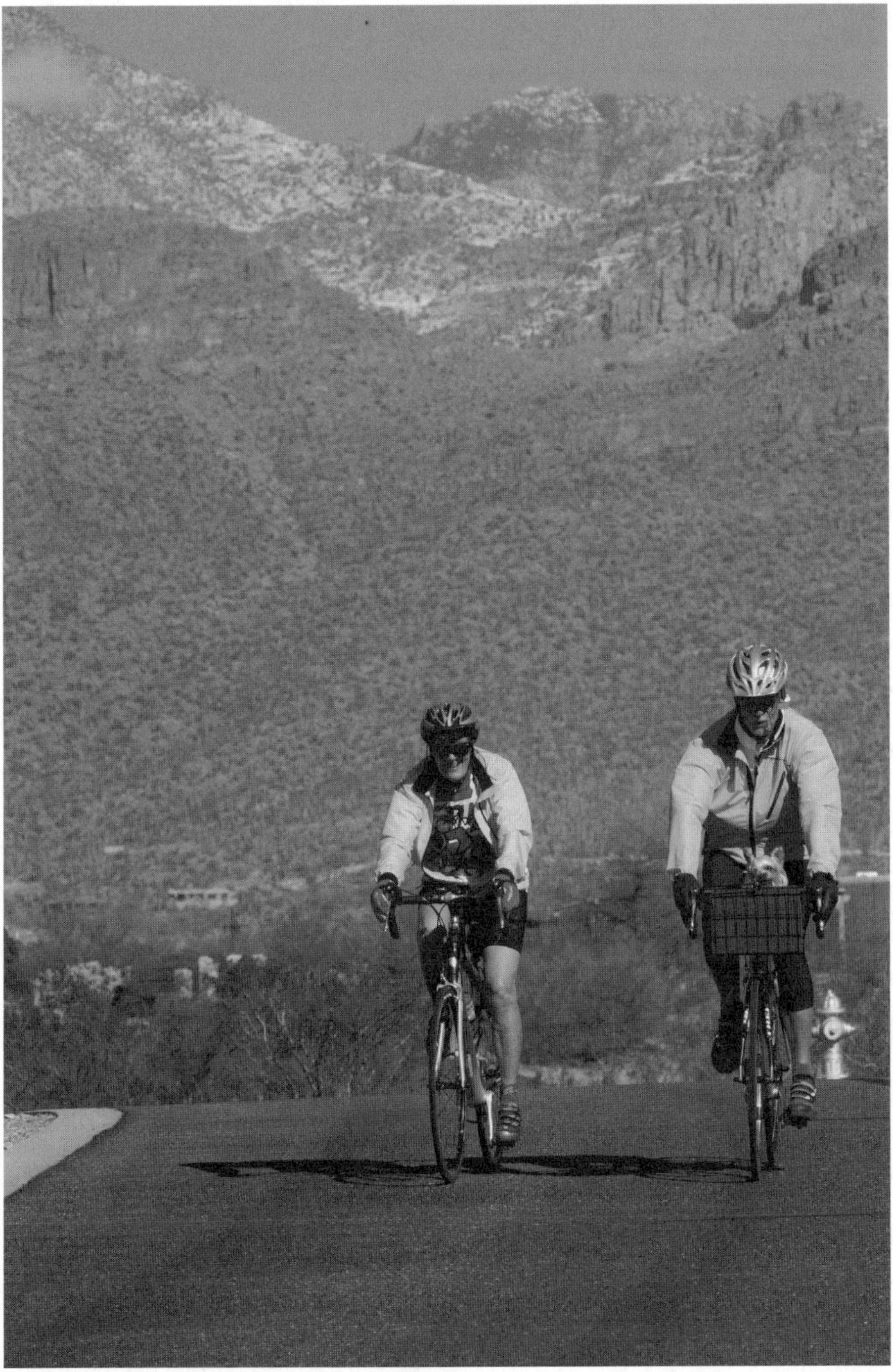

Bicycling in Tucson is a popular sport, owing to plentiful bike lanes and magnificent views. PHOTO BY KATE REYNOLDS

In 2006 the Tucson region received the gold award from the League of American Bicyclists as a Bicycle Friendly Community. The level of cooperation among the various regional jurisdictions is exceptional.

THIRD STREET BIKE BOULEVARD

The Third Street bike boulevard is an east-west connector route that provides bicycle access to and from the university and midtown areas. It includes special arterial street crossings, traffic calming devices, and other bicyclist-friendly enhancements. West of campus, the bikeway continues along University Avenue through Main Gate Square shopping district to the Fourth Avenue historic shopping district in downtown Tucson.

TUCSON DIVERSION CHANNEL BIKE PATH

At the present time these two bikeways are separate paths, but plans to link them are in the works. One part, which is only 1 mile long, offers beautiful desert scenery and interesting artwork along the way. The other part, which stretches for 3 miles, borders a city park and Kino Memorial Hospital. There's some up-and-down riding (on ramps) as you travel along. Sam Lena Park offers the best access and car parking from the east, although you can start at any of the overpasses along the route. Catch the western start just on the other side of I-19.

RIVER PARKS

The banks of Tucson's river systems have been in the process of being turned into recreational facilities since the first River Park Master Plan was introduced in 1976.

Since the first section of the river park was completed in 1987 along the Rillito River between Campbell Avenue and Flowing Wells Road, the city and county have been determined to build a pedestrian, in-line skating, bicycle, and equestrian trail network. These well-marked two-lane, 10-foot-wide minihighways will connect all the major watercourses along the Santa Cruz and Rillito Rivers, Tanque Verde Creek, Julien Wash, and Panatano Wash and serve as an alternate route for bike riders to weave through the metropolitan area.

Today two major sections of the river park system exist—Rillito River Park and Santa Cruz River Park. Both parks open at sunrise and close at sunset, and each has amenities including restrooms, drinking fountains, parking, artwork, picnic areas with bike racks, and frequent switchbacks that lead down to the sandy riverbeds. At major intersections cyclists are given the choice to go under the streets or cross them. Either way, using the river park system can be either an adventure or a tranquil way of crisscrossing the urban sprawl of Tucson.

Rillito River Park

This east-west river park runs between Craycroft Road and Interstate 10. It's made of a combination of paved and unpaved pathways.

The north bank is designated for walkers, joggers, cyclists, and in-line skaters; the south bank is reserved for walkers, joggers, and horseback riders. Don't make the mistake of riding your bike on the south bank—the park rangers will stop you, and you could be fined. And remember: When it comes to yielding on this well-kept path, bike riders are at the bottom of the food chain and are required to yield to everybody. Parking and easy access can be found at any of the major cross streets. (See the Parks and Recreation chapter for more information on Rillito River Park.)

Santa Cruz River Park

This is a very well-kept river park and the nicest way to transit the heart of Tucson. The park runs from Grant Road, north of downtown, south through the downtown area, and around Congress Street to Irvington Road. There is a break from Silverlake Road south to Ajo Way, but it is easily bypassed and worth the temporary detour along Mission Road to pick up the river trail farther south to Irvington Road.

On the west bank of the Santa Cruz, near the corner of Riverside Drive and Huron Street, you'll pass a playground, ramadas, picnic tables, and restrooms. There's a set of arches designed by local artist Susan Gamble that tell the history of the river and its ancient inhabitants.

Farther south along the west bank is the Garden of Gethsemane, featuring religious statuary by sculptor Felix Lucero (see the Attractions chapter). The statues were made from materials found in the Santa Cruz.

As you ride south and emerge from under the Congress Street Bridge, a huge eucalyptus tree will come into view. At 4 feet in diameter, it is Tucson's largest tree. On the ride farther south are restrooms, drinking fountains, and opportunities to cut down into the riverbed to explore. (See the Parks and Recreation chapter.)

MOUNTAIN BIKING

The entire Tucson vicinity is within easy proximity to mountain and desert parks that offer great chances for off-road riding. The area's splendid scenery, moderate climate, and range of elevations, from the desert floor to the 9,100-foot-high Mount Lemmon, make the surrounding area ideal.

If you plan to enter any mountain bike races, we suggest you contact the nonprofit **Mountain Bike Association of Arizona** (P.O. Box 41255, Mesa, AZ 85274; 602-351-7430; www.mbaa.net). This organization is the sponsor of many area races sanctioned by NORBA.

For maps and information on trails, check the local bike shops for a copy of the Tucson Bicycling Map. It includes designated trails in both Saguaro National Park East and West. The parks also have trail maps, which can be found at the visitor centers in each park. Keep in mind that there are trails specifically designated for mountain biking.

The most important thing to remember when spending any time in the parks is the "Leave No Trace" ethic that has kept these areas pristine. Keep your riding groups small, and stay on the trails to avoid scarring the landscape and plant life everyone comes to admire.

Here are some of the area's best and most scenic trails, which are highly recommended by Sonoran Desert Mountain Bicyclists, who have kindly provided this information and who list other trails, maps, and helpful advice on their Web site at www.sdmb.org.

FANTASY ISLAND

Fantasy Island is a mountain bike playground in southeast Tucson. It features over 16 miles of twisty singletrack in natural Sonoran Desert and was built by mountain bikers for mountain bikers. It is located off Irvington Road, just east of Harrison Road. Mountain bikers love this place.

Saguaro National Park East

CACTUS FOREST LOOP

Though there are more than 75 miles of trails in Saguaro National Park East (some of which head into the nearby Rincon Mountains), the 8.0-mile Cactus Forest Loop in Saguaro East is the only section of the park's trail system that is legal for mountain bikes.

To get there, take Broadway Boulevard east to Old Spanish Trail and follow the signs to Saguaro National Park East. You will pay a day fee of about $3 per bike. Because the trail is a paved loop, you will find the trailhead no matter which way you turn past the guardhouse. Be sure to stop at the visitor center for trail maps.

The trail heading north is one-way in that direction, while the loop heading south is two-way for bicycle traffic. Heading south, you'll hit the Javelina picnic area along a slight detour. This is the point where traffic becomes one-way again—from the opposite direction. Some riders take this 1.3-mile route, have a snack, and then head back the other way past the visitor center to travel the entire loop. Others prefer to go north and stop at this picnic area during the final leg of the trip to reflect on what they've seen over the last 7.0 miles.

Either way, this trip through the desert forest of cacti is enjoyable, and you're bound to see a number of desert creatures lurking in the bush. The trail is accessible to beginners, but more experienced riders will enjoy it as well.

North of Tucson

CATALINA STATE PARK

This is certainly one of the nicest, in-close areas to ride. Catalina State Park is located north on Oracle Road about 6 miles from the intersection of Ina and Oracle. Golder Ranch Road, which leads to much of the 50-plus-year-old trail and the Chutes, is around 10.5 miles north on Oracle from the intersection of Ina and Oracle Roads. Both are on the right (east) side of Oracle Road.

There is plenty of singletrack and some technical areas, along with a whole bunch of beginner to intermediate rides. This area has something for everyone. You can arrange your ride to be virtually any distance or time you would like. There is a 2.0-mile introductory fun ride, up to 30 miles of killer climbs, and technical challenges. All of this, and it is beautiful.

There is a loop of singletrack that will definitely convince people that riding is fun! Go to the parking area at the end of Golder Ranch Road and pick up the singletrack down the road on your right. There are two tracks, one about 50 yards down on the right and another about 300 yards along, also on the right. These will eventually join up at a dirt road. You can't miss with these trails. You can do about a 3.0-mile loop and will really have a ball. Watch out for the cacti, however!

Mount Lemmon

MEADOW AND ASPEN DRAW TRAIL

This is a wonderful, cool ride—7.0 miles, with the uphill mostly on asphalt. There is singletrack for almost all of the return downhill. This is a loop you will probably want to do twice. Ride it, eat, and ride it again. It is 30 degrees cooler than the Tucson basin and feels all of it. The elevation is 8,000 to 9,000 feet, so the air is a lot thinner and you will most definitely take notice of this. The uphill on the little-used road to the observatory is fairly tough. The singletrack has some technical challenges (logs, wet roots, tree stumps, switchbacks, etc.), but it is rideable by an intermediate who is cautious. If you are out of shape, blow this ride off.

Directions: Take the Mount Lemmon Highway to the top (Summerhaven) and park in the dirt parking area on your right as you enter the village. Get on your bike and head back the way you came in to the turn to the Mount Lemmon ski area and go left. Take this road to the observatory on the top of the mountain. Take the trail from the parking area to the left of the gate on the road to the observatory. The trail is at the west end of the lot. It's a short climb, roughly parallel to the road, and then a slight downhill. Bear to the right at an intersection, and skirt the south side of the observatory. You'll encounter some rocks and roots on the singletrack, but it's rideable. You will come out on a jeep road. Turn left and follow the road, climbing back toward the observatory. When you return to the parking area, find the trail dropping down to the south, and take it a short distance to a gate on the road that goes behind the ski area. (This is close to the road you came up.) Follow that road about 0.25 mile and look for a trail on the left. This is the Aspen Draw Trail (do not go on the Aspen Trail!).

i Click on over to http://tucsonbiketrails.wikispaces.com. You'll find a helpful wiki that lists popular trails and even a downloadable mountain biking map.

South of Tucson (Santa Rita Mountains)

GARDNER CANYON—KENTUCKY CAMP

This area has literally miles upon miles of singletrack and four-wheel-drive roads. You can find any type of ride that interests you. It is fairly close to Tucson, much cooler, has beautiful scenery, is well marked (mostly), has caves and lots of history—has just about everything—and some can hike while others ride.

The ride that is featured here is one that brings into play most of the singletrack in the area, uses very little of the four-wheel-drive roads, and passes through Kentucky Camp (an ill-fated gold-mining venture just after the turn of the twentieth century with restored adobe structures). This will let you experience many different riding levels (you can walk parts if you want) and can take as long as you wish because it is an out and back.

Directions: From I-10 and the Sonoita, turn onto Highway 83, head south until you get almost to Sonoita, and go right (west) on the Gardner Canyon turnoff. Take your first right (Y in the road), and stay on that road until you get to the large parking area on your left (a couple of miles). Good maps are posted in this area. Ride up (left/west) the Forest Service road for a couple of miles to a gate on your left at the top of the ridge. Turn left and head down to Kentucky Camp.

INFORMATION PLEASE!

Whether you need maps or information on trails, local rider clubs, or Tucson bicycle laws, the following quick reference list will help you get started.

CITY OF TUCSON BICYCLE COORDINATOR
201 North Stone Avenue, Sixth Floor
(520) 791-4372
www.ci.tucson.az.us
This full-time, paid position handles the promotion and coordination of bike- and pedestrian-related projects, including the annual Bike Fest, for the city of Tucson. Call for updates on bikeways, legislation, and special events.

Close-up

Cycling with Others

Tucson is truly a bicyclist's paradise, with great weather and lots of scenic rides. If you're looking for a group to ride with, there are lots of bike clubs in town. Here's a sampling:

DooDah Road Club

This is a great group of people dedicated to promoting enjoyable cycling for the whole family and for all levels of cycling enthusiasts. Annual dues are $18, but it isn't necessary to join to ride with the group. For more information, contact the Head Doo at www.doodahroadclub.org.

Greater Arizona Bicycling Association

GABA rides, competitive to leisurely, are open to anyone. All riders must have a helmet, and all bikes must be in good working order. Check www.bikegaba.org for a schedule of day rides, or call (520) 760-0458.

Oro Valley Bike Club

No fee for this one either. Riders meet at the Oro Valley Bike Shop on Oracle Road. Call (520) 825-2751 or check www.orovalleybicycle.com (click on "Lounge" for details and maps).

Southern Arizona Mountain Biking Association

SAMBA organizes bike rides and related events every week. Rides are for varied skill levels in the mountains and desert country around town. Helmets are required. Nonmembers are welcome at all events. If you like what you see, then you can become a member for an annual fee of $15. For more information, call (520) 323-0571. A detailed schedule is posted at www.sambabike.org.

EPIC RIDES
2609 East Broadway Boulevard
(520) 745-2033
www.epicrides.com
An offshoot of PBAA, this organization sponsors mountain bike gatherings in Tucson and throughout Arizona. Their comprehensive Web site offers listings of rides and gatherings and an e-newsletter to keep you up to date.

GREATER ARIZONA BICYCLING ASSOCIATION—TUCSON CHAPTER
4590 North Via Noriega
www.bikegaba.org
The Tucson chapter of this state organization promotes interest and involvement in all aspects of bicycling. To this end it publishes a free monthly newsletter with comprehensive tour and racing listings, legislation updates, and other bicycling news. Their Web site offers a great list of local rides and maps. The newsletter is distributed by most of the bike shops listed under Retail Shops and Repair in this chapter.

THE PERIMETER BICYCLING ASSOCIATION OF AMERICA
2609 East Broadway
(520) 745-2033
www.pbaa.com
The PBAA is a national group located in Tucson. It organizes El Tour de Tucson every November as well as a number of other smaller events. The association publishes *Tail Winds,* a full-color, tabloid-size free newspaper, six times a year. It's crammed with information and advertising and is distributed at area bike shops. PBAA is a membership-driven organization. Annual membership includes a year's worth of *Tail Winds* plus discounts on any PBAA-sponsored event and many other benefits.

REGIONAL BICYCLE COORDINATOR
Pima Association of Government
177 North Church Avenue, Suite 405
(520) 792-1093
www.pagnet.org
The Pima Association of Governments (PAG) coordinates the regional bicycle planning process among local jurisdictions and produces several area bicycle maps. Contact these folks with any and all questions about biking rules and regulations.

SONORAN DESERT MOUNTAIN BICYCLISTS
P.O. Box 65075, Tucson, AZ 85728-5075
(520) 750-8222
www.sdmb.org
This organization is devoted to the promotion of the sport of mountain bicycling by providing fun, safe biking experiences and social events for the mountain bicycling community.

SOUTHERN ARIZONA MOUNTAIN BIKING ASSOCIATION
2720 East Third Street
(520) 323-0571
www.sambabike.org
This nonprofit, locally based club schedules mountain bike rides on both weekends and weekdays for riders of various skill levels, leading rides into some of the most beautiful and remote country found in southern Arizona.

SUN TRAN CUSTOMER SERVICE CENTER
4220 South Park Avenue, Building 10
(520) 792-9222
www.suntran.com
City buses are equipped with bike racks. The *Sun Tran Ride Guide* lists the times and routes of these buses, as well as other useful info for the city bike commuter. (See the Getting Here, Getting Around chapter for more information about Sun Tran.)

TUCSON–PIMA COUNTY BICYCLE ADVISORY COMMITTEE
(520) 791-4372
www.dot.pima.gov/tpcbac/index.html
Established in 1987, this joint committee of Pima County and the city of Tucson is a citizen advisory group of approximately 21 people who meet each month to provide direction in decisions affecting the bicycling community. The committee also provides a strong voice in advocating for cyclists needs.

For a fully digitized version of any of the Tucson-area bike maps, go to http://dot.tucsonaz.gov/bicycle/. Here you can access a very cool multicolored version of the paper copies available at most bike shops.

MAJOR EVENTS

A weekend hardly goes by without some group of riders teaming up for short or long rides as a riding club. Here we list a few of the standout events that draw large numbers of people and add some millions to the local economy. Keep in mind that an industry-approved bike helmet is always required to participate in these events.

April

CLEAN AIR FAIR
City of Tucson
(520) 740-3947
Every year at the beginning of April, the city of Tucson sponsors Clean Air Fair. The idea is to promote bicycle commuting and alternative forms of transportation good for both personal health and the health of the local environment. The event includes fun rides, classes, and a Bike to Work Day.

TOUR OF THE TUCSON MOUNTAINS
Various locations
(520) 745-2033
www.pbaa.com
Organized by the PBAA, this event draws some 1,000 cyclists of all ages and abilities to participate in the 58-mile, 29-mile, and Kids Fun Ride events held in April. Starting points vary every year. The event routes riders around the Tucson Mountains.

July

TOUR FOR TUCSON'S CHILDREN
Tucson Convention Center
260 South Church Street
(520) 791-4870
www.cityoftucson.org/parksandrec
Usually held on July 4 and organized by the Tucson Parks and Recreation Department, Tour for Tucson's Children is a 27-mile ride, as well as a 10.5- and 6.5-mile Family Ride and 0.5-mile FunRide for kids. Each race starts at the Tucson Convention Center. The money raised from these rides benefits the Tucson Safe Kids Coalition Helmet and Bike Fund.

September

CORONA DE MARANA MS BIKE TOUR
National Multiple Sclerosis Society, Southwest Chapter
44400 East Broadway, Suite 600-0
(520) 747-7472
www.nmss.org
This scenic one-day loop tour usually takes place the last Saturday in September and starts in Marana, just a few miles north of Tucson. The event is part of a national series of rides designed to raise funds for the Multiple Sclerosis Society. With several rides, it's a great outing for the whole family. There is a registration fee and a minimum donation required to participate. Riders receive free breakfast and lunch. This is a fully supported ride with rest stops, SAG vehicles, and a bike patrol.

November

EL TOUR DE TUCSON
The Perimeter Bicycling Association of America
2609 East Broadway
(520) 745-2033
www.pbaa.com
Since 1983 cyclists have turned out for this tour, considered the oldest and largest perimeter cycling event in the United States, that actually circles the Tucson area. El Tour is always held the Saturday before Thanksgiving. Every year the proceeds from the race are given to a different local charity.

This is a fun ride, and all participants receive medallions. There are 109-, 81-, 66-, and 35-mile routes and fun rides for adults and kids. The event is a big deal in Tucson, with strong police traffic support along the route for safety, as well as aid stations and medical personnel. More than 8,000 cyclists, ranging from celebrated athletes from around the world to casual bikers, come out to compete or at least participate. Processing and registration fees apply, depending on when you sign up. The ride begins and ends in downtown Tucson.

El Tour de Tucson has been named by *Bicycling Magazine* as one of the 10 best century courses (that's 100 miles for all you nonbikers) in America, and the city folk who come out to watch are very supportive.

RETAIL SHOPS AND REPAIR

AJO BIKES
1301 East Ajo Way
(520) 294-1434
www.ajobikes.com
This shop promises to provide "wheels for everyone," offering a large selection of kids' trikes, BMX, freestyle, adult road and mountain bikes, and adult trikes. They are also the largest recumbent (reclining bike) dealer in the Southwest. Repairs and service are provided by master mechanics.

ARIZONA BICYCLE EXPERTS
2520 East Sixth Street
(520) 881-2279
www.abecycling.com
Not your average bike shop, this small shop is geared toward the avid cyclist. Staff research and stock high-quality products that are durable and dependable. They carry Santa Cruz, Moots, Rocky Mountain, Orbea, Felt, Race Face, and Chris King and Kona; do service and repairs; and will accept and hold bikes shipped from out of town. Rentals are available here as well.

BROADWAY BICYCLES
140 South Sarnoff Drive
(520) 296-7819
www.broadwaybicycles.com
One block south of Broadway Boulevard on the east side, this shop has been around since 1975 and offers a full line of biking clothing, accessories, parts, tools, car racks, and expert repairs on all makes. Broadway rents mountain bikes for a 24-hour period.

FAIR WHEEL BIKES
1110 East Sixth Street
(520) 884-9018
www.fairwheelbikes.com
Located in the heart of the university area, this store specializes in pro and custom bikes—road, mountain, and BMX—and used bikes. Fair Wheel offers a complete service department and rentals with pickup and delivery. Mountain bikes and road bikes are available for daily and other rentals.

ORDINARY BICYCLE SHOP
311 East Seventh Street
(520) 622-6488
This shop sells new road, touring, hybrid, mountain, cruiser, and tandem bikes and a selection of used bikes. You'll find full repair services and all accessories here, too. No rentals.

i **BICAS (Bicycle Intercommunity Art and Salvage) is a nonprofit community bike shop that offers terrific rides, repair classes, advocacy, and events for bicyclists of all ages. Located at 44 West Sixth Street, on the northwest corner of Sixth Street and Ninth Avenue, they sponsor community rides on the last Saturday of each month and a series of bike-in movies. Call (520) 628-7950 or go to www.bicas.org for details.**

ORO VALLEY BICYCLE
12985 North Oracle Road
(520) 825-2751

2850 West Ina Road
(520) 544-5999
www.orovalleybicycle.com
A family-owned business since 2001, the staff has over 25 years of experience in the bicycling industry. They offer models from Raleigh,

Specialized, Lemond, Gary Fisher, Diamondback, Giant, Co-Motion, Moots, and more and carry an extensive selection of parts, clothing, and cycling accessories. Buy your bike here and get personalized service and free lifetime adjustments on any bicycle sold. They also sell new and reconditioned bicycles, take trade-ins, and offer rentals.

PERFORMANCE BICYCLES
7204 East Broadway Boulevard
(520) 296-4715

3302 East Speedway Boulevard
(520) 327-3232
www.performancebike.com
Part of a larger chain based in California, these stores offer every kind of bicycle imaginable, from tricycles to cross-comfort styles. You'll also find clothing, electronics, equipment, and more.

PIMA STREET BICYCLES
5247 Pima Street at Rosemont
(520) 326-4044
ww.pimastreetbicycle.com
Do you have an old bike you'd like to get rid of, or not enough cash to afford a brand-new shiny bike? This is the place for you! It's a consignment-only shop dedicated to getting you the best price for your bike, minus their 20 percent commission. Bicycles of all shapes and sizes are welcome—you set the price.

R&R BICYCLE SUPERSTORES
2830 North Campbell
(520) 795-1099
You'll find southern Arizona's largest selection of bicycles and accessories at R&R along with lots of maps and friendly advice on where to bike. Trade-ins are also considered on purchases.

SABINO CYCLES
7045 East Tanque Verde Road
(520) 885-3666
www.sabinocycles.com
Sabino Cycles offers a full-service repair department, parts, accessories, clothing, rentals, and bikes for all ages.

TUCSON BICYCLES
4743 East Sunrise Drive
(520) 577-7374
www.tucsonbicycles.com
In the foothills near Swan Road and Sunrise Drive, this full-service shop is open seven days a week and offers a large selection of custom frames, repairs, parts, rentals with pickup and delivery, and even wheelchair repair. Tucson Bicycles also rents mountain and road bikes. Call ahead, as they have a limited fleet and get booked early.

SPECTATOR SPORTS

Tucson is a terrific venue for spectator sports. You'll find just about every outdoor and indoor sport here, from professional baseball and competitive swimming and diving to horse racing and ice hockey. The ideal year-round weather attracts pro baseball teams for spring training, and the University of Arizona offers nearly every sport imaginable, including top-ranked Pac-10 teams in men's baseball and basketball and women's softball. And Tucson plays host to two major-league teams during the spring training season. At press time, a third major-league team, the Chicago White Sox, was scheduled to practice in Tucson in 2009 and move to Glendale, Arizona, in 2010.

The university's nickname is the Wildcats, and you won't be in Tucson long before seeing signs, T-shirts, hats, or publications touting the Cats. UA competes in at least 18 varsity sports, most of which are very spectator oriented and provide great viewing and great fun for Tucsonans, who are faithful and supportive fans of their college teams. Unless otherwise noted, tickets for all UA games can be obtained at the ticket office at McKale Center, which is on National Championship Drive just west of Campbell Avenue and a block north of Sixth Street (520-621-2287; www.arizonaathletics.com). Just remember that any of the ticket prices given in this chapter are subject to change.

In addition to profiling the pro teams that play here and the major college sports you can watch in Tucson, this chapter covers other spectator sports offered in Tucson, such as racing and golf. We also take a slight detour to the north to tell you about the major sports teams based in Phoenix, because it's not uncommon for Tucson residents or visitors to travel there for a pro or bowl game. And finally, we also provide a primer on the major sports playing fields in both cities so you know how to get there, where to park, and what to expect.

TUCSON

Baseball/Softball

CACTUS LEAGUE

Each year, the boys of spring descend upon Tucson. We're Cactus League home to the championship Arizona Diamondbacks and the Colorado Rockies. At press time, the Chicago White Sox have plans to remain in Tucson for the 2009 season before moving to Glendale, Arizona, for spring training. The Diamondbacks and White Sox headquarter at Tucson Electric Park, while the Rockies hit homers at Hi Corbett Field in Reid Park. The spring training season lasts from early March to the first of April, and tickets will cost anywhere from $5 to $20. For Diamondback tickets call (866) 672-1343 or visit www.arizonadiamondbacks.com. Colorado Rockies fans can call (800) 388-ROCK (7625) or visit http://coloradorockies.com. For 2009 Chicago White Sox tickets, call (520) 434-1367 or visit chicago.whitesox.mlb.com.

i Looking to spot a ballplayer? You might find a few chowing down at Daisy Mae's, a spring training dinner hangout. Players luuuuuve the rib and chicken platter. Daisy Mae's is at 2735 West Anklam Road. Call (520) 792-8888.

The Arizona Diamondbacks take on the Chicago White Sox at Tucson Electric Park. PHOTO BY KATE REYNOLDS

UNIVERSITY OF ARIZONA WILDCATS—MEN
Jerry Kindall Field at Frank Sancet Stadium
640 North Warren Drive
(520) 621-4102
www.arizonaathletics.com

A testimony to the quality of UA's baseball program is the fact that plenty of professional baseball players have come from the team over the past 20 or so years. With its excellent sports reputation, UA can recruit good players, and with weather conditions conducive to lots of practice opportunities, the result is a good team and fans who come out to watch the games. The Wildcat baseball players were NCAA champs in 1976, 1980, and 1986, and play fine baseball every season, which runs from February to May. Ticket prices vary. The playing field is at North Warren and East Enke Drives just across from McKale Center, where tickets can be obtained. The closest parking is at the Cherry Garage to McKale Center's west or another pay parking lot just north of that.

UNIVERSITY OF ARIZONA WILDCATS—WOMEN
Hillenbrand Stadium
East Second Street and North Warren Drive
(520) 621-4920
www.arizonaathletics.com

The women's softball team is hot, hot, hot. Winners of many national titles, including the 2007 NCAA national championship, their home games are packed, and they've definitely elevated the profile of the sport nationwide. The season runs from February to May, and games are played at the 2,000-seat Hillenbrand Stadium on campus. Tickets range from $3 to $10 at the McKale Center ticket office.

Basketball

TUCSON FIESTA BOWL BASKETBALL CLASSIC
McKale Center
1 National Championship Drive
(520) 621-2287
www.tostitosfiestabowl.com/tucson

This basketball event is played at McKale Center in Tucson during the week before the New Year's

Day football game. It's an invitational tournament, but the UA basketball team is always one of the teams playing. On the first day there are two games between four teams, and on the second day a consolation and a championship game. Ticket prices vary; call for details. They usually go on sale around the first week of December at the McKale Center ticket office or by phone.

i Low on funds but love sports? You're in luck! Admission to the following Arizona Athletics sporting events is always free—just show up: cross-country, golf, gymnastics, soccer, swimming and diving, tennis, and track and field.

UNIVERSITY OF ARIZONA WILDCATS—MEN
McKale Center
1 National Championship Drive
(520) 621-4813, (520) 621-2287 (tickets)
www.arizonaathletics.com

Tucson has one of the best college teams, compliments of UA and coach Kevin O'Neill. Since the 1987–88 season, UA owns the best winning percentage in collegiate basketball. This Pac-10 team has been conference champions for 7 of the last 12 years, reached the Final Four in the NCAA tournament four times, won the NCAA championship in 1997, and were 2001 NCAA runner-up. The season runs from November to April and opens with the annual Red/Blue intrasquad scrimmage.

Home games are played at McKale Center at the university, which seats more than 14,500. Your best chance for a ticket is to befriend a season ticket holder who can't get to the game. Individual game tickets may be available at the McKale Center ticket office, online or by phone. As in all urban university towns, parking is at a premium and can be almost as tough to get as a ticket to the game. The closest option is the Cherry Garage immediately west of McKale Center, but those spots are for reserved season ticket holders.

UNIVERSITY OF ARIZONA WILDCATS—WOMEN
McKale Center
1 National Championship Drive
(520) 621-4813, (520) 621-2287 (tickets)
www.arizonaathletics.com

The women's basketball team was the 2003–2004 Pac-10 co-champion. And their popularity is growing, with several WNBA draft picks from the team. They play at McKale Center from early November through early March, with the NCAA tournament games immediately after. Ticket prices vary and are available from the McKale Center ticket office.

Football

UNIVERSITY OF ARIZONA WILDCATS
Arizona Stadium
East Sixth Street and North Warren Drive
(520) 621-4917
www.arizonaathletics.com

When September rolls around in Tucson, it may not seem like fall with temperatures still hovering in the low 100s, but that's what greets the university's Wildcat football players and fans in Arizona Stadium. Sunscreen is mandatory if you're going to a day game, but fortunately most are at night. The Wildcats are in the Pac-10 and play teams such as UCLA, USC, and Washington. But the biggest rivalry each year is against our neighbors to the north, the Arizona State University Sun Devils. Ticket prices vary. Parking on or near campus can be tough, so the easiest option may be the shuttle buses from the eastern end of El Con Mall at Broadway and Dodge Boulevards and also from the Tucson Mall.

Golf

The World Golf Championship—Accenture Match Play Championship made its first appearance in Tucson in 2007. Since eligibility is limited to the top 64 available players in the world, you can count on seeing the finest golfers work their magic. Past champions include Tiger Woods, Jeff Maggert, and Steve Striker. The February match is played at Marana's Gallery Golf Club at Dove Mountain, a challenging 7,351-yard, par 72 course. Each year the five-day tournament is sponsored by the Conquistadores, a civic group that supports local charities with the proceeds. You can purchase tickets online by visiting www.worldgolfchampionships.com or by calling (866) 942-2672. (For details on the tournament, see the Festivals and Events chapter.)

Ice Hockey

UNIVERSITY OF ARIZONA ICECATS
Tucson Convention Center
Church Avenue and Cushing Street
(520) 791-4266 (tickets)
www.uaicecats.com

The university's Icecats games are usually packed with a wildly uproarious audience reaching 6,000 to 8,000. One of the top club teams in the country (meaning they are not NCAA-affiliated but play in a league), the Icecats play at the Tucson Convention Center from October through February. Ticket prices vary for single games. Parking is available at the TCC for a fee or is free on neighboring side streets.

Racing

Horses

Rillito Downs
Rillito Park
4502 North First Avenue
(520) 293-5011

Rillito Downs is Tucson's only venue for horse racing, which takes place Saturday and Sunday afternoons, usually January through March, but the season length varies. The 88-acre racetrack is just off First Avenue, south of River Road, and is adjacent to the (usually dry) Rillito River, making it a pretty spot to watch the thoroughbreds and quarter horses run. And it's right next to Rillito Park, so you can take a picnic lunch and make a day of it. The racetrack features outside and inside seating with admission around $2, pari-mutuel wagering, and a full bar and restaurant. In addition to live races, there are simulcast races, and Rillito Downs races are played at about seven or eight off-track betting sites around Tucson. Call the racetrack or check with the Tucson Convention & Visitors Bureau for free season passes. Parking is free and usually ample.

i **The Copper Bowl, a top-rated national junior tennis event, is held annually at the Tucson Hilton El Conquistador Golf and Tennis Resort. Boys and girls aged 12 to 14 play on the 31 courts. For further information contact Dickinson Sports (520-742-2204).**

Greyhounds

TUCSON GREYHOUND PARK
36th Street at Fourth Avenue
(520) 884-7576
www.tucdogtrak.com

When the horses aren't running at Rillito, and even when they are, you can still watch races of the four-legged variety at Tucson Greyhound Park, which is open year-round (except Thanksgiving and Christmas) and has pari-mutuel wagering. Live races are run six days a week—Monday through Saturday evenings at 7:40 p.m. Greyhound Park also simulcasts races, both horse and dog. For the general admission fee, you'll watch the greyhounds streak along from a large air-conditioned grandstand, with bars, concession stands, and a nonsmoking area, or from the trackside rail. The park also offers a clubhouse, where a full-service restaurant and bar are available; reservations are advised. Call for race schedules, post times, or clubhouse reservations. Parking is free at the track.

Cars

SOUTHWESTERN INTERNATIONAL RACEWAY
Pima County Fairgrounds
Exit 275 just south of I-10
(520) 762-9700
www.sirace.com

Throughout the year Tucsonans can head to this drag racing track at the county fairgrounds

Close-up

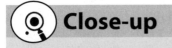

Tucson Sports Stadiums

Arizona Stadium

This is the University of Arizona's football stadium, located on East Sixth Street a couple of blocks west of Campbell Avenue. It seats about 55,000. Spectators cannot bring in any containers or alcoholic beverages, nor are they sold here during any college activity. There are a few unusual things about this stadium that the average spectator may never notice. One is that two sides of the stadium, the south and east, actually are built over dormitories. (We hope no students are trying to snooze or study during a game.) You can enter this stadium from just about any side, but wheelchair patrons are advised to use Gate 1. The will-call trailer is at the southeast corner near Gate 9. You'll find the typical stadium concessions on all levels and the Scoreboard Cafe on the north side of the stadium at street level. If you're not lucky enough to find parking in one of the university's nearby garages, try the neighborhood streets to the south.

Hi Corbett Field

This Tucson baseball field is situated in the middle of a multiacre city complex called Reid Park that houses golf courses, parks, and the zoo and can be accessed from Broadway Boulevard or 22nd Street to 900 South Randolph Way. It's home to the Colorado Rockies during spring training. There's a shuttle bus from the east side of El Con Mall during spring training. For information call Tucson Parks and Recreation at (520) 791-4873.

McKale Center

This copper-roofed circular structure seating 14,500 is home to a number of Wildcat sports, including men's and women's basketball, volleyball, and gymnastics. Located just north of Sixth Street and west of Campbell Avenue on National Championship Drive, it's surrounded by other university sports fields, including the stadium, Jerry Kindall baseball field, and Hillenbrand Aquatic Center. McKale is wheelchair accessible, and entry for all spectators is on the south side facing National Championship Drive. Concession stands are on Level 3, and no containers can be brought into the center. McKale also houses the university's main ticket office, where tickets for all sport games can be purchased. The ticket booths are outdoors on the south side facing National Championship Drive, and there are metered parking spaces right there for picking up or inquiring about tickets. Phone numbers for inquiring about or charging tickets are (520) 621-CATS (2287) or (800) 452-CATS (2287). There's a pay parking garage just to the west, but don't count on getting in during a game.

Tucson Electric Park

This baseball stadium is part of a Pima County facility called Kino Sports Complex that also houses practice and playing fields for baseball, soccer, and basketball. Located on Ajo Way near I-10, the baseball stadium was named to reflect the support of Tucson Electric Power Company in taking the complex from dream to reality. It debuted for 1998 spring training and is now Tucson's spring training home for the Arizona Diamondbacks. The 150-acre complex includes an 11,000-seat ballpark, 12 practice fields, 3 practice infields, 2 major-league clubhouses, a minor-league clubhouse, batting tunnels, and pitching mounds. For baseball games there are five seating levels and corresponding prices ranging from lawn seating to club seats. For information call (520) 434-1367 or (866) 672-1343 or go to www.kinosportscomplex.com.

and see everything from professional fuel cars to novice street cars race around a quarter-mile drag strip. Events at this NHRA-sanctioned facility take place at various times, including Friday evenings. Check the schedule for specifics. Spectator tickets are $5, with kids younger than 10 always free. Spectators are not allowed to bring in alcohol or any glass containers, but the raceway has a full line of concessions, including beer. Parking is ample and free.

TUCSON RACEWAY PARK
11955 South Harrison Road
(520) 762-9200
www.tucsonracewaypark.com
Spectators who like to see stock cars speeding around a track and possibly smashing into one another or the walls should head to the raceway in southeast Tucson for the NASCAR races. It has a 0.375-mile high-banked asphalt track famous for its three grooves that allow three-abreast racing. The main season is April to October, with races every Saturday, but racing now takes place year-round. Tickets are $10 for adults, $7 for kids older than 11 and seniors, with kids younger than 11 free. The raceway has ample free parking and all the typical concessions (spectators can only bring in water in its original container). Gates open at various times throughout the year, so check the Web site.

Rodeo

There aren't many spots in the states where you can see an authentic rodeo, but Tucson is one of them. The biggest—also one of the oldest in the nation—is **Fiesta de los Vaqueros,** which takes place over several days in late February at the Tucson Rodeo Grounds, 4823 South Sixth Avenue. (For all the details, see the Festivals and Events chapter.) Another is the **Desert Thunder Pro Rodeo** held the third week in October at the Tucson Rodeo Grounds. It's the third-largest PRCA/WPRA-sanctioned rodeo and offers live music and a chili cook-off in addition to all the roping, riding, and bronco busting. Ticket prices vary but it's free for kids with one general admission ticket. Call (520) 721-1621 for information, or check www.desertthunder.com. Parking at the Rodeo Grounds is a fee per vehicle, or park for free on neighboring streets.

Seniors

Each year the Tucson Parks and Recreation Department holds the Tucson Senior Olympics. For about one week near the end of January, seniors from all over the area gather at a variety of sites including senior centers, city parks, and adult residential communities to compete in games such as track, tennis, bicycling, boccie, swimming, shuffleboard, golf, and many more. Many of them go on to the state Senior Olympics held in Phoenix and even the nationals (in 1997 Tucson was the site of the national Senior Olympics). For information on how to participate or when and where to go to watch the games, call Parks and Recreation at (520) 791-3244. (See the Festivals and Events chapter.)

PHOENIX

For faithful fans of spectator sports, Phoenix isn't all that far away—less than a two-hour drive or bus trip and half that by plane. Even though most of Arizona's major sport teams are based in Phoenix, they're still considered Arizona teams; many even have adopted "Arizona" as part of their name rather than "Phoenix" to signify their statewide affiliation. So if Tucson doesn't satisfy all your cravings for sports, head on up to Phoenix.

Baseball

ARIZONA DIAMONDBACKS
Chase Field, Phoenix
(602) 514-8400, (888) 777-4664 (tickets)
www.azdiamondbacks.com
Winners of the 2001 World Series against the powerful New York Yankees, the Diamondbacks, a National League expansion team, play in the state-of-the-art Chase Field in downtown Phoenix. Ticket prices vary and are available for individual games, for the season, and monthly. Tucsonans can leave the driving to them by tak-

ing the Diamond Express bus trip from Foothills Mall to Chase Field for $18 round-trip ($15 for kids 12 and under). The bus trip is offered only for Saturday and Sunday games and reservations are a must at (520) 434-1367.

CACTUS LEAGUE BASEBALL SPRING TRAINING

Arizona is heaven for folks from other parts of the country who are die-hard baseball fans and a bit sun-starved. For about a month each spring from early-March to the first of April, they can watch their favorite major-league baseball teams practice and spar with other teams during spring training. Ten teams currently practice in Phoenix and its suburbs: the Chicago Cubs at Hohokam Park in Mesa, the San Diego Padres and the Seattle Mariners at Peoria Sports Complex in Peoria, the Los Angeles Angels at Tempe Diablo Stadium in Tempe, the Milwaukee Brewers and Oakland Athletics at Maryvale Sports Complex in Maryvale, the San Francisco Giants at Scottsdale Stadium in Scottsdale, the Chicago White Sox, beginning in 2010, at the new Goodyear stadium, and the Texas Rangers and Kansas City Royals at Surprise Recreation Park. With each of these teams playing about 15 home games, baseball fans have about 150 games to choose from during the month. Tickets are reasonably priced, usually ranging from about $5 to $20, but vacant seats are not easy to come by, especially for the more popular teams. For information on schedules or how to get tickets for any of the games check the Cactus League Web site at www.cactus-league.com.

Basketball

PHOENIX MERCURY
US Airways Center
201 East Jefferson Street, Phoenix
(602) 252-9622, (602) 514-8333 (office)
www.wnba.com/mercury

The Phoenix Mercury was one of the initial charter teams in the WNBA and played their first season in the summer of 1997 at the air-conditioned America West Arena (since renamed US Airways Arena) in downtown Phoenix. And they're good—in 2007 they won the WNBA championship. Attendance exceeds expectations, with home games averaging 10,000-plus fans who pay $10 to $200 a ticket. (It's a way for basketball devotees who can't get into the arena for a Suns game to see pro basketball and maybe even afford a ticket for the kids.) The season runs from September to May.

PHOENIX SUNS
US Airways Center
201 East Jefferson Street, Phoenix
(602) 379-7900 (office), (602) 7867 (box office)
www.nba.com/suns

If you don't recognize this championship NBA basketball team, you may recognize their furry mascot, "Go" the Gorilla, who is as athletic and entertaining as the more famous team members and has risen to dean of NBA mascots. The Suns are a winning team, so tickets to their home games during the October to June season at US Airways Center sell out quickly. They can be obtained through the Suns' ticket office or through Ticketmaster at (800) 4NBATIX (462-2849).

i **For definitive information on the shuttle buses that go from El Con Mall to various sport venues, call Sun Tran at (520) 792-9222.**

Football

ARIZONA CARDINALS
University of Phoenix Stadium
Loop 101 & Glendale Avenue, Glendale
(602) 379-0102 (office),
(602) 379-0102 (box office)
www.azcardinals.com

The Cardinals, founded in 1898 and a charter member of the National Football League, are the oldest continuously run professional football franchise in the nation. The NFC West division team plays home games at the gorgeous University of Phoenix Stadium, which played host to the 2008 Super Bowl. Ticket prices range widely from single-game tickets to season tickets, and they're fairly easy to get.

TOSTITOS FIESTA BOWL
University of Phoenix Stadium
Loop 101 & Glendale Avenue, Glendale
(480) 350-0900
www.tostitosfiestabowl.com

Every New Year's Day or thereabouts, one of the major college bowl games is played outside Phoenix at Glendale's University of Phoenix Stadium. The Fiesta Bowl is usually played between two top college teams selected by the Fiesta Bowl Committee. This bowl is now part of the College Football Bowl Alliance, so once every four years it will be the site of the national championship playoff, the first of which was right here in the early days of 1999. Ticket prices run up to $350 and can be obtained from various sources. A number of other events take place as part of Fiesta Bowl, including the Fiesta Bowl Basketball Classic played in Tucson during the week before the bowl game (see the previous listing in this chapter).

Ice Hockey

PHOENIX COYOTES
Jobing.com Arena
9400 West Maryland Avenue, Glendale
(623) 463-8800 (office),
(480) 784-4444 (box office)
http://coyotes.nhl.com

From September through April, Arizonans can go to the Jobing.com Arena in Glendale and watch the National Hockey League Coyotes slip and slide around on the ice, coached by former pro Wayne Gretzky. During the season more than 80 games are played at the arena, and fans love them. Tickets sell out fast. They can be obtained from Ticketmaster outlets or by calling (480) 563-7825. Occasionally the Coyotes play a game in Tucson at the Tucson Convention Center, so call for information.

DAVIS-MONTHAN AIR FORCE BASE

Since 1927, some of America's most famous (and infamous) flying machines have flown the skies of Tucson. The ***Spirit of St. Louis*** and its pioneering pilot were here to participate in the opening ceremonies of the air base. Bombers like the B-17 Flying Fortress, the B-24 Liberator, and the B-29 Superfortress (used to drop the atomic bomb on Japan) flew overhead during the World War II years.

When the jet age was ushered in around 1953, Tucsonans could glance skyward and spot a new B-47 Stratojet or a squadron of F-86-A Sabre jet fighters. And then came the cold war era with its Titan II missiles and silos and U-2 reconnaissance planes that flew global missions out of our Air Force base. Later years brought the F-4 Phantom fighter, and today A-10 Thunderbolts shine against our blue skies.

But long before "U.S. Air Force" was even a glimmer in anyone's eye, what is now known as Davis-Monthan Air Force Base in south-central Tucson got its humble start as a municipal airfield—really just a two-man refueling station and a dirt runway. The year was 1919 when Tucson officials voted to create an airport. It all began on an 82-acre site where the rodeo grounds are today. (A plaque on the rodeo grounds on South Sixth Avenue marks the spot.) First called Macauley Field and then Fishburn Field, it became Tucson Municipal Flying Field in 1923. Tucson officials definitely had vision. Not only had they established the first municipal airport in Arizona, but hoping that it would be selected as the site for an Army air base, they also began building it to military specifications under guidance from the Army Air Corps.

By 1927 their dreams were coming true. Col. Charles A. Lindbergh, fresh from his triumphant solo flight across the Atlantic aboard the ***Spirit of St. Louis,*** came to town to dedicate the air field as an Army Signal Corps base. It was the largest municipal airport in the United States and the first to be converted to a military base. By this time the airfield had been relocated from South Sixth Avenue—still a good way from where the heaviest concentration of Tucson's population of 32,000 was concentrated—to a location farther southeast where city fathers had already bought up 1,280 acres of homesteaded ranch land. This was the Davis-Monthan Air Force Base of the future.

It was also at the 1927 dedication that two Tucson military aviators became immortalized when the airfield was officially named Davis-Monthan Airfield. The two young men may never have even met each other, but it would turn out they had a lot in common. One was born in England, the other in Tennessee, but both would eventually live in Tucson. One attended Tucson High School and the University of Arizona and served in the Army at Fort Huachuca, Arizona. The other worked on his family's Tucson ranches before joining the Army. Both were military pilots when aviation was still in its infancy, and both ultimately would perish in the flying machines they loved—Lt. Samuel H. Davis in Florida in 1921 and Lt. Oscar Monthan in Hawaii in 1924. Their names would grace a municipal airport, an Army air base, and eventually a U.S. Air Force base.

For more than 10 years after its conversion to an Army Signal Corps base, Davis-Monthan Field continued to serve both military and commercial flights. Among the pilots who landed here were Amelia Earhart, Wiley Post, and James Doolittle, along with Standard Airlines, which later was absorbed by American Airlines.

During the 1930s the Army built the base's first hangar and operations building and added paved roads and runways. By the end of the decade, with war clouds building in Europe and the Pacific, the Army wanted to station some men and planes at the field. At the same time city leaders wanted the federal government to take over the field in order to get additional funds for construction and the soldiers who would be stationed there. Agreement was reached—the city would move its airport to a new site (where Tucson International Airport is today) and the Army would take over Davis-Monthan Field.

i **La Zarzuela B&B offers a 50 percent discount (subject to availability) to Davis-Monthan military personnel as a way of saying thanks. If you get the chance to take your sweetie to this romantic spot on the far west side of town, grab it. Call (888) 848-8225 for details.**

WARTIME EXPANSION

When Pearl Harbor was attacked on December 7, 1941, the population of Davis-Monthan Field was 2,175. One year later the base's military population had jumped to 9,642, and the field was being expanded to the tune of $3 million by the federal government. The base's war mission was to train light and heavy bombardment aircrews who then would be deployed overseas. It had the reputation as the best heavy bombardment station in the nation. As the base workload increased and aircraft personnel were dispatched to distant shores, women from the area took on base chores ranging from driving dump trucks to serving in the Women's Army Auxiliary Corps. And for a time, the base also held a German prisoner-of-war camp.

With the war's end, the base became a "separation center," processing nearly 10,000 returning soldiers for transition to civilian life. When that job was done, the base was deactivated and the field became a storage location for B-29 bombers and C-47 cargo planes, better known as "Gooney Birds." But this respite would not last long. With the official creation of the U.S. Air Force shortly after the war, the base was turned over to the new branch of the service and got its official name—Davis-Monthan Air Force Base—in early 1948.

In the years that followed, Davis-Monthan served as a home base for Titan II missiles, U-2 reconnaissance forces, and a series of fighter jets. Following the Strategic Arms Limitation Treaty, Russian satellites flew overhead taking photographs of the nuclear arms and aircraft dismantled by Davis-Monthan personnel and placed in open view on the base for the satellite cameras to see. Davis-Monthan planes and personnel were dispatched to serve in three more wars—the Korean War, Vietnam, and Desert Storm—as well as many real or potential trouble spots around the globe.

Today Davis-Monthan occupies 17 square miles (almost 9 percent of the city), employs military and thousands of civilian personnel, and trains thousands of pilots and support personnel. But Tucsonans seem to either love it or hate it. For some residents the thunderous drone of massive cargo and transport planes or low-flying fighter jets is nothing more than an intrusion. For others the sound is a welcome one, signifying our nation's military might and the streamlined beauty of the world's most sophisticated flying machines. For some—like land developers—Davis-Monthan means only that valuable land cannot be turned into commercial or residential profit. For others the lost land value pales in comparison to the base's contributions to Tucson's economy, estimated to be in the millions.

Fortunately for the air base and for Tucsonans who welcome its presence here, the bulk of our residents favor it. When federal rumors of its possible closing were rampant in the early 1990s, supporters far outnumbered the picketers, and it was easy to make a case for Davis-Monthan's significance not only as a military installation but also as an integral part of the city's lifestyle and economy.

Close-up

AMARC Tour

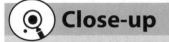

You can tour the amazing aircraft storage and warehouse facility, known as AMARC (Aerospace Maintenance and Regeneration Center) and nicknamed the "boneyard." Home to over 5,000 aircraft, the 2,600 acres of open storage hold more than 70 different types of aircraft, including post–WWII aircraft from the Korean War, B-52 bombers, helicopters, fighter jets, and much, much more. Tucson's low humidity, nonalkaline soil, and hot weather are perfect for the long-term storage of these miracles of modern engineering, and you won't see anything like it anywhere else in the world.

The tours are organized by the Pima Air and Space Museum and run Monday through Friday (except for holidays and military alerts). Starting times are seasonal, so call ahead. There are several tours a day, and they last one hour. The tour takes place by bus that boards in front of the museum. Photo ID is required for everyone over 16. Due to increased security, only one small carry-on item is allowed, and that is subject to search. Adults $6, children 12 and under $3. Reservations are strongly recommended; call (520) 574-0462.

With 27,000 people connected with Davis-Monthan (including military, dependents, civilians, and retirees), it's not difficult to see the base's significance to Tucson and Arizona. They eat in Tucson restaurants, shop in Tucson stores, attend Tucson's events and art programs, hook up to Tucson's utilities, and enroll their kids in Tucson's day-care centers and schools, adding to the city's and state's tax base with every purchase or service they consume. And if the base weren't here, many of Tucson's 13,000 or more military retirees (and their pensions) might not be either. Over the years the government has pumped many millions into Davis-Monthan, often hiring local contractors for the work done on the base, from paving runways and roads to erecting hangars and housing.

Nor is the impact of the base purely economic. Davis-Monthan makes a big deal out of encouraging volunteerism. One office on the base works exclusively to help match base personnel with community volunteer assignments. Military dependents, and sometimes the military personnel as well, spend many hours volunteering in Tucson's schools, youth organizations, and other agencies. And if a natural disaster or emergency occurred in the area, you can be sure the base's people and resources would be there to help the community out.

Behind its 25 miles of fence and restricted-access gates, Davis-Monthan has everything from fast food to the Air Force's version of M*A*S*H, and from an 18-hole golf course to "the world's largest parking lot." The average visitor to Tucson, and even most residents, may only be aware of the runways, airplanes, and air traffic control tower—the trappings of Davis-Monthan that can easily be seen by driving along Golf Links Road or merely looking skyward. But these are just the tip of the iceberg.

Inside this city within a city, over 5,000 people live within multiunit and single-family housing (the rest live off base), two elementary schools are run by the Tucson Unified School District, and a base hospital serves thousands of patients annually. There are restaurants, officer and enlisted clubs, a base exchange (BX), a commissary, a post office, a youth center, and a service station. For entertainment, base personnel can choose from an 18-hole golf course, a pool, movie theater, bowling alley, parks, and sports fields, plus a library and fitness center for improving mind and body. Military retirees who call Tucson home also have access to this vast array of facilities.

i Jim Click auto dealerships offer free oil changes and tire rotations to vehicles owned by immediate family members of active military—even if you didn't buy the car from Jim Click. Other vehicle maintenance repairs are given at employee rates. Call (520) 407-4850

AVIATION GRAVEYARD (AMARC)

Although much of this military complex is out of view, even the Air Force can't hide "the world's largest parking lot" from the public eye. Only it's not for vehicles; it's for aircraft (and related equipment). Perhaps you caught a glimpse of it as your plane descended toward Tucson—endless airplanes lined up in perfect rows on the desert floor, as if waiting to launch a fearful invasion. They stretch for miles—colossal B-52s and Gooney Birds; scores of helicopters; and sleek, fearless fighter jets. If the planes parked here belonged to another country, they would be one of the largest air forces in the world. But up close you could see that these are old aircraft, often partially covered with a skin of plastic to protect them from the elements. These 2,600 acres on the east end of Davis-Monthan hold over 5,000 aircraft and tons of related equipment. It's the only storage depot like it in the world.

Tucsonans tend to call it the airplane boneyard or graveyard, but officially it's the Aerospace Maintenance and Regeneration Center, or AMARC, run by the Department of Defense. In 1965 the Defense Department consolidated all U.S. Army, Navy, and Air Force storage locations into this one. They picked Davis-Monthan because of the Sonoran Desert—the air is dry and the ground so hard and alkaline that even a 180,000-pound B-52 can be towed over it without sinking.

And what about the fate of these flying machines? A small percent are returned to flight status. Many are gradually picked over for spare parts. Some are flown to remote places and used for target practice. Some are purposely kept untouched so they could be put into battle on short notice if need be. Even several Boeing 707s banned by the FAA rest here, their powerful engines that were too noisy for commercial airports now stripped off for use in Air Force tanker planes. Some of the aircraft could be sold intact to a foreign government, but only after lots of red tape and only to "friendly" buyers. The majority of the planes are sold for scrap, but only after their navigational equipment and weaponry are removed. So the next time you lift up that can of soda or that garden rake, you may be holding all that's left of a 1950s military bomber or fighter.

It's quite a sight to see, this final resting place for Uncle Sam's warplanes. It even has its own celebrity row—a line of rare and one-of-a-kind aircraft, each with a sign designating its name—worthy of the history books and a spot in anyone's photo album. You can catch a glimpse of AMARC by driving south on Kolb Road. Or better yet, if you want to see "the boneyard" planes up close or in the lens of your camera, or see a captured Iraqi tank or some of the spiffy planes on the base's tarmac, take a tour of the base.

AMARC is only one of the many missions going on at Davis-Monthan. Nearly every major air command, the Air Force Reserve, and the Air National Guard are represented here. The 355th Wing is the base's primary activity and occupant, responsible for training pilots on the A-10 Thunderbolt, a low and slow and highly maneuverable tank destroyer. (It also happens to be a relatively quiet jet, which pleases Tucsonans who are picky about the noise level.) The 355th also conducts training for other aircrews, provides airborne command and communications, and helps with Strategic Arms Limitation Treaty (SALT) compliance. It also operates one of only five air transportable hospitals (the Air Force version of a M*A*S*H unit), which can be deployed on a moment's notice to trouble spots around the globe.

Davis-Monthan also houses the 12th Air Force Command and the people assigned to it, who are responsible for the combat readiness of all tactical air forces west of the Mississippi. The base is the site of an Air National Guard unit that flies the F-16 Fighting Falcon, an Air Force Reserve unit that flies search and rescue helicopters, and the West Coast Combat Search and Rescue unit. Other federal agencies using the base include the Federal Aviation Administration, the U.S. Customs Service Air Service Branch, the U.S. Army Corps of Engineers, the Federal Law Enforcement Training Center, and a detachment of the Naval Air Systems Command. With one of the longest runways in the Air Force—13,643 feet—Davis-Monthan is equipped to handle just about any job in the airborne military.

DAY TRIPS AND WEEKEND GETAWAYS

It's difficult to imagine wanting to leave Tucson, but the reality is that southern Arizona has much to offer, including its proximity to Mexico. In this chapter we give you some ideas on great day and weekend trips not to be missed!

The choices are so great that we've really only scratched the surface here. We've selected some destinations that both visitors and residents consider to be must-sees if they get the chance, plus a few others that are relatively undiscovered. Most of the weekend getaways included here are within a three-hour drive of Tucson. A few are a bit farther, but we include them because they're especially appealing destinations.

For most of the weekend getaways, we've mapped out an itinerary that highlights a number of locations, attractions, and activities. You may not get to them all, but at least you'll be informed enough to make a choice about what you absolutely can't miss and what can wait until next time. Even if you're just searching for a day trip, be sure to read the sections on getaways as well—they contain lots of ideas for day trips. Conversely, the day trips described here can easily be turned into getaways—we even give a few tips on how best to do that.

Whatever your destination or its duration, it's always best to call ahead and confirm the seasons and hours they're open, prices, and any age restrictions so that you won't be disappointed on arrival. Likewise, contact the chambers of commerce or visitor centers for your destinations; they'll provide lots of useful information, even if you're making last-minute plans. And last but not least, get a good map.

DAY TRIPS

Boyce Thompson Southwestern Arboretum

This combination state park/museum/nature preserve is less than two hours from Tucson and can easily be a day trip, or it can be combined with other sights east of Phoenix for a weekend getaway (we map out such a trip under Phoenix and Environs). Either way, plan on at least a couple of hours to see this site that most people fall in love with. It's a fascinating collection of arid land plants from all over the world—3,200 different desert plants to be more exact. It's also a rich riparian habitat that supports more than 300 species of mammals, birds, reptiles, and amphibians thanks to Queen Creek, which flows through the property.

The Arboretum (520-689-2811; arboretum.ag.arizona.edu) is located near the mining town of Superior and was endowed in 1924 by William Boyce Thompson, the founder of two major mining companies in the Superior area. He established it as a research facility, but much of it is now open to the public, along with a visitor center and gift shop, self-guided nature walks, miles of easy trails, a desert lake, a picnic area, and restrooms. It's open daily (except Christmas) from 8:00 a.m. to 4:00 p.m. (6:00 a.m. to 3:00 p.m. May through September) at $7.50 for adults and $3 for kids 5 to 12. From Tucson, take Oracle Road (Highway 77) north to Highway 79, then go east on U.S. Highway 60. Highway 79 is also called the Pinal Parkway, a scenic drive along which the native vegetation is identified with markers.

Safford

A great day or even a weekend camping trip, Safford in Graham County, just two and a half hours from Tucson, is worth the drive. Take Interstate 10 east past Willcox to U.S. Highway 191 north 25 miles right into Safford.

Kids of all ages will love Discovery Park, part of the Eastern Arizona College campus. It's open to the public from 9:00 a.m. to 5:00 p.m. Monday through Friday and 4:00 to 10:00 p.m. every Saturday for stargazing (928-428-6260; www.discoverypark.com). You can explore 200 acres of riparian and natural habitat and peek inside a pond through a glass window. The park is also home to the world's largest camera obscura. On Saturday you can sign up for tours of the Mt. Graham International Observatory, which take place from early May through mid-November, or until weather prohibits them. The tour, which leaves the park by van at 9:30 a.m., features a trip up scenic Mount Graham, lunch near the summit, and a guided tour of the observatory facility, including the world's most powerful optical telescope, the Large Binocular Telescope.

When your feet get tired, head to the hidden Roper Lake State Park in the shadow of Mount Graham, located off US 191, 6 miles south of Safford. You'll find a beautiful, scenic lake surrounded by reeds, picnic sites, and campsites. Only small electric motorboats are allowed here, so you can swim, paddle a canoe, or sail or row a boat along the lovely shores, and there is a natural hot springs pool on the grounds. Call (928) 428-6760 for details on fees and to reserve a campsite. The park is open daily 6:00 a.m. to 10:00 p.m. For more information check the Web at www.pr.state.az.us/parks/parkhtml/roper.html.

If you don't like to soak in the great outdoors, Safford is home to several other hot springs that are more commercial. Check out Essence of Tranquility at 6074 Lebanon Loop (928-428-9312, 877-895-6810; www.azhotmineralspring.com) and Kachina Hot Springs Artesian Mineral Spa at 1155 West Cactus Road (928-428-7212).

Madera Canyon

Nature lovers will be enthralled by this spot 60 miles south of Tucson in the Santa Rita Mountains. It's a popular day trip destination for Tucsonans escaping the heat in summer and for birders all year long. About 400 species of birds have been sighted here, including hummingbirds and elf owls. There are about 200 miles of scenic trails, some of which hug the meandering Madera Creek, so there's something here for casual walkers as well as serious hikers wanting to explore the upper reaches of the mountains. At an elevation of 5,600 feet, Madera Canyon is covered with thick pines and is significantly cooler than the desert floor below.

At the entrance to the recreation area is a small visitor center, though it's usually open only on weekends. There's also a small store that may or may not be open, so it's best to have your own supplies. Nearby is a small campground with toilets and drinking water. The canyon's Santa Rita Lodge Nature Resort (520-625-8746; www.santaritalodge.com) caters to birders—all cabins and casitas have bird feeders outside the windows. Madera Canyon is under the purview of the Coronado National Forest, so call the Nogales District Office at (520) 281-2296 for information. There is a $5 daily parking fee.

i **Another beautiful canyon to visit is Ramsey Canyon, near Sierra Vista. While you're there, stop in for a good old time at the Arizona Folklore Preserve, where state balladeer Dolan Ellis (a founding member of the New Christy Minstrels) cranks out a mighty fine yarn and tune. Specializing in cowboy songs and tales of the Old West, Ellis entertains just about every Saturday and Sunday afternoon at 2:00 p.m. with old-fashioned jokes, stories, and pictures in a cozy cafe setting. Tickets are $15. Call in advance to make reservations (520-378-6165), or go to www.arizonafolklore.com.**

Mariachi bands are just part of the experience over the border in Nogales, Mexico. COURTESY OF THE METROPOLITAN TUCSON CONVENTION & VISITORS BUREAU, GILL KENNY

To find Madera Canyon, take exit 63 off Interstate 19, then go east on White House Canyon Road, which becomes Madera Canyon Road. The road winds up the mountainside for about 15 miles, but it's easy to traverse by car. Just remember that this is an outdoor recreation area in the middle of a mountain, so you won't find much here beyond the bounties that nature provides.

Nogales, Mexico

This is a favorite destination for visitors and newcomers to Tucson, especially those who have never been to Mexico. Located in Sonora, it's close and an adventure for first-timers. Be aware, however, that Nogales is not necessarily representative of the rest of Mexico. As a border town, it's crowded, congested, and focused almost exclusively on selling merchandise. In fact, people often have mixed reactions to Nogales. Some view it as great fun, while others are put off by the hubbub and the constant hawking of vendors trying to lure customers. One advantage to Nogales, however, is that many people speak English, so you won't have a language barrier.

Nogales is less than two hours by car, straight down I-19. It's an easy day trip, and you'll still have several hours to shop and eat. It also can be combined into a great weekend getaway with Tubac and Tumacacori (described in this chapter). It's so much easier to cross into Nogales on foot than by car that we won't even discuss taking your vehicle into Mexico here, other than to say it simply isn't worth the hassle when your destination is Nogales. As you drive south on I-19 and near the border, follow the signs to the international border, which actually will take you into Nogales, Arizona. The freeway ends, and in less than a mile you'll begin seeing parking lots—and attendants trying to wave you in. (An easy landmark is the McDonald's restaurant. Consider it a sign that you're in the right spot and can park nearby.) All of these lots are within a couple blocks of the border crossing, so any will do, and you can expect to pay about $5 for the day, even if you won't be there but a few hours. The parking lot attendant, or anyone else who happens to be around, will point you in the direction of the border crossing. You'll soon see the signs guiding the way for foot traffic, and before you know it, you're in a foreign country. There are no border checks until your return, at which point you'll go through U.S. Customs. (See the Close-up in this chapter so you'll be familiar with the border process ahead of time.)

Now that you've arrived, get ready to be bombarded by vendors and by more Mexican goods than you've ever seen, all crowded together in small shops and lining alleys and sidewalks. It wouldn't hurt to practice shaking your head to signal "no" or saying "no gracias" or "no thanks"—you'll be doing it often unless you plan to buy out Nogales.

Begin walking the sidewalks and alleys looking for regional items such as rugs, blankets, glassware, tinware, wrought metal, pottery, silver jewelry, leather, and so on. Most items don't have price tags, but if they do, it's usually in dollars, not pesos, and dollars are the accepted currency. A few shops will not bargain and let you know they don't; otherwise, bargaining with shopkeepers is customary and even expected.

i Mexico uses the metric system, so miles and speed limits are posted in kilometers. If you're buying the Gulf of California's famous shrimp, you'll pay by the kilo, not the pound (a kilo equals 2.2 pounds).

Another rule of thumb: If you've done a good job negotiating the price, the item will cost you less—sometimes significantly—than if you purchased it stateside. As you shop in Nogales, all the streets may look similar, but don't worry about getting lost; anyone will be able to point you back to the starting place. Just relax and enjoy your adventure.

If you need a break from the shopping spree, here are two restaurants in Nogales to try. Tourist-friendly **Elvira's Restaurant and Bar** is a funky, wildly decorated place to grab a bite, sip a margarita, and rest your feet after a day of shopping. It's conveniently located just over the border, before you get to the center of town. Once you cross the border on foot, take an immediate right and walk about 3 blocks. **La Roca** (meaning "the rock," and indeed it's built into the rock in the side of a cliff), at 91 Calle Elias, is probably Nogales's finest restaurant, but it's off the beaten path and will be a walk of at least several blocks, some of it up a steep hill. Ask for directions, but if you don't think you can find it, you can probably find a friendly person who will gladly be your guide (but tip your guide a dollar or two, please). At La Roca you'll have a fine meal in a lovely old building that also has a number of shops that are more upscale than many in Nogales. Restaurants and the few hotels in Nogales are also the only places you're likely to find a restroom. For more details check the **Nogales Chamber of Commerce** Web site at www.nogaleschamber.com or call (520) 287-3685.

Before taking your trek to a foreign country, here are a few final tidbits. It's best to plan your trip so that you leave Mexico by about 5:00 p.m. because many of the stateside parking lots all but shut down as day's end draws near. However, if you want to stay in Nogales for dinner, just check with the parking lot before leaving your car to make sure you'll be able to retrieve it on your return. Keep in mind that, like Tucson, the busy season in Nogales is late fall to early spring, and weekends are busier than weekdays. Most businesses do accept credit cards. And finally, you'll notice the word *Sonora* on lots of things; Sonora is the name of the state in Mexico in which Nogales is located.

Patagonia Lake State Park

Water-deprived Tucsonans and their visitors will be glad to hear that the damming of Sonoita

Creek more than 30 years ago created the largest recreational lake in southern Arizona. And there's more good news—it's less than two hours away. The 265-acre lake and the 645-acre park in which it sits combine to offer just about every type of outdoor recreation. For folks who like to catch their dinner or just fish for sport, the lake is stocked with trout in winter and with bass, crappie, catfish, and bluegill the rest of the year. If you didn't bring your own, a concession at the general store rents paddleboats, canoes, and rowboats at hourly rates, plus deposit. The lake even has a sandy beach for swimmers and sunbathers who just want to be reminded of the ocean. You can windsurf here, as well as water- or jet-ski, but not on weekends from May through September, because that's when desert dwellers come here in droves. There are picnic areas, restrooms, and showers, plus plenty of places for casual hikes through the rolling hills around the lake. (See the Campgrounds and RV Parks chapter for information on the campsites.) The park is also home to the Sonoita Creek State Natural Area, a riparian oasis. There is a day-use fee per vehicle. For swimming, surfing, boating, and fishing in southern Arizona, take I-10 east to Highway 83, go south to Highway 82, and continue south 7 miles on Highway 82 past the town of Patagonia. To reach the park by phone, call (520) 287-6965, or check out their Web site at www.pr.state.az.us/parks/parkhtml/patagonia.html.

Taliesin West

Admirers of one of the twentieth-century's greatest architects, Frank Lloyd Wright, won't want to miss visiting his personal winter residence and architectural school. Located in Scottsdale (the outskirts of Phoenix), Taliesin West is only about two hours from Tucson, so it's an easy day trip. But there's so much else to do in this area that it could also be included in a weekend getaway (you'll find ideas for that elsewhere in this chapter). Perched on 600 acres of rugged Sonoran Desert at the base of the McDowell Mountains, Taliesin West is a National Historic Landmark. Like most of Wright's structures, it's both amazing and unique. He and his apprentices gathered rocks from the desert floor and sand from the washes to build this set of structures that includes his former residence, a school, and an architectural firm, all linked by dramatic terraces, gardens, and walkways.

If you plan to visit Taliesin West, take one of the tours. Each season, different types of tours are offered at different times of the day and for various prices, so call ahead for recorded tour information. For example, a morning panorama tour lasts one hour and includes the Cabaret Cinema, Music Pavilion, and Wright's private office, but not the residence. Another tour—Insights—lasts 90 minutes and includes the dramatic Taliesin West living room with furniture Wright designed and living quarters. In addition to the various scheduled tours during each season, private and group tours are available but must be arranged in advance. Walking shoes and sun protection are recommended, and toddlers must be in strollers or carried. There's a bookstore with an extensive selection of Wright books and prints, works by Taliesin artists, and souvenirs. For additional information call (480) 860-2700 or go to www.franklloydwright.org. The entrance to Taliesin West is at the intersection of Cactus Road and Frank Lloyd Wright Boulevard in northeast Scottsdale.

Tubac

Just 45 miles south of Tucson off I-19 at exits 40 and 34 is a lovely little village that once was the second-oldest European settlement west of the Mississippi. Today it's a sophisticated artists' colony.

Tubac and the surrounding areas are filled with history. In the 1700s the Spanish came north from Mexico and built a presidio (or fort) here, and the settlement of Tubac became the first European settlement in Arizona. **Tubac Presidio State Historic Park** (520-398-2252; www.pr.state.az.us/Parks/parkhtml/tubac.html) marks the site of this small fort and is open daily from 8:00 a.m. to 5:00 p.m. From October to March a living history program reenacts eighteenth-century life.

In the heart of Old Town Tubac (which is just east of the present-day shopping area), you'll also see **Placita de Anza,** historic **St. Ann's Church,** an 1885 one-room schoolhouse, and the **Tubac Historical Society,** which offers a research library, visitor guides, and self-guided tour maps. It's difficult to visit Tubac without taking in some of the shopping opportunities, but there are plenty of alternatives if shopping isn't on your top-10 list of things to do. In addition to all the historical sites, there's a 4.5-mile trail that winds south along the Santa Cruz River, and in this part of the river, you'll actually see water flowing year-round. The trail begins at the picnic grounds south of the presidio museum in Old Town Tubac. Throughout the year Tubac conducts many events and performances featuring music, dance, song, and art. In December, for example, there's Fiesta Navidad and Luminaria Night, which celebrates the holiday season in the Mexican tradition, and in February Tubac holds its Annual Festival of the Arts, now more than 40 years old.

Intermingled with all this history and natural beauty are shops, restaurants, and inns that occupy old adobe and newer whitewashed brick structures reminiscent of the earliest settlers' housing. Most of the artists and craftspeople who sell their wares in Tubac also live here, so it's truly an artists' colony. There are only about a half dozen small streets in this entire village, but they are lined with about five dozen shops carrying everything from jewelry and pottery to sculpture and clothing. The shops offer anything and everything made by Mexican and American Indian crafters and artists, plus creations in metal, jewelry, ceramics, and glass, and on canvas by local as well as internationally known artisans.

The dining choices are nearly as vast as the shopping choices. At **DeAnza Restaurant and Cantina** you can dine on Mexican food and margaritas indoors or out on a lovely patio. For a taste of Italy, try **Melio's Trattoria.** At **Old Tubac Inn,** diners can play darts or pool while waiting for their meal or for carryout food to enjoy at the picnic grounds in Old Town Tubac. Or take the footbridge to **Shelby's Bistro**. The **Chile Pepper** has cappuccino, ice cream, and fountain drinks if you're just too busy to take the time for sit-down dining. For a fancy Mexican/Southwest sit-down meal, try the upscale **Dos Silos** restaurant at the Tubac Golf Resort.

Although Tubac can easily be a day trip because it's so close to Tucson, it's also a great spot for an overnight or weekend getaway. There's certainly plenty to do in the form of shopping, gallery gazing, hiking, history learning, and golfing (see the Golf chapter). If you decide to turn your day trip into a getaway, here are a few places to bunk out. For authentic charm, try either the **Tubac Country Inn** (520-398-3178; www.tubaccountryinn.com) or **Tubac Secret Garden Inn** (520-398-9371). Both are in the historic district and across the street from the presidio park. The Secret Garden Inn has a wall surrounding three acres of green oasis. Another spot to stay is the lovely, intimate **Tubac Golf Resort** (520-398-2211; www.tubacgolfresort.com) just a quarter mile out of town. For more information check the Web site at www.tubacaz.com, or call the chamber of commerce at (520) 398-2704.

i **If you're heading to Tubac for a day of shopping and art gallery hopping, make a reservation at the Tubac Culinary School for "Dinner with the Chef." You'll be wowed by delicious food prepared right before your eyes by top area chefs. Five-courses, champagne, and wine pairings make this an elegant dining experience. Call (520) 398-8501 for reservations; check the Web at www.tubacculinaryschool.com for the schedule.**

Tumacacori

If you're going to visit Tubac, it's only a short drive to Tumacacori, the "town" that's too tough to pronounce. (Actually, it's neither a town nor tough to pronounce if you do it slowly and phonetically—*too-mah-kah-core-ee.*) It's the site of a Franciscan mission built in the 1700s that was regularly besieged by the Apache Indians. The ruins that are visible today include a chapel and graveyard. Visitors can also walk through an adobe mission church built between 1800 and 1822. The site has been converted into a National Historic Park with a visitor center where you can learn all about the mission. This is a very picturesque and tranquil spot with lots of mesquite trees and a 0.5-mile trail. On weekends there's often a craft demonstration.

Nearby is the **Santa Cruz Chili and Spice Company,** in business since 1943 and famous for their Santa Cruz chili paste (520-398-2591; www.santacruzchili.com). Open Monday through Friday from 8:00 a.m. to 5:00 p.m. and Saturday 10:00 a.m to 5:00 p.m., you'll find spices, herbs, salsas, and cookbooks plus a Western museum. Just to the north of the park is **Wisdom's Café** (520-398-2397; www.wisdomscafe.com), which offers Mexican fare.

Like Tubac, Tumacacori can be a day trip from Tucson, or you can stay in this area for a weekend full of history, hiking along the river, bird-watching, and shopping. Tumacacori is just south of Tubac at exit 29 off I-19, or simply take the frontage road between the two.

WEEKEND GETAWAYS

Cosanti and Arcosanti

If you're heading north to Scottsdale and beyond, these are two unusual attractions you might want to include in your itinerary. Because Cosanti is in the heart of Paradise Valley, a close-in suburb of Phoenix, it could be a day trip from Tucson, but there's so much else to do in the Phoenix area that including Cosanti in a weekend getaway would be a much better alternative. Arcosanti, on the other hand, is a bit too far for a comfortable day trip but could easily be combined with a weekend visit to the Prescott, Jerome, and Sedona areas (and we guide you to and around these areas elsewhere in this chapter). Both of these attractions were founded by Paolo Soleri and are now operated by the nonprofit Cosanti Foundation. Soleri is an Italian architect who moved to Arizona in 1956 and has become famous for his unusual project called Arcosanti and for his spectacular bronze wind chimes.

A state historic site, **Cosanti** is the residence and sculpture studio of Paolo Soleri and his staff. It is located at 6433 East Doubletree Ranch Road (480-948-6145, www.cosanti.com) in upscale Paradise Valley (just northeast of the Phoenix city limits). Except for major holidays, it's open daily from 9:00 a.m. to 5:00 p.m., 11:00 a.m. to 5:00 p.m. on Sunday, and it's free. Cosanti's essence is a gallery of Soleri art, but it's much more than that: a blend of desert landscaping of cacti, paloverde, and olive trees with earth-formed concrete architectural structures. Suspended amid courtyards, terraces, and garden paths is the work of Paolo Soleri and his artisans—a spectacular array of bronze and ceramic wind bells. Visitors can see how these art forms are crafted on-site and purchase them as well. There is also a line of "cause bells," all of which represent issues of national or global concern and sales of which go to help nonprofit organizations. (For ways to make this part of a weekend getaway, see Phoenix and Environs in this chapter.)

While Cosanti is a place, **Arcosanti** is a vision turned almost into reality. It could even be thought of as a prototype of Biosphere 2. Arcosanti represents a term that Soleri coined, arcology, to describe the concept of architecture and ecology working as one integral process to produce new urban habitats. Thus this strange-looking project of ultramodern structures built into the basalt cliffs 60 miles north of Phoenix was created as an urban "city" to epitomize Soleri's concept of arcology. It combines housing (originally for 5,000 people but never fully realized), large-scale solar greenhouses, a music center, and artist workshops and galleries. Today it's a place for students and professionals to study architecture, ecology, and art in the Soleri fashion and for visitors to view this 4,000-acre experiment in urban architecture. Visitors can see the creation of Soleri wind bells and purchase them, take tours, and snack at the cafe or bakery. Be prepared to do some walking and stair climbing, because Arcosanti is built into cliffs. The access road to Arcosanti is mostly dirt and very rough riding.

For information on Arcosanti or its tours, workshops, Elderhostel, or frugal overnight accommodations, call (928) 632-7135 or check the Web site, www.arcosanti.org. It's open daily except Thanksgiving, New Year's Day, and Christmas, and a donation is suggested per person. Hourly tours between 10:00 a.m. and 4:00 p.m. are $12 per person, and a variety of special tours are also available: agriculture, architecture, and birdwatching. Take Interstate 17 north from Phoenix to exit 262. To make this site part of a weekend getaway, consider staying overnight in the Verde River Valley towns of Prescott or Sedona, which we describe elsewhere in this chapter.

Today driving from Tucson to Tombstone on the interstate takes a little over one hour. In the 1800s travel to Tombstone was by stagecoach only. It would have taken Big Nose Kate two to three days, traveling about 3 to 5 miles per hour (assuming no Indian attacks or robbery attempts) to get from Tucson's railroad station to Tombstone to see her lover, Doc Holliday.)

Cochise County

Southeast of Tucson is an area filled with history, beauty, and tons of things to do and see. (Both Rhode Island and Connecticut would fit within Cochise County's 6,200 miles.) It includes the farmlands and ponds of Willcox; some of the premier birding spots in the country; Tombstone, the "town too tough to die"; and the mountains where the famous Apache Indian chief Cochise made his stronghold and where his successor, Geronimo, finally surrendered. Many of these sites could be individual day trips from Tucson, or the area can be visited in one or two weekend getaways. For one weekend getaway, we recommend taking Highway 80 south and visiting Benson, Tombstone, and Bisbee. A second getaway lies a bit farther east and takes in Willcox and the Chiricahua and Dragoon Mountains. Read on for trips that explore Cochise County.

Benson to Bisbee

About 70 miles south of Tucson is Tombstone, the "town too tough to die," which can be a day trip from Tucson or combined with the other sites outlined in the following paragraphs to make a weekend getaway. From Tucson, take I-10 east to exit 302 to Highway 90 south and watch for signs for one of the world's most interesting natural wonders, **Kartchner Caverns** (see also our Parks and Recreation chapter). Located in Kartchner Caverns State Park, the cave is a wet, or live, cave, meaning that the calcite formations are still growing. There are several sections, each more spectacular than the last. There are several tours offered: A Throne Room tour is available year-round, and a Big Room tour provides historic detail (October 15 through April 15; under age 7 not permitted). The tours will give you a close look at the variety of formations and colors. Reservations are strongly recommended, as the tours sell out very quickly. Avoid disappointment and call (520) 586-CAVE (2283) for reservations several weeks in advance. For information call (502) 586-4100.

Tombstone

Continue about 20 miles south on Highway 90, then west on Highway 82 another 25 miles to one of southern Arizona's most popular and famous family attractions, Tombstone. This is where, in 1881, the Earp brothers and Doc Holliday battled it out with the Clanton boys near the OK Corral. But there's more to the old silver mining town than the OK Corral, including Courthouse State Historic Park, the Rose Tree Inn Museum (displaying the world's largest rosebush, planted in 1885 and covering 8,000 square feet), the Birdcage Theater, the Crystal Palace Saloon, wooden sidewalks, preserved historical buildings, and even a stagecoach ride down the main drag, Allen Street. Shops, saloons, and eateries flourish here as well. A must-see on the outskirts of Tombstone is Boot Hill, the famous graveyard where the victims of the OK Corral shoot-out are buried, along with lots of other folks. It's perhaps too commercialized now, but you'll be able to ignore that as you walk through the cemetery reading the fascinating tombstones, which range from humorous to touching.

Go back in time in Tombstone, where gunfights still take place on the streets. COURTESY OF METROPOLITAN TUCSON CONVENTION & VISITORS BUREAU, GILL KENNY

If your visit to Tombstone is part of a weekend getaway, some good choices for lodging include the **Best Western Look-Out Lodge** (520-457-2223, 877-652-6772; www.bestwestern tombstone.com), a motel with a lot of Old West character and great views, and the **Tombstone Boarding House,** a bed-and-breakfast in two meticulously restored adobe buildings in a quiet residential neighborhood (520-457-3716, 877-225-1319; www.tombstoneboardinghouse .com). Stop by the visitor center at 315 Allen Street for maps, information, and ways to save a few bucks on local sights. Their Web site, www.cityof tombstone.com, is a good information source.

Bisbee

From Tombstone continue south on Highway 80 toward Bisbee. Along the way, the hikers and bird-watchers among you might want to detour onto Highway 90 west, then Highway 92 south to see **Ramsey Canyon Preserve,** managed by The Nature Conservancy and open daily from 8:00 a.m. to 5:00 p.m. March through October and 9:00 a.m. to 4:00 p.m. Monday through Thursday, November through February. The preserve attracts more than 170 species of birds and dozens of species of butterflies.

i Don't miss breakfast in Bisbee. The Bisbee Breakfast Club (75A Erie Street; 520-432-5885; www.bisbeebreakfastclub .com) offers it from 7:00 a.m. to 3:00 p.m., and even *Gourmet* magazine writers Jane and Michael Stern were impressed with the homemade biscuits and Blue Wally Cakes bursting with blueberries and walnuts and topped with real maple syrup. Save room for pie—fresh daily it's not to be missed.

Many varieties of hummingbirds summer here, while coatimundis and white-tailed deer are among the year-round residents. The parking lot is small (23 spaces) and available on a first-come, first-served basis. Admission is $5 per person; under age 16 free. There's a visitor center and bookstore, and a bed-and-breakfast adjacent to the preserve has six guest rooms and two separate apartments. Call (520) 378-3010 for reservations. Call (520) 378–2785 for more information on the preserve, or visit www.nature.org/arizona.

After your commune with nature, continue south on Highway 80 through Mule Mountain Tunnel to the former copper-mining town of Bisbee, a pretty little town that hugs the steep mountainside. At one time this old mining camp was one of the richest mineral sites in the world, and in the early 1900s Bisbee was the largest city between St. Louis and San Francisco. Eventually the mines played out, and Bisbee became an artists' colony and retirement area characterized by its Old World charm and restored Victorian and European-style buildings. Turquoise is big here, since it's a by-product of copper mining. To get a glimpse of what mining was like, go just beyond downtown to the **Lavender Pit Mine,** a huge hole that is one of the world's largest open-pit mines. Or for a more authentic sample of mining, visit the **Copper Queen Mine** (520-432-2071; www.queenminetour.com). Plan on taking one of the tours offered daily and lasting about one to one and a half hours. You'll be outfitted in miner's garb and enter the shaft via a small train like the real miners rode. (The underground temperature is a cool 47 degrees on average, so be prepared.) If the underground tour sounds a bit too scary, take a surface tour by van. And if you still haven't had your fill of mining, there's the **Mining and Historical Museum** across the street in town.

Bisbee has lots to offer besides its former industry. One of its most popular attractions is the fully restored **Copper Queen Hotel,** built in 1898, in the heart of downtown Bisbee. You need not book a room here to wander in and enjoy its grand lobby, saloon, and dining room from yesteryear. The hallways are lined with photos of the Copper Queen's early days, some depicting the celebrities who have stayed here, including John Wayne and Teddy Roosevelt. Another must-see is the historic **St. Patrick's Catholic Church** built in 1917 on Higgins Hill. The stained-glass windows here are considered one of the 10 best examples of Victorian glass in the nation. In fact, all over the downtown area you'll find well-preserved turn-of-the-twentieth-century brick buildings that today house a variety of boutiques, craft shops, and restaurants. It's easy to park the car in one spot and then see the town on foot, stopping whenever the urge strikes for a bite to eat or a memento to buy. Stop by the visitor center on Main Street any day for maps and walking tour guides.

Although a day trip from Tucson to Bisbee is long but not impossible at 100 miles, Bisbee is also a great weekend getaway by itself or via the itinerary described earlier. Unique places to stay besides the Copper Queen Hotel (520-432-2216, www.copperqueen.com) include the **School House Inn,** which is just what its name indicates, a schoolhouse transformed into a bed-and-breakfast (520-432-2996, 800-537-4333; www.schoolhouseinnbb.com), or the **Letson Loft Hotel**, located in the oldest remaining commercial building in Bisbee (520-432-3210, 877-432-3210; www.letsonlofthotel.com). For a sumptuous meal, the award-winning **Cafe Roka** offers sophisticated Italian and California dishes. It's always full and hours are seasonal, so be sure to make a reservation before you go (520-432-5153; www.caferoka.com). For more information about Bisbee, go to www.discoverbisbee.com or call (520) 432-3554.

Willcox

As a great day trip or to start out another weekend getaway that will take you into the mountains of Cochise County, visit the farming area of Willcox. Willcox is about two hours east of Tucson off I-10, and along the way you'll go through the dramatic boulder area of the Dragoon Mountains called Texas Canyon. Be sure to stop for a close-up view, a bit of hiking, or photos amid this unusually beautiful terrain. Nearby at the Dragoon Road exit just south of I-10 is the

Amerind Foundation (a contraction of *American* and *Indian*), a research facility and museum housed in a beautiful Spanish Colonial Revival building displaying high-quality exhibits that give an overview of Southwestern cultures. It's open Tuesday through Sunday, with an admission of $5 (520-586-3666; www.amerind.org).

Continue heading for Willcox on I-10 to exit 336 north, then take Fort Grant Road, which will lead to nearly a dozen farms where kids and parents have a great time picking all manner of delicious fruits and vegetables. If you're not into picking your own, many have already done it for you and sell it freshly harvested. Willcox is most famous for its apple crops and some of the best-looking apple pies you've ever seen, but lots of other things will entice the farmer in you, including corn, tomatoes, chilies, peaches, pecans, pumpkins, melons, and more. In other areas around Willcox, you'll find about another dozen farms, including a couple specializing in pistachios. The harvests usually run from July through October or early November, so summer and fall are the best times to head for Willcox. The farms are well marked from the road, or you can stop at the easy-to-spot **Chamber of Commerce Visitor Center** (520-384-2272, 800-200-2272; www.willcoxchamber.com), at 1500 North Circle I Road, exit 340 off I-10, to pick up a list of where the farms are and what they offer. The chamber of commerce will also send out a brochure on request.

While you're in Willcox, stop at the Rex Allen Cowboy Museum (520-384-4583; www.rexallen museum.com), located in one of Willcox's oldest commercial buildings. This was the famous cowboy's birthplace, and the museum focuses on his life and the pioneer settlers and ranchers who shaped the West. It's open daily from 10:00 a.m. to 4:00 p.m. Willcox also happens to be about the only place is southern Arizona where it's possible to see waterfowl such as geese, ducks, and cranes, especially in the winter months. You'll spot them at the Willcox ponds south of the interstate and west of town.

The Chiricahuas

From Willcox head south on Highway 186 (the "Apache Trail") to the Chiricahua (*chee-ree-CAH-wah*) Mountains for an outdoor adventure, but don't plan on combining this with Willcox in one day; find a spot to stay in Willcox overnight or camp out in the mountains. Two lodging options in Willcox are **Days Inn** (520-384-4222, 800-329-7466) and **Best Western Plaza Inn** (520-384-3556, 800-262-2645). Both Willcox and the Chiricahua Mountains also have places for RVs. You can drive into much of these mountains on paved roads or well-graded dirt roads, but to really explore you'll want to do some foot travel. Your first stop might be the turnoff to **Fort Bowie,** an 8-mile gravel road that ends in a parking lot. From here you'll take an easy 1.5-mile footpath to the fort ruins, along the way passing several well-marked historic sites, including a cemetery where Geronimo's baby son is buried and a picturesque 4-foot waterfall at Apache Spring. For details check www.nps.gov/fobo.

i When in Willcox, stop by Apple Annie's Orchard, where they sell fantastic sky-high apple pies, cider, and fresh apples (in season). You can pick your own, take a hayride through the orchard, grab a burger at the snack bar, and buy all kinds of apple-themed gifts at the gift shop. You'll find them 5.5 miles from exit 340, off I-10. Call (520) 384-2084 or visit www.appleannies.com for more information.

Back on Highway 186, continue south to the **Chiricahua National Monument,** with its thousands of rock spires and stone columns reaching skyward. Travel through the park along a winding 8-mile road to Massai Point for a spectacular view of the unusual rock formations. Throughout the area you'll find streams, maybe even a waterfall, and plenty of trees, along with breathtaking views. There are places to camp and restrooms but little else in the way of modern amenities. In summer this getaway will be cooler than Tucson, but carry water and sunscreen; in winter it will probably be too cold for comfort. To continue along the Apache Trail, take Highway 181 to US 191 north to Ironwood Road, then west 9.1 miles to the campground entrance. Part of this road is rough and rocky and leads to Cochise's Stronghold (www.cochisestronghold.com) in the Dragoon Mountains, where the famous Apache Indian leader and his warriors evaded the cavalry easily in the canyons and cliffs of the terrain. It's now a year-round park with picnic areas, lots of historical information, and hiking and nature trails. Admission fee for day use (hiking and picnicking) is $3. The Cochise Stronghold Bed and Breakfast in Pearce (520-826-4141, 877-426-4141; www.cochisestrongholdbb.com) is a really great place to stay. This romantic retreat in the heart of Cochise Stronghold Canyon offers luxury suites, casitas, and even a secluded tepee.

For more information on the attractions in these mountains, including camping areas, call the Coronado National Forest in Tucson at (520) 388-8300 or go to www.fs.fed.us/r3/coronado. For information about the Chiricahua National Monument, call (520) 824-3560, ext. 302, or go to www.nps.gov/chir.

New Mexico

If you're looking for a getaway that not everyone else in southern Arizona is flocking to, consider crossing the border, but this time into another state. Take I-10 east to Lordsburg, New Mexico, then Highway 90 north to Silver City, a drive of about three hours. It's an old mining town full of history—Billy the Kid roamed the streets in his youth, and miners and merchants built elegant Victorian homes here during its mining heyday. But on this getaway we're going a bit northward, via U.S. Highway 180, to a place called **Glenwood** in one of the least-populated counties (Catron) in the Southwest. Its climate parallels the Arizona high country, so it's an ideal summer destination and great in spring and fall as well. This is land once occupied by gold and silver miners, Apaches, and even Butch Cassidy and his Wild Bunch.

This getaway is truly an escape and definitely leans toward outdoor fun—canyon hikes, ghost towns, and hot springs—peppered with some good old-fashioned food and hospitality. It's been called New Mexico's best-kept secret, and we're letting you in on it.

Glenwood is a pastoral community of about 200 year-round residents. For lodgings try the scenic **Double T Homestead** (505-539-2812; www.doublethomestead.com) with its fantastic views of the Mogollon Mountains. Choose from a historic restored adobe, rustic cabin, or guesthouses on the property. There's even a horse motel fully equipped with a corral and water for your equine friends. Just south of the center of Glenwood is a USDA Forest Service office where you can get maps and recreation information on the area's hiking trails, 186 miles of trout streams, riding trails, and camping sites.

A must-see attraction is the **"catwalk" of Whitewater Canyon,** about 5 miles east of Glenwood. The canyon was reportedly once a hideout for Indians and desperadoes such as Butch Cassidy, while the catwalk was built by miners in the 1800s to carry water to a remote mill site. It was rebuilt in 1961 by the Forest Service as a recreation attraction. As you walk along the very safe and easy-to-navigate metal "sidewalk" that clings to the sides of the steep canyon walls, 25 feet below you'll see Whitewater Creek as it tumbles over boulders and winds through a forest of trees. At one point on the 1.0-mile catwalk, stairs lead down to the creek, where you can enjoy a tiny sandy beach, a waterfall, and wading pools. Looking skyward, you might be lucky enough to spot a bighorn sheep or two grazing near the canyon's peaks. At several spots, trails depart from the catwalk and wind up and down along the canyon. Be sure to take a picnic along and a good book—the picnic area near the entrance offers great shade and the relaxing sound of the tumbling creek.

After this visit with the beauty of nature, you might want to take a drive to the restored mountain ghost town of **Mogollon,** once the site of one of the largest gold mines in the country. But don't make this trip unless you feel comfortable navigating narrow switchback roads, because that's the only way to reach Mogollon. Traffic, however, will be almost nonexistent. No more than a few dozen people live in Mogollon today, and they've opened up shops and even a guest lodge to attract tourists. The nearby forest of the Gila Wilderness offers fishing, hiking, bird-watching, and observing the wildlife. For more information about Glenwood, check www.glenwoodnewmexico.com or call the chamber of commerce at (505) 539-2711.

Phoenix and Environs

There's no shortage of things to do and see in the Phoenix area and no shortage of places to find information on them—tourist materials abound at the airport, nearly every hotel, and the visitor bureau (602-254-6500; www.phoenixcvb.com). Instead of reinventing the wheel, we'll concentrate on mapping out a weekend getaway that consists of some of the attractions described in this chapter with a few others tossed in. For starters, as you head northward on I-10 (actually I-10 west), take a slight detour to the **Casa Grande Ruins National Monument** (www.nps.gov/cagr), which is accessible from exit 194 heading toward Coolidge. Here you'll see the ruins of a Hohokam Indian settlement built in 1350 and learn what archaeologists and historians know today about this now-extinct tribe. (This is true desert with little natural shade, so be prepared for the sun and heat.) After this step back into history, return to I-10 toward Phoenix.

In Phoenix your first stop should be one of the most exquisite museums in the state, the **Heard Museum** at 2301 North Central Avenue in the downtown area (602-252-8848; www.heard.org). The Heard exhibits hundreds of outstanding historic Native American works, some dating back 1,000 years and representing almost every tribal group, past and present, of the Southwest. They also have an exquisite gift shop focusing on Native American items and culture.

For a luxurious stay, consider the **Arizona Biltmore Resort and Spa** (2400 East Missouri; 602-955-6600, 800-950-2575; www.arizonabiltmore.com). This gorgeous historic hotel, known as the "jewel of the desert," has been host to many celebrities and politicians. Built in 1929, its unusual architecture was influenced by Frank Lloyd Wright. The giant checkers and chess set, nightly s'mores parties, outdoor pool movies, and waterslide will keep the kids happy, while the perfect landscaping, poolside bar, excellent restaurants, and cushy robes will keep adults relaxed.

Scottsdale

Downtown you'll find Scottsdale's **Arts District** located on the west side of Scottsdale Road from Main to Third Avenue. This area is packed with galleries and museums featuring a wide variety of amazing art. The **Old Town District,** on the east side of Scottsdale Road, from Second Street to Indian School Road, is home to historic buildings and numerous shops featuring Western ware, Southwestern jewelry, and more. You'll also find the sleek **Scottsdale Museum of Contemporary Art** (7374 East Second Street; 480-874-4666; www.smoca.org), featuring modern and contemporary art, architecture, and design from around the globe. Designed by award-winning architect Will Bruder, SmoCA's minimalist building (formerly a movie theater) includes a public "skyspace" by the acclaimed artist James Turrell. And don't miss Frank Lloyd Wright's incredible **Taliesin West** at 12621 North Frank Lloyd Wright Boulevard (see the comprehensive listing under Day Trips earlier in this chapter).

To continue on our getaway, head back to the interstate (I-10) east to the Superstition Freeway, also known as US 60. In Apache Junction take Highway 88 north, aka the Apache Trail (one of several carrying this name in the state). Here you'll see the spectacular Superstition Mountains, where legend has it the hidden fortune of the Lost Dutchman Mine has yet to be discovered. Stop at the **Goldfield Ghost Town** (4650 North Mammoth Mine Road; www.goldfieldghosttown.com) to see the area's only historic ghost town and try your luck at gold panning.

Farther north along the Apache Trail, you'll arrive at **Canyon Lake,** one of three lakes created by dams in the Salt River. This is a gorgeous spot for just admiring the water and its surrounding canyon cliffs or enjoying a lakeside picnic. Better yet, try something totally unexpected in Arizona—a cruise on a steam-operated paddle wheeler. The **Dolly steamboat** glides along the lake and its secluded inner waterways for about 90 minutes as the guide recounts legends of the Superstition Mountains. It operates daily. Ticket prices vary, with kids younger than 6 admitted free. Call (480) 827-9144 (www.dollysteamboat.com) for tour times, and be sure to allow several hours at Canyon Lake if you plan to include the boat cruise. For the perfect finale to this getaway, head back south on Apache Trail and east on US 60 to **Boyce Thompson Southwestern Arboretum** (see the earlier listing under Day Trips).

For places to stay on this getaway, consider Scottsdale or nearby Paradise Valley as a good midpoint. For budget accommodations, there's **Days Inn at Fashion Square Mall** (480-947-5411, 800-329-7466). Or try a resort that has great amenities, including a huge pool with a swim-under waterfall, but is more reasonable than most in this upscale area—the **Doubletree Paradise Valley Resort** (480-947-5400, 800-222-8733). These are but two possibilities from hundreds of places to stay that are easy to locate in Phoenix-area tourist guides or by just driving along the roadways. For a comprehensive guide to Phoenix, log onto www.phoenixcvb.com.

Close-up

Tips on Visiting Mexico

Traveling to Mexico is a great experience, whether you just set foot over the border to Nogales (just an hour south of Tucson) or venture farther south to the beach town of Puerto Peñasco/Rocky Point (three hours from Tucson), both in the state of Sonora, or beyond. Tourism is a big business here, and all visitors are warmly welcomed. There's lots to see and do.

According to U.S. Customs and Border Protection, travelers returning to the United States through a land port of entry (like Lukeville, Nogales, Douglas) must present documents at the border, not simply state their citizenship. The following single documents are acceptable: a U.S. or Canadian passport, U.S. military identification with military travel orders, Trusted Travel cards such as NEXUS, SENTRI, or FAST, state enhanced or provincial issued enhanced driver's license that denotes identity and citizenship. Two-document options include a driver's license or ID card issued by a federal, state, provincial, county, territory, or municipal authority **PLUS** a U.S. or Canadian birth certificate, U.S. Certificate of Citizenship, or U.S. consular report of birth abroad.

There are restrictions on what you can bring back into the states. For example, only one bottle of liquor per adult is allowed, fruits and vegetables are taboo, but seafood is OK, and you're required to have a prescription for certain medications that you buy in Mexico, even if they're sold over the counter there. U.S. Customs permits each adult to bring $800 in goods duty-free every 30 days. If you're not sure, check with customs officials at the border before you cross into Mexico, or you'll have to relinquish the "contraband."

The border crossing at Nogales Deconcini is open 24 hours a day. Keep in mind that during daylight saving time, Sonora will be an hour behind Arizona.

Going to Rocky Point is a bit more complicated because you'll be in a vehicle and driving in Mexico, and no doubt staying for days rather than only hours.

It's a good idea to buy gas on the U.S. side of the border. You'll be able to get it in Mexico, of course, but quality and prices vary.

Mexican law requires liability insurance for foreign-registered vehicles driven anywhere in Mexico. Insurance agents also recommend comprehensive and collision insurance—check with your carrier to see if your policy covers this. Without insurance, if you get into an accident, you can be jailed. You can purchase Mexican car insurance, either in Tucson before you start out or on the U.S. side of the border, where many signs will proclaim where it's available. It's sold in 24-hour chunks, and cost varies by type of vehicle. Be sure to have your driver's license and vehicle documents with you. Taking a rental car across is another story, so ask at the rental agency whether they'll permit it and what you'll need.

If you plan to be in Mexico for less than 24 hours and within the Border Zone, which includes Nogales and Rocky Point, you won't need a tourist permit. The "Sonora Only" program allows United States travelers to drive through most of the state of Sonora (primary attractions are Hermosillo and San Carlos) without a car permit, but you must still purchase a tourist visa at ports of entry. For longer trips you'll need a tourist permit, requiring a birth certificate or passport, and a vehicle permit. Call or visit the Mexican Consulate's Office at 553 South Stone Avenue in downtown Tucson (520-882-5595) for information or to get one.

If you plan on traveling with a minor who isn't your child, you need to have a copy of the child's birth certificate and a letter of consent signed by both parents. Also, if a child is traveling with just one parent, that parent should have a notarized letter from the other parent stating permission to take the child to Mexico or a custody document. If Fido is coming along for the journey, you'll need an International Certificate of Health (Form 77-043) and proof of vaccination against rabies and distemper issued at least 15 days and not more than 12 months before you enter Mexico.

The border crossing at Lukeville, Arizona, is open from 6:00 a.m. to midnight, Nogales/Mariposa is open from 6:00 a.m. to 10:00 p.m., and Douglas is open 24/7. If you are driving, border wait times can be long due to increased regulations. Check the Web at http://apps.cbp.gov/bwt for a listing of all delays and wait times.

While crossing, you may be asked to pull over by Mexican officials to check what you're bringing into the country. Searches are completely random: If the red light goes on, pull over; if the green light comes on, just drive through. Most of the Mexican border officials speak English, and usually they'll just want to look in the trunk. About the only thing you should absolutely not take into Mexico is a gun; it may put you in jail.

Speed limits and mileage are posted in kilometers, and your speedometer will usually have kilometers calibrated. Otherwise, driving in Mexico is no different, but watch for livestock crossing the roads. Stop signs, however, say *alto.*

If you have an emergency in Rocky Point, there's a Red Cross ambulance and a hospital in town. In restaurants and hotels, it's perfectly safe to drink the water and use ice, which are purified. But it's best not to drink from the tap, so carry or buy bottled water.

If you're calling a phone number within Mexico, it'll be just five digits. To call from Tucson you have to preface it with 011, representing the international code; the Mexico code; and the area code. Calling in the opposite direction is a bit trickier. You may not be able to use a calling card from a hotel room, so you'll either need to look for signs advertising long distance service available here, or purchase a local calling card, which is the easiest method.

If you have any other questions or concerns, contact the Mexican Consulate's Office in Tucson (listed above), one of Tucson's AAA offices, an agency that deals in Mexican insurance such as Sanborn's (520-327-1255), or call (800) 4-SONORA (476-6672). For specific border information, check the U.S. Customs Web site at www.cbp.gov. As the border crossing requirements change frequently, it's best to check with the U.S. Customs and Border Protection Agency before you travel.

Florence

Instead of riding I-10 all the way to Phoenix, take a scenic detour north out of Tucson on Highway 79 (which you'll pick up past Oro Valley). Also known as the Pinal Pioneer Highway, this will take you to Florence, the fifth-oldest town in the state. Just 45 minutes northwest of Tucson, it was founded in 1866 and hasn't changed much since.

On your way you can stop at the **Tom Mix Memorial** at Milepost 116. This is the spot where Mix, Hollywood's first "King of the Cowboys," who appeared in over 300 movies, had his fatal car accident in 1940.

Downtown Florence has been designated an official historic district and has over 140 homes and commercial buildings on the National Register of Historic Places, more than any other town in Arizona. Some of the notable historic sites are the first and second county courthouses, both completely different in architectural style. The first was built in 1877 and is open to the public as **McFarland State Park.** It holds the papers of hometown boy Ernest W. McFarland, who held the three highest offices in Arizona—chief justice of the Arizona Supreme Court, governor, and U.S. senator—and was known as the "Father of the GI Bill." The second was built in 1891 of American-Victorian architecture and is still in use today. The fully restored **Brunenkant Building,** built in 1889, serves as the Greater Florence Chamber of Commerce. The **Pinal County Visitor Center** is at 330 East Butte. Florence is also the location of a state prison, built by inmates and opened in 1908, replacing the old Territorial Prison at Yuma.

For a real look at life in territorial Arizona, stop by the **Pinal County Historical Museum** at 715 South Main Street (520-868-4382), which houses an eclectic collection including information about the WWII POW camp located here (surrounded by an Army Air Corps practice bombing range), period furnishings, the first lethal gas chamber chair, and ropes utilized in hangings.

For a bite to eat, head to family-owned **L&B Inn** at 695 South Main Street (520-868-9981; www.lbinn.com) for fresh Mexican fare.

Rocky Point, Mexico

Although it's quite a stretch including this Mexico destination as a weekend getaway, it just wouldn't do to keep southern Arizonans' favorite (and closest) beach a secret. **Puerto Peñasco** is its real name, Rocky Point the literal translation, and it's about four hours from Tucson near the tip of the Gulf of California (or Sea of Cortez)—that body of water separating Mexico's mainland from its Baja Peninsula. If you have three days to call a weekend, or better yet four, a drive to Rocky Point will put you on the ocean in a resort town, sort of (it's not Acapulco or Puerto Vallarta, folks, but it'll more than do for desert dwellers). U.S. citizens will need a passport or a birth certificate AND a picture ID in order to reenter the United States. (Read all about the ins and outs of getting in and out of Mexico in this chapter's Close-up.)

Like Nogales, Rocky Point is in the Mexican state of Sonora, and to reach it via the scenic route take Highway 86 west from Tucson to Highway 85 (at Why, Arizona) heading south, which will put you at the border. From there Mexico Highway 8 goes to Puerto Peñasco. Along the way you'll go through **Organ Pipe Cactus National Monument,** a 500-square-mile preserve of huge organ pipe cacti and lots of other desert wildlife on the Arizona side of the border.

Another similarity to Nogales is that Rocky Point is very Anglicized—English is spoken by many, U.S. currency is accepted, and most signage is in English, so it's easy to find your way around. Because Rocky Point has really become a tourist attraction, there are plenty of hotels and other amenities. In addition to hotels, lodging choices include RV parks and rentals of condos and homes, some of them quite luxurious beachside vacation homes.

Before getting into the specifics of where to stay and what to do in Rocky Point, we'll provide an overview of the town. The weather is about the same as Tucson's, sometimes a few degrees warmer, which means that it may not be beach weather in December or January, but spring and fall are perfect, and summer will actually feel hotter because of the oceanside humidity. But there's

Close-up

Tohono O'odham Nation Cultural Center and Museum

The **Tohono O'odham Cultural Center and Museum** is worth a stop on the way to Rocky Point or as a day-trip destination itself. Located in the tiny town of Topawa just off Highway 86, the $15.2 million facility showcases Tohono O'odham life and culture. The second-largest tribe in the United States, the Tohono O'odham (Desert People) are less well known than other tribes. The fascinating exhibits at the museum offer a window into the world of these amazing people who have made their home in the Sonoran Desert for centuries. In addition to the exhibit and gallery space, an outdoor patio offers a fabulous view of sacred Baboquivari Peak. Nature trails, an outdoor amphitheater, and covered armadas are great for walking and picnicking. There are no food vendors here, so bring your own. The museum is open Monday through Saturday 10:00 a.m. to 4:00 p.m. For more information call (520) 383-0201.

Signage for the museum is limited. To get there take Highway 86 to Sells, follow the business loop toward the hospital, and turn south at the sign reading TOPAWA AND SAN MIGUEL, which takes you onto BIA Route 19. Travel approximately 9 miles south and turn left onto the dirt road at the sign for Baboquivari Peak, which is Fresnal Canyon Road. The museum will be on your right about 1,000 yards ahead.

Eight feet in diameter, this etched Man in the Maze window is one of the centerpieces of the Tohono O'odham Cultural Center and Museum. PHOTO BY M. PAGANELLI VOTTO

a solution to that problem—jump in the water. Water is all around, along with miles of white beaches, and they're all public. To the town's north is an area called **Cholla Bay.** With lots of beach, small beachfront houses, and nightlife, this area is a favorite of vacationing college students and young adults. To the town's east is more beach, miles of it, along with a gated upscale community called **Las Conchas,** with homes and condos.

As for where to stay, choices range from a tent or sleeping bag on **Sandy Beach,** for a daily fee, to the midlevel **Playa Bonita** (www.playabonitaresort.com). There are also RV parks north and east of town starting at about $25 a night. Another choice is to rent a condo or home in Cholla Bay or Las Conchas. There are also numerous luxury time-shares in town and along the beach. Reserving a hotel in advance is a good idea, and reserving an RV space or private rental in advance is a necessity. For assistance call the **Sonora Tourism Office** at (800) 476-6672, check the Web site at www.gotosonora.com, or look up

Tucson travel agencies that specialize in Rocky Point. Another good source is the Sunday travel section of the *Arizona Daily Star,* which always has ads for Rocky Point reservation services that book private rentals and hotels.

i While in Rocky Point, stop by the CETMAR aquarium. Not a fancy aquarium by most standards, it features giant tubs and slightly opaque tanks. Kids, however, will love the hands-on tide pools and feeding the resident sea turtles and sea lions. You'll find it at 43 Las Conchas Road, just before you enter the main guard gate for Las Conchas. Hours can vary, but it is usually open Monday through Friday 10:00 a.m. to 2:30 p.m. and Saturday and Sunday 10:00 a.m. to 6:00 p.m. There is a small entry fee plus the cost of food to feed the sea creatures.

Once you're checked into your getaway quarters, the fun begins. Seaside, you can frolic in the salt water or on the beach, search for seashells, snorkel, fish, parasail, and scuba dive. You also can rent just about any kind of fun you didn't bring with you—personal watercraft, ATVs, parasail rides, scuba dives, and even a banana boat ride in the shallow surf. (Look for the large tourist information sign for places that rent equipment, fishing boats, and so forth.) Even when tourists flock in, the beaches are so broad that people aren't crammed like sardines. In town or on Cholla Bay, you can shop for all the regional goods Mexico is famous for, including blankets, jewelry, carvings, and more. But don't miss a visit to the fish market in the scenic **Old Port** area. Whether you're doing your own cooking or merely want to take some of the sea's bounty back to Tucson, you'll find large shrimp for about $9 a pound and all kinds of freshly caught fish for about $3 a pound. Seafood is a staple of many restaurants, but there's also Italian food, burger and pizza places, and of course Mexican food. For more information call the visitors bureau at (877) 843-3717.

Verde Valley

North and a bit west of Phoenix is an area called Verde Valley (named for the Verde, meaning "green," River) that houses some of the state's most popular spots: the mountainside former mining town of Jerome, the historic and lovely city of Prescott, and the breathtaking red-rock country of Sedona. Because this area has so much to offer and is quite different from Tucson and the Sonoran Desert, we'll map out a weekend getaway to take you there, but you'll need a long weekend—three or four days—to fit it in. The driving time alone from Tucson to Sedona, the farthest point of this trip, is four hours, and that doesn't include some must-see stops along the way.

Begin this multifaceted weekend getaway by taking I-10 west to Phoenix, where you'll catch I-17 north. For your first stop, consider **Arcosanti,** the urban habitat founded by Paolo Soleri (described previously in this chapter under Day Trips). But be sure to allow enough time to drive a bit farther up I-17, to exit 289, for **Montezuma Castle** (www.nps.gov/moca). Don't be fooled or put off by this attraction's moniker—it's not a castle, but an Indian ruin, one of the best-preserved prehistoric cliff dwellings in Arizona. If you only have time to see one Indian ruin in the southern half of the state, this should be it. The Sinagua (Spanish for "without water") Indians built Montezuma Castle around A.D. 1125. A peaceful farming people, they cultivated the valley using water from the Verde River and its tributaries and sometimes built cliff dwellings as a way to live protected from the more aggressive inhabitants of the area. What today is called Montezuma Castle was such a dwelling. (Later settlers erroneously thought it was built by the Aztec Indians and, thinking it looked like a castle, named it for the Aztec leader.) Today it's a national monument and a sight to behold. After parking your vehicle and entering the visitor center, you'll still have no idea what lies ahead until you walk down a pathway with a creek coursing nearby—the same water that centuries ago provided the sustenance for this small group of cliff dwellers who disappeared.

The first sight of the five-story cliff dwelling is breathtaking, and the 500-acre monument itself is a lovely place of huge old trees and pathways lined with the story of these people. Montezuma Castle (928-567-3322) is open daily from 8:00 a.m. to 5:00 p.m. (6:00 p.m. in summer) and costs $5 for anyone older than 16.

If you'd like to see more examples of ancient dwellers, both Sinagua and Hohokam, take I-17 a few miles farther north to exit 293 and visit **Montezuma Well.** This is an oasis of lush vegetation, including huge Arizona sycamore trees, where you'll see remains of a Sinagua cliff dwelling and pueblo and a Hohokam pithouse. From the Indian ruins you'll probably want to find a spot to rest for the night before tackling the rest of this getaway. Prescott is the closest spot, Jerome the most difficult to get to, and Sedona the farthest, but any will do as a base from which to explore the exciting and varied Verde Valley.

Highway 69 west will take you into **Prescott,** a scenic city that combines the Old West and 1860s Victorian charm. Prescott was founded when gold was discovered in nearby hills and was the Arizona Territory's first capital. By then rowdy gold miners were frequenting Prescott's now-famous Whiskey Row, and European gentry were living in grand Victorian houses. More than 500 buildings in Prescott are on the National Register of Historic Places, so history and architecture buffs will find much to explore in this city, including the territorial governor's residence built in 1864. The downtown area is where you'll find most of the historic sites, along with Whiskey Row, museums, and a lovely square called Courthouse Plaza, where many art shows and special events take place.

Prescott is also a great place for outdoor fun. It actually has four seasons, but they're mild; in other words, it's minus the extreme heat of the desert in summer and the extreme cold and snow common to the north. In and around Prescott visitors can play golf, hike, climb on some of the state's best rock formations, fish, ride horses, pan for gold, watch and wager on the horse races at Prescott Downs, and see the world's oldest rodeo in July. If you choose to make Prescott an overnight stop, there are many choices of hotels and bed-and-breakfasts, among them the historic **Hotel St. Michael** (928-776-1999, 800-678-3757; www.hotelstmichael.net) and the quaint **Hotel Vendome** (928-776-0900, 888-468-3583; www.vendomehotel.com).

Another spot you might want to consider visiting in Verde Valley is **Jerome.** Although most ghost towns in Arizona have remained just that, Jerome is one of the rare exceptions. The mines around this old mining town clinging to the side of Mingus Mountain once produced $125 billion worth of copper ore, and Jerome had 15,000 residents. For several decades it was almost totally abandoned (earning it the reputation of a ghost town), but today it is an enclave of artists and a National Historic Landmark.

At its 5,000-foot elevation, Jerome offers some spectacular vistas of mountains, the Mogollon Rim, and the red-rock country. The downside of Jerome is the road one must traverse to reach it. This narrow and winding switchback road up the mountain, although paved, is not for everyone. But once in Jerome, you'll find a quaint and scenic village with shops, restaurants, museums, galleries, and old-time saloons. Dining options are limited in number but varied. Grills and hamburger joints join the upscale **Asylum Restaurant** (928-639-3197; www.theasylum.biz) with its spectacular views. For lodging there are several bed-and-breakfast inns, but it's best to contact the chamber of commerce (928-634-2900; www.jeromechamber.com) in advance to find out what's open and the price of a room. From I-17 take Highway 260 west to Cottonwood, then Highway 89A to Jerome.

To round out your Verde Valley getaway, we've saved what many people believe is the best for last: the red-rock scenery of **Sedona** and **Oak Creek Canyon.** From either Prescott or Jerome, Highway 89A will take you to Sedona; otherwise, from I-17 take Highway 179 to the Sedona exit. Be sure to include some time for seeing the surroundings because, although the town is picturesque and can keep you very busy, a walk in the wild here is like nothing you will experience elsewhere. That's because this pocket of the state was blessed with vibrant red sandstone cliffs and rock formations that display their dramatic spires and odd shapes amid pines, sycamores, buttes, and a beautiful rushing stream, Oak Creek.

Some highlights of the red-rock country you'll want to include in your sightseeing are **Red Rock Crossing,** which is a bit off the beaten path for most tourists and therefore a more peaceful spot for frolicking in Oak Creek or hiking along an easy trail to the base of Cathedral Rock; **Bell Rock,** a landmark formation southeast of Sedona on Highway 179; the Frank Lloyd Wright–designed **Chapel of the Holy Cross**; and the popular **Oak Creek Canyon** north of town, where slide rocks provide some serious rides down the creek for kids and adults alike. No matter where you may choose to drive, bike, or walk around the Sedona countryside, however, you'll be treated to nature at its finest.

Sedona is a mecca for shopping, the arts, dining, and lodging—and it all leans toward upscale. **Tlaquepaque** (www.tlaq.com), for instance, is a lovely shopping center with the architecture and flavor of Old Mexico and about two dozen shops (pronounce it *tla-keh-pah-keh*). Throughout Sedona you'll find shops selling everything from Southwestern items to fine clothing and home accessories. The town is dotted with scores of art galleries, while art exhibits, live theater, and music events are regular happenings here. Sedona also has a vast array of eateries, from delis and ice-cream shops to some very fine dining. And if this is where you plan to rest for a night or two, the accommodation choices are almost dizzying. There are motels, such as **King's Ransom** (928-282-7151; www.kingsransom.com) and **Sedona Super 8** (928-282-1533) that, while not cheap in this neck of the woods, are at least affordable. Or choose from among many bed-and-breakfasts, including two that travel writers often call among the best in the Southwest: **Grace's Secret Garden** (928-284-2340, 800-579-2340; www.gracessecretgarden.com) and the **Casa Sedona** (928-282-2938; www.casasedona.com). If you really want to splurge on a resort stay, Sedona offers some of the best. Two choices for luxurious accommodations are the **L'Auberge de Sedona** (928-282-1661, 800-905-5745; www.lauberge.com) and **Enchantment Resort** (928-282-2900, 800-826-4180; www.enchantmentresort.com).

At an elevation of 4,400 feet, Sedona is cooler than Tucson and a favorite playground of both Arizonans and tourists. It's a busy place year-round but especially in summer when desert dwellers need an escape. In addition to attracting tourists for all the obvious reasons, Sedona also is said (by those who know these things) to be a "vortex" of spiritual rejuvenation; for the uninitiated, that's something like having a mystical energy, making Sedona a mecca for meditation types. But whatever your reason for visiting Sedona—its spectacular beauty, art offerings, mystical energy, or the cool running waters of Oak Creek—you'll be enchanted.

For information contact the chamber of commerce (928-282-7722, 800-288-7336; www.sedonachamber.com) or stop by the visitor centers at 331 Forest Road in uptown Sedona for maps, tour information, accommodations, and more. Open daily except Christmas, Thanksgiving, and New Year's Day.

NEIGHBORHOODS, NEIGHBORING TOWNS, AND REAL ESTATE

Tucson is made up of a variety of eclectic and fast-growing neighborhoods, ranging from upscale new housing and condo developments to historic, artsy, downtown communities. You'll find a little bit of everything here.

The Tucson metropolitan area was slammed as hard as the rest of the country by the 2006/2007 housing downturn. House prices fell and fewer new homes were built. At the end of 2007, supply-and-demand factors remained unfavorable, according to the Eller College of Management. In December 2007 the Tucson Association of Realtors put the average home sale price at $260,000, while the median price for the same time period was $210,000, down from the previous two years. But the news isn't all bad. Buyers can find real gems at decent prices, and the buyer pool is expected to grow in coming years. Young families are attracted to Tucson for the excellent business climate, while retiring baby boomers come for the sun. But how soon the housing market will recover is anybody's guess.

Even with the housing market slowdown, land is still scarce in the Tucson area. When the market begins to turn around, land values should continue their upward swing, so if you are thinking of moving to Tucson, now is the time. The areas of most growth include downtown, where many new homes are being built and renovated as a result of Rio Nuevo, a multimillion-dollar revitalization effort (see the Area Overview chapter). The northwest (Oro Valley and Marana) and southeast (Rincon Mountain) areas of town are bursting with available new single homes and developments, and the Green Valley area continues to expand with luxury housing developments and active adult communities (see the Retirement chapter).

Tucson, unlike many cities of its size or larger, does not have suburbs in the customary sense. There's Tucson (the city) and there's Pima County (surrounding the city), and within both are numerous neighborhoods and towns, each with something a little different to offer. This chapter presents a primer on the metro area—from its fascinating historic areas to the sprawling newer ones. We try to convey the character and lifestyle, distinguishing architectural features, a few major points of interest, and what the real estate scene is like in select areas.

If you're a visitor to Tucson, you'll find great information about specific neighborhoods to visit for their historic, cultural, and design significance. If you're a new resident or plan to be, this chapter will help you get an overview of the many options Tucson offers in the more established neighborhoods and where the growth is.

NEIGHBORHOODS

Historic and Old Neighborhoods

El Presidio

The Hohokam Indians were the first human inhabitants of Tucson. Long after they disappeared, Spanish settlers arrived from Mexico and created what is Tucson's first neighborhood—El Presidio. They may not have known it, but they settled very near a Hohokam site. The first neighborhood started out as a fort (or presidio) called San Augustin del Tucson, covering approximately 12 acres and enclosing two plazas, a chapel, a cemetery, stables for horses, and quarters for officers, soldiers, and settlers. Gradually houses were built outside the presidio walls, and eventually the walls came tumbling down.

As with the other downtown historic areas, the neighborhood really took off with the arrival of the railroad and Anglo-Americans in the early 1880s, their Victorian, Tudor, and bungalow-style houses supplanting the Sonoran row houses of the first settlers. Meyer and Court Streets offer examples of the original Sonoran architecture, with adobe row houses built to the front property line and open courtyard spaces in the interior. In contrast, the houses along Main Avenue reflect architectural styles introduced from the East and Midwest by Anglo-Americans—these houses are set back from the street, surrounded by yards and lush vegetation, and Victorian in architectural style. The grand homes along Main and Granada Avenues and Paseo Redondo earned this area the name "Snob Hollow" in the 1920s and 1930s, coined because Tucson's movers and shakers lived there and the area was in a topographical hollow.

Designated the El Presidio Historic District in 1975, it covers a 12-block area immediately north of today's downtown, bounded roughly by Alameda, Church, and Sixth Streets and Granada

The Eliza Rockwell House was once part of exclusive Snob Hollow. PHOTO BY KATE REYNOLDS

Avenue. The district is rich with old structures, many of which have been converted into museums or professional buildings. The oldest is **La Casa Cordova,** now housing a Mexican heritage museum. Nearby is the **Edward Nye Fish House,** a typical prerailroad Sonoran row house that now houses the **Tucson Museum of Art's Pavilion of Western Art.** The **Steinfeld Mansion** at 300 North Main Avenue was built for $10,000 in 1899. The 12,000-square-foot **Manning House,** at 450 West Paseo Redondo, was built in 1907 and occupied by a one-time mayor. Other historic residences are the Corbett House, Romero House, and Stevens House.

i Many of the historic districts in and around the downtown area make for some excellent walking tours, complete with historic buildings, houses converted into museums, churches, and even a shrine. Stop by the Metropolitan Tucson Convention & Visitors Bureau at 100 South Church Avenue for tour information and lots more on the Tucson area (including discount offers on accommodations, travel, attractions, and more).

If your tour of the area makes you a bit weary of concrete and buildings, visit a lovely little oasis in the midst of it all—the **Alene Dunlap Smith Memorial Garden,** on the east side of Granada Street just north of Franklin Street. If you'd like to get in a bit of shopping or dining with your history, visit **Old Town Artisans,** an adobe-walled structure on Washington and Meyer Streets, parts of which date back more than 150 years. The half dozen shops here include items handmade by local artists and a collection of folk art. Directly across Alameda Street (the historic district's southern boundary) are **El Presidio Park** and the **Pima County Courthouse,** built in 1928 in an elaborate Moorish style with a tile mosaic dome that's a Tucson landmark.

El Presidio has been undergoing a residential renaissance as a result of multimillion-dollar initiatives aimed at revitalizing the downtown area. Historic adobes have been renovated and lovely new single-family and town homes constructed, some designated for lower income residents. Paving projects and other roadwork are improving access and traffic flow. It's a friendly, intimate neighborhood with a strong neighborhood association committed to preserving the look and feel of this historic area. There are not a lot of services here; commercial and historic buildings are the norm. The area attracts a variety of people from artists to professionals. It might not be a first choice for families with school-age children. Homes here range from $185,000 to more than $900,000; new developments like Franklin Court, a nine-unit upscale residential development at the northeast corner of Franklin and Court, start at $340,000. The area falls within Tucson Unified School District, Tucson's largest school district.

Armory Park

Way back when, the area now known as Armory Park began as the original military plaza of Camp Lowell. (Later the military camp was moved to the Rillito River area and renamed Fort Lowell, discussed separately in this chapter.) From 1880, when work on the transcontinental railroad reached Tucson, until about 1920, the Armory Park area transformed into a residential area inhabited by prominent railroad executives, affluent entrepreneurs, and working-class people. Anglo-Americans began migrating in and, with the help of the railroad, imported building materials typically used in eastern housing. Also typical of the Anglo style, their houses were built in the center of lots with spacious yards all around.

Today you'll still see an eclectic mix of Victorian, Queen Anne, California bungalow, Mission, and Spanish Colonial Revival styles. Designated a historic district in 1974 (Tucson's first), Armory Park covers about 30 blocks just southeast of the central business district. It extends from 12th Street south to 19th Street and from about Second Avenue on the east to Stone Avenue on the west.

In addition to an actual park—named, what else, Armory Park—and a senior center adjacent to it, some of the highlights of the district are the **Temple of Music and Art,** a handsomely restored structure now housing the Arizona Theatre Company; the original Tucson Carnegie Library, now home to the **Tucson Children's Museum**; and the **Tucson Center for the Performing Arts,** formerly a Catholic church. **Safford Middle School** is an excellent example of the Mission Revival style, with plastered walls, an elaborate ornamental entry, and portals.

Along with turn-of-the-twentieth-century hotels, converted office buildings, and even a bed-and-breakfast or two, the outer edge of this neighborhood is growing rapidly as a result of the development of **Armory Park del Sol** (www.armoryparkdelsol.com) at South Third Avenue and 16th Street. This attractive development includes two parks, a community garden, and landscaped common areas. The well-designed homes are energy efficient and, although modern, incorporate historic elements from the Queen Anne, Mission Revival, territorial, and bungalow styles found in the neighborhood. Homes start at $396,000 and jump dramatically.

The Armory Park area has few services and attracts primarily young professionals. Several historic buildings in the area, including a former convent and an icehouse, have been converted into upscale lofts with apartments both for rent and for sale. A lovely historic area within the Tucson Unified School District, it may not be the ideal place for families, however, because of the dense traffic, the commercial businesses intermingled with residences, and the homeless population that often occupies Armory Park.

Barrio Historico

In sharp contrast to the contemporary concrete edifice right across the street known as the Tucson Convention Center, Barrio Historico dates from the mid-1850s. Also known as Barrio Viejo, this historic district covers about 20 blocks from Cushing Street on the north to 18th Street on the south and from the railroad tracks on the west to Stone Avenue on the east. Although working-class Mexicans were the predominant settlers, Chinese, African-American, Anglo-American, and Native American settlers made it a somewhat ethnically diverse area.

Unlike for some of the other central historical neighborhoods, the influx of Anglo-Americans and the railroad had less impact on the barrios, and they retained much of their Spanish culture and heritage, as well as the name "barrio." What did have an impact on the barrios, however, was urban renewal in the late 1960s; about half the barrio neighborhoods in the downtown area gave way to parking lots, government buildings, the convention center, and other commercial structures. Barrio Historico is one of a handful of barrios that were saved from the bulldozers.

Designated a historic district in 1975, Barrio Historico is an excellent example of Sonoran style, which relied on the use of native materials—mud adobe, mesquite, and saguaro—and ingenuity to adapt to the desert climate. Houses were tightly clustered, often with shared walls, to gain protection from the desert heat. They were built close to the front property line so that interior courtyards would be protected from the sun by the surrounding structure. Another characteristic of the barrios is that they were self-contained—local merchants set up shop to sell groceries and staples, provide furniture and other craft works, and even give credit.

A visit to Barrio Historico is a journey back in time not only to early Tucson, but also to Mexican villages or Mediterranean villages, whose architecture strongly influenced the Sonoran style. It contains the largest and best-preserved collection of old adobes in the West. Today the restored row houses are used for residences as well as offices and studios for artists and designers. But the most unusual site in Barrio Historico may well be **El Tiradito,** meaning "the little castaway" but commonly called the Wishing Shrine.

Legend has it that this outdoor adobe shrine with a soot-scarred image of the Virgin of Guadalupe was erected for a man murdered in a love triangle before the turn of the twentieth century. It is believed to be the only one of its kind in the United States dedicated to a sinner buried in unconsecrated ground. Now on the National

Register of Historic Places, it is said that if you light a candle there at night and it burns until morning, your wish will come true. This makeshift shrine, common in the Mexican culture, stands as a lonely reminder of the past set amid modern paved roads and restaurants, and within throwing distance of the TCC. You'll find the shrine on Main Avenue just south of Cushing Street and right next to a more modern neighborhood landmark, yet still one of the older family-run Mexican restaurants in the city, El Minuto Cafe (see the Restaurants chapter).

i For a cool way to learn about Barrio Viejo, let a student docent show you around. Head over to La Pilita Museum at 420 South Main Avenue. From September though May, students at Carillo Magnet School conduct museum tours and offer historical perspectives on the area. No tours are offered on Wednesday, and it's best to call ahead to arrange a tour (520-882-7454).

This area too is being upgraded and renovated as part of the improvements to the downtown and El Presidio areas. Attractive elderly and mixed housing developments and new adobe and territorial-style homes are recent additions to the neighborhood. Home prices here have escalated to the $200,000 range and are expected to climb. This area is in the Tucson Unified School District but may not be an ideal area for families with kids because houses have no yard areas and are very close to the street. Commercial businesses are intermingled with residences, and it's very close to the congestion and heavy traffic of the Tucson Convention Center.

West University

The 60-block area located between the University of Arizona and downtown is historically significant because it exemplifies the pattern of middle- and upper-class residential development in Tucson from 1890 to 1930. Thus it was designated a historic district by the city in 1984. Although some buildings reflect the Mexican style, the neighborhood's architecture is mostly European and California bungalow styles because it was settled by Anglo-Americans after the arrival of the Southern Pacific Railroad.

Strolling pedestrians will pass restored bungalows and Victorian-style houses on tree-lined streets, the **Fourth Avenue shopping district** (and Tucson's trolley line), and, just beyond the east boundary of the district, the university's first building, Old Main. The district extends roughly from Sixth Street north to Speedway Boulevard and from Seventh Avenue on the west to Euclid Avenue. Today it's a mixture of older homes occupied by longtime residents and more transient student rentals, peppered with a few fraternity houses, bed-and-breakfast inns, restaurants, and shops catering mostly to students. Home prices vary widely here, ranging from the low $200,000s to over $600,000 for renovated properties.

Middle-school kids in this neighborhood can attend the very first elementary school ever built in the state, which is now **Roskruge Middle School** on East Sixth Street, a handsomely restored building that obviously still has old-world charm and appeal. This school and the neighborhood are in the Tucson Unified School District.

i Every Tuesday at 8:00 p.m., there's a community bike ride that's great fun. The ride is usually 5 to 8 miles, and everyone is welcome. People show up on unicycles, cruiser bikes, or even old three-speeds. Bring a light and a rear reflector. The group meets by the flagpole in front of the University of Arizona's Old Main. Learn more at www.tucsonbikelawyer.com.

Fort Lowell

There's something about the Fort Lowell area that just seems to silently shout "history." Maybe it's the ghosts of the Hohokam, or the imagined sounds of the battles between the cavalry post's soldiers and the Apaches, or the generations-old adobe homes handmade by early Mexican settlers. Or perhaps it's the juxtaposition of uniformed six-year-olds playing soccer games on the very parkland where more than a hundred years ago uniformed soldiers may have played, or where more than a thousand years ago Hohokam Indians tilled the ground to farm. Whatever the reason, this area, located just south of the confluence of the Pautano and Tanque Verde washes, is often said to reflect where Tucson's soul resides.

Hohokam Indians first settled and farmed this area about A.D. 300. They were long gone by 1873, when the military began building a cavalry post to protect Arizona settlers from Apache raids—a fort that was 7 miles away from "Tucson" and connected to it by the "Fort Lowell Road." Under the safety of the fort, Mexicans migrated here to farm and ranch the fertile bottomlands, and they were soon followed by Mormons.

Only 0.25 square mile in size, the district is rich in 1,500 years of history. Fort Lowell Park contains the **Fort Lowell Museum** (part of the Arizona Historical Society), some remaining ruins of fort buildings, and even a Hohokam archaeological site. Fort Lowell Road, to the west of the park, offers some rambling Sonoran ranch adobes nearly hidden by lush vegetation. Just west of the district boundary is **San Pedro Chapel,** built in Mission Revival style and designated as the city's first historic landmark in 1982 (and also on the state and national registers). Very nearby is a tiny chapel called **La Capillita,** originally built in 1915 by the Mexican settlers but reduced to a pile of rubble until a group of local volunteers led the effort to rebuild it in 1997.

The Fort Lowell Neighborhood Association opens it doors to the past once a year in February for **La Reunion de El Fuerte,** which is open to the public and free (see the Festivals and Events chapter). The one-day event takes its name from the Mexican settlement that grew up among the abandoned military buildings and was named El Fuerte, or "the fort." Visitors can get a rare view of the cavalry corrals and stables, or at least what's left of these fragile adobe ruins, which are now protected by chain-link fencing and metal roofs under the purview of the Fort Lowell Museum. Other events at La Reunion include cavalry drills, music, and walking tours of the district.

In recent years vacant land in this area has been gobbled up by home builders, but even the new developments seem to reflect the character of the old—mostly stucco houses with lots of vegetation that retain the sense of quiet calm of the neighborhood. Today the area contains an eclectic mix of residences, from starter and patio homes in the low $200,000s to luxury adobes selling for as much as $600,000-plus and from turn-of-the-twentieth-century adobe houses to contemporary architecture. The narrow and curving East Presidio Street is lined with newer homes but feels like an old hacienda-lined street of Mexico, with walled courtyards, lush vegetation, and hundreds of mesquite trees.

Located in the Tucson Unified School District, this is a great neighborhood for families—quiet, filled with history, mostly large properties, and fairly removed from commercial businesses but within easy access of them. One of Tucson's foremost private preparatory schools, **St. Gregory,** is at the north end of the neighborhood.

i Tucson locals often drop by Rincon Market in the Sam Hughes neighborhood for breakfast on Saturday or Sunday mornings. It's a great way to meet people. Rincon Market is at 2513 East Sixth Street; (520) 327-6653.

Sam Hughes

First there was Sam Hughes, local pioneering merchant and civic leader. Then there was Sam Hughes Elementary School. Then there was the Sam Hughes neighborhood, bounded by Speedway Boulevard, Campbell Avenue, Broadway Boulevard, and Country Club Road. Originally homesteaded by five landowners, this square mile east of the university was eventually subdivided into numerous housing projects and then combined under the rubric "Sam Hughes neighborhood." It contains some of the Old Pueblo's finest examples of charming Mission Revival and Spanish Colonial homes.

This is a neighborhood that has become very popular with upscale city dwellers—people who prefer the city life to the outskirts (and the accompanying commute), along with quiet streets, older homes both restored and still needing fixing up, the proximity of the university and all it has to offer, and friendly sidewalks and streets for jogging or bike riding. A neighborhood association was formed in 1971 to preserve the residential character of the area and fend off undesirable development. Long a Tucson treasure, the neighborhood became a national treasure with its National Historic District designation in 1994.

Highlights of the neighborhood, in addition to the many lovely homes and relative peace and quiet, include **Himmel Park** and its namesake library and the **Rincon Market** on Sixth Street and Tucson Boulevard, a favorite gathering and shopping place for the residents for years.

Among the neighborhood's famous residents are Frank Borman, who lived here before going on to orbit the moon and become president of Eastern Airlines, and Hiram "Hi" Corbett, a civic leader who brought Cactus League baseball to Tucson and whose name the baseball stadium bears.

The nostalgia, the historically preserved homes, and the proximity of town combine to make Sam Hughes pricey and its residents a largely liberal mix of attorneys, professors, architects, and a surprising number of retirees. The biggest change to this historic neighborhood is the development of **Sam Hughes Square** at the southeast corner of Campbell Avenue and Sixth Street. The three-story building is home to commercial and office buildings and condominiums, a first for this area. Served by Tucson Unified schools, this is a good family neighborhood, as long as your family conforms to the association rules and preservationist philosophy. Prices range from the mid-$200,000s to upwards of $1,500,000 for the large, beautifully restored homes on Third and Fourth Streets. Houses do go on the market here, but not many and not frequently. You can buy a whole lot more space for the same money elsewhere, but not in a central neighborhood with this kind of commitment to the past and the future.

Pie Allen

This neighborhood owes its unusual name to pies made by one of its earliest settlers. Made from dried apples because fresh fruit was scarce here then, John "Pie" Allen's pies were a big hit and started Allen on the road to becoming a local entrepreneur and eventually mayor of Tucson. Bounded by Park and Fourth Avenues and by Sixth Street and Broadway Boulevard, the neighborhood covers 24 blocks just west of the university. Residents formed an association in 1980, primarily to protect themselves and their historic homes from university expansion.

A building boom in the 1880s transformed the former ranch land into homes occupied largely by railroad workers. Almost every architectural style popular between the 1860s and the 1940s is represented in Pie Allen, and many have been restored. Several were designed by one of Tucson's most famous and distinctive architects, Josias Joesler. One of the area's vintage buildings, a Spanish Colonial Revival–style structure dating from 1928, is the **Colonial Hotel** at 410 East Ninth Street.

Within the Tucson Unified School District, Pie Allen boasts the oldest high school in the state, now **Tucson Magnet High,** which recently underwent a major renovation. Today homes in this neighborhood are less expensive than, say, Sam Hughes homes and start in the mid-$200,000s.

El Encanto

This hidden neighborhood just west of the sprawling El Con Mall boasts some of the most elegant homes—almost mansions—in central Tucson. Sometimes referred to as the "Beverly Hills of Tucson," this neighborhood developed in the late 1920s has a strong California influence, beginning with its geometric street pattern that was a major departure from the grid pattern of all prior neighborhoods in Tucson. From a central circle, streets fan out in a diagonal pattern, making the neighborhood a bit difficult for the uninitiated to traverse. Another obvious California influence is the landscaping—hundreds of Mexican fan palms and date palms were planted during the initial layout, along with many citrus, olive, and eucalyptus trees. The street pattern, combined with the lush landscaping and many walled yards and courtyards, gives the neighborhood a sense of mystery and privacy.

Given the value of this real estate today, it's astonishing that the land was actually acquired free from the federal government by a homesteader more than 90 years ago. The first home built here and its surrounding 10 acres were purchased for $3,700 by Leroy "Jessie" James (no, not the famous outlaw), who was ridiculed for buying worthless desert land so far from town. Jessie no doubt had the last laugh when a few years later he got offers of 10 times that amount.

Today this neighborhood bounded by Fifth Street and Broadway Boulevard and Country Club Road and Jones Avenue is city living at its finest. Emanating from the center circle, which boasts more than 150 saguaro cacti, are nearly 150 homes on one-acre lots in styles including Moroccan, Spanish, Italian, Mexican, and early California. About 50 are on the National Register of Historic Places. Home prices here can easily reach or exceed $1.5 million, and there is not much turnover. It's in the Tucson Unified School District.

Winterhaven

Added to the National Register of Historic Places in 2006, two things are most noticeable in this 0.5-square-mile neighborhood that extends from Tucson Boulevard to Country Club Road and Prince Road to Fort Lowell Road. One is the lush green grass surrounding every home, unusual in the Tucson desert; the other is the street named Christmas Avenue. The former no doubt results from the fact that a fertilizer company once occupied much of the land, its huge manure piles making for rich soil underneath. The latter signifies the neighborhood's real claim to fame—the Festival of Lights, which started in 1949, the same year the development opened, and has been held annually every Christmas since then (see the Festivals and Events chapter).

Winterhaven remains an attractive residential neighborhood with ranch-style homes, located fairly close to the university and downtown areas. It's a peaceful and comfortable middle-class neighborhood that looks like it was transplanted from back East—explained by the fact that the developer reportedly patterned it after Shaker Heights, Ohio.

In 1949 homes sold for $9,000 to $16,000. Today homes on good-size lots covered with green grass and mature vegetation start at about $255,000. It has a strong neighborhood association and lies within the Tucson Unified School District boundary. More details are available at www.mywinterhaven.net.

i Take a stroll through one of Tucson's secret delights, Poet's Corner. It got its name from all the streets named for poets. The area is bordered by Swan Road on the east, Columbus Boulevard on the west, Sixth Street to the north, and Broadway to the south. See streets named for Poe, Burns, Whitman, and the famous poet, Ninth Street. Oh, wait. That's not a poet.

Tucson Country Club

At one time this enclave was considered way out in the boondocks, but with continual expansion to the east, it's actually quite convenient to downtown and nearly all points in the valley. This is old-world country-club living at its finest amid mature vegetation, lots of mesquite trees, large flat lots, and some of Tucson's most prominent residents.

An exclusive, upscale neighborhood bounded by the Tanque Verde and Pantano washes on the south and west and by Tanque Verde Road on the east, Tucson Country Club is almost an island in a sea of recent development, most of it commercial. Hidden behind service stations, restaurants, and all manner of shops, the neighborhood of 300 to 400 homes begins on a street called Camino Principal and winds westward to a private golf and country club. And unless you drive through the entrance area, you'll have no idea this neighborhood exists.

Many of the club's homes were built in the 1950s. The price for resales starts at more than $600,000 and goes way up from there. It's within Tucson Unified School District boundaries.

i If you're a student or anyone else planning to rent in the university area, the university publishes a free annual *Off-Campus Housing Guide*. It contains some great advice on leasing plus the complete Arizona Residential Landlord and Tenant Act, useful forms and maps, and lots more. Call (520) 621-5859 for information on where to pick one up, or download it at www.union.arizona.edu/csil/csa/offcampus.php.

Other Neighborhoods

In the 1920s Tucson's population topped out at 20,000. By the '60s we were just passing the quarter-million mark. Today we're close to a million in the metropolitan area. Where do all these people homestead? In every direction they can, including up the mountainsides.

The Catalina Foothills

Today the word *foothills* designates any area rising into any one of the mountain ranges surrounding Tucson, and as the population swells, so too do the mountainside homes. But the original foothills growth was to the city's north at the base of the Santa Catalina Mountains, an area close to the city center and offering views over the entire Tucson valley. It's a very popular area that attracts wealthy retirees and families.

The Catalina foothills area extends from River Road on the south to as high or far as anyone can build on the north and from about Craycroft Road on the east to about Campbell Avenue on the west. Here you will find exclusive gated communities such as Finisterre, Skyline Country Club, and Cobblestone; the Westin La Paloma Resort and its country club housing; many custom homes on one-acre lots; luxury apartment complexes; kid-friendly developments; and mansions. This area is also home to famous artist Ted DeGrazia's studio on North Swan Road. (See the Arts and Culture chapter for details on the studio and its founder.)

Catalina foothills land is scarce, and one-acre lots can command upwards of $1 million plus. A smaller semi-custom home, built in the '70s and probably without a city view, can be purchased for just over $500,000, while the most exclusive homes in the upper regions can go for millions. These desert homes are far removed from the traffic and bustle of the valley below yet close enough for a quick commute. Their appeal is bolstered by the school district. Much of the area lies within District 16, usually reputed to be the best in the metro area. Many families choose to live in the foothills just for the school district, which boasts the highest test scores in the city, and homes within the District 16 boundary (versus foothills homes in the Tucson Unified School District) typically command a higher price.

Sabino Canyon

Nestled into the lower Santa Catalina Mountains but farther east than the Catalina foothills, the Sabino Canyon area is still definitely foothills land and much in demand. And it has another major draw—the Sabino Canyon recreation area. Extending north from River Road and east from Sabino Canyon Road, it is lovely desert land on the northeast side of the metro area, much of it still being developed. Although primarily residential with very few commercial businesses, major services are within easy reach.

Homes right along Sabino Canyon Road start in the low $400,000s, while those farther east and around the world-famous Canyon Ranch Spa can cost in the millions. This is a booming area with choices ranging from homes built in the 1970s to high-end condos and townhomes to golf course homes. The Sabino Canyon area is a great place for families—traffic is fairly light except for the few major roads, many neighborhoods are "neighborhoody" with homes in close proximity, commercial establishments are almost nonexistent, and much of it lies within the realm of the popular District 16 schools. (Homes south of Snyder Road are in the Tucson Unified School District but within the boundary for Fruchthendler Elementary School on Cloud Road, one of that district's finest.)

Ventana Canyon

The posh Loews Ventana Canyon Resort was the forerunner of development in this exclusive and pricey area in the foothills of the Catalina Mountains that falls between the Catalina foothills and Sabino Canyon areas and north of Sunrise Drive. This is incredible desert land with home prices that often match. For folks who can afford it, this is the most desirable spot in the entire metro area.

Driving along Sunrise Drive near Kolb Road, you can look north into the mountains and see houses so far up, they look minuscule but in reality are contemporary mansions hugging the granite mountainside. On a more down-to-earth level, lovely patio homes and single-family homes surround the golf courses of the resort, occupied by families and retirees who appreciate the golf course views and recreation and can afford upward of $300,000. To the east along Sunrise Drive are many developments with attractive family-oriented homes selling from the high $200,000s and up.

Ventana Canyon offers nearly every housing choice, but it's all high-end—condos, townhomes, patio homes, single-family homes, and mansions. Many of the communities are gated, and they tend to be more affordable than the gated communities in the more established Catalina foothills. This is strictly residential land with several commercial businesses and shopping malls along Sunrise Boulevard. It's accessible to all of the east side of Tucson and about a 30- to 40-minute commute to downtown or the university. And it lies within the highly desirable District 16 for schools.

East

This area is growing by leaps and bounds, with large tracts of single-family housing developments and chain store retailers taking over what was, until fairly recently, virgin desert land. Just about anything in the vast area east of Alvernon Way and extending north to the Catalinas, east to the Rincons, and south to the Santa Rita Mountains can be considered the "Eastside." The close-in Eastside has some affordable housing, while the closer the mountains the higher the home sites and the prices.

Nearly all the neighborhoods would be considered family oriented; there are numerous housing developments in the area, particularly along Houghton Road, where new single-family homes start in the low to mid-$200,000s. Other choices include townhomes and patio homes, manufactured homes, and a multitude of apartment complexes. Most of the Eastside is served by TUSD except for the far east, which is served by the Tanque Verde School District.

Some of the more exclusive areas on the Eastside include Old Spanish Trail near Saguaro National Park, the Bear Canyon and Agua Caliente areas in the northeast, and the Reddington Pass area winding into the base of the Rincon Mountains. Here you will still find expanses of virgin desert, along with homes built on large acreages, retirement communities, luxury developments, and even some horse properties.

One of the older Eastside neighborhoods with unique lots is the Forty-Niner Country Club Estates on Tanque Verde Road just east of Tanque Verde Loop Road. Built in the '70s around a private golf course, this neighborhood features a mesquite bosque, lush vegetation due to the fertile floodplain soil, lakes, and grass. There are four subdivisions here, from gated communities and single-family homes right on the edge of the golf course to townhomes. Single-family homes range from the high $400,000s to more than $1 million, while townhomes start in the mid-$200,000s. The neighborhood is in the Tanque Verde School District, ranked one of the best in metro Tucson.

Dorado Country Club

An oasis in the midst of Tucson's close-in eastern commercial sprawl near Speedway Boulevard and Wilmot Road, Dorado is a lovely community surrounded by a wall that keeps it private and quiet yet within biking or walking distance of stores, restaurants, movie theaters, and more. At one time this was a gated community with a private golf course. The two gated entrances are now purely decorative, and the golf course is open to the public. The streets wind around the golf course and are lined with a variety of home types—from roomy patio homes and townhomes to exclusive single-family homes on large lots—often situated with views of the golf course. Many retirees and professionals live here.

Housing prices start in the mid-$200,000s and go to the high $500,000s. The only rentals available are private homes.

Southeast

This region, south on Houghton Road from Old Spanish Trail to just past Interstate 10, is growing rapidly, and housing developments are sprouting up faster than weeds. There are lots of single-family homes, manufactured homes, master-planned communities, and older ranch-style neighborhoods. Most of the new developments are south of Golf Links Road near Rita Ranch, one of Tucson's largest master-planned communities. Practically a city unto itself with its own parks, ball fields, and stores, Rita Ranch with 4,500 homes takes up a huge swath of property on the west side of Houghton. The master-planned community of Civano (www.civano.com) is also here, on the east side of Houghton Road, south of Golf Links. A huge development of energy-efficient, environmentally friendly homes built in various styles, Civano has many activities and numerous amenities. The attractive development is very popular with young families, despite its distance from central Tucson. Homes here range from the mid-$200,000s to the $500,000s. Farther south, 7 miles past I-10, is the unincorporated community of Corona de Tucson, an older, more established subdivision. Overall, prices can range widely here, from the high $100,000s to upwards of $500,000.

This part of town is fairly far from central Tucson, but easy access to I-10 makes it a popular area for commuters going into town. Several major retailers have set up shop on Old Spanish Trail and Broadway, and more are coming as this area continues to grow. Traffic and congestion here have increased exponentially and are a topic of great debate. This area of town is within the Vail School District.

Tucson Mountains and the West

The jagged Tucson Mountains forming Tucson's western edge are literally surrounded by real estate, even though the west side traditionally had been less popular and less populated than Tucson's east and northwest. This may be the result of the mountains themselves posing an obstacle to infrastructure development and travel. Or it may be that it's too close to downtown and some of the "less desirable" areas surrounding it. But change is in the air, and this area is starting to boom, with major developers moving in fast. With Catalina foothills lots scarce and home prices out of reach for many, the Tucson Mountains are becoming popular. All of the Tucson Mountains area is within TUSD until it reaches the Marana School District in the far north.

For a bird's-eye view, let's go first to the western base of the range, where there are several large manufactured home communities as well as both older and newer houses, some in tract housing developments and others on large rural plots. Although close to major attractions like Saguaro National Park West, Tucson Mountain Park, the Arizona-Sonora Desert Museum, and Old Tucson Studios, this area is somewhat of a trek from Tucson and accessible only by two roads—Ajo Highway to Kinney Road on the south end and the narrow, winding Gates Pass Road in the middle of the range.

At the southern and southeastern tip of the mountain range our view takes in the Pascua Yaqui Reservation and the growing area around Ajo Way and Valencia Road, where housing options include modest single-family homes and apartment complexes. Traveling north to Gates Pass Road, there are more exclusive homes on large properties, many with spectacular views of the valley and the mountains. At the far north end of the mountains, around Picture Rocks Road, housing opportunities include manufactured homes, family-oriented developments with attractive tract homes, large contemporary custom homes built into the mountainside, and lots of vacant land.

Our final destination is the eastern side of the mountains, closest to downtown Tucson, and the most built-up side of this mountain range. Housing here includes the area around Silverbell and Anklam Roads and Pima Community College's west campus, where neighborhoods are older and family-oriented and homes are affordable, starting around $100,000. Here we also see the hot housing area called Starr Pass, anchored by a golf course and the Starr Pass Marriott, the largest resort hotel in Tucson. This luxury residential community offers saguaros and city views from golf course villas, luxury apartments, and custom homes on sites from $200,000 to $500,000. Townhomes start in the mid-$200,000s, while luxury homes run to over $2 million. Starr Pass has an eclectic mix of residents, from families to retirees to vacation home owners.

Northwest

Tucson's sprawl north of the Rillito River and across 80 square miles of desert is the vast northwest. The population is growing by leaps and bounds. Very little existed here before 1960, but you'd never know that driving north on Oracle Road or west on Ina Road. The number of housing developments is mind-boggling, not to mention the golf courses, shopping centers, schools, churches, retirement communities, restaurants, banks, and every imaginable kind of commercial enterprise. Much of the area considered northwest is unincorporated Pima County land, while other areas have incorporated into towns like Oro Valley and Marana.

Here you will find Tohono Chul Park, the Sheraton El Conquistador Resort, Foothills Mall, Rancho Vistoso (Tucson's Sun City), Catalina State Park and its Romero Falls, Omni Tucson National Golf Resort, Heritage Highlands Golf Club, Northwest Hospital, Miraval—Life in Balance Resort, Green Fields Country Day School, Continental Ranch, the retirement community of Saddlebrook, and the area called Catalina that runs along U.S. Highway 89 to the Pima County northern boundary.

The northwest used to be an area where affordable homes, priced at less than $100,000, were plentiful. Not so anymore. The market is maturing, and available land is going the way of the dinosaur. Although they're around, finding a single-family home at $100,000 or less takes some digging. The more typical price is in the high $200,000s, and some high-end properties reach the millions, especially in the western foothills of the Catalina Mountains. But the choices are almost infinite—golf course communities, manufactured housing, new apartment complexes, condos, townhomes, retirement communities, custom mountainside homes with fabulous views, and down-to-earth typical family-oriented neighborhoods with attractive tract homes and nearby schools.

The northwest is popular for several reasons. Land is still available for new housing, and home buyers have a broad choice among both older homes in established neighborhoods and brand-new homes. For folks who commute often to Phoenix for business or for air travel, the proximity of I-10 is a great attraction. Likewise, the proximity of the freeway for commuters to downtown Tucson and the university means not having to battle crosstown traffic each day. And the Amphitheater School District, which serves the bulk of the northwest, draws families to this side of town.

Midvale Park

This was Tucson's first completely planned community, carved out of 1,300 acres known as Midvale Farms between the Santa Cruz River on the east, Mission Road on the west, Irvington Road on the north, and the San Xavier Reservation on the south. It was designed in the early 1980s to provide a complete mix of commercial, residential, educational, and recreational offerings—shopping centers, office buildings, schools, parks, and a variety of housing styles. Groves of cottonwood and pecan trees were left untouched by the builders, and landscaped boulevards and bike paths were integral to the design.

Annexed by the city in 1983, Midvale Park is an affordable area with single-family, multifamily, and manufactured housing options. Close to Interstate 19, it's accessible to downtown, the airport, and major employers such as Raytheon and Burr-Brown. Homes can be purchased here in the low $100,000s and up, and kids attend either Tucson Unified School District or the Sunnyside School District. More details are at www.midvalepark.com.

TOWNS AND A CITY

City of South Tucson

This is a small town surrounded by a city, a place where to be a minority is to be in the majority. It's 1 square mile of people with a strong sense of independence, pride, and perseverance. After one thwarted attempt to incorporate to prevent the city of Tucson from annexing it, area residents successfully incorporated in 1939 and now have their own political structure and emergency services. South Tucson's population of 5,500 is about 81 percent Hispanic and 10 percent Native American. Businesses tend to be small and family run. Some of the best Mexican restaurants in Tucson are in South Tucson, particularly along South Fourth Avenue. Two of Tucson's main attractions are located here—Tucson Greyhound Park and La Fiesta de los Vaqueros, or the annual rodeo, in February.

Generally, the people and Spanish-style houses of South Tucson have populated the area for generations. The residents fix up the homes, add to them, or perhaps move to better housing, usually in the same area. Much residential property has been converted into small businesses—bakeries, restaurants, and a variety of shops. Real estate is not in demand here except by existing residents of South Tucson, recent immigrants from Mexico, or small-business owners. Most of the housing is small and Spanish style, typically starting in the low $100,000s and probably in need of repair. A renovated or new house can be had for $200,000 or less. Its schools are part of the Tucson Unified School District.

Oro Valley

Home to the massive communities of Rancho Vistoso (8,000 housing units) and Copper Creek, Oro Valley is experiencing tremendous growth. Six miles north of Tucson's city limits along Oracle Road (Highway 77), the valley is formed by the juncture of the Santa Cruz River and Gold Creek in the Santa Catalina Mountains. Originally incorporated in 1974, the town has grown to more than 34 square miles through annexation, with a population of about 40,000. With additional annexations in the works, the town expects to more than double its size by 2010. Named one of "America's Top-Rated Smaller Cities," Oro Valley has the image of being a small, sleepy bedroom community nestled in the western foothills of the Catalinas, but in reality it's a growing town in a booming area of metro Tucson.

Housing in Oro Valley runs the gamut but tends toward the high end, because much of it is situated in the foothills, which is pricey property with a view. Very nice family-size houses average over $260,000, while homes in exclusive developments go for well over a million dollars. The Amphitheater School District serves this area. Check www.ci.oro-valley.az.us for more details.

Marana

Marana is mushrooming! It is one of the closest things to a suburb in Pima County. U.S. Census Bureau population estimates rank Marana as Arizona's fastest-growing town outside of Maricopa County, growing 31.1 percent in just one year. Home to only 2,100 residents in 1990, the town has grown to just over 20,000. It is packed with developments with housing prices starting in the $180,000s.

Large-scale housing developments in town include the vast master-planned communities of Continental Ranch and Continental Reserve. Very popular with young families, this middle-class community offers kid-friendly neighborhoods with wide streets and parks. Marana is also home to the luxury resort community Dove Mountain, where homes sell for as high as $1 million. Additional large-scale developments are in the planning and review stages. Growth here is so phenomenal that a $57 million interchange at Twin Peaks Road and Linda Vista Boulevard is planned to ease congestion and access to I-10. Construction should be completed in 2008. More information about Marana is at www.marana chamber.com.

Green Valley

Often called one of the most successful retirement communities in the country, Green Valley is about 25 miles south of Tucson off I-19. This isn't a city or town, but you'd never know it. It's an unincorporated area of Pima County that took off in 1970 and continues to grow dramatically. The permanent population of about 26,000 swells up to 40,000 during the months of January through March with the arrival of winter visitors and seasonal homeowners. It has the atmosphere of a small town but provides all the services and commercial establishments anyone would need.

Although primarily a retirement community (the median age here is 72.2) and home to several active adult communities, a number of housing developments have no age restrictions, and kids attend the Continental School District. Housing prices range from the low $70,000s to over half a million. Spanish Colonial and territorial architectures prevail in Green Valley. It's famous for its golf courses (see the Golf chapter) and for its proximity to nearby attractions including the Titan Missile Museum, Madera Canyon, Tubac, and Nogales, Mexico. (Look for more on Green Valley in the Retirement chapter.) Go to www.greenvalleychamber.com for additional information.

Sahuarita

This town (pronounced *saw-wah-ree-ta*) just north of Green Valley in the Santa Cruz Valley was established in 1994. About 15 miles from Tucson, it's also booming. Less of a retirement community than Green Valley, the major development here is the master-planned community of Rancho Sahuarita, which has a lake, recreation facilities, and hiking trails. Townhomes with nice amenities start at $140,000 and climb fast. There are also two retirement communities in town (see the Retirement chapter for details). Although a bit far from Tucson proper, Sahuarita is family friendly and offers lots of recreation facilities and a Wal-Mart Super Center. The town is served by the Sahuarita Unified School District. Go to www.ci.sahuarita.az.us for details.

Vail

Named for the Vail brothers Edward and Walter, who arrived in the late 1870s, this area is on the far southeastern part of town. Although Vail was christened as a town in 1893, it was never incorporated and thus has no official boundaries or legal status. Still small with a population of several thousand, it is growing rapidly, attracting young families and professionals with its relatively low housing prices, sense of community, and excellent school district. Housing here is mostly new single-family developments starting in the $200,000s. It's close to the University of Arizona Science and Technology Park, Raytheon, and Davis-Monthan Air Force Base but fairly distant from retailers and services. It is served by the Vail School District.

REAL ESTATE

Companies

Although Tucson certainly isn't one of the largest cities in the country, you'd never know that by looking up "real estate agents" in the phone book. The number of listings here probably rivals the Big Apple or the Bay Area or L.A. This is a boomtown in the desirable Southwest, and nothing signals a boomtown more than real estate.

All the major national real estate companies are represented here, and most have multiple offices across the metro area. In addition, there are a couple hundred local realty companies ranging in size from small to huge. Given the geographical size of Tucson and the size of its real estate market, it's almost a necessity to rely on a real estate professional, especially if you haven't zeroed in on a neighborhood you want or are unfamiliar with Tucson's many hidden communities.

If you select one of the major companies, you can be assured that at least one of the many agents in one of their many offices will be a specialist in a given neighborhood. The Tucson Association of Realtors at 1622 North Swan Road (520-327-4218; www.tucsonrealtors.org) can be a resource for inquiring about real estate companies.

The many real estate publications available nearly everywhere (grocery stores, shopping centers, libraries) for free will also help you choose a real estate agent. They often identify agents who specialize in, for example, adult and golf communities, the Catalina foothills, or the northwest. Another clue to finding an area specialist is the location of the office; for example, the Century 21 office at 7780 North Oracle Road specializes in properties in Oro Valley and northwest Tucson. There's also a company that deals only in helping buyers find a new home in one of Tucson's 150-plus new subdivisions. You can also find real estate companies that specialize in modular or manufactured homes. And nearly every one of the major companies also has listings of lots if your choice is to build.

A. P. BROWN
601 North Craycroft Road
(520) 795-2500, (800) 280-2700
www.apbrownrealtors.com
This agency provides residential sales, land sales, and relocation assistance to both buyers and sellers. The office is independently owned and takes pride in good personalized service.

CENTURY 21
4842 East Broadway Boulevard
(520) 886-7334

2125 South Craycroft Road
(520) 790-7311

7740 North Oracle Road, Suite 106
(520) 881-8110

4641 East Pima Road
(520) 795-7031

7360 East 22nd Street
(520) 296-7143

8830 East Speedway Boulevard
(520) 296-5491

81-A West Esperanza Boulevard, Green Valley
(520) 648-3100
www.century21.com
Although a national company, each office of Century 21 is independently owned and operated. All of the offices listed are full-service real estate agencies. As part of the nationwide referral network of Century 21, they all deal with relocations to or from other places in the country. The company also has an extensive rental listing, including apartments, condos, and homes.

COLDWELL BANKER RESIDENTIAL REALTY
2890 East Skyline Drive, Suite 250
(520) 577-7433

5460 East Broadway Boulevard, Suite 350
(520) 745-4545

6970 North Oracle Road
(520) 544-4545

8872 East Tanque Verde Road
(520) 749-8925

180 West Continental, Suite 100, Green Valley
(520) 625-1112
www.coldwellbanker.com
With offices strategically located around the metro area and beyond, this national company provides full-service real estate services to buyers and sellers across Tucson. They also represent a number of new home developments and handle relocations nationally for people moving to or from Tucson.

DEL ORO REALTY
2292 West Mage Road
(520) 744-1121, (800) 884-5663
www.delororealty.com
This realty company in the northwest is operated by a couple who are both brokers and owners and specialize in the northwest area of the valley. They deal in residential sales, land sales, and property management, so they also have a list of rentals available in the northwest.

FIRST TUCSON REAL ESTATE
4340 West Ina Road
(520) 572-6220
www.firsttucson.com
This small, highly personalized agency specializes in properties in the Marana and Oro Valley areas. They pay great attention to detail and thoroughly research all market options and pricing.

LONG REALTY COMPANY

Home Office
900 East River Road
(520) 888-8844

Relocation Division
900 East River Road
(520) 888-8844

Broadway/East
7810 East Broadway Boulevard
(520) 790-7320

Casas Adobes
6875 North Oracle, Suite 125
(520) 297-1186

Central
3130 East Broadway Boulevard
(520) 326-1122

Foothills
5683 North Swan Road
(520) 299-2201

Northwest
3580 West Ina Road, Suite 100
(520) 544-4444

Oro Valley
10445 North Oracle, Suite 121, Oro Valley
(520) 825-7227

River/Campbell
1890 East River Road
(520) 577-7400

Southwest
3185 South Kinney Road
(520) 883-2446

Tanque Verde
6410 East Tanque Verde
(520) 886-7500

Green Valley
275 West Continental Road, Suite 101, Green Valley
(520) 625-5000
www.longrealty.com
The largest realty company in the Southwest, Long has been in business since 1926. Agents cover the entire metro Tucson area as well as Green Valley. They also provide comprehensive relocation services nationally and internationally.

NORTHWEST PROPERTIES
7632 North La Cholla Boulevard
(520) 544-9927
As its name suggests, this agency specializes in the northwest. They offer full residential real estate services (including the multiple listing service) as well as short- and long-term rentals and property management.

PRUDENTIAL FOOTHILLS REAL ESTATE
64 North Harrison Road, #160
(520) 577-8333
www.prudentialfoothillstucson.com
This full-service real estate agency was founded by Gary and Robyn Hardy. With 100 full-time associates, they have a centrally located main office and several service centers around town.

REALTY EXECUTIVES OF SOUTHERN ARIZONA
1610 North Kolb Road
(520) 721-3171

1849 North Kolb, Suite 101
(520) 886-8282

6760 North Oracle Road
(520) 297-7300

6872 East Sunrise Drive
(520) 529-5100

1745 East River Road, Suite 245
(520) 615-8400
This national company has offices around Tucson plus another in Green Valley and is one of the area's major realty companies. The corporate office at Sunrise Drive also has an international relocation services division.

RE/MAX
7090 North Oracle Road, #160
(520) 297-4545

1985 East River Road
(520) 202-5400
www.remaxpremiertucson.com
The offices of this national company are independently owned and operated and offer full-service real estate, including residential, commercial, and relocation assistance through the national network.

Rentals

Apartments are as plentiful in Tucson as sunshine. And it's largely because of our abundant sunshine that Tucson attracts so many visitors and newcomers who seek rental housing. There simply is not an area of Tucson—north, south, east, or west, in the hills or in the flatlands—that doesn't have something to rent.

The average monthly rent for apartments in the metro area ranges from $550 to nearly $1,500 depending on size and location. Luxury condos in neighborhoods like the Catalina foothills or Sabino Canyon can easily approach $1,500 for two or three bedrooms. Conversely, nice one- and two-bedroom apartments can be found for $550 but in less desirable neighborhoods and often on a main thoroughfare.

But apartments are not the only option for leasing. Many privately owned condos, town houses, patio homes, and single-family homes are available for rent, often at not much more than a high-end apartment. The four best ways to find these rentals are to drive around neighborhoods and look for signs, check out the Sunday real estate section of the *Arizona Daily Star*, or contact realty companies that also handle or locate rentals. (See the following listing of real estate companies for ones handling rentals.) Also take a look at Tucson.craigslist.org for current listings.

With the mind-boggling array of rental choices, you might need a few good places to start. First, cruise around Tucson and decide on some areas where you'd prefer to live; this will make your selection chore much easier no matter which resource you rely on. Next, read the real estate section of the Sunday *Arizona Daily Star* (the Sunday edition is most comprehensive), where rentals are broken down by type and geographic area. For another resource, look for the various apartment guide booklets, like *For Rent Magazine* and the *Tucson Apartment Showcase*, which can be found (free) at most local supermarkets, major drugstores, and corner quick marts.

Here are a few of the apartment-finder services in the Tucson area to help your search.

ADOBE PROPERTY MANAGERS INC.
2122 North Craycroft Road, Suite 120
(520) 325-6971
www.adobepropertymgrs.com
This agency provides strictly rentals and property management. The choices include apartments, condos, town houses, and single-family homes but not mobile homes. Most rentals require a six-month or annual lease and are unfurnished.

APARTMENT LOCATORS
5460 East Speedway Boulevard, Suite B103
(520) 323-2200, (800) 955-7545
www.apartmentsarizona.com
This service is free to renters and boasts more than 45,000 apartments, condos, townhomes, and houses listed for rent, both furnished and unfurnished and month to month or longer term.

FOOTHILLS PROPERTIES
6262 North Swan Road, Suite 165
(520) 299-2100
www.tucsonfoothills.com

Despite the company's name, they don't focus just on the foothills but cover the entire northern section of the valley. This is a full-service property management firm with nearly 600 properties in their portfolio. They manage unfurnished long-term rentals, as well as furnished vacation rentals. Rental costs for houses and town houses range from $800 to $5,000 a month.

PEACH PROPERTIES HM, INC.
299 South Park Avenue
(520) 798-3331
www.peachprops.com

Specializing in rentals, this small company headquartered in Tucson offers all sizes and styles of rentals, from the funky to the standard. Located in the Lost Barrio, its Web site provides extensive listings, photos, and price ranges.

RELOCATION

Welcome to Tucson! You've made a great choice. With a metro population of just over one million, Tucson was voted "friendliest city" and one of the "top ten U.S. cities to visit" by the readers of *Condé Nast Traveler* magazine. The second-largest city in Arizona and one of the fastest-growing metropolitan areas in the country, Tucson offers low-key living in the beautiful Sonoran Desert surrounded by five mountain ranges.

There's something here for everyone. Love to golf? Tucson is consistently rated one of the best golfing destinations in the western United States. Into bicycling? *Bicycling Magazine* has ranked Tucson one of the top three cities in North America for cycling. Thinking of retiring? Tucson is one of best places to retire, according to CNNMoney.com.

There are few places that offer the sophistication of a small city with nearby wilderness areas that are still home to mountain lions, javelinas, and bears. You can attend a Broadway show or throw on your hiking gear and walk miles into pristine desert or forestland in a matter of minutes. With spectacular weather; hundreds of city, county, state, and national parks; a symphony; a ballet; and a top-rated university, Tucson has it all.

Multicultural with a strong mix of Spanish, Mexican, and Native American heritage, Tucson has a distinct personality.

Moving to any new area has its share of challenges, and Tucson is no exception. Here we aim to make things a little bit easier by offering a mini resource guide for newcomers packed with important phone numbers and local information.

UTILITIES AND BASIC SERVICES

Everyone needs water, gas, electricity, and a phone. Here's who to call:

TUCSON WATER DEPARTMENT

(520) 791-3242
www.ci.tucson.az.us/water
Services most of Tucson and Pima County. Plan to call at least a week ahead of your move-in date to set up services.

SOUTHWEST GAS CORPORATION

(520) 889-1888
www.swgas.com
Founded in 1931, Southwest Gas is the major supplier of natural gas in the area. It serves over 1.8 million households, businesses, and industries in Arizona, Nevada, and portions of California.

TUCSON ELECTRIC POWER COMPANY

(520) 623-7711
www.tucsonelectric.com
Arizona's second-largest investor-owned electric utility, Tucson Electric Power Company (TEP), the principal subsidiary of UniSource Energy (publicly traded on the NYSE under the symbol UNS), serves more than 1.5 million customers in Arizona.

QWEST COMMUNICATIONS

(800) 244-1111
www.qwest.com
Handles phone service installation for Pima County.

CABLE TELEVISION

Is there life without cable? There are two major cable companies in town, Cox Communications

(520-884-0133) and Comcast Digital Cable (520-744-1900), or you can splurge on satellite. (See the Media chapter for more details).

AREA CODE

Just so you know, Tucson and Pima, Pinal, Santa Cruz, and Cochise Counties all use the 520 area code.

DAYLIGHT SAVING TIME

Unlike the rest of the country (except Hawaii), the state of Arizona doesn't observe daylight saving time, so forget about spring forward/fall back. Our time is the same as Pacific daylight time (three hours earlier than the East Coast) during April through October. The rest of the year we are two hours earlier than the East Coast.

VOTER REGISTRATION

There are several organizations in town that assist with voter registration. For starters, contact the Pima County Recorder's Office voter registration line at (520) 740-4330 or check office locations online at www.recorder.pima.gov.

CITY GOVERNMENT

Got a problem or a concern? Contact Mayor Bob Walkup at (520) 791-4201.

DRIVING LAWS

Be safe and follow the rules! The state of Arizona requires that all front-seat passengers and drivers have their seat belts fastened, and children under age 5 must ride in car seats. Bicycle riders 17 years old and younger must wear a helmet, and motorcycle drivers under 18 must wear a helmet.

CAR REGISTRATION

If you live in Arizona more than seven months in one calendar year, you must title and register your car here. You will need to have an emissions test, certificate of title, and proof of insurance. There are five motor vehicle divisions in town. For locations and hours call (520) 629-9808 or visit www.dot.state.az.us/mvd.

EMISSIONS TESTING

There are three inspection locations in town. For the nearest location, current wait times, and best times to test, call the Car Care Hotline at (800) 284-7748, 24 hours a day, or visit the Web site at www.myazcar.com. Note that only cash and checks are accepted, no credit cards.

HEALTH CARE

There are 15 major hospitals and more than 2,000 physicians here. In addition, Tucson is home to numerous clinics, urgent care facilities, alternate health care providers (there are more than 4,000 holistic medicine providers), and specialty practices. Check the Health Care chapter for comprehensive listings.

LIBRARIES

Looking for a good book? There are library branches all over town, and all Pima County residents are eligible for a free library card with proof of ID and residency. Just stop in at any location, or you can sign up online. For a list of library locations and other details go to www.lib.ci.tucson.az.us.

MAIN LIBRARY INFOLINE
(520) 791-4010

Reference librarians will answer your questions and search for information Monday through Saturday.

EDUCATION

The University of Arizona and Pima Community College are the major advanced learning centers here. You'll also find 15 school districts, many private schools, and charter schools along with several specialty (including the Arizona State Schools for the Deaf and Blind) and technical schools. Detailed listings are in the Education and Child Care chapter.

CHILD CARE

The Education and Child Care chapter provides listings of local day-care centers, preschools, and babysitting services, but here are two useful resources to have at hand:

CHILD AND FAMILY RESOURCES
(520) 881-8940
www.childfamilyresources.org
Offers a variety of referral services.

TUCSON OFFICE OF CHILD CARE LICENSURE
(520) 628-6540
www.azdhs.gov/als/childcare
Maintains records for every state-licensed child-care facility.

REAL ESTATE

As the second-largest city in Arizona, the Tucson area and Pima County are rapidly expanding. There are many neighborhoods and towns here, all with distinct personalities and price ranges, and things are growing and changing fast. Here are some housing resources, but for much more detail, read the Neighborhoods, Neighboring Towns, and Real Estate chapter.

LONG REALTY
www.longrealty.com
The largest commercial agency in town (and in southern Arizona), these skilled agents know Tucson and Pima County like the back of their hand. Their Web site also offers helpful information about relocating.

TUCSON METROPOLITAN CHAMBER OF COMMERCE
(520) 792-1212
www.tucsonchamber.org
A great resource for housing and economic data about Tucson and Pima County. Nonmembers can get lots of information from their Web site.

RETIREMENT

Pima County is attracting seniors in droves, especially to the Green Valley area located just south of town. Sunny weather, great facilities, and needed support services make Tucson an ideal retirement destination. Check out the Retirement chapter for details and listings of retirement services and communities of all types, from active senior to assisted living. A terrific central resource is the Pima Council on Aging, (520) 790-7262, www.pcoa.org.

HOUSING

There are a number of ways to find out about housing in Tucson. The *Arizona Daily Star* prints a supplement in the Sunday edition that provides new home information. *Tucson Lifestyle* publishes a free magazine called the *Tucson New Homes Guide*, also available online at www.tucsonnewhomesguide.com. *Tucson Homes Illustrated* (www.homesillus.com) offers comprehensive information about new homes and rentals. The *Tucson Relocation Guide* at www.nxtbook.com/nxtbooks/rg/tucson07/index.php provides community profiles, facts and figures, and useful information for newcomers.

VISITOR INFORMATION

METROPOLITAN TUCSON CONVENTION & VISITORS BUREAU VISITOR CENTER
100 South Church Avenue
(520) 624-1817, (800) 638-8350
www.visittucson.org
The Metropolitan Tucson Convention & Visitors Bureau maintains a terrific visitor center chock-full of valuable information for visitors and residents alike. Their Web site also offers tons of Tucson facts and information.

EDUCATION AND CHILD CARE

Keeping up with Tucson's growth is probably the biggest challenge the education system faces. Nearly all of the school districts serving Pima County are financially strapped and in need of new facilities to serve the growing population. On top of this, Arizona spends less on education than most other states do. As a result, Tucson has a vast number of private and charter schools as alternatives to public education.

Despite underfunding of public education, however, Tucson has some fine public schools and school districts. It also has some of the nation's best private schools and leads the nation in number of charter schools.

For youngsters who are not yet ready for school, Tucson has a vast array of child-care options, from day-care centers operated by religious organizations or private businesses to preschools affiliated with the YMCA or local school districts. We also have nanny and babysitting services as well as excellent resources for finding the child care that's right for you and your child.

Opportunities for higher education in Tucson are almost limitless. Whether you're looking for a degree from a top-notch university, career training, or just some courses to improve yourself, you'll find it here. We have the University of Arizona, ranked as one of the top in several fields of study, including anthropology, astronomy, pharmacy, and creative writing. We have one of the nation's largest multicampus community colleges. And we have a slew of schools that offer training and degrees in nearly every career imaginable.

Here we provide a general overview of the school districts that serve Tucson as well as some of the private schools and charter schools in the area. You'll also find profiles of colleges, universities, and other institutions of higher learning. Finally, we wrap up the chapter with a look at the child-care scene in Tucson.

PUBLIC SCHOOL DISTRICTS

AMPHITHEATER UNIFIED SCHOOL DISTRICT

701 West Wetmore Road
(520) 696-5000
www.amphi.com

Its first school was a five-room adobe building in 1893. Today the district has 22 schools and is growing by leaps and bounds along with the population of the Oro Valley and Catalina areas of the valley. The 109-square-mile district extends as far south as Grant Road, to the north it reaches the Pima County line, on the west is Shannon Road, and east is Campbell Avenue. Over 16,000 students attend 13 elementary, 3 middle and 3 high schools. Two of the elementary schools contain kindergarten through eighth grade.

Also within this district is a privately operated extension program called PAL (520-888-2727) that offers before- and after-school programs for students in the elementary schools. It's conducted at the elementary school sites and costs include a registration plus hourly fees. PAL is also available at selected school sites during holiday breaks and the summer.

Amphi is known as one of the best public school districts in the valley. On standardized test scores that compare it with other districts, Amphi students score among the highest. Their high schools also have outstanding athletic programs.

Some of the schools operate on a traditional calendar year that ends in late May and starts in mid-August, while others are on a modified year with a shorter summer vacation and several intersession breaks.

If your kids don't appreciate the benefits of today's education, take them to Fairbank just south of Benson to see one of the oldest schoolhouses in Arizona. Dating from the 1920s, the schoolhouse is part of a museum and information center. Open from 9:30 a.m. to 4:30 p.m. Friday through Sunday; free admission. For more information and directions, call (520) 439-6400 or check www.blm.gov/az/cultural/san_pedro/fairbank.htm.

CATALINA FOOTHILLS SCHOOL DISTRICT
2101 East River Road
(520) 299-6446
www.cfsd16.org

As the population of the foothills has grown, particularly on the eastern end of the district around Sabino Canyon and Ventana Canyon, the school populations have skyrocketed. This district traditionally has boasted an average class size that's the lowest in the state.

Bounded roughly by the mountains to the north, Camino Seco to the east, Snyder Road and Sunrise Drive to the south, and First Avenue on the west, Catalina Foothills School District (CFSD), also commonly known as District 16, now has one preschool and, four elementary, two middle, and one high school. Bus transportation is provided for most of the district's students.

CFSD's schools emphasize academics and the arts and have strict discipline policies. Students score in the top 10 percent of the nation and are among the highest in the state on standardized tests. The average CFSD student reads and computes one full year above grade level. Spanish-language instruction is provided starting in kindergarten.

The district operates an intergenerational orchestra—the Foothills Phil—open to all interested musicians. Its CARE program, based at each elementary school, is open to enrolled elementary students for before- and after-school enrichment and is especially valuable to families with both parents working. Like most of the valley school districts, school starts in early-August and ends in late May. The district offices on East River Road formerly housed its first school designed by famous local architect Josias Joesler.

FLOWING WELLS UNIFIED SCHOOL DISTRICT
1556 West Prince Road
(520) 696-8800
www.flowingwellsschools.org

Surrounded by the Amphitheater, Tucson, and Marana School Districts, Flowing Wells is geographically much smaller than the others. It covers 13 square miles between Grant and Ina Roads and the Santa Cruz and Rillito Rivers on Tucson's northwest side. It has six elementary schools, one junior high, and one high school, plus one alternative school for kids who can't adjust or perform in a regular school setting.

About 6,000 kids are in the district, and buses transport all kindergarten students plus others who live more than a designated distance from their school (1.0 mile for elementary, 1.5 miles for junior, and 2.0 miles for high school). Students have access to a comprehensive special-education program plus Army Junior ROTC, a center for academically talented students, summer school, and after-school activity programs. Innovative curriculum offerings include vocational agriculture, fine arts, anthropology, and environmental education. All the elementary schools offer an on-site daycare program.

At Flowing Wells High School, the district operates a resource and wellness center to assist teens and their families with health, social, and educational services. They provide pregnancy and teen-parent counseling, referrals to community services and medical care, and emergency food boxes.

The district has a good reputation for academics, and many of its schools have won state and national awards over the years. All schools are on the traditional school-year calendar, beginning in early August and concluding in late May.

MARANA UNIFIED SCHOOL DISTRICT
11279 West Grier Road
(520) 682-3243
www.az.maranausd.org

Geographically, this school district covers a large area of the west and northwest valley—550 square miles—about 16 miles northwest of downtown Tucson. It extends east from Shannon Road and the Tucson Mountains, north to the county line, and south to where the Tucson Mountains end. It encompasses the town of Marana, the rapidly growing northwest residential areas along Interstate 10 and west of downtown, and the largely desert areas west and north of the Tucson Mountains.

Approximately 13,000 students attend 11 elementary, 1 intermediate, 2 middle, 2 high, and 2 alternative schools. The student achievement scores are typically well above county, state, and national norms. The district has innovative programs in math, reading, spelling, and written expression, plus special, gifted, migrant, ELL, and Native American education programs. After-school tutoring is available at all secondary and most elementary schools, and the high schools have strong athletic programs.

Marana also offers a preschool program for handicapped children ages 3 to 5. A year-round LEAP (learn and play) program operates for preschool and kindergarten through sixth graders from 6:00 a.m. to 6:00 p.m. at most of the elementary schools for a fee. The district offices on West Grier Road are west of exit 236 off I-10. The school year runs from early August to late May.

SUNNYSIDE UNIFIED SCHOOL DISTRICT
2238 East Ginter Road
(520) 545-2000
www.sunnysideud.k12.az.us

This growing and dynamic district covers 96.3 square miles in the south part of Tucson, including 2 miles of the Tohono O'odham Indian Reservation. More than 16,000 students attend 14 elementary, 5 middle, and 3 high schools, plus 1 alternative school for grades 9 through 12. It's the third-largest district in the county, with a majority of Hispanic students. And like most districts in the booming Tucson area, its schools are overcrowded.

Despite the strains, it operates many good educational and enrichment programs. They include an all-day kindergarten, ELL, special education, a gifted and talented program, and middle school intramural athletics. One of its elementary schools is not a neighborhood school but instead accepts students who want a more challenging and stringent educational environment (on a first-come basis). The district also has dropout prevention, a teenage parent program, and health services that include immunization clinics in every school during October.

Other unique offerings include family literacy programs. District headquarters on East Ginter Road are north of Valencia Road and west of Tucson Boulevard. The school year runs from early August to late May.

TANQUE VERDE UNIFIED SCHOOL DISTRICT
11150 East Tanque Verde Road
(520) 749-5751
www.tanq.org

This district (District 13) was organized in 1886, when this part of town was considered remote from Tucson. Today over 1,300 kids attend one high school, one junior high, and two elementary schools in the district.

Tanque Verde has the reputation of being one of the best districts in the area. Academically, students score above the norms, and the tax base for school funding enables small class sizes and top-notch instructional resources. Its boundaries encompass the upscale neighborhoods east of Sabino Canyon, the Forty-Niner Country Club, and the Redington Pass and Old Spanish Trail areas.

The curriculum includes all the basics plus Spanish (grades 1–9), fine arts, computers, and chorus. Special education, gifted education, remedial reading, and speech and language therapy are offered as needed. The Community Schools program offers after-school classes, summer programs, and activities. District offices are

Close-up

Ventana Vista

Ventana Vista Elementary School, located in the Catalina foothills, was designed by internationally noted architect and native of the Southwest, Antoine Predock. Designed as a "children's city," the unusual structure is set against the backdrop of the Santa Catalina Mountain Range. In the architect's own words, "Spaces and elements throughout the school were designed to create unique learning environments for children. Educational icons are strategically placed throughout this children's city as landmarks and learning tools." The stunning design features a mystery light monitor, a solar solstice wall, and a natural periscope for viewing the mountains. Wonderful tiled murals and private courtyards found around every corner are complemented by desert landscaping, children's gardens, and play areas. Lucky kids! Ventana Vista is located at 6085 North Kolb Road just north of Kolb and Sunrise Drive.

on the corner of Tanque Verde Road and Tanque Verde Loop Road. Students attend classes from early August to late May.

TUCSON UNIFIED SCHOOL DISTRICT
1010 East 10th Street
(520) 225-6000
www.tusd.k12.az.us

Tucson Unified School District (TUSD) was one of the first public school districts established in Arizona and today is the second largest in the state, encompassing the most populated part of the metropolitan area. It covers 231 square miles; has more than 60,000 students enrolled in 75 elementary, 21 middle, and 11 high schools; and transports about 13,000 children to school every day. It's also one of the largest employers in Pima County.

All of the district's schools operate on a traditional school-year calendar coinciding with the University of Arizona's academic calendar, which also ends by late May and resumes in mid-August. In addition, the district offers all-day kindergarten in its elementary schools. Reflecting the diversity of Tucson itself, the student population includes Anglo, African-American, Hispanic, Native American, and Asian American students. Sensitive to its varied communities, TUSD provides a range of services including academic and cultural programs through its Mexican American/Raza, Native American, African-American, and Pan-Asian studies departments. With over 40 languages spoken among the student population, TUSD offers more than 420 teachers and professionals with bilingual education endorsement and support professionals in 35 elementary, 4 middle, and 3 high schools.

Among the district's most unique and popular features are its 19 magnet schools, which offer special curricula from kindergarten through high school. Examples of these special curricula include math and science, engineering and technology, creative and performing arts, law, international studies, health, and aviation and aerospace.

Another unique option provided to TUSD students is the opportunity to apply to University High School, which specializes in college-prep course work for very high-achieving students. Please note that students must meet admission criteria and pass an entrance exam to be selected to attend.

A comprehensive support system for students with special needs is also available through the district. About 7,600 students ages 3 to 22, or almost 12 percent of the district enrollment, receive special education services, which are available at all schools. Most students receive special education services at their home school; however, there are specialized programs for students with complex needs. About 1,000 gifted students in the district have access to self-contained classes, including bilingual classes, for gifted and talented education, also known as GATE, at several elementary and middle schools. They also have access to itinerant teachers.

Programs continue to be offered after school lets out for the summer break. About 18 percent of the district's students attend the Summer Enrichment and Academic Success programs. Another summer enrichment program is the Summer Academy for English language learners. More details regarding these and other TUSD programs can be viewed at the district's Web site: www.tusd.k12.az.us.

VAIL SCHOOL DISTRICT
13801 East Benson Highway
(520) 879–2000
www.vail.k12.az.us
Situated in the far southeast and extending east from Wilmot Road and south from Irvington Road, the Vail School District covers a sparsely populated area but one that has seen a huge increase in housing. Its eastern boundary is the Rincon Mountains, and to the south it reaches the Santa Rita Mountains. It encompasses the Rita Ranch area as well as Corona de Tucson.

Founded in 1903, the Vail School District was once a ranching community with a one-room schoolhouse. Now over 20,000 people from all walks of life call the community of Vail home. Only 20 minutes southeast of downtown Tucson, the Vail School District is one of the fastest-growing districts in Arizona. The district has five elementary, three middle, and two charter, two comprehensive, and one alternative high school, with more than 9,000 students in grades K through 12. The district projects enrollment to continue to grow exponentially.

PRIVATE SCHOOLS

In addition to the schools among the eight public school districts covered here, Tucson has many private schools, some of which have a religious affiliation, with tuition ranging from around $1,000 to $13,000 a year. So if your neighborhood public school doesn't suit your needs, there's a vast array of private schools to choose from. Some are considered among the top in the nation. Here we provide a brief profile of a variety ranging from those with special programs to serious college prep.

Unless otherwise noted, all the schools listed here operate on the same school calendar (mid-August to late May) as most Tucson schools and offer some type of financial assistance.

CASAS CHRISTIAN SCHOOL
10801 North La Cholla Boulevard
(520) 297-0922
www.casaschristianschool.com
Started in 1970, Casas is a Christian school that incorporates Bible study and prayer into the curriculum. Its academics emphasize problem solving, critical thinking, and research skills. Emphasis is on math, science, language, music, art, and spiritual growth. The school also has Bible and computer technology classes. About 500 students attend grades kindergarten through 8 with a class size of 20 or fewer.

GREEN FIELDS COUNTRY DAY SCHOOL
6000 North Camino de la Tierra
(520) 297-2288
www.greenfields.org
Founded in 1933 as a residential ranch school for boys, Green Fields is one of Arizona's oldest independent day schools for grades 1 through 12. Its 21-acre campus includes an extensive library, modern science labs, a computer lab, tennis, swimming, ball fields, and a center for the performing arts that seats 300. Kids here can learn desktop publishing, pottery, printmaking, drama, and darkroom photography along with algebra, calculus, journalism, Spanish, and French. They can participate in several interscholastic sports or intramural tennis. It's an outstanding college preparatory school with about 240 students and a teacher-to-student ratio of about 1 to 9.

KINO SCHOOL
6625 North First Avenue
(520) 297-7278
www.kinoschool.org
Located on 10 acres just north of the city limits, Kino is a highly eclectic, loosely structured independent coed school for grades kindergarten through 12. Younger students learn language arts, environmental responsibilities, social and motor skills, and self-expression. Older kids learn to think critically and creatively, be self-directed, and take responsibility for their community. Kino considers the world to be a classroom and regularly exposes students to the environment and the arts through local and extended field trips. Students are involved in setting their own goals and evaluating their progress. Enrollment numbers about 80, with a ratio of one teacher to seven students. At present, limited financial aid is available through the school.

i Each year the *Arizona Daily Star* publishes an annual survey of private schools in Tucson. It offers good at-a-glance information, including tuition, so call the newspaper, (520) 573-4400. The newspaper also publishes a similar profile of charter schools.

SALPOINTE CATHOLIC HIGH SCHOOL
1545 East Copper Street
(520) 327-6581
www.salpointe.org
This coed school for grades 9 through 12 has about 1,200 students representing a broad socioeconomic mix, about 22 percent of whom are not Catholic. This excellent college preparatory school requires courses in English, foreign language, math, theology, science, and social studies, as well as volunteerism. Electives include the fine arts, humanities, physical education, and practical arts. Class size is about 27, and 98 percent of Salpointe graduates go directly to college, many on grants and scholarships. More than half the students participate in interscholastic sports, including baseball, basketball, cross-country, football, golf, soccer, tennis, volleyball, and swimming. Parish families get discounts on tuition.

SATORI SCHOOL
3801 North First Avenue
(520) 887-4003
www.satorischool.org
Satori, a Japanese word describing the pursuit of learning, offers a preschool through eighth grade program for gifted children. The second through eighth grade is a charter school that is tuition-free. The self-directed curriculum, which includes math, art, dance and movement, drama, humanities, foreign language, and computers and science, is designed to challenge the intellectual, emotional, behavioral, and social needs of these children. Enrollment is about 230, with an average class size of 10. The school also offers summer camps for children with science exploration, hands-on learning, and field trips.

ST. GREGORY COLLEGE PREPARATORY
3231 North Craycroft Road
(520) 327-6395
www.stgregoryschool.org
This is a nonsectarian coed day school for grades 6 through 12 located along the bank of the Rillito River near the Fort Lowell historic area. The campus includes a theater that seats 375, a gymnasium, a 7,000-volume library with computer labs and a darkroom, and outdoor athletic facilities. Nearly all courses offered at the school are advanced placement or honors. In the sophomore year, students begin a college-planning program and, in their junior and senior years, meet with up to 100 college representatives during the school's annual college day. Students are encouraged to volunteer or take internships in the community. During summer the school has enrichment programs of two to six weeks, some of which include studies abroad. Enrollment is over 300, and class size is about 18. About 25 percent of the students receive financial assistance.

TUCSON HEBREW ACADEMY
3888 East River Road
(520) 529-3888
www.tucsonhebrew.org
Located adjacent to the Jewish Community Center, the day school for grades 1 to 8 is a modern

building facing the Santa Catalina foothills. It includes an auditorium for dining and theater events, a library, outdoor courtyard, and state-of-the-art classrooms with science, computer, and art labs, and students have access to all the facilities at the community center. The general academic curriculum is integrated within a Judaic framework to provide both a secular and religious education. Enrollment averages about 200 with a class size of 14. The community center, a separate facility, operates a preschool during the regular school year that includes early-morning and late-afternoon hours.

TULLER SCHOOL
5870 East Fourteenth Street
(520) 747-1142
www.tullerschool.com

In operation since 1956, this private co-educational school known officially as the Abbie Loveland Tuller School, uses the Tuller Method, a "correlated pattern system devised to give all students the opportunity to achieve their highest potential." Very small classes from kindergarten to eighth grade make this an intimate school experience. The grounds are lovely with fountains and old-growth trees. Uniforms are required, as well as attendance at chapel. Tuition assistance is available.

TURNING POINT SCHOOL
200 East Yavapai Road
(520) 292-9300
www.turningpointschool.com

Turning Point is the only private nonprofit day school specifically for learning disabled children in grades 1 through 8. It accommodates 75 students. The school accepts students who have reading, writing, or spelling difficulties, are average or above in intelligence, and have no behavioral problems. Students receive the full range of academics along with special education in their particular learning disability. The school also offers a morning summer program during the month of June. Turning Point usually has a waiting list.

CHARTER SCHOOLS

In 1994 Arizona's legislature passed one of the nation's most lenient charter laws, and the state leads the nation in the number of charter schools. These are "alternative" schools that are allowed to operate without the rigid educational requirements attached to public schools except regarding health, safety, civil rights, special education, insurance, and student assessment testing. Essentially they are public schools under contract—or charter—from a public agency to a group of parents, teachers, a business, or others who want to create alternatives and choice in education. Charters may be granted by the state or by individual school districts. The charter school then receives a per-student allocation (equivalent to the district's average cost per pupil) for each student enrolled, plus some state monies allocated for capital needs.

The number of charter schools in Pima County continues to grow and includes a wide range of schools from small ones in temporary facilities to established Montessori schools. On the whole, parents who choose this option are pleased with both the quality and professionalism of these institutions, and public schools are finding the need to be competitive with them to retain students.

For more information on charter schools in Tucson, contact the Department of Education at (520) 628-6794, or check the Web site at www.ade.state.az.us/charterschools/info. Here we offer just a sampling.

BASIS TUCSON
3825 East 2nd Street
(520) 326-6359
www.basistucson.org

The recipient of numerous academic awards, this middle and high charter school (grades 5 through 12) has a rigorous liberal arts curriculum and high academic standards. A system of yearly comprehensive exams ensures that all students have accomplished their academic goals. Courses include language, literature, history, art, philosophy, mathematics, and science. Sports and fine arts courses are offered to all students, and middle school students take physical education. After-school sports and band are also available. Enrollment is just over 200 students.

KHALSA MONTESSORI ELEMENTARY SCHOOL
3701 East River Road
(520) 529-3611

This school is geared to parents who want a Montessori education for their kids without the private-school price tag. The Montessori philosophy holds that teachers need to give children the tools, environment, and nurturing in which they can learn and grow.

SONORAN SCIENCE ACADEMY
2255 West Ina Road
(520) 572-0586
www.sonoranacademy.org

Sonoran Science Academy (SSA), a K–12 tuition-free public charter school, is a college preparatory school that emphasizes science, math, and computer science. There numerous extracurricular academic clubs including robotics, anime, chess, and drama. PE, art, and music are part of the rigorous curriculum, and free tutoring is offered to students in all subjects. Class sizes are around 20.

i **Take some time to help others learn how to read by volunteering at the nonprofit Literacy Volunteers of Tucson (520-882-8006; www.lovetoread.org). Here you can help adults improve their reading, writing, and speaking skills through one-on-one and group tutoring**

TUCSON COUNTRY DAY SCHOOL
9239 East Wrightstown Road
(520) 296-0883
www.tcdcharterschool.com

One of the more established charter schools in town, the school serves students from preschool through eighth grade and has an enrollment capacity of 700. The student-teacher ratio is about 1 to 19. Curriculum includes technology, Spanish, art, music, and PE, along with extracurricular athletic teams. Summer prep courses and a summer day camp are also available.

HIGHER EDUCATION

UNIVERSITY OF ARIZONA
University Boulevard and Park Avenue
(520) 621-2211
www.arizona.edu

Although designated by the territorial legislature in 1885 (before Arizona was a state), the school existed only on paper until a saloon owner and two gamblers donated 40 acres. It opened in 1891 in its first building, Old Main, with 32 students in agriculture and mining. Today it's one of the top-20 public research universities in the country, with an enrollment of about 37,000 and covering 378 acres. It offers undergraduate, master's, doctoral, and professional degrees. It boasts University Medical Center, a leading research and teaching hospital.

The university is tops in the country in astronomy, optical sciences, and applied mathematics. It's ranked in the top 10 in anthropology, East Asian studies, ecology and evolutionary biology, higher education, hydrology, linguistics, MIS, nursing, pharmacy, philosophy, planetary science, respiratory science, speech and hearing, radiology, and sociology. It has multiple colleges, ranging from agriculture and architecture to medicine and law, and numerous schools ranging from music and dance to public administration. A number of degrees can be obtained through the university's evening and weekend program.

The school year consists of two semesters—August to December and January to May—with two five-week summer sessions available.

UA also has an Extended University that offers regular university credit courses off campus, noncredit courses, workshops both on and off campus, and high school and university correspondence courses. Call (520) 621-8632 for details. The university's library system, which is also available to the public, contains an amazing seven million items, including three million

The University of Arizona is Tucson's largest and most prestigious educational institution. PHOTO BY M. PAGANELLI VOTTO

books. In addition to the main library, at Fourth Street and Cherry Avenue, there are separate science and engineering, music, and medical libraries, the last located at University Medical Center.

The university's athletic accomplishments rival its academic ones. It has multiple varsity sports teams, many of which have placed in the top 15 nationally. Wildcats hold national titles in men's basketball, baseball, women's softball, women's golf, and synchronized swimming. The school is ranked in the top 10 overall in athletic program ratings.

And if it weren't for the university, Tucson's cultural and educational community would face a serious void. The school houses the Museum of Art, with one of the best collections of Renaissance art in the Southwest. Centennial Hall, a major venue for performances in Tucson, is part of the university, as is the Arizona State Museum. Flandrau Science Center and Planetarium and its mineral museum are available to Tucsonans compliments of the university. UA also houses the Center for Creative Photography.

The university's presence benefits the community far beyond its cultural offerings. The Cooperative Extension, which has offices in every county in Arizona, assists farmers and supports natural resources statewide. UA operates southern Arizona's Public Broadcasting Station (KUAT) as well as one AM and two FM radio stations. For kids, UA's Extended University offers a variety of enrichment programs.

It's highly unlikely that you can visit Tucson, or live here, without somehow being touched by the university. Maybe you'll use the university's library, attend performances at Centennial Hall, or visit a museum. Perhaps you'll get medical care at UMC or one of several university physician clinics around Tucson. Or you might visit the Admissions Office for publications on the university. Maybe you'll take the kids to Spring Fling, a carnival on the mall featuring rides, eats, and other fun. And most likely, you'll be watching the Wildcats compete in football, basketball, and many other sports at McKale Center, Arizona Stadium, Frank Sancet Field, or Hillenbrand Stadium.

Visitors, including Tucson residents, should stop by the campus visitor center, which has an enormous amount of helpful information about UA and its facilities. Located at 811 North Euclid Avenue, on the northwest corner of Euclid and University, the center is open Monday through Friday. Call (520) 621-5130.

The center also offers a walking tour, led by UA alumni docents, by appointment. Tours are also offered on a regular basis by the Admissions Office. Call (520) 621-3641. While you are on campus, remember that pedestrians have the right-of-way and that finding parking can be difficult, especially if there are special or sporting events taking place.

Prospective students interested in attending the university can contact the UA Admissions Department at (520) 621-3237 or visit www.admissions.arizona.edu for specific information about admissions policies and procedures.

PIMA COMMUNITY COLLEGE
4905 East Broadway
(520) 206-4500
www.pima.edu

Opened in 1969, Pima is one of the nation's largest multicampus community colleges. The college has six campuses: Community Campus, Downtown Campus, East Campus, Desert Vista Campus, Northwest Campus, and West Campus. In addition, classes are offered at other sites throughout Pima and Santa Cruz Counties.

The college offers hundreds of program areas leading to associate of arts, associate of business, associate of science, associate of general studies, associate of applied arts, and associate of applied science degrees and basic, advanced, and technical certificates. Pima Community College is a two-year institution that serves residents of Pima and Santa Cruz Counties. Each year the college meets the educational needs of its students through credit and noncredit courses. Pima has six campuses that offer university transfer programs, occupational and developmental education, and special interest courses.

Pima students have access to free academic and career counseling, tutoring, financial aid and veterans assistance, basic skills assessment, disabled-student resources, and other special programs. Libraries are located at multiple campuses and contain a collection of more than a quarter-million multimedia items and books. Financial aid may be available in the form of scholarships, loans, grants, and part-time employment.

Pima's traditional semester courses cover 16 weeks, with semesters beginning in August and January. In addition, the college offers summer sessions, a winter intersession, and short-term classes (eight weeks or less). Students may also choose self-paced, accelerated, day, evening, weekend, online, and televised classes. Pima offers college success courses for those wanting to improve their college experience, free workshops on subjects ranging from taking tests to career planning, and job fairs that are open to the public.

The college plays a significant role in local economic development by providing customized training and on-site classes to business and industry throughout Pima and Santa Cruz Counties. A state-of-the-art computer training center specializes in cost-effective training for employees of local companies and is available for employers to conduct their own training.

Extracurricular activities include a student newspaper and literary magazines; student chorale, jazz band, and other music ensembles; and student drama productions. Pima also offers intramural and junior college intercollegiate athletic programs in sports such as baseball, basketball, cross-country, football, golf, soccer, softball, tennis, track, and volleyball.

Pima's Community Education Office (520-206-6574) offers hundreds of personal development courses at learning centers throughout the area. Pima for Kids, a youth program, offers fun and educational activities and summer camps for children; call (520) 206-6579.

The college's West Campus also houses the Center for the Arts, where exhibits and performances by students, local production companies, and national troupes are presented throughout the year.

Free parking is available at all campuses, and most have cafeterias that are open all day during the week. Sun Tran buses stop at all PCC campuses.

Other Colleges and Technical Schools

Tucson has a number of smaller colleges and specialty schools that offer degrees or career training. The **University of Phoenix**'s Tucson locations at 300 South Craycroft Road and 555 East River Road (520-881-6512 and 520-408-8202, respectively; www .phoenix.edu) are part of the nation's largest private university. This is where working adults can get an undergraduate or graduate degree by going to class evenings and weekends and online. They have degree programs in business, education, technology, management, criminal justice, and nursing plus nondegree graduate courses and teacher certification for school educators and administrators.

Tucson Open University, 838 East Prince Road (520-293-5557; www.emol.org/tou), offers noncredit community education classes. Its focus is on self-improvement, with offerings such as arts and crafts, languages, computers, and wellness.

Prescott College at Tucson, 2233 East Speedway Boulevard (520-319-9868; www .prescott.edu), offers an adult degree program where students of any age can earn a bachelor's or master's degree in a unique individualized program that combines tutorial and traditional independent study. Areas of study include teacher education/certification, management, human services, psychology, counseling, and environmental studies.

Brown Mackie College, 4585 East Speedway Boulevard, Suite 204 (520-327-6866; www .chap-col.edu), offers bachelor's degrees in business administration as well as several associate's degree and certificate programs. Tracks of study include accounting, legal assistant, criminal justice, and computer networking and security. Students have a choice of day or evening classes, and financial aid is available.

Apollo College, 3550 North Oracle Road (520-888-5885; www.apollocollege.com), has diploma programs for medical, veterinary, and dental assistants; massage therapy; and pharmacy technicians in addition to associate's degree programs for several health-related technicians.

For a school that specializes in health fields, contact **Pima Medical Institute,** 3350 East Grant Road (520-326-1600; www.pmi.edu). It offers associate's degrees in a number of health fields, including respiratory therapy and radiography, and career training in numerous medical, dental, and veterinary assistant positions.

Two other schools that offer career training in business and technical fields are **ITT Technical Institute,** 1455 West River Road (520-408-7488; www.itt-tech.edu), and **International Institute of the Americas,** 5441 East 22nd Street, Suite 125 (520-748-9799; www.iia.edu). The former offers associate's, bachelor's, and master's degree programs in fields such as electronics, information systems, and digital game design. The latter offers certificates, diplomas, associate's, and bachelor's degrees in medical, business, corrections, and criminal justice.

Several schools provide career training in office skills such as word processing, computer software, legal secretarial, court reporting, and transcription.

For people pursuing a career in art, the **Art Design Center College** at 2525 North Country Club Road (520-325-0123; www.theartcenter .edu) is a design college offering associate's and bachelor's degrees and training in illustration, animation graphics, and interior design.

And if the food and beverage industry strikes your fancy, you can attend the **Bartending Academy,** 2723 North Campbell Avenue (520-325-6300), for training in bartending during the day or evening. Or perhaps you want to become a personal chef and hone your skills at **Culinary Concepts,** 2930 North Swan Road (520-321-0968; www.culinaryconcepts.net), which is located in Plaza Palomino.

CHILD CARE

Tucson is a boomtown, and, like most comparable metropolitan areas, there is a significant demand for child care because of single-parent families and households with both parents working. Schools, churches, nonprofit organizations, and private businesses all help meet this demand with a variety of day-care and preschool programs. Although there are too many to list here, we can describe some of the options available to parents and resources for tracking down others.

Day-care facilities include **Kids Forever Learning Centers,** with multiple locations and pickup services (520-325-1365); **Kindercare,** which accepts children as young as six weeks (520-296-9087; www.kindercare.com); **La Petite Academy,** with various locations around town (www.lapetite.com); and the **Sandbox,** which offers both full and after-school care from 6:30 a.m. to 6:00 p.m. for kids ages 1 to 8 (520-795-9595; www.thesandbox2.com).

i **Sometimes we just have to take our kids with us! Don't despair—cool kidlets will love Baby Club Congress at the ultrahip Congress Hotel (311 East Congress Street). They welcome kids of all ages for live music, face painting, petting zoo, play area, and snacks while you are sipping a brewski at the bar. Call (520) 622-8848 for details and schedule.**

KIDCO is a recreation program designed for kids in kindergarten through fifth grade. Offered during the school year and the summer, it takes place in schools around Tucson. A comprehensive list of locations is published twice a year in the Tucson Parks and Recreation Department's program guide. Funded by Parks and Rec, this innovative program offers kids a safe, comfortable place to be after school and during the summer with a variety of activities. There is a registration fee for KIDCO. For more information and to register, call the registration line at (520) 791-4877.

i **The Parent Connection (www.theparentconnectionaz.org) is a great spot for parents and kids, from newborns to toddlers. The center provides all sorts of classes and activities, as well as outreach programs at their child-friendly center at 5326 East Pima in Tucson. You'll find organized play groups, music classes, support groups for new parents, and all sorts of resources here. Your first class is free, but after that you will need to join for a nominal fee, and there are charges for some programs. But it's a great way to meet other parents and to introduce your child to new experiences and other kids. For more information, call (520) 321-1500.**

Childcare Resource and Referral, 2800 East Broadway Boulevard (520-325-5778; www.childfamilyresources.org), provides information on child care, sitters, preschools, and how to search for quality care as well as a child-care center. You can also search for child-care centers and providers at www.arizonachildcare.org. And each year, *Inside Tucson Business* publishes a book of the 20 largest child-care providers in the metro area. The *Arizona Daily Star* publishes special sections throughout the year about summer programs, schools, and special kids' activities.

The **Choice Care Agency** (520-322-6966; www.choicecareagency.com) provides experienced nannies for four-hour minimums plus transportation costs. Expect to pay about $9 an hour, more for an infant under 3 months or multiple children. Nannies will come to your house or hotel. Another service is the **A-1 Sitting Service** (520-881-1578; www.a-1sitterservice.com), which provides sitters on short notice and long term. There's a four-hour minimum, hourly rates, and an agency fee, and you can prescreen the candidates.

HEALTH CARE

Back in 1880 when Arizona was still a territory and every small town and settlement had its neighborly doc or two (who no doubt made house calls), St. Mary's Hospital opened in Tucson, the state's first. That same year the Sisters of St. Joseph of Carondelet began their work to provide health care to the settlers of the area, eventually opening another hospital.

Things have changed a great deal since then. Today both of those early hospitals are part of the nationwide Carondelet Health Care System, and Tucson now has about a dozen hospitals plus several HMOs, medical clinics, mental health and substance abuse facilities, hospices, alternative medical services, and health spas.

The world of health care today is fraught with confusion for just about anyone and everyone. And if you're a visitor or newcomer to an area, the thought of facing a medical or dental emergency or just getting relief from a common illness can be daunting. So we've included this chapter in the book to help put you at ease. We can't cure what ails you, but we can help point you in the right direction. We offer here the major players, as well as some phone numbers you'll want to keep handy during your stay in the Old Pueblo. (For information on Tucson's two health spas, Canyon Ranch and Miraval, go to the Accommodations chapter.)

URGENT CARE CLINICS

Although we earnestly hope you won't need health care during your stay in Tucson, if you do, you may want to turn to an urgent care center as a first stop. Sometimes called "docs in a box" or, more commonly, walk-in clinics, these centers typically provide care for anything that's not life threatening (for which you'll want to seek an emergency room, which we cover in the hospital section of the chapter). Usually you need not worry about whether your insurance will cover the treatment as long as you have the cash or a major credit card. Most are open extended hours—from about 8:00 a.m. to 8:00 p.m. or longer. Although no appointment is necessary, you may have a long wait, so it's best to call ahead.

NEXTCARE
6238 East Pima
(520) 290-0022
www.nextcare.com
Open 8:00 a.m. to 8:00 p.m. weekdays; 8:00 a.m. to 4:00 p.m. weekends and holidays.

NORTHWEST MEDICAL CENTER URGENT CARE
2945 West Ina Road
(520) 469-8295
Open 9:00 a.m. to 9:00 p.m., seven days a week.
13101 North Oracle Road
(520) 818-2000
Open 9:00 a.m. to 9:00 p.m., seven days a week.
8333 North Silverbell Road, Marana
(520) 202-7700
www.northwestmedicalcenter.com
Open 10:00 a.m. to 8:00 p.m., seven days a week.

UNIVERSITY MEDICAL CENTER URGENT CARE
1501 North Campbell Avenue
(520) 694-4750
Open 8:00 a.m. to 1:00 a.m., seven days a week.

THE UNIVERSITY PHYSICIANS HEALTHCARE HOSPITAL AT KINO
2800 East Ajo Way
(520) 874-2800
Open 10:00 a.m. to 10:00 p.m., seven days a week.

URGENT CARE ASSOCIATES
1622 North Swan Road (just south of Pima Street)
(520) 795-8888
www.urgentcaretucson.com
Open 9:00 a.m. to 9:00 p.m. weekdays, 9:00 a.m. to 6:00 p.m. weekends.

URGENT CARE SATELLITE CLINIC
9348 East Rita Road
(520) 382-8000
Open noon to 8:00 p.m. Monday through Friday, 10:00 a.m. to 4:00 p.m. Saturday; closed Sunday.

REFERRAL SERVICES

Several agencies help consumers find medical and dental services. Keep in mind that those operated by a hospital are most likely to make referrals to medical practitioners who are affiliated with their facilities. There is no charge for using these referral services.

ARIZONA DENTAL REFERRAL
(800) 866-2732
www.azda.org

BANNER HEALTH REFERRAL AND RESOURCE LINE
(602) 230-2273
www.bannerhealth.com
For physician and specialist referrals in the Phoenix area.

NORTHWEST MEDICAL CENTER
(520) 544-2000

PIMA COUNTY MEDICAL SOCIETY
(520) 795-7985

i **UMC's Child Life Activity Center has a new $15,000 playhouse for pediatric patients and siblings. It was donated to the Steele Children's Research Center by kind-hearted, anonymous donors.**

UNIVERSITY HEALTH CONNECTION
(520) 694-8888

PHYSICIANS

The days of the sole practitioner have all but gone by the wayside as doctors and other medical practitioners have joined together in large practices, most of which are affiliated with one or more hospitals or HMOs. Typically you'll need to belong to a major insurance plan or Medicare to use these facilities, and you're not likely to get a prompt appointment unless you're a prior patient. In lieu of attempting to list some of the thousands of physicians practicing in Tucson, check the Yellow Pages under "Physicians." There you'll find physicians listed by type of practice, such as internal medicine, family practice, obstetrics, cardiology, and tons more specialties. There are separate listings for homeopathic and naturopathic doctors as well. Or check out the physician referral services listed earlier.

HOSPITALS

Tucson has a number of specialty hospitals, such as rehabilitation and psychiatric, as well as acute-care hospitals—those most likely to have an emergency room and a full spectrum of medical and surgical services. (Most of the hospitals listed in this section are acute care.) Many have physician office complexes; some have a hospice, psychiatric unit, substance abuse unit, or nursing home on the campus.

CARONDELET ST. JOSEPH'S HOSPITAL
350 North Wilmot Road
(520) 296-3211
www.carondelet.org
This 300-plus–bed facility on the Eastside offers a full range of comprehensive inpatient and outpatient services, an emergency room, and a regional hospital eye center. Their labor and delivery unit is the largest in Tucson.

Need Help?

Ambulance, Fire, or Police • 911

Alcoholics Anonymous • (520) 624-4183

American Cancer Society • (520) 321-7989

American Diabetes Association of Southern Arizona • (520) 795-3711

American Heart Association • (520) 795-1403

American Parkinson Disease Association • (520) 326-5400

Arizona Kidney Foundation • (520) 882-7604

Arthritis Foundation • (520) 917-7070

Catholic Community Services of Southern Arizona • (520) 623-0344

Community Outreach Program for the Deaf • (520) 792-1906 (voice or TDD)

Crisis Counseling Help On Call • (520) 323-9373

Muscular Dystrophy Association, Greater Tucson • (520) 795-3434

National Multiple Sclerosis Society, Southern Arizona Chapter • (520) 747-7472

Pima County Health Department • (520) 243-7770

Pima County Medical Society • (520) 795-7985

Planned Parenthood of Southern Arizona • (520) 624-1761

Southern Arizona AIDS Foundation • (520) 628-7223

Southern Arizona Association for the Visually Impaired • (520) 795-1331

Southern Arizona Center Against Sexual Assault • (520) 327-1171, information; (520) 327-7273, crisis

Tucson Centers for Women and Children • (520) 795–8001

CARONDELET ST. MARY'S HOSPITAL
1601 West St. Mary's Road
(520) 872-3000
www.carondelet.org

St. Mary's, the state's oldest hospital, is just west of downtown. The 402-bed facility has comprehensive inpatient, outpatient, and home-care medical services. The facility also operates a hospice. St. Mary's is home to Arizona's only dedicated burn unit and Tucson's busiest emergency room.

KINDRED HOSPITAL
355 North Wilmot Road
(520) 584-4500
www.khtucson.com

Kindred Hospital Tucson is a 51-bed facility licensed by the state of Arizona as a specialty hospital providing long-term acute care. The hospital is certified by Medicare and accredited by the Joint Commission on Accreditation of Healthcare Organizations. Kindred Hospital Tucson offers a full range of services to medically complex and catastrophically ill patients. Most of Kindred's patients are referred from local hospitals and require acute care for an extended time. Specialized services include ventilator weaning, wound care, and rehabilitation.

NORTHWEST MEDICAL CENTER
6200 North La Cholla Boulevard
(520) 742-9000
www.northwestmedicalcenter.com
A 300-bed hospital in the valley's northwest, Northwest Medical Center offers emergency room services and features a women's center, cardiopulmonary services, and oncology facilities. It also hosts many wellness and health classes for the local community, particularly for seniors. The medical center operates an urgent care service.

i Stop by the new Peter and Paula Fasseas Cancer Clinic at 3838 North Campbell to see a collection of inspiring paintings by artist and patient Janie Cohen. The collection, called Renewal of Spirit, can be seen on the stairwell between the first and second floors.

NORTHWEST MEDICAL CENTER ORO VALLEY
1551 East Tangerine Road, Oro Valley
(520) 901-3500
www.northwestmedicalcenter.com
Established in 2005, this 96-bed facility offers emergency services, cardiology, orthopedics, general surgery, oncology, and an inpatient rehabilitation unit. Specialized services include high-definition, state-of-the-art radiological and diagnostic equipment and operating suites.

SOUTHERN ARIZONA VA HEALTH CARE SYSTEM
3601 South Sixth Avenue
(520) 792-1450
www.tucson.va.gov
The Southern Arizona VA Health Care System comprises a 283-bed teaching hospital in Tucson. The 83,000-square-foot ambulatory wing houses outpatient clinics, including primary care clinics, a women's health clinic, eye clinic, pharmacy, and diagnostic unit. A new 45,000 square-foot mental health outpatient building, scheduled to open in late 2008, will house most of the mental health-related services. The Medical Center provides medical, surgical, neurological, psychiatric, geriatric, hospice, and rehabilitation services and the Southwestern Blind Rehabilitation Center. SAVAHCS is located on 116 acres of land about 6 miles south of downtown Tucson. The Tucson Vet Center, offering readjustment counseling services, is located about 7 miles from the VA Medical Center. The Southern Arizona VA Health Care System operates Community-Based Outpatient Clinics (CBOCs) in Casa Grande, Sierra Vista, Yuma, Green Valley, and Northwest Tucson. A new CBOC was scheduled to open in southeast Tucson in 2008.

TUCSON HEART HOSPITAL
4888 North Stone Avenue
(520) 696-2328
www.tucsonhearthospital.com
This hospital, now part of the Carondelet Health network, offers a total heart-care environment for cardiac patients, from prevention and wellness through surgery and rehabilitation, all with the latest technology. The emergency department, however, is ready to treat not only acute coronary conditions but also any emergency. A variety of wellness programs are offered, including screenings for cholesterol levels and cardiac risk.

TUCSON MEDICAL CENTER
5301 East Grant Road
(520) 327-5461
www.tmcaz.com
Founded as a tuberculosis sanitarium in 1927, the facility was donated to the city in the 1940s to be run as a community hospital. Today it's a full-service facility spreading over 40 acres. It operates the city's most-visited emergency department. With 609 beds, it's southern Arizona's largest hospital. TMC operates Palo Verde Mental Health Services at 2695 North Craycroft Road, which is a full-service psychiatric facility (inpatient and outpatient) for adults ages 18 to 64. A new $280

million multistory building will replace the current facility in 2010. The hospital serves more than 30,000 inpatients and 122,000 outpatients yearly and has several emphasis areas, including maternal child health, cardiac care, hospice care, neuroscience, oncology, orthopedics, diagnostic services, behavioral health, and senior services. TMC also has the region's only emergency department dedicated specifically to kids and the only hyperbaric chamber in southern Arizona. Future plans include the opening of a 90-bed community hospital at Civano, to be called Rincon Community Hospital, on the east side of town. The consumer health library at TMC's Health Resources Center is available to the public for free, providing current medical and health information.

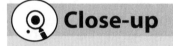

Close-up

The First of Its Kind

On August 4, 1994, the Program for Integrative Medicine debuted as part of the University of Arizona's College of Medicine. The first of its kind in the United States, the center was founded by Andrew Weil, M.D., best-selling author of *8 Weeks to Optimum Health, Spontaneous Healing,* and several other books on natural health. For many years Harvard-trained Dr. Weil has graced the covers of national magazines—from *Time* to *New Age Journal*—as America's best-known proponent of integrative medicine.

The approach melds the best of both conventional and alternative therapies and accepts the body's inherent ability to heal itself. At the clinic patients are examined and interviewed for one hour about their lifestyles, diet, exercise, spiritual and emotional states, and family-health history. The examining rooms have natural wood floors, vases of fresh flowers, and soft lighting from floor lamps so patients will feel comfortable and secure.

At a follow-up appointment, patients receive the collective recommendations of the medical director and other physicians attending the fellowship program. From those recommendations an integrative combination of specific conventional and alternative holistic healing is suggested and overseen by Dr. Weil's staff. Dr. Weil does not see patients.

As a leader in integrative medicine, Weil believes conventional medicine does some things very well, especially in the treatment of trauma and acute bacterial infections. In other words, conventional medicine is good at managing crises, but Weil's books are known for promoting prevention and wellness living that he believes in the long run can prevent many illnesses.

The clinic is intent on training physicians in the whole range of alternative and natural therapies not currently taught in medical schools. There is a huge waiting list for appointments, however. A two-year residential fellowship is the cornerstone of the program to train physicians who can later direct similar programs at other institutions. Because of the training aspect of the center, this is not a high-volume clinic, but the detail with which they look at the patient's mind/body connection makes this one of the most important institutions in the United States health care system.

The program also sponsors an annual Nutrition and Health Conference, open to the public, which brings together physicians, nutritionists, dieticians, scientists, and journalists to discuss and review the relevance of nutrition to our growing health problems today.

The Program for Integrative Medicine is on the sixth floor of University Medical Center, 1501 North Campbell Avenue (520-626-6489; www.integrativemedicine.arizona.edu).

UNIVERSITY MEDICAL CENTER
University of Arizona
1501 North Campbell Avenue
(520) 694-0111
www.azumc.com

A private, nonprofit hospital, UMC is located in the Arizona Health Sciences Center, next to the University of Arizona. The center includes the Colleges of Medicine, Nursing, Pharmacy, and Public Health and the University Physicians medical group. These affiliations allow UMC to offer the latest treatments as well as routine medical care and wellness. University Medical Center was ranked among the nation's best hospitals in 10 areas of specialty care in *U.S. News & World Report*'s annual guide to "America's Best Hospitals" in 2005.

The Peter and Paula Fasseas Cancer Clinic, at 3838 North Campbell Avenue, is the new home for clinical activities of the famous Arizona Cancer Center. UMC is also the only Level 1 trauma center in the city and is one of the most highly rated in the country.

As the primary teaching hospital for the University of Arizona College of Medicine, UMC is affiliated with several research projects, including the Arizona Cancer Center, University of Arizona Sarver Heart Center, Arizona Arthritis Center, Arizona Emergency Medicine Research Center, Respiratory Center, and Arizona Center on Aging.

i The Cortiva Desert Institute of the Healing Arts is a Tucson-based massage school that opened in 1982. In addition to teaching massage therapy and bodywork, the institute offers bargain massages done by students of all levels. A 50- to 55-minute massage by any student is only $25. The student clinic is located at 6390 East Broadway and is open Monday through Saturday. Call (520) 792-1191 to make an appointment.

THE UNIVERSITY PHYSICIANS HEALTHCARE HOSPITAL AT KINO
2800 East Ajo Way
(520) 294-4471, (520) 874-2000
www.uphkino.org

The University Physicians Healthcare Hospital at Kino is the only hospital serving southern Tucson. The 197–bed facility is open 24 hours a day, 365 days a year. Facilities include an emergency room, UPH Urgent Care (open 10:00 a.m. to 10:00 p.m.), and a Children's Multi-Specialty Center, now at 535 North Wilmot Road. Primary care includes doctors in family practice, internal medicine, pediatrics, and adolescent medicine.

Areas of specialty care include audiology; additional doctors in general surgery, neurology and urology; and a stroke clinic. University Physicians, in partnership with the University of Arizona and Pima County, is building Arizona's next academic medical campus. The new campus will be developed on 70 acres of land surrounding the hospital and will include teaching and research facilities for UA Health Science Colleges of Medicine, Nursing, Pharmacy, and Public Health, along with physician offices and specialized medical treatment centers, including a Women's Health and Resource Center.

As part of an ongoing expansion, University Physicians plans to double the number of physicians to approximately 600, subsequently increasing the number of graduate medical residents, staff, and patients they are able to serve over the next 10 years.

ALTERNATIVE THERAPY AND WELLNESS

Tucsonans have a unique health advantage with a large community of alternative and wellness therapists to choose from, including naturopaths, homeopaths, holistic healers, chiropractors, and integrative medicine and Eastern medicine practitioners. In fact, Arizona is considered to be in the vanguard of alternative medicine, both in the open atmosphere and in the number of practitioners. Here are a few. (Also see the chapter Close-up.)

COMPLEMENTARY MEDICINE ASSOCIATION
4649 East Malvern Street
(520) 323-6291
www.compmed.com

This holistic organization will help you find an alternative therapist. It also publishes journals for the layperson and medical profession and offers a variety of workshops on alternative medicine and therapies.

SWAN CLINIC OF NATURAL HEALING
1001 North Swan Road
(520) 323-7133

The Swan Clinic offers personalized, empathic alternative medicine treatments and therapies. The goal of the practice is to identify the problem sources of a condition, not simply remove its symptoms. The clinic offers women's health care, acupuncture, massage and colon therapies, and chiropractic services. They also dispense holistic and herbal remedies.

WHOLISTIC FAMILY MEDICINE
1601 North Tucson Boulevard, Suite 37
(520) 322-8122

The doctors at this clinic provide naturopathic care, nutrition counseling, allergy testing, women's health care, acupuncture, alternative cancer therapy, chelation, and metabolic vitamin therapy.

RETIREMENT

Ahhhhhh, retirement. No more punching the time clock, fighting the rush-hour traffic, dealing with office politics, or waiting endlessly for that two-week vacation to roll around. You're finally free from decades of the workday world. But what to do with all that time? Well, if you're living or wintering in Tucson, your choices are almost infinite. Stroll through the many historic neighborhoods and parks, or hike or bike along the rivers and washes. Play golf or tennis every day of the year if you want. Visit the many museums and art galleries around town. Explore fascinating attractions like Tucson Botanical Gardens, Pima Air and Space Museum, or Colossal Cave. Mingle with the wildlife at Arizona-Sonora Desert Museum or Reid Park Zoo. Go to a nearby senior center and make new friends. Volunteer at a local hospital or school. No wonder ***Money*** magazine ranked Tucson as one of the country's top six places to which to retire!

And if you really want to get into the lifestyle of an active older adult, consider one of the many retirement communities for which Tucson is famous. They offer carefree living (as in "leave the driving and cooking to us"). Take your meals in elegant dining rooms, leave the housecleaning to the maids, forget about any household repairs or yard work, and simply hop on the van for weekly trips to the grocery store. But beyond that, they have activities galore—swimming; walking; playing shuffleboard, billiards, or cards; dancing; learning crafts; putting on the green; working out in the exercise room; taking a group excursion; or just finding a good book in the library—and lots of neighbors to share them with. All of this awaits you in one of Tucson's retirement apartment communities.

Or maybe you like the idea of having lots of activities and people to share them with but still want to own your own home. In that case, the Tucson area is a mecca of retirement communities and subdivisions. The Del Webb Corporation, famous for its Sun City (near Phoenix), created similar communities here, including Sun City Vistoso and Sunflower. And don't forget about Green Valley just south of Tucson. It's a huge community with most subdivisions exclusively for older adults. (And heaven if you're a golfer.)

Still another option is adult communities that feature manufactured or prebuilt homes where you buy the house, lot, and a carport or garage as a package, and pay home owner fees for maintenance of the common areas and facilities. You're still a homeowner, but the cost is usually less than buying in a regular senior subdivision.

There's even another alternative for adults who like the active lifestyle—living or wintering in your mobile home or RV. Tucson has many mobile communities exclusively for adults, complete with lots of activities and amenities to fill up your days and evenings. And if you don't own your own home on wheels, you can usually rent one of theirs.

Whatever retirement lifestyle you choose, rest assured that retirement housing is big business in Tucson. The number of seniors (age 55 and older) in Pima County is increasing rapidly. According to the U.S. Census and city and state forecasts, the population over 65 years of age in Arizona will grow to 23.3 percent by 2030. In this chapter we focus on retirement options for people living independent lifestyles.

But that is by no means all there is. Many seniors can no longer live independently, and Tucson has a number of residential options for them. For example, some of the independent-living

apartments covered in this chapter also offer assisted living, in-home care, or other related services. So you can choose to live in a retirement apartment and still get some daily help. There are many adult-care homes and nursing homes available here as well.

Whatever lifestyle you're in search of—independent or assisted or just some ideas on how to spend your time constructively—be sure to read the Resource Roundup section of the chapter. We present some important resources for older adults—places to contact for everything from Meals on Wheels to exercise classes and from nursing homes to in-home care. Older adults can often be the target of unscrupulous businesses, so it's critical to make informed choices and get advice and referrals from credible and upstanding sources.

RETIREMENT HOUSING

Retirement housing choices in Tucson consist of apartments to rent or homes to buy (or privately owned homes their owners rent out). Apartment communities are in all parts of the metro area. Tucson has well over two dozen adult communities, and the demand for them is high—many of the retirement apartments are usually full, and housing subdivisions for adults sell out rather quickly. So once you've decided which one is right for you, get on a waiting list if the community is full. Also, be aware that in most of the communities, existing residents often have priority when a larger or more desirable unit opens up.

i The Tucson Prunes and Pruners are fun-loving 50+ people who put on shows for reunions or birthdays or just about any group. The Prunes and Pruners are always looking for fresh dancing, singing, and comedic talent. Call (866) 778-6372 or visit www.tucsonprunes.com.

The apartment communities differ in many ways but have many similarities as well. Some are very secure, some are not. All meals may be included in the rent or some meals or none. Rules on owning pets vary. All offer cable TV hookups but may or may not include cable TV in the rent. Rents may include all utilities (except phone) or some or none. Although one-year leases are typical, some communities rent monthly. Be aware also that most of the rent prices quoted here are for one person in an apartment; a second occupant may mean a higher monthly rent. Rents change frequently (up is the way they usually go), so consider the rents given here as merely a guide. With all the variables, be sure to ask very specific questions when considering an adult community, including minimum age for occupancy.

One thing is fairly constant across all the communities: They want residents to have an array of both indoor and outdoor activities and amenities on-site, and they make it very easy to remain active, socialize, and lead a nearly carefree lifestyle.

THE ACADEMY VILLAGE
13701 East Old Spanish Trail
(520) 647-0900, (866) 647-0900
www.theacademyvillage.com

This fast-growing, attractive adult community (55-plus) on the far east side of town attracts active seniors with a focus on lifelong learning and community involvement. There are townhomes and single-family homes, with starting prices in the $300,000-plus range. Like most active adult communities, they offer myriad activities and programs. What makes them unique is the on-site Academy, a nonprofit organization devoted to lifelong learning, thinking, and doing, which offers ongoing educational and cultural programs, seminars, and concerts. A wellness center, pool, and tennis courts keep the body active, too.

ATRIA BELL COURT GARDENS
6653 East Carondelet Drive
(520) 886-3600
www.atriaseniorliving.com

Opened in 1984 and one of three communities in Tucson owned by Atria, this is a luxury resort community conveniently located near several shopping areas and major medical complexes. Accommodations include one- and two-bedroom apartment homes with full kitchens and an emergency call system in every apartment. A full restaurant offers daily continental breakfast and choice of a chef-prepared lunch or dinner. Amenities include a heated pool, spa, exercise rooms, and more. Rents start at just over $2,000 per month.

ATRIA CAMPANA DEL RIO
1550 East River Road
(520) 299-1941
www.atriaseniorliving.com

If villa living is your cup of tea, this community may be one to consider. In addition to studio, one-, and two-bedroom apartments in a three-story building, Campana del Rio has two-bedroom villas with one or two baths. The property has a total of 190 independent apartments, plus another 64 units for assisted-living and memory-impaired residents. Although the community is not gated, security is on duty 24 hours. Fine dining, complete with linens and flowers on the tables, is another hallmark of Campana del Rio, but they're not too formal to refuse diners a doggie bag for the delicious leftovers. And a private dining room can be reserved by residents who want a special gathering of friends or family.

Monthly rent includes breakfast and one main meal daily, weekly maid and linen service, free laundry facilities, scheduled van transportation, a pool, utilities, and access to scads of activities such as aqua therapy, billiards, excursions, and exercise equipment. Each apartment is equipped with emergency call buttons, and all the assisted-living units are wheelchair accessible with sit-in showers. The apartments and grounds are comfortable and clean, and the courtyard offers a tropical setting for walking, relaxing, or swimming in the pool. The minimum age is 55, leases are required, and small pets are OK.

Although Campana del Rio is in a scenic and convenient foothills area, it's also a congested area for traffic—something to keep in mind if you drive a lot. But it's also only about a furlong away from Rillito Downs if you're a horse race aficionado. The property itself is set back off River Road and hugs the north side of the Rillito "River" (for an explanation of the quotation marks here, see the Natural World chapter).

ATRIA VALLEY MANOR
5549 East Lee Street
(520) 886-7937
www.atriaseniorliving.com

Built in the mid-1960s, this complex has undergone several transformations. Although old, the buildings are spacious with wide hallways and large patios off the 64 apartments surrounding a pleasant courtyard. Valley Manor is located on a residential street 1 block south of Pima Street and east of Craycroft Road, a close-in Eastside neighborhood with major services nearby.

For apartments ranging from 400-square-foot efficiencies to 1,380-square-foot two-bedroom, two-bath units, monthly rents start at just over $1,000 and include two full hot meals daily in the dining room, utilities, and scheduled transportation. Maid and laundry services are available. Pets are allowed for an additional cost. Home health care is available also.

i **The Senior Trekkers Club, for folks 50 and over, offers weekly local hikes on Thursday at 8:00 a.m. Hikes are about two hours long, and the group has lots of fun. For more information call (520) 296-7795.**

BROADWAY PROPER
400 South Broadway Place
(520) 296-3238
www.leisurecare.com

"The Reuben sandwich is out of this world" might be a plaudit heard from residents of this 232-unit apartment complex, who generally speak highly of the dining hall's lunch offerings. But Broadway Proper has more going for it than the eats. Housed in a peach Southwestern-style three-story stucco elevator building are 10 floors of studios and one- and two-bedroom apartments surrounding a central courtyard and a beautifully landscaped 0.33-mile walking path. It isn't a gated community, but it is staffed around the clock. All of the typical retirement apartment amenities are here: an elegant dining room, emergency call system in each apartment, lots of activities, weekly housekeeping and linen services, and cable TV hookups. The staff puts out a great little newsletter that profiles all the upcoming activities for the next month or two, both on-site and excursions.

The grounds are pleasantly green and palm-tree covered, and amenities include a library, beauty salon, pool and Jacuzzi (this is Arizona), free laundry facilities, and off-street parking. A luxury air-conditioned and wheelchair-accessible 26-passenger bus takes residents to scheduled activities. And right next door is a YMCA that residents can use for free. Four-footed friends can live here with owners who are age 62 or older.

Rents are monthly and include just about everything described here plus basic utilities, breakfast, and one additional meal daily. Assisted-living services, for additional fees, are available to residents who need them.

This complex is located in a busy area with lots of shopping, churches, and hospitals nearby, but it's set back from the main roads enough to allow for privacy and quiet. The downside is that it's typically all filled up and has a waiting list of about six months. When you go searching for Broadway Proper, ignore the street address—it's not much help. Instead, look for the Hilton Hotel on Broadway Boulevard about 2 blocks east of Kolb Road and pretend you're going into the Hilton. It happens to be located behind the Hilton and shares the Hilton's entrance. Leisure Care, Inc., owns this property along with another one in Tucson and several dozen around the country.

CASCADES OF TUCSON
201 North Jessica Avenue
(520) 886-3171
www.cascadestucson.com

This may be one of the few privately owned, as opposed to corporately owned, retirement communities in the area. An older but well-maintained complex of 240 apartments, the Cascades offers two types of apartments: independent and assisted. One-bedroom apartments of 400-plus square feet with balconies rent for over $2,100 a month on a year's lease. This includes two meals a day in the dining room, biweekly maid service, scheduled transportation, and all on-site activities. Assisted-living apartments are 284-square-foot studios renting at monthly rates. These residents get three meals, daily maid service, and "lots of TLC." The apartments are small but are wheelchair accessible with wide doorways and roomy showers.

The building is four stories with elevators and a central entrance. Apartments have emergency call buttons, and a security guard patrols at night. Amenities include a pool, game and activity rooms, and a beauty salon. The minimum age is 65, and small pets are allowed. This is a convenient location in close-in east Tucson just off Broadway Boulevard between Wilmot Road and Kolb Road. The apartment complex is close to shopping and dining and nearly all other services but off the main road enough for quiet living. Oh, and it's very shaded—somewhat of a phenomenon in Tucson.

COPPER CREST
7700 West Bopp Road
(520) 883-6670
www.coppercrest.com

This is a luxury senior (55-plus) community where you buy both the manufactured home and the lot it's on. It's much like being a home owner in Sun City or Green Valley, except the home itself is prebuilt. Opened in 1989, Copper Crest has 357 sites of various sizes on its 80 acres. Complete packages—home, lot, and carport or garage—start in the $190,000s with a maximum size of one-fifth acre. You'll also pay a monthly home owner fee for maintenance of the common areas and facilities.

Among the facilities you'll find here for recreation and entertainment are a lap pool, spa, shuffleboard, boccie, horseshoes, library, dance floor, exercise room, billiards, crafts center, and a kitchen in the clubhouse for social gatherings.

And because Copper Crest lies at the southwestern edge of the Tucson Mountains, there's plenty to do and see at the Arizona-Sonora Desert Museum, Old Tucson Studios, and Tucson Mountain Park, all of which are nearby.

COUNTRY CLUB OF LA CHOLLA
8700 North La Cholla Boulevard
(520) 797-8700
www.lacholla.us

The name is apt for this resort-style retirement community—it's adjacent to Omni Tucson National Golf Course (in northwest Tucson), and it boasts a 30,000-square-foot clubhouse. And it's exclusively for independent active adults older than 55. Monthly rents vary in price. Lots of amenities and basics accompany the rent, including a few you'll find nowhere else in the Tucson area, but first you need to be lucky enough to be selected from the list of standbys, which is usually full with a waiting list.

For starters, you can choose from about 200-plus bright apartments of 600 to 1,100 square feet, including casitas, but you'll need to sign a year's lease. Access is through a gated entrance that's locked at night, plus 24-hour security is on duty. The basics include breakfast and one meal daily, utilities, housekeeping, scheduled transportation, emergency call systems, and either a patio or balcony with every unit. Country Club of La Cholla has not one but two dining rooms and an English pub, complete with Friday happy hours. Contributing to your independent and active lifestyle are pool and spa, lots of on-site activities and outings, shuffleboard, a greenhouse available to residents, billiards, ballroom, exercise room, library, chapel, and beauty salon. About the only drawback to this place is its lack of wheelchair-accessible apartments.

DESERT POINT-LA RESERVE
10701 North La Reserve Drive, Oro Valley
(520) 498-1111
www.leisurecare.com

This is an upscale senior community nestled in the foothills of the Catalina Mountains. You'll find studio, one-, and two-bedroom apartments that range in size from 417 to 1,437 square feet, all on a month-to-month plan. Dining facilities are elegant, and when the weather is right, you can even dine outside. In the mornings a full breakfast is served, and residents are offered a choice of lunch or dinner. Lots of activities here will keep you busy. They have classes, a library, lap pool, movie theater, spa, Jacuzzi, putting green, and other amenities. A full-time guest services supervisor provides a comprehensive activity program. Desert Point provides independent and assisted living in an integrated environment to those aged 62 and over.

THE FOUNTAINS AT LA CHOLLA
2001 West Rudasill Road
(520) 797-2001
www.thefountains.com

It would be possible to live here and never leave the 16 acres of grounds, so complete are the services and amenities at the Fountains. It also happens to be a beautiful setting—Southwestern-style buildings surrounded by the natural beauty of the desert and enhanced by lots of greenery, trees, flowers, and fountains of course. Living here is not cheap, but if you can afford the best, this is one place to find it. You can choose from over 300 apartments, including one- and two-bedroom apartments and casitas.

The clubhouse is elegant, the corridors are wide, and pets are not merely allowed, they're absolutely encouraged. That's because the Fountains subscribes to the "Eden alternative," which seems to prove that pets are indeed a boon to the elderly, emotionally as well as physically. But even if you don't have a furry friend, there's lots going on at the Fountains. In addition to all the standard amenities, there's a dance floor and stage, on-site banking, wellness clinic, art gallery, spa and pool, library, beauty salon, outdoor gardening, and an on-site home-health agency.

Rents at this award-winning community are monthly for independent-living apartments or casitas. The Fountains also has assisted living, called the Inn, and an Alzheimer's unit called the Gardens, with monthly rates. The apartments are typically full, and wannabes are placed on a waiting list. The Fountains at La Cholla was built in 1987 and is owned by Sunrise Senior Living. It's in the northwest of town, with two hospitals and two nursing homes about a block away.

Several groups in town offer excellent events. Activities often include lectures, classes, and local tours. Three of the best programs can be found at Tohono Chul Park (520-742-6455), the Tucson Botanical Gardens (520-326-9686), and the Arizona Historical Society (520-628-5774). You don't have to be a member, but members get priority.

THE MANOR AT MIDVALE
6250 South Commerce Court
(520) 294-3200

You can read all about Tucson's first master-planned community of Midvale Park, which is where the Manor at Midvale is located, in the Neighborhoods, Neighboring Towns, and Real Estate chapter. Specifically, Commerce Court is a squiggly street off Midvale Road north of Valencia Road on Tucson's southwest side and not far from Interstate 19. One of its most desirable features is its proximity to services—major stores are a walk across the street and nearly everything else is nearby.

Managed by XL Management, the Manor is a retirement complex with Southwestern-style architecture and lovely landscaping. Four two-story elevator apartment buildings and the clubhouse building form a square around a courtyard, all of which are connected with covered walkways and are wheelchair accessible. You need to be 55 or retired to live here but won't need to sign a one-year lease. You can choose from 137 studio, one-, or two-bedroom apartments of 500 to 980 square feet. The rents start at just over $2,000, but you won't even have to cook one meal at home. It includes three dining-room meals daily, weekly housekeeping, laundry facilities, local transportation, all utilities, emergency call buttons, and amenities such as exercise classes, pool, spa, and a homey and friendly atmosphere.

SADDLEBROOKE
63395 East Flower Ridge Drive
(520) 825-3030
www.robson.com

With more than 5,000 residents and still growing, Saddlebrooke is one of the largest retirement communities in the Tucson area. Unlike most of the other retirement properties in this chapter, this is a sprawling master-planned development, and the housing is for sale rather than rent. Although only 14 miles north of Tucson, it's actually situated in Pinal County, not Pima County, and abuts the northeast end of the Santa Catalina Mountains.

Buying a home here means you're likely to have great mountain views from nearly any spot plus an elevation of 3,300 feet, where temperatures are somewhat cooler than the city to the south. Although the setting is spectacular, the location is somewhat remote, but growing rapidly. Except for the few services available in Saddlebrooke, you'll be driving about 16 miles to the nearest hospital and at least half that far for groceries, restaurants, doctors, and other services. Saddlebrooke does have a fire station with paramedics, however.

Robson Communities, the developer, labels it a resort paradise, and that it certainly is. It's been listed as one of the top 100 places to retire by *Where to Retire* magazine. A multimillion-dollar rec center offers billiards, dining, a library, indoor/outdoor lap pool, weight room, tennis courts, spa, and even massage and facial pampering. An 18-hole championship golf course with pro shop is strictly for Saddlebrooke residents and guests. Residents can hit the links every day of the year or can pay as they play.

SANTA CATALINA VILLAS
7500 North Calle Sin Envidia
(520) 742-6242
www.arclp.com

Rancho Sin Vacas is an exclusive gated community in the Catalina foothills on Tucson's north side, which should tell you something about this retirement complex located there. It's exclusive, pricey, and lovely. And there's almost always a waiting list to rent one of its 158 independent-living apartments that range from studios to two-bedroom, two-bath units.

The apartments are located in 15 two-story buildings, each with only 4 to 16 apartments, so it resembles a villa (American Retirement Corporation, the owner, terms it campus style). All have a patio or balcony, emergency call system, full kitchens, oversize bathrooms, and weekly maid and linen services, but utilities and parking are extra. Some units are wheelchair accessible. The monthly rent includes 20 meals a month in the elegant dining room plus daily continental breakfast and amenities including scheduled van transportation, fitness center, free laundry rooms, pool, Jacuzzi, beauty salon, and 24-hour security. The minimum age is 62, and one-year leases are required.

Because Santa Catalina Villas also has a nursing home on-site, couples with one person needing nursing care and the other capable of independent living can still live in the same complex. The nursing center has 70 units that provide Alzheimer's, memory impairment, and skilled nursing care. The community also operates its own in-home and companion services for independent-living residents who may need these services.

To reach Santa Catalina Villas, go north on either Campbell Avenue or Pima Canyon Road from Sunrise Drive, but be sure to call ahead. Rancho Sin Vacas is a gated area, and you'll need an appointment to get by the guard.

SPLENDIDO AT RANCHO VISTOSO
13500 North Rancho Vistoso Boulevard, Oro Valley
(520) 229-8889, (888) 381-8889
www.splendidotucson.com

Splendido has received not one, but two "Best of 50–" housing awards and is beautifully designed. The community offers 245 luxurious villas and terrace homes for independent living in addition to assisted living, skilled nursing, and memory support care. Amenities include three dining areas, a fitness and wellness center and spa, two swimming pools, an 18-hole putting course, cybercafe, billiards room, library, on-site health-care center, and many social activities. In addition to a rental fee, there is a monthly fee that covers a wide range of services.

i **If you're not quite ready for a retirement community but need a little help, check out Catalina In-Home Services (520-327-6351, www.catalina-in-home.com). This private-duty adult home-care company provides services such as personal care, meal preparation, light housekeeping, transportation, companionship, and errand running from 4 to 24 hours a day, seven days a week.**

SUN CITY VISTOSO COMMUNITY
1565 East Rancho Vistoso Boulevard, Oro Valley
(520) 825-3711
www.suncity-vistoso.com

In early 1987 Del Webb opened Sun City Tucson within the larger master-planned community of Rancho Vistoso about 10 miles northwest of Tucson in what is now the town of Oro Valley. Within 10 years the 2,500 homes covering Sun City Tucson's 1,000 acres were sold out, but resales are on the market if you choose to live here.

Del Webb is renowned for the amenities and activities they offer adults 55 and older, and Sun City is no exception. Multimillion-dollar recreation facilities include pools, eight tennis courts, an 18-hole golf course, restaurants, and countless arts, crafts, and sports offerings available to residents who own a home there and pay homeowner association fees. And surrounding Sun City is the larger community of Rancho Vistoso, with shopping centers, medical and professional offices, shops, restaurants, churches, schools, and additional sports and recreation facilities. (Rancho Vistoso's 7,555 acres contain developments by many builders, but only Sun City has an age qualification.)

Although Sun City is a bit remote from Tucson, this area of town is growing rapidly and nearly everything short of a hospital is available in Rancho Vistoso. Mountain views abound, as do wide streets, miles of walking paths, golf course views, and a low crime rate. If you're an active adult who still wants to own (and care for) a house, contact an area real estate agent for homes available in Sun City Tucson. To find it, go north on Oracle Road to Rancho Vistoso Boulevard.

SUNFLOWER
7759 Goldbrook Drive, Marana
(520) 572-9780
www.sunflower.com

The word *sun* in the community's name is a good clue it's another Del Webb venture. The company's adult development in the Tucson area is located in the master-planned community of Continental Ranch in the town of Marana to Tucson's northwest. Groundbreaking took place in late 1997, and there are 1,000 homes on Sunflower's 245 acres. Currently sold out, homes are available for resale only through real estate agents or homeowners.

Like its sister communities, active lifestyle is the byword. A central clubhouse area, with clusters of homes emanating from it like spokes of a wheel, offers a pool, spa, tennis, and tons of activities. The grounds are abundant with walking and bicycling paths, and the wide streets are lined with hundreds of mesquite and paloverde trees along with all the customary desert vegetation. Although Sunflower is quite distant from the city of Tucson, both Continental Ranch and Marana are rapidly growing areas and will no doubt soon have major services to offer. To reach Sunflower, go west on Cortaro Farms Road from Interstate 10 to Silverbell Road, then north to Twin Peaks Road, and watch for the entrance.

Tucson Environs

GREEN VALLEY

Southern Arizona's most famous retirement community lies 25 miles south of Tucson off I-19. Although its population of over 25,000 is not strictly older adults, Green Valley is considered primarily a retirement community and continues to grow by leaps and bounds. There are several active adult communities here, including Robson's Quail Creek (800-732-9949; www.robson.com). Monterey's the Legends (www.montereyhomes.com), La Posada at Park Centre (www.laposadagv.com), and Las Campanas Village (www.retireinaz.com). More and more developments are being built to keep up with the high demand.

Shuttle buses, golf carts, bicycles, and wheelchairs bound about the streets, which feature specially designated "traffic" lanes. At 8 miles long and 2 miles wide, Green Valley isn't a town or city per se (it's unincorporated Pima County), but it sure seems like it. Nearly all the major services are right here—shopping, recreation, restaurants, medical and dental care—more than 400 businesses, in fact. It's also a golfing mecca, with at least seven of southern Arizona's finest courses.

Green Valley has many appealing features for seniors. At an elevation slightly above Tucson's, the summer temperature is usually more tolerable and the rest of the year is lovely, so outdoor activities are often possible year-round. Another plus is the beautiful environment—it's desert tempered with lots of lush landscaping and spectacular mountain views. Swimming pools, tennis courts, walk and bike paths, and recreation centers throughout the community contribute to a fun lifestyle for active adults. And many older adults like this retirement area because it's not "big city" but big-city facilities and services are a mere 30-minute drive away.

You'll find many types of housing, including seasonal, rentals, single-family homes, apartments, condos, and villas (or patio homes), new and resale. Housing prices range from the low $150,000s to over half a million dollars. Many housing subdivisions are located around golf courses. The best way to locate a place in Green Valley is through a local real estate agent or the Green Valley Chamber of Commerce (520-625-7575; www.greenvalleychamber.com). Another source is Long Realty Rental (520-625-6608), one of the larger agencies in the area. Or just drive around and look for signs that signal something's for sale or for rent.

SAHUARITA

Sahuarita, just north of Green Valley, is booming with housing options for active adults and retirees. Communities for the 55-plus set include Del Webb's Las Brisas and Sonora (www.delwebb.com), two communities with multiple home designs ranging from the low $190,000s and up, and virtually sold out. The housing boom has resulted in the upgrading of local roads and an influx of retailers. Very popular, the town has a man-made lake for sailing and swimming, parks, and many other amenities. Find out more about the community at www.ci.sahuarita.az.us.

Mobile Home and RV Communities

Because Tucson is such a popular travel and retirement destination for older adults, many mobile home communities and RV resorts cater to this group. Retirees come here as winter visitors or permanent residents and set up housekeeping for the season or for good in one of Tucson's many mobile home or RV parks for adults. They get the benefits of a great climate without the responsibilities of maintaining a house or land and often can save money compared to renting one of the area's retirement apartments. Most of these mobile and RV parks have all the trappings of a resort and offer residents ample activities and amenities along with the opportunity to make new friends with similar interests and lifestyles.

Mobile home communities differ from RV resorts (or parks) in that the homes and the residents tend to be more permanent, while the RV parks tend to be more seasonal and more like resorts. Many of the mobile home and RV communities profiled here both sell and rent mobiles already set up on a space, or residents can wheel in their own and merely lease the space. Read on for a profile of some of the major mobile communities for adults.

FAR HORIZONS TUCSON VILLAGE

555 North Pantano Road
(520) 296-1234
www.tucsonvillage.com

Far Horizons has been offering RVers age 55 and older a lovely spot to visit or winter for some 20 years. It's an excellent park on Tucson's east side, close to major services and attractions. More than 500 RV spaces are situated amid beautiful desert landscaping, paved streets, and views of the Rincon and Catalina Mountains. Activities include arts and crafts, fashion shows, monthly dances with live entertainment, Saturday-morning jam sessions, hiking, miniature golf, exercise classes, billiards, Ping-Pong, and shuffleboard. For water fun, there's a pool and Jacuzzi. And if you need a break from the fun, you can always do the laundry.

There are daily, weekly, monthly, and annual spaces available at varying rates.

MISSION VIEW MOBILE HOME AND RV RESORT

31 West Los Reales Road
(520) 741-1945
www.missionviewrv.com

This is an adult community that offers both a mobile home park and an RV park—the former is called Club Estates and the latter Mission View RV Resort. (There's even a third section, Mission View Manor, but it's a family mobile home park, so we don't have to confuse you further by covering it here; suffice it to say that the adult sections are off-limits to the youngsters.) The community is located on the part of the Tohono O'odham Reservation that's called the San Xavier Reservation, although it's not operated by the Indian tribe and is directly east of the San Xavier Mission. (Hence the name Mission View, and a lovely view it is.)

The adult mobile home park has nearly 200 spaces that lease for a monthly rate plus utilities, but you're not likely to get a spot here unless you're on a waiting list and someone vacates. The RV park has 150-plus spaces that are 40 feet by 60 feet, big enough to accommodate just about anything; they have gravel, cement patios, and picnic tables. These spaces rent daily, weekly, monthly, and annually, but the months of January through March are usually reserved by the previous September. Both the mobile and RV parks are surrounded by a fence and have a single entrance, but it's not secured. Desert landscaping and paved streets surround the rental spaces.

The two adult communities are for people age 55 or older and share facilities and amenities—most notably an indoor tropical pool and spa and a library with two Internet connections. There are shower and laundry facilities in addition to the customary clubhouse and outdoor activities.

If you'd like to check out Mission View, ignore the address. Instead, take I-19 south from Tucson to exit 92, which is San Xavier Road. Go east about a mile to the RV resort.

QUAIL RIDGE ESTATES
15301 North Oracle Road
(520) 825-9088

The Catalina or Tortolita Mountains are the backdrops for the terraced homesites in this manufactured-home community situated in Tucson's far northwest on gently sloping desert land. It boasts a layout in which 91 percent of the 130 homesites are corner lots and a 1996 national award as "manufactured-home community of the year." All the homes are double-wide and are only available as resales.

To qualify for Quail Ridge, each home must have one person 55 or older and no one younger than 18. The residents are active adults who take advantage of the community's offerings—pool and spa, putting green, shuffleboard, horseshoes, crafts, and lots of social gatherings. Quail Ridge is off Oracle Road north of the Rancho Vistoso area, so it's quite a trek from Tucson. But the area of Catalina is nearby with shops, restaurants, and medical services.

RINCON COUNTRY RV RESORT EAST
8989 East Escalante Road
(520) 401-8989
www.rinconcountry.com

Located on Tucson's southeast side near the eastern end of Davis-Monthan Air Force Base, this is the smaller of the two Rincon Country resorts, so it only has one Jacuzzi. Otherwise, activities and amenities rival its sister resort on the west side. Here you will find 460 spaces that rent for weekly, monthly, and annual rates. Spaces are usually unavailable in the high season without reservations years in advance. Amenities include a pool, basic cable TV, a library, and three laundry rooms. This resort also rents and sells park-model RVs. Don't be frightened off by the proximity to the base—the airstrips are miles away on the base's west end. But you probably will have a view of the aircraft graveyard on Davis-Monthan's eastern end.

RINCON COUNTRY RV RESORT WEST
4555 South Mission Road
(520) 294-5608, (800) 782-7275
www.rinconcountry.com

This is the sister resort to Rincon Country East but is much larger, probably the second-largest RV resort in Tucson. It's on Tucson's southwest side in a still somewhat rural area but within easy reach of major roads and all the west-side attractions, including San Xavier Mission, Tucson Mountain Park, Arizona-Sonora Desert Museum, and Old Tucson Studios. Its 80 acres contain 1,100 spaces that usually are filled in the high season of January through March. Both short-term visitors and year-round residents are welcome, but you must be 55 or older. Pets are allowed, but there are restricted areas where they can be walked. Spaces go for daily, monthly, and yearly rates, with some utilities extra. The resort has a perimeter fence, and gated entry at night is by card or code.

With Rincon Country's amazing array of amenities and activities, boredom should never be a factor. An activities director arranges crafts, classes, and social gatherings to suit just about anyone. Or you can swim in the pool, bask in the indoor or outdoor Jacuzzi, practice on the putting green, throw horseshoes, or play tennis, shuffleboard, or billiards.

Rincon Country rents and sells "park models," which are 400 square feet with one bedroom, or you can wheel in your own RV for as short or long a time as you want. Opened in 1983, it's an attractive RV park with active and community-spirited residents.

SWAN LAKES ESTATES
4550 North Flowing Wells Road
(520) 887-9292

At first glance you may be put off by the neighborhood surrounding this mobile home community—it's older and definitely not upscale. But if you look closer, you'll see a lovely and well-maintained community with a beautiful lake in its center, complete with ducks and fish and maybe even a swan. And residents can fish in it, too. There are 279 spaces, but not many are available. Swan Lakes sells mobile homes but doesn't rent them and leases sites monthly for a single-wide. Utilities are extra. The community is fenced in, and a nightly security guard controls access through the entrance gate. For fun and recreation there's an extensive social and activities calendar plus two heated pools and a Jacuzzi.

VOYAGER RV RESORT
8701 South Kolb Road
(520) 574-5000, (800) 424-9191
www.voyagerrv.com

Voyager has been voted best in the nation and has as much if not more to offer than the poshest resort anywhere. And you need not be older than 55 to live here, just 19 or older. You can bring in your own RV or buy one of their 400-square-foot park models and lease one of the 1,500-plus spaces for the night or annually (plus electricity). As you might guess, however, Voyager is full during the high season and mighty popular the rest of the year as well.

And here are some of the things that make it so popular. Start off with 150 acres of lush landscaping, well-lighted streets and walkways, plenty of parking, and spacious lots with cement patios. Toss in a nine-hole golf course with a lake, putting green, driving range, and pro shop. Add 3 heated swimming pools; 2 heated spas; 2 saunas; 16 shuffleboard courts; lighted tennis courts; volleyball courts; square, round, and ballroom dancing with instructions; billiards; card rooms; a slew of arts and crafts; lots of special-interest clubs; and deep-pit barbecues complete with cookouts. Round it out with a restaurant and general store (in-season), chapel, library, and more. There's not much more anyone could want except possibly mountain views, and Voyager has those as well.

WESTERN WAY RV RESORT
3100 South Kinney Road
(520) 578-1715
www.wwrvresort.com

Kinney Road winds along the western side of the Tucson Mountains, and that's where Western Way is. With the mountains as a backdrop, the adult RV park offers residents and visitors a heated swimming pool, spa, ballroom (and dancing), card and game rooms, library, billiards, and bingo. Directly across the street is Tucson Estates, a huge mobile home community with two private nine-hole golf courses where residents of Western Way can play for a fee. Also within walking distance are several restaurants, beauty salons, stores, and a post office. Nearby are some of Tucson's most popular attractions: Arizona-Sonora Desert Museum, Old Tucson Studios, and San Xavier Mission. And Tucson Mountain Park is great for desert hiking and picnicking.

RVs must be full hookups; no pop-up campers are allowed. Spaces lease daily, weekly, and monthly with water, sewage, and garbage pickup included. Annual spaces are available. Of the park's 300 spaces, however, only about 80 are not occupied by year-round renters. The busy season is fall through spring, and the peak is January through March. The park has a perimeter wall with only one entrance, but it's not secured.

RESOURCE ROUNDUP

Arizona is second only to Florida in the number of seniors who move to the state. So you might surmise, and correctly so, that Tucson has lots of resources and services for older adults. For example, Tucson has over two dozen nursing homes, at least a dozen assisted-living centers, and over 200 adult-care homes licensed by the state's Department of Health Services. Whether you're seeking a place to ballroom dance or swim in a heated pool, or whether you're in need of Meals on Wheels, housing, or in-home health care, this section of the chapter will point you in the right direction.

Senior Resource Network, which is part of a nonprofit agency called Information and Referral Services, may be your best single source for senior information and assistance in town. They can help you find anything—from a place to dance or swim or socialize with other seniors to a place to live if you can't live independently. There's no charge to use the service. This is a private nonprofit agency that knows what's available or will find out for you. Their expertise is especially valuable if you're looking for some type of health care or a place to live that provides daily assistance and don't want to make a wrong choice. They're wise and they're willing, so call them at (520) 795-7480 for assistance or check the Web at www.azinfo.org/snr.html.

The **Pima Council on Aging** (520-790-7262; www.pcoa.org) is a private nonprofit agency that offers a variety of information and help for seniors. Their many services include advocacy on senior issues, legal services, respite care, Medicare insurance counseling, housing referrals, places to socialize, how to get meals delivered, and a free mature workers' placement center for those over 50. Most of their services are free (with donations welcomed) or available on a sliding scale. They have excellent knowledge of the area's senior resources and can usually lend a helping hand. Seniors needing information or assistance can also call the **Northwest Interfaith Council** (520-297-6049; www.icstucson.org).

There are several private agencies that make referrals to adult-care homes, nursing homes, and retirement communities. One of these is **Adult Care Home Placement Services** (520-529-0911; www.adultcaretucson.com), which specializes in matching residents to one of Tucson's many adult-care homes. When choosing this type of referral agency, look for one that's staffed by health professionals (registered nurse or social worker, for example).

For seniors looking for a place to socialize, exercise, play bingo, learn arts and crafts, or maybe even get a noon meal, both the city of Tucson and Pima County operate senior citizens programs (or centers) around town, and they're free. There are many such programs held at park buildings, plus one in Green Valley. Your best source for locating one of these senior programs and finding out what it offers is the **Pima Council on Aging** (520-790-7262; www.pcoa.org).

The nonsectarian **Handmaker Jewish Services for the Aging** (520-881-2323; www.handmaker.com) operates an adult-care home, assisted-living apartments, day programs, a nursing home, and home health services. **Home Instead** (520-770-9943; www.seniorcare-tucson.com) is one of a number of Tucson agencies providing a variety of in-home services for people who still live independently but need assistance with daily or weekly activities of a nonmedical nature. The nonprofit **Caregiver Consortium** (520-795-0300; ext. 210; www.arizonacaregivers.org) offers a wealth of information for older adults as well as caregivers. The agency's Web site is a terrific resource, providing comprehensive information on area services and events.

MEDIA

Tucson has an astonishing number of free or inexpensive publications covering all manner of topics, from poetry to music to parenting to bicycling, not to mention a slew of papers devoted to tourism and entertainment. This is good news, because wherever you are you'll find something to help you enjoy Tucson. Tucson also has two dailies, a morning and afternoon version, that are distinctly different in scope and political leanings. And if you prefer listening over reading, there's a radio station geared to every taste.

This chapter covers the major papers, magazines, and radio and television stations available in Tucson. The list is fairly complete, but remember that things change: Publications come and go, radio stations switch formats, and cable companies get new names.

NEWSPAPERS

Dailies

THE ARIZONA DAILY STAR
4850 South Park Avenue
(520) 573-4400
www.azstarnet.com

Considered the state's first daily newspaper, the roots of the *Star* date back to 1877 when the *Daily Bulletin* began publishing with a firm Democratic slant. After going through a triweekly stage, the paper became known as the *Arizona Daily Star* in 1879. It is now a product of Lee Enterprise.

The city's morning newspaper is published seven days a week, with a Thursday "Caliente" section that serves as a weekly arts and entertainment guide. The Sunday edition includes "Home," "Travel," book review, and editorial comment sections. Watch for regular supplements geared toward everything from wedding planning to senior health. It also operates *AzStarnet,* the Web version of the paper and home to many other local sites. The paper is 50 cents on the street, but the *Star* offers a variety of subscription packages for weekly, monthly, and annual issues and daily and weekend editions. Daily circulation is more than 140,000, higher on Sunday.

ARIZONA DAILY WILDCAT
University of Arizona
(520) 621-3551
www.wildcat.arizona.edu

First published in 1899, this daily (Monday through Friday) college paper has a following off campus as well. It can be found around the university area. The *Wildcat* is free and contains well-written articles and editorials on local, state, and national politics as well as campus news. It's also a great source for information and schedules regarding games, seminars, and concerts at the university.

THE DAILY TERRITORIAL
3280 East Hemisphere Loop, Suite 180
(520) 294-1200
www.azbiz.com

This is Pima County's legal newspaper of record and contains some business and legal news. But primarily it's a list of legal notices filed within the county. The paper was started in 1966 and currently has a circulation of 1,000. A year's subscription is $115, or you can purchase a single issue at newsstands or newspaper boxes for $1.

TUCSON CITIZEN
4850 South Park Avenue
(520) 573-4400
www.tucsoncitizen.com

Established in 1870 by Republican Richard McCormick, the original *Arizona Citizen* was published as a weekly and went through several name changes. The final name change came in 1977 when the owners dubbed it the *Tucson Citizen*. Now the city's afternoon paper publishes six times a week under the ownership of the Gannett Company. Although both the *Arizona Daily Star* and *Tucson Citizen*, Tucson's morning and afternoon dailies, share the same building and marketing arm (Tucson Newspapers, Inc.), they are actually owned by two different publishing companies.

There is no *Tucson Citizen* on Sunday, but the Saturday edition acts as a weekend paper and is available Saturday morning with comics and other trappings of a "Sunday paper." On Thursday it publishes the "Calendar," a weekly guide to entertainment, the arts, and activities. Issues are 35 cents on the street. Weekly subscriptions include the Sunday edition of the *Daily Star*. Daily circulation is about 27,000.

Other Papers—Weekly, Semiweekly, Semimonthly, Monthly

ARIZONA GOURMET LIVING
1877 North Kolb Road
(520) 721-1300
Published locally four times a year and available by subscription and at select restaurants and gourmet stores, this magazine focuses on the local dining scene, offering in-depth profiles of local chefs, restaurants, and recipes.

ARIZONA JEWISH POST
5546 East Fourth Street
(520) 319-1112
www.jewishtucson.org
Published since 1946, this biweekly Jewish-interest paper keeps the community up to date on events, news, and people. The *Post* is only distributed through patron contribution in lieu of subscription, but newcomers can receive three months for free on request.

ARIZONA TOURIST NEWS
105 Grant Road
(520) 622-7008, (800) 462-8705
www.aztourist.com
Published monthly and distributed free in hotels, stores, and libraries among many other places, this newspaper is packed with information: guides to dining, shopping, hotels, historical sites, art galleries, and nightclubs, plus a map.

AZTEC PRESS
Pima Community College
2202 West Anklam Road
(520) 206-6800
http://aztecpress.pima.edu
Aztec Press is the student-run weekly paper printed eight times a year at the city's community college. It's free and covers news pertinent to the campus.

BEAR ESSENTIAL NEWS FOR KIDS
1037 South Alvernon Way, Suite 150
(520) 792-9930
www.bearessentialnews.com
This lively free monthly is a great kids' publication, especially if your child likes to work puzzles, play games, enter contests, or actually write articles. Parents will find a lot of useful information about day care, events, and even places to eat with the little guys. There is also a "Kid Times" section that is written mostly by middle-school students and by members of a local Young Reporters Program. This paper can be found all over town at eating establishments, bookstores, and the Children's Museum.

DESERTLEAF
3968 East Fort Lowell Road
(520) 881-5188
www.desertleaf.com
DesertLeaf is more magazine than award-winning tabloid-size paper, running only feature stories. Targeting the Catalina foothills and northwest communities, the monthly paper is delivered free to more than 50,000 households in that area as well as distributed free at select bookstores, libraries, restaurants, and coffee shops. The regular features include travel, arts, nature, history,

people, restaurant listings, gallery listings, and desert gardening. People outside the distribution area can subscribe for a yearly fee via bulk mail.

DOWNTOWN TUCSONAN
110 South Church Avenue, Suite 6140
(520) 547-3338
www.downtowntucson.org
Published by the Tucson Downtown Partnership, a nonprofit corporation charged with improving business conditions downtown, this free newspaper comes out the first of every month. It covers the arts, entertainment, business news, and events happening in the rapidly developing downtown area.

EL IMPARCIAL
1661 North Swan Road, Suite 208
(520) 792-2114
www.elimparcial.com
This daily Spanish-language newspaper, published in Mexico, covers Tucson, Nogales, and Douglas. Only $1 a copy, it can be found at supermarkets, newsstands, and local merchants, primarily on the south side of town.

EL INDEPENDIENTE
P.O. Box 210158B, Tucson, AZ 85721-0158
(520) 621-7556
www.journalism.arizona.edu/publications/independiente
This free English/Spanish newspaper covering the city of South Tucson is published monthly by the University of Arizona Journalism Department students. Political, community, and sports articles of interest to South Tucson are included, as well as a helpful list of community resources. You'll find it in South Tucson government offices and retail outlets and online.

GOOD NEWS
3755 East 34th Street, Suite 107
(520) 792-6650
www.goodnewstucson.com
Published by Media Solutions Group, this weekly tabloid paper focuses on local issues related to family spirituality and wholesome entertainment. Copies are available at all major grocery stores, libraries, places of worship, and retail locations around the city.

INSIDE TUCSON BUSINESS
3280 East Hemisphere Loop, Suite 180
(520) 294-1200
www.azbiz.com
Inside is the weekly business publication of professionals in Tucson. The paper is the only one devoted entirely to business news. It costs $1 from street boxes, convenience stores, or at newsstands. A one-year subscription is $50.

THE NORTHWEST EXPLORER
7235 North Paseo del Norte
(520) 797-4384
www.explorernews.com
This weekly community newspaper targets the residents of the fast-growing northwest corridor, providing a local focus of news, politics, reviews, and meeting updates as well as a variety of columnists, both local and national. The paper is primarily delivered by subscription, but you can buy individual copies at libraries, restaurants, and City Hall.

SUN TENNIS
1540 East Maryland Avenue, Suite 102, Phoenix
(602) 242-5045
www.sunmagazines.com
Although published in Phoenix and covering the Southwest, this is a great free bimonthly for tennis buffs who want to read articles about the sport or find out what's going on where. There's a listing of Tucson tennis clubs, Arizona tennis organizations, a calendar of Southwest events, and even summer camps for kids. Find it at tennis venues and sports stores.

TAIL WINDS
2609 East Broadway
(520) 745–2033
www.perimiterbicycles.com/TailWinds/TailWinds.html
Published six times a year by the Perimeter Bicy-

cling Association of America, this upbeat newspaper covers everything related to biking in Arizona and neighboring states, including races and equipment. You can find it free at most bicycle shops.

TUCSON WEEKLY
3280 East Hemisphere Loop, Suite 180
(520) 294-1200
www.tucsonweekly.com
Tucson's free alternative weekly paper is published on Thursday, distributed through street boxes and various retail stores, and contains articles on local politics as well as music reviews, club listings, and restaurant guides and reviews. The *Weekly* also publishes an annual reader's poll of the Best of Tucson each September. A one-year subscription is available for $110.

MAGAZINES

FITNESS PLUS
4474 East Fifth Street
(520) 881-6696
www.fitplusmag.com
As the title suggests, this free monthly magazine covers all aspects of keeping fit, including nutrition and health. Packed with ads from fitness clubs, the publication is very advertiser-driven but contains a full range of articles covering the fitness lifestyle in Tucson. It's available at hundreds of retail locations and through a paid annual subscription.

SOUTHERN ARIZONA TEE TIMES
PMB 327
7320 North La Cholla Boulevard, #154
(520) 575-0025
Arizona's only bimonthly golf publication, this magazine highlights golf throughout southern Arizona, including golf vacations and resorts. An annual subscription is available, or you can pick up a complimentary copy at area golf shops and resorts.

TUCSON GUIDE QUARTERLY
1650 East Fort Lowell Road, Suite 100
(520) 322-0895
www.maddenpreprint.com
From the largest magazine-publishing house in Arizona, Madden Preprint, *TGQ* is a classy, full-color quarterly guide to the city that has excellent feature articles, such as a regular "101 Things to Do" column and a "Festivals and Fiestas" calendar. The publication is $3.95 at newsstands and anywhere magazines are sold. A one-year subscription is $13.95.

TUCSON HOME MAGAZINE
1650 East Fort Lowell Road, Suite 100
(520) 322-0895
www.tucsonhomemagazine.com
This quarterly magazine, published by Madden Preprint Media, focuses on home and interior design and offers tips and articles about gardening and home decorating trends. A handy resource directory offers contact information for local businesses ranging from caterers to accessories. Annual subscriptions are available; the publication is also distributed free to select zip codes.

TUCSON LIFESTYLE MAGAZINE
7000 East Tanque Verde Road
(520) 721-2929
www.tucsonlifestyle.com
Owned by Conley Magazines, this monthly "City Book" covers Tucson's lifestyle, real estate, fashion, and society-related topics. A regular feature is the city guide "Where to Shop—Where to Dine—What to See." The annual "Newcomers" edition is very handy for residents and transplants alike. Annual subscriptions are available and also include six issues of the companion publication *Tucson Lifestyles Home & Garden.*

TUCSON'S FILM INDUSTRY

The film industry has had a solid foothold in Tucson with Old Tucson Studios, dubbed "Hollywood in the Desert." Since it was built in 1939 as a re-creation of 1860s Tucson for the movie *Arizona,* the 160-acre site has been the location of more than 200 movies, TV shows, and commercials (see the Attractions chapter). The facility is the most popular Old West location in the United States. But southern Arizona in general is popular as well, with film crews shooting movies, TV shows, and several acclaimed features and documentaries.

Exemptions, tax incentives, tax credits, and rebates offered by the state, including the Motion Picture Production Tax Incentives Program, should bring additional film productions into town. This statewide program requires that at least 25 percent of full-time employees on a film be Arizona residents—a boon to actors in the area.

The **Tucson Film Office** (520-770-2151) coordinates filming activities and offers professional support services for filmmakers. Recent productions set in the Tucson area include *Redemption* and the independent films *Coyote* and *Red 71*.

Tucson also has an active independent film community with its own **International Film Festival** (see the Festivals and Events chapter); art films shown regularly at the Loft, 3233 East Speedway Boulevard (see the Nightlife chapter); and several popular film series at the University of Arizona.

For those making videos, the not-for-profit Tucson Community Cable Corporation (Access Tucson) has one of the best production facilities in the country due to generous funding from the local commercial cable operators, and the company is always looking for volunteer producers!

i Wanna be an actor? Head straight to www.azcommerce.com/Film/Hotweb.htm, the Arizona Film Offices' up-to-the minute listing of productions casting in Arizona for actors and crew.

TELEVISION

Present-day KOLD, Tucson's first TV station, went on the air February 1, 1953, as KOPO. The station was owned by Gene Autry, and the population of the city was 48,774. It took a while for the unrefined electronic stranger to catch on in Tucson. At the time TVs were selling for between $199 and $599, not much different from today until you consider a solid middle-class income was $5,000.

Today Tucson not only has a full complement of network affiliates and independent stations, but also several cable operators that provide the means to view the local stations as well as numerous national ones. Here are the television stations operated in Tucson:

KGUN Channel 9 (ABC)
KHRR Channel 40 (Telemundo)
KMSB Channel 11 (Fox)
KOLD Channel 13 (CBS)
KQBN Channel 14 (Telenoticias)
KTAZ Channel 40 (Telefutura)
KTTU Channel 18 (UPN)
KUAT Channel 6 (PBS)
KVOA Channel 4 (NBC)
KWBA Channel 58 (WBN)

In addition to all the typical television offerings, Tucson boasts one of the best public-access production facilities in the country. City, county, and FCC agreements mandate that the commercial operators in the city provide funds for a nonprofit, public-access operation. **Tucson Community Cable Corporation (Access Tucson),** at 124 East Broadway Boulevard (520-624-9833; www.access.tucson.org), is a training ground for up-and-coming TV and video producers, offering classes, digital editing booths, sound stages, and even equipment loans to members. Tucsonans who want to see the fruits of this local labor can do so on Cox Communications cable TV's public-access channels 97, 98, and 99, and on channels 72, 73, and 74 for Comcast subscribers.

Cable Companies

The cable TV companies serving Pima County have their own distinct geographical areas, so depending on where you stay in town—or where you choose to live—you'll be somewhat limited as to which company will serve you.

COMCAST DIGITAL CABLE
8251 North Cortaro Road, Marana
(520) 744-1900
www.comcast.com
Servicing Pima County residents, including Marana and Oro Valley, Comcast offers cable, digital cable, and high-speed Internet access.

COX COMMUNICATIONS
1440 East 15th Street
(520) 884-0133
www.cox.com
The nation's fourth-largest cable provider, Cox services residents of Tucson, South Tucson, Davis-Monthan, Patagonia, Green Valley, and parts of Sahuarita. Cox offers broadband, digital cable, cable and Internet services, and PPV along with several local specialty channels, including the city of Tucson channel and several public-access channels produced at Tucson Community Cable Corporation.

RADIO

Tucson is unusual in that, for a city this size, there isn't much format-war-type competition among radio stations. That's because for each major format—rock, Top 40, country hits, etc.—there is usually only one station, or at most two or three.

For those desiring an alternative to the commercial, KAMP-AM, a student-run station at the University of Arizona, offers eclectic fare, as does the community station KXCI-FM. The University of Arizona also runs a professional public radio jazz station and a classical station, both of which also broadcast National Public Radio programs.

Here is a complete list of the stations on the dial in Tucson.

Adult Contemporary

KCEE 1030 AM (pop classics)
KHYT 107.5 FM (classic hits)
KGMG 104.9 FM (Motown, funk)
KMXZ 94.9 FM
KSZR 97.5 FM
KWMT 92.9 FM
KZPT 104.1 FM

Christian

KFLT 830 AM
KGMS 940 AM

Classical

KUAT 90.5 FM

College Radio

KAMP 1570 AM

Community Radio

KXCI 91.3 FM

Country

KIIM 99.5 FM

Hip-Hop/R&B

KOHT 98.3 FM

Jazz

KUAZ 89.1 FM and 1550 AM (plus NPR)

Latin

KQTL 1210 AM
KTKT 990 AM
KTZR 97.1 FM
KXEW 1660 AM
KZLZ 105.3 FM

News/Talk

KCUB 1290 AM
KFFN 1490 AM (sports talk)
KJLL 1330 AM
KNST 790 AM (plus sports and UA games)
KTKT 990 AM (Arizona Cardinals)
KVOI 690 AM (talk, news)

Oldies

KGMG 106.3 FM (mega oldies)
KGVY 1080 AM (Big Band)
KSAZ 580 AM
KTUC 1400 AM ('50s and '60s hits)
KWFM 1450 AM

Rock

KFMA 92.1 FM (alternative)
KLPX 96.1 FM (classic)

Top 40

KRQQ 93.7 FM

WORSHIP

Tucson is home to an amazing variety of religious groups and denominations. A drive through just about any neighborhood reveals a mix of faiths. You'll find large churches that fill whole blocks located just blocks from tiny storefront fellowships. You'll see the tall spires of a Western church in the same glance as a golden-domed mosque. You may even find our one and only drive-in church (more about that later). A convent, wishing shrine, and Benedictine monastery round out Tucson's eclectic houses of worship, many designed to showcase the desert vista, incredible sunsets, and works of God and nature that make Tucson a special place to live and visit.

A BRIEF HISTORY

Tucson is one of the few cities in the United States that proudly displays a religious structure, San Xavier del Bac, on its city seal. The "White Dove of the Desert," as the church is called, is as much a symbol of Tucson as the saguaro cactus (which is also on the seal). A visit to the mission church (see the Attractions chapter) is a must—especially now that the interior has been restored to its original beauty. It's not surprising that a religious symbol would've found its way to the city's seal; Tucson has long been considered a spiritual place.

As early as 800 B.C., Native American tribes developed settlements near the base of what is now known as "A" Mountain. The natural beauty of the desert was much revered by the various tribes and as such was an integral part of their religious ceremonies. Father Eusebio Francisco Kino, the founder of so many missions in the Southwest, always considered the mission at the village of Bac (near what is now Tucson) his favorite.

Tucson eventually became the Diocese of Tucson, which served as the center for the Catholic Church in the Arizona Territory. Tucson was also the site of the only synagogue in the Arizona Territory, **Stone Avenue Temple,** built in 1910. The temple, now a historic site and museum (The Jewish Heritage Center), located at 564 South Stone Avenue, is open for tours and events. Call (520) 670-9073, or go to www.jewishheritage-center.net.

During the wars with Mexico, the Mormon Battalion—a large group of Mormons who helped with the war effort—marched through town. And although they did not stay long enough to establish a congregation, today more than 20,000 Mormons call Tucson home. (You can see a memorial to the Mormon Battalion in El Presidio Park behind the county courthouse downtown.)

As the town grew, other religious groups arrived and established congregations. Methodists, Episcopalians, and those of other faiths found their place in the Old Pueblo. By the turn of the twentieth century, Tucson had become home to some 13,000 people, with all Western religions being well represented.

The University of Arizona has added to the mix. With faculty and students from around the world, Eastern religions have also found a place in Tucson. Today you'll find Muslims, Baha'is, Buddhists, Sufis, and members of any number of other Eastern faiths in town.

A wide range of religious services is offered citywide. Services can be found in Spanish, Mandarin Chinese, various Native American languages, and of course English. At **St. Augustine Cathedral** (520-623-6351; www.diocesetucson.org), built in 1896, you can even attend a mariachi

St. Philip's in the Hills

St. Philip's in the Hills Episcopal Church is worth a stop. The beautiful church was designed in 1936 by one of Tucson's most famous architects, Josias Joesler. The interior has carved beams, pews, and an altar made from cedar logs from Mexico; gorgeous handcrafted stained-glass windows; and a 12-foot arched window behind the altar that looks out at the Santa Catalina mountain range. A cloistered patio with fish pond and water lilies is a super place to meditate or just take a break from the hustle and bustle of daily life. The church and grounds, located at 4440 North Campbell Avenue (at River Road) are open during daylight hours. Call (520) 299-6421 for more information.

St. Philip's Church. PHOTO BY M. PAGANELLI VOTTO

Mass where guitarists, fiddlers, and horn players accompany the service with traditional Mexican religious songs, and the Mass is held in Spanish.

For a slightly different twist to the usual Sunday routine, the **Park Avenue Christian Church** (520-294-7571) holds services at a local drive-in theater at 4635 South Park Avenue. Church members can stay in their cars and listen to the sermon over the car speakers. (Sorry, the snack bar is closed.)

For those with a more contemplative side, **Grace St. Paul's Episcopal Church** (520-327-6857; www.grace-stpauls.org) has a meditation garden where you can quietly reflect either alone or in a group. And if spending some time with Mother Nature is more to your liking, Sanctuary Cove at Safford Peak—15 miles northwest of the city—features a hand-built stone chapel and several paths leading through the desert. **Picture Rocks Retreat** (520-744-3400; www.desert

Labyrinths have been part of ancient mysticism for centuries; traverse Tucson's own at Westward Look Resort.

PHOTO BY M. PAGANELLI VOTTO

renewal.org), staffed by the Redemptorist Fathers and Brothers, is another beautiful place to have a private service (groups may also reserve time there) or take the scenic trail that leads you past the 14 stations of the cross. The Man in the Maze labyrinth at Westward Look Resort is another soothing place to relax and walk off your troubles. The resort offers guided meditation walks for $5 (reservations recommended), or you can just take your own walk around the concentric circles for free. The resort is located at 245 East Ina Road (520-917-2467).

But there is much more to the spiritual side of Tucson than hundreds of churches and interesting services.

The **Jewish Community Center** (520-299-3000; www.tucsonjcc.org) plays a major role in not just local Jewish life, but also the life of the entire community. The modern facility offers a long list of activities, including recreation, athletics, child care, classes for all ages, and a fine arts gallery, as well as camps, senior programs, and even a dating service.

i **El Tiradito (the Castaway), also known as the Wishing Shrine, is a local legend in Tucson and a National Historic Site. Located just down the block from El Minuto Cafe at 354 South Main, this shrine memorializes a love triangle turned tragic and is the only shrine in the United States dedicated to a sinner. It is said your prayers and wishes can be granted with a small prayer or offering at the site.**

Located in front of the center is the Holocaust Memorial. Its tall shattered column represents the shattered lives of those touched by the Holocaust. A stone from Auschwitz is embedded in the memorial.

Next door is the Jewish Federation of Southern Arizona (520-577-9393; www.jewishtucson.org), which was organized in 1946. The federation serves as the umbrella organization for the Jewish Community Center, Handmaker Jewish

Services for the Aging, Jewish Family and Children's Services, B'nai B'rith Hillel Foundation at the University of Arizona, and the Tucson Hebrew Academy. Serving some 20,000 Jews in the area, the federation also raises funds to assist Jews in eastern Europe and elsewhere and provides opportunities for travel to Israel. The biweekly *Arizona Jewish Post* is another service of the federation. The *Post,* the only Anglo-Jewish newspaper in southern Arizona, has a circulation of approximately 6,500.

Catholic Community Services of Tucson (520-623-0344), which began in 1933, offers counseling for adults, children, and families; immigration, migration, and refugee services; residential care for mothers and infants; adoption services; and case management, nutrition, and socialization services for the elderly and for people with disabilities.

The Pima County Interfaith Council (520-903-2333) has representatives from all faiths and works toward building a better community with programs to improve the lifestyles of many Tucsonans.

Many other area churches provide counseling, hospice services, camps, preschools, and after-school programs. **St. Philip's in the Hills** (520-299-6421; www.stphilipstucson.org) and St. **Francis in the Foothills** (520-299-9063; www.stfrancisumc.org), both offer gay and lesbian spirituality groups. **The Little Chapel of All Nations** (520-623-1692), on the UA campus at 1401 East First Street, has a library available for study and research and holds spiritual events.

Historically and architecturally speaking, there are some magnificent religious structures in Tucson, the most famous of which is the **Mission San Xavier del Bac** (see the Attractions chapter) on the Tohono O'odham Reservation. This magnificent structure has undergone an intense renovation in recent years. With the help of hundreds of volunteers and thousands of dollars in donations, restoration experts have removed countless years of grime, dirt, and candle smoke to reveal some beautifully detailed Spanish colonial–period baroque artwork.

At the opposite end of the spectrum in size and decor is La Capillita, which was rebuilt on the site of the original **La Capillita** (the center of the village of El Fuerte) thanks to the efforts of the Old Fort Lowell Neighborhood Association. This tiny structure (it measures 8 feet by 12 feet with 10-foot walls), made of adobe bricks and covered with lime stucco, can be found near Fort Lowell Park at 5230 East Fort Lowell Road on the same property as the restored San Pedro Chapel (520-318-0219), the city of Tucson's first landmark.

Dove of Peace Lutheran Church, 665 West Roller Coaster Road (520-887-5127), designed in the 1960s by architect W. Kirby Lockard, was honored by the American Association of Architects for its unique design. Unlike most churches, the altar is in the middle, with pews surrounding it and a skylight above.

Those worshipping Islam will find sanctuary at the **Islamic Center of Tucson,** located at 901 East First Street, near the University of Arizona. Call (520) 624-3233 or visit www.ictucson.com for details. Downtown, adherents of the Baha'i faith will find the **Baha'i Information Center** at 531 North Fourth Avenue (520-623-4090). Buddhists are served by the **Tara Mahayana Buddhist Center** at 1701 East Miles Street (520-296-8626; www.meditationintucson.org).

We cannot possibly list every worship service and religious center here. But we do have a few suggestions on where to look for places of worship and religious information during your stay in Tucson.

i You may think you're in Europe when you see the Spanish Renaissance style Benedictine monastery at 800 North Country Club. Home to 19 nuns of the Benedictine Sisters of Perpetual Adoration, the beautiful and soothing chapel, open to all faiths, is a lovely place for quiet contemplation and prayer. Check www.tucsonmonastery.com for hours.

The Saturday edition of the *Arizona Daily Star* has a section devoted to area houses of worship and the times of their services. Check our Media chapter for information on publications such as *Good News* and the *Jewish Post*. Also, several radio stations (see the Media chapter) offer music and information with a religious message.

Several stores, such as **Gospel Supplies** at 5611 East Speedway (520-722-1441) and 6032 North Oracle (520-797-7491) and **Trinity Bookstore** at 3801 East Fort Lowell Road (520-326-3466), offer complete lines of religious supplies as well as books, music, and cards with religious themes.

INDEX

R

ABOUT THE AUTHORS

MARY PAGANELLI VOTTO

A graduate of Vassar College and the New School Culinary Arts Program, Mary is a food writer, editor, and chef. She moved to Tucson from New York City in 2001 and enjoys the wide-open spaces, natural beauty, and terrific weather in southern Arizona. Mary works with the nonprofit organization Tohono O'odham Community Action to document and promote traditional Tohono O'odham foods and contributes locally to *Tucson Lifestyle* magazine.

KATE REYNOLDS

Kate Reynolds is an Arizona native who lives in Tucson with her husband and four well-behaved cats. In addition to visiting the small corners of Tucson, she spends a great deal of time up north working on the *Insiders' Guide to Phoenix*. In her free time she writes novels and articles—and trains her cats. She loves to hear what readers have to say and can be reached at kate@word doctor.net.